Van Eyck to Bruegel

1400-1550

Dutch and Flemish [illegible]
in the collection of the
Boymans-van Beuningen

Museum Boymans-van Beuningen
Rotterdam 1994

KPMG

Foreword

Johan R. ter Molen

Interim director of the Boymans-van Beuningen Museum

Few museums in the world today can boast the illustrious names of both Van Eyck and Bruegel in the title of a catalogue of their own collection. Yet many will have heard these names in combination before. In 1921, a book was published called *Von Eyck bis Bruegel. Studien zur Geschichte der niederländischen Malerei.* The work was compiled by the Berlin art historian Max J. Friedländer, a pioneer of studies in fifteenth and sixteenth-century Netherlandish painting. His fourteen-volume *Die Altniederländische Malerei*, which appeared between 1924 and 1937, has remained a seminal work on the early masters to this day. The structure of the Boymans-van Beuningen catalogue is based on Friedländer's standard work.

The Museum received many of its paintings by this celebrated group of early painters with the collection of D.G. van Beuningen. Friedländer and Van Beuningen maintained close ties with one another, and in 1949 Friedländer wrote the preface to the catalogue of the collector's paintings. This is therefore an ideal opportunity to pay tribute to Friedländer, by echoing the title that he himself chose.

The Boymans-van Beuningen project was initially launched in 1979, when Jeroen Giltaij, head of the Old Masters Department, contacted Dr J.R.J. van Asperen de Boer, professor of scientific examination of works of art at Groningen University, to propose a study of the painting by Van Eyck. The project was soon under way. The painting was examined by x-radiography and infrared reflectography, and samples of paint were taken for analysis. The results were published in 1987. This partnership, formed over fifteen years ago, has proved beneficial to both parties ever since. Van Asperen de Boer has found the Museum a willing source of subject matter for his students, while the Museum has continued to profit from the fruits of their studies. Their findings are now published here.

Dr Peter Klein, an expert on wood biology at Hamburg University has conducted dendrochronological analyses of many of the panels. His results are also published in this catalogue. The Museum is deeply grateful for Dr Klein's article and the comprehensive table that accompanies it. Thanks are also due to Ms Annetje Boersma for her illuminating report on the restoration of Quinten Massys's exquisite painting, and to Ms A. van Grevenstein-Kruse for her authoritative account of the restoration of the Norfolk triptych.

The catalogue was produced by Friso Lammertse, deputy keeper of Old Masters and the author of many of the entries. Jeroen Giltaij has also made an important contribution to the text and was largely responsible for reporting on paintings which were researched and restored early on in the project. I should like to commend them both on this achievement and thank them for their dedication. A word of thanks is also due to the other contributors to the catalogue: Liesbeth Helmus, Suzanne Laemers, Cunera Vergeer, Julien Chapuis, Margreet Wolters, Ron Spronk, Esther Darley and Jeltje Dijkstra.

Once again, we have been able to discover and publish some of the secrets of a particularly beautiful part of our collection of Old Master paintings and sculptures.

Scientific examination at the Boymans-van Beuningen Museum

The Boymans-van Beuningen Museum has encouraged the scientific examination of works of art since the early 1970s. At that time, several small interdisciplinary committees were set up to provide guidance and supervision in important restorations (Master of Aix, Bosch shutters (cat. nos. 17-18) Titian, etc.).

University involvement in scientific examinations probably began in 1977, when a group of art history students under Dr. Ilja Veldman of the University of Amsterdam was allowed to study four Pieter Aertsen paintings, in a project which made use of methods of scientific examination. The results were later published in the *Netherlands Yearbook for History of Art (NKJ)* 40 (1989). A small exhibition held in 1990, with a catalogue by Yvette Bruijnen, made the technical data of the Rotterdam paintings accessible to a wider public.
Collaboration between the Museum and Groningen University's Institute for Art History on a more regular basis was initiated in 1979 with the scientific examination of Van Eyck's *Three Maries at the Tomb* (cat. no. 2). For the first time, a student (Lilian Blauwkuip) was able to write a minor thesis 'Scientific examination of works of art' based on actual examination in a museum. The results of this work were published in 1987.

Since then, and especially in recent years, paintings in the Museum have been assigned to some thirty students as subjects for minor theses. Often this has also meant a first opportunity to – carefully – handle a painting, and take a look behind the scenes at a museum. By financing the production of infrared reflectograms and the taking of x-radiographs by the Röntgen Technische Dienst of Rotterdam and by facilitating the transport of equipment, the Museum has promoted scientific examination to the benefit of both research and teaching in art history.
Occasionally, students were also able to watch Dr. P. Klein of Hamburg at work on his dendrochronological examinations at the Museum. His dating results have been included in the present catalogue entries and are a very important complement to the results of other methods of examination.

In preparing this exhibition, the curators endeavoured to have all the paintings on display x-radiographed and scanned using infrared reflectography. The selection of paintings for students was somewhat biased on didactic grounds: those not showing any underdrawing or in rather poor condition were not chosen. Data from stereomicroscopic examination and paint sample analysis are therefore not available for all the paintings exhibited.
The scope of this catalogue did not permit extensive reporting of the results of scientific examinations. In some cases summaries were judged adequate because of the availability of a separate publication (Van Eyck, cat. no. 2, Master of the gathering of the Manna, cat. no. 8, Pieter Aertsen, cat. nos. 89-92).

The many illustrations showing infrared reflectograms and x-radiographs underline the importance attached to what is rightly becoming a distinct aspect of modern museum catalogues.

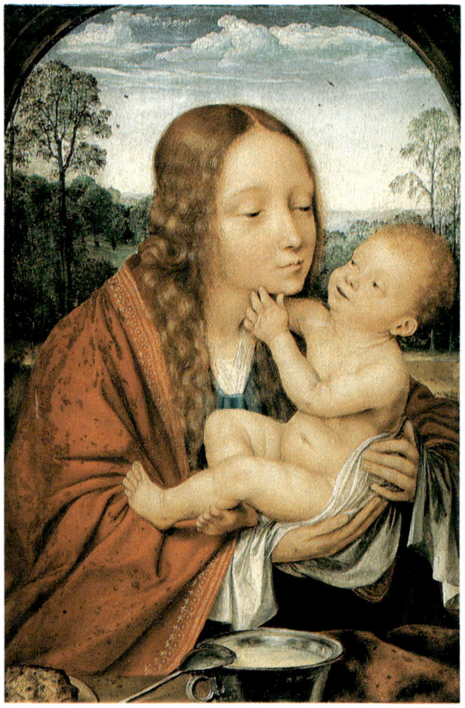

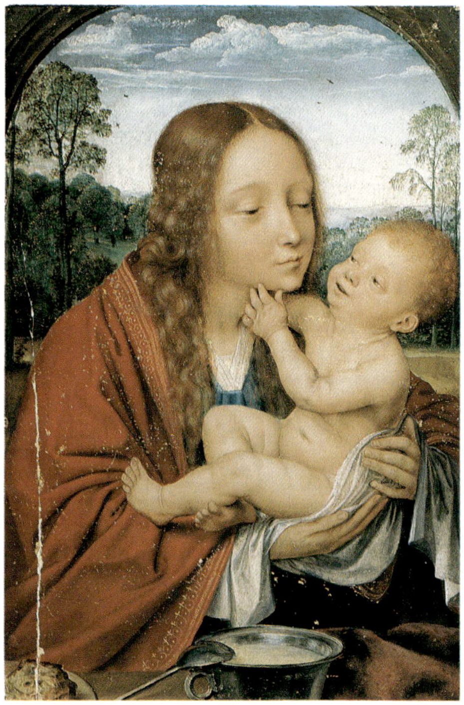

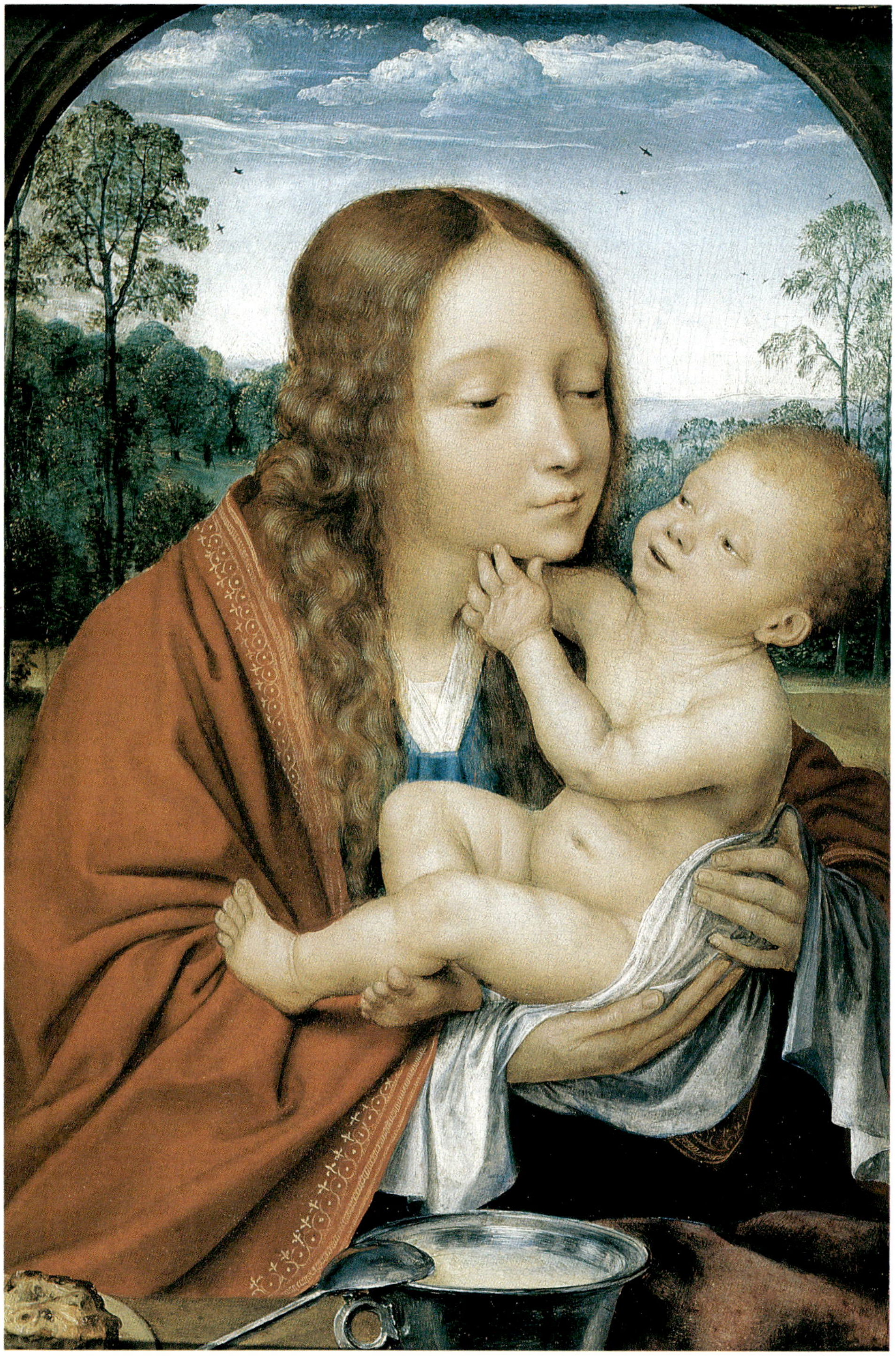

1. Condition before restoration.

2. Condition after cleaning and before retouching.

3. After restoration

Quinten Massys's *Virgin and Child in a landscape* re-examined

The *Virgin and Child in a landscape*, which Quinten Massys painted around 1520, was restored in 1993-1994.[1] The initial reason were the many discoloured overpaintings which were very disturbing to the eye. An old yellowed varnish on the surface of the paint changed the original contrast of colour and was producing tensions in the original paint layers. The restoration will be discussed below, after technical aspects of the work have been explained.

How did the painter go about his work?

Massys and his contemporaries usually used oak supports for their paintings.[2] Before the painter could start working, the planks had to be allowed to dry out completely, after which they were planed to achieve the required thickness. Usually the panel would then be framed, although sometimes the panel and frame were made from the same piece of wood.[3] Next, the painter, or one of his assistants or pupils, would apply a thin coat of glue size, which served to seal the wood. The moisture from the ground layer, when still wet, might otherwise penetrate the wood and cause it to warp. The ground usually consisted of a mixture of chalk and animal glue. The ground was then scraped down and polished until smooth. Often, a light-coloured, intermediate oil-based layer would be applied to the ground to seal it and thus make it more suitable for painting.

The composition was then usually drawn on this intermediate layer with black chalk or black aqueous paint. Sometimes, artists would make their first drawing on the ground itself and add the intermediate layer afterwards. Thanks to the technique of infrared reflectography, it is now possible to study such underdrawings.[4] Some artists worked in a different way by making not an underdrawing but an underpainting – that is to say, by modelling the figures in paint and taking account of the final colour which they planned for a particular area. This modelling often plays an important role for creating the final colour. Most artists used oil-bound paint, made by grinding pigment (colour in dry form) with oil. An alternative used was tempera, using egg yolk as a medium. Tempera was especially popular in fourteenth-century Italian art and earlier. Tempera gives a more matt surface after drying and the colours are more opaque, whilst oil-bound paint gives the artist greater scope in creating transparency and depth of colour when glazed in several successive layers. In the fifteenth and sixteenth centuries, tempera was also used for underpainting in the Netherlands.

The Massys painting has an oak support. The small panel consists of a single plank 5 mm thick. The grain of the wood runs vertically and the back of the panel is roughly planed. The original frame has not been preserved. The fact that the painting was already in its frame when the ground and paint layers were applied can be seen from the so-called *barbe* which is still present on the left, right and top edges. If a panel is painted in its frame, a raised edge or ridge of paint is formed where the panel meets the frame. If the frame is removed, the edges of the panel which have not been treated with ground become visible, as does the slightly raised rim of paint. This rim is called the *barbe*. Our painting does not have a *barbe* along the lower edge, which indicates that the bottom of the panel was sawn down at some stage in the past. During a later restoration the edges which had been exposed when the frame was removed were coated with a thick ground and painted.

Few of Massys's paintings are extensively underdrawn. He more often applied an underpainting directly onto the ground. X-radiographs clearly show that he used lead white to underpaint the flesh areas.

Painting technique
Massys used two types of blue for the sky. For the underpainting he used a paint which contained the slightly greenish-coloured pigment azurite. In order to deepen the tone, he then applied a paint containing the very expensive pigment ultramarine, which was made from the semi-precious stone lapis lazuli.[5] There is a transition of colour in the sky from a dark grey-blue at the top to white on the horizon.[6] The sky was painted with loose brushstrokes. In order to make the small white clouds transparent, Massys scratched lines in the wet paint with the blunt end of his brush or another hard object to expose the blue colour underneath (fig. 4).

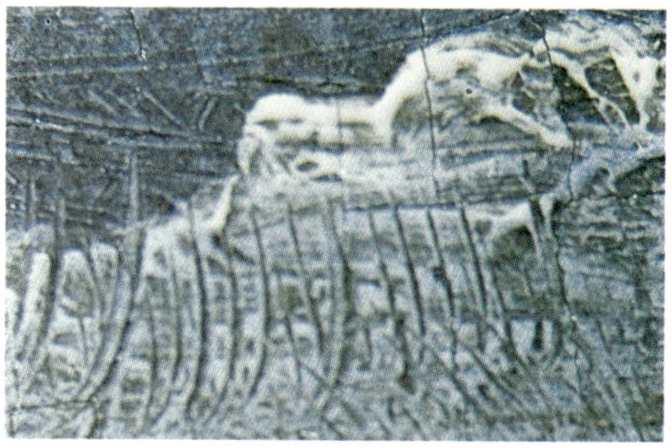

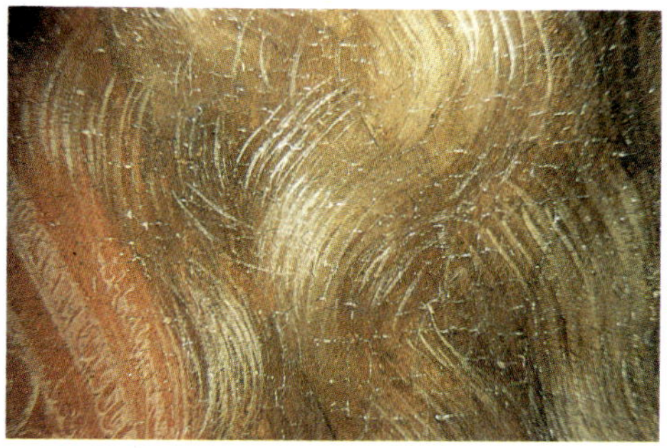

4. Detail of the sky with scratches in the clouds

5. Detail with locks of the Virgin's hair

The foliage and trees in the foreground of the landscape were painted with a fine brush in green-turquoise shades. The trunks and branches were rendered with a single stroke of black paint. Massys painted the distant background with a broader brush and in light-blue. The green of the landscape is in excellent, original condition. There could be some discolouration of the paint where the bright green has turned brown due to oxidisation. This is explained by the painter's use of copper resinate green as a pigment.

The flesh areas of the naked child and of the head and hands of the Virgin were rendered in various hues of opaque pink and ochre in different tonal values. The artist modelled the shadows of the body with a thin, transparent layer (glaze) of darker brown paint. The Virgin's hair is painted in minute detail. The blond locks are painted with a very thin brush as light ochre-coloured lines on brown, in a regular, twisting movement (fig. 5).

In Massys's day, a great deal of attention was given to the painting of clothing, particularly the intensities and tonality of colour in the folds of drapery. The Virgin's red cloak takes up a large part of our painting, and Massys painted the red in several layers to work out the structure of the textile with great care. On top of a light red paint layer, he applied a darker, transparent red glaze to give the colour a deep tone and to characterise the material of the cloak. When this top layer was studied under a stereo-microscope it was found to contain tiny dark-red dots forming a regular pattern. It would seem that the artist stippled this layer with a brush or used a kind of 'lattice' to achieve as regular a red as possible. Massys painted the shadows of the draperies to this layer with black brushstrokes.[7] In this he departed from the practice of many of his contemporaries who began modelling the folds at an earlier stage. The darker areas are often made up of many layers of paint creating a relief on the surface of the paint.[8] The Virgin's cloak is decorated with pink and ochre-coloured ornaments which protrude from the red surface.

Craquelure
The entire paint surface is marked with the craquelure which formed as the paint layers were drying. Because these layers consisted of a variety of substances, tensions were produced during the drying process, leading to cracks (premature crackle). Fluctuations in moisture and temperature often have a strong impact on the formation of craquelure. Especially in the sky different forms of cracks due to age can be seen.

The form of the craquelure on our painting – small horizontal and vertical fractures – is typical of works made in this period. Cracks can also appear in a layer of varnish due to ageing as could be seen in our painting before restoration. The old varnish had darkened somewhat and displayed a network of fine cracks.

Restoration

The panel has a vertical crack in the wood at the bottom left which runs through the ground and paint layers. This crack was rather excessively overpainted during a previous restoration. The overpainting had become discoloured with time. In addition, small retouches were visible over the entire surface of the painting. These had been painted in during previous restorations in order to hide small gaps in the paint surface. Small particles of the original paint were detached from the ground probably due to fluctuations in moisture and temperature.

The retouches and the old, thick varnish layer were causing tensions in the original paint layers, which made restoration essential. The yellowed varnish was removed, as were the discoloured retouches.[9]

Besides the crack mentioned above and some other minor damage, the surface of the paint proved to be in much better condition than had previously been assumed. Much of the surface was still in its excellent original condition. The upper, transparent layer of paint (glaze) in the cloak was still completely intact. Only in a few places had small particles become detached, which in fact made it possible to study the structure of the paint and how it was built up. After cleaning, all the damaged areas were once more retouched.[10] This process was kept to a minimum to avoid adding more new material than was necessary. Although the retouches are reversible, that is, they could easily be removed at a later date, any new material will one day show signs of age and may discolour. Before and after retouching, the paint surface was given a thin coat of varnish.[11]

1 See for this painting also cat. no. 35.

2 Dutch and Flemish painters in particular made use of this type of wood. In Italy, poplar was mainly used. In other parts of Europe, limewood, walnut and softwood were also used. See R.H. Marijnissen, *Schilderijen. Echt, fraude, vals*, Brussels-Amsterdam 1985, pp. 61-79. H. Verougstaete-Marcq, R. Van Schoute, "Painting technique: supports and frames", in: *Scientific examination of easel paintings, Pact* 13 (1986), pp. 13-34.

3 See J. Dunkerton, S. Foister, D. Gordon, N. Penny, *Giotto to Dürer: Early Renaissance Painting in the National Gallery*, London-New Haven 1991, pp. 154-160.

4 See J.R.J. van Asperen de Boer, "An introduction to the scientific examination of paintings", *Nederlands Kunsthistorisch Jaarboek* 26 (1975), pp. 6-12.

5 The painting was examined with a stereo microscope under the guidance of J.R.J. van Asperen de Boer. No paint samples were taken. The pigments were thus not identified.

6 The dark grey-blue in the upper part of the sky could have been caused by a discolouration of the paint medium. Alternatively, it could be the result of green azurite underpaint coming through. Residues of old varnish can discolour a paint film. No paint samples were taken to prove any of these points.

7 The restorations carried out and published by the National Gallery in London provide interesting material for comparison of the painting techniques and pigments used. See A. Roy, "The technique of a 'Tüchlein' by Quinten Massys", *National Gallery Technical Bulletin* 12 (1988), pp. 36-43 and D. Bomford, A. Roy & A. Smith, "The techniques of Dieric Bouts: two paintings contrasted", *National Gallery Technical Bulletin* 10 (1986), pp. 39-57.

8 See for example cat. no. 63.

9 The varnish was "rolled off" with cotton wool sticks using a mixture of isopropanol and ethanol.

10 The retouches were built up from a watercolour underpainting, followed by a layer of loose pigment mixed with a medium of dammar (see also note 11). Subsequently, a glaze of oil paint with most of the oil filtered out was applied with a medium of dammar, in order to make it transparent.

11 The varnish also consists of a dammar-resin solution thinned with white spirit.

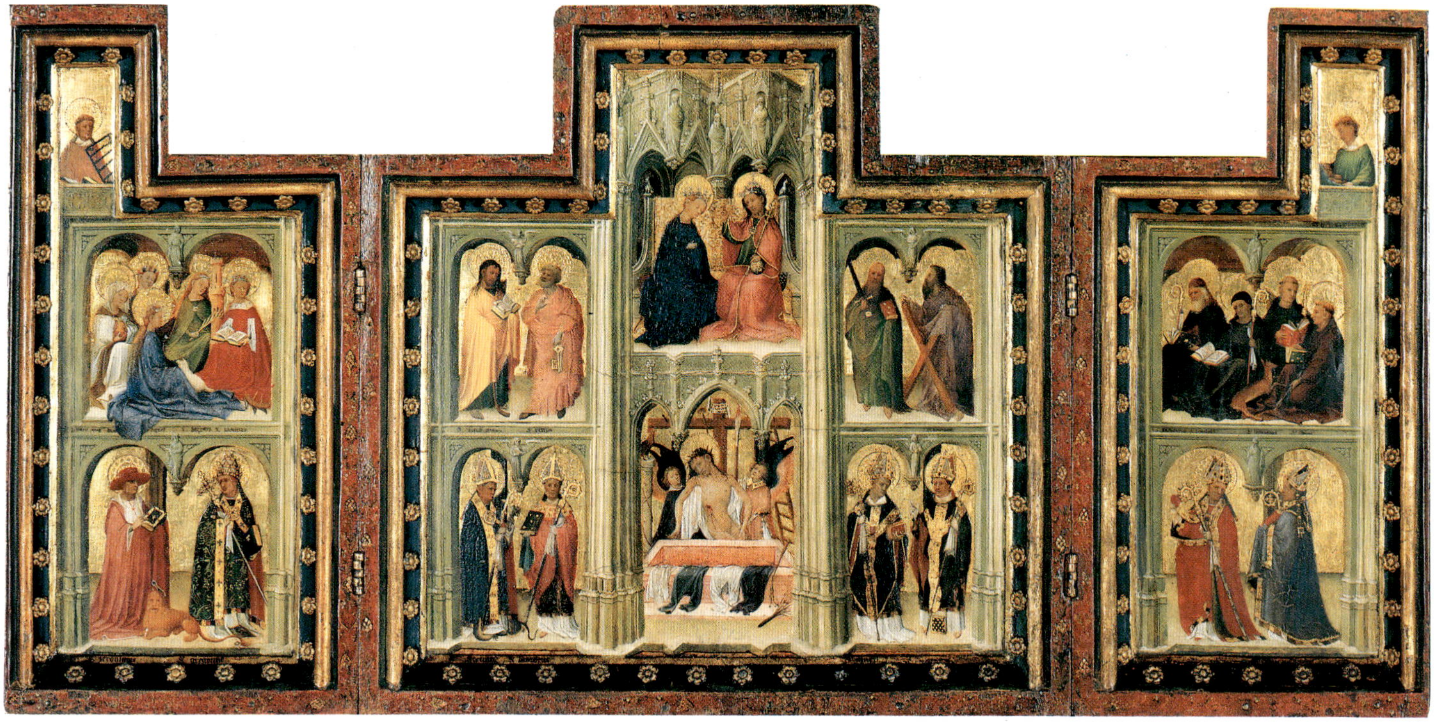

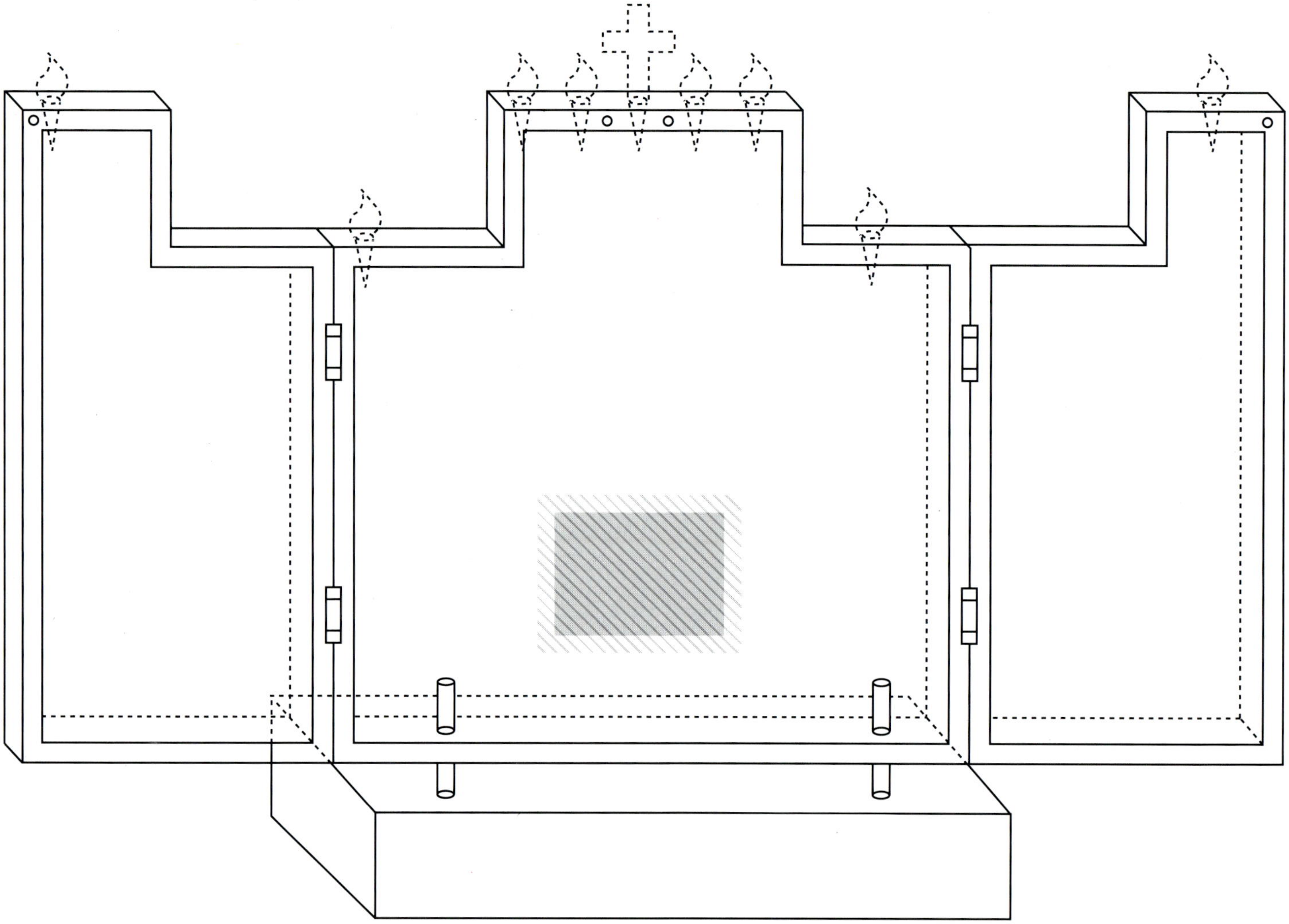

Report on the treatment of the Norfolk triptych

The so-called 'Norfolk triptych', one of the rare examples of early Netherlandish painting before Van Eyck, was restored in 1993-1994. This article will discuss aspects of the materials and techniques used for the triptych which came into focus during the restoration. Overall, the painting was in very good condition. The reason for intervening was a disturbing loss of paint, which was flaking where it overlaps the gold leaf.

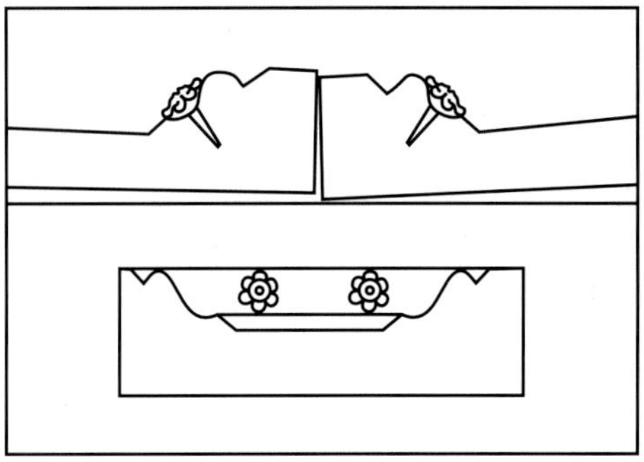

1. Plan of the frame profile.

2. The painting and an illustration showing a reconstruction of the triptych.

Physical characteristics

The support consists of three small oak planks which together form a triptych. Measured from the edge of the frame, the centre panel is 2.45 cm thick, and the shutters 2.30 cm. When closed, the triptych is therefore 4.75 cm thick. It is 33 cm across and 33 cm high measured from the highest point, and 26 cm from the step. The frame (fig. 1) is cut from the same thick plank, which was hollowed out to a thickness of 1.20 cm. The grain runs vertically, which means that the horizontal profile of the frame had to be cut across the grain of the wood. This method, generally associated with eastern icons, is more difficult than cutting and planing each component of the panels and frame separately and then reassembling them. It was also an expensive method because wood was cut away across the entire width of the panel.[1]

The x-radiograph (fig. 3) of the centre panel reveals that a further recess was cut into the thickness of the wood, into which a thin plank of softwood (11.5 x 9 cm) was inlaid.[2] The grain runs across that of the oak panel. This piece of wood was covered with a very thin and loosely woven piece of textile that extended approximately 1 cm beyond the edges of the inlay. This served as a bridge between the inlay, the panel and the ground. The reverse of the centre panel shows no sign of this treatment: the grain is straight and regular and there is no indication of a knot in the wood. There is therefore no obvious technical reason for the insertion of this extra piece of wood.[3]

The ground was applied after the panel and frame had first been coated with glue size. This white chalk/animal glue layer was then scraped down, after which a preparatory underdrawing was made on the smooth surface. Infrared reflectography reveals on the outside of the shutters an underdrawing executed with a black pigment and probably applied with a fine brush[4]. It is quite sketchy with many hesitant lines. The central panel and the inside of the shutters also have a black preparatory drawing, though using a less hesitant technique, with thin nervous lines sometimes ending in a small loop as if they had been executed with a quill instead of a brush (figs. 5, 6). A compositional change in the foreground of the centre panel meant that instruments of the Passion (nails and a hammer) which had been included on the underdrawing were ultimately omitted (fig. 6). Parts of the centre panel and the inside of the shutters were gilded. Light incisions defined the areas where gold leaf was to be applied. Before the metal leaf sections could be burnished to produce a high gloss these areas had to be underpainted with a layer of reddish-brown bole in an aqueous medium. The ground for the gold leaf had to be entirely free of grease so that it could be burnished, which is why the gilding was always carried out before painting. The inside edge of the frame was gilded at the same time. The gold leaf was burnished using agate which, if the stone was not perfect, sometimes left tiny scratches on the surface (fig. 4). The contour lines remained visible

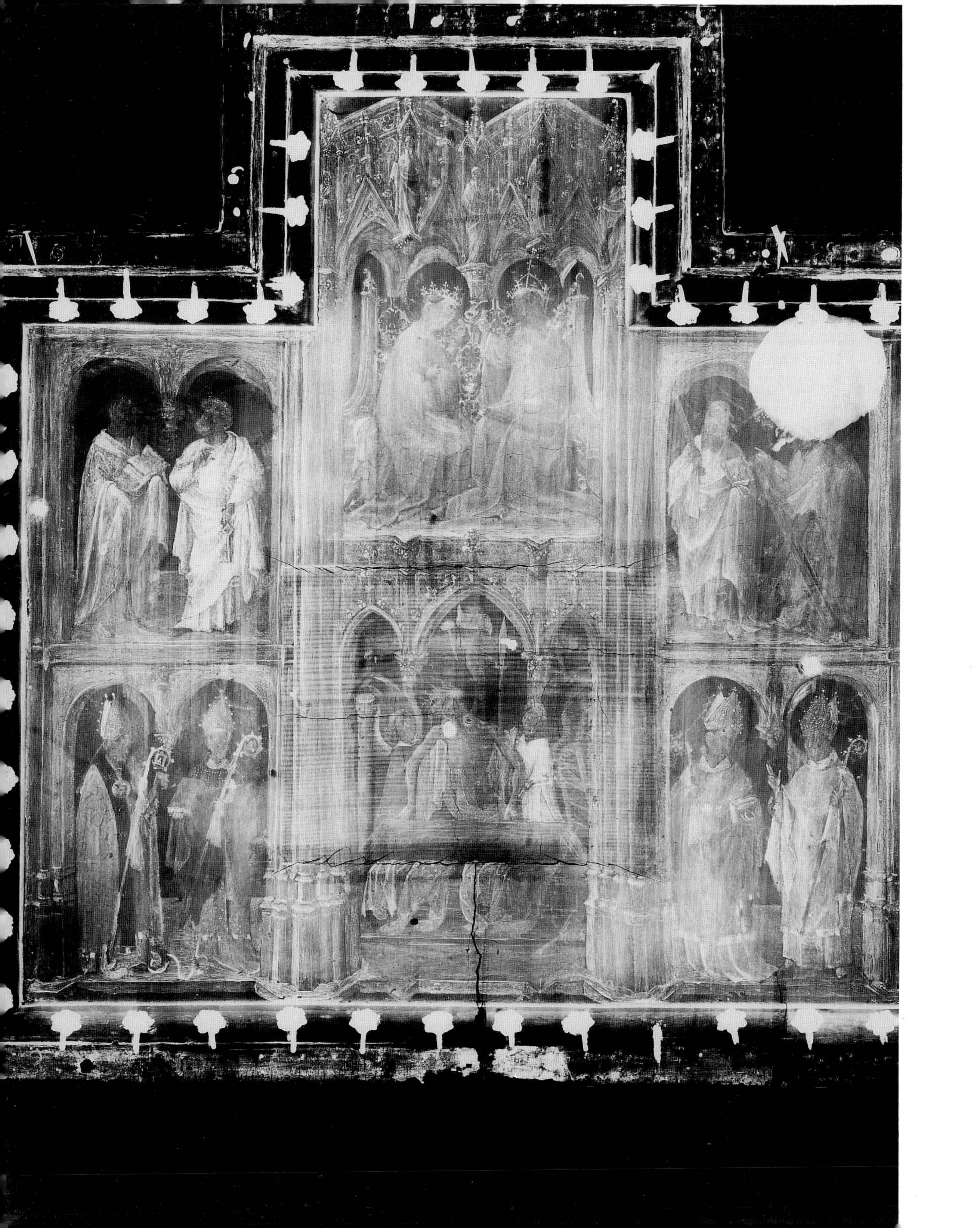

after the application of the metal leaf, which would not have been the case with a normal black drawing. The incised lines show up white on the x-radiograph because lead white-based paint from the paint layers has accumulated in the tiny grooves. The round arches in the architecture may have been marked using a compass with a radius of 1.6 cm for the centre panel and 2.2 cm for the shutters. However, it is possible that the circular segments were traced around a model, because there are no obvious marks left by a compass point. The vertical construction lines seem to have been drawn freehand.

3. X-radiograph of the centre panel.

The painting technique[5] is an excellent example of pre-Eyckian painting on panel. Paint cross-sections show a thin white-lead layer over the drawing to prevent the medium penetrating into the ground. An unpigmented oil layer is found in Eyckian painting.[6] The paint partly overlaps the gold leaf, particularly along the contours of the composition and the edges of the panel. At these junctures, the adhesion of the paint is poor, which has led to repeated loss of paint and flaking. It seems that the upper layers of paint dried too quickly, which resulted in premature crackle (fig. 9). This is particularly true of the blue areas of azurite and lapis lazuli which may have been applied in an aqueous medium. A very fine maze of premature drying cracks over the whole painted surface points to the eventuality of the use of an emulsion over an isolation layer of white lead in oil.

After burnishing, the gold leaf was decorated with simple, small punches, the outline of the nimbi with slightly larger punches (or the same punches struck more firmly along an indented line (fig. 8). The contours of the nimbi, and of other areas of gold leaf, were indented with a metal stylus after burnishing (figs. 7, 9). In the case of the gold brocade hanging behind the Virgin's throne, this was done after the white pomegranate motif had been painted, thus producing the effect of threads in the precious textile.

Gold was also used for decorations on top of the paint. These areas were probably first underpainted with an oil-based adhesive (so-called mordant gilding) before the gold leaf was applied: once it had dried, the excess gold was brushed away. However, it is also possible that powdered gold mixed with an aqueous medium was used for this very fine detail (the powdered gold was known as 'shell gold' because it was traditionally stored in shells). Both techniques produce a matt and somewhat grainy surface (figs. 8, 9).

Other metals seem also to have been used for the decoration of, for example, St Servatius's key and the shaft of the bishop's staff. One might think of oxidised silver or even tin leaf (fig. 9). The burnished gold leaf of the background was subsequently adorned with a thin floral motif such as is often found in manuscript illumination. A translucent, probably non-pigmented, medium was applied with a fine brush, which gave the gold leaf a slightly matt appearance as described in the Strasbourg manuscript where the use of gum arabic is advised (fig. 10).[7]

The highly refined play of surface and variations in luminosity which cause the light to be reflected or diffused depending on the technique used, is familiar from Italian painting, manuscript illumination and, most importantly, from polychromed sculpture. The polychroming of statues was also often carried out by painters. In other cases there was close collaboration between painters and sculptors, as for example between Melchior Broederlam and Jacques de Baerze, in the production of altarpieces.[8]

It is in the treatment of the frame that the parallels with techniques used in polychromed sculpture are most obvious. The frame which, as was discussed above, is part of the panel, was overpainted at a later date on a brown ground layer.[9] Under this overpaint the original polychromy of the frame is slightly damaged but in places perfectly preserved. On a thin chalk/glue ground, the inner bevel edge was covered with burnished gold. Then follows matt azurite-blue on a black underpaint in the hollow profile as a background for the oil-gilded lead-cast rosettes. The round profile is oil-gilded on a black underlayer. The next bevel is green with a brown glaze.[10] The outer flat ridge was painted with a translucent red (probably water-soluble madder) over a layer of vermilion. This ridge was decorated with a continuous painted green stalk with

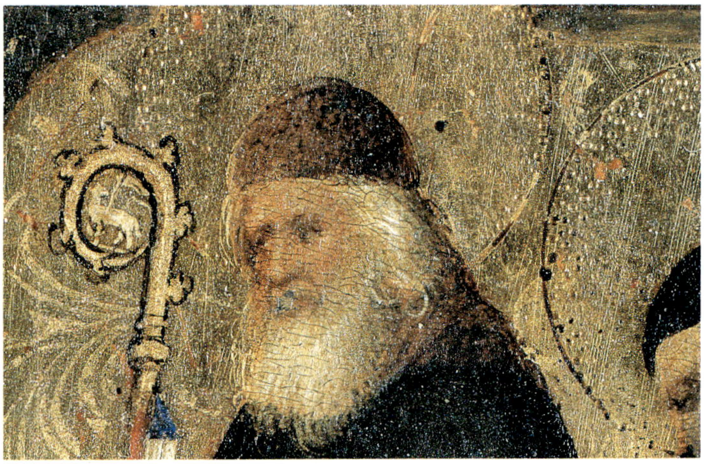
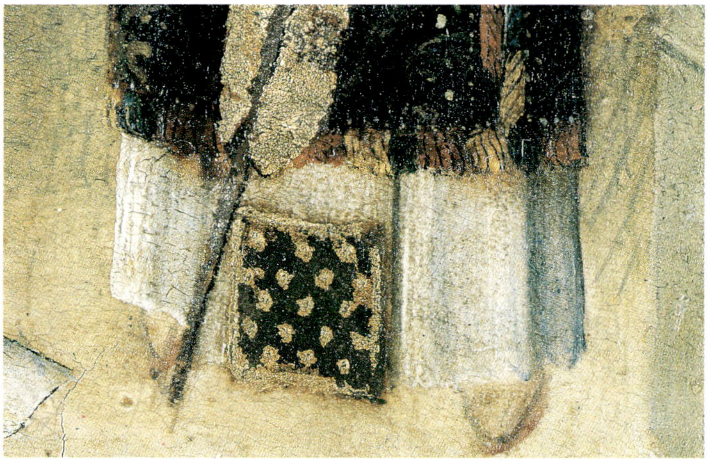
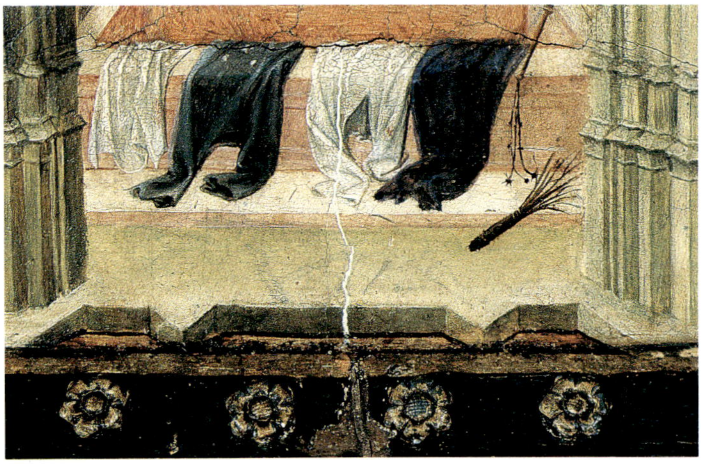
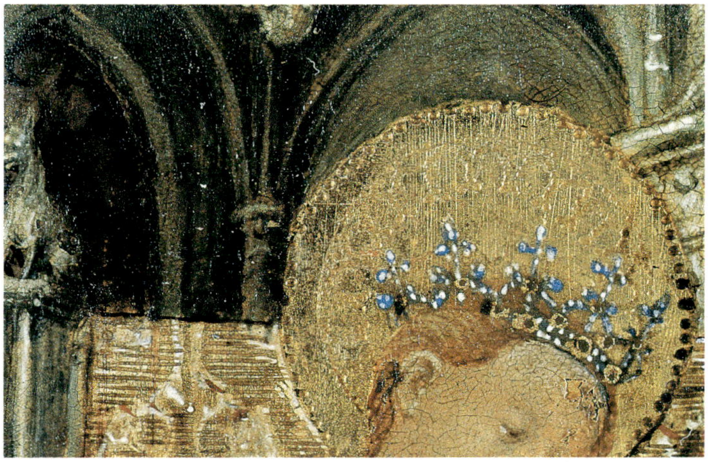
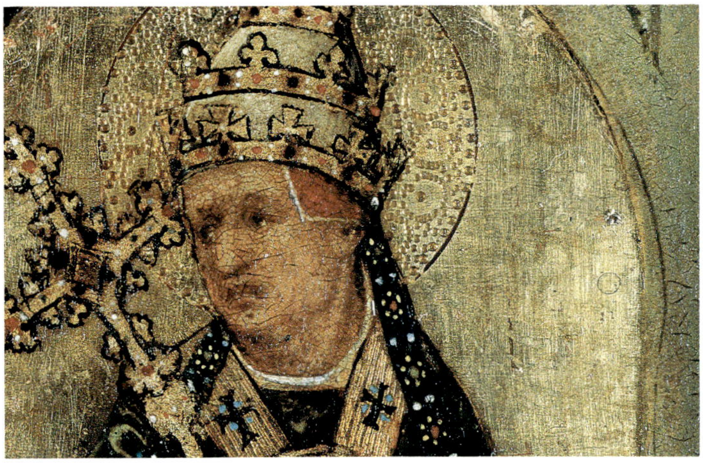
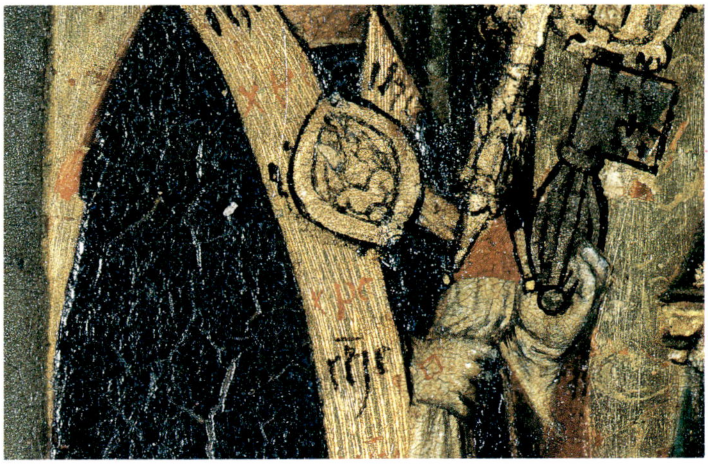

pairs of violets (?) and curly green leaves ending in a pine cone motif (?) of mordant gold with a black contour. The motif is repeated eight times on the stiles. The pine cone motif points upwards and the two garlands meet at top centre in two pairs of violets.

A *trompe l'oeil* painted version of a rosette frame can be seen on the pre-Eyckian panels of Walcourt.[11] It is also noteworthy that the Broederlam/De Baerze altarpiece in Dijon has rosettes in the frame of the altar case and painted floral garlands on the gilded frame of the shutters, a motif which is comparable to that of the Norfolk triptych but finished using a different technique (painted and punched on a burnished gold underground).[12]

The slanting sill at the bottom of the triptych is decorated with a band of burnished gold leaf on which the basements of the pillars of the architecture are completed. Then follows a band of blue with raised rosettes and then a band of green, separated from the former by a very thin white line. At the top of the centre panel and of the shutters are several holes, some of which still contain broken-off metal pins. This could indicate that the decorative elements, beyond the frame continued. It is possible that the painted architecture above the Virgin and Christ on the heavenly throne may have been extended with three-dimensional pinnacles or finials (fig. 2). There are also two holes in the bottom edge of the centre panel, 7 cm from the corners, in the middle of the plank. These holes are 0.6 cm in diameter and 4 cm deep, suggesting that wooden pins were once used to secure the triptych on a lost base. The whole triptych probably originally looked like an altar on a pedestal. In that light it may be said that, with the architectonic decoration at the top, the representation looks orderly, recalling statues in the recesses of a sculpted retable. In this context of exchange between two- and three-dimensional representation the *trompe l'oeil* details are masterful, such as the blue cloak of St Agnes extending out of the painted niche in the architecture, or the Star of Bethlehem on the flat painted frame on the outside of the left shutter.

The fastenings consist of four hinges sunk into the sides of the centre panel and the shutters. The front faces of the spills are covered with mordant gilding. The round heads of copper tacks protrude from the front of the outside corners of the shutters. When the shutters are closed, the heads touch those of similar tacks at the top and bottom of the centre panel. These act as stops to prevent damage to the painting.

The outside edges of the shutters show the remains of locks. In the centre of the right edge of the left shutter is a rosette-shaped, embossed copper plate fastened by a nail through the centre. Four small holes at the four tips of the petals may point to reinstatement or re-use (textile decoration?). Traces of lost round plates, likewise fixed with nails through the centre, are visible at the top and bottom edges of the left shutter. At the corresponding point on the edge of the right shutter was a wooden pin, which has since broken off. These fragments suggest a fastening system. A piece of metal is still visible in the lower left corner of the right-hand shutter, as are two holes and a mark which may have been scratched by a hook at the same level on the left shutter. These traces of old fastenings should prompt a search for similar objects with the aim of establishing the appearance of the original attachments.

The restoration work carried out in 1994

Except for the overpainting of the frame on the inside of the triptych and the outside of the shutters, the paint is in very good condition, with a few, very small old retouches. The overpainting of the frame follows the original polychromy, except the matt azurite and the green which have both been overpainted in glossy black. The reason for intervening was a disturbing loss of paint, which, as mentioned above, was flaking where it overlaps the gold leaf.

A vertical crack 6 cm long from the bottom of the centre panel was strengthened using a thin piece of wood whose grain runs across that of the oak. The front and bottom of the fracture were filled with wax and gesso and overpainted. This crack does not appear in an old photograph. More recent pictures taken in 1990 show no signs of deterioration.

4. Gold leaf with traces of burnishing, tooling, impressed aureoles and unpigmented matt decoration of the background: 'musieren'.

5. Black preparatory drawing showing through on the centre panel.

6. Instruments of the Passion in the preparatory drawing, not included in the painting.

7. Gold brocade on the Virgin's throne; indented lines.

8. Punching; mordant gilding on the mitre and staff.

9. Indented lines, mordant gilding, premature crackle and oxidised silver on the key of St Servatius.

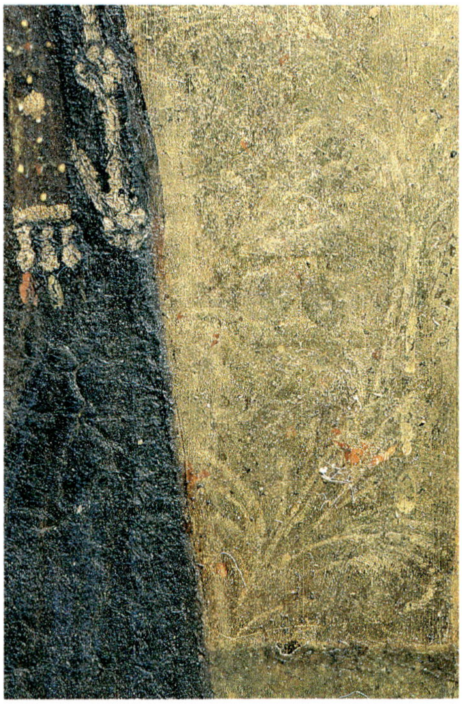

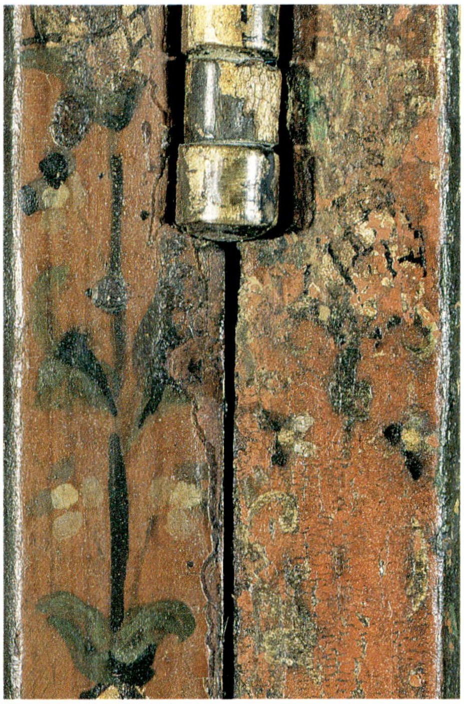

10. 'Musieren' or 'florieren': delicate decoration painted on gold leaf in translucent paint (glacis).

11. Left: imitative overpainting. Right: traces of the original garland.

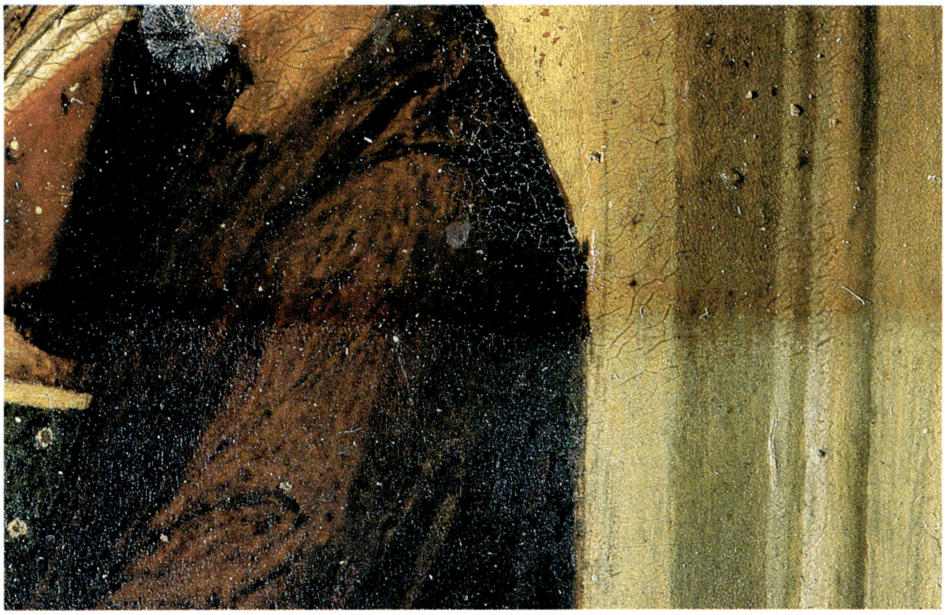

12. During the reduction of the varnish layers.

After several months of observation it was decided to leave well alone, although the crack was closed with a thin slice of balsa-wood. A non-aqueous glue was used to avoid any swelling of the wood fibres leading to a "wedge effect". The crack was then filled with a mixture of wax, chalk and pigment, applied with an electrically heated spatula. As well as reducing the visible damage, this reduced the penetration of moist air which could cause the inlaid softwood plank to swell, so producing additional internal tensions. The flaking paint was fixed using a synthetic resin.[13] In view of their great fragility, work on these areas was carried out with the help of a surgical stereo microscope.

The old, oil-based layers of varnish were covered with a thin layer of probably synthetic resin and had turned distinctly brown.[14] The risk that a contraction of these layers of varnish would cause further flaking of the already fragile areas could not be discounted. For this and aesthetic reasons – the illusion of space and the reproduction of colours were badly impaired – it was decided to attempt to reduce the thickness of the varnish. The microscope was again used, as were very thin sticks of cotton wool and various solvents to dissolve the different kinds of varnish (fig. 12).[15] The paint on the frame was partly removed using solvents, and partly mechanically. After cleaning, the paint layer was fixed for a second time using the same synthetic resin. Small retouches were made with dry pigment and Paraloid B72. It was decided not to varnish the triptych.

1 Another example of this method, which was rare in this part of the world, is a small triptych from the end of the fourteenth century in the Our Lady Basilica in Tongeren. This pre-Eyckian panel contains a relic from the Virgin's headscarf. See: H. Verougstraete-Marcq, R. van Schoute, *Cadres et supports dans la peinture Flamande aux 15e et 16e siècles*, Heure-Le-Romain 1989, pp. 321-322.

2 X-radiographs taken by the Röntgen Technische Dienst in 1991 and the Stichting Restauratie Atelier Limburg in 1994, see also note 4.

3 By analogy with the pre-Eyckian reliquary panel from the Our Lady Basilica in Tongeren, this recess could have been intended for a relic: the softwood itself might, for example, represent a piece of the true Cross. This piece would then have had an intrinsic, but not directly visible sacred value, as is the case with icons.

4 See the unpublished minor thesis by Geraldine van Heemstra, *Methoden en technieken van materieel onderzoek van kunstvoorwerpen*, which was written under the supervision of J.R.J. van Asperen de Boer. See also cat. no. 1.

5 See also Geraldine van Heemstra's thesis (note 4).

6 See for the painting technique of the Van Eycks: P. Coremans et. al., *L'Agneau Mystique au Laboratoire, Contributions a l'histoire des Primitifs Flamands*, Antwerp 1953; see also J.R.J. van Asperen de Boer, "A scientific reexamination of the Ghent altarpiece", in *Oud Holland* 93 (1979), pp. 141-214.

7 See R.E. Straub, "Tafel- und Tüchleinmalerei des Mittelalters", in: *Reclams Handbuch der Kunstlerischen Techniken*, Volume 1, Stuttgart 1984, pp. 131-259, especially pp. 186-187 "Musieren oder Florieren".

8 See E. Panofsky, *Early Netherlandish painting*, Cambridge, Mass. 1953, p. 86. He also discusses at length the stylistic connections between pre-Eyckian painting and manuscript illumination: pp. 91-129.

9 See Van Heemstra (note 4), paint sample no. A302/11.

10 Layer 3 of paint sample no. A 302/11 contains green and yellow particles. See Van Heemstra (note 4).

11 P. Colman, "Les panneaux pre-Eyckiens de Walcourt", *Bulletin Koninklijk Instituut voor het Kunstpatrimonium, Brussel* III (1960), pp. 35-54.

12 For the rosette motif in architecture, in ivory carving and sculpture and in book illumination (notably the rendering of frames) see Panofsky, (note 8), p. 92.

13 20 g Paraloid B72 in 100 ml xylene. This acrylic resin is classified as a class A material due to its stability.

14 See Van Heemstra (note 4), sample no. A302/8.

15 Dimethyl formamide, ethyl alcohol, isopropyl alcohol.

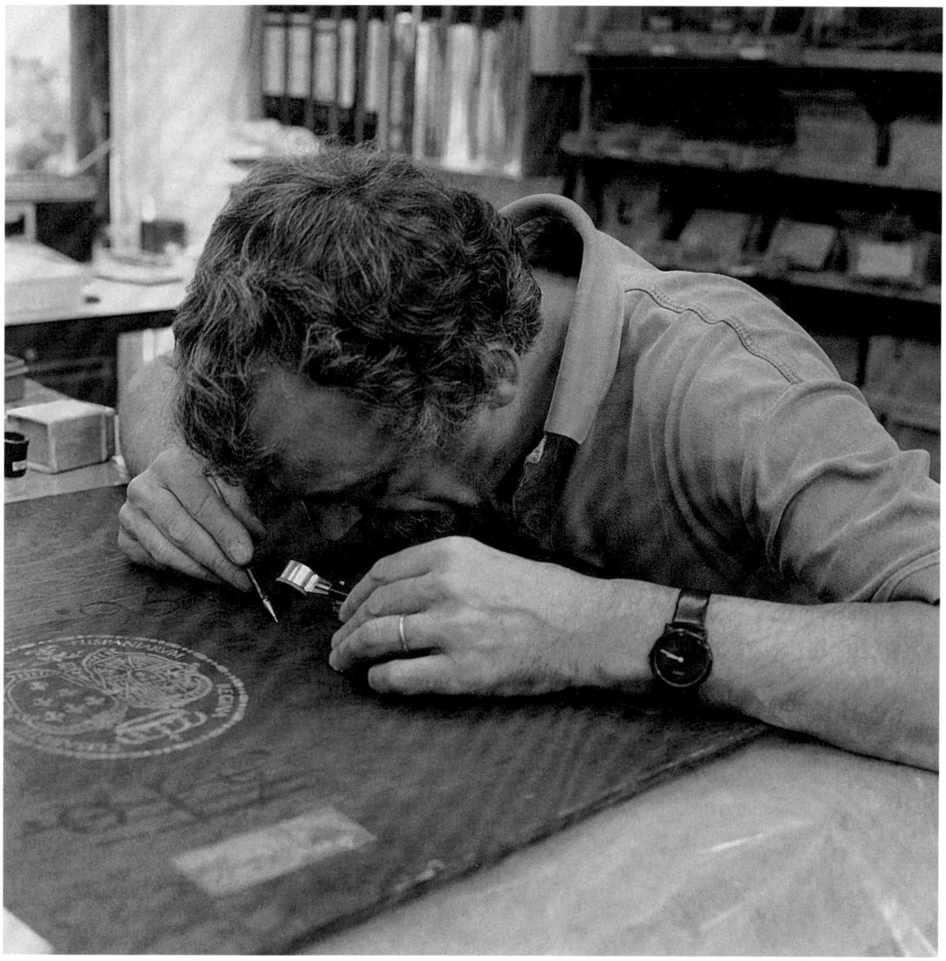

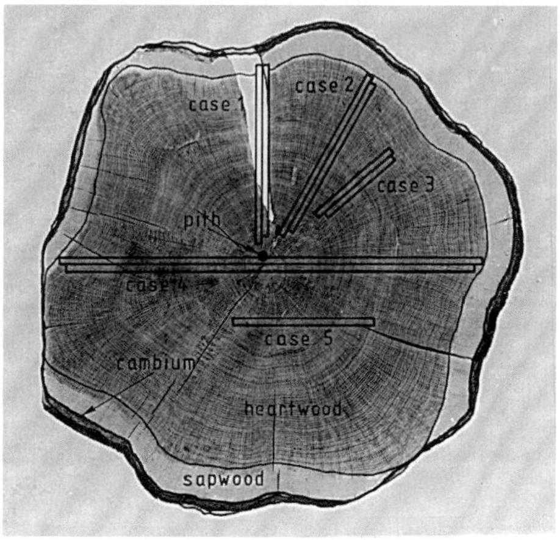

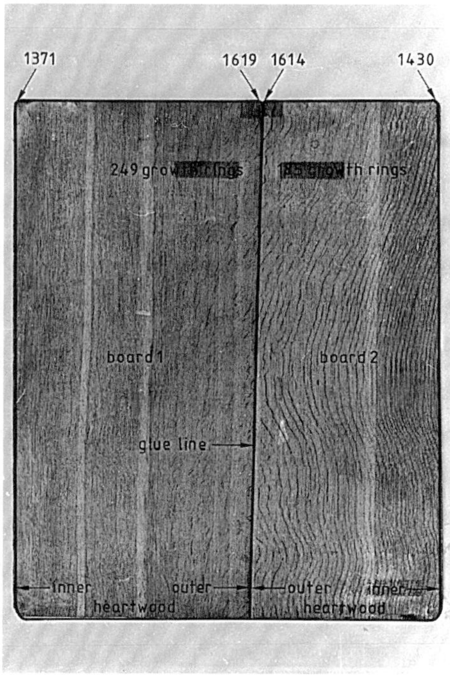

1. Peter Klein measuring Bruegel's *Tower of Babel*

2. Various methods of extracting planks from an oak tree

3. A seventeenth-century oak panel made of two planks; size 62.2 x 50 cm, thickness 1 cm

Dendrochronological analyses of panels from the fifteenth and sixteenth centuries

Dendrochronological analysis which can determine the age of wooden objects is used in art history as a dating tool for panels. The objective of dating is to ascertain at least the *terminus post quem* for a painting by determining the felling date of the tree, i.e. the point in time after which the wood for the panel could have been sawn. The principle of this method is to measure the width of the annual growth rings in the wood of the panels and to compare the growth ring curve produced by this measurement with the dated master chronologies. Comparing the characteristics of the growth ring curve over centuries, for trees from different countries, can produce a dating which is exact to the year.

Panel makers usually cut planks radially with regard to the cross section of the tree (fig. 2). The bark and the light and perishable sapwood were cut off. A determination of the exact felling year is therefore not possible. Only the latest measured growth ring of the panel can be determined exact to the year (fig. 3).

On the other hand, the number of sapwood rings (which must be added to the number of heartwood rings to achieve a reliable dating) can be estimated using statistical evaluation which must consider each case separately. The provenance of the oak wood is significant for the sapwood statistic. The number of sapwood rings found in trees varies between 7 and 50 in western Europe and between 9 and 36 in eastern Europe. This knowledge helps us to determine the sapwood allowance, as does the fact that most of the wood used for Netherlandish panels came from the Baltic region (fig. 4).

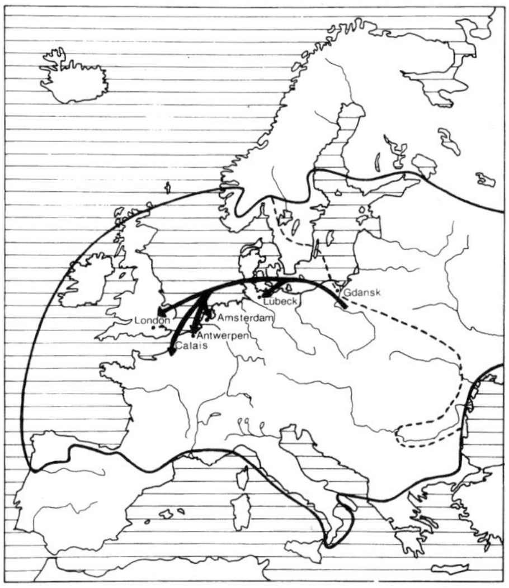

4. The areas of the natural distribution of oak. The distribution of Quercus robur L. (European oak) is shown as a continuous line; the distribution of Quercus petraea Liebl. (sessile oak) is shown as a broken line. European oak originates further to the north-east than does sessile oak. The source of oak timbers of type II three-ring patterns and the places of their utilisation as panels are indicated by arrows.

An analysis of the number of sapwood rings found in 179 oak trees from northern Poland resulted in a median value of 15 with 50% of all values lying between 13 and 19, a minimum of 9 and a maximum of 36. In addition, the number of sapwood rings also depends on the age of the tree. More sapwood rings can normally be expected in a tree 300 years old than in a tree 100 years old (fig. 5).

To determine the earliest felling date – i.e. the point in time before which the painting could not have been made – a minimum of 9 sapwood rings must be added to the latest measured growth ring in the panel. The felling date of an oak panel with sapwood rings can be estimated by the addition of the median of 15 growth rings to the sapwood-heartwood boundary with an error margin of between −2 and +4 years. On panels with only heartwood rings the felling date can be narrowed down with the addition of 15 years with an error margin of between −2 and +X, where 'X' is an unknown number of sapwood and heartwood rings lost during the manufacture of the panels. Therefore, the felling date cannot be fixed exact to the year.

The next problem is to determine how much time elapsed between the felling of the tree and the initial painting of the panel. For signed and dated panels from the sixteenth and seventeenth centuries, the interval can be estimated with an error margin of between 2 and 8 years in most cases. The problem for fifteenth century early Netherlandish paintings is that only a few signed and dated panels exist. From these few examples it can be concluded that the interval amounts to about 10 years and more. It is evident that this period of 10 years' storage time is also a purely statistical figure and can differ widely in particular cases.

These problems notwithstanding, dendrochronological analysis is often an aid to pinpointing the date and origin of a painting. This is demonstrated by the results obtained for the paintings of the Boymans-van Beuningen Museum (fig. 10).

5 Analysis of sapwood rings

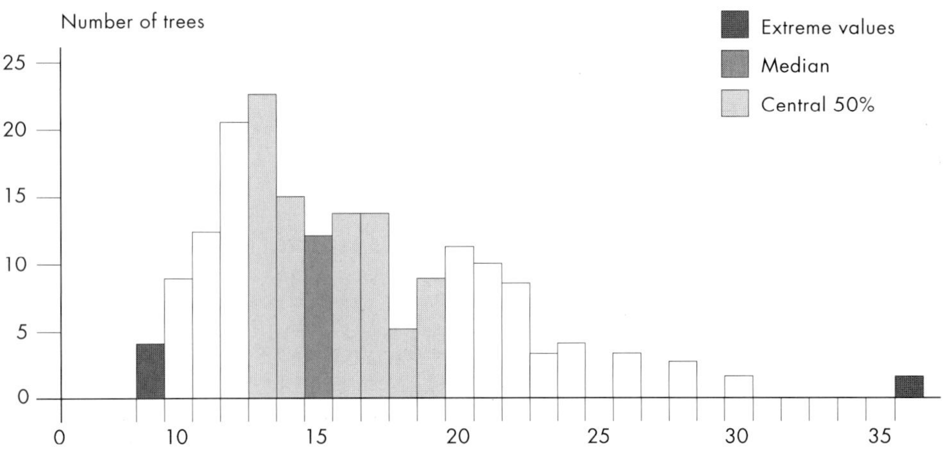

5. Distribution of the number of sapwood rings in 179 oak trees from northern Poland.

Some examples are discussed in detail below. From the dendrochronological results (fig. 6) of the analysis of the painting of the *Three Maries at the tomb* by Jan van Eyck (cat. no. 2) it is evident that this painting could have been created in Van Eyck's lifetime. By adding 15 sapwood rings and 10 years' storage time to the youngest heartwood growth ring, a dating is plausible from 1430 onwards. The same formula for the painting *Lucca Madonna* (Frankfurt, inv. no. 944) produces a dating about 5 years later.

Fig. 7 demonstrates the value of the dendrochronological method in distinguishing copies from originals. The theme of the Adoration was often used by Jheronimus Bosch and members of his studio. It is sometimes impossible to differentiate between the original and later copies on the basis of style alone. Dendrochronological analysis showed that the version of the *Adoration* (cat. no. 23) in the Boymans-van Beuningen collection was made around 1540 at the earliest. The style of Bosch was also copied in the seventeenth century, as another version of an *Adoration* in a private collection shows.

Growth ring analysis gives not only a felling date for the tree but it can also shows which planks were cut from the same tree. In the case of the panel *The pedlar* (cat. no. 16), all four planks originated from the same tree. Moreover, both planks used for the *Death and the miser* (Washington, National Gallery) were also cut from this tree. The dating of the youngest heartwood ring (1477) of the Washington panel should therefore also be applied to the Rotterdam panel.

6 Jan van Eyck

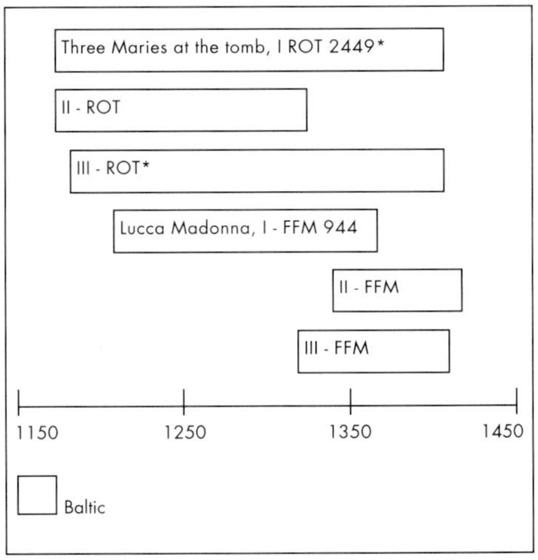

6. Dendrochronological determination of the felling date of two paintings by Van Eyck. The asterisks indicate that planks are from the same tree. (FFM - Städelsches Kunstinstitut, Frankfurt, Frankfurt am Main; ROT – Boymans-van Beuningen Museum, Rotterdam).

7 Jheronimus Bosch and Follower 'Adoration'

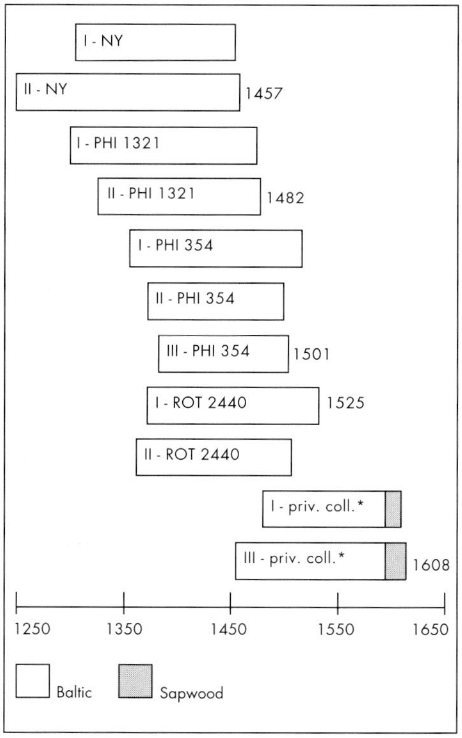

7. Dendrochronological determination of the felling date of five paintings from the Bosch group. All paintings are titled *Adoration*. The asterisks indicate that planks are from the same tree (NY - The Metropolitan Museum of Art, New York; PHI - Museum of Art, Philadelphia; ROT - Boymans-van Beuningen Museum, Rotterdam)

For three paintings by the Master of St John Altarpiece, the *Birth of St John, Elizabeth fleeing with her son* (Rotterdam, cat. nos. 25, 26) and *St John Preaching* (Philadelphia) it was shown that all the planks came from three separate trees (fig. 8):

Tree A:	Birth of St John:	planks I and III
	Elizabeth fleeing with her son:	planks I and III
Tree B:	Birth of St John:	plank II
	Elizabeth fleeing with her son:	plank II
	St John Preaching:	planks I and III
Tree C:	St John Preaching:	plank II

Three panels attributed to the Master of the Gathering of the Manna (*The Gathering of the Manna* and *The Crucifixion*, Douai, Musée de la Chartreuse and *The Offering of the Jews* (cat. no. 8, Rotterdam) were dendrochronologically examined (fig. 9). It was determined that the two planks of *The Crucifixion* and one each from *The Offering of Jews* and *The Gathering of the Manna* are from the same tree, while the remaining two planks of the latter panels are from a single, different tree. This irrefutably establishes that the three panels belonged to one altarpiece.
Finally, the wood used for the *Virgin with the infant Christ holding an apple* (Master of the Legend of the Magdalen (?), cat. no. 63) was identified as 'fir' (Abies sp.). The use of this kind of wood is very rare in Netherlandish paintings. Some 700 Netherlandish paintings from the fifteenth and sixteenth centuries were examined and only one panel, the *Adoration* by Jacob Cornelisz van Oostsanen (Chicago, Institute of Art, Inv. no. 1953.3) was found to be on a panel made from the same species of wood. Fir was sometimes used in the 15th and 16th centuries by the Cologne School and in southern Germany. It is quite probable that fir was sold to the Netherlands because it was used for the masts of ships.

Conclusion

Dendrochronological studies of panels can give a *terminus post quem* for the planks of panels. Furthermore, a comparison of the growth ring series of the single planks often enables us to determine whether or not they came from the same tree. It may be then be surmised that certain planks came from the same carpenter, which has consequences for the attribution. This means of dating the panels attributed to a painter makes it possible to establish a relative chronology.

8 Master of the St. John Altarpiece

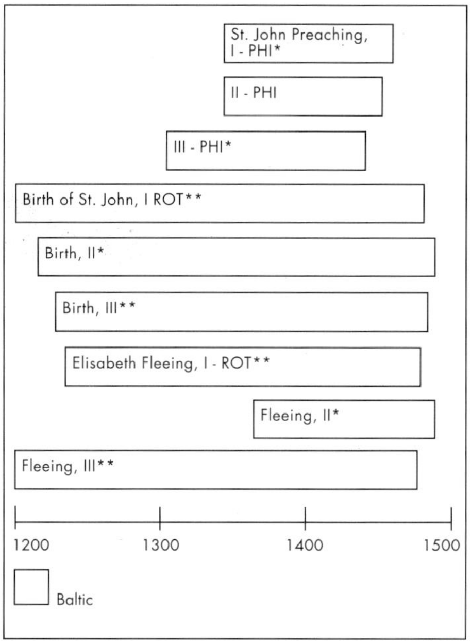

8. Dendrochronological determination of the felling date of three painting by the Master of the St John Altarpiece. The asterisks indicate that planks are from the same tree (PHI - Museum of Art, Philadelphia; ROT - Boymans-van Beuningen Museum, Rotterdam)

9 Master of the Gathering of the Manna

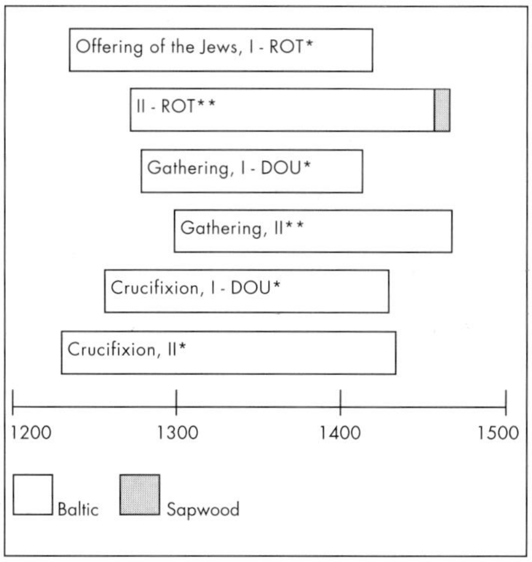

9. Dendrochronological determination of the felling date of three paintings by the Master of the Gathering of the Manna. The asterisks indicate that planks are from the same tree. (DOU - Musée de la Chartreuse, Douai; ROT - Boymans-van Beuningen Museum, Rotterdam)

Artist	Painting/Inv. - no.	Plank	No. of growth rings/ sapwood	Youngest growth ring	Earliest felling date 9 sapwood rings	Estimated felling date 15 sapwood rings
Pieter Aertsen	The pancake bakery (1006) cat. no. 90	I	182/8	1543	1544	1550
		II	146	1535		
		III	155/5	1539		
	Worship of the statue of Nebuchadnezzar (1007) cat. no. 91	I	144/5	–		
		II	212/4[1]	1546	1551	1557
		III	170[1]	1533		
Anonymous Netherlandish Master	Adoration of the Christ Child* (S27/BrF 2) cat. no. 28	I	–	–	1471	1477
		II	99	1460		
		III	116	1458		
	Ecce Homo* (S28/BrF 3) cat. no. 29	I	75	1462	1471	1477
		II	103	1461		
		III	110	1461		
Anonymous North Netherlandish Master	Christ before Pilate (S32) cat. no. 30	I	232/3	1452	1458	1464
Anonymous South Netherlandish (?) Master	Two figures wearing mitres (fragment) (1177) cat. no. 24	I				
		II	77	1366	1375	1381
Anonymous South Netherlandish Master, Bruges (?)	St. Catherine being led away (2468) cat. no. 33	I	163	1415	1424	1430
Anonymous South Netherlandish Master	Virgin and Child in a courtyard (2478) cat. no. 44	I	286	1462	1471	1477
Anonymous South Netherlandish Master, Brussels	Crucifixion, with the Virgin and St. John (2477) cat. no. 64	I	138	1446	1455	1461
Jheronimus Bosch	St. Christopher carrying the Christ Child (St 26) cat. no. 15	I	159	1441	1488	1494
		II	141	1469		
		III	88	1461		
		IV	132	1479		
	The pedlar (1079) cat. no. 16	I	222[2]	1473	1486	1492
		II	86[2]	1367		
		III	91[2]	1476		
		IV	225[2]	1476		
	The Hell (St. 27) cat. no. 17	I	79[3]	1393	1506	1512
		II	212[4]	1497		
	The Flood (St. 28) cat. no. 18	I	225[4]	1491	1506	1512
		II	113[3]	1404		
Jheronimus Bosch, after	Marriage at Cana (St. 25) cat. no. 20	I	177[5]	1544	1553	1559
		II	155/2	1538		
		III	185[5]	1542		
	The temptation of St Anthony (2441) cat. no. 21	I	248	1515	1531	1537
		II	249	1522		

10. Dendrochronological analyses: paintings of the 15th and 16th century.

Boards with the same index are originating from the same tree.
* = formerly front- and backside; therefore the same felling date.
** = this panel is made of fir wood (Abies sp.). A dating is not possible.

Artist	Painting/Inv. - no.	Plank	No. of growth rings/ sapwood	Youngest growth ring	Earliest felling date 9 sapwood rings	Estimated felling date 15 sapwood rings
Jheronimus Bosch, manner of	**Christ before Pilate (2438) cat. no. 22**	I II	36 172	1412 1497	1506	1512
	The adoration of the magi (2440) cat. no. 23	I II	173[4] 160[4]	1525 1518	1534	1540
Dirk Bouts	**Head of Christ (2442) cat. no. 6**	I	170	1439	1448	1454
Dirk Bouts, circle of	**St John writing the Gospel (1083) cat. no. 7**	I II III	85 164 192	1420 1440 1440	1449	1455
Pieter Bruegel	**The tower of Babel (2443) cat. no. 95**	I II	141 166	1539 1539	1548	1554
Petrus Christus	**Virgin and Child in an archway (3316) cat. no. 3**	I	200/7	1426	1428	1434
Gerard David	**Virgin and Child in a landscape (2446) cat. no. 34**	I	144	1475	1484	1490
Jan van Eyck	**The three Maries at the tomb (2449) cat. no. 2**	I II III	223[6] 136 213[6]	1407 1319 1408	1417	1423
Geertgen tot St Jans	**The glorification of the Virgin (2450) cat. no. 13**	I	101	1443	1452	1458
Jan Gossaert	**The metamorphosis of Hermaphrodite and the nymph Salmacis (2451) cat. no. 36**	I	162	1480	1489	1495
Maerten van Heemskerck, studio	**The entombment of Christ (1291) cat. no. 87**	I II III	177 152 152	1509 1506 1516	1525	1531
Lucas van Leyden	**Potiphar's wife displays Joseph's garment (2455) cat. no. 57**	I	164	1426	1435	1441
Quinten Massys	**Virgin and Child in a landscape (2460) cat. no. 35**	I	256	1500	1509	1515
Master of the Amsterdam Death of the Virgin	**Portrait of Dirck Borre van Amerongen and Maria van Snellenberg (2464) cat. no. 59**	I	182	1487	1496	1502

Artist	Painting/Inv. - no.	Plank	No. of growth rings/ sapwood	Youngest growth ring	Earliest felling date 9 sapwood rings	Estimated felling date 15 sapwood rings
Master of the St John Altarpiece	Birth of John the Baptist (2118) cat. no. 25	I	290^{8}	1489	1504	1510
		II	271^{9}	1495		
		III	255^{8}	1492		
	Elizabeth fleeing with her son (2117) cat. no. 26	I	245^{8}	1489	1504	1510
		II	136^{9}	1495		
		III	285^{8}	1487		
Master of the St John Altarpiece, circle	Christ bearing the Cross (S 25) cat. no. 27	I	245	1452	1472	1478
		II	160	1463		
Master of the Gathering of the Manna	The offering of the Jews (2349) cat. no. 8	I	172	1418	1445	1451
		II	160/4	1440		
Master of the Legend of the Magdalen (?)	The Virgin with the infant Christ holding an apple** (2481) cat. no. 63	I	140			
Master of the Virgo inter Virgines	The Annunciation (1568) cat. no. 14	I	224^{10}	1457	1469	1475
		II	215^{10}	1460		
Hans Memling	Two horses in a landscape (2470) cat. no. 31	I	131	1446	1474	1480
Joachim Patinir	Landscape with the destruction of Sodom and Gomorrah (2312) cat. no. 46	I	132	1504	1513	1519
	Landscape with grazing donkey (2474) cat. no. 47	I	250	1471	1480	1486
Joachim Patinir, circle of	Landscape with the Flight into Egypt (2473) cat. no. 48	I	137	1481	1490	1496
Joachim Patinir, follower of	Rest on the Flight into Egypt (2476) cat. no. 49	I	190	1496	1505	1511
Jan van Scorel	A young scholar (1797) cat. no. 73	I	179/5	1525	1529	1535
Jan van Scorel, studio	St. Sebastian (2342) cat. no. 74	I	248^{11}	1519	1530	1536
		II	264^{11}	1519		
		III	243^{11}	1513		
		IV	168	1521		
Jan van Scorel, circle of	Virgin and Child (1798) cat. no. 75	I	120	1500	1509	1515

For further information about dendrochronological analysis, see:

D. Eckstein et al., "New Evidence for the Dendrochronological Dating of Netherlandish Paintings", *Nature* 320 (April 3, 1986), pp. 465-466.

J. Bauch, D. Eckstein, and P. Klein, "Dendrochronologische Untersuchungen an Gemäldetafeln des Wallraf-Richartz-Museums, Köln", in: F.G. Zehnder, *Katalog der Altkölner Malerei* (Kataloge des Wallraf-Richartz-Museums 11), Cologne 1990, pp. 667-683

P. Klein, "The Differentiation of Originals and Copies of Netherlandish Paintings by dendrochronology", in: H. Verougstraete-Marcq and R. van Schoute (ed.), *Le Dessin sous-jacent dans la peinture: Dessin sous-jacent et copies*, Louvain-la-Neuve 1991, pp. 29-42.

P. Klein, "Dendrochronological analysis of German Panels in the National Gallery of Art", in: *German Paintings of the 15th through the 17th centuries, National Gallery*, Washington 1993, pp. 195-197.

P. Klein, "Dendrochronological analysis of panels attributed to Petrus Chistus", in: exhib. cat. *Petrus Christus, Renaissance Master of Bruges*, New York, The Metropolitan Museum of Art, 1994, pp. 213-215.

Contributors:

AdB J.R.J. van Asperen de Boer
JC Julien Chapuis
ED Esther Darley
JD Jeltje Dijkstra
JG Jeroen Giltaij
LH Liesbeth Helmus
FL Friso Lammertse
SL Suzanne Laemers
RS Ron Spronk
CV Cunera Vergeer
MW Margreet Wolters

Abbreviated literature:

Cat. 1962:
(J.C. Ebbinge Wubben), *Museum Boymans-van Beuningen Rotterdam. Catalogus schilderijen tot 1800*, 1962

Friedländer, I-XIV, 1924-1937:
M.J. Friedländer, *Die Altniederländische Malerei*, I-XIV, Berlin-Leiden 1924-1937

Friedländer, I-XIV, 1967-1976:
M.J. Friedländer, *Early Netherlandish Paintings*, Leiden-Brussels 1967-1976

Hannema, 1949:
D. Hannema, *Catalogue of the D.G. van Beuningen Collection*, Rotterdam 1949

Notes on the scientific examinations

Scientific examinations involving various techniques and methods were carried out at the Museum. The Röntgen Technische Dienst in Rotterdam came to the Museum to examine our paintings on the premises. The company acted as a sponor to the Museum by spending one day a year taking x-radiographs of our paintings in exchange for an ektachrome to be used for a Christmas card.

Peter Klein of the department of wood biology, University of Hamburg, made periodic visits to the Museum, at our convenience, to conduct his dendrochronological analyses. A note on his findings appears in the entry on each of the panels he examined. These sections include a dating for the most recent heartwood growth ring and, in some cases, for that of the sapwood growth ring as well. They also mention the earliest year in which the panel would have been ready for painting, and the year after which it is most likely to have been painted. In the case of both fifteenth and sixteenth-century panels, the former date is arrived at by adding 9 sapwood year rings to the last heartwood year ring and allowing for a two-year storage period. The formula for calculating the year after which a fifteenth-century panel is most likely to have been painted is to add fifteen sapwood year rings to the youngest heartwood year ring with an additional storage period of ten years. In the case of sixteenth-century panels, the date is calculated by adding 15 sapwood year rings to the most recent heartwood growth ring and allowing for a two-year storage period. The results of Klein's studies are summarised in an article in the first section of the catalogue.

Most of the infrared reflectographic examinations were carried out by students, who were also responsible for cutting and assembling the reflectograms. In addition, they examined the paintings under a stereomicroscope. These projects were always supervised by Professor J.R.J. Van Asperen de Boer, who kindly provided the equipment. All paint samples were taken by Professor Van Asperen de Boer. The students' task was to embed and grind the samples to prepare paint cross-sections for further microscopic study. The infrared reflectograms are the property of Professor Van Asperen de Boer, as are the samples and paint cross-sections.

Glossary

The definitions listed below, with a few amendments, are cited from the outstanding glossaries in the catalogues by David Bomford, Christopher Brown and Ashok Roy, *Art in the making. Rembrandt*, London, National Gallery, 1988-1989, p. 144 ff, and by David Bomford, Jo Kirby, John Leighton and Ashok Roy, *Art in the making. Impressionism*, London, National Gallery, 1990, p. 211 ff.

Cross-section

By examining minute samples of paint in cross-section under the miscrocope, the layer structure of the painting, including the ground layers, can be determined for that sample point. Many pigments can be identified by their colour and optical properties in a cross-section. Samples are mounted in a block of cold-setting resin, then ground and polished to reveal the edge of the sample for examination in reflected light under the optical microscope.

Dendrochronology

A technique used to date wooden objects, including panel paintings, by examining annual growth rings in the wood. Trees grow faster in favourable summers, giving wider rings than those formed in bad summers. A sequence of ring widths has been worked out reaching many centuries in the past, so that dates can usually be calculated for when a tree was alive. The year in which it was cut down can be known precisely only if the final ring, just under the bark, is present, but an estimation of the felling date can usually be made.

Infrared reflectography, reflectogram

Infrared is similar to visible light, but slightly too long in wavelength for the eye to see. In conventional infra-red photography, an image is recorded using film sensitive to infrared radiation in an ordinary camera.

Infrared reflectography is a technique in which a television camera provided with an infrared vidicon sensitive to somewhat larger infrared radiation is connected to a television monitor. The image is seen instantaneously and is photographed from the screen. The individual reflecograms are printed and pasted together into an infrared reflectogram assembly. Infrared reflectography is mainly used to reveal the underdrawing – a first sketch – beneath covering paint layers.

X-rays

A form of radiation which passes through solid ojects, but is obstructed to differing degrees by different materials.
The larger the atoms of which a substance is made, the more opaque it is to X-rays. Lead compounds are particularly opaque, those containing lighter metals less so. Thus in an X-ray image (known as an X-radiograph) of a painting, areas of paint containing lead pigments will appear almost white, areas containing iron pigments will be in an intermediate grey, and areas containing lighter materials will appear dark. In interpreting X-rays it should be remembered that all layers are superimposed: thus the image of the wooden panel, cradling and features on the back of a painting may seem to overlie the image of the paint itself.

Register of artists

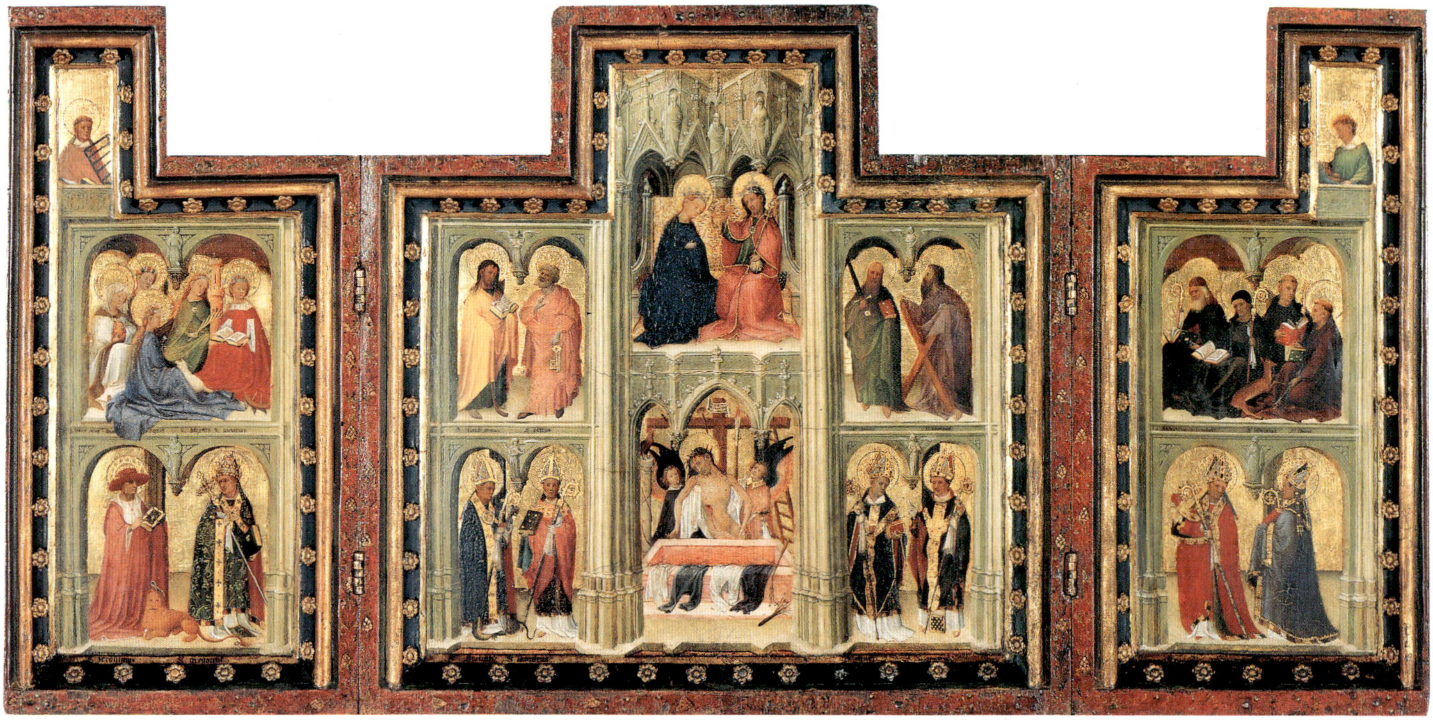

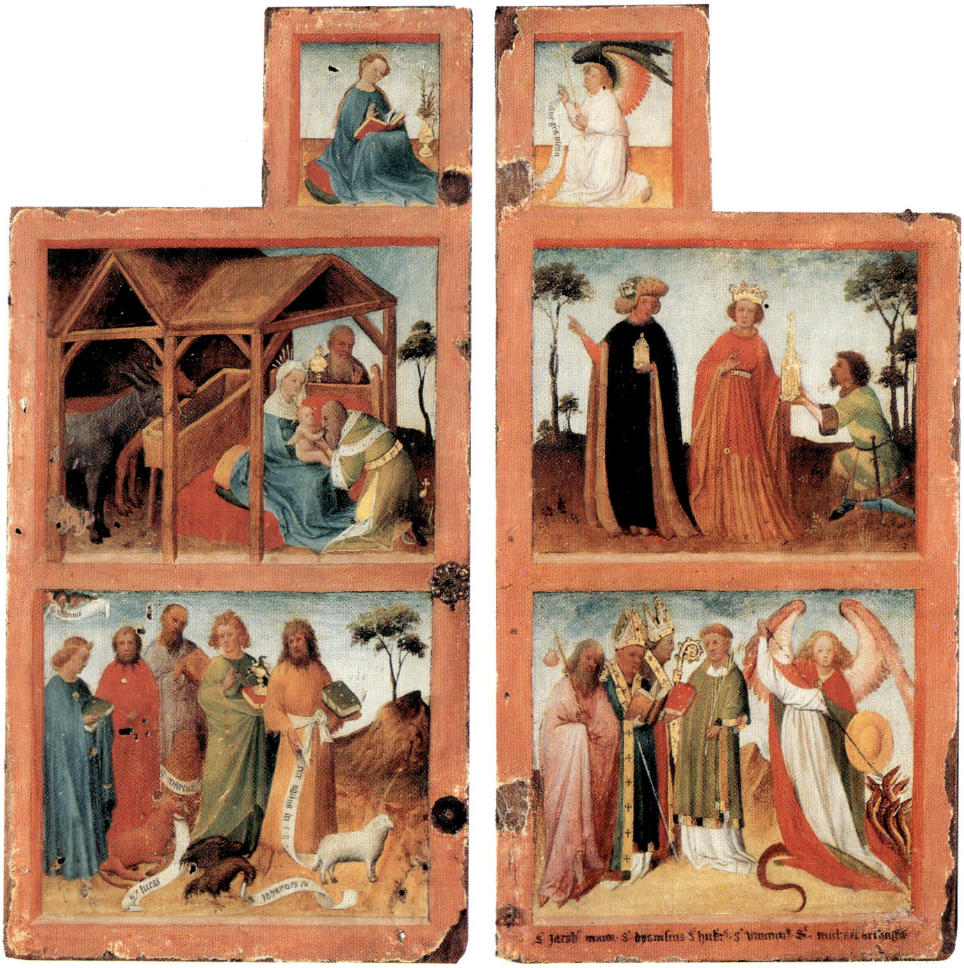

Christ as the Man of Sorrows, with a multitude of saints

Anonymous
South Netherlandish master, Liège?
c. 1415-1420

Centre panel; 33 x 32 cm; side panels; 33 x 13 cm

Inscriptions:
Inside:
Left:
top: S Laur...(?)
middle: marie mag dorot agnes s.barbara s.katharina
bottom: S jeronimus S gregorius

Middle:
upper left: S Jacob minor S.petrus
lower left: S.servati S Lambtus
upper right: S.paulus S.andreas
lower right: S.marti.. S...(letters missing)

Right:
top: S.stephan
middle: S.Anthonius S.benedict S.Leonardus S.egidius
bottom: S...(letters missing) an (?) (letters missing)

Outside:
Left, on the banderole: S Matheus S.Lucas S.Marcus S.Johannes ev. ecce agnus dei c (?) r (?)
Lower right: S Jacob maior S dyonisius S hubt s S vincenti S michael.....(?).
The inscription above the cross is undecipherable.

Centre panel, reverse: part of a gummed label with the letters: A.J.B.Ho (A.J.Beresford-Hope?); D.G. van Beuningen's seal.

Physical characteristics:[1] the three parts consist of three panels; the frame forms part of the panel.

Infrared reflectography:[2] a detailed, fairly linear underdrawing can be seen on the outward-facing side of the shutters. It was rendered on the ground layer and is covered by a thin, white intermediate layer with only a single layer of paint on top. The inside of the triptych is covered with gold leaf. The simple paint structure would support the proposal that the artist was also a manuscript illuminator (see entry).

Paint samples: large quantities of lapis lazuli were used on the front.

Provenance: possibly taken from the Netherlands to England by the banker Hope;[3] A. Beresford-Hope; Duke of Norfolk, sale London, Christie's, 11 February 1938, no. 85 (French school, £4,305, or 4,100 guineas, to Max Rothschild); purchased by J. Goudstikker, Amsterdam; acquired there by D.G. van Beuningen, Rotterdam and Vierhouten, on 31 August 1938 for 172,000 guilders; acquired with the D.G. van Beuningen Collection, 1958; inv. no. 2466.

Exhibitions: *Catalogue of the art treasures of the United Kingdom*, Manchester, 1857, no. 382 (as Cologne master); *Oude Kunst tentoonstelling*, Maastricht, Stedelijk Museum, 1939, no. 1, fig.; *Kersttentoonstelling. Schilderijen, teekeningen en beeldhouwwerken uit particuliere Nedelandsche verzamelingen*, Rotterdam, Boymans Museum, 1938-39, no. 22, figs. IV-VIII; *Nederlandsche Kunst van de XVde en XVIde eeuw*, The Hague, Mauritshuis, 1945, no. 1; *Les Primitifs Flamands*, Paris, Musée de l'Orangerie, 1947, no. 61, fig. XLIII; *Honderd jaar Museum Boymans Rotterdam. Meesterwerken uit de verzameling D.G. van Beuningen*, Rotterdam, Boymans Museum, 1949, no. 18; *Chefs d'œuvre de la collection D.G. van Beuningen*, Paris, Petit Palais, 1952, no. 58, fig. 12; *Kunst der Maasvallei*, Rotterdam, Boymans Museum, 1952, no. 258, fig. 49.

Literature: Waagen, *Galleries and cabinets of art in Great Britain*, IV, London 1857, p. 190; J.A. Crowe, G.B. Cavalcaselle, *The early Flemish painters*, London 1872, p. 348; Ch. Sterling, *La peinture Française. Les primitifs*, Paris 1938, p. 61, note 45 bis, fig. 62; "A little triptych sold for £ 4305: the Norfolk picture sale surprise", *The Illustrated London News*, 19 February 1938, p. 315; K.G. Boon, "Rotterdam", *Pantheon* XXIII (1939), pp. 142-143; J. van Waas (pseudonym of J. Borms), "Een vroeg-Nederlandsch drieluik", *Nieuwe Rotterdamsche Courant*, 6 January 1939; A. Kessen, in *De Maasgouw* 59, vol. 4, July-August 1939, pp. 44-46; G. Hulin de Loo, "Traces de Hubrecht van Eyck, empreintes contemporaines en Suisse et en Allemagne", *Jaarboek der Koninklijke Museums voor Schoone Kunsten van België* IV (1943-44), p. 22, fig. 16; A. Glavimans, "Notities bij de primitieven in het Mauritshuis", *Phoenix* I (1946), p. 47, figs. 46-49; S. Gudlaugsson, "Aanvullingen omtrent de Norfolk-triptiek", *Kunsthistorische mededeelingen van het Rijksbureau voor Kunsthistorische Documentatie* I (1946), pp. 17-22, figs. 1-3; Hannema, 1949, p. 23 and no. 18; M.J. Friedländer, "Bilder und Zeichnungen in der Sammlung Van Beuningen", *Phoenix* 4 (1949); exhib. cat. *Art Mosan et arts anciens du pays de Liège*, Liège 1951, p. 109; E. Panofsky, *Early Netherlandish painting. Its origins and character*, Cambridge Mass. 1953, pp. 92-94, 97, 128, 181, figs. 106, 107; J.Q. van Regteren Altena, "D. Hannema, Catalogue of the D.G. van Beuningen Collection", *Oud Holland* LXVIII (1953), p. 226, figs. 1, 3; L. van Puyvelde, *La peinture Flamande au siècle des Van Eyck*, Paris 1953, pp. 53-54, fig. p. 61; L. Ninane, "Un calvaire sur fond or de l'ancienne collection E. Renders peut-il être attribué à un maître italien de l'Ecole d'Avignon?", *Revue Belge d'Archeologie et d'Histoire de l'Art* 23 (1954), p. 61, note 1; J. Lejeune, *Les Van Eyck, peintres de Liège et de sa cathedrale*, Liège 1956, pp. 23-27, note 32, figs. 5-7; A. Châtelet, "Les étapes de l'enluminure des manuscrits dits de Turin et de Milan-Turin", *Revue des Arts* VI (1956), p. 204; cat. 1962, pp. 80, 81; E. Schiltz, *Les ecriteaux infamants de Jan van Eyck*, Antwerp 1963, p. 6 ff.; H. Schulte Nordholt, "Norfolk triptiek", *Openbaar Kunstbezit* 7 (1963), no. 9, fig.; G.J. Hoogewerff in H.E. van Gelder et al., *Kunstgeschiedenis der Nederlanden, II. De Middeleeuwen*, Zeist-Antwerp 1963, pp. 244, 256-259, figs. 5, 6; F. Winkler, "Die Vermählung der Hl. Katharina im Germanischen Nationalmuseum", *Anzeiger des Germanischen Nationalmuseum*, Nurenberg 1964, pp. 24-31, figs. 2, 3, 5, 7, 9; E. Schiltz, *Les Ecriteaux Infamants de Jan van Eyck*, III, Antwerp 1965, p. 5; E. Schiltz, *Ontdekking van een onbekend schilderij van Jan van Eyck*, Antwerp 1965, p. 2, fig.; M. Meiss, *French painting in the time of Jean de Berry*, London-New York 1967, p. 399, note 1; J.G. van Gelder, "An early work by Robert Campin", *Oud Holland* LXXXII (1967), p. 15; C.D. Cuttler, *Northern painting. From Pucelle to Bruegel*, New York 1968, pp. 70-71, fig. 85; E. de Jongh, "Speculaties over Jan Gossaerts Lucas-Madonna in Praag", *Bulletin Museum Boymans-van Beuningen* XIX (1968), p. 50, fig. 27; L. van Puyvelde, *La peinture Flamande des Van Eyck à Metsys*, Brussels 1968, p. 37, fig. 10; J. Lejeune, exhib. cat. *Liège et Bourgogne*, Musée de l'art Wallon, Liège 1968, p. 149, no. 156, pl. XXV; J.L. Ward, "A proposed reconstruction of an altarpiece by Rogier van der Weyden", *The Art Bulletin* LIII (1971), p. 32, note 21; L. Brand Philip, *The Ghent altarpiece and the art of Jan van Eyck*, Princeton 1971, pp. 80, 81, 91, figs. 76, 80; J. Stiennon, exhib. cat. *Rhein und Maas. Kunst und Kultur 800-1400*, Cologne, Schnütgen-Museum, Brussels, Koninklijke Musea voor Kunst en Geschiedenis, 1972, p. 31, fig.; B.G. Lane, "Depositio et elevatioe: The symbolism of the Seilern Triptych", *The Art Bulletin* LVII (1975), p. 29, fig. 12; Ch. Sterling, "Jan van Eyck avant 1432", *Revue de*

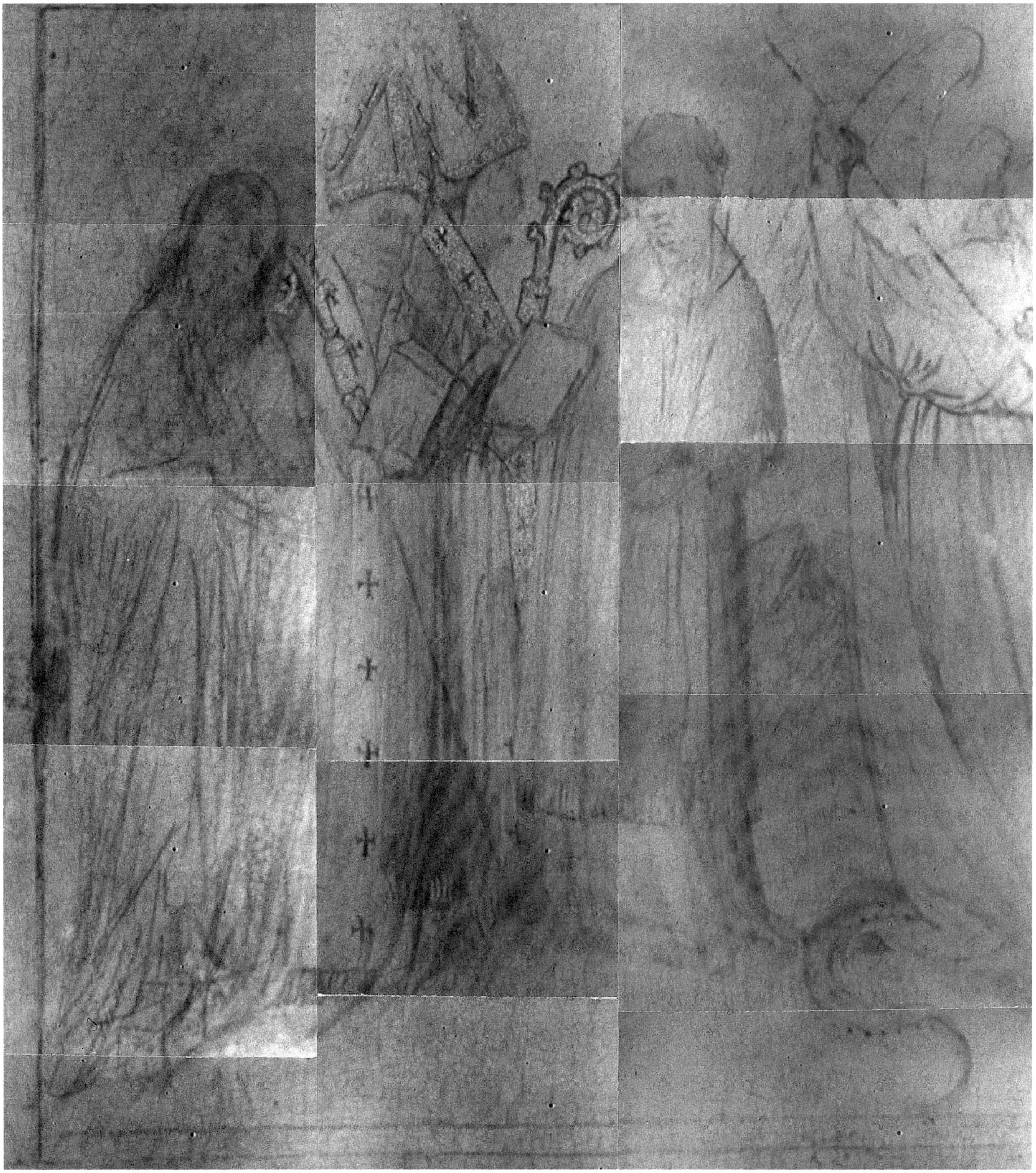

a. Infrared reflectogram assembly showing St James the Greater, St Dionysus, St Hubert, St Vincent and the archangel Michael on the outside of the right shutter.

D.G. van Beuningen parted with an exorbitant sum for this small triptych, one of the lesser known treasures of the Boymans-van Beuningen Museum. He bought the work from the Goudstikker Gallery, which had in turn purchased it at the Duke of Norfolk's sale. Since that time it has informally been known as the Norfolk Triptych.

The scene in the middle section of the centre panel is set in a church-like structure. Christ and the Virgin Mary are seated on the heavenly throne at the top; lower down is the *Imago Pietatis*, or Christ as the Man of Sorrows, depicted in the French manner showing the dead Christ rather than the resurrected Saviour.[4] Surrounding these figures are saints, with their names inscribed beneath them. Some of the inscriptions have been damaged, however, and a few have been lost completely, making it difficult to identify the figures. In the top gallery, their names clearly legible, are four of the twelve apostles: James the Less and St Peter on the left, and St Paul with St Andrew on the right. In the next row down are the saints Servatius and Lambert, whose names can also be read. The inscriptions under the two figures on the right are missing. One has been variously identified as St Martin,[5] St Medardus[6] and Martin of Tours.[7] The figure to his right might be St Hubert[8] or St Remaclus.[9] In the top section of the left panel is Lawrence with his gridiron; his counterpart on the right is St Stephen. In the gallery below them are five seated saints with inscriptions identifying them as Mary Magdalene, Dorothy, Agnes, Barbara and Catherine. The four portrayed in the corresponding position on the right panel are the saints Antony, Benedict, Leonard and Egidius. The figures in the lowest scene on the left are two of the four church fathers, Jerome and Gregory. The inscriptions under those in the corresponding frame on the right panel have been lost, but they must certainly be the other two church fathers, Augustine and Ambrose. Returning to the centre panel, above Christ and the Virgin are five figures painted in grisaille. J. van Waas describes them as the patriarchs, whereas Gudlaugsson identifies them, from left to right, as the prophets Elijah, Isaiah, Jeremiah, Ezekiel and Elishah.[10] Between the arches in the outermost scene of the centre panel are four grisaille angels with musical instruments. J. van Waas identifies the four figures in the same position on the outside shutters as patriarchs and prophets. However, in Gudlaugsson's opinion they represent the Greek patriarchs Basil, Gregory of Nazianz, Chrysostom and Athanasius. When the shutters are closed, the two upper scenes combine to form a representation of the Annunciation, with Mary on the left and the angel on the right. Beneath them, likewise covering the two panels, is the Adoration of the Magi. The Virgin and Child with Joseph and one of the kings can be seen in the stable on the left. The other two kings are painted on the right-hand panel. An interesting detail is that the star which has led the kings to the child is rendered on the painted frame above the stable. A kneeling knight can be seen on the far right, offering the child a model of a tower. This figure is discussed in more detail below. Five more figures are portrayed at lower left. They are the evangelists Matthew, Luke, Mark and John, together with John the Baptist. The evangelists' banderoles simply give their names; John the Baptist's proclaims in Latin, "Behold the Lamb of God". Finally, the five saints on the right panel are named as James the Greater, Dionysius, Hubert, Vincent and the archangel Michael, who is depicted slaying a dragon. The portrayal of so many saints on the triptych suggests that it may be a representation of all saints. The central images are Christ and the Virgin and Christ as the Man of Sorrows. Also shown are the apostles, the church fathers and the evangelists, as well as the Annunciation and the Adoration of the Magi. However, it is difficult to establish why the remaining figures were chosen.

The triptych was initially thought to have been made in Cologne, but later scholars suggested Maastricht or Liège. J. van Waas observes that many of the saints, including Servatius and Lambert, were especially popular in Liège. This is confirmed by Gudlaugsson, who adds that even more of the saints portrayed on the triptych had special ties with Liège. The datings proposed are ca. 1415, ca. 1420 and ca. 1419-1420.[11] Hence we may conclude that the altar was probably made in Liège around 1415-1420. Several attempts have also been made to identify the donor. He has been named as Jan van Beyeren, a bishop of Liège, and Johannes VIII of Heinsberg, who was bishop of the city from 1419 to 1455.[12] Returning to the knight with the model of a tower on the outside of the right-hand panel: the two figures on his right were initially thought to be a king and queen offering a chapel,[13] but the supposed queen is in fact

l'Art 33 (1976), pp. 24-25, 46, figs. 29, 30; J.H. Marrow, *Passion iconography in Northern European art of the late Middle Ages and Early Renaissance*, Courtrai 1979, p. 175, note 739, fig. 126; J.J.M. Timmers, *De kunst van het Maasland*, II, Assen, 1980, pp. 272-274, figs. 462, 463; J.K. Steppe, "De voorstelling van de heilige Benedictus in de beeldende kunst", *Benedictus, Pater Europae*, Antwerp 1980, p. 66, fig. 34; L.F. Jacobs, "The inverted T-shape in early Netherlandish altarpieces. Studies in the relation between painting and sculpture", *Zeitschrift für Kunstgeschichte* 54 (1991), p. 35, fig. 3.

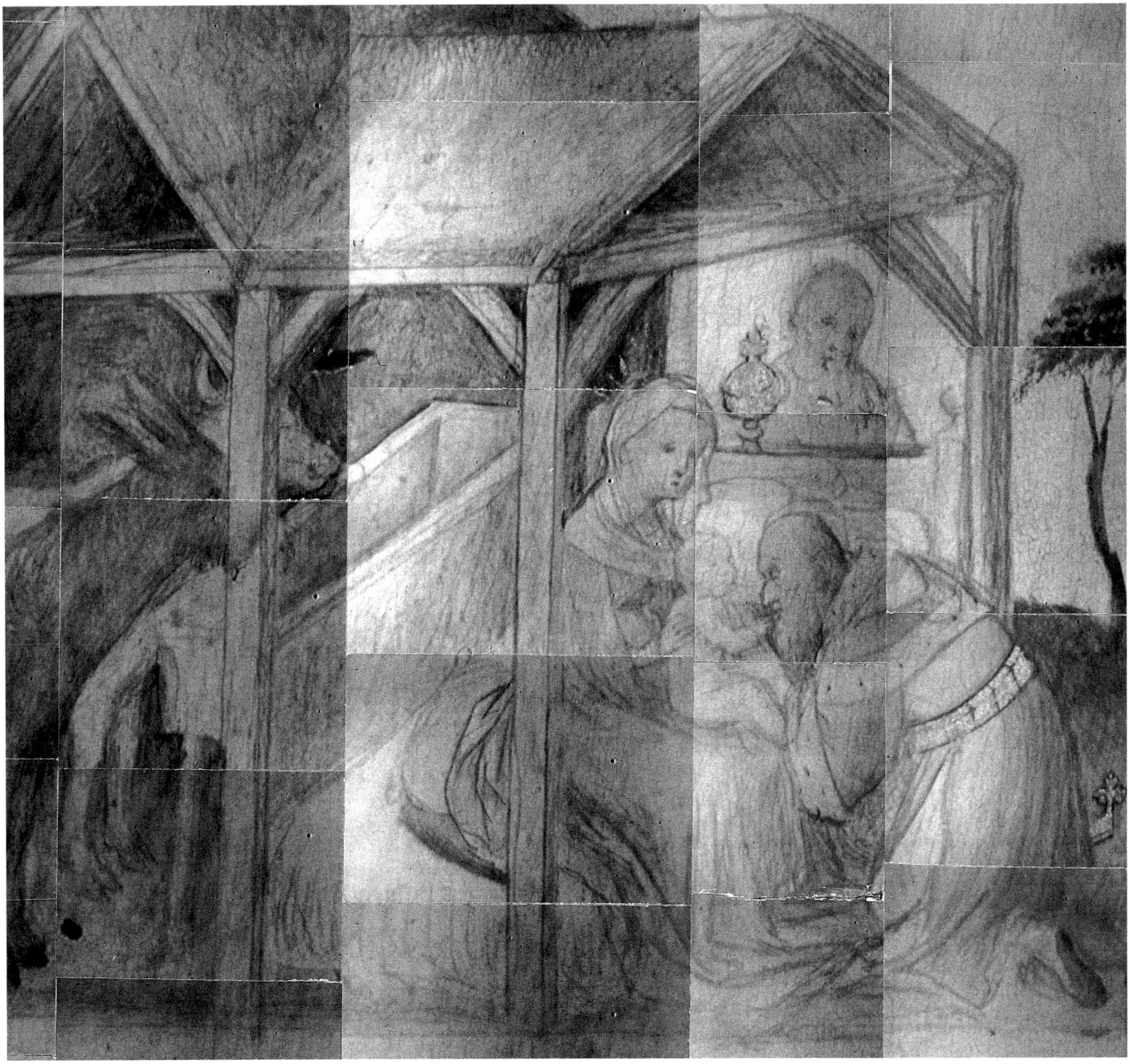

b. Infrared reflectogram assembly showing a detail of the Adoration of the Magi on the outside of the left shutter.

one of the magi. Gudlaugsson read the figure on the far right as a servant presenting the king's gift, which he described as a gold monstrance. However, the costume is decidedly not that of a servant. The 1938-1939 catalogue was probably correct in identifying the figure as a king offering a model of a chapel. In that case, it would probably represent the donor of the triptych. On the other hand, the fact that the figure appears not to be a clergyman argues against the theory that the donor was a bishop from Liège. A mark of some kind can be seen to the right of the figure, but it is unfortunately undecipherable. It may originally have been a letter, and was perhaps meant to identify the figure.

The letters at the end of the text on John's banderole have been read as "E.G." or "C.G.", while a third letter has also been interpreted as a "C". Though it has been suggested that they were part of the artist's signature, it is highly improbable that a triptych from this period would be signed.

Boon described the painting as a derivative of early works, such as those made by the Van Eycks in the Maas valley.[14] Yet given the outstanding quality of the triptych, this theory is highly improbable. Since it is dated no later than ca. 1415-1420, the piece should probably be seen as a culmination of the achievements of painting before the Van Eycks. The extraordinary delicacy and precision of the piece suggest that it may be the work of an artist who also made illuminated manuscripts.

The flaking paint was treated in a recent restoration and the triptych was subsequently cleaned. On close examination it transpired that part of the panel, mainly the section with Christ as the Man of Sorrows, had been replaced by a new piece of wood, but the reason for this is unknown. The restoration also revealed some of the miniature-like details in the almost invisible decoration of flowers on the gold background behind the saints. The overpainting on the frame on the inside of the piece was removed to expose the exquisite original colours underneath. Once the back was cleaned it was also possible to see where the hinges had originally been. The methods and techniques used to restore this triptych are described in Anne van Grevenstein's article elsewhere in this catalogue.
JG

1 The examination was conducted by Geraldine van Heemstra under the supervision of J.R.J. van Asperen de Boer. A copy of her minor thesis in the Museum's file on the painting. See also Anne van Grevenstein's article in this catalogue. Paint samples: A 302/1-11; infrared reflectograms: AB 1152/1-1155/10.
2 Examined by J.R.J. van Asperen de Boer.
3 Suggested by Boon (1939), p. 142.
4 According to E. Panofsky, "Imago Pietatis", *Festschrift für Max J. Friedländer zum 60. Geburtstage*, Leipzig 1927, p. 280.
5 Suggested by J. van Waas (1939), A. Kessen (1939) and S. Gudlaugsson (1946).
6 Suggested by G.J. Hoogewerff (1963).
7 Suggested by Lejeune (1956).
8 According to J. van Waas (1939) and A. Kessen (1939).
9 According to S. Gudlaugsson (1946).
10 Van Waas (1939), Gudlaugsson (1946).
11 Sterling (1938), Boon (1939) and Hoogewerff (1963) respectively.
12 Proposed by Hoogewerff (1963).
13 In exhib. cat. Rotterdam 1938-1939.
14 Boon (1939).

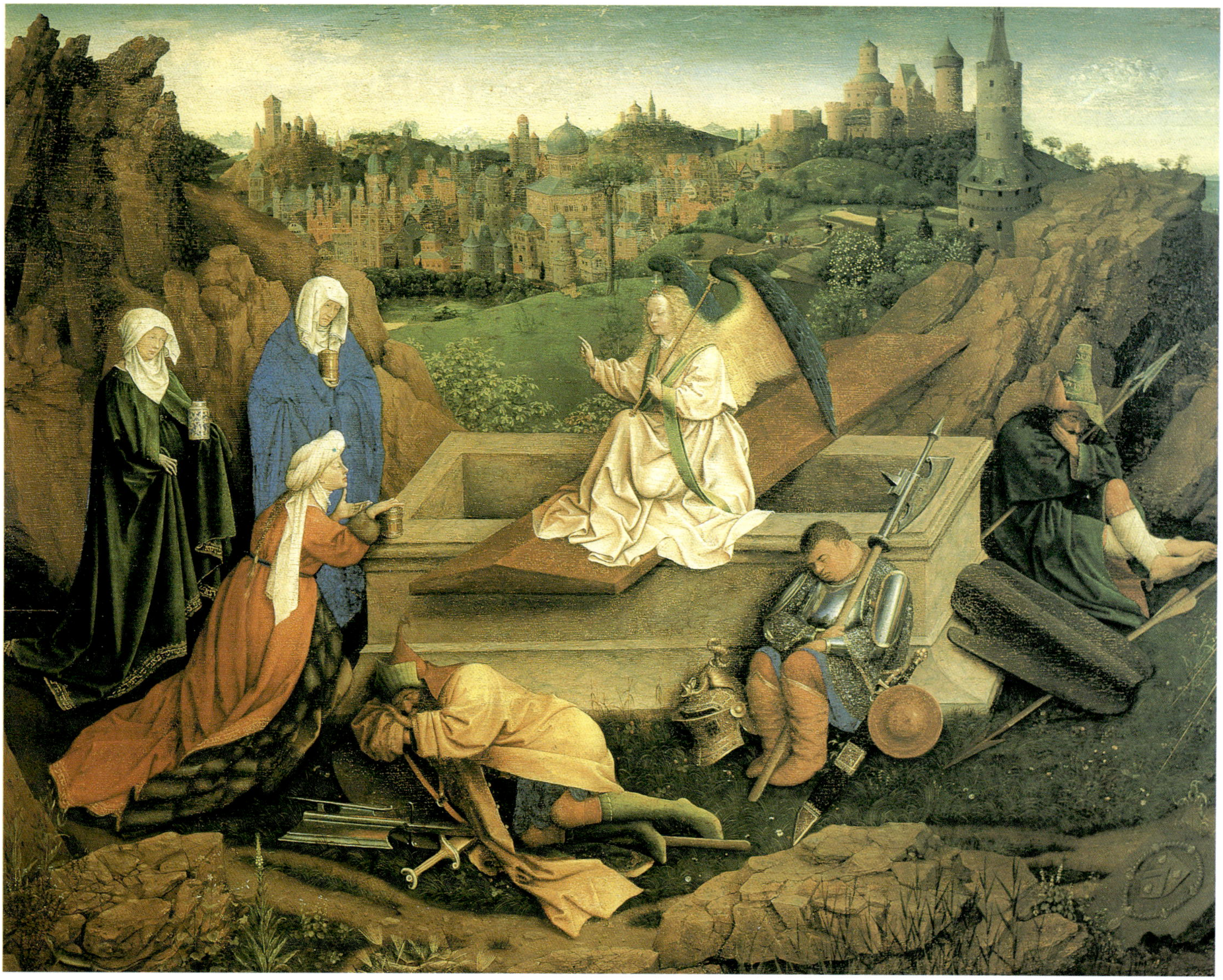

The three Maries at the tomb

Jan van Eyck (group)
(Maaseyck(?) c. 1390-Brugge 1441)

Panel; 71.5 x 90 cm

Physical characteristics:[1] the panel consists of three planks joined together horizontally with dowels. There is no *barbe* or unpainted edge.

Infrared reflectography: there is an extensive underdrawing. See entry.

Dendrochronology: the youngest heartwood growth ring dates from 1408. The panel could not have been painted before 1419; it was more probably painted in or after 1433. See article by P. Klein.

Provenance: Philippe de Commines (1447(?)-1511) is suggested by the insignia added to the painting later, although another aristocratic family is possible;[2] contrary to Weale, 1912 (reprint 1928), pp. 69, 251, the panel was not in the J. Winckelmann sale, Bruges, 4 May 1770, no. 68 ("Un grand tableau anticq, répésentant les trois mages, par Hemmelyck"); nor is there any evidence of B. Bauwens sale, Bruges, 8 August 1826, no. 90, also mentioned by Weale; discovered in 1871 by James Weale in a coach house in Belgium;[3] private collection in Antwerp;[4] collection of W. Middleton, Brussels; sale at Christie's, London, 26 January 1872, no. 140 (Johnson £335); Sir J.C. Robinson;[5] Sir Francis Cook, Doughty House, Richmond; Sir Frederick Cook; Sir Herbert Cook; bought by D.G. van Beuningen, Rotterdam and Vierhouten, on 30 April 1940 for £250,000; acquired by the Museum with the D.G. van Beuningen Collection, 1958; inv. no. 2449.

Exhibitions: *Exhibition of the Works of the Old Masters*, London, Royal Academy of Arts, Burlington House, 1873, no. 171; *Exhibition of Pictures by Masters of the Flemish and British Schools, including a selection from the works of Sir Peter Paul Rubens*, London, The New Gallery, 1899-1900, no. 9; *Exposition des Primitifs flamands et d'art ancien*, Bruges, 1902, no. 7; *Exhibition of a Selection of Works by the Early Flemish Painters*, London, Guildhall Gallery, 1906, no. 1, fig.; *A Catalogue of the Pictures and Drawings in the National Loan Exhibition*, London, 1909-1910, no. 75, fig.; *Exhibition of Flemish and Belgian Art 1300-1900*, London, Royal Academy of Arts, 1927, no. 7; *Nederlandsche Kunst van de XVde en XVIde eeuw*, The Hague, Mauritshuis, 1945, no. 50; *Honderd jaar Museum Boymans Rotterdam, Meesterwerken uit de verzameling D.G. van Beuningen*, Rotterdam, Boymans Museum, 1949, no. 11; *Bourgondische pracht van Philips de Stoute tot Philips de Schone*, Amsterdam, Rijksmuseum, 1951, no. 292; *Chefs-d'œuvre de la collection D.G. van Beuningen*, Paris, Petit Palais, 1952, no. 46, fig. 1.

Literature: J.A. Crowe, G.B. Cavalcaselle, *The Early Flemish Painters*, London 1872, p. 113; H. von Tschudi, "London. Die Ausstellung altniederländischer Gemälden im Burlington Fine Arts Club", *Repertorium für Kunstwissenschaft* 16 (1893), p. 101; L. Kaemmerer, *Hubert und Jan van Eyck*, Bielefeld-Leipzig 1898, pp. 50-52, fig. 34; O. Seeck, "Die charakteristischen Unterschiede der Brüder van Eyck", *Abhandlungen der königlichen Gesellschaft der Wissenschaften zu Göttingen* N.F.III, Berlin 1899, pp. 22, 68; K. Voll, *Die Werke des Jan van Eyck, eine kritische Studie*, Straatsburg 1900, pp. 103-106; M.J. Friedländer, "Die Leihausstellung der New Gallery in London, Jan-März 1900", *Repertorium für Kunstwissenschaft* XXIII (1900), p. 246; W.H. James Weale, "Hubert van Eyck", *Zeitschrift für bildende Kunst* N.F. XI (1900), p. 254, fig. p. 252; W.H. James Weale, "Hubert van Eyck", *Gazette des Beaux-Arts* XXV (1901), p. 475; G. Hulin de Loo, *Bruges 1902, Exposition de tableaux Flamands des XIVe, XVe et XVIe siècles, Catalogue Critique*, Ghent 1902, no. 7; W. Vogelsang, "Tentoonstelling van oud-Vlaamsche kunst te Brugge", *Bulletin Nederlandsche Oudheidkundige Bond* 3 (1901-02), pp. 296-297; M.J. Friedländer, "Die Brügger Leihausstellung von 1902", *Repertorium für Kunstwissenschaft*, XXVI (1903), p. 68; W. James Weale, "The Early Painters of the Netherlands as illustrated by the Bruges exhibition of 1902", *The Burlington Magazine* I (1903), p. 42, fig.; Le Comte Paul Durrieu, *Les débuts des Van Eyck*, Paris 1903, pp. 10-12; A. Marks, *Hubert and John van Eyck: The question of their collaboration considered*, London 1903, pp. 8, 10; W.H. James Weale, "Popular opinions concerning the Van Eycks", *The Burlington Magazine*, IV (1904), pp. 35-36; H. Fierens Gevaert, *Etudes sur l'Art Flamand. La Renaissance septentrionale et les premiers maîtres des Flandres*, Brussels 1905, pp. 115, 120, fig. opp. p. 136; Maurice W. Brockwell, *A Catalogue of the Paintings at Doughty House Richmond*, III, London 1915, no. 453, pl. VIII; K. Voll, *Die Altniederländische Malerei von Jan van Eyck bis Memling*, Leipzig 1923 (ed. princ. 1906), p. 48; W.H. James Weale, *Hubert and John van Eyck*, London-New York 1908, pp. 153-157, cat. no. 28, pp. 201-202, fig. opp. p. 152; E. Heidrich, *Alt-Niederländische Malerei*, Jena 1910, p. 14, fig. 11; L. van Puyvelde, *Schilderkunst en toneelvertooningen op het einde van de Middeleeuwen*, Ghent 1912, p. 162, fig. 38; G.J. Kern, "Perspektive und Bildarchitektur bei Jan van Eyck", *Repertorium für Kunstwissenschaft* 25 (1912), p. 48, fig. 16; W.H. James Weale, M.Brockwell, *The Van Eycks and their Art*, London 1928 (reprint of 1912 edition), pp. 69-74, cat. no. III, fig. X; M. Conway, *The Van Eycks and their Followers*, London 1921, pp. 59, 61-62; P. Durrieu, "Le temple de Jérusalem dans l'art français et flamand du XVe siècle", *Mélanges offerts à Gustave Schlumberger*, Paris 1924, II, p. 508; Friedländer, I, 1924, pp. 77-78, 167, fig. XXI; M. Dvorak, *Das Rätsel der Kunst der Brüder Van Eyck*, Munich 1925, pp. 120-124; F. Dülberg, "Niederländische Malerei der Spätgotik und Renaissance", *Handbuch der Kunstwissenschaft* 9 (1929), p. 14, fig. 11; M.W. Brockwell, *Abridged*

Catalogue of the Pictures at Doughty House Richmond, London 1932, p. 61, fig. XXI; K. Smits, *De iconografie van de Nederlandsche Primitieven*, Amsterdam 1933, p. 122, fig. 49; E. Renders, *Hubert van Eyck, personnage de légende*, Paris-Brussels 1933, pp. 100-101; H. Beenken, "Zur Entstehungsgeshichte des Genter Altars, Hubert und Jan von Eyck", *Wallraf-Richartz-Jahrbuch* II/III (1933-34), p. 198, fig. 174, 179; E. Renders, *Jean van Eyck, son œuvre, son style, son évolution et la légende d'un frère peintre*, Bruges 1935, p. 75, pl. V; E. Panofsky, "The Friedsam Annunciation and the problem of the Ghent Altarpiece", *Art Bulletin* XVII (1935), p. 437, note 7, fig. 2; G.J. Hoogewerff, *Vlaamsche Kunst en Italiaansche Renaissance*, Mechelen-Amsterdam, s.a. (1935), p. 25; J.A.B.M. de Jong, "Mag het paneel, voorstellend de "Drie Maria's aan het H. Graf" wel aan Van Eyck worden toegeschreven?", *Handelingen van het 3e Congres voor Algemeene Kunstgeschiedenis*, Ghent 1936, pp. 21-24; W. Schöne, "Ueber einige Altniederländische Bilder, vor allem in Spanien", *Jahrbuch der Preussischen Kunstsammlungen*, 58 (1937), p. 156; E. Panofsky, "Once more "The Friedsam Annunciation" and the Problem of the Ghent Altarpiece", *Art Bulletin*, 20 (1938-39), p. 419; Ch. de Tolnay, *Le Maître de Flémalle et les frères Van Eyck*, Brussels 1939, pp. 23, 74, fig. 29; A. Heppner, "Sir Herbert Cook's verzameling te Richmond", *Historia* 5 (1939), p. 310, fig. 1; H. Beenken, *Hubert und Jan van Eyck*, Munich 1941, pp. 14, 15, fig. 21, 22; H. Beenken, "Jan van Eyck und die Landschaft", *Pantheon* 28 (1941), p. 177, fig. p. 178; L. van Puyvelde, *Les Primitifs Flamands*, Paris-Brussels 1947, p. 18, fig. 6, 7; Th. Musper, *Untersuchungen zu Rogier van der Weyden und Jan van Eyck*, Stuttgart 1948, pp. 88-89, fig. 116; H. Gerson, "Overzicht van de Litteratuur betreffende Nederlandsche Kunst", *Oud Holland* 63 (1948), pp. 88-89, fig. 116; Hannema, 1949, no. 11; M.J. Friedländer, "Bilder und Zeichnungen in der Sammlung Van Beuningen", *Phoenix* 4 (1949), pp. 141-142, figs. 2-4; L. Baldass, "The Ghent Altarpiece of Hubert and Jan van Eyck", *The Art Quarterly* XIII (1950), pp. 187-189; E. Renders, *Jean van Eyck et le polyptique, deux problèmes résolus*, Brussels 1950, p. 68, figs. 17-18; L. Baldass, *Jan van Eyck*, Cologne 1952, pp. 22-23, figs. 1-6; E. Panofsky, *Early Netherlandish Painting, its origins and character*, Cambridge Mass. 1953, pp. 230-231, figs. 285-286; J.Q. van Regteren Altena, "Catalogue of the D.G. van Beuningen Collection", *Oud Holland* LXVIII(1953), p. 226; M.W. Brockwell, *The Van Eyck Problem*, London, 1954, pp. 54-58, fig. X, XVI; W. Schöne, "Die drei Marien am Grabe Christi, ein neugewonnenes Bild des Petrus Christus", *Zeitschrift für Kunstwissenschaft* 8 (1954), p. 136, fig. 4; J.S. Held, "Erwin Panofsky, Early Netherlandish Painting", *The Art Bulletin* 37 (1955), p. 222; J. Squilbeck, "Une œuvre énigmatique, "les Trois Marie au Tombeau" du Musée Boymans à Rotterdam", *La Revue Belge d'Archéologie et d'Histoire de l'Art* XXVIII (1959), pp. 3-27, fig.; F. Lyna, "L'œuvre présumée de Jean van Eyck et son influence sur la miniature flamande", *Scriptorium* 16 (1962), p. 94; F. van der Meer, "Hubert en Jan van Eyck, De vrouwen aan het Graf", *Openbaar Kunstbezit* 5 (1961), no. 19, fig.; cat. 1962, p. 49; E.K.J. Reznicek, *Quo vadimus? Splitsing of synthese bij het kunsthistorisch onderzoek*, public lecture, Utrecht, 1964, pp. 10-17; G.J. Hoogewerff, "De Schilderkunst in de Noordelijke Nederlanden tot omstreeks 1440", N. Beets, "De Nederlandse Schilderkunst van de vijftiende eeuw", in *Kunstgeschiedenis der Nederlanden*, II, Zeist-Antwerp 1963, p. 272, fig. 14, pp. 330-331; M.J. Friedländer, *Landscape, portrait, still-life, the origin and development*, New York 1963, pp. 26-27, 158-159, fig. 3, 24; A. Dohmann, *Die Altniederländische Malerei des fünfzehntes Jahrhunderts von Van Eyck bis Bosch*, Leipzig 1964, p. 25, fig. 29; L.J. Bol, *Jan van Eyck*, Utrecht 1965, pp. 8, 76, figs. pp. 44-45; K.S. Egorova, *Jan van Eyck*, Moscow 1965, figs. 14-17; M.J. Friedländer, *Die frühen niederländischen Maler von Van Eyck bis Bruegel*, Cologne 1965, p. 15, fig. 11; R. Genaille, *L'art flamand*, Paris 1965, p. 32; S. Thalheimer, *Der Genter Altar*, Munich 1967, p. 84; Friedländer, I, 1967, pp. 51-52, fig. 37a; J. Lejeune, Exhib. cat. *Liège et Bourgogne*, Liège, Musée de l'art Wallon, 1968, no. 158; J.L. Ward, "A new look at the Friedsam Annunciation", *The Art Bulletin*, L (1968), p. 185, fig. 4; R. Brignetti, G.T. Faggin, *L'opera completa dei Van Eyck*, Milan 1968, p. 87, no. 1, fig.; C.D. Cuttler, *Northern Painting from Pucelle to Bruegel*, New York e.a., 1968, p. 86, fig.; L. van Puyvelde, *La peinture flamande des Van Eyck à Metsys*, Brussels 1968, pp. 49-50, fig. 25-26; C. Peman y Pemartin, *Juan van Eyck y España*, Cadiz, 1969, p. 38, fig. 13; C. Versini, "Le Métier des Pays-Bas des Van Eyck à Rembrandt", *Les Cahiers de l'Academie Anquetin* 12 (1970), pp. 21-60, fig.; C. Krinsky, "Representations of the temple of Jerusalem before 1500", *Journal of the Warburg and Courtauld Institutes* XXXIII (1970), pp. 13-16, fig. 4b; Ch. Sterling, "Observations on Petrus Christus", *The Art Bulletin* 53 (1971), p. 24; L. Brand Philip, *The Ghent Altarpiece and the Art of Jan van Eyck*, Princeton 1971, p. 184, fig. 182; S. Urbach, *Frühniederländische Tafelbilder, Museum der Bildenden Künste*, Boedapest 1971, with no. 1; M.B. McNamee, "The Origin of the Vested Angel as a Eucharistic Symbol in Flemish Painting", *The Art Bulletin* 54 (1972), p. 268, fig. 13; K. Strauss, "Keramikgefässe, insbesondere Fayencegefässe auf Tafelbildern der deutschen und niederländischen Schule des 15. und 16. Jahrhunderts", *Keramikfreunde der Schweiz* 84 (1972), Table 41.7; J. Snyder, "The Chronology of Jan van Eyck's paintings", *Album Amicorum J.G. van Gelder*, 's-Gravenhage 1973, p. 296; O. Pächt, "René d'Anjou - Studien I", *Jahrbuch der Kunsthistorischen Sammlungen in Wien* 69 (1973), p. 92, note 16, pp. 94-95, figs. 92-93; C. Gould, *Failure & Succes, 150 years of the National Gallery 1824-1974*, London (1974), p. 11, fig.; Ch. Sterling, "Jan van Eyck avant 1432", *Revue de l'Art* 33 (1976), pp. 15, 29, 43, 46, 52-53, figs. 34, 76; J.R.J. van Asperen de Boer, "A Scientific Re-examination of the Ghent Altarpiece", *Oud Holland* 93 (1979), p. 208; H. Guratzsch, *Die grosse Zeit der niederländischen Malerei*, Freiburg-Basle-Vienna 1979, p. 35, fig. 4; A. Châtelet, *Van Eyck*, Bologna 1979, no. 1, fig.; A. Châtelet, "Un collaborateur de Van Eyck en Italie", *Relations artistiques entre les Pays-Bas et l'Italie à la Renaissance, études dédiées à Suzanne Sulzberger, Etudes d'Histoire de l'art publiées par l'institut historique belge de Rome* IV, 1980, p. 56, note 30; E. Dhanens, *Hubert en Jan van Eyck*, Antwerp 1980, pp. 355, 358, fig. 222; A. Tzeutschler Lurie, "A Newly Discovered Eyckian St John the Baptist in a Landscape", *The Bulletin of the Cleveland Museum of Art* LXVII (1981), p. 102, fig. 33; H. Belting, D. Eichenberger, *Jan van Eyck als Erzähler*, Worms 1983, p. 135, fig. 45; J.R.J. van Asperen de Boer, J. Giltaij, "Een nader onderzoek van de "Drie Maria's aan het H. Graf" - een schilderij uit de "Groep Van Eyck" in Rotterdam", *Oud Holland* 101 (1987), pp. 254-276; H. van Os, "Opstanding of Heilig Graf, enkele opmerkingen over de ikonografie van *De drie Maria's aan het Graf* uit de Groep van Eyck", *Oud Holland* 105 (1991), pp. 39-40; Francis Haskell, *History and its Images, Art and the Interpretation of the Past*, New Haven-London 1993, pp. 451-452, fig. 247.

Following Christ's entombment, Mary Magdalene, Mary the mother of James and Mary Salome bought herbs to preserve the body. When they came to the tomb, they saw that the stone had been moved back and an angel told them that Christ had awoken (Mark 16:1-8).

The painting shows the three Maries approaching from the left holding unguent jars. They are addressed by the angel seated on the empty tomb. The three guardians of the tomb, equipped with lances, helmets and shields, have fallen asleep.

In the foreground a variety of flowers and a lizard are depicted in extremely fine detail. A broad landscape, including rock formations, stretches away into the background. A small fox can be made out on the outcrop at the far right. The city of Jerusalem, with its Dome of the Rock, rises in the background.

The painting's provenance can only be traced back as far as 1871, when it was discovered in a coach house in Belgium. In 1872 Crowe and Cavalcaselle wrote that it had, a few years earlier, been in the possession of a gentleman in Antwerp.

The coat of arms in the lower right-hand corner has been identified as that of Philippe de Commines who may have had it added to the painting between 1469 and 1472. Since it was done in shades of brown and grey, it is not possible to ascertain to whom it belonged.

In the period immediately after 1872 the painting was attributed to Jan van Eyck. Since the beginning of the twentieth century, however, his brother Hubert has generally been regarded as a more likely candidate. A few authors, such as Marks and Panofsky, have also considered the possibility of a joint work by both artists, as in the case of the Ghent altarpiece. For various reasons, other experts, including Voll, Krinsky, Squilbeck and Dhanens, expressed doubts about this attribution and felt that the painting was from a later period.[6]

Following the restoration carried out by Joseph van der Veken in Brussels in 1947, another problem arose. On the right of the painting, a number of golden rays had become visible, giving rise to speculation that the work had originally had a different form. It could, for example, have been part of some sort of frieze or the centre panel of a triptych whose wings have been lost.

At the request of the present author, J.R.J. van Asperen de Boer conducted a scientific examination of the painting in 1979-80 which was published in 1987, together with a general critical analysis. What follows is only a very brief summary of this article, which illustrated X-radiographs, infrared reflectogram assemblies, paint cross-sections and stereo micrographs of specific details.

Dr P. Klein was asked to carry out a dendrochronological analysis of the panel. This showed that the tree from which the panel was made was probably felled no earlier than 1417 and that the painting could have begun in the middle of the 1430s.

Infrared reflectography revealed a comprehensive underdrawing. In keeping with Van Eyck's normal practice, very few differences were made in the final work. The underdrawing is closely related to that on the *Mystic Lamb* polyptych in Ghent. X-ray photographs showed that only minor changes were made during the painting process and that the underpainting, too, is similar to that in the *Mystic Lamb*.

The stereomicroscope enabled details to be seen which are scarcely visible to the naked eye, such as the horsemen and the small figures in the city square.

The paint cross-sections show that the paint was built up in two to four layers. Its structure and composition are fairly similar to those in the Ghent altarpiece. Although the quality of execution of different parts of the painting varies, negative conclusions should not be drawn concerning the work as a whole.

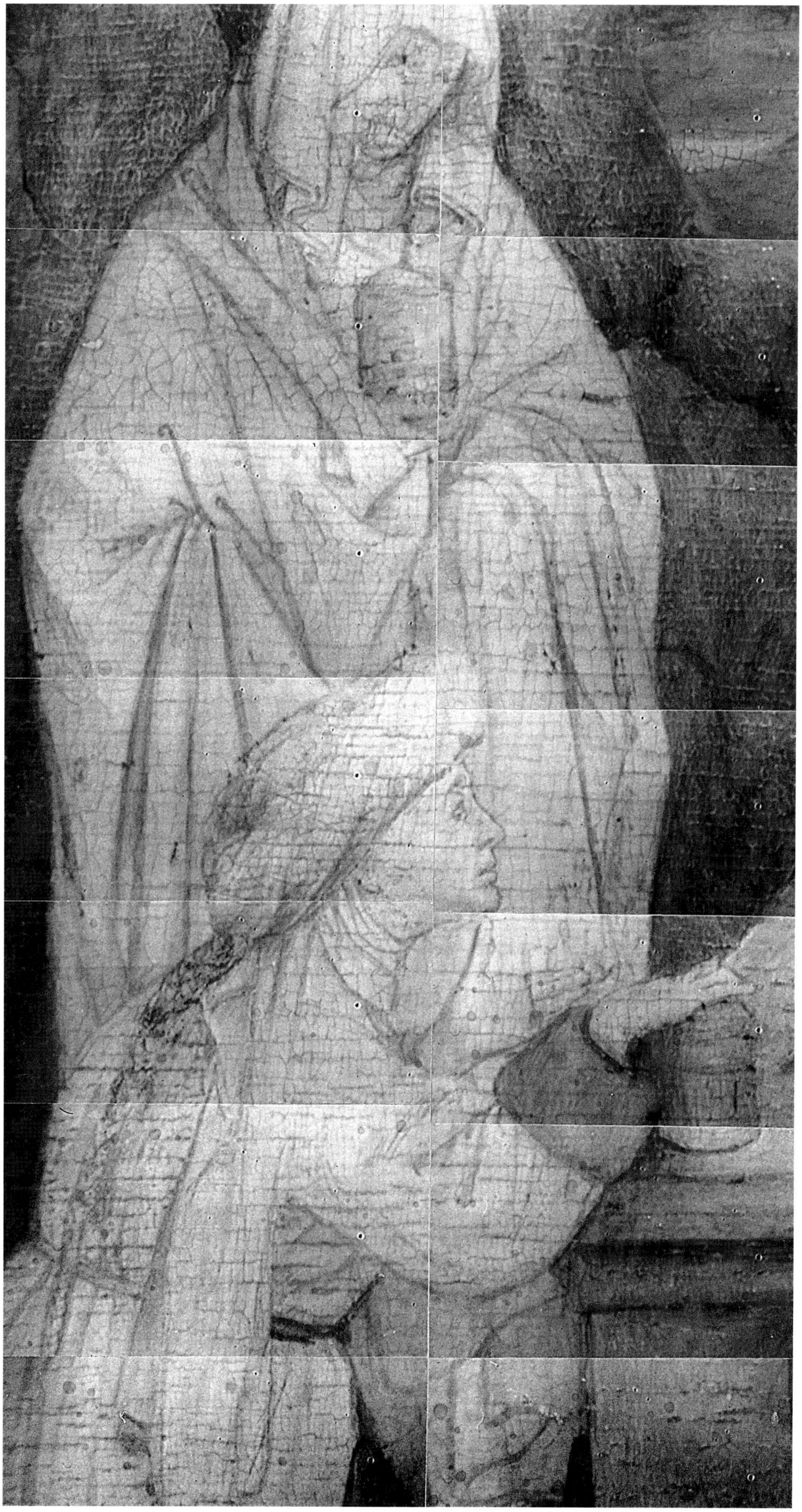

a. Infrared reflectogram assembly.
Detail of two Maries.

Analysis of the samples has also established that both the gilded rays on the right and the coat of arms were painted on layers of varnish, showing that they were later additions. This removes the need to reconstruct a hypothetical complete original version which included the gilded rays.

Other aspects of the painting were also studied, in addition to the technical examination described above. Most experts date the soldiers arms later than the period in which Van Eyck lived and worked, although there is some disagreement concerning specific parts of their equipment. It has also been suggested in the literature that the view of Jerusalem suggests that the painting was made later in the fifteenth century, since such an accurate rendering of the city is not known to have existed at an earlier date.

Apart from the Dome of the Rock, the building on the right behind the hill can perhaps be identified - as the Church of the Sepulchre - whilst the gate with the golden statue to the left of the Dome of the Rock could be the Golden Gate.

No sense can be made of the Hebrew letters on the hems of two of the Maries' cloaks and on the sleeping soldier's cap.

We can conclude that the painting is a relatively early work from the group Van Eyck which, on the basis of dendrochronological analysis, should be dated around 1425-35. Despite their differences, it is most closely related to parts of the Ghent altarpiece. The unusual craquelure on the surface of the Rotterdam painting has caused several authors to query the attribution to Van Eyck.
JG

1 Published in Van Asperen de Boer, Giltaij (1987). Paint samples A 161/1-17. Infrared reflectograms: AB 273-AB 278/12.
2 Letter from T.N. Schelhaas, Centraal Bureau voor Genealogie, 10 Decembre 1980.
3 Brockwell (1954), p. 54.
4 According to Crowe, Cavalcaselle (1872), p. 113.
5 According to James Weale (1908), p. 153.
6 Marks (1903); Panofsky (1953); Voll (1900); Krinsky (1970); Squilbeck (1959); Dhanens (1980).

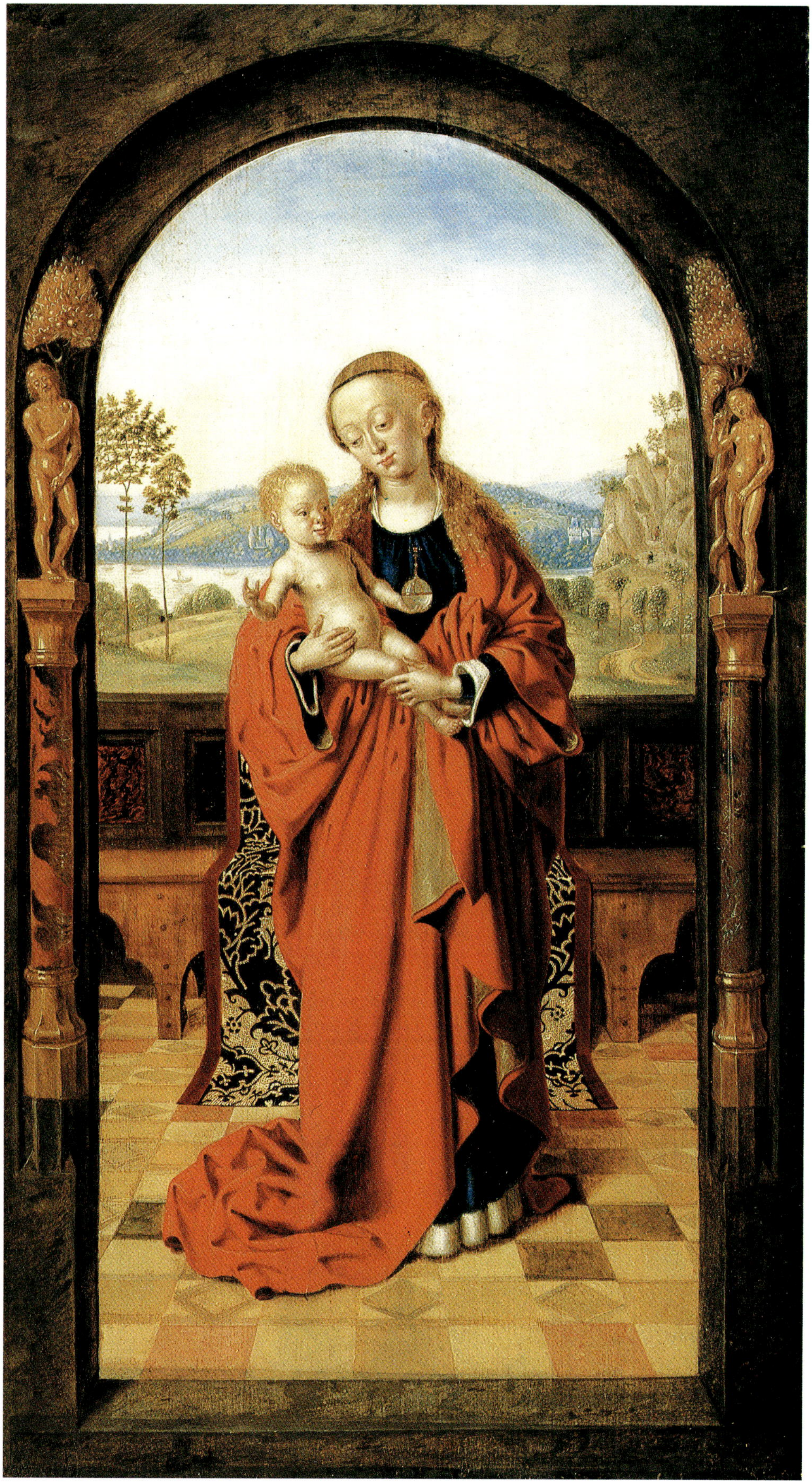

Virgin and Child in an Archway

Petrus Christus (group)
(? - Bruges 1475/76)

Panel; 56.6 x 31.6 cm

Physical characteristics: panel, thinned, transferred to a second panel and cradled.

Infrared reflectography: underdrawing only visible in the columns.

Dendrochronology: the youngest heartwood growth ring dates from 1419. The youngest sapwood growth ring dates from 1426. The panel could not have been painted before 1430; it was more probably painted in or after 1444. See article by P. Klein.

Paint samples: the pigments identified are natural ultramarine, azurite, vermillion, lead white and lead-tin yellow.

Provenance: vere probably the picture mentioned by Friedländer as sold in the Sellar auction, Paris 1892, no. 9, the Dollfus auction, Paris 1912, no. 80 and finally at an auction in Paris on 14 February 1914, no. 4.[1] In the 1967 edition its whereabouts were unknown. According to a letter from the 'Oberfinanzdirektion München' to (Count) George Stroganoff Sherbatoff dated 8 April 1968 the picture was returned to Amsterdam on 5 November 1946 (recovered after the war, when it had been destined for Hitler's museum at Linz) instead of a similar but larger picture (60.5 x 47 cm) from the Stroganoff Collection.
The Stroganoff picture is mentioned by Friedländer as the first replica of the painting in Budapest (fig. a, Szépmüvészeti Museum, inv.no. 4324).
When the picture was first examined by the present writer in 1976 several labels were pasted on to the back. These were removed and lost in a recent restoration. One of these bore the inscription: "Cirkers' Warehouses. Lot P5177. Piece M1." This is an American firm and the label testified to the picture's transport to the USA in 1966 where G. Stroganoff-Sherbatov was living at the time.
Two other labels showed that it had been in two exhibitions: "Kunstmuseum Basel Ausstellung 'Fals(ch)) oder Echt? Kat.nr. 38 Januar-Februar 1953" and "Gemeentelijke Musea van Amsterdam. Tentoonstelling Vals en Echt..."
It is unclear when and why the picture was dismissed as a fake. An extant label on the reverse from the Netherlands Office for Fine Arts (RBK) states: 'Christus, Petrus. Vervalsing Madonna met Kind. NK 1841. Inv. 1305.'
On the upper right-hand corner of the reverse of the painting the number '4995' is written in black ink. This is the number cited in the aforementioned letter from the 'Oberfinanzdirektion München' as "Mü Nr. 4995". It is likely that this was the number of the projected Linz museum, which suggests that our picture and not the Stroganoff painting arrived there; Netherlands Office for Fine Arts (RBK), The Hague (inv. 1305, NK 1841); on loan to the Kunsthistorisch Instituut der Rijksuniversiteit Utrecht, until 21 July 1966; on loan to the Boymans-van Beuningen Museum, Rotterdam, since 1994; inv. no. 3316.

Exhibitions: *Vals of Echt?*, Amsterdam, Stedelijk Museum, 1952, no.96; *Falsch oder Echt?*, Basel, Kunstmuseum, 1953, no. 38; *Kijken en verder kijken*, Groningen, Instituut voor Kunstgeschiedenis der Rijksuniversiteit, 1984.

Literature: Friedländer I, 1924, p. 151; Friedländer I, 1967, p. 85; *Rijksdienst Beeldende Kunst. Old Master Paintings. An illustrated summary Catalogue*, Zwolle-The Hague 1992, p. 67, no. 431.

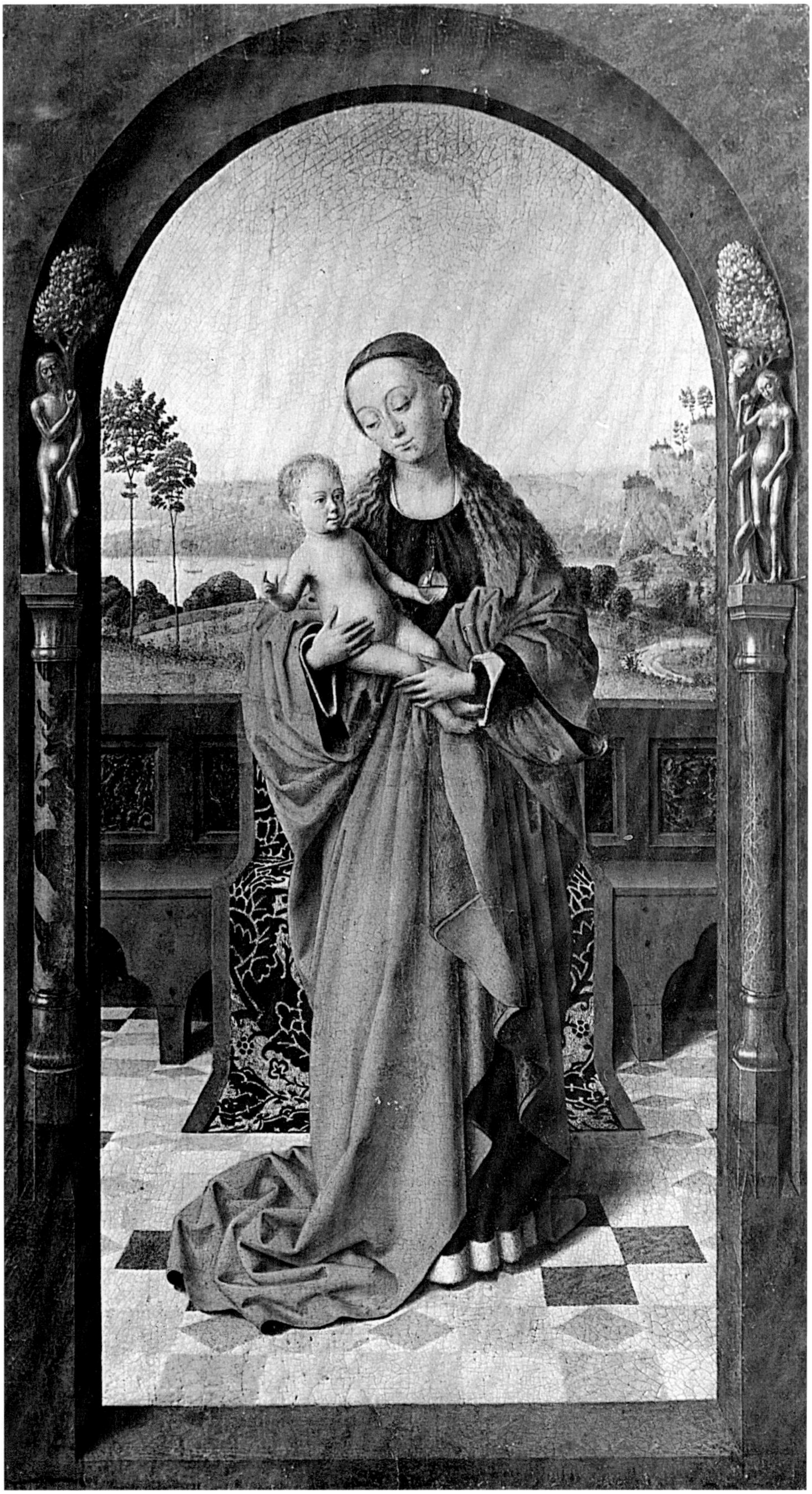

a. Petrus Christus, Virgin and Child in an archway
Panel; 55.8 x 31.6 cm
Budapest, Szépmüvészeti Museum

The painting was received by G. Stroganoff Scherbatoff from the Netherlands Office for Fine Arts, The Hague (Dienst voor 's Rijks Verspreide Kunstvoorwerpen) on 22 July 1966 as he had bought the panel (assuming it to be the one from his St Petersburg collection) together with two Lucas Cranach paintings (NK 1693 and NK 1694) from the Dutch State for 60,000 guilders. Dr H. Kühn of Munich examined the picture in 1967 at the request of Count Stroganoff who rightly believed that the work he had bought back as his own was a different painting. This must have been immediately obvious as the original Stroganoff version was larger (60.5 x 47 cm) and had two coats of arms, the right one with the "signature": I.P.C. A° 1441 (Invenit Petrus Christus?). As a result Stroganoff took legal action against the State of the Netherlands. A settlement was reached and the painting was returned to the Netherlands Office for Fine Arts, The Hague.

Kühn was able to examine the Budapest panel (fig. a) as well and could thus compare the two paintings in his unpublished report of 21 August 1967. Not only are the dimensions almost identical (Budapest: 55.8 x 31.6 cm) but the pigments identified in both paintings were found to be the same: natural ultramarine, azurite, vermilion, lead white and lead-tin yellow (I) – a pigment no longer used in the eighteenth century.

In 1976 the present writer independently examined the present picture – not believing it to be a fake – and could corroborate Kühn's findings. Paint cross-sections (not made by Kühn) moreover showed a two-layer structure on top of a greyish flesh-coloured intermediate layer (visible in x-radiographs as well) on the ground. This structure is somewhat simpler than in Eyckian paintings and quite compatible with works from the Petrus Christus group.

The panel was examined with infrared reflectography in 1976 and 1993; underdrawing was found only in the columns.

In February 1994 Dr P. Klein of Hamburg carried out a dendrochronological examination. He established a felling date of 1432..1434...1438, sapwood rings being present. The panel was probably used after 1444. The oak used for this panel is thus earlier than that in Budapest where Klein found a felling date of 1437..1439..1443+x suggesting the panel could have been used from 1449 on.

It is quite probable that the present picture was made in the Petrus Christus workshop. Petrus Christus is the first (and only) Flemish Primitive painter known from historical sources to have produced several versions of the same image.[2]
Dendrochronological dating and the painting technique support this hypothesis.
AdB

1 Friedländer, I, 1924, p. 151; Friedländer, I, 1967, p. 85.
2 P. Rolland, "La Madonne Italo-Byzantine de Frasnes-les-Buissenal", *Revue Belge d'Archéologie en d'Histoire de l'Art* XVII (1948), 97-106.

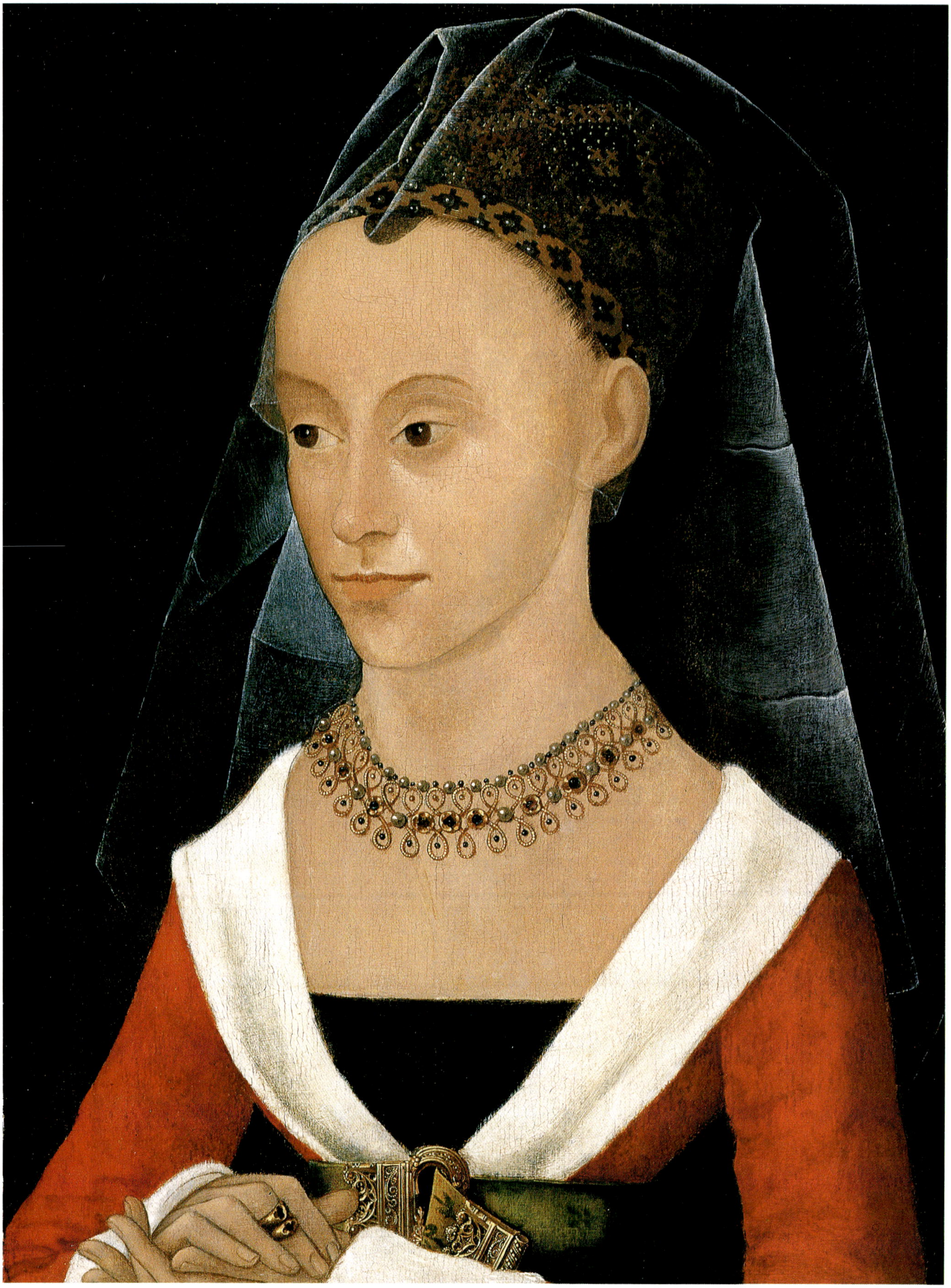

Portrait of a young woman

Rogier van der Weyden, follower of
(Tournai c. 1399-Brussels 1464)

Panel; 38 x 28.5 cm

The painting is an imitation of Rogier van der Weyden. A comparable example by the painter is the *Portrait of a woman* in the National Gallery in Washington, whose dimensions correspond quite closely to those of the painting in the Frederiks Collection. The posture, clothing and hands in the two works match and the two belts are virtually identical. The Rotterdam painting appears to have been inspired by the Washington piece and may date from the end of the fifteenth century. It was restored in 1976, when earlier additions were removed.[2] The woman's veil was initially longer, falling over her forehead and breast.

In the Washington catalogue, the Rotterdam painting is described as another version of a work which was in the collection of Lord Rothermere in London in 1938[3] and was auctioned with the Halifax collection in 1947.[4] The current whereabouts of this painting are unknown. However, comparison with a photograph of the work in *Pantheon* in 1938 prompts the question whether the painting in the Frederiks collection is not the work once owned by Rothermere and Halifax. The basis for the comparison is a photograph taken before the restoration of the Rotterdam piece (fig. a) and another showing the other painting in the magazine *Pantheon* of 1938 (fig. b). The only difference seems to be that in the present painting the upper lip is slightly thinner and the lower lip slightly thicker. This leads to the conclusion that the two photographs in fact show the same painting at different times, with minimal differences which could be the result of restorations carried out in the intervening period. In that case, the provenance of the painting in the Frederiks collection would be the Rothermere and Halifax collections.
JG

Physical characteristics: the panel consists of a single plank. The *barbe* can be seen on all sides. The painting is in poor condition and much of it has been overpainted.

Infrared reflectography: no underdrawing could be discerned.[1]

Provenance: J.W. Frederiks Collection, on loan to the Boymans-van Beuningen Museum since 1968; inv. no. S 29.

Not exhibited.

Literature: M. Wolff in J.O. Hand, M. Wolff, *The collections of the National Gallery of Art systematic catalogue, Early Netherlandish Painting,* Washington 1986, p. 245, note 16.

1 Scanned on 24 January 1994 by J.R.J. van Asperen de Boer.
2 Carried out by P.F.J.M. Hermesdorf.
3 Dénes Csánsky, "Ausstellung der Leihgaben aus der Sammlung Lord Rothermere", *Pantheon* 22 (1938), p. 395, fig. opposite p. 367.
4 Halifax, auction London, Christie's, 12 December 1947, no. 23.

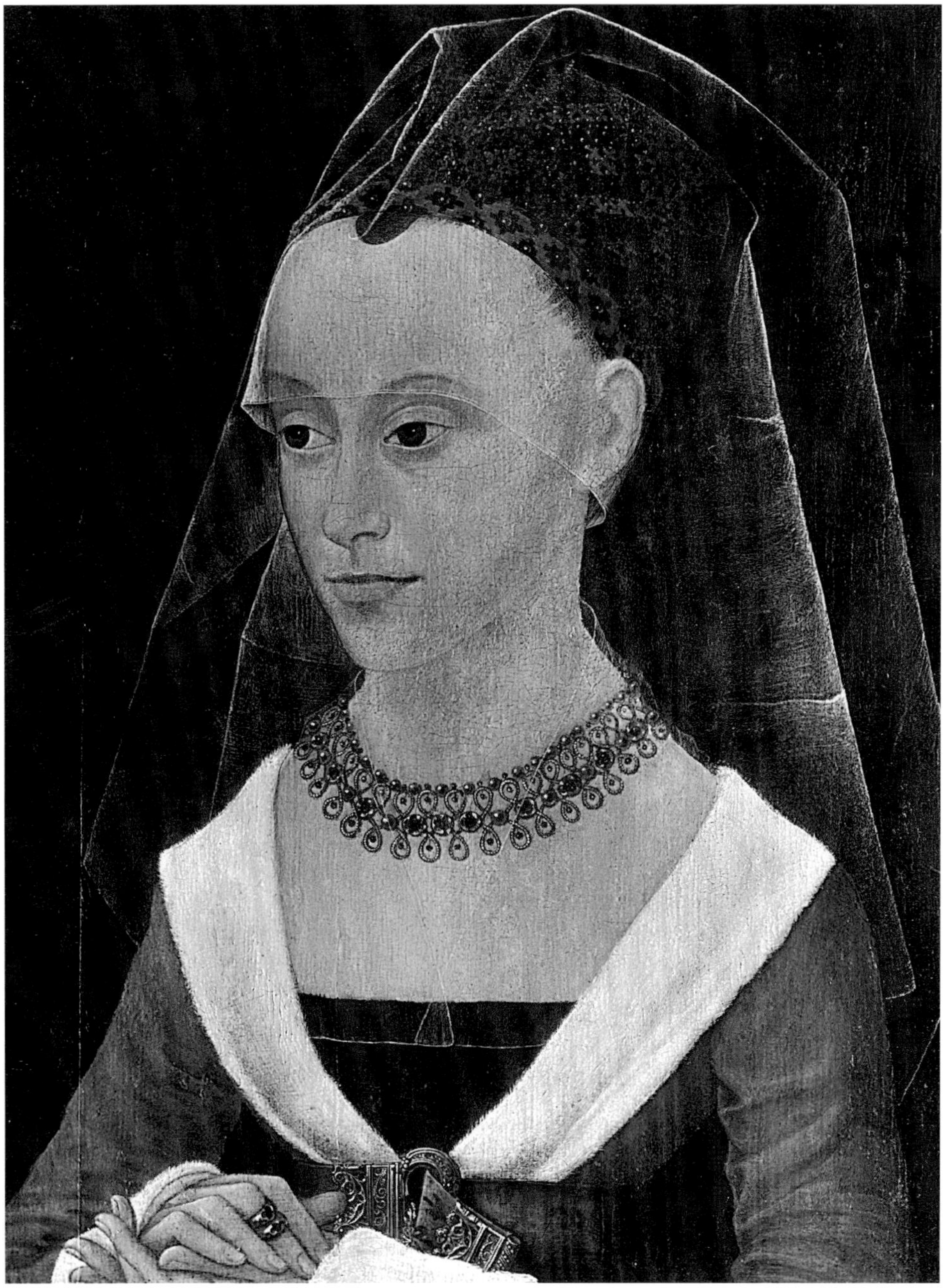

a. Follower of Rogier van der Weyden, Portrait of a young woman.
Condition before restoration.

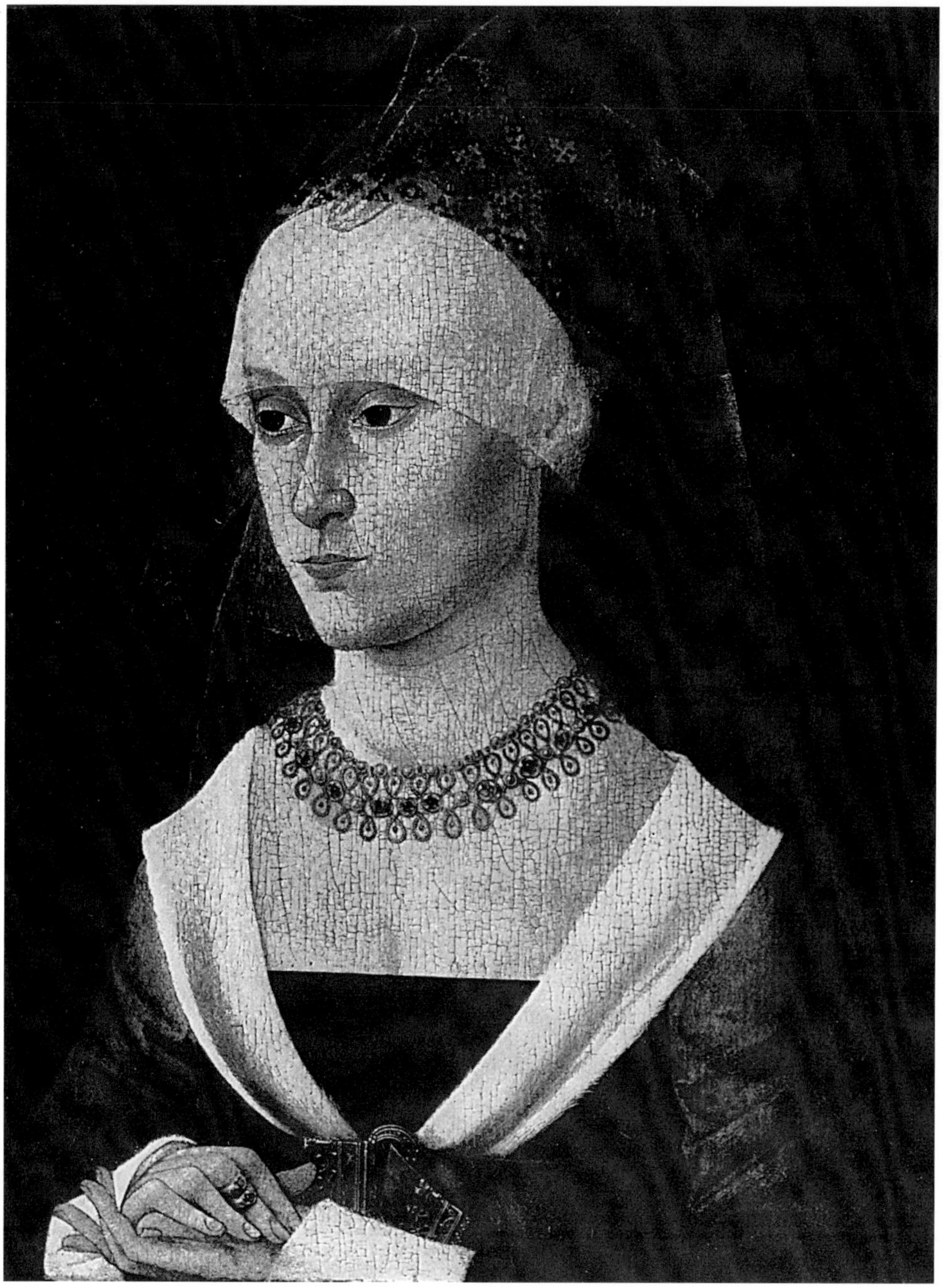

b. Follower of Rogier van der Weyden, Portrait of a young woman.
Photograph from the magazine *Pantheon* 1938.

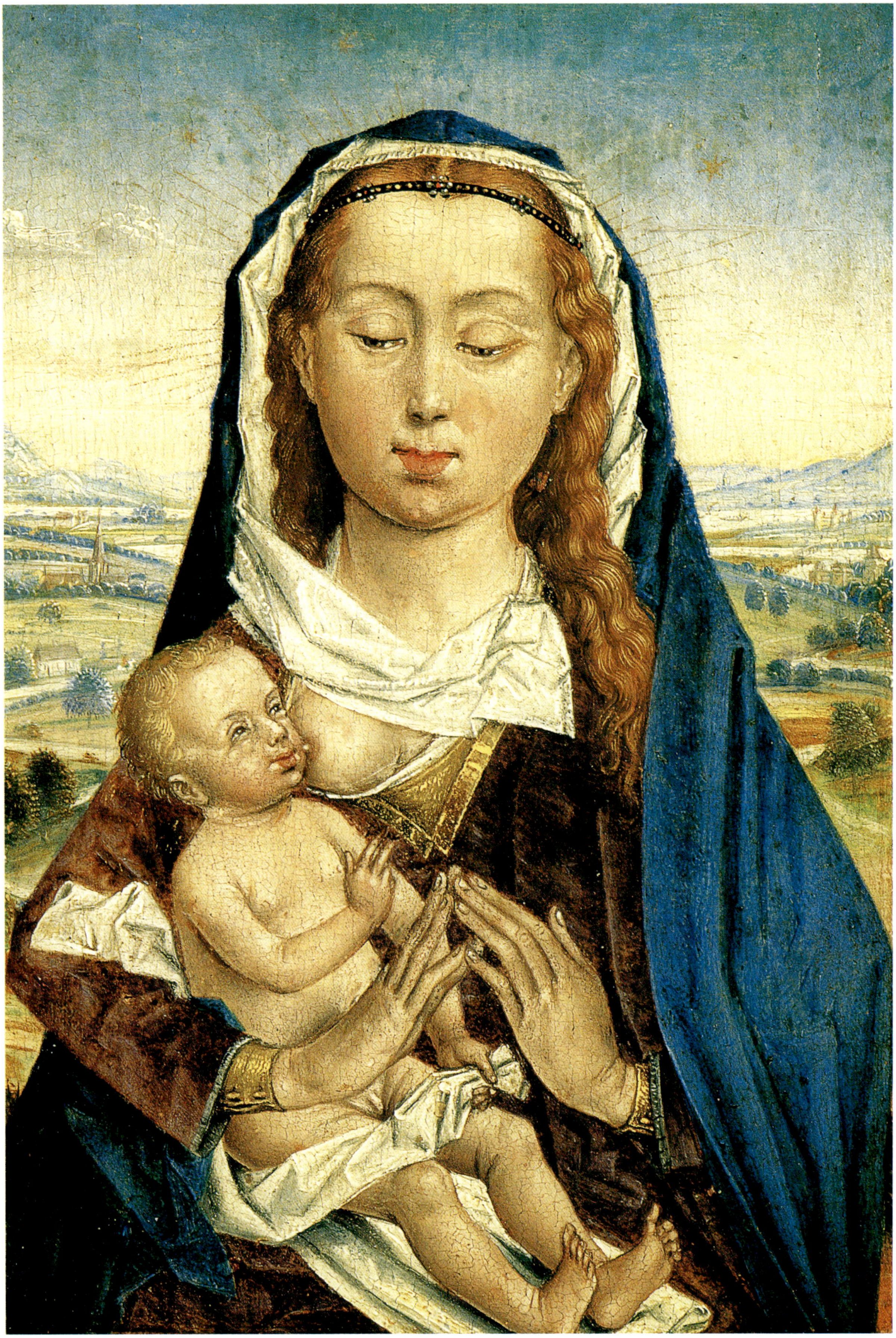

Virgin and Child in a landscape
Reverse: Still life with books, water jug and basin

5

Anonymous
South Netherlandish master, Brussels
c. 1470-80

Panel; 21 x 14 cm

Physical characteristics: the panel consists of a single plank.

Infrared reflectography:[1] no underdrawing could be discerned.

Provenance: bought by H. Vieweg[2] from Guggenheim, Venice, in 1885 on the advice of W. Bode; Goudstikker Gallery, Amsterdam; bought from the gallery in 1934 by D.G. van Beuningen, Rotterdam and Vierhouten, for 15,000 guilders; acquired by the Museum in 1958 with the Van Beuningen Collection; inv. no. 2469.

Exhibitions: *Catalogue des Nouvelles Acquisitions de la Collection Goudstikker*, Amsterdam, 1930 (no. 38), no. 31, fig.; *Wereldtentoonstelling van koloniën, zeevaart en oud-Vlaamsche kunst*, I, Antwerp, 1930, no. 28; *Het Stilleven*, Amsterdam, Goudstikker Gallery, 1933, no. 338, fig. on cover; *Catalogus van de tentoonstelling van 115 stillevens 1480-1933*, Rotterdam, Boymans Museum, 1933, no. 106, fig. I; *Nederlandsche Kunst van de XVde en XVIde eeuw*, The Hague, Mauritshuis, 1945, no. 9; *Honderd jaar Museum Boymans Rotterdam. Meesterwerken uit de verzameling D.G. van Beuningen*, Rotterdam, Boymans Museum, 1949, no. 35; *Chefs-d'œuvre de la collection D.G. van Beuningen*, Paris, Petit Palais, 1952, no. 48, pl. 14; *La Nature Morte de l'Antiquité à nos jours*, Paris, Orangerie des Tuileries, 1952, no. 7, pl. II; *Stilleben in Europa*, Münster, Westfälisches Landesmuseum, 1979-80, p. 480, fig. 246.

Literature: D., "Versteigerungen in März", *Kunst & Künstler* XXVIII, no. VI (1929-30), p. 263; O. von Falke, "Die Sammlung Vieweg", *Pantheon* V (1930), p. 78, fig.; W. Schöne, *Dieric Bouts und seine Schule*, Berlin-Leipzig 1938, p. 217, no. 152; Hannema, 1949, no. 35, figs. 26, 27; E. Panofsky, *Early Netherlandish Painting, its origin and character*, Cambridge Mass. 1953, p. 414, note 137, 6; I. Bergström, *Dutch Still-life Painting in the Seventeenth Century*, London 1956, p. 12, fig. 8; Ch. Sterling, *La Nature Morte de l'Antiquité à nos jours*, Paris 1959, p. 27, fig. 9; cat. 1962, p. 160; P.J.J. van Thiel, "Vlaamse school (omstreeks 1475)", *Openbaar Kunstbezit* 9 (1965), no. 9; Friedländer, III, 1968, Add. 121, pl. 89; E. Snoep-Reitsma, "De waterzuchtige vrouw van Gerard Dou en de betekenis van de lampetkan", *Album Amicorum J.G. van Gelder*, The Hague 1973, p. 287, fig. 4; G. de Werd, "Een handdoekrek door de Kalkarse beeldhouwer Arnt van Tricht (ca. 1540)", *Antiek* 16 (1981-82), p. 45, fig. 13; E. Greindl, *Les peintres Flamands de nature morte au XVIIe siècle*, Sterrebeek 1983, p. 6.

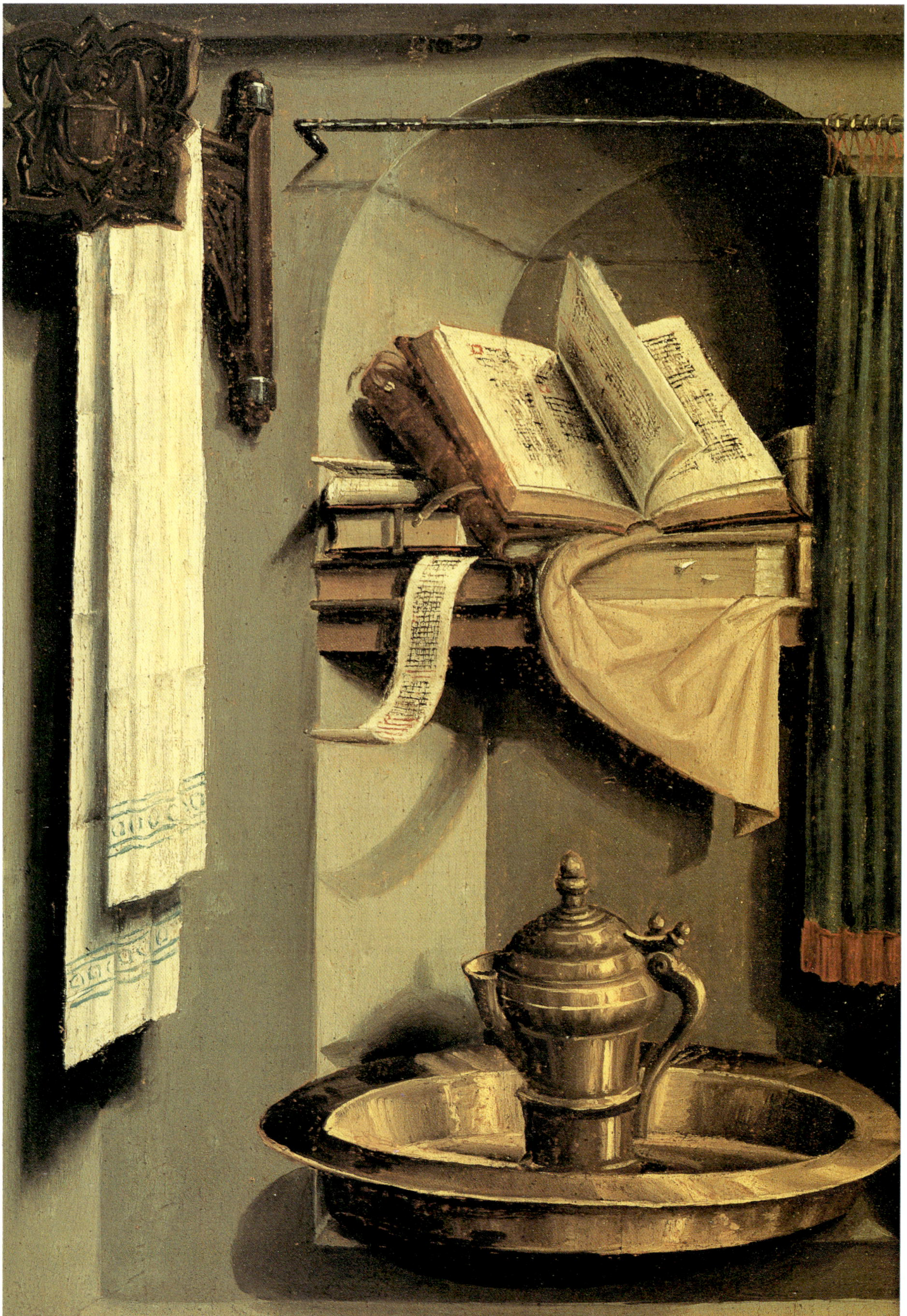

In the small painting of the Virgin and Child the infant's hand is raised in benediction. The Virgin's hands are folded in prayer and she offers the child the breast. The figures are shown against a wide background landscape.

The painting on the reverse is a still life of a niche containing a water jug and basin and, on a shelf, a pile of books with the top book lying open. An open curtain is suspended from a rail before the niche. A towel hangs on a rail affixed to the wall at the left.

The painting was published by F. Winkler in a comprehensive description in the 1930 Vieweg auction catalogue, in which he states that it was earlier listed in the *Verzeichnis der national wertvollen Kunstwerke* whose export was prohibited, and was wrongly attributed to Dieric Bouts. He also states that it was acquired from Guggenheim in Venice in 1885 on the advice of Bode.[3] He considers the painting from the circle of Bouts, formerly in the Pourtalès Collection, which Bode used as a comparison, to be more alike in appearance than in style.[4] He was more inclined to place it in the circle of Rogier van der Weyden. In his view, the painting can be traced back to the *Virgin and Child* in the Musée des Beaux-Arts in Caen, the left wing of a diptych whose right wing, *Portrait of Laurent Froimont*, is in the Koninklijke Musea voor Schone Kunsten, Brussels.[5] The author considers the still life, however, to be quite unique, and adds that Friedländer associated it with an artist such as the Master of the St Catherine Legend, whom he thought could be Pieter van der Weyden, son of Rogier. Finally, he states that this magnificently painted reverse is not from the same hand as the Virgin and Child.

Like the panels in Caen and Brussels, the Rotterdam panel was probably also part of a small diptych, and the missing right wing would likewise have been the portrait of a donor. As Winkler observes, the *Virgin and Child* is an early copy of the Caen painting, and the remarkable still life is a masterpiece. The objects are symbols relating to the Virgin on the other side. The books denote her piety, the white towel her purity, and the water jug and basin her virginity. A towel rail such as that in the painting can be seen in Xanten. It was made in 1523.[6]

Formerly attributed to Dieric Bouts, the panel is ascribed by Winkler to the immediate circle of Rogier van der Weyden as a work by "a Brussels Master, ca. 1470-1480". The Master of the St Catherine Legend to whom Friedländer refers (and so called by him in association with a panel depicting the legend in the Baron J. van der Elst Collection) worked in Brussels at the end of the fifteenth century. Problems attach to the attribution, however, because the *Virgin and Child* is a copy, while the still life can hardly be compared with the artist's known works. Some of the still-life elements in the *Last Supper* in the Bisschoppelijk Seminarie, Bruges, display a certain affinity with the Rotterdam panel.[7] For the moment, however, uncertain though it is, the attribution must be the Brussels School (circle of Rogier van der Weyden).
JG

1 Scanned by J.R.J. van Asperen de Boer on 10 January 1994.
2 See Vieweg auction catalogue (1930).
3 "Auf Empfehlung Bode's 1885 von Guggenheim in Venedig erworben. Bode, der das Bild dort zuerst gesehen und immer sehr hoch gestellt hat – weshalb es wohl auch in das 'Verzeichnis' aufgenommen wurde – hat sich in seinen Briefen an H. Vieweg wiederholt damit beschäftigt. So schreibt er u.a.: 'Hätten wir nicht für so und so viele Jahre noch Schulden und hätten nicht unsere Berliner Bankiers durch die russischen Papiere gar zu grosse Verluste gehabt, um in diesen Jahre ans Schenken denken zu können (obenein habe ich schon die meisten von ihnen, soweit sie sich für Kunst und fürs Museum interessieren, mit ziemlich grossen Summen gekränkt), so würde ich das Bildchen sofort für unsere Galerie genommen haben...ein sehr ähnliches Bild hatte Graf Pourtalès...einen Vorrang vor diesem hat das Guggenheim'sche durch seine bemalte Rückseite..." (15.5.1885). "Mir erscheint sie ein noch zweifelloserer Bouts als die etwas breitere und..., auch in braunerem Tone gehaltene Madonna bei Pourtalès. Ob sie wirklich von Bouts herrührt, würde ich hier am besten sagen..." (14.6.1885).
4 Friedländer, III, 1967, p. 66, nos. 30 and 31, plates 52 and 53.
5 Friedländer, II, 1967, p. 66, nos. 30 and 31, plates 52 and 53.
6 See De Werd (1981-82).
7 See exhib. cat., *Anonieme Vlaamse primitieven. Zuidnederlandse meesters met noodnamen van de 15de en het begin van de 16de eeuw*, Bruges, Groeninge Museum, 1969, pp. 87-95.

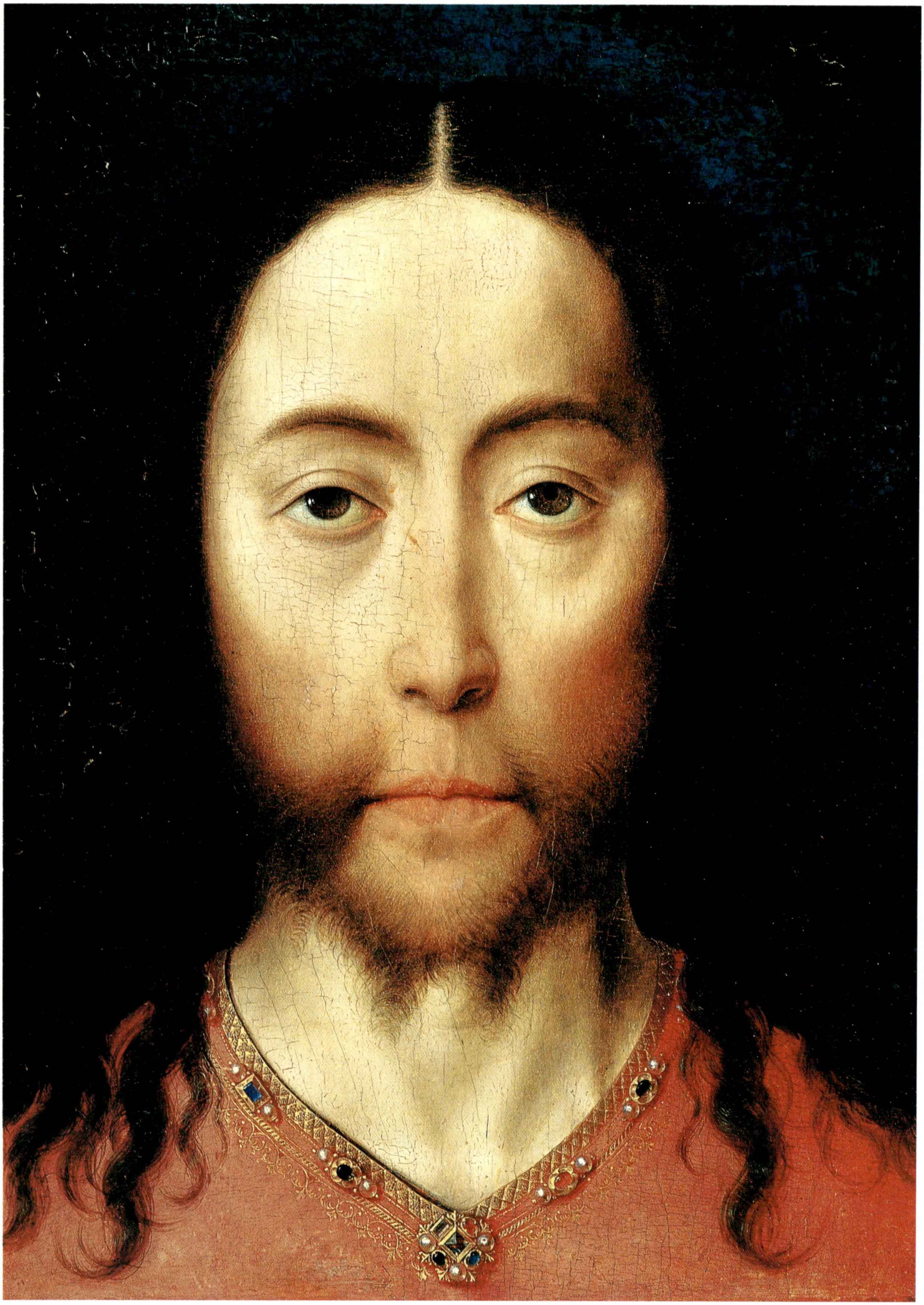

Head of Christ

6

Dirk Bouts
(Haarlem c. 1415/20-Leuven 1475)

Panel; 36 x 27 cm (painted surface: 33.5 x 24.5 cm)

Physical characteristics: the panel consists of a single plank. A strip of wood has been added on three sides of the original panel.

Infrared reflectography:[1] no underdrawing could be discerned.

Dendrochronology: the youngest heartwood growth ring dates from 1439. The panel could not have been painted before 1450; it was more probably painted in or after 1464. See article by P. Klein.

Paint samples: analysis has shown that lapis lazuli was applied to an underpainting of azurite. The background was painted over later; the overpainting contains the nineteenth-century pigments synthetic ultramarine and viridian.

Provenance: J. Goudstikker Gallery; acquired from the gallery by D.G. van Beuningen, Rotterdam and Vierhouten, in 1939 for £10,000; acquired with the D.G. van Beuningen Collection, 1958; inv. no. 2442.

Exhibitions: *Catalogus tentoonstelling van schilderijen, beeldhouwwerken en teekeningen uit particuliere verzamelingen in Nederland*, Rotterdam, Boymans Museum, 1939-40, no. 3, fig. X; *Les Primitifs Flamands*, Paris, Musée de l'Orangerie, 1947, no. 15, pl. XVII; *Honderd jaar Museum Boymans Rotterdam, Meesterwerken uit de verzameling D.G.van Beuningen*, Rotterdam, Boymans Museum, 1949, no. 8; *Bourgondische pracht*, Amsterdam, Rijksmuseum, 1951, no. 294; *Chefs-d'œuvre de la collection D.G.van Beuningen*, Paris, Petit Palais, 1952, no.42; *Dieric Bouts*, Brussels, Paleis voor Schone Kunsten, Delft, Prinsenhof Museum, 1957-58, no. 21, fig.; *Geert Grote en de Moderne Devotie*, Utrecht, Catharijneconvent, 1984, no. 113.

Literature: M.J. Friedländer, "De Kersttentoonstelling in Museum Boymans te Rotterdam", *Maandblad voor Beeldende Kunsten* 17 (1940), p. 37, fig.; Hannema, 1949, no. 8, fig. 23; J.Q. van Regteren Altena, "Catalogue of the D.G. van Beuningen Collection", *Oud Holland* LXVIII (1953), p. 229; F. Baudouin, "Kanttekeningen bij de catalogus van de Dieric Bouts-tentoonstelling", *Bulletin Koninklijke Musea voor Schone Kunsten*, Brussels, 7 (1958), p. 120, fig. 9; J. Bialostocki, exhib. cat. *Malarstwo Niderlandzkie w Zbiorach Polskich 1450-1550*, Warsaw, Muzeum Narodowe, 1960, p. 25, no. 9; cat. 1962, p. 30; R. van Schoute, *La Chapelle Royale de Grenade*, Brussels 1963, p. 55; J. Bialostocki, *Les Musées de Pologne (Gdansk, Krakow, Warszawa)*, Brussels 1966, p. 35; Friedländer, III, 1968, p. 76, Add. 119, pl. 74; J. Lafon, *Musée du Petit Palais, catalogue sommaire illustré des peintures*, Paris, 1981, at no. 102.

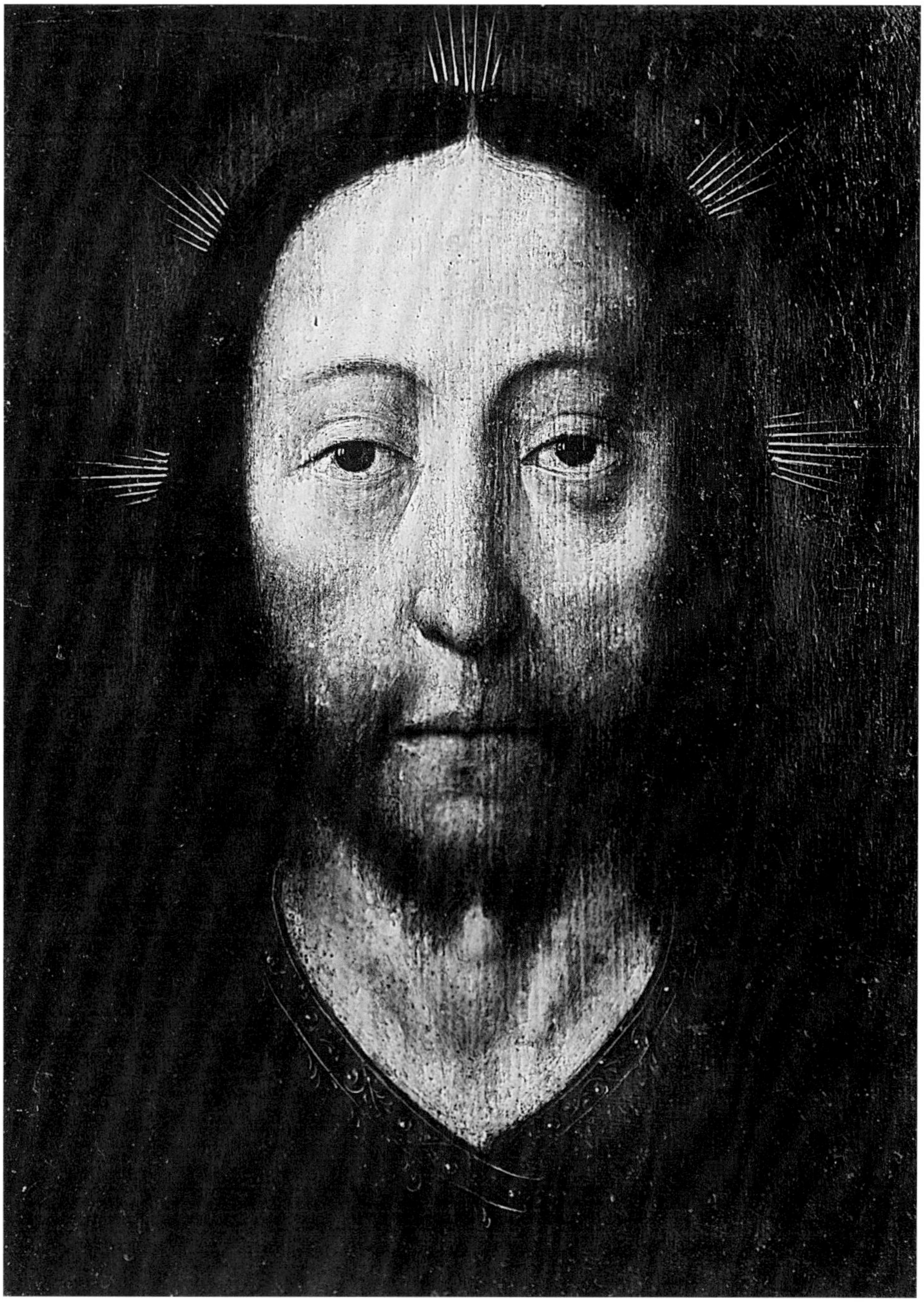

a. After Dirk Bouts, Head of Christ
Panel; 34 x 25 cm
Cracow, Czartoryski Museum

The portrayal of Christ's face dates back to the medieval legend about how Publius Lentulus described Jesus's appearance to the Roman emperor ("Vera Effigies"). This painting is a frontal view of the Saviour. The neckline of his garment is beautifully decorated with precious gems.

Very little is known of the painting's history. The earliest mention is a certificate by M.J. Friedländer dated 26 November 1937.[2] Schöne, whose book on Bouts was published in 1938, was not aware of this painting.[3] He describes the picture at the Czartoryski Museum in Cracow as the best preserved copy of a lost original, and refers to seven more copies. Friedländer published Van Beuningen's painting in 1940 as "the well-preserved original". Baudouin dated it in the same period – around 1450 – as *The resurrection of Christ* by Bouts in the Alte Pinokothek in Munich. Van Schoute believed the Rotterdam painting to be the original.[4]

The painting is in good condition and technically of high quality, as Frieländer observed, although most of the blue background has been painted over.

Schöne also mentions a painting which, in 1505, was in the possession of Jan van der Winckele, a notary in Leuven, and was described then as a head of Christ by Dieric Bouts.[5] Since the Rotterdam painting is now the only known original work of this subject by Bouts, it is tempting to conclude that it was once owned by Jan van der Winckele.
JG

1 Scanned by J.R.J. van Asperen de Boer on 20 December 1993. Paint samples: A 387/1-2.
2 The text reads: "Das umstehend photographierte Bild, dessen Komposition in der Bouts-Werkstätte mehrmals wiederholt worden ist, halte ich nach genauer Prüfung der ausserordentlichen Qualität für ein eigenhändiges Werk von Dieric Bouts – Max J.Friedländer, Berlin, d. 26.XI.1937."
3 W. Schöne, *Dieric Bouts und seine Schule*, Berlin-Leipzig, 1938, pp. 127-129.
4 Baudouin (1958); Van Schoute (1963).
5 W. Schöne, *op. cit.* (note 3), p. 156, no. 37.

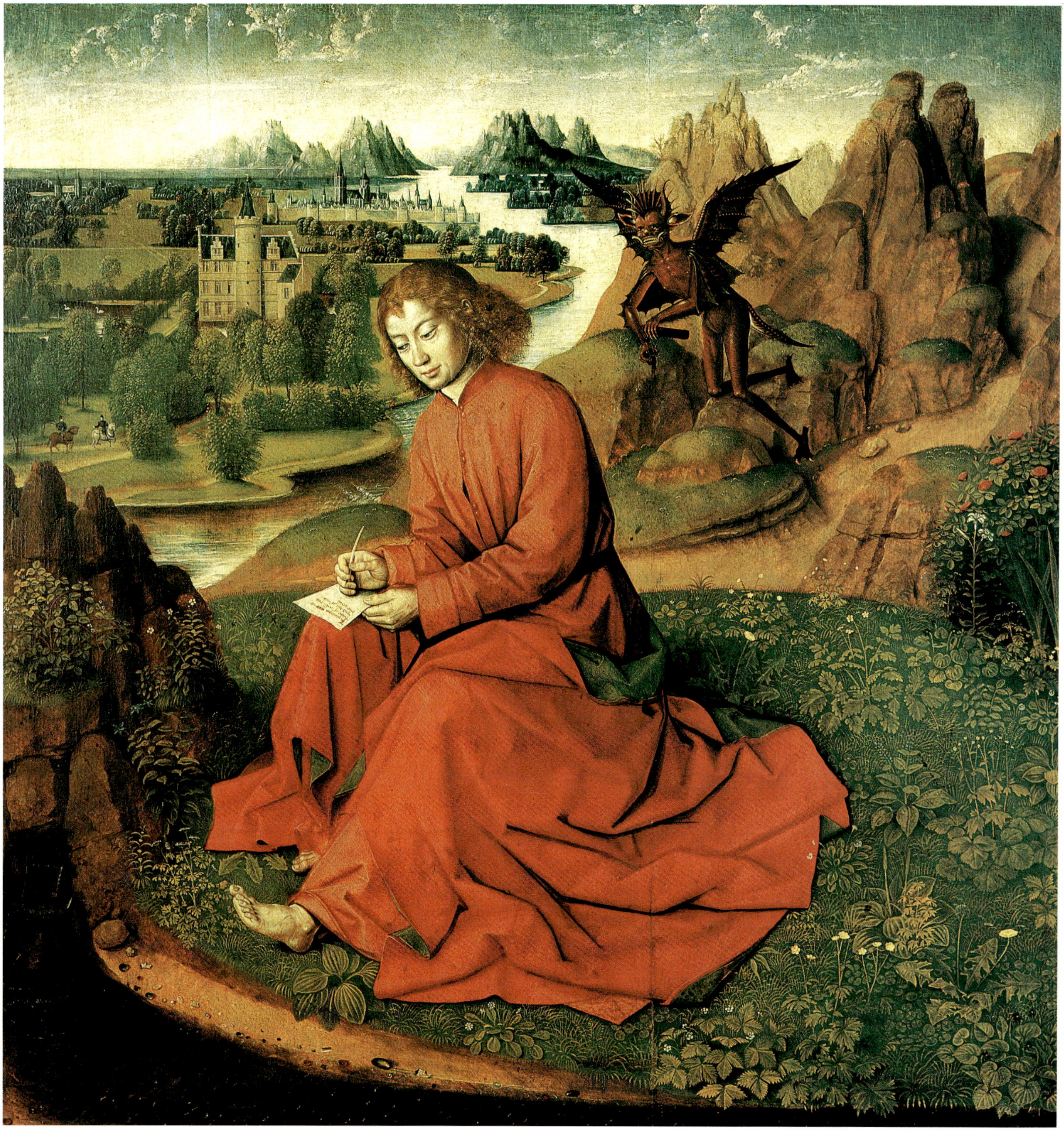

St John writing the Gospel
Reverse: St Agnes

Dirk Bouts, circle of
(Haarlem c. 1415/20-Louvain 1475)

Panel; 70 x 65 cm
Inscription on the front: In principio er..ve/rbum et verbu erat/ apud deu (?) et deus/ erat verbu.

Physical characteristics: the panel consists of three vertical planks. The original *barbe* is present on all sides.

Infrared reflectography:[1] no underdrawing could be discerned.

Dendrochronology: the youngest growth ring dates from 1440. The panel could not have been painted before 1451; it was more probably painted in or after 1465. See article by P. Klein.

Provenance: F.J.O. Boymans, auction Utrecht, 31 August 1811, no. 54; legacy F.J.O. Boymans, 1847; inv. no. 1083.

Exhibitions: *Nederlandsche kunst van de XVde en XVIde eeuw*, The Hague, Mauritshuis, 1945, no. 35; *De Jerome Bosch à Rembrandt*, Dijon, Musée de Dijon, 1950, no. 2; *Flemish Art 1300-1700*, London, Royal Academy of Arts, 1953-54, no. 35; *Dieric Bouts*, Brussels, Paleis voor Schone Kunsten, Delft, Prinsenhof Museum, 1957-58, no. 69, fig.

Literature: *Catalogus van schilderijen enz. in het museum te Rotterdam gesticht door mr. F.J.O. Boymans*, 1849, no. 157; L. Viardot, *Les Musées d'Angleterre, de Belgique, de Hollande et de Russie*, Paris 1852, p. 218; *Beschrijving der schilderijen enz. in het museum te Rotterdam gesticht door mr. F.J.O. Boymans*, 1859, no. 371; W. Burger, *Musées de la Hollande*, II, Paris 1860, pp. 327-330; *Beschrijving der schilderijen en beeldhouwwerken in het museum te Rotterdam gesticht door mr. F.J.O. Boymans*, 1880, no. 338; G. Lafenestre, E. Richtenberger, *La Hollande*, Paris 1898, p. 9; *Verslag omtrent den toestand en de aanwinsten van het Museum Boijmans over het jaar 1913*, p. 4; M.J. Friedländer, *Von Eyck bis Bruegel*, Berlin 1921, p. 186; F. Winkler, *Die Altniederländische Malerei*, Berlin 1924, p. 99; Friedländer, III, 1925, p. 106, no. 6, fig. XI; G. Hulin de Loo, "Sur la biographie de Dieric Bouts, avant 1457", *Mélanges offertes à Henri Pirenne*, I, 1926, pp. 257, 262; G. Glück, "M.J. Friedländer..", *Kunstchronik und Kunstliteratur* 60 (1926-27), p. 20 (Beilage *Zeitschrift für Bildende Kunst*); O. Pächt, "M.J. Friedländer, Dieric Bouts-Joost van Gent", *Kritische Berichte zur Kunstgeschichtlichen Literatur*, 1927, pp. 42-45, fig. 2; L. Baldass, "Die Entwicklung des Dirk Bouts", *Jahrbuch der Kunsthistorischen Sammlungen in Wien* NF VI (1932), pp. 112, 113; W. Schöne, *Dieric Bouts und seine Schule*, Berlin-Leipzig 1938, p. 50; M.J. Schretlen, *Dieric Bouts*, Amsterdam, no date (1946), p. 24, fig. p. 33; H. Gerson, "Overzicht van de Litteratuur betreffende Nederlandsche Kunst", *Oud Holland* 68 (1948), p. 139; L. van Puyvelde, "Les Primitifs Portugais et la peinture Flamande", *XVI Congrès International d'Histoire de l'Art*, Lisbon-Porto 1949, p. 33; L. van Puyvelde, *De Vlaamse Primitieven*, Brussels 1959, p. 65, fig. 67; cat. 1962, pp. 30, 31; J. Bruyn, "H. Adhémar, Le Musée National du Louvre...", *Oud Holland* 78 (1963), p. 154; A. Dohmann, *Die Altniederländische Malerei des fünfzehnten Jahrhunderts von Van Eyck bis Bosch*, Leipzig 1964, p. 65, fig. 161; Friedländer, III, 1968, p. 60, no. 6, figs. 12, 13, p. 87, note 30; L. van Puyvelde, *La Peinture Flamande de Van Eyck à Metsys*, Brussels 1968, fig. 93; J.G. van Gelder, "Der Teufel stiehlt das Tintenfass", *Kunsthistorischen Forschungen Otto Pächt zu ehren*, Salzburg 1972, pp. 173-188; A.P. de Mirimonde, "Le symbolisme du rocher et de la source chez Joos van Cleve, Dirk Bouts, Memling, Patenier, C. van den Broeck, Sustris et Paul Bril", *Jaarboek van het Koninklijk Museum voor Schone Kunsten Antwerpen* 1974, p. 81, fig. 5; D. de Vos, "Nieuwe toeschrijvingen aan de Meester van de Lucialegende, alias de Meester van de Rotterdamse Johannes op Patmos", *Oud Holland* 90 (1976), pp. 137-161, figs. 1, 2, 7, 8, 10, 12, 17, 19, 22; A. Châtelet, *Les primitifs Hollandais*, Freiburg 1980, p. 81, fig. 70, p. 214, no. 57; W.S. Gibson, *Mirror of the Earth*, New Jersey 1989, p. 7.

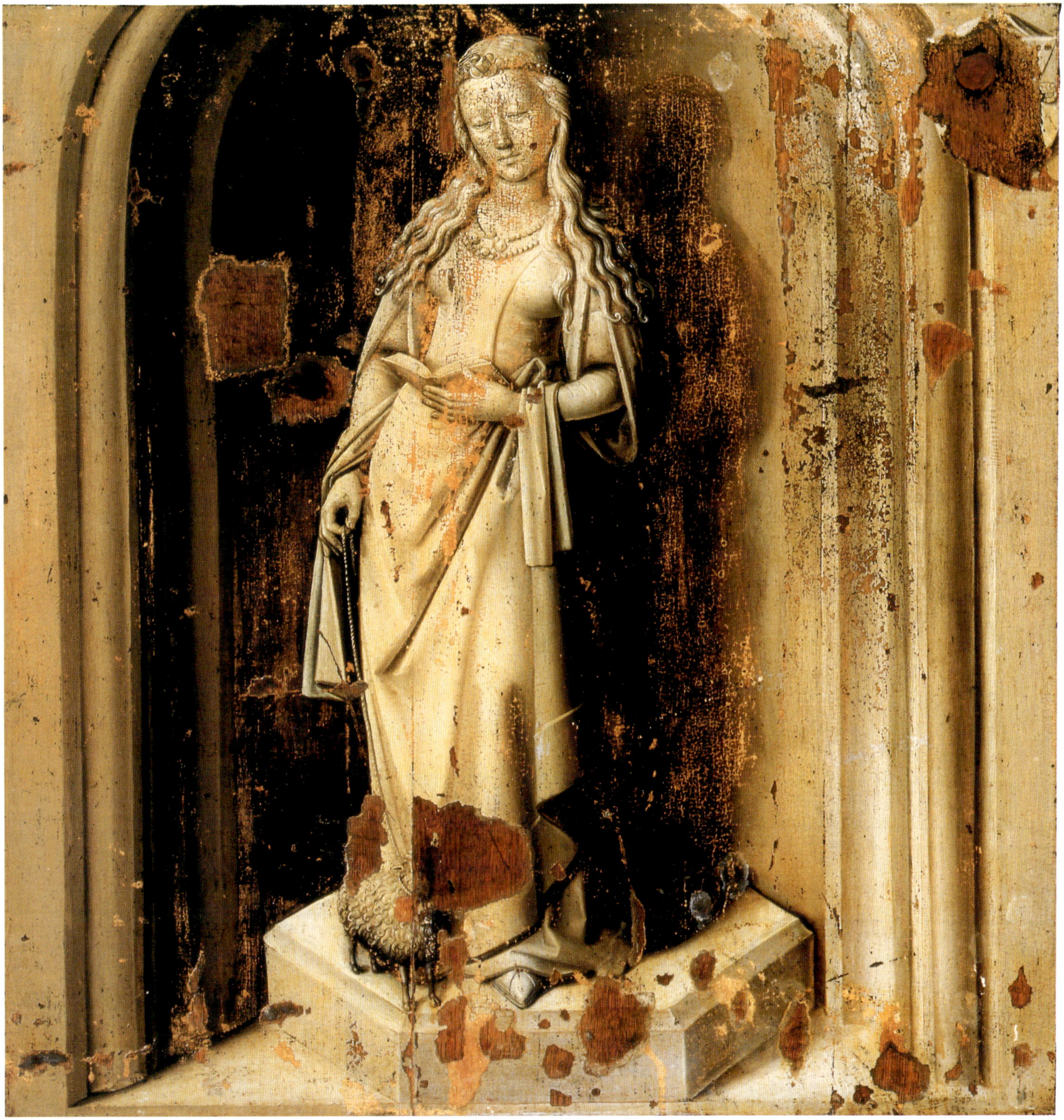

St John is seated in a rocky landscape, writing the Gospel. The first words, in Latin, can be read on the page in front of him: "In the beginning was the Word, and the Word was with God, and the Word was God". The foreground is beautifully elaborated with plants and shells, and a wide landscape with a castle stretches into the distance. An interesting detail is the devil behind St John. With a fiendish grin, he is emptying the evangelist's inkpot in order to prevent him from writing the Gospel. It is a motif also occurring in other works, as discussed in an article published by Van Gelder in 1972.

First attributed to Lucas van Leyden (1811 auction catalogue), the painting was listed by the Museum in 1849 as a work by Memling. Viardot ascribed it to an unknown Hemling or Memmelink of Munich, and in 1859 the artist was thought to be Rogier van der Weyden, whose dates were given as 1480-1529. Burger thought the person thus referred to must be a son of Rogier's, which he considered to be an extraordinary attribution. He himself thought the work to derive from the circle of Memling. In the 1880 catalogue it was listed, with a question mark, as a work by Dirk Bouts.[2]
It is undeniably reminiscent of Bouts. As Pächt observed in 1927, the rocks on the right are an exact replica of the lowest section of the right wing of the Bouts altarpiece in Sint Pieterskerk, Louvain, depicting Elijah in the wilderness. He also noted that the stretch of grass in the foreground appears to be based on the left wing of the altarpiece known as the Pearl of Brabant in the Alte Pinakothek, Munich. Schöne named the artist the Master of the Rotterdam St John in Patmos, and attributed various other works to him. He tentatively identified the painter as Jan Bouts, the eldest son of Dirk (active ca. 1498-1520). Châtelet calls the artist the Master of the taking of Christ, after the painting in the Alte Pinakothek, Munich.[3]

De Vos, on the other hand, ascribes the painting to the Master of the St Lucy Legend on the grounds of the following characteristics:[4] the even line of blue separating the landscape from the sky; the horizon bordering on this line, which sometimes seems to have been painted with the aid of a ruler; the structure of the landscape; the dandelion with one dead flower and one flower in bloom; the stippling on the flowers in the central section; and the ear showing through the saint's hair.

What is interesting, however, in our view, is the rigid, dry quality of the work of the Master of the St Lucy Legend. He was obviously an uncomplicated painter who emulated the masters, but had few capacities of his own. The Rotterdam panel, however, is notable for its superior qualities, its refinement and expressiveness, as in the detail of the devil, so that it is difficult to sustain its identification with the Master of the St Lucy Legend.

Given the fact that the rock formation is obviously copied from Dirk Bouts, the work must be provisionally attributed to his circle.

On the reverse is a grisaille representation of St Agnes and the lamb, which was discovered during a restoration in 1913. As the upper part of the arch in which she stands is missing, it was assumed that part of the top of the panel had been removed. But as the original edges are still intact, this cannot be so.
It was also thought at one time that the panel had formed the left wing of a diptych or polyptych. But according to Van Gelder, the grisaille on the reverse shows it to have been the right wing of a diptych, triptych or polyptych, presumably because the figure of St Agnes is turned to the left. The theory of an original polyptych is however by no means proven.

The largely indistinct coat of arms in the grisaille painting is thought by De Vos to be *in saltire*, corresponding to the coat of arms of the Bruges Van der Lende family. If his hypothesis is correct, the donatrix who would then have been portrayed on the reverse of the missing left wing would be Agnes van der Lende.

Despite these numerous attempts, the artist has not yet been identified. In view of the quality of the painting and of the similarities with Bouts, it must provisionally be assumed that he was a gifted follower of the master, which means dating the work to the last quarter of the fifteenth century.
JG

1 Scanned by J.R.J. van Asperen de Boer on 20 December 1993.
2 Viardot (1852); cat. 1859; Burger (1860); cat. 1880.
3 Schöne (1938); Châtelet (1980).
4 De Vos (1976).

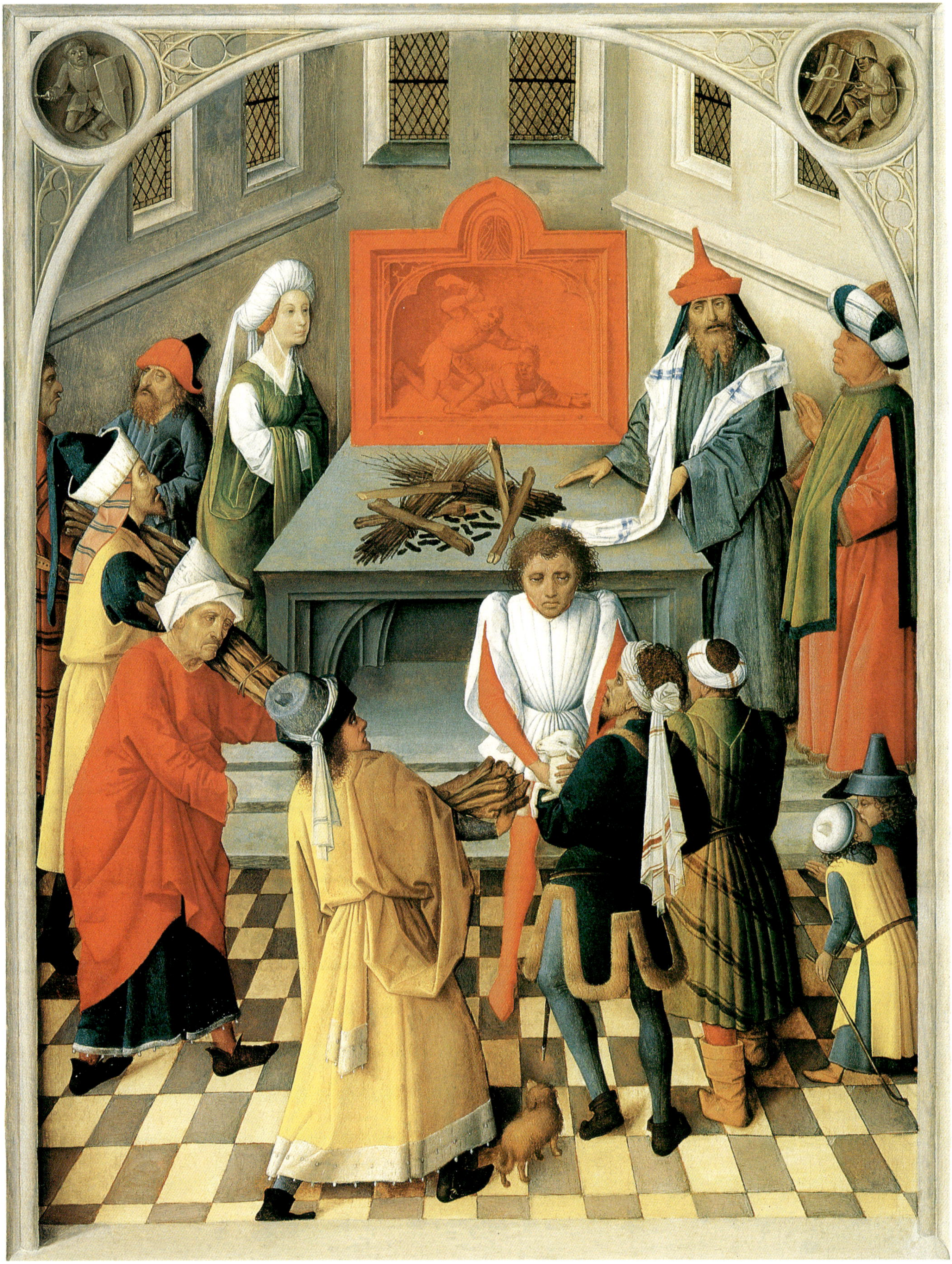

The offering of the Jews
Reverse: St Peter

Master of the gathering of the Manna
(active c. 1470)

Panel; 69 x 51 cm
Inscription on reverse: S PIETER (only the upper half of the letters are legible)

Physical characteristics:[1] the panel consists of two vertical planks. The *barbe* is present on all sides.

Infrared reflectography: underdrawing detectable only in the architecture and on the figure of St Peter on the reverse. There is no underdrawing for the figures on the front, although some indications of colour were found there; see text.

Dendrochronology: the youngest heartwood growth ring dates from 1436. Four sapwood growth rings were also found. The panel could not have been painted before 1447; it was more probably painted in or after 1461. See article by P. Klein.

Paint samples: the pigments lead white, vermilion, azurite and lapis lazuli were identified.

Provenance: Earl of Mount Edgcombe; Duits Gallery, London; Mr. N. Beets, Amsterdam; acquired with the support of the Erasmus Foundation and an interest-free loan from the Rembrandt Society, 1951; inv. no. 2349.

Exhibitions: *Middeleeuwse kunst der Noordelijke Nederlanden*, Amsterdam, Rijksmuseum, 1958, no. 9, fig. 21; *Le Maître de la Manne*, Douai, Musée de la Chartreuse, 1990, p. 13, fig. 11 en 14.

Literature: K.G. Boon, "Een Hollands altaar van omstreeks 1470", *Oud Holland* LXV (1950), pp. 207-215; E. Haverkamp Begemann, "Een Noord-Nederlandse primitief", *Bulletin Museum Boymans Rotterdam* II (1951), pp. 50-57, figs. 2-3; E. Haverkamp Begemann, "Een aanwinst bij een aanwinst", *Bulletin Museum Boymans Rotterdam* IV (1953), pp. 9-11; N. Beets, "De Nederlandse Schilderkunst van de vijftiende eeuw", in: *Kunstgeschiedenis der Nederlanden*, I, 1954, p. 256, fig. 11; J.E. Snyder, "The early Haarlem school of painting", *The Art Bulletin* XLII (1960), pp. 48-49, fig. 10; cat. 1962, p. 85; M. Kahr, "Titian's old testament circle", *Journal of the Warburg and Courtauld Institutes* 29 (1966), p. 197, fig. 44d; Friedländer, III, 1968, p. 77, add. 129, figs. 54-55; L. Brand Philip, *The Ghent Altarpiece and the Art of Jan van Eyck*, Princeton 1971, p. 102, fig. 110; Robert G. Calkins, "Parallels between Incunabula and Manuscripts from the Circle of the Master of Catherine of Cleves", *Oud Holland* 92 (1978), p. 147, fig. 12; M.L. Wurfbain, "De Meester van de Manna-Inzameling: Broeder Tymanus?", *Boymans bijdragen*, Rotterdam 1978, pp. 24-35, figs. 1-2; Ruth Mellinkhof, "Cain and the Jews", *Journal of Jewish Art* 6 (1979), p. 38, fig. 34; A. Châtelet, *Les Primitifs hollandais*, Fribourg 1980, p. 87, no. 63C, fig. 76; Colin T. Eisler, "A Nativity signed PETRUS XPI ME FECIT 1452", *Liber Amicorum Herman Liebaers*, Brussels 1984, p. 461; Françoise Baligand, "La Crucifixion par le Maître de la Manne", *La Revue du Louvre* 38 (1988), p. 340, fig. 1, 2; M. Grams-Thieme, *Lebendige Steine, Studien zur niederländischen Grisaillemalerei des 15. und frühen 16.Jahrhunderts*, Cologne-Vienna 1988, p. 435, fig. 65; J.R.J. van Asperen de Boer, François Baligand, J. Giltaij and Luuk Pijl, "The enigmatic underdrawing of the Master of the Gathering of the Manna", *Les dessin sous-jacent dans la peinture, Colloque VIII*, Louvain-la-Neuve 1991, pp. 103-107, fig. 52.

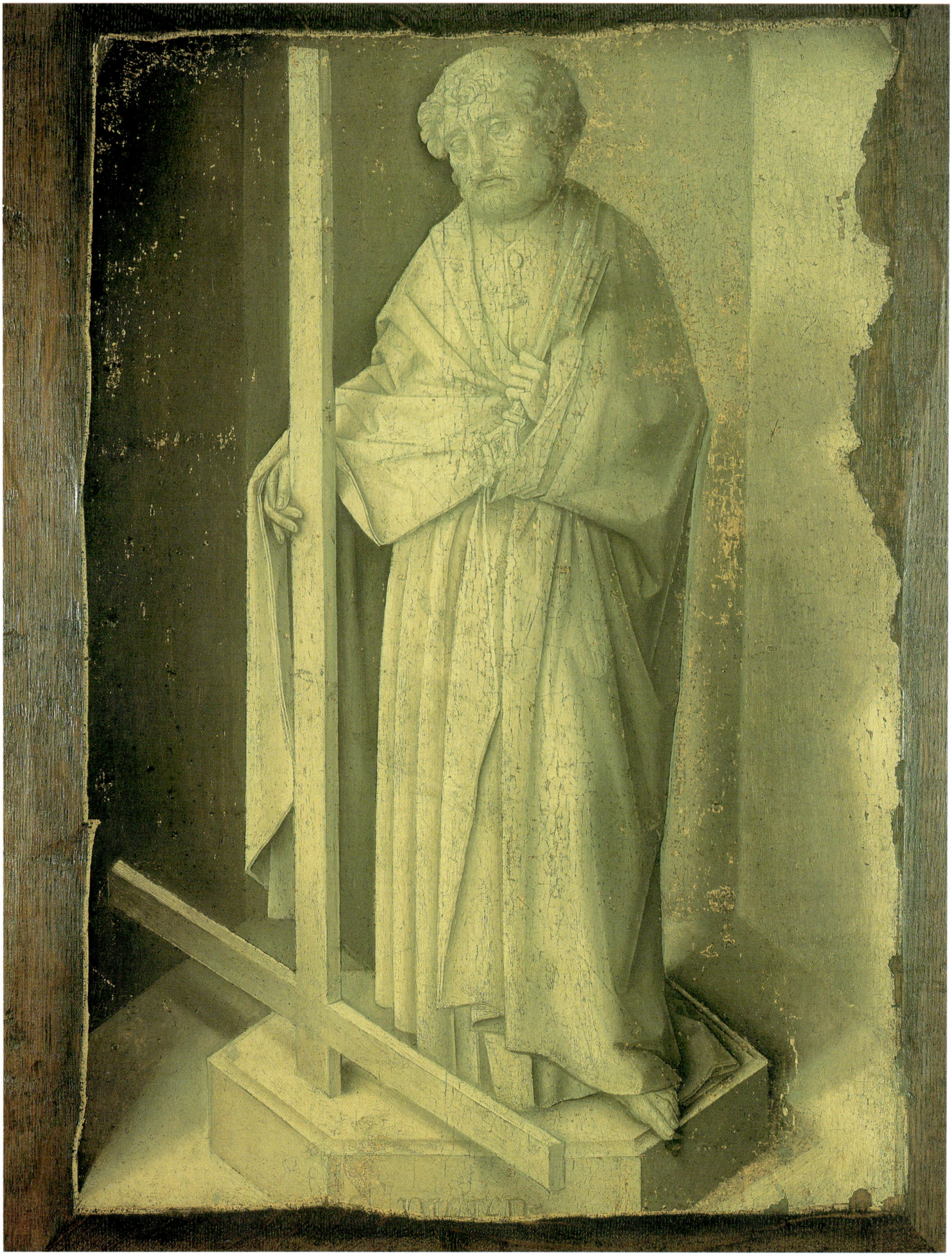

This painting was published by Boon in 1950 when it was still at the Duits Gallery in London. It was apparently acquired by the Beets Gallery in Amsterdam, where it was bought by the Museum. Boon also mentioned paintings depicting *The gathering of the Manna* in Douai (on loan from the Louvre) and *The crucifixion of Christ*, then in a private collection in Paris. He assumed that together they formed the three panels of a single altarpiece. As a result he named the artist the Master of the gathering of the Manna, locating him in South Holland, and dated the altar at around 1470. The painting still bore the signature of Israhel van Meckenem, which had been added some time after the painting was made. It was, however, removed by the restorer when the painting came to the Museum.

Boon thought that the painting depicted the sacrifice of the Paschal lamb at the Jewish Passover or perhaps a ritual animal sacrifice in the Temple in Jerusalem of the kind described in the third book of Moses (Leviticus 3).

We see several figures in a temple around an altar on which some wood has been laid. Two men are bringing more wood, whilst the man in the centre is holding the sacrificial lamb. Behind the altar is a relief depicting Cain's murder of Abel. Boon writes that the sacrifice of the Paschal lamb was seen as a prefiguration of Christ's sacrifice, as was the murder of Abel by Cain. The two remarkable figures in medallions in both upper corners seem to be fighting like soldiers – an archer conquering evil, in J.G. van Gelder's opinion,[2] or a representation of *Discordia* according to Eisler.[3]

In 1951 Haverkamp Begemann produced an article in connection with the new acquisition, and two years later wrote that the reverse of the panel had been covered with a layer of black paint which was, however, removed by the restorer. This revealed the grisaille depicting St Peter, confirmed by the half-preserved letters: S Pieter.
Whilst it was still in a private collection, Wurfbain had incorrectly ascribed the panel with the *Crucifixion* mentioned above to another master. He then identified the painter of the present work as Brother Tymanus, the leading master of the Hieronymusdal (or Lopsen) monastery in Leiden.[4]

In 1987 the Musée de la Chartreuse succeeded in acquiring the panel which was in a private collection in Paris.

At my suggestion an exhibition of the three panels was organised in Douai, with Van Asperen de Boer carrying out the scientific examination. An inspection of the panel with *The gathering of the manna* in Douai showed that the reverse was painted black, as had been the case with the painting in Rotterdam. My proposal that the back should be cleaned resulted in a fragment of grisaille being found depicting St Barbara, tower included. Dendrochronological analysis was performed by Dr P. Klein, who concluded that both planks of the *Crucifixion*, one plank of the *Gathering* and one plank of *The offering of the Jews* came from the same tree and that the two remaining planks originated from another tree. He believed that the panel would have been ready for painting from 1461.

Some underdrawing was exposed in the architecture, as well as the words "root", "purp", "ghel" or "gh", which were colour indications – red, purple and yellow – written on the ground.

The painter cannot as yet be localised with any great degree of precision. The bright and powerful colours would certainly indicate a northern Netherlandish artist, and Boon's rather vague suggestion that he was from South Holland seems for the present to be the most acceptable proposition. The original form of the altar also poses a problem. One would obviously be inclined to place the *Crucifixion* in the middle. The arch-shaped decorations of the other two panels are not, however, identical, and it is, therefore, not clear if they really were left- and right wings, although the fact that they both have grisailles on the reverse does make this quite likely. If that is the case, then a centre panel must be missing. It is also unclear whether the St Peter in grisaille and the newly revealed St Barbara can provide any further clues regarding an original ensemble.
JG

1 The results of the scientific examination were published in Van Asperen de Boer, Baligand, Giltaij and Pijl (1991) and in exhib. cat. Douai 1991. Paint samples A 273/1-9. Infrared reflectograms: AB 1073/16-AB 1076; AB 1100/30-AB 1101/18.
2 See Boon (1950), p. 210, note 1.
3 Eisler (1984).
4 Wurfbain (1978).

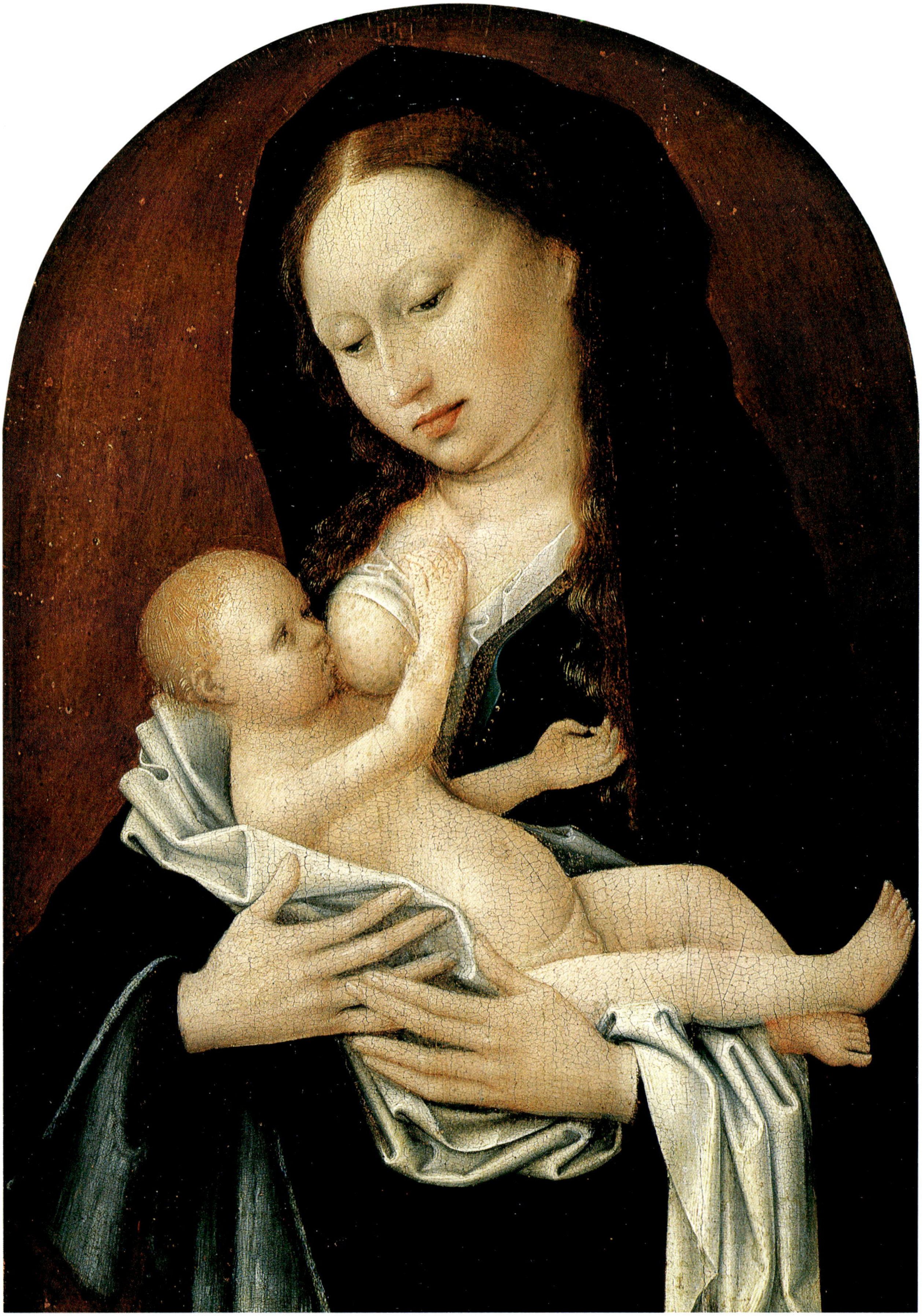

The Virgin and Child

Master of the Khanenko Adoration
(active at the end of the fifteenth century?)

Panel; 33 x 25.5 cm

In this finely-executed painting, the Virgin Mary is nursing the infant Christ. The Child is pressing its left forefinger and thumb together. The Virgin's hands are ingeniously laid together. The frame around this painting is part of the panel. Unfortunately, little is known about the painting. It may already have been attributed to the Master of the Khanenko Adoration by the time Frederiks acquired it from the art dealer Beets in 1940.

The Master of the Khanenko Adoration was thus named by Friedländer in 1926.[2] The author brought together several paintings whose styles were influenced by Hugo van der Goes. He saw the painter not as a copyist or a slavish imitator, but rather as a worthy follower of Van der Goes. Friedländer's starting point was a diptych in the Khanenko Collection at the National Museum of Fine Arts, Kiev, which explains the name given to the artist.[3] Characteristic of the painter is that the heads are proportionately large and the hands lively in their movement. The forms are softer and rounder than those of Hugo van der Goes. Boon tried to identify the Master of the Khanenko Adoration with the Master of the Turin Crucifixion.[4] Winkler disagreed with the composition of Friedländer's small group of paintings.[5] D. de Vos gives a summary of the state of affairs, reporting that we know nothing about the dates of the painter or where he was from, but that the link with Hugo van der Goes suggests a painter active in Ghent.[6]

The attribution of this painting from the Frederiks Collection to our master deserves consideration. There seem to be similarities to a painting, also of the *Virgin and Child*, in the Staatliche Galerie in Dessau, particularly in the quite broad face with the high forehead. The hands in the two paintings, with their long, stretched fingers also correspond to some extent.[7]
JG

Physical characteristics: the panel and frame consist of a single arched plank.

Infrared reflectography: underdrawing with thin, fine lines (fig. a).[1]

Provenance: N. Beets, Amsterdam; acquired by J.W. Frederiks, The Hague, in 1940; on loan from the J.W. Frederiks Collection to the Boymans-van Beuningen Museum since 1968; inv. no. S 30.

Not exhibited.

Unpublished.

1 Scanned and recorded on 20 December 1993 and 17 January 1994 by J.R.J. van Asperen de Boer. Infrared reflectograms: AB 1561/14A-20A.
2 Friedländer, IV, 1926, p. 77.
3 See also Friedländer, IV, 1969, pp. 44, 97, note 235, pl. 48 and 49.
4 K.G. Boon, "Meester van de Khanenko-aanbidding of Meester van de Kruisiging te Turijn", *Oud Holland* 68 (1953), pp. 209-216.
5 F. Winkler, *Das Werk des Hugo van der Goes*, Berlin 1964, p. 291.
6 D. de Vos in exhib. cat. *Anonieme Vlaamse primitieven*, Bruges, Groeningenmuseum, 1969, p. 65, and M. Baes-Dondeyne and P.G. Chabert, pp. 216-220.
7 Compare Friedländer, IV, 1969, pl. 48, no. 44.

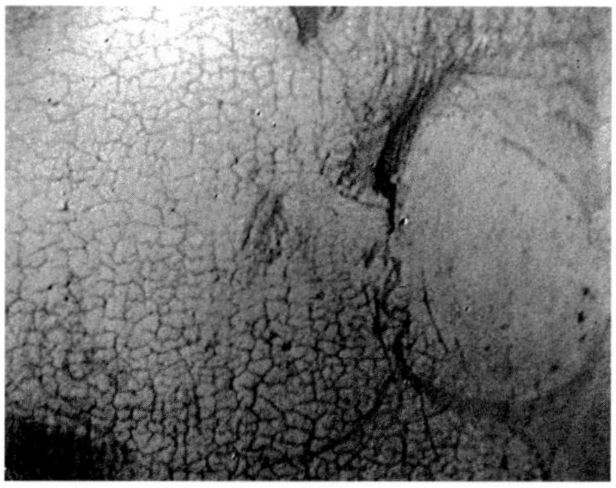

a. Infrared reflectogram assembly. Detail of the head of the infant Christ.

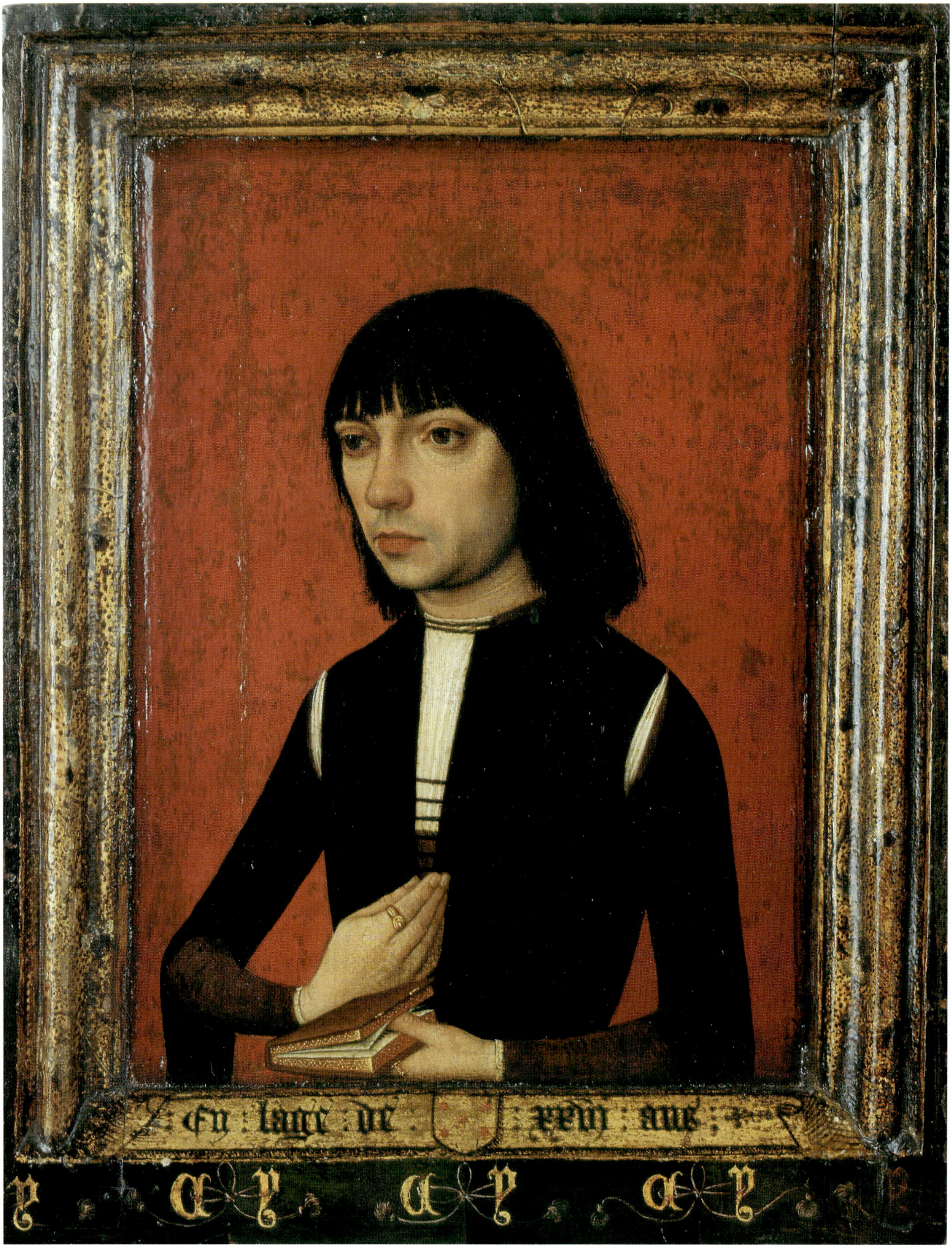

Portrait of a young man

Master of the Portraits of the Princes
(active c. 1490)

Panel; 39 x 29.5 cm

Physical characteristics: the panel consists of a single plank. The frame is original.

Infrared reflectography:[1] underdrawing is discernible on the right of the face, the lip, under the chin and on the hands (figs. b and c).

On the inside of the lower edge of the frame is the inscription "En: lage: de: XXVI: ans" (at the age of 26 years); between "de" and "XXVI" is a coat of arms (five red six-cornered stars on a gold background, with a so-called label on top); on the outside of the frame at the bottom are the letters: y, cy, cy, cy and y; the outermost edge is decorated with violets; on the left of the frame are the letters y and c above one another.
The coat of arms is repeated on the reverse; above it is a helmet with a plume; at the top are the words "A dieu", on the left and right at the bottom are the letters c and y; on the left and right are the letters y and c; on the outer edge of the back of the frame are the letters c and y, and in the middle on the left are the letters d and b intertwined.

Provenance: Johann Peter Weyer, sale in Cologne, Heberle, 25 August 1862, no. 213 (as Jan van Eyck, Porträt eines Herzogs von Burgund; 731 francs to Mireur Souillé); Fürst Karl Anton von Hohenzollern, Sigmaringen (1811-1885); Fürstlich Hohenzollern'sches Museum, Sigmaringen;[2] F. Koenigs, Haarlem, acquired in 1928 from the Sigmaringer Sammlungen; from 1935 on loan to the Boymans Museum; Stichting Nederlands Kunstbezit; from 1948 on loan from the Netherlands Office for Fine Arts (RBK); inv. no. 2311.

Exhibitions: *Kurzes Verzeichnis der im Staedelschen Kunstinstitut ausgestellten Sigmaringer Sammlungen* Frankfurt am Main, 1928, no. 4; *Verzameling F. Koenigs, Schilderijen*, Rotterdam, Boymans Museum, 1935, no. 6, fig. VII; *Herwonnen Kunstbezit*, The Hague, Mauritshuis, 1946, no. 5; *Herwonnen Kunstbezit*, Utrecht, Centraal Museum, 1946, no. 16, fig. 2; *Herwonnen Kunstbezit*, Eindhoven, Van Abbemuseum, 1946-47, no. 2; *De Jerôme Bosch à Rembrandt*, Musée de Dijon, Dijon, 1950, no. 8; *Bourgondische pracht*, Amsterdam, Rijksmuseum, 1951, no. 22; *Anonieme Vlaamse primitieven*, Bruges, Groeningemuseum, 1969, no. 61, fig.

Literature: *Fürstlich Hohenzollern'sches Museum zu Sigmaringen, Verzeichnis der Gemälde*, Sigmaringen 1883, no. 100; F. Rieffel, "Das Fürstlich Hohenzollernsche Museum zu Sigmaringen Gemälde und Bildwerke", *Städel-Jahrbuch* 3/4 (1924), p. 59, fig. XVIb; Friedländer, VI, 1926, p. 106; G. Swarzenski, "Der Verkauf der Sigmaringer Sammlung", *Zeitschrift für bildende Kunst* 62 (1928-29), p. 274;[3] J. Tombu, "Le Maître de la Légende de Marie-Madeleine", *Gazette des Beaux-Arts* 71 (1929), 2, pp. 281-282; P. Wescher, "Das höfische Bildnis von Philipp dem Guten bis zu Karl V", *Pantheon* 28 (1941), p. 274; G. Ring, *A Century of French Painting 1400-1500*, London 1949, p. 223, no. 203; G. Ring, "Le Grand Siècle des Ducs de Bourgogne at Dijon", *The Burlington Magazine* 93 (1951), p. 297, note 10; cat. 1962, p. 88; Friedländer, IV, 1969, p. 59, note 20, fig. pl. 104; Catheline Périer-D'Ieteren, "Une œuvre retrouvée du Maître des Portraits Princiers",*Annales d'Histoire de l'Art & d'Archeologie* (Université Libre de Bruxelles) VIII (1986), pp. 43-56, fig. 4.

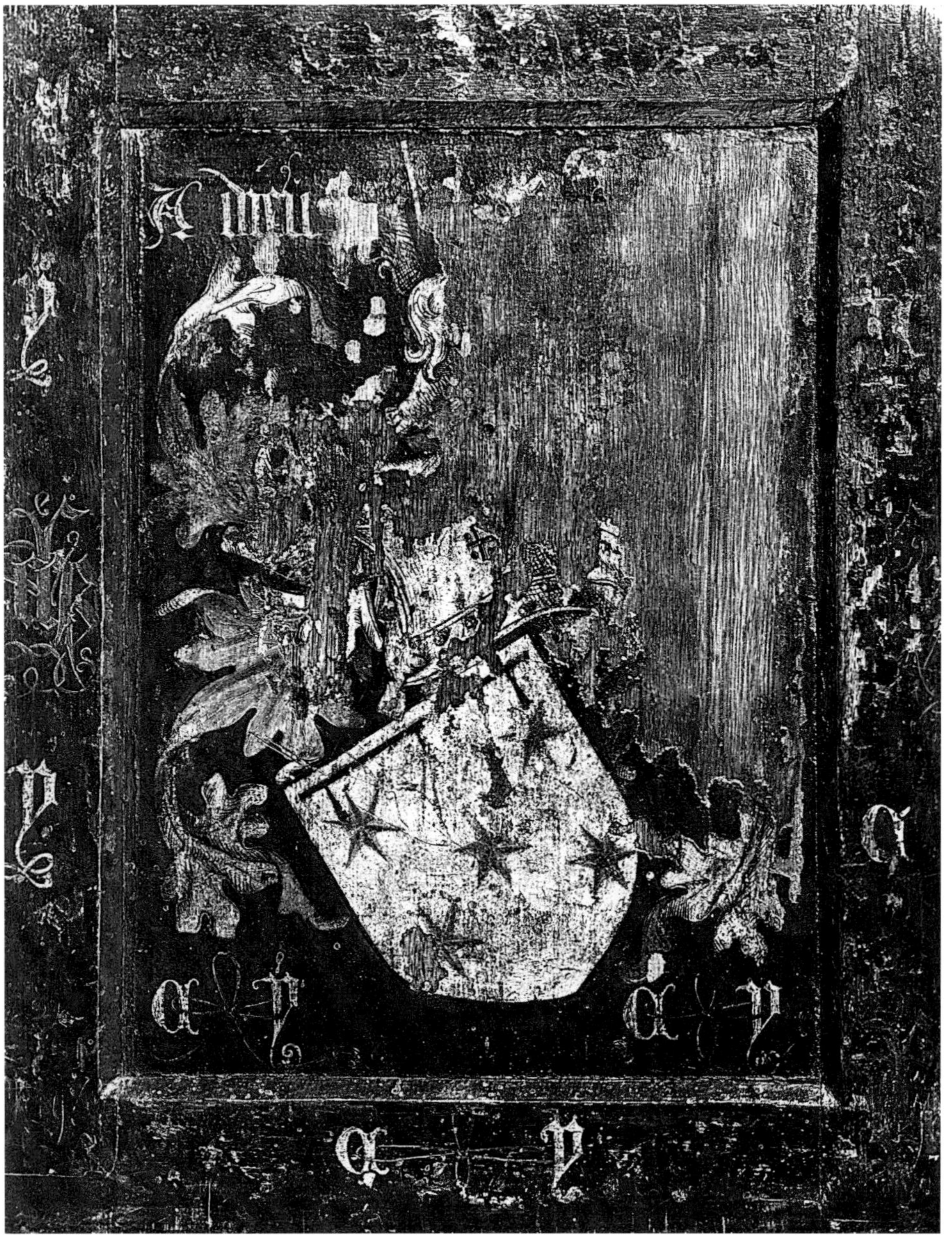

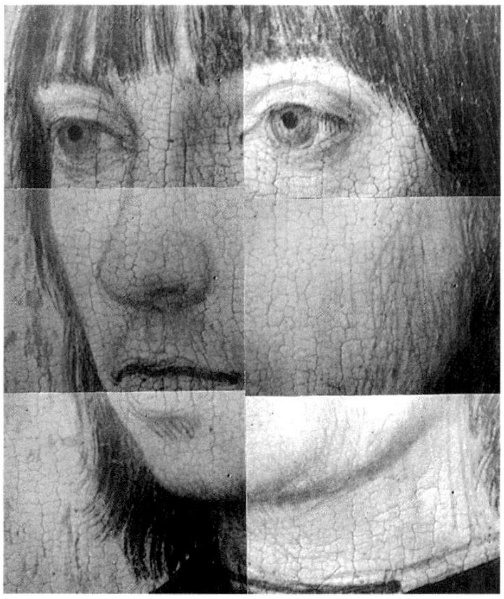

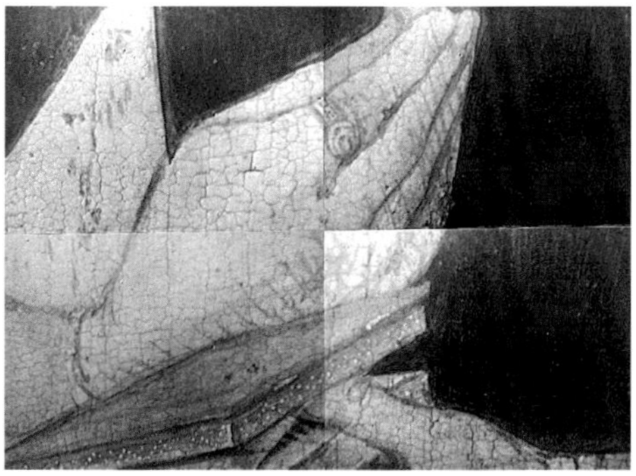

a. Reverse of the panel

b. Infrared reflectogram assembly (face)

c. Infrared reflectogram assembly (hands)

The young man portrayed here has a book in his left hand, with his thumb between two pages, whilst his right hand is held in front of his chest. He is twenty-six years old according to the French inscription. The meaning of the letters c and y, joined by a so-called lovers' knot, is not clear. Tombu has associated the coat of arms on the front with the Spanish Fonseca family.[4]

The same coat of arms is represented on the reverse (fig. a), this time embellished with a helmet. Of the inscription written above the coat of arms – evidently the family motto – only the words "A Dieu" remain. The letters c and y are found here too. Half-way to the left is what appears to be a monogram in which the letters b and d have been deciphered.

During the last century, when the painting formed part of the renowned Weyer Collection and, later, that of the Hohenzollerns in Sigmaringen, it was attributed to Jan van Eyck. When Riefel wrote about the latter collection in 1924, he considered the painting to be the portrait of one of the dukes of Burgundy by a master of the Burgundian school. It was acquired by Franz Koenigs in 1928, when the large Hohenzollern Collection was sold.

In trying to identify the painter, Friedländer started with the left wing (depicting the *Marriage at Cana*) of a triptych in Melbourne portraying the *Miracles of Christ*.[5] He believed that it was by the same artist as the portrait of Engelbert van Nassau, which has been at the Rijksmuseum in Amsterdam since 1933,[6] and that he was also the painter of a portrait which was then in the Poznan Museum in Poland, which was for a long time missing, but which was eventually traced in 1986 to a private collection in Belgium[7] and, finally, that he was the painter of the present work, then still in Sigmaringen. He named the artist the "Meister des Fürstenporträts". He presumed that the portrait in the Rijksmuseum mentioned above had been made in Brussels and, hence, located the master in that city. The Amsterdam painting is dated 1487, giving an idea of the period in which he was active. In Tombu's opinion, the artist was in fact the Master of the Legend of the Magdalen. Ring, on the other hand, considered that the Rotterdam painting was more closely related to the works of the Burgundian school than to those of the Master of the Portraits of Princes, to whom it was persistently attributed.[8] Duverger identified the painter of the portrait of Lodewijk van Gruuthuse in the Groeninge Museum in Bruges, which had also been attributed to the Master of the Portraits of Princes, as Lieven van Lathem.

Although one can certainly detect the hand of the same artist in this group of portraits, identifying the painter concerned is less straightforward. Even though the portraits were included in the fascinating exhibition of anonymous Flemish Primitives held in the Groeninge Museum in Bruges in 1969, we should perhaps consider the possibility that the artist was in fact a Burgundian master, as Ring believed.
JG

1 The painting was scanned and recorded by J.R.J. van Asperen de Boer on 20 December 1993 and 17 January 1994. Infrared reflectograms: AB 1561/21A-32A.

2 For more information about the sale of this collection, see A.L. Mayer, "Die Fürstlich-Hohenzollernschen Sammlungen in Sigmaringen", *Pantheon* 1 (1928), pp. 59-65. For details of the collection itself, see H. Vey, "Johann Peter Weyer, seine Gemäldesammlung und seine Kunstliebe", *Wallraf-Richartz-Jahrbuch* XXVIII (1966), pp. 159-254.

3 "Das französische Porträt wählte Herr Koenigs".

4 Tombu (1929).

5 For details of this painting, see Ursula Hoff and Martin Davies, *Les Primitifs Flamands, The National Gallery of Victoria Melbourne*, Brussels, 1971, p. 131 ff.

6 Inv. no. A 3140.

7 The painting had been stolen from the museum in 1949. See Périer-D'Ieteren (1986).

8 Ring (1949).

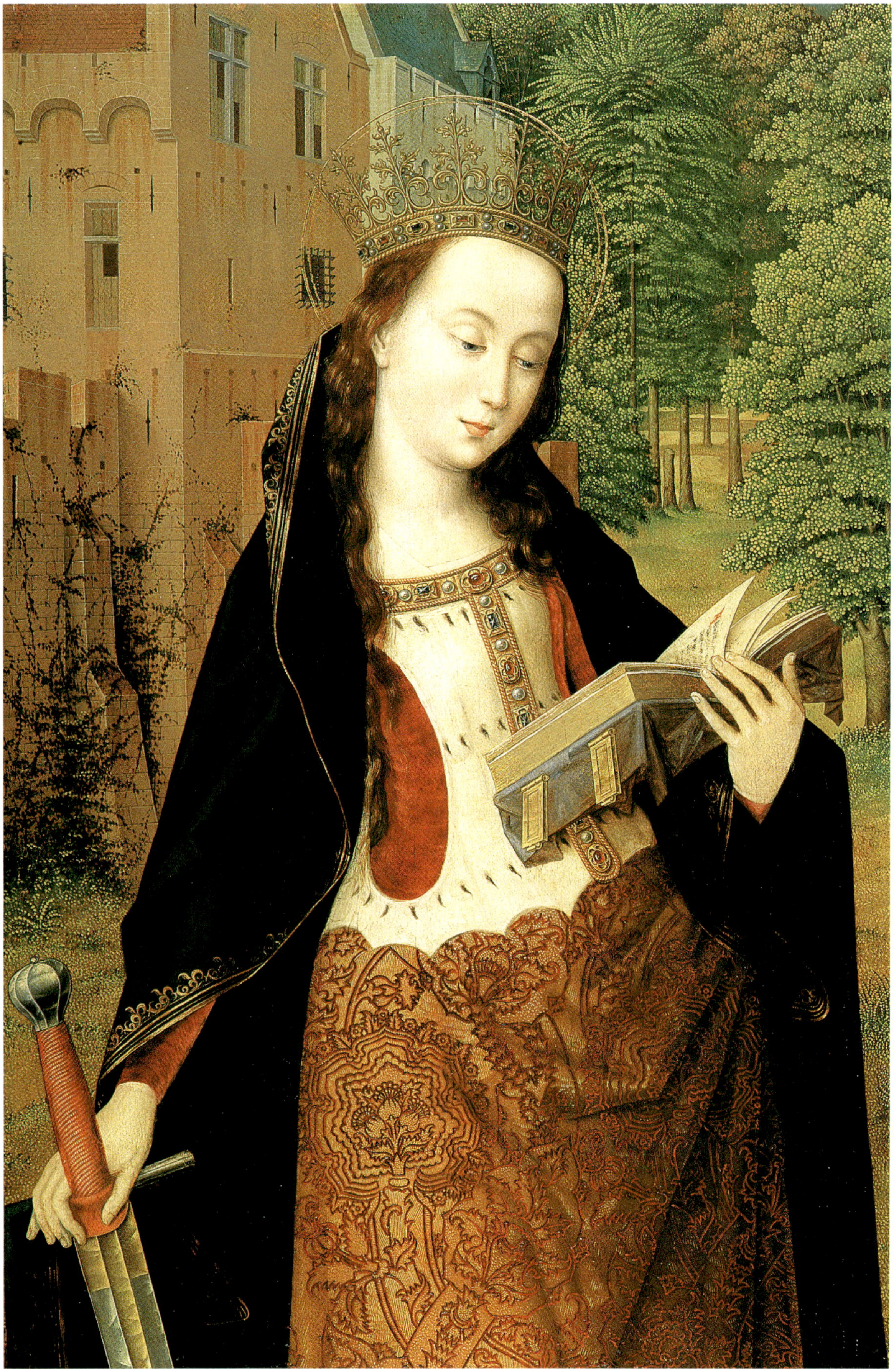

St Catherine
St Barbara

Master of the Embroidered Foliage
(active Brussels (?) c. 1500)

Panels; 96 x 63 cm

The first known reference to the paintings is in the catalogue of the exhibition in Bruges in 1902, which attributes them to an anonymous artist. The catalogue of another Bruges exhibition, in 1907, lists them as the work of Hans Memling.

In 1926 Friedländer associated them with a group of six paintings by an artist he thought was active around 1500, possibly in Brussels, whose work was characterised by a pedantic style of painting foliage in stipples. He therefore dubbed the painter "Der Meister mit dem gestickten Laub", or Master of the Embroidered Foliage, after the "embroidered" effect of the foliage in his paintings.

De Vos discerns in this master a last surge of the tremendous influence exercised by Rogier van der Weyden. He is not impressed by the artist's qualities, describing the figures as lacking in depth and purely decorative.[2]

The left panel depicts St Catherine of Alexandria with the sword which is her attribute. According to the legend, this saint was beheaded with a sword. Holding a Bible in her left hand, she stands before a castle in a wooded landscape.

The second figure is now named St Barbara. In the catalogue of the 1907 exhibition she was referred to as Clothilde, whose attribute was a shield bearing three lilies, which is not in the painting. St Barbara's attribute is the tower in which she was imprisoned by her father. It may be represented by the architecture in the background, but this is uncertain. Both works appear to have been sawn off along the lower edge, so it is likely that the figures were originally full length. They were undoubtedly wings of a triptych whose central panel is lost.

Attention has been drawn to their correspondence to the wings of a triptych by the same artist in the Chiesa Madre, Polizzi Generosa, Sicily (fig. a),[3] in which St Catherine of Alexandria is also portrayed in the left wing, and St Barbara (with what is plainly a tower) in the other. It gives us some idea of what is missing from the Rotterdam panels. The central panel in Polizzi Generosa depicts the Virgin and Child with four angels, which may also have been the subject of the central panel of the Rotterdam wings.

The low rating accorded the artist is justified on some points: the reproduction of the foliage is rather mechanical and the work as a whole is somewhat superficial, especially in comparison with his great predecessors like Rogier van der Weyden. On the other hand, the detail displays considerable craftsmanship, and the artist has achieved a monumental quality that entitles him to be classed as a fairly important figure in Flemish art around 1500.
JG

Physical characteristics: the original *barbe* can be seen on the left edges of both paintings (cat. nos. 11 and 12).

Infrared reflectography: no underdrawing could be discerned.

Provenance: L. Harris, London, 1902; Léo Nardus, Suresnes, 1907; Onnes van Nijenrode, Nijenrode Castle, auction Amsterdam, Mensing, 10 July 1923, no. 17, fig.; Van Wickevoort Crommelin Collection, The Hague; in 1984 bequeathed to the State by Mrs M.L.J.D. van Wickevoort Crommelin-Teixeira de Mattos, who expressed the wish that they were to be on permanent loan to the Boymans-van Beuningen Museum, Rotterdam;[1] (cat. 11) inv. no. 3168; (cat. 12) inv. no. 3169.

Exhibitions: *Exposition des Primitifs Flamands et d'Art ancien*, Bruges, 1902, nos. 404 and 405; *Exposition de la Toison d'Or à Bruges*, Brussels, 1907, nos. 198 and 199.

Literature: M.J. Friedländer in auction catalogue 1923, p. X; Friedländer, IV, 1926, p. 145, no. 86, fig. LXV, LXVI; G. Carandente, *Les Primitifs Flamands, Collections d'Italie, I, Sicile*, Brussels 1968, p. 30, no. 16; Friedländer, IV, 1969, p. 82, no. 86, fig. 81; *Old Master Paintings, An Illustrated Summary Catalogue, Rijksdienst Beeldende Kunst*, Zwolle-The Hague, no date (1992), p. 193, nos. 1624 en 1625.

1 The testator wished the paintings to be exhibited at the Rijksmuseum, Amsterdam. If that was not possible, they were to go on permanent loan to the Mauritshuis, The Hague, the Frans Hals Museum, Haarlem, or the Boymans-van Beuningen Museum, Rotterdam, in that order, subject to the condition that they were to be exhibited to the public. The Boymans-van Beuningen Museum accepted the condition.
2 D. de Vos, in exhib. cat., *Anonieme Vlaamse primitieven*, Bruges, Groeninge Museum, 1969, p. 150.
3 See Carandente (1968).

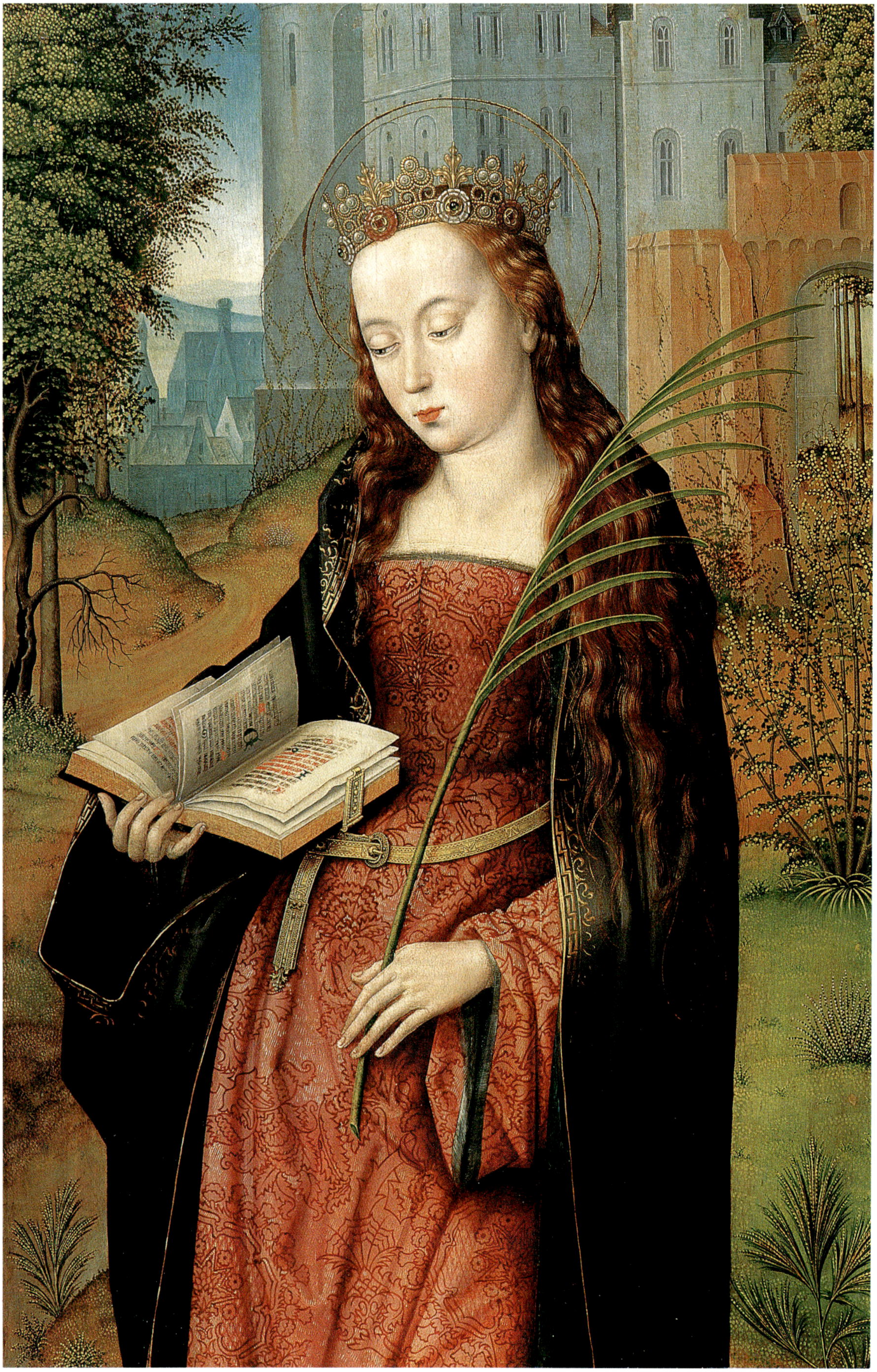

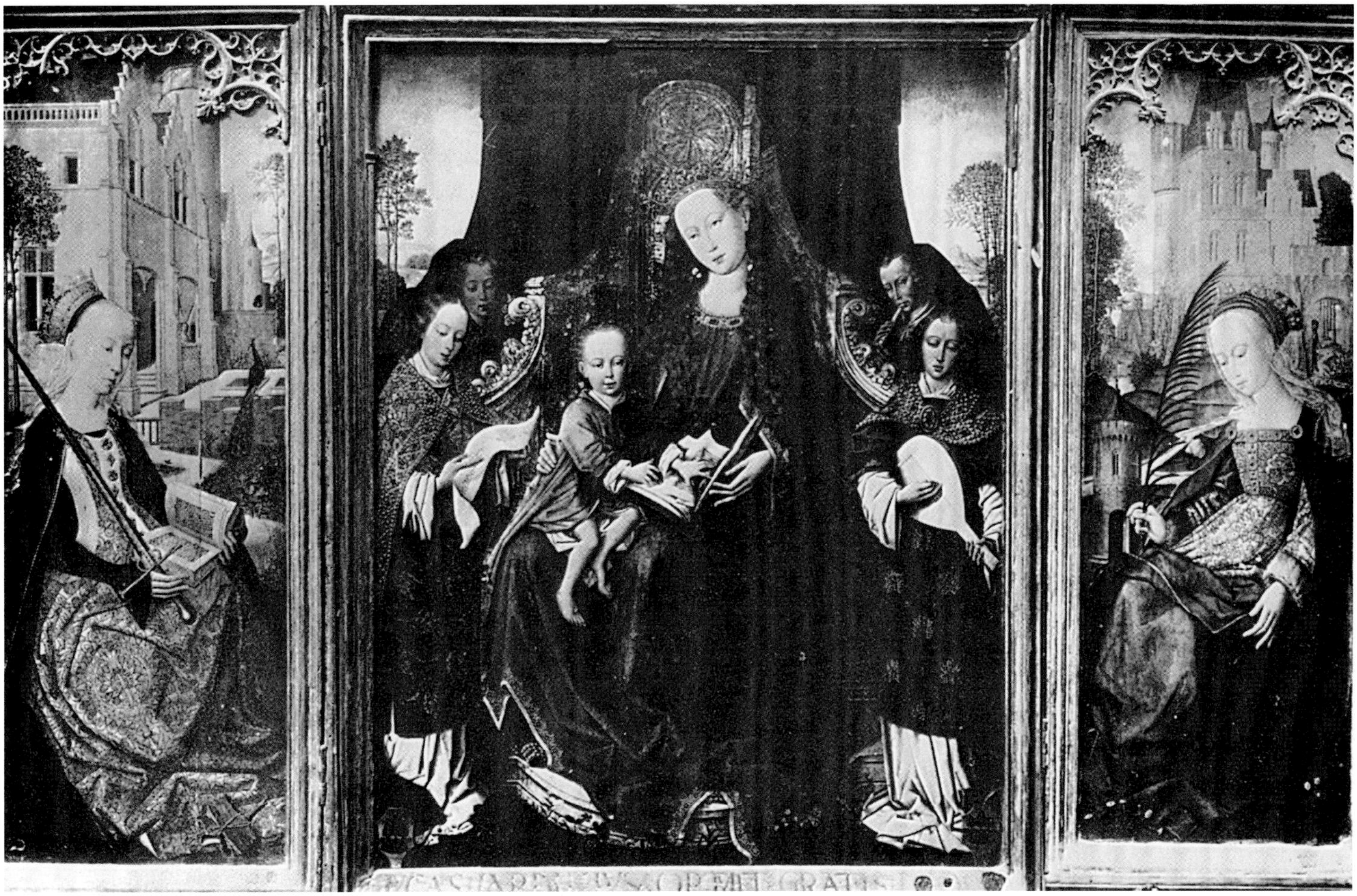

a. Master of the Embroidered Foliage, triptych portraying the Virgin and Child on the central panel, and St Catherine and St Barbara on the wings
Central panel: 158 x 123 cm
Wings: 162 x 57 cm
Polizzi Generosa, Chiesa Madre

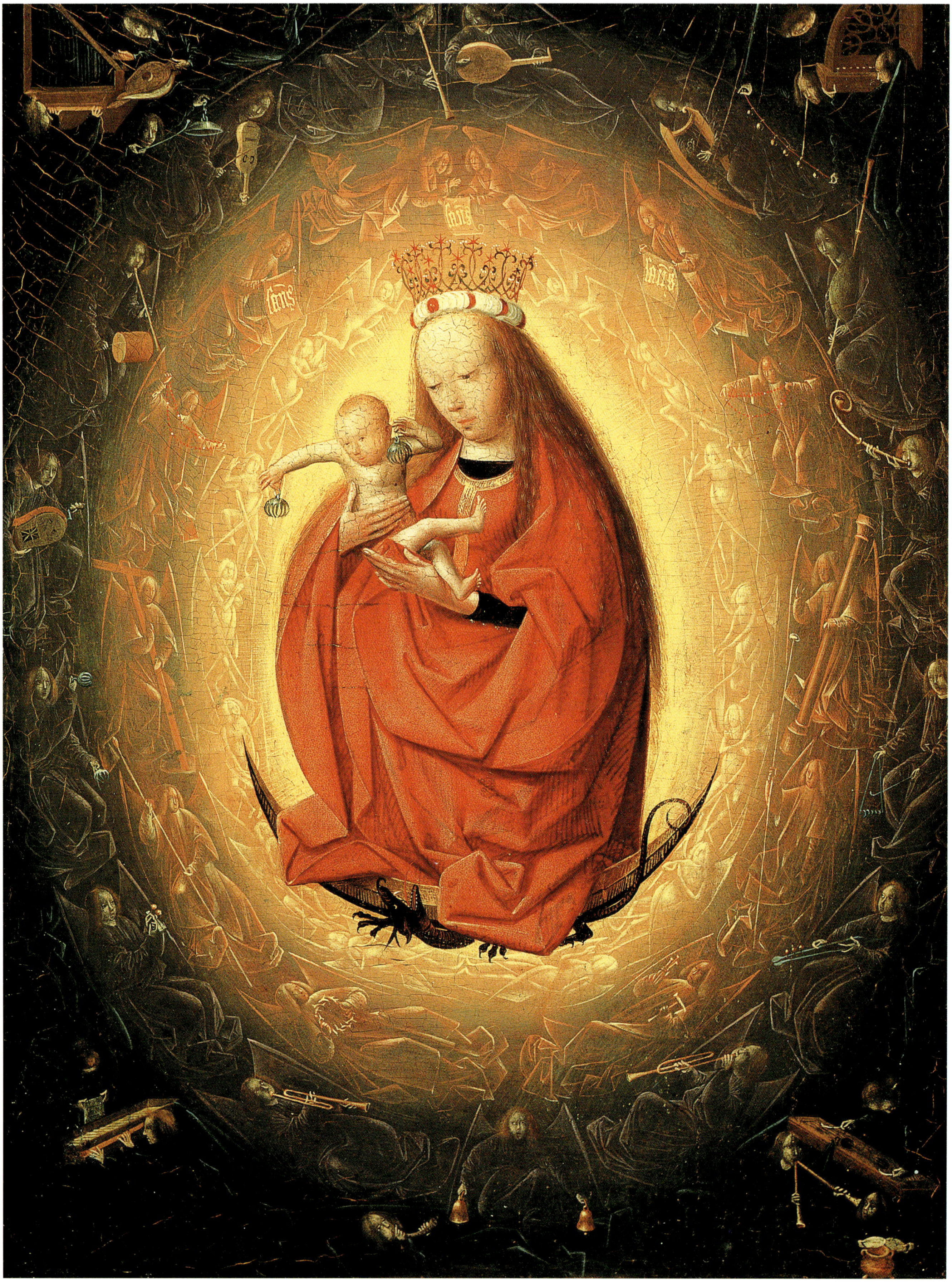

The glorification of the Virgin

Geertgen tot St Jans
(Leiden (?), c. 1460/65-Haarlem, c. 1490/95)

Panel; 26.8 x 20.5 cm (with gilt border)
24.6 x 18.1 cm (without gilt border)
Inscription on three scrolls: SAÑS

Physical characteristics: the panel consists of a single plank. The picture is surrounded by a gilt border which is part of the plank itself.

Infrared reflectography:[1] the underdrawing is possibly in pen. It is detectable only in Mary's dress (fig. a). See description.

Dendrochronology: the youngest heartwood growth ring dates from 1443. The panel could not have been painted before 1454; it was more probably painted in or after 1468. See article by P. Klein.

Provenance: Cardinal Fesch Collection; sale of his collection in Rome, Palazzo Ricci, 17 March 1845, no. 264; bought here by Mr Therry for 28; V.D. Spark Gallery, New York (1949-1950); G. Wildenstein Gallery; in 1952 exchanged by Wildenstein with D.G. van Beuningen, Rotterdam and Vierhouten, for the *Cypresses* attributed to Vincent van Gogh;[2] acquired by the Museum with the D.G. van Beuningen Collection; inv. no. 2450.

Exhibitions: *Bourgondische pracht*, Amsterdam, Rijksmuseum, 1951, no. 43, fig. 16; *Chefs-d'œuvre de la collection D.G. van Beuningen*, Paris, Petit Palais, 1952, no. 49. fig. 2; *Kunstschatten uit Nederlandse verzamelingen*, Rotterdam, Boymans Museum, 1955, no. 10, fig. 7; *Middeleeuwse Kunst der Noordelijke Nederlanden*, Amsterdam, Rijksmuseum, 1958, no. 14, fig. 4; *In het licht van Vermeer/Dans la lumière de Vermeer*, The Hague, Mauritshuis, Paris, Musée de l'Orangerie, 1966, no. 5, fig.

Literature: M.J. Friedländer, "Zu Geertgen tot St. Jans", *Maandblad voor Beeldende Kunsten* 25 (1949), pp. 186-188, fig.; D.M. Hoffmann, "A little known masterpiece; our lady of the sanctus, *Liturgical Arts* XVIII (1950), p. 43 ff.; H. Gerson, *De Nederlandse schilderkunst I, Van Geertgen tot Frans Hals* (De Schoonheid van ons land), Amsterdam 1950, p. 14, fig. 12; G. Ring, "Attempt to reconstruct a lost Geertgen composition", *The Burlington Magazine* XLIV (1952), p. 147; E. Panofsky, *Early Netherlandish Painting*, Cambridge Mass. 1953, p. 495; J.E. Snyder, *Geertgen tot Sint Jans and the Haarlem school of painting*, (diss.), Princeton 1957, no. XIV, pp. 270-272; S. Sulzberger, "Gérard de Saint Jean et l'art de la miniature", *Oud Holland* LXXIV (1959), pp. 167-168, fig. 2; S. Sulzberger, "La glorification de la vierge de Gérard de St. Jean, *Oud Holland* LXXIV (1959), p. 169; J.Q. van Regteren Altena, "Postscriptum", *Oud Holland* LXXIV (1959), pp. 169-173; S. Sulzberger, "Juste de Gand et l'école de Harlem", *Revue Belge d'Archéologie et d'Histoire de l'Art* XXIX (1960), p. 58; J.E. Snyder, "The early Haarlem school of painting II, Geertgen tot St. Jans", *Art Bulletin* XLII (1960), pp. 125, 131-132, fig. 20; J. Bruyn, "Geertgen tot St. Jans ±1464-±1495), De verheerlijking van Maria met het kind" *Openbaar Kunstbezit* 4 (1960), no. 5, fig.; E. Winternitz, "On angel concerts in the 15th century: a critical approach to realism and symbolism in sacred painting", *Musical Quarterly* XLIX (1963), pp. 450-63; J.H.A. Engelbregt, "'Het glorievolle rozenkransgeheim van Maria's kroning in de hemel' door Geertgen tot St. Jans", *Album discipulorum J.G. van Gelder*, Utrecht 1963, pp. 31-44, fig. 1; H. van Os, "Coronatio, Glorificatio en Maria in sole", *Bulletin Museum Boymans-van Beuningen* XV (1964), pp. 22-38; J.H.A. Engelbregt, "Enkele opmerkingen n.a.v. het artikel van H.W. van Os over Coronatio, Glorificatio en Maria in Sole", *Bulletin Museum Boymans-van Beuningen* XVII (1966), pp. 37-38; J.Q. van Regteren Altena, "Wanneer verbleef Geertgen tot St. Jans in Vlaanderen?", *Oud Holland* LXXXI (1966), p. 76 ff.; G.Th. M. Lemmens, "Geertgen tot St. Jans' 'Kruisiging met de Heilige Dominicus'", *Oud Holland* LXXXI (1966), p. 73, fig. p. 85; K.G. Boon, "Cross-currents in early northern painting", *Apollo* 1967, July, p. 8, fig. V; K.G. Boon. *Geertgen tot St.Jans* (Beeldende Kunst en Bouwkunst in Nederland), Amsterdam 1967, pp. 9-10; E. Guldan, *Eva und Maria. Eine Antithese als Bildmotiv*, Graz-Cologne 1966, pp. 104-105, 209; E.M. Vetter, "Ernst Guldan, *Eva und Maria. Eine Antithese als bildmotiv* (Rezension)", *Kunstchronik* 20 (1967), p. 83; E. Winternitz, *Musical instruments and their symbolism in Western Art*, London 1967, pp. 106, 139-142, 147-148, fig. 64, 65b; W. Elders, *Studien zur Symbolik in der Musik der Alten Niederländer*, Bilthoven 1968, pp. 126, 195, fig. on p. 5; Friedländer, V, 1969, p. 94, fig.; *National Gallery of Scotland. Shorter Catalogue*, 1970, pp. 37-38; L. Wuyts, "De madonna en de stralenkrans van Geertgen tot Sint-Jans, een ikonologisch onderzoek", *Annalen van het XLIII congres der federatie van kringen voor oudheidkunde en geschiedenis van België*, 1974, pp. 348-357, fig. 1; U. Zsuzsa, *Geertgen tot St. Jans*, Boedapest 1976, fig. 45, 46; *National Gallery of Scotland. Shorter Catalogue*, 1978, pp. 41-42; A. Châtelet, *Les Primitifs Hollandais*, Fribourg 1980, pp. 134-136, no. 99a, fig. 115; O. ter Kuile, "Onderdelen van een kerkkroon en van twee kandelaren uit de St. Jacobskerk te Den Haag", *Bulletin van het Rijksmuseum* 28 (1980), p. 127, fig. 7; J. Snyder, *Northern Renaissance Art*, New York 1985, pp. 178-79, fig. 30; L. van Dijck en T. Koopman, *Het klavecimbel in de Nederlandse kunst tot 1800*, Amsterdam 1987, no. 5, fig.; R.H. Marijnissen, *Hieronymus Bosch, Het volledige oeuvre*, Antwerp 1987, fig. p. 286; J.M. Upton, *Petrus Christus, his place in fifteenth-century Flemish painting*, London 1990, pp. 65, 108, fig. 61.

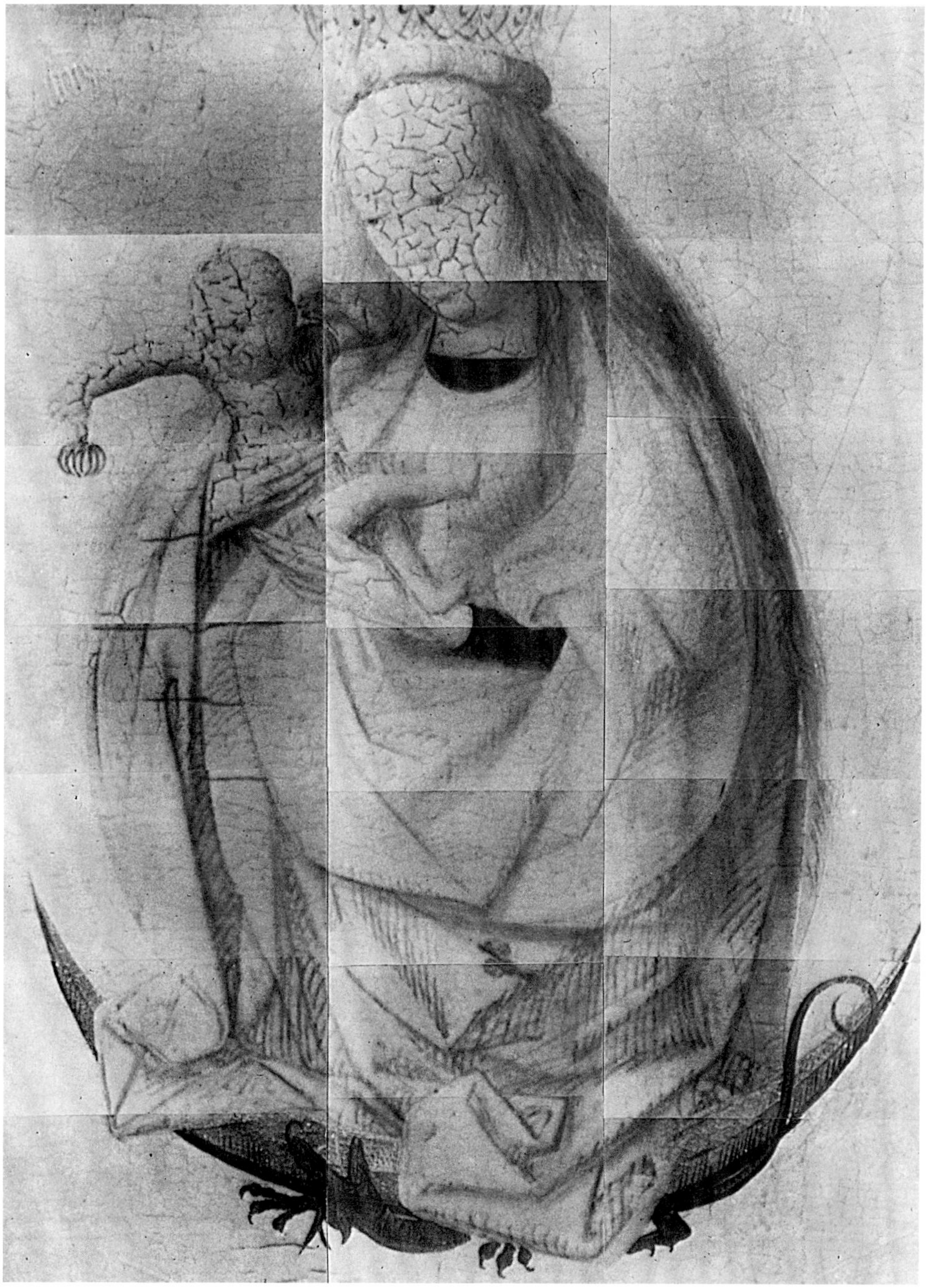

a. Infrared reflectogram assembly. (Infrared reflectography by Molly Faries)

"Whenever I visit your museum, I always go and see Geertgen tot St Jan's painting "The Glorification of the Virgin". I know of no other work of art in which a non-material, irrational idea is so effectively expressed by means of material attributes. (The musical instruments circling her in the firmament send me into a state of rapture and, given the dwindling strength of my organ of balance, a slight state of dizziness too.)" So wrote Gerard Reve when requesting a photograph of the painting in 1982.[3]

Since its discovery in 1949, many authors have written, some in quite lyrical terms, about the panel's exceptional qualities. Several have also attempted to unravel its complex iconography.

They are all agreed that the picture is, in the first instance, a reference to the vision of St John the Evangelist, described in the twelfth chapter of the Book of Revelations. John saw a woman "clothed with the sun, and the moon under her feet, and upon her head a crown of twelve stars." A dragon wrapped around the crescent moon represents the conquered devil.

Angels swirl in a series of three concentric rings around Mary and the infant Christ. The first, most brightly illuminated, ring consists of the "six-winged" seraphim, two of which are holding Mary's crown. The second ring is formed by six angels carrying the instruments of the Passion, two angels each with a rosary, and four angels carrying three scrolls bearing the inscription "sans" (sanctus). The outermost ring consists of an entire orchestra of angels making music.[4]

Mary's crown is resting on a chaplet, a garland made from a sequence of five white roses and one red. This headdress, together with the two angels with rosaries, indicate that the work was commissioned by an adherent of the cult of the rosary. Further evidence for this is provided by the pendant to the present painting, a *Crucifixion*, now in the National Gallery of Scotland in Edinburgh (fig. b). In the foreground on the right St Dominic is shown.[5] The Dominican order was the chief propagator of the prayer of the rosary.

There is some disagreement about the extent to which the ideas surrounding the cult of the rosary are represented. In 1964 Van Os expressed the view that this aspect should not be taken too far, and that the painting was intended for quite general devotional purposes. This was in reaction to the view of Father Engelbregt (1963), who saw in the panel an image of the "glorious mystery of the rosary".

The prayer of the rosary consists of saying 150 Hail Marys, divided into three groups of fifty. Each group is centred on a "mystery". One starts with the "joyful mysteries", events from Christ's youth, such as the Annunciation and Birth. Next come the "sorrowful mysteries", associated with the Passion. The last stage includes the "glorious mysteries" which deal with such transcendental themes as the Resurrection and the Ascension. The conclusion to these "glorious mysteries" is provided by the Assumption and the Coronation of the Virgin. This is, according to Engelbregt, shown on the panel, whilst the Edinburgh painting depicts the "sorrowful mysteries". He infers that a third painting must have existed, with the Annunciation representing the "joyful mysteries". An objection to this theory is that nothing comparable is known to exist.

Wuyts (1974) regards the painting as an example of the portrayal of the "Immaculata". He considers it unnecessary to make any connection with the rosary since, according to him, the chaplet and rosaries refer to the immaculate Virgin Mother.

It does seem clear, however, that the Rotterdam and Edinburgh panels are connected in some way with the cult of the rosary, which indeed had a great following in Haarlem, where they were both made. The first Dutch brotherhood of the rosary was established there in 1478. A painting of the legend of the rosary – now known only from two copies – was probably commissioned by a member of this brotherhood.[6] It is generally accepted that the original artist was Geertgen tot St Jans.[7] In the background of this painting, St Dominic is shown semi-clad kneeling before an altar, in an attitude strikingly

1 Carried out by Molly Faries in 1993.

2 Verbal account by the former director of the Museum, J.C. Ebbinge Wubben. The Van Gogh later transpired to be a fake, as a result of which Van Beuningen's widow paid the sale price valid at the time of the exchange. For further details on the *Cypresses*, see Hannema, 1949, no. 143, fig. 186 and W. Feilchenfeldt, "Van Gogh fakes. The Wacker affair, with an illustrated catalogue of the forgeries", *Simiolus* 19 (1989), no. 30.

3 Museum archive, letter received on 1 April 1982. "Steeds wanneer ik Uw museum bezoek, ga ik het schilderij van Geertgen tot St Jan "Verheerlijking van Maria" bekijken. Ik ken geen kunstwerk, waarin een niet-materiële, irrationele gedachte doormiddel van materiële attributen zo doeltreffend is uitgedrukt. (Die om Haar heen in de wereldruimte cirkelende muziekinstrumenten brengen mij in verrukking al word ik er, met mijn minder wordende evenwichtsorganen, ook wel ietwat duizelig van.)"

4 Both Engelbregt (1963), pp. 33-36 and Van Os (1964), p. 27 observe that the division of the three rings is based on a hierarchical classification going back to Dionysius the Areopagite. Seeking a deeper significance in the three rings, however, Engelbregt recognises the three "secrets" of the rosary. He also identifies all the musical instruments represented (note 17).

5 Inv. no. 1253. Panel; 24.4 x 18.4 cm (painted part). In addition to St Dominic, St Jerome is portrayed at the Crucifixion. Other episodes from the Passion are depicted as small scenes in the background. Van Regteren Altena (1959) was the first to associate the Edinburgh panel with the one in Rotterdam. X-radiographs show evidence of hinges at exactly the same height on both panels. In Cardinal Fesch's collection the paintings were listed in succession (nos. 263 and 264) as "manière de Henry de Bles", by which time they had already been separated. At the sale of Fesch's collection, the Edinburgh painting was sold to Marini for 31. In 1886 it was listed amongst the collection of F. Locker Lampson in Rowfant. Lemmens (1966) has published a painting in the Episcopal Museum in Vich, which bears a close resemblance to the panel in Edinburgh.

6 See Van Os (1964).

7 See Friedländer, V, 1969, fig. 13 and app. 141. The most complete copy is in the Museum der Bildenden Künste in Leipzig; a copy of the right-hand part is in a private collection in Britain. Also see Châtelet (1980) for further information on the painting.

8 Van Os (1974), pp. 32-34. The two paintings concerned are *The tree of Jesse* and *The Holy Family*, both in the Rijksmuseum in Amsterdam.

9 See Friedländer, V, 1969, fig. 9. Snyder (1960), observed that the Madonna in the present work closely resembles a panel that has come down to us in two versions, one in the town hall in Pretoria and the other at the G. Wildenstein Gallery in New York (for an illustration, see exhib. cat. *Middeleeuwse kunst der Noordelijke Nederlanden*, Amsterdam, Rijksmuseum, 1958, no. 31, fig. 16).

10 For example, Van Os (1964) en Lemmens (1966).

11 The underdrawings of the paintings in Vienna were published by Truus van Bueren and Molly Faries, "The 'Portraits' in Geertgen tot Sint Jans' Vienna Panels", in: H. Verougstraete-Marcq and R. Van Schoute (eds.), *Dessins sous-jacent et copies* (Le dessin sous-jacent dans la peinture, colloque VIII), Louvain-la-Neuve, 1991, p. 141-150.

12 For example, Van Os (1964) and Van Regteren Altena (1966).

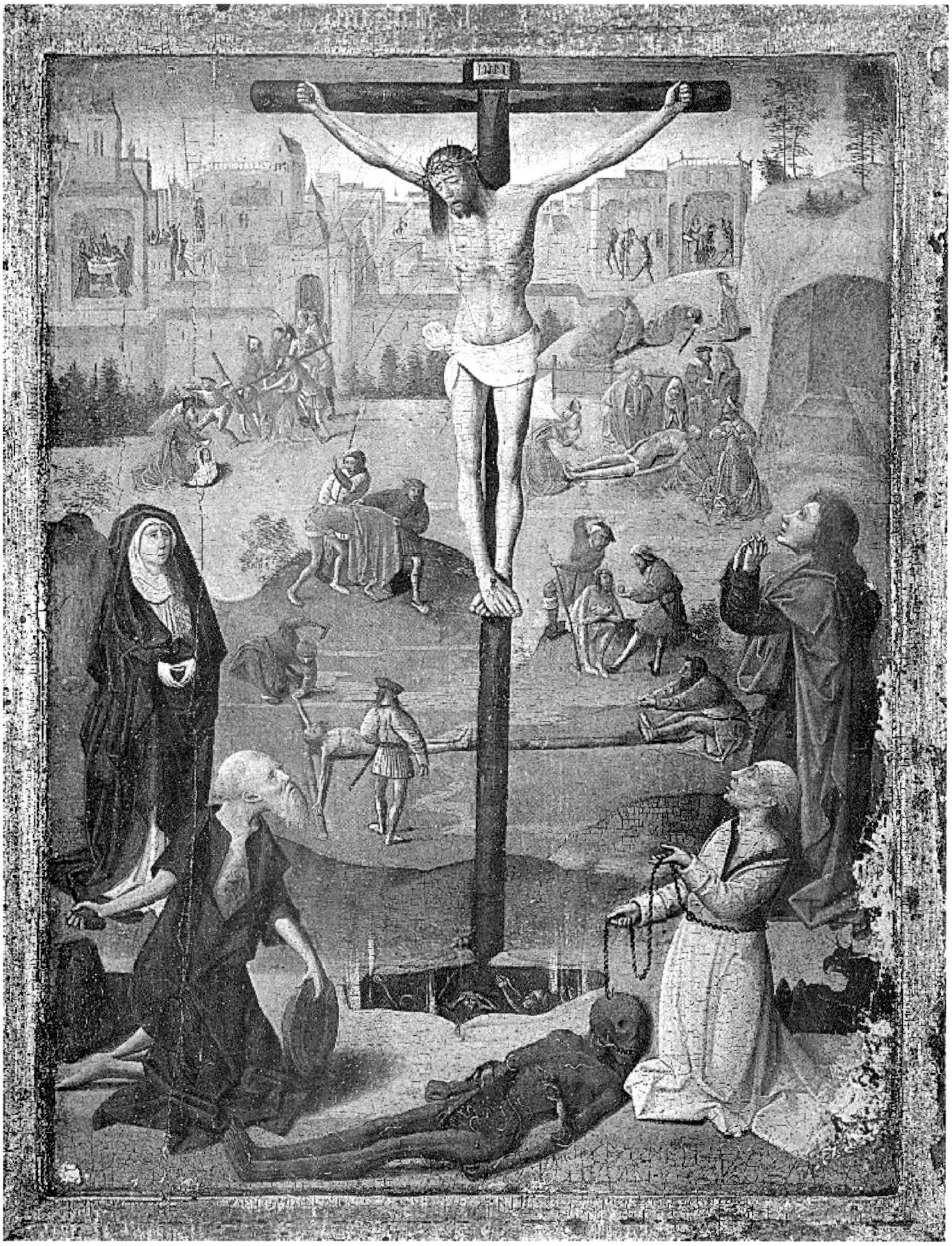

b. Geertgen tot St Jans, circle of, Crucifixion
Panel; 24.4 x 18.4 cm
Edinburgh, National Gallery of Scotland

similar to that shown on the panel in Edinburgh. Van Os observed, moreover, that two other paintings often attributed to Geertgen can also probably be associated with the Dominican order in Haarlem.[8]

In addition to the painting's iconography, its dating and attribution have been the subject of much discussion. A major problem in connection with the attribution is the evident difference in calibre between the Rotterdam painting and the one in Edinburgh. The rather wooden figures and gloomy composition, as well as the way in which the figures are positioned would seem to exclude Geertgen as the painter of the Edinburgh panel. The panel in Rotterdam, on the other hand, with its lucid composition and splendid treatment of light is accepted as original by most authors. Reference has repeatedly been made to its affinity with the *Madonna and child* in the Ambrosiana in Milan – a work whose authorship has never been in doubt.[9] A large number of authors have resolved the whole issue by assuming the existence of two different masters.[10]

It is not certain, however, that this is in fact the case. The damned under the cross in the Edinburgh panel have much in common with the angels in the painting in Rotterdam. The treatment of the folds in Mary's dress is also similar. It is, therefore, likely that both panels were made by a direct follower, and not by Geertgen tot St Jans himself. There is, nevertheless, a striking difference between the rather stiff panel in Edinburgh and the exceptionally fine painting in Rotterdam. Châtelet's (1980) attribution of both panels to the Master of the Antwerp triptych is not very convincing. The style of the underdrawing (fig. a) is different from those of the paintings of Geertgen in Vienna. A comparison is, however, extremely difficult to make, since these are much larger works.[11]

Most authors prefer an early dating – that is, before 1489.[12] They all, however, regard the Rotterdam panel as original. But if both are by the same artist, then the end of the fifteenth century would be more plausible, particularly in view of the eclectic nature of the painting in Edinburgh.[13]
FL

13 In a letter dated 13 January 1967 to the National Gallery of Scotland S.M. Newton wrote that, in her judgement, the clothing in both panels indicated the beginning of the sixteenth century. Comparable clothing can be found in two paintings attributed by Hoogewerff to Cornelis Buys and his studio. See G.J. Hoogewerff, *De Noord-Nederlandse schilderkunst*, II, The Hague 1937, figs. 170, 174. Lemmens (1966), p. 74, observed that the Lamentation in the background of the Edinburgh panel was a mirror-image copy of the famous painting by Geertgen in Vienna.

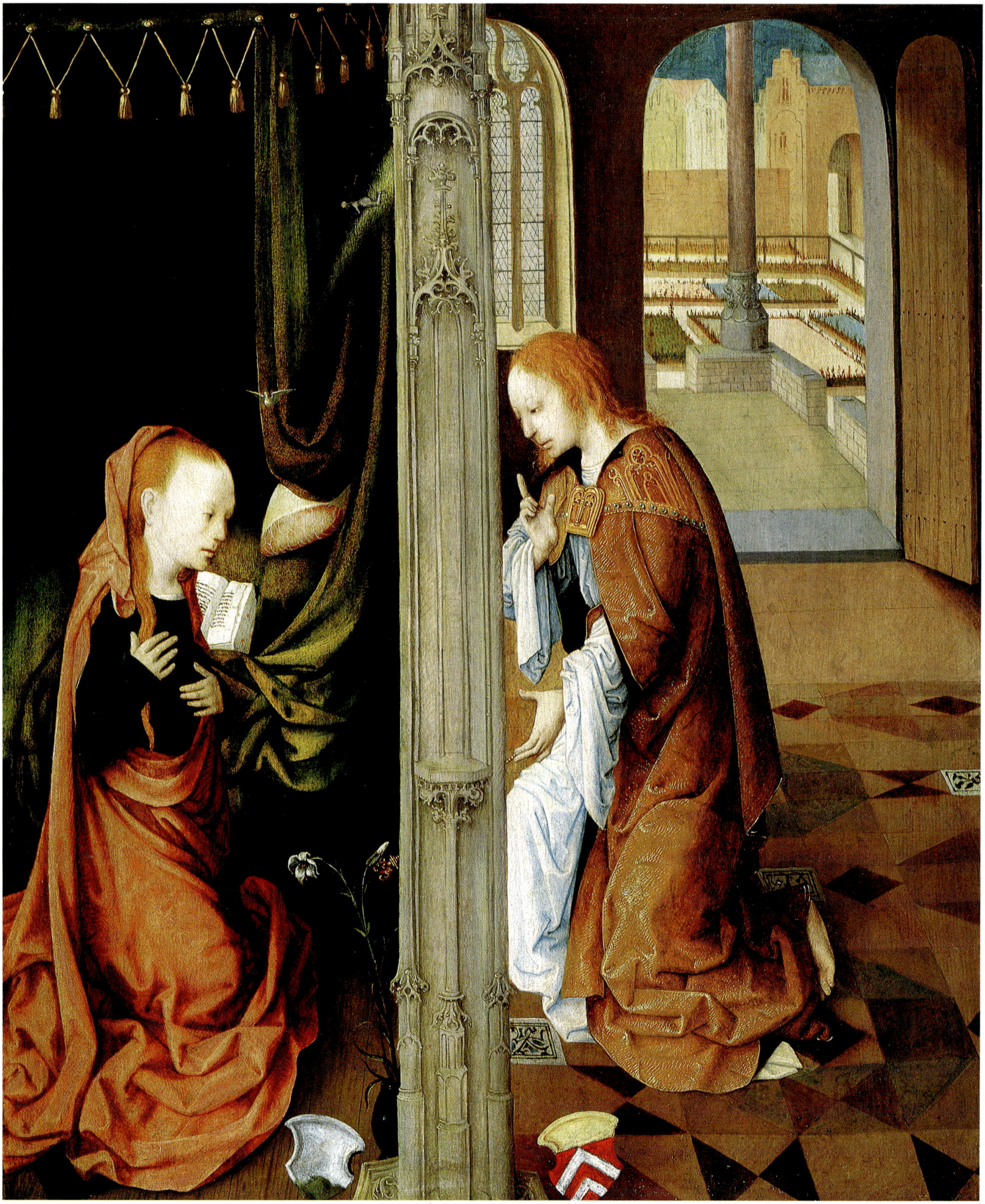

The Annunciation

Master of the Virgo inter Virgines
(active Delft c. 1470-1500)

Panel; 57 x 48 cm

Physical characteristics:[1] the panel consists of two vertical planks. The *barbe* can be seen on the left side and along the lower edge.

Infrared reflectography: only parts of the underdrawing are discernible. See description.

Dendrochronology: the youngest heartwood growth ring dates from 1460. The panel could not have been painted before 1471; it was more probably painted in or after 1485. See article by P. Klein.

Paint samples: five samples were analysed. The bed hangings were originally green. The present shade of brown results from the irreversible discoloration of the pigment copper resinate.

Provenance: private collection, Berlin (Schöneberg-Berlin);[2] De Burlet Gallery, Berlin;[3] Stefan von Auspitz, Vienna; purchased in 1932 by D.G. van Beuningen, Rotterdam and Vierhouten, through the K.W. Bachstitz Gallery, The Hague, for 20,000 guilders; on loan from that date to the Boymans Museum; acquired by the Museum in 1958 with the Van Beuningen Collection; inv. no. 1568.

Exhibitions: *Exhibition of Dutch Art 1450-1900*, London, Royal Academy of Art, 1929, no. 9; *Jeroen Bosch*, Rotterdam, Boymans Museum, 1936, no. 21, fig. 40; *Nederlandsche Kunst van de XVde en XVIde eeuw*, The Hague, Mauritshuis, 1945, no. 30; *Honderd jaar Museum Boymans Rotterdam. Meesterwerken uit de verzameling D.G. van Beuningen*, Rotterdam, Museum Boymans, no. 23; *Chefs-d'œuvre de la collection D.G. van Beuningen*, Paris, Petit Palais, 1952, no. 60; *Middeleeuwse kunst der Noordelijke Nederlanden*, Amsterdam, Rijksmuseum, 1958, no. 50.

Literature: F. Winkler, *Die Altniederländische Malerei*, Berlin 1924, p. 150; Friedländer, V, 1927, p. 69, no. 45, fig. table 31; F. Dülberg, *Niederländische Malerei der Spätgotik und Renaissance* (Handbuch der Kunstwissenschaft), Potsdam-Wildpark 1929, p. 104; H. Gerson, "Jerome Bosch and the North-Netherlandish Primitives", *The Burlington Magazine* LXIX (1936), p. 137; cat. 1937, no. 279; Friedländer, XIV, 1937, p. 98; G.J. Hoogewerff, *De Noord-Nederlandsche Schilderkunst*, II, The Hague, 1937, pp. 265-268, fig. 128; Hannema, 1949, no. 23, pl. 50; G. Knuttel, *De Nederlandse schilderkunst van Van Eyck tot Van Gogh*, Amsterdam 1950, p. 93, fig. p. 94; H. Gerson, *Van Geertgen tot Frans Hals*, Amsterdam 1950, p. 19, fig. 34; R. van Luttervelt, "De herkomst van de Meester van de Virgo inter Virgines," *Bulletin Museum Boymans* III (1952), pp. 57-71, fig.; M.J. Friedländer, *From Van Eyck to Bruegel*, London 1966, p. 57, fig. 133; G. Heinz, "Das Bild der Verkündigung Mariae vom Meister der Virgo inter Virgines im Salzburger Museum Carolino Augusteum", *Salzburger Museum Carolino Augusteum, Jahresschrift 1960*, Salzburg 1961, pp. 52, 54, note 4, fig. 11; cat. 1962, p. 87; J. Bruyn, "Meester van de Virgo inter Virgines", *Openbaar Kunstbezit* 2 (1958), no. 24, fig.; L. Reis-Santos, *Masterpieces of Flemish Painting of the Fifteenth and Sixteenth Centuries in Portugal*, Lisbon 1962, p. 65; E.G. Grimme, "Das Suermondt-Museum", *Aachener Kunstblätter* 28 (1963), p. 188, note 2; K.G. Boon, P.J.H. Vermeeren, *De Meester van de Virgo inter Virgines, Delftse verluchte Handschriften*, Oud Delft, 2, Rotterdam-The Hague 1963, pp. 17, 31, no. 4, p. 34, note 12; M.J. Friedländer, F. Grossmann, *Von Van Eyck bis Breugel*, Cologne 1965, fig. 133; Friedländer, V, 1969, p. 79, no. 45, fig. 29; A. Châtelet, *Les Primitifs Hollandais*, Freiburg 1980, pp. 148, 232, no. 124; D. Hammer-Tugendhat, *Hieronymus Bosch, eine Interpretation seiner Gestaltungsprinzipien*, Munich 1981, pp. 68, 88, fig. 66; J. Snyder, *Northern Renaissance Art: painting, sculpture, the graphic arts from 1350 to 1575*, New York 1985, p. 450, fig. 520.

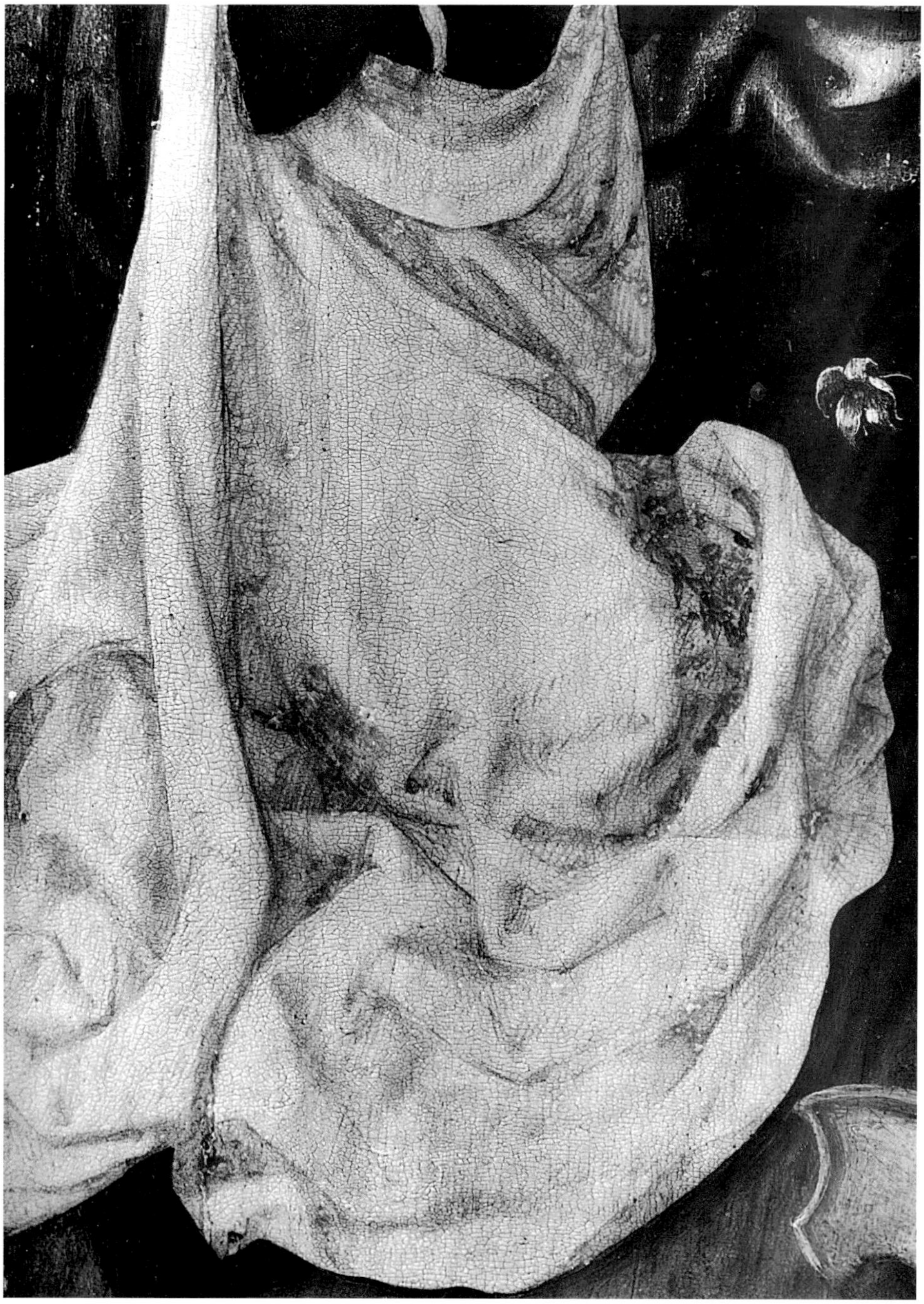

a. Infrared photograph of the Virgin's mantle.

The Master of the Virgo inter Virgines is named after a painting in the Rijksmuseum, Amsterdam, *Virgin and Child, with St Catherine, St Cecilia, St Barbara and St Ursula*. The artist, whose name is unknown, probably worked in Delft at the end of the fifteenth century. He also designed woodcuts, some of which were printed in books published in 1486 and 1487. As Boon states, in the Boymans-van Beuningen painting, as in the *Adoration of the Kings* in Berlin, the *Lamentation of Christ* in Liverpool and the *Crucifixion* in the Uffizi, Florence, he was at the height of his formidable powers.[4]

The angel, depicted kneeling with the right hand raised and a staff in the left hand, has entered through the open door. The Virgin, on the left, is also kneeling. The lily in the foreground symbolises her virginity. The dove, the symbol of God, and the Child Jesus, bearing the Cross, descend from the upper right. The angel is announcing the birth of Christ to the Virgin.

A remarkable feature, one that is characteristic of this painter, is the figures' hair, set so far back as to give them extremely high brows. It falls in strands over their shoulders. Endowing his figures with a deep expressiveness, it renders the Delft master immediately identifiable. It is perhaps in this quality that the influence of the Flemish artist Hugo van der Goes is perceptible.

The coats of arms at the foot of the painting were thought to be those of the Delft Van den Berg family, but this conclusion has proved controversial.[5] The composition exhibits a close affinity with the far left wing of the altarpiece with the *Adoration of the magi* in the Carolino Augusteum Museum, Salzburg, in which the figures are similarly represented.[6]

An examination conducted in 1986 revealed some parts of an underdrawing which, though faint (fig. a), is comparable to the underdrawing of the work in Amsterdam. The master's works are extremely difficult to date. Boon dates the Rotterdam panel around the same time as the woodcuts in *Evangelien ende Epistelen*, a book published in 1487.
JG

1 Examination in 1986 by J.R.J. van Asperen de Boer with the assistance of Patty van der Jagt. Infrared reflectograms: AB 903/6-35. Paint samples: A 242/1-5.

2 See Hannema (1949).

3 Note by E. Haverkamp Begemann in the Museum's file: "Winkler said the painting was discovered by De Burlet in Berlin. As he was leaving a gallery, he passed in the doorway a man carrying a parcel under his arm. He asked if he could see it; it proved to be dirty and broken in two (from top to bottom along the 'buttress'), but he perceived its age and good quality and bought it for next to nothing".

4 Boon (1963).

5 Suggested by Van Luttervelt (1952), termed uncertain by Boon (1963), and rejected by W.H. van Seters in a letter written to the Museum in 1972.

6 See the article by Heinz (1961).

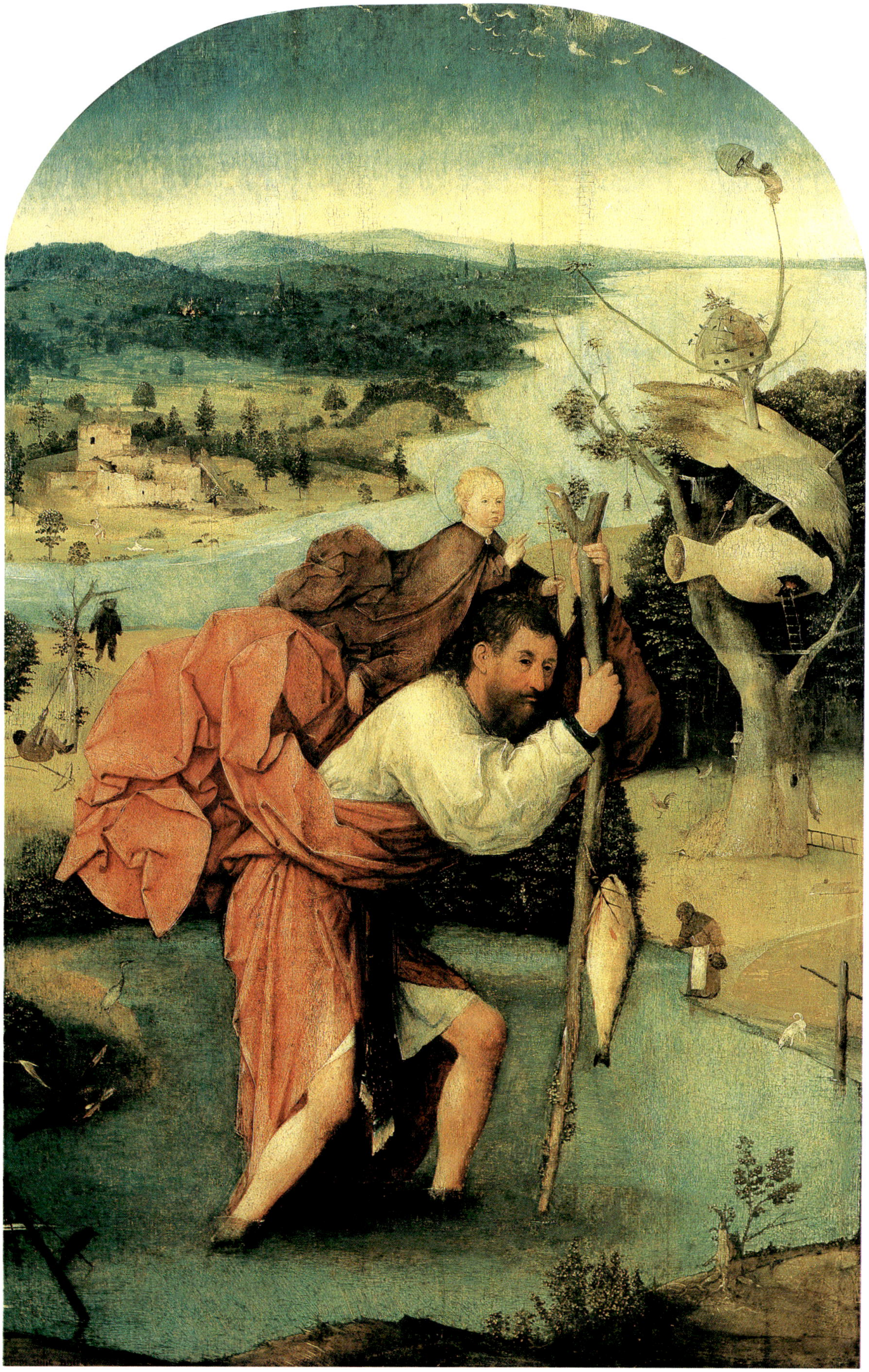

St Christopher carrying the Christ Child

Jheronimus Bosch
('s-Hertogenbosch c. 1450-'s-Hertogenbosch 1516)

Panel; 113 x 71.5 cm
Signed below left: Jheronimus Bosch

Physical characteristics:[1] the panel consists of four vertical planks. The *barbe* has been preserved showing that the arched shape must be original.[2]

Infrared reflectography: brush underdrawing. See text.

Dendrochronology: the youngest heartwood growth ring dates from 1479. The panel could not have been painted before 1490; it was more probably painted in or after 1504. See article by P. Klein.

Paint samples: the underdrawing was possibly painted directly onto the ground and an intermediate layer only applied afterwards. There are at most two layers of paint. The pigment azurite was detected.

Provenance: private ownership, Italy; F. Koenigs, Haarlem; on loan to the Boymans Museum, Rotterdam, 1935-1940; purchased by D.G. van Beuningen in April 1940 with the Koenigs Collection; donated by him in 1941 to the Boymans Museum Foundation, Rotterdam; inv. no. St. 26.

Exhibitions: *Tafelbilder des 15. und 16. Jahrhunderts*, Zurich, Kunsthaus, 1934, no. 95, fig. XXXVI; *Verzameling F. Koenigs, schilderijen*, Rotterdam, Boymans Museum, 1935, no. 2, fig. I; *Jeroen Bosch. Noord-nederlandsche primitieven*, Rotterdam, Boymans Museum, 1936, no. 60, fig. 61; *Meesterwerken uit vier eeuwen, 1400-1800*, Rotterdam, Boymans Museum, 1938, no. 1, fig. 37; *La peinture Hollandaise de Jerome Bosch à Rembrandt*, Brussels, Paleis voor Schone Kunsten, 1946, no. 12, fig. 4; *Les primitifs Flamands*, Paris, Musée de l'orangerie, 1947, no. 6, fig.; *Middeleeuwse Kunst der Noordelijke Nederlanden*, Amsterdam, Rijksmuseum, 1958, no. 69, fig. 41; *Jheronimus Bosch*, 's-Hertogenbosch, Noordbrabants Museum, 1967, no. 9, fig.

Literature: Friedländer, XIV, 1931, p. 101; A. Vermeylen, *Hieronymus Bosch*, Amsterdam 1939, pp. 19-20, fig.; F.M. Huebner, *Hieronymus Bosch*, Berlin 1939, fig. 30; J. Combe, *Jérome Bosch*, Paris 1946, p. 32, no. 75, fig.; J. Mosmans, *Jheronimus Anthonis-zoon van Aken alias Hieronymus Bosch. Zijn leven en zijn werk*, 's-Hertogenbosch 1947, pp. 16, 58-59, fig. 31; D. Bax, *Ontcijfering van Jeroen Bosch*, The Hague 1949, pp. 231-235, fig. 57; W. Fraenger, *Die Hochzeit zu Kana. Ein Dokument Semitischer Gnosis bei Hieronymus Bosch*, Berlin 1950, pp. 110-114; G.J. Hoogewerff, *Het landschap van Bosch tot Rubens*, Antwerp 1954, p. 12; D. Bax, *Beschrijving en poging tot verklaring van het Tuin der Onkuisheiddrieluik van Jeroen Bosch, gevolgd door kritiek op Fraenger* (Verhandelingen der Koninklijke Akademie van Wetenschappen, Afdeling letterkunde, n.r. LXIII, 2), Amsterdam 1956, pp. 169-170; L. Baldass, *Hieronymus Bosch*, Vienna-Munich, 1959 (1943), pp. 43, 82, 84, 238-239, fig. 78; C. Linfert, *Hieronymus Bosch. The paintings*, London 1959, p. 117, fig. 56; C.A. Wertheim Aymès, *Die Bildersprache des Hieronymus Bosch*, The Hague 1961, p. 62; J. de Boschère, *Jérôme Bosch et le fantastique*, Paris 1962, p. 233; L. van Puyvelde, *La peinture Flamande au siècle de Bosch et Breughel*, Brussels 1962, p. 38; M. Gauffreteau-Sevy, *Jérôme Bosch*, Paris 1965, pp. 219-220, no. 26; F.H. Huebner, *Jérôme Bosch*, Brussels 1965, p. 26; D. Buzzati, M. Cinotti, *L'Opera completa di Bosch*, Milan 1966, nr 36, fig. XXXVIII-XL; P. Gerlach, "Studies over Jeronimus van Aken (alias Bosch) II", *Spiegel der Historie* 2 (1967), p. 628; J. Bruyn, "Jheronimus Bosch (omstr. 1450-1516), De Heilige Christophorus", *Openbaar Kunstbezit* 11 (1967), no. 5, fig.; H. Read, *Art and alienation. The role of the artist in society*, London 1967, p. 81; V.M. Nieto Alcaide, *Bosch*, Novara 1968, p. 9, fig. XXXV; Friedländer, V, 1969, p. 91, fig. 114; P. Reuterswärd, *Hieronymus Bosch*, Uppsala 1970, p. 270, no. 25, fig. 51; N. van den Blom, "De vork aan de staf van de Christophorus van Jeroen Bosch", *Bulletin Museum Boymans-van Beuningen* 21 (1971)/1, pp. 35-36; O. Benesch, "Hieronymus Bosch and the thinking of the late Middle Ages", in: *Collected Writings* II, London 1971, p. 22; J.P. Filedt Kok, "Underdrawing and drawing in the work of Hieronymus Bosch: a provisional survey in connection with paintings by him in Rotterdam", *Simiolus* 6 (1972-73), pp. 138-140, fig.; W.S. Gibson, *Hieronymus Bosch*, London 1973, pp. 136, 154, 159, fig. 119, 120; G. Dogaer, "Jeroen Bosch. De Heilige Christophorus", *Openbaar Kunstbezit* 17 (1973), pp. 149-152, fig.; R. Schuder, *Hieronymus Bosch*, Berlin 1975, p. 59, fig. 54; W. Fränger, *Hieronymus Bosch*, Dresden 1975, pp. 221-223, 475, fig. 63-66; H. Holländer, *Hieronymus Bosch*, Cologne 1975, p. 105, fig. 25; Ch. de Tolnay, *Hieronymus Bosch*, Baden Baden 1975 (1st ed. 1937), pp. 38, 278-281, no. 27, fig.; J. Chailley, *Jérôme Bosch et ses symboles. Essai de décryptage*, Brussels 1978, pp. 197-199, no. 36, fig. XXVIII; M. Bergman, *Hieronymus Bosch and alchemy. A study on the St. Anthony triptych*, Stockholm 1979, p. 92, fig.; G. Unverfehrt, *Hieronymus Bosch. Die Rezeption seiner Kunst im frühen 16. Jahrhundert*, Berlin 1980, pp. 12, 27, 29, 34, 55, 57, 170, 178, 189-197, 200, nrs. 16, 39, 68, 74; I. Bango Troviso, F. Marias, *Bosch, reality, symbol and fantasy*, 1982, p. 212.; R. Genaille, "Le paysage Flamand et Wallon au XVIème siècle avant Patenir", *Jaarboek van het Koninklijk Museum voor Schone Kunsten, Antwerpen* 1986, p. 65; H. Marijnissen, *Hiëronymus Bosch. Het volledig oeuvre*, Antwerp 1987, pp. 402-409, fig.; R.L. Falkenburg, *Joachim Patinir. Landscape as an image of the pilgrimage of life*, Amsterdam-Philadelphia 1988, p. 67, fig. 31; P. Gerlach (samenstelling en redactie P.M. LeBlanc), *Jheronimus Bosch. Opstellen over leven en werk door drs. P. Gerlach O.F.M. cap*, The Hague 1988, pp. 57, 92, 99; W.S. Gibson, *"Mirror of the earth", The world landscape in sixteenth-century Flemish painting*, Princeton, New Jersey 1989, pp. 6,92 (note 102).

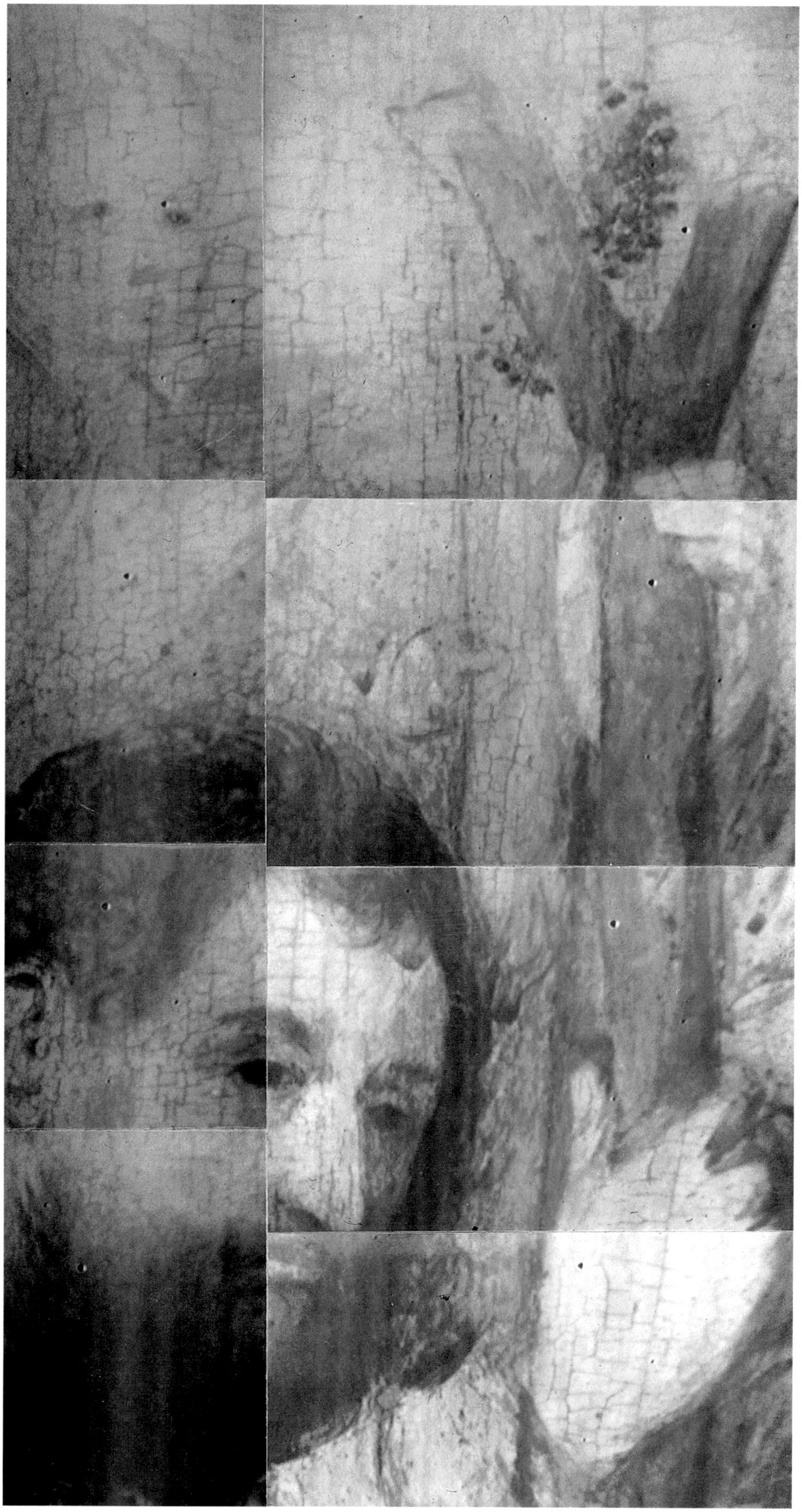

a. Infrared reflectogram assembly. Detail of St Christopher's staff.

Little is known of the provenance of this panel before it became part of the collection of Franz Koenigs. A "St Christopher" by Bosch is mentioned in a number of seventeenth-century inventories, such as those of Rudolph II, Philip IV and Melchior Wyntgis.[3] The descriptions are, however, too cursory to allow any of the panels mentioned to be identified as the painting under consideration. There is no documentary evidence to substantiate Mosman's conjecture that the work was produced for the chapel of the 's-Hertogenbosch Brotherhood of St Anne.[4] There is unanimous agreement that the work is original. It is usually dated in the artist's middle period, that is, somewhere between 1490 and 1505.

The underdrawing, which can be detected using infrared reflectography, is limited to the figure of Christ and the clothing of the saint (figs. a, b). Outlines and folds are indicated using a broad brush, whilst shadows are given by shading with short thin lines.[5] When painting, Bosch only departed from his drawings to alter a few details, such as the giant's right hand and staff, both of which were reduced in size. Bosch used quite a thin layer of paint for the larger areas of sky and landscape. Details, on the other hand, were pastose. The artist made only a small number of changes whilst painting the panel. For example, the giant's left index finger was initially placed over the staff rather than along it, the right thumb was originally larger and the right river bank probably continued further.

Several versions of the story of St Christopher have been related, the best known of which is in the *Golden Legend*. Reprobus, the "damned", was searching for the most powerful man on Earth. He at first served a king who feared the devil, after which he entered the service of the devil who, in turn, turned out to be afraid of a cross. A hermit advised him to serve Christ by carrying travellers over a dangerous river. One night a small child asked the giant to take him to the other side. During the crossing the ostensibly light burden became almost too heavy to support, and the child revealed himself to be the Saviour. To prove it, he told the giant that, if he planted his staff in the ground, it would bloom the next day. This duly happened and the giant was, from that day on, a devout Christian and took the name of Christopher – he who carries Christ.

Bosch painted the giant in an expansive riverine landscape, carrying the infant Christ as he supported himself with a long staff. The mast of a sunken ship is protruding from the water.[6] On the left a winged fish is flying and, on the bank, there is a man with a small dog. On the left behind the giant a man is hanging a bear in a tree. The animal has been hit by an arrow. On the right some chickens are running around a large tree, at the bottom of which there is small chapel and a fox hanging by its tail. A huge jug is hanging above the chapel; a burning fire is visible through a hole in its side. A small figure is standing on the rim hoisting up a lantern. Above the jug we can see a skewer with roast meat and a drying shirt, over which a canopy has been placed. Higher still there is a dovecote and a beehive, towards which a small figure is climbing. On the far bank of the river a small naked man is fleeing and a dragon is emerging from a deserted ruin. There are a few settlements in the distance, one of which is on fire.

The way the saint and the infant Christ are depicted here is in keeping with a long-established tradition,[7] although Christ is usually shown holding a globe instead of a staff. The are some leaves sprouting from St Christopher's staff. This would appear to contradict the *Golden Legend*, but is consistent with a German version of the story, in which the branch starts blooming during, rather than after, the crossing.[8]

The hermit who drew the giant's attention to God appears in the background of virtually every portrayal of St Christopher. Although Bosch depicts him with a jug in his hand, he is generally shown holding a lantern. In the German version of the story mentioned above, St Christopher meets the hermit for the first time when he is collecting water.[9]

Iconographers are hampered by the scarcity of material with which to compare some of the smaller details. The fish on the staff, which could be a reference to Christ, has also been interpreted as a symbol of the giant's conversion.[10] The bear being hoisted up might possibly refer to an earlier episode in the giant's story in which he gave assistance

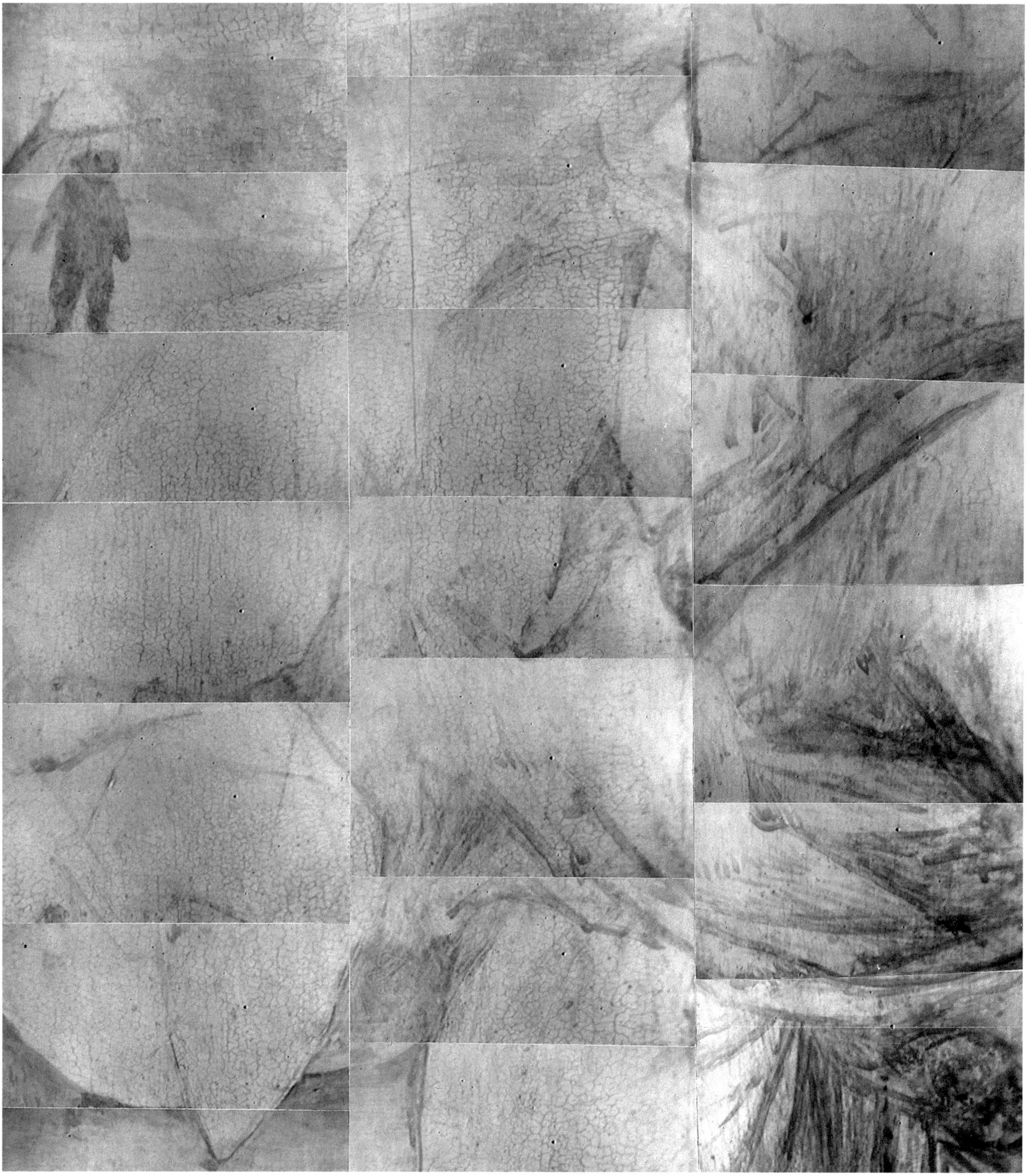

b. Infrared reflectogram assembly. Detail of St Christopher's cloak.

to hunters.[11] The act of hoisting has also been interpreted as symbolising the defeat of chastity.[12] It is difficult to find a satisfactory explanation for the strange tree on the right, which is apparently the hermit's dwelling. Bax believes that it is possessed by the devil and that the beehive and dovecote are symbols of gluttony and lechery.[13] Marijnissen observed that the jug is probably a 'starling-pot' for trapping birds.[14] There is a rather less bizarre tree serving as the hermit's dwelling in a painting of St Christopher by Patinir in the Escorial in Madrid.[15] The small naked man climbing towards a beehive also appears in different versions of Pieter Huys's *Temptation of St Anthony*.[16] Most authors tend to regard the details in the tree and the dragon in the ruin, for example, as evil threats which the giant must withstand.[17] This interpretation is sometimes combined with the more general idea of St Christopher representing each individual's need to overcome the many dangers and temptations obstructing his or her path through life.[18]
FL

1 Scientific examination conducted in 1991 by R.J. James under the supervision of J.R.J. van Asperen de Boer. A copy of his minor thesis in the Museum's file on the painting. Paint samples A 321/1-6. Infrared reflectograms: AB 1202/6-AB 1204/5.

2 Tolnay (1975) thought that the arched shape could not be original.

3 The collection of Rudolph II included, in 1619, "Ein Taffel, gar alt, sanct Christophoro mit allerlei wunderbarlichen sachen von Jan Boss" and in 1621, "Sanct Christophorus, wie er übers Meer gehet von Hieronymus Bosch (orig.)"; see P. Vandenbroeck, "Rudolf II als verzamelaar van werk van en naar Jheronimus Bosch", *Jaarboek van het Koninklijk Museum voor Schone Kunsten Antwerpen* 1981, pp. 127-128. In 1636 the inventory of Philip IV listed "S. Cristobal que va pasando un rio con varias invenciones de figuras y dos fuegos"; see C. Justi, "Die Werke des Hieronymus Bosch in Spanien", *Jahrbuch der Königlich Preussischen Kunstsammlungen* X (1989), p. 144. Melchior Wyntgis owned "een orgineel stuck olieverwe synde een Sint Christoffels tempatie, van Jeronymus Bosch. In een groote lyst...60 gulden", see G. Glück, "Peter Bruegel the elder and the legend of St. Christopher in early Flemish painting", *The Art Quarterly* XIII (1950), p. 45 (note 8).

4 Mosmans (1947).

5 The underdrawing corresponds with that of *St John on Patmos* (Berlin), *St Jerome* (Ghent) and *John the Baptist* (Madrid), see Filedt Kok (1972-73).

6 Bax (1956) claims that it is a trap.

7 See, for example, Unverfehrt (1980).

8 Bax (1949). There are other cases of St Christopher holding a branch in bloom. The Frangipani altarpiece by van Scorel in Obervellach is an example. See Friedländer, XII, no. 298.

9 See note 8.

10 See Bax (1949) about the fish as a symbol of Christ and Tolnay (1975) about the fish as a token of conversion.

11 See note 8.

12 Baldass (1959).

13 See note 8.

14 Marijnissen (1987).

15 Apart from Patinir, many other painters followed Bosch in placing the hermit's dwelling in a tree. Some of these dwellings also have sparrow-pots around them, but of normal dimensions. See Unverfehrt (1980) and Gibson (1989), fig. nos. 1.26 and 3.11.

16 For example, in the painting kept in the Koninklijke Musea voor Schone Kunsten in Brussels.

17 Bax (1949) and Baldass (1959), for example.

18 Unverfehrt (1980). Also see Falkenburg (1989), p. 106.

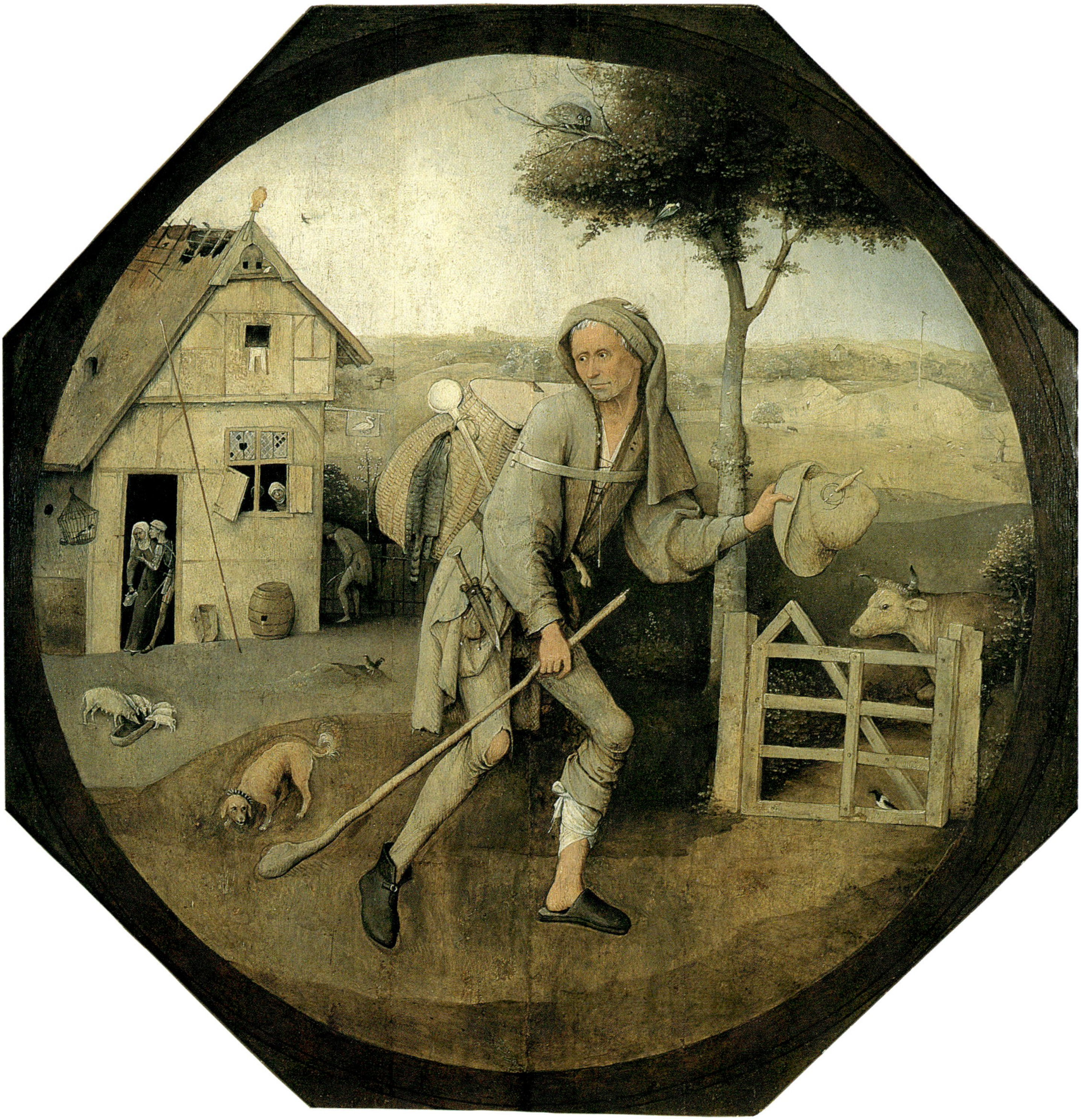

The pedlar

Jheronimus Bosch
('s-Hertogenbosch c. 1450-
's-Hertogenbosch 1516)

Panel; 71 x 70.6 cm
Diameter of circle 64.6 cm

Physical characteristics: the panel originally consisted of three planks. The centre plank was sawn through vertically, with the result that the painting now consists of four planks. It is not known when this occurred.

Infrared refectography:[1] there is an extensive brush underdrawing. The figure of the pedlar is particularly detailed. Shadows are indicated by cross-hatching. The final painting differs little from the underdrawing, with a few details, such as the dagger and the dog, being reduced in size. Some birds, included in the underdrawing, were not painted (fig. a).

Dendrochronology: The four planks come from the same tree. The youngest heartwood growth ring dates from 1476. The panel could not have been painted before 1488; it was more probably painted in or after 1502. Also see the text and article by P. Klein.

Provenance: Théodor Schiff Collection, Paris; Albert Figdor Collection, Vienna; auctioned in Berlin, P. Cassirer, 1930, cat. III, no. 41, fig.; purchased by Goudstikker Gallery, Amsterdam for DM 385,000; purchased from the gallery in 1931 by the Museum for 262,000 guilders; inv. no. 1079.

Exhibitions: *Nouvelles acquisitions de la collection Goudstikker*, Amsterdam, Herengracht 458, Rotterdam, Kunstkring 1930-31, no. 3, fig.; *Jeroen Bosch. Noord-Nederlandsche primitieven*, Rotterdam, Boymans Museum, 1936, no. 57, fig. 76; *Tentoonstelling bijbelsche kunst*, Amsterdam, Rijksmuseum, 1939, no. 124a, fig. 5; *La peinture Hollandaise de Jerome Bosch à Rembrandt*, Brussels, Paleis voor Schone Kunsten, 1946, no. 13, fig. 5; *Middeleeuwse kunst der Noordelijke Nederlanden*, Amsterdam, Rijksmuseum, 1958, no. 71, fig. 42; *Jheronimus Bosch*, 's-Hertogenbosch, Noordbrabants Museum, 1967, no. 36, fig.

Literature: G. Glück,"Zu einem Bilde von Hieronymus Bosch in der Figdorschen Sammlung in Wien" *Jahrbuch der Königlich Preuszischen Kunstsammlungen* 25 (1904) pp. 174-184; M.G. Gossart, *Jérôme Bosch. La peinture de diableries à la fin du Moyen-Age*, Lille 1907, p. 290; P. Lafond, *Hieronymus Bosch Son art, son influence, ses disciples*, Brussels-Paris 1914, pp. 48, 76, 77, no. 37, fig. 65; E. Heidrich, *Altniederländische Malerei*, Jena 1910, p. 41, fig. 105; L. Baldass, "Die Chronologie der Gemälde des Hieronymus Bosch", *Jahrbuch der Königlich Preuszischen Kunstsammlungen* 38 (1917), pp. 193-194; M. Conway, *The Van Eycks and their followers*, London 1921, pp. 341-342, fig. XVI. 3; K. Pfister, *Hieronymus Bosch*, Potsdam 1922, p. 28, fig. 36; W. Schürmeyer, *Hieronymus Bosch*, Munich 1923, pp. 68-69, fig. 40; L. Baldass, "Betrachtungen zum Werke des Hieronymus Bosch", *Jahrbuch der Kunsthistorischen Sammlungen in Wien* N.F. 1 (1926), p. 117, fig. 63; Friedländer, V, 1927, pp. 102, 152, no. 103; G. Glück, "Dr. Albert Figdor und seine Sammlung, *Zeitschrift für Bildende Kunst* 61 (1927-28), p. 256, fig.; L. Baldass, "Die Gemälde der Sammlung Figdor", *Pantheon* IV (1929), p. 467, fig.; M. Conway, "The literature of art: dr. Friedländer on Flemish painting" *The Burlington Magazine* LVI (1930), p. 166; *Jaarverslag Museum Boijmans, Rotterdam* 1931, pp. 2-5, fig.; D. Hannema, "De verloren zoon van Jheronymus Bosch", *Vereeniging Rembrandt. Jaarverslag over 1931*, pp. 8-11, fig.; W. Cohen, "Rundschau: Rotterdam", *Pantheon* 8 (1931), p. 440; P. Koomen, "Een Bosch in Boymans", *Maandblad voor Beeldende Kunsten* 9 (1932), pp. 45-49; *Beknopte catalogus van de schilderijen en beeldhouwwerken in het Museum Boymans te Rotterdam*, 1935, no. 51; A.M. Hammacher, "Jeroen Bosch" *De Vrije Bladen* 13 (1936), fig.; G.J. Hoogewerff, "Hieronymus Bosch", *Elsevier's geïllustreerd maandschrift* 46 (1936), pp. 10-11; L. Baldass, "Zur Entwicklungsgeschichte des Hieronymus Bosch", *Jaarboek der Koninklijke Museums voor Schoone Kunsten van België* 1 (1938), pp. 68-69; M. Brion, *Bosch*, Paris 1938, p. 32, fig.; W. Schöne, *Die grossen Meister der Niederländischen Malerei des 15. Jahrhunderts. Hubert van Eyck bis Quentin Massys*, Leipzig 1939, pp. 20-22, fig.; A. Vermeylen, *Hieronymus Bosch*, Amsterdam 1939, pp. 48-49, fig.; F.H. Huebner, *Hieronymus Bosch*, Berlin 1939, fig. 10; D.Th. Enklaar, *Uit Uilenspiegels kring*, Assen 1940, pp. 77-85; F.M. Huebner, *Jeroen Bosch als mensch en kunstenaar*, The Hague 1942, p. 19; L. von Baldass, *Hieronymus Bosch*, Vienna 1943, pp. 17-18, 60, 73, 91, 232, figs. 5-7; E.R. Meijer, "Hieronymus Bosch en de verloren zoon", *Phoenix* 1, no. 7 (1946), pp. 1-7, fig.; J. Combe, *Jerome Bosch*, Paris 1946, p. 42, figs. 112-115; J. Mosmans, *Jheronimus Anthonis-zoon van Aken alias Hieronymus Bosch. Zijn leven en zijn werk*, 's-Hertogenbosch 1947, p. 41; D. Bax, *Ontcijfering van Jeroen Bosch*, 's-Gravenhage 1949, pp. 222-231; A. Pigler, "Astrology and Jerome Bosch", *The Burlington Magazine* 92 (1950), pp. 132-36; W. Fränger, *Die Hochzeit zu Kana*, Berlin 1950, p. 110, fig. 12,28; H. Gerson, *Van Geertgen tot Frans Hals* (De schoonheid van ons land), Amsterdam 1950, p. 60, fig. 25; W. Fraenger, "Hieronymus Bosch. Der verlorene Sohn", *Castrum Peregrini* 32 (1951), pp. 27-39, fig.; D. Bax, "Bosschiana. Verloren Zoon-Johannes op Patmos-Wellusttuin-Doornenkroning", *Oud Holland* LXVIII (1953), p. 200; K. Seligmann, "Hieronymus Bosch. The peddler", *Gazette des Beaux-Arts* 42 (1953), p. 97-104; G. van Camp, "Autonomie des Jerome Bosch et récentes interprétations de ses œuvres", *Bulletin Koninklijke Musea voor Schone Kunsten* III (1954), p. 137; D. Bax, *Beschrijving en poging tot verklaring van het tuin der onkuisheid drieluik van Jeroen Bosch* (Verhandelingen der Koninklijke Nederlandse Akademie van Wetenschappen, afd. letterkunde, n.r. LXIII, no. 2), Amsterdam 1956, pp. 34 (note 14), 81, 169, 178-179, 180-181; L. van Puyvelde, "De bedoelingen van Bosch", *Mededelingen der Koninklijke Nederlandse Academie van Wetenschappen*, n.r. vol. 19 (1956), pp. 101, 103-104; L. Brand Philip, "The peddler by Hieronymus Bosch. A study in detection", *Nederlands Kunsthistorisch Jaarboek* 9 (1958), pp. 1-81; L. Baldass, *Jheronimus Bosch*, Vienna-Munich 1959,

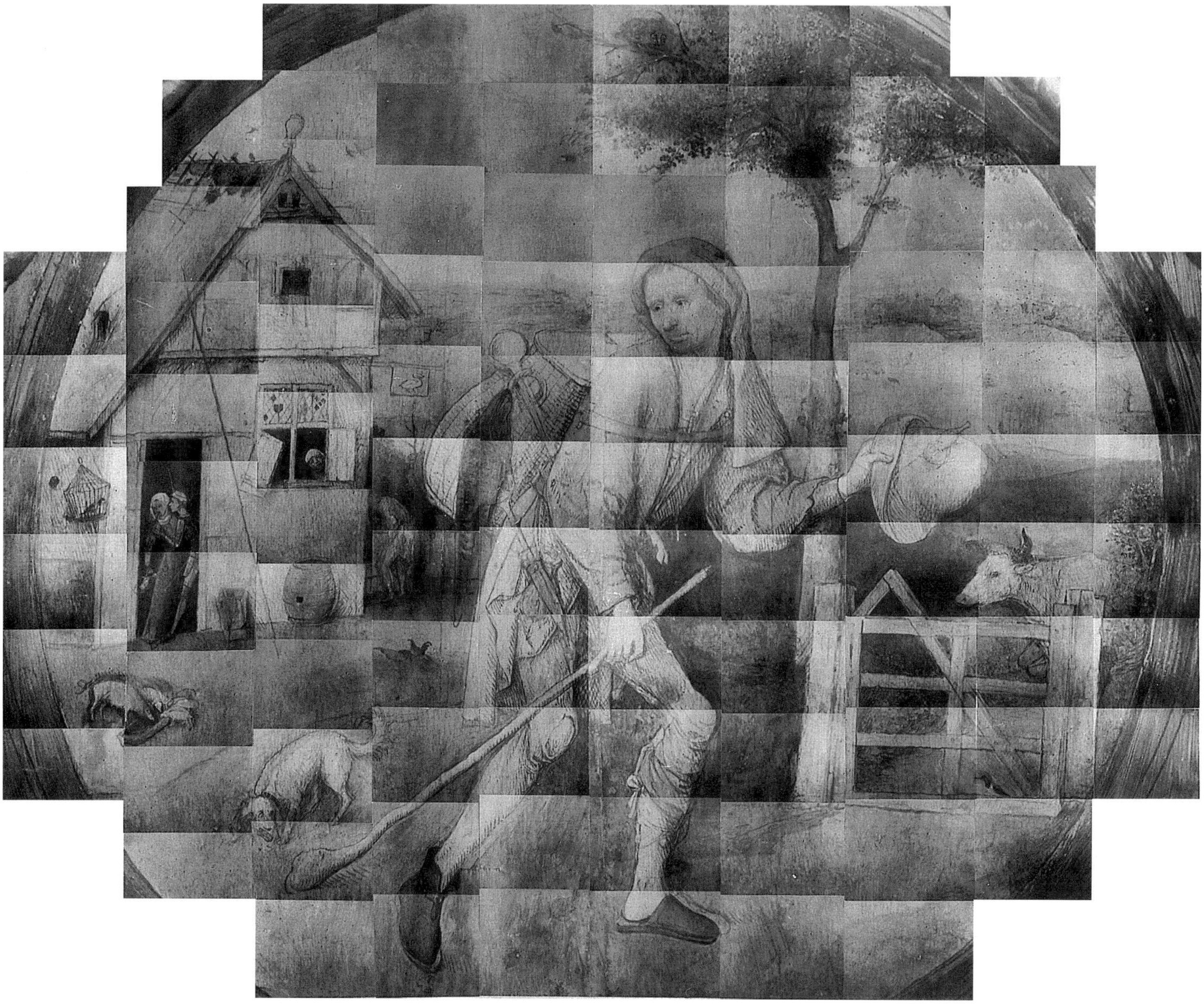

a. Infrared reflectogram assembly.

pp. 19-20, 227, figs. 14-16; C. Linfert, *Hieronymus Bosch. The paintings*, London 1959, p. 118, figs. 78-79; H. Schulte Nordholt, "Jeroen Bosch (ca. 1450-1516), De Verloren Zoon" *Openbaar kunstbezit* 3 (1959), no. 1, fig.; R.L. Delevoy, *Bosch*, Geneva 1960, pp. 38-39, fig.; C. Peman, "Sobre la interpretacion del viandante al reverso del Carro de heno de El Bosco", *Archivo Espaòl de Arte* 34 (1961), pp. 125-139, fig.; C.A. Wertheim Aymes, *Die Bildersprache des Hieronymus Bosch*, The Hague 1961, pp. 7-31; C.T. Eisler, *New England Museums* (Les primitifs flamands. Corpus de la peinture des anciens Pays-Bas méridionaux au quinzième siècle, 4), Brussels 1961, p. 46; J. de Boschère, *Jérôme Bosch et le fantastique*, Paris 1962, p. 78-82, fig. 11; L. van Puyvelde, *La peinture Flamande au siècle de Bosch et Breughel*, Brussels 1962, pp. 38, 42, 60, fig. 10; D. Bax, "Bezwaren tegen L. Brand Philips interpretatie van Jeroen Bosch' marskramer, goochelaar, keisnijder en voorgrond van hooiwagenpaneel", *Nederlands Kunsthistorisch Jaarboek* 13 (1962), pp. 1-54; cat. 1962, p. 28; C. Linfert, "Hieronymus Bosch-halb Rätsel, halb Enthüllung", *Blick auf Beckmann. Dokumente und Vorträge*, Munich 1962, p. 191, fig. 102; S. Sulzberger, "Notes sur la grisaille", *Gazette des Beaux-Arts* 59 (1962), p. 120; N. Beets, "De Nederlandse schilderkunst van de vijftiende eeuw", *Kunstgeschiedenis der Nederlanden*, II, Zeist-Antwerp 1963 (1st ed 1937), p. 366, fig. 22; K. Arndt, "C.T. Eisler, *New England Museums*, Brussels 1961", *Zeitschrift für Kunstgeschichte* 27 (1964), p. 174; M.J. Friedländer, *Von Van Eyck bis Bruegel*, Cologne 1965 (1st ed. 1921), p. 67, fig. 158; Ch. de Tolnay, *Hieronymus Bosch*, Baden-Baden 1965 (1st ed. 1937), pp. 45-46, 282, no. 28, fig.; M. Gauffreteau-Sevy, *Jérôme Bosch*, Paris 1965, pp. 120-121, 210-212, no. 34; F.H. Huebner, *Jérôme Bosch*, Brussels 1965, p. 26, fig. 20; D. Buzatti, M. Cinotti, *L'Opera completa di Bosch*, Milan 1966, pp. 111-112, no. 61; H. Read, *Art and alienation. The role of the artist in society*, London 1967, pp. 78-81, fig. 16; Friedländer, V, 1967, p. 56, no. 103, fig. 94; S.K. Scher, "Hieronymus Bosch: An exercise in attribution", *Bulletin of Rhode Island School of design, Museum notes* 1967, pp. 3-5, fig. 2; K.G. Boon, "Bespreking van Ch. de Tolnay, *Hieronymus Bosch*, Baden-Baden 1965", *The Burlington Magazine* CX (1968), p. 156; V.M. Nieto Alcaide, *Bosch*, Novara 1968, p. 9; J. van Lennep, "A propos de Jérôme Bosch. Polémique, Tarot et Sang-dragon", *Gazette des Beaux-Arts* 71 (1968), pp. 189-190; R. Peeters, "Rondom een paar thema's bij Jeroen Bosch", *Taxandria* n.r. XL (1968), pp. 1-20; I.L. Zupnick, "Bosch's representation of acedia and the pilgrimage of everyman", *Nederlands Kunsthistorisch Jaarboek* 19 (1968), pp. 115-132; K. Renger, "Versuch einer neuen Deutung von Hieronymus Boschs Rotterdamer Tondo", *Oud Holland* LXXXIV (1969), pp. 67-76, fig.; H.G. Franz, *Niederländische Landschaftsmalerei im Zeitalter des Manierismus*, Graz 1969, p. 26; G. von der Osten, H. Vey, *Painting and sculpture in Germany and the Netherlands: 1500-1600* (Pelican history of Art), Harmondsworth 1969, p. 160; K. Renger, *Lockere Gesellschaft*, Berlin 1970, p. 27, 90, 102, 114; P. Reutersward, "The face in the rock", *Art News Annual* 36 (1970), pp. 101-102, fig.; P. Reuterswärd, *Hieronymus Bosch*, Uppsala 1970, pp. 41, 122, 139-148, no. 21, fig. 38; C. Linfert, *Jheronimus Bosch*, Cologne 1970, p. 35, fig. 52; J. Traeger, "Der 'Heuwagen' des Hieronymus Bosch und der eschatologische Adventus des Papstes", *Zeitschrift für Kunstgeschichte* 33 (1970), p. 308; O. Benesch, "Hieronymus Bosch and the thinking of the late Middle Ages", in: *Collected Writings* II, London 1971, p. 26; R.H. Marijnissen, K. Blockx, P. Gerlach e.a., *Jheronimus Bosch*, Brussels 1972, pp. 23, 36, 42, 44, 48, 53-54, 62-63, 86-87, 93 (note 12), 99 (note 119), 100 (note 124), 157, 170, 192, 205, 209; J.P. Filedt Kok, "Underdrawing and drawing in the work of Hieronymus Bosch: a provisional survey in connection with paintings by him in Rotterdam", *Simiolus* 6 (1972-73), pp. 140-145, fig.; W.S. Gibson, *Hieronymus Bosch*, London 1973, pp. 103-106, 154-155, 158-159, fig. 85-86, 141; D. Hannema, *Flitsen uit mijn leven als verzamelaar en museumdirecteur*, Rotterdam 1973, pp. 39, 42-44, 60, 62, 78; G. von der Osten, *Deutsche und Niederländische Kunst der Reformationszeit*, Cologne 1973, p. 169, fig. 136; J. Chailley, *Jérôme Bosch*, Brussels 1973, pp. 119-120, 273-274, fig.; W. Fränger, *Hieronymus Bosch*, Dresden 1975, pp. 257-267, fig.; R. Schuder, *Hieronymus Bosch*, Berlin 1975, pp. 40-41, figs. 20-21; H. Holländer, *Hieronymus Bosch*, Cologne 1975, pp. 40, 110, fig. 12; R.H. Marijnissen, "Bosch' zogeheten "Verloren Zoon"", *Taxandria* n.r. XLVIII (1976), pp. 217-24; J. Chailley, *Jérôme Bosch et ses symboles. Essai de décryptage*, Brussels 1976, pp. 273-274, no. 6; G. Martin, *Hieronymus Bosch*, London 1978, no. 31, fig.; M. Bergman, *Hieronymus Bosch and Alchemy. A study on the St. Anthony Triptych*, Stockholm 1979, p. 81, fig.; G. Unverfehrt, *Hieronymus Bosch. Die Rezeption seiner Kunst im frühen 16. Jahrhundert*, Berlin 1980, pp. 12, 27, 29-31, 34, 36, 46, 131, 158, no. 21; A. Boczkowska en A. Wiercinski, "Hieronymus Bosch's self-portraits", *Ars Auro Prior* 1981, pp. 193-199; V.G. Tuttle, "Bosch's image of poverty", *The Art Bulletin* 63 (1981), pp. 88-95, fig. 2; R. Graziani, "Bosch's wanderer and a poverty commonplace from Juvenal", *Journal of the Warburg and Courtauld Institutes* XLV (1982), pp. 211-216, fig. 34b; P.S. Beagle, *The garden of earthly delights*, New York 1982, p. 65, fig.; I. Bango Troviso, F. Marias, *Bosch, reality, symbol and fantasy*, 1982, pp. 170-171, fig.; G. Vallese, "Il tema della follia nell'arte di Bosch: Iconografia e stile", *Paragone* 405 (1983), p. 41, figs. 29-30; A. Cook, *Changing the signs. The fifteenth-century breakthrough*, Lincoln-London 1985, pp. 86-88, fig. 30; P. Vandenbroeck, "Bubo significans. Die Eule als Sinnbild von Schlechtigkeit und Torheit, vor allem in der Niederländischen und Deutschen Bilddarstellung und bei Jheronimus Bosch. I", *Jaarboek van het Koninklijk Museum voor Schone Kunsten Antwerpen* 1985, p. 22; J. Snyder, *Northern Renaissance Art*, New York 1985, p. 206, fig. 196; J.O. Hand, M. Wolf, *Early Netherlandish Painting* (The collections of the National Gallery of Art, Washington, systematic catalogue), 1986, p. 259; R. Genaille, "Le paysage Flamand et Wallon au XVIème siècle avant Patenir", *Jaarboek van het Koninklijk Museum voor Schone Kunsten, Antwerpen*, 1986, p. 67; H.J. Raupp, *Bauernsatiren*, Niederzier 1986, p. 200; R.L. Falkenburg, *Joachim Patinir. Landscape as an image of the pilgrimage of life*, Amsterdam-Philadelphia 1988, pp. 88-90, fig. 44; R.H. Marijnissen, P. Ruyffelaere, *Hieronymus Bosch. Het volledige oeuvre*, Antwerp 1987, pp. 410-420, fig.; P. Vandenbroeck, *Jheronimus Bosch, tussen volksleven en stadscultuur*, Berchem 1987, pp. 62-69; M. Tóth-Ubbens, *Verloren beelden van miserabele bedelaars, leprozen-armen-geuzen*, Leiden-Ghent 1987, p. 48; W. Bosing, *Hieronymus Bòsch*, Cologne 1987, pp. 61-65, fig.; P. Gerlach (samengesteld en redactie door P.M. Le Blanc), *Jheronimus Bosch. Opstellen over leven en werk, door drs. P.Gerlach O.F.M. CAP.*, 's-Hertogenbosch-The Hague 1988, p. 26, fig.; P. Vandenbroeck, "Jheronimus Bosch' zogenaamde Tuin der lusten. I", *Jaarboek van het Koninklijk Museum voor Schone Kunsten Antwerpen* 1989, pp. 72, 92; exhib. cat. *From Pisanello to Cezanne, Master drawings from the Museum Boymans-van Beuningen, Rotterdam*, New York, Pierpont Morgan, Library, Forth Worth, Kimbell Art Museum, Cleveland, The Cleveland Museum of Art, 1990-91, pp. 51-53; P. Reuterswärd, *The visible and the invisible in art*, Vienna 1991, pp. 191, 198; exhib. cat. *David Teniers de Jonge*, Antwerp, Koninklijk Museum voor Schone Kunsten, 1991, p. 118, fig. 35b.

Dirk Hannema lost a night's sleep thanks to this famous painting. He was the Museum's director when it was put up for auction in Berlin in 1930. He wanted to buy it, but could not possibly afford the price it would fetch. Fortunately, however, the panel found its way to the Goudstikker Gallery. He was eventually able to gather together the necessary funds, although this did present some problems, as the reply from Sir Henry Deterding to a request for a contribution shows: "I do not feel inclined to make the Museum a gift of that ugly vagabond; I will give it something a good deal better, when the time comes".[2]

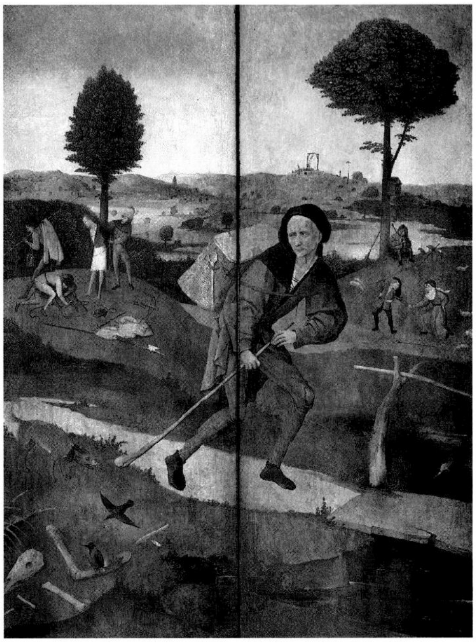

b. The rear of the Haywain Triptych. Museo del Prado, Madrid.

The panel is painted predominantly in shades of grey, together with green, brown, white, yellow and pink.

The paint is thin and the number of layers applied appears to be small. In places the underdrawing is visible through the painted surface of this well-preserved tondo. The brush strokes are most clearly visible in the highlights.

The painting's present octagonal shape is not original. During restoration work in 1931 it was found that the corners had been sawn off later and that the panel must also once have been thicker. It was therefore assumed that there must originally have been paintings on both the front and reverse of the panel, which had at some time been separated from each other.[3]

On the basis of the subdued colours used, it is reasonable to assume that the painting was originally on the reverse.[4] Having accepted this, the question nevertheless remains as to whether the painting was the reverse of one (left-hand) panel or the reverse of both wings of a triptych. The second possibility is suggested by the joint running exactly down the middle of the panel. Attention should also be drawn to the reverse of the *Haywain Triptych* (Museo del Prado, Madrid) on which a very similar picture was painted across two panels (fig. b). Another possibility is that the joint comes from the painting being sawn in two. This could have occurred when the front and rear were separated since, if there was not a long enough saw available to complete the separation in one go, the painting would first have had to be sawn in half.[5]

There has never been any doubt about the painting's authenticity and it is regarded by the vast majority of authors as one of Bosch's late works. Study of the underdrawing has, however, cast some doubt on the accuracy of this dating. Although Bosch's underdrawings have been divided into a number of groups, specific periods have not been found for them.[6] It is striking that the painting's underdrawing is extremely similar to that of a number of works which have traditionally been placed in the artist's middle period: the *Ship of fools* in Paris, the *Allegory of gluttony and lust* in New Haven and the *Death of a miser* in Washington. The planks on which the latter was painted are now known to come from the same tree as the present work.[7]

The painting has had a broad appeal ever since its discovery in 1904, speaking to us in an unusually direct way for the late Middle Ages. The exact meaning of the panel still, however, needs to be answered. It was initially construed as depicting the prodigal son (Luke 15:11-32) on the point of repenting.[8] This was justified by the house in the background – clearly a brothel – where the son had squandered his money and by the pigs, supposedly referring to his period as a swineherd. Doubts were soon expressed about this interpretation, particularly in view of the advanced age of the main figure,[9] who could just as easily have been a vagrant, hawker, vagabond or beggar. Various authors remarked on his resemblance to the fool in a pack of tarot cards.[10]

Pigler, the first person to make a connection with astrology, thought that the man was a child of Saturn.[11] Lotte Brand Philip developed this hypothesis further in an article which was as ingenious as it was implausible. She sees the figure as symbolising melancholy and the element earth. The painting is, in her view, a fragment of a triptych with the four elements – standing at the same time for the four humours – depicted on the outside.[12] A number of authors have followed Hannema in claiming to recognise the man as a self-portrait of Bosch.[13]

In general, though, attempts to discover a deeper meaning behind all the painting's components have not been very convincing. Most of the details can be interpreted in completely different, and often contradictory, ways. They are of necessity based on literary sources and old sayings and only seldom on relevant visual material.[14]

Nevertheless, as Marijnissen has correctly observed, if we allow for a few exceptions, many of the more general interpretations do not actually diverge significantly.[15] A large proportion of authors assume that, in addition to any specific connotation, such as the prodigal son or a vagrant, Bosch's design also had a more general purpose.

The figure stands for mankind; he is a 'homo viator', making his way through life, sin threatening to ensnare him at every turn. Most authors see the figure as a man coming to his senses who, aware of his unsatisfactory existence, wishes to improve his life.[16] Whether this is in fact the case is a matter of speculation. This reading ultimately relates to the first interpretation – that he represents the prodigal son. These authors are persuaded by the man's expression and posture, combined with a positive explanation of the details at the right of the painting. His expression is, however, far from unambiguous. Art historians have variously described his face as shy, disturbed, confused, full of life, profoundly serious or as displaying a melancholy smile of self-knowledge.[17] The details on the right, such as the cow, magpie, fence and tree admit both positive and negative interpretations.

The common interpretation of the main figure as "mankind" is based on the assumption that Bosch's patrons, the wealthy bourgeoisie and aristocracy, would have been able to identify with a poor pedlar. Given that this cannot be stated with any certainty, the interpretations offered by Renger, Raupp and Vandenbroeck are more convincing.[18] Renger associates the figure with personifications of "Alberoyt" (Penniless) and "Sorgheloos" (Carefree) which are to be found on some sixteenth-century prints.

An objection to his account is that the examples provided were all produced later and none displays any direct resemblance to the painting itself. Renger's interpretation was adopted by Raupp who compared the picture with the composition on the rear of the *Haywain Triptych*. He concluded that the figure signifies sin and represents the antithesis of bourgeois ethics. Vandenbroeck observes that contemporary sources and literature show that pedlars were seen in an extremely negative light. Both Renger and Vandenbroeck regard the main figure as a swindler.

Since none of the different interpretations is entirely convincing, it is perhaps best to refer to the painting by the neutral title of "pedlar".
FL

1 The painting has been examined twice using infrared reflectography. The first examination was conducted by J.R.J. van Asperen de Boer and J.P. Filedt Kok in 1971-72 and was published by Filedt Kok in 1972-73. A report on the second examination, made in 1988-89, by U.I. Nürnberger is in the Museum's file on the painting. Infrared reflectograms: AB 1079/2-AB 1082.

2 "Ik denk er niet aan om die lelijke landloper cadeau te doen aan het Museum; dat krijgt wel wat beters van mij, te zijner tijd." Hannema (1973), p. 62, writes that the painting "went" for 264,000 guilders at the Berlin sale, but that it later transpired that the painting had been withdrawn. After Koenigs had promised that he would act as guarantor, Hannema was able to procure the necessary funds within a year, during which time the painting remained with Goudstikker. The largest share of the money, 180,000 guilders, came from the Van der Schilden bequest, whilst Van Beuningen and Koenigs each contributed 20,000 guilders. The remainder was donated by the Rembrandt Society and various private individuals. In 1936 Sir Henry Deterding donated two paintings – by David Teniers and Gerard Dou (inv. nos. 2039 and 1186). Hannema's claim that they were sold by the Alte Pinakothek to raise funds to buy the *Pedlar* is incorrect. Bosch's panel had been in the Boymans Museum for a long time when the two works were sold.

3 Details concerning the restoration have been taken from the Museum's file on the painting.

4 Bosch often made circular paintings in a grisaille-like technique on the reverse of his panels. See, for example, the *Bearing of the Cross* in Vienna and the *St John on Patmos* in Berlin.

5 This was suggested during the restoration in 1931. See the Museum's file on the painting.

6 See D.R. van Schoute, "Over de techniek van Jeroen Bosch", *Jheronimus Bosch. Bijdragen bij gelegenheid van de herdenkingstentoonstelling te 's-Hertogenbosch*, pp. 72-79 and Filedt Kok (1972-73).

7 See P. Klein's article in this catalogue.

8 Glück (1904)

9 See, for example, Baldass (1926), Friedländer (1927), Bax (1949) and Van Camp (1954).

10 Seligmann (1953) and Van Lennep (1968), for example.

11 Pigler (1950)

12 Brand Philip (1958).

13 Hannema (1931), Boczkowska and Wiercinski (1981).

14 See Marijnissen (1987) for a review of the different interpretations of the details.

15 Marijnissen (1987).

16 For example, Seligman (1958), Zupnick (1968), Peeters (1968), Beagle (1982), Falkenburg (1988), Snyder (1985).

17 Friedländer (1927), Fraenger (1951), De Tolnay (1965), Baldass (1943), Schulte Nordholt (1959) and Bax (1949) respectively.

18 Renger (1969), Raupp (1986), Vandenbroeck (1987).

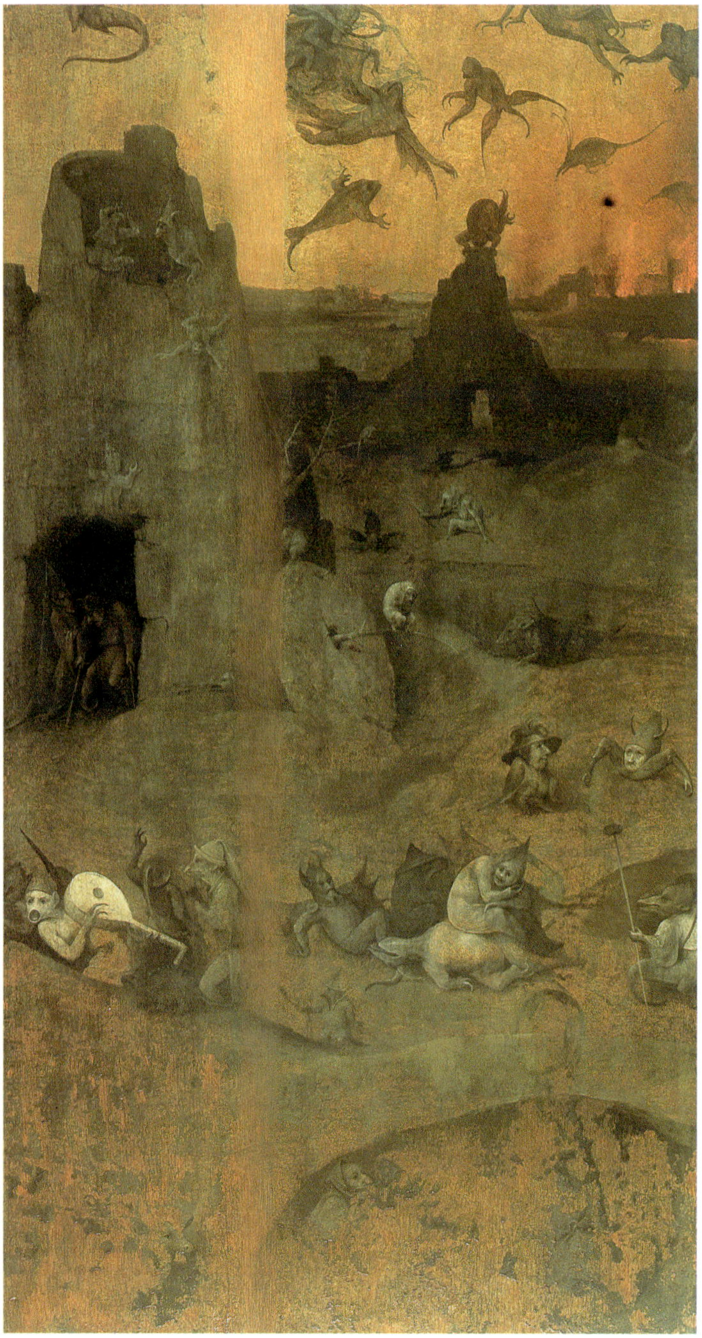

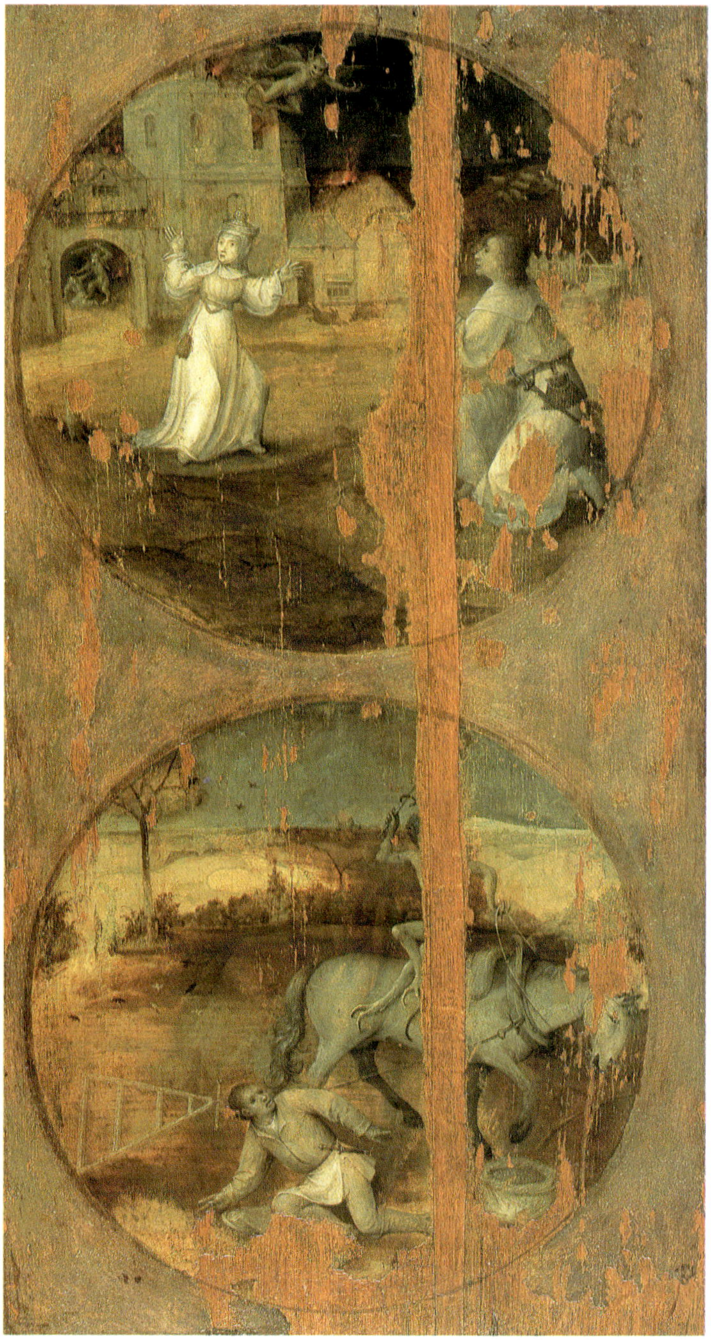

Hell
The Flood

Jheronimus Bosch
('s-Hertogenbosch c. 1450-'s-Hertogenbosch 1516)

Panels; 69 x 36 cm / 69 x 38 cm

Both panels were discovered at the end of the 1920s by the art dealer N. Beets at the residence of the Marquis de Chiloedes in Madrid, and were sold by him to Koenigs. Friedländer was the first to mention the paintings. In 1927, when they were still privately owned in Madrid, he wrote, "Bedeutende Erfindung, sicherlich von Bosch. Über die Ausführung kann ich nicht urteilen, da ich nur kleine Abbildungen von diesen Flügeln gesehen habe." Ten years later, he reported, "Original, schlecht erhalten." On a less positive note, that same year, De Tolnay expressed the view that they were not by Bosch.

Not long after that, Von Baldass made the first detailed study of the paintings.

The front of the right panel (which was actually thought to be the left one initially) shows the biblical story of Noah and his family leaving the ark after the Flood (Genesis 8:15-22). We see Noah and his family on the stranded ark. They have opened the hatch and a great procession of animals – lions, giraffes, camels and many other species – is descending to the land. At the bottom of the mountain lie the bodies of the drowned people and animals.

The other panel is given over to demonic figures. One of them is passing the time playing the lute. The sky is filled with fantastic flying creatures and, in the distance, a city stands in flames.

The scene is generally regarded as representing hell, or the state of mankind before the Flood, when God saw that the world was full of human wickedness (Genesis 6:5).

On the reverse sides of the panels are four circular pictures which have been interpreted in a variety of ways. The upper scene on the back of the *Flood* shows a virtually naked man being attacked by three demons. At the bottom of the picture, there is a spectacular, monstrous animal, exactly like one in a drawing by Jheronimus Bosch in the Kupferstichkabinett in Berlin (fig. a). The lower scene presents Christ in the foreground. He appears to be blessing the same man, who has his hands joined in prayer. An angel in the background is offering him a garment. In the distance, in the water, lies a shipwreck. In the upper scene on the other panel, we see a large farm in the background being laid waste by the devil. He is attacking a figure on the left and, in front of the farmhouse, cattle lie dead. An elegantly-dressed person raises his or her arms to heaven and takes flight. On the right a man is kneeling with his hands clasped together. Beneath that is a portrait of the devil. Seated on a horse, he is harrowing a field. He has taken over from the farmer, who has either fallen over or been thrown on the ground.

Although a considerable amount of attention has been paid to the interpretation of these scenes, the relatively simple analysis provided by Von Baldass in 1943 probably captures the essence of the matter. He interprets the naked man in the first two scenes as representing the soul being attacked by demons, then kneeling before Christ and, in the background, being clothed. In the other pair, he sees an exorcism of the devil above, and possibly an interpretation of the parable of the sower (Luke 8) below. Von Baldass further observed – correctly – that both sides of the panels had been painted in grisaille,

Physical characteristics:[1] both panels (cat. nos. 17 and 18) consist of two vertical planks.

Infrared reflectography: both panels have extensive brush underdrawings. See text.

Dendrochronology: the youngest heartwood growth ring dates from 1497. The panels could not have been painted before 1508; they were more probably painted in or after 1514. See text and article by P. Klein.

Provenance: Marquis de Chiloedes, Madrid, 1927 (discovered there by N. Beets); Mr. N. Beets; F. Koenigs, Haarlem, on loan to the Boymans Museum, 1935-40; in 1941 donated by D.G. van Beuningen to the Boymans Museum Foundation; (cat. no. 17) inv. no. St. 27; (cat. no. 18) inv. no. St. 28.

Exhibitions: *Catalogus van de tentoonstelling van oude kunst*, Amsterdam, Rijksmuseum, 1929, no. 10; *Verzameling F.Koenigs schilderijen*, Rotterdam, Boymans Museum, 1935, nos. 4, 5, figs. III-VI; *Jeroen Bosch Noord-Nederlandsche Primitieven*, Rotterdam, Boymans Museum, 1936, nos. 58, 59, figs. 72-75.

Literature: Friedländer, V, 1927, p. 143, fig. 64; Friedländer, XIV, 1937, p. 100, no. 64; Ch. de Tolnay, *Hieronymus Bosch*, Basle 1937, pp. 31, 67, note 94, 92, nos. 13, 14, figs. 24-27; L. von Baldass, *Hieronymus Bosch*, Vienna 1943, pp. 22, 28-29, 69, 232, 235, figs. 8, 9, 26, 27; J. Combe, *Jerome Bosch*, Paris 1946, nos. 34-37, fig.; W. Fraenger, *Die Hochzeit zu Kana, ein Dokument semitischer Gnosis bei Hieronymus Bosch*, Berlin 1950, pp. 97-107, figs. 24, 25; J. Mosmans, *Maria en Sint Jan, onbekend en laat schilderwerk van Jheronimus Bosch bewaard in zijne vaderstad*, 's-Hertogenbosch 1950, p. 20; D. Bax, *Beschrijving en poging tot verklaring van het tuin der onkuisheidsdrieluik van Jeroen Bosch*, Amsterdam 1956, pp. 151-153, 166-169, 173, 179, 181; O. Benesch, "Hieronymus Bosch and the Thinking of the Late Middle Ages", *Konsthistorisk Tidskrift* XXVI (1957), p. 113, fig. 25; L. Brand Philip, "The Peddler by Hieronymus Bosch, a Study in Detection", *Nederlands Kunsthistorisch Jaarboek* 9 (1958), p. 21, fig. 16; L. Baldass, *Jheronimus Bosch*, Vienna, Munich 1959, pp. 33-34, 82-83, 231, figs. 17, 18, 42, 43; C. Linfert, *Hieronymus Bosch, The Paintings*, London 1959, nos. 30-32; cat. 1962, p. 28; J. de Boschère, *Jérôme Bosch et le fantastique*, Paris 1962, pp. 165-168, figs. IX, X.; M. Gauffreteau-Sévy, *Jérôme Bosch*, Paris 1965, pp. 86, 217, no. 13, fig. p. 163; D. Buzzati, M. Cinotti, *L'opera completa di Bosch*, Milan 1966, p. 97, nos. 25A-F, figs. X, XI; Friedländer, V, 1969, p. 81, no. 64,

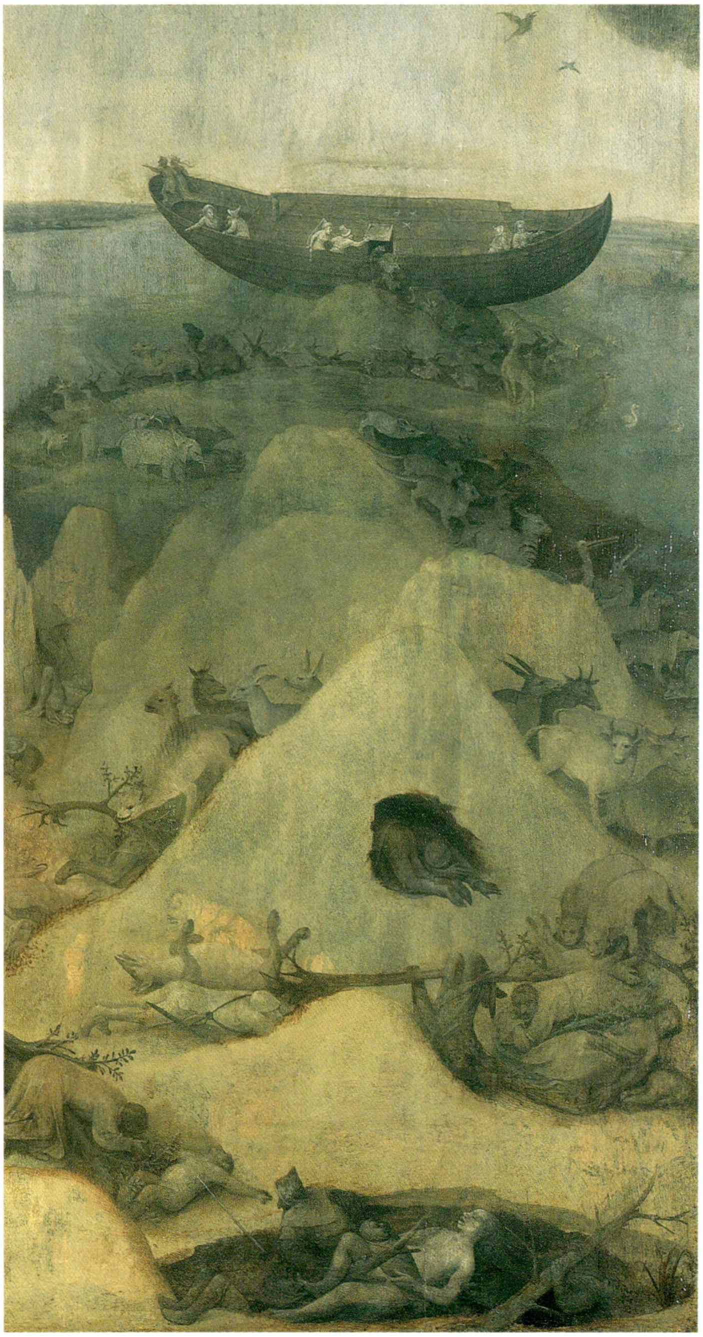

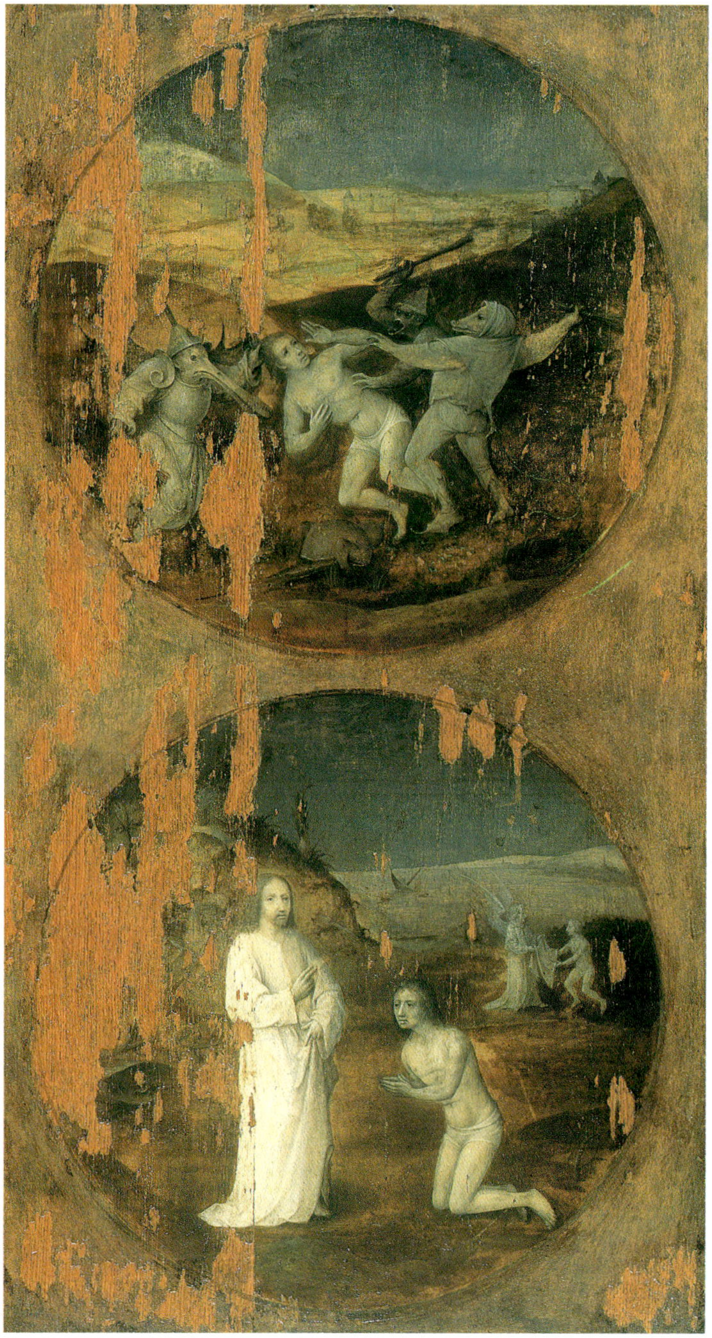

rather than one side as in the case of an altarpiece. He inferred that they originally formed the wings of an altar depicting the *Last Judgement*.

Fraenger expressed the view that this altarpiece was a work by Bosch entitled "Sicut erat in diebus Noë" (As it was in the days of Noah), acquired by Archduke Ernst in 1595.[2] He associates the picture of hell with the "Nephilim" family, which is not, however, listed in any lexicon. He explains the four scenes as follows. First we have the young Tobias healing the possessed daughter of Rachel. Then, in agreement with Baldass, comes the parable of the sower. The third and fourth pictures give a rendition of the story of the Good Samaritan. Together they signify the four ages of man.

Wittrock, for her part, recognises the first scene as an episode from St Augustine's *De civitate Dei*. She believes that the second one was based on a text of Peregrinus.[3] The sermon of Peregrinus is the subject of the third, whilst, for the fourth, she can offer no explanation.

However, the interpretation of the four scenes need not perhaps be so very complicated. If we return to the order the paintings were in shortly after their discovery, we would first of all find the scene depicting a woman or – more probably – a man being driven from his farm by demons. In the scene underneath he is also being chased by the devil from his land. He is then far from hearth and home and, virtually naked, is attacked by fiends. Finally he is saved by Christ. This makes it a straightforward story of salvation.

It has always been assumed that the paintings are the wings of a triptych – with the centre panel depicting the *Last Judgement*, according to Von Baldass. That would imply that both the front and reverse of the side-panels were in grisaille, which, as he observed, would be unusual.

It is far from certain that the paintings were, in fact, originally side-panels. It is also conceivable that they performed a particular function as part of a larger altarpiece: as small wings, for example, such as the Adriaen van Wesels Lady altar must have possessed.[4]

There was, at first, a lack of agreement as to whether the panels were painted by Bosch. Friedländer was certain that they were original, De Tolnay thought they were not, and Von Baldass, although he considered their condition too poor to make a definite judgement one way or the other, agreed to accept his attribution. The literature has reflected this state of uncertainty for a long time.

The panels' state of preservation had for a long time been so bad that the decision was eventually taken in 1981 to have them restored.[5] The extremely intricate process of restoration took five years to complete.

Some new, quite spectacular infrared reflectograms were made to assist in the restoration.[6] A bird-like creature, for example, was drawn in the middle of *Hell* (fig. b), but never painted; and the witch at the bottom left of the painting was originally seated on a barrel with feet. Two figures – a monk on his knees on top of an animal and a man kneeling in front of them – were drawn in the *Flood* (fig. c). They are both now visible with the naked eye through the paint. On the right, other figures appear to have been drawn which were also left unpainted. These underdrawings were made with a fairly broad brush. Although the strokes on the circular pictures are considerably narrower and more delicate, brush was probably used here too.

Starting with the scene where a figure is being driven from his house, only a few architectural alterations are in evidence (fig. d). In the picture below (fig. e), the complete figure of the devil on horseback was originally drawn some five centimetres to the left. We can also form an impression of the devil's head which, although it has disappeared from the painting with the vertical strip, is clearly visible in the underdrawing. Radical changes were also made to the upper scene on the other panel (fig. f). Where today we

figs. 42, 43; E.H. Gombrich, "Bosch's 'Garden of Earthly Delights': a Progress Report", *Journal of the Warburg and Courtauld Institutes* 32 (1969), p. 170, fig. g; P. Reuterswärd, *Hieronymus Bosch* (Acta Universitatis Upsaliensis, Figura Nova Series VII), Uppsala 1970, pp. 19, 262, figs. 13, 15, 16; A.P. de Mirimonde, "Le symbolisme musical chez Jérôme Bosch", *Gazette des Beaux-Arts* 77 (1971), p. 38, fig. 42; J.P. Filedt Kok, "Underdrawing and drawing in the work of Hieronymus Bosch: a provisional survey in connection with the paintings by him in Rotterdam", *Simiolus* 6 (1972-73), pp. 145-149, figs. 10-13; W.S. Gibson, *Hieronymus Bosch*, New York (1973), p. 108, figs. 88-94; R. Schuder, *Hieronymus Bosch*, Berlin 1975, p. 70, figs. 77, 78; W. Fraenger, *Hieronymus Bosch*, Dresden 1975, pp. 146-150, figs. 44-52, 75; J. Chailley, *Jérôme Bosch et ses symboles*, Brussels 1978, pp. 134-139, no.25; I. Wittrock, "Die sogenannte Sintflutflügel des Hieronymus Bosch", *Oud Holland* 93 (1979), pp. 52-60, figs. 1-4; G. Unverfehrt, *Hieronymus Bosch, Die Rezeption seiner Kunst im frühen 16. Jahrhundert*, Berlin 1980, pp. 24, 26, 42, 57, 144, 146, 179; R.H. Marijnissen, P. Ruyffelaere, *Hieronymus Bosch, Het volledig oeuvre*, Antwerp 1987, pp. 292-299, fig.; P.F.J.M. Hermesdorf, "Het technische en het al te technische in de restauratie van schilderijen", *Die Kunst und ihre Erhaltung, Rolf E. Straub zum 70. Geburtstag gewidmet*, Worms 1990, pp. 134-147, fig. 18.

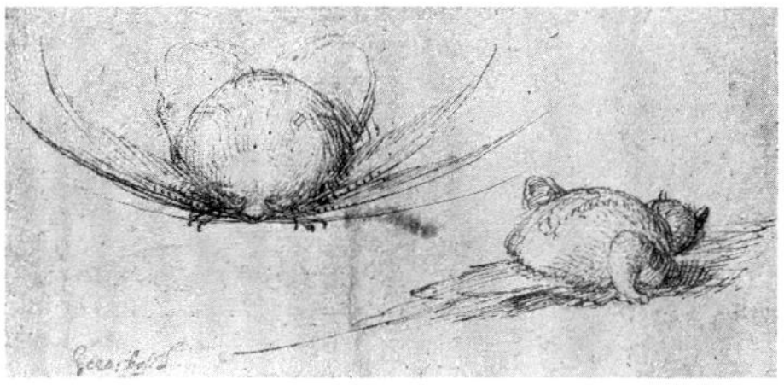

a. Jheronimus Bosch, Two monsters
Pen; 8.5 x 18.2 cm
Berlin, Kupferstichkabinett

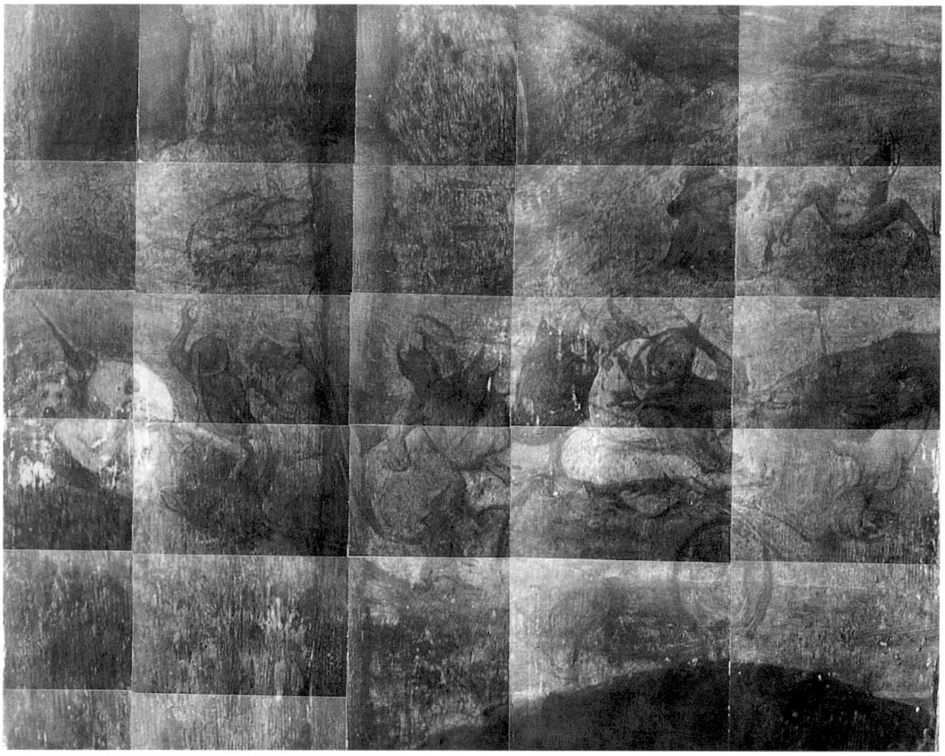

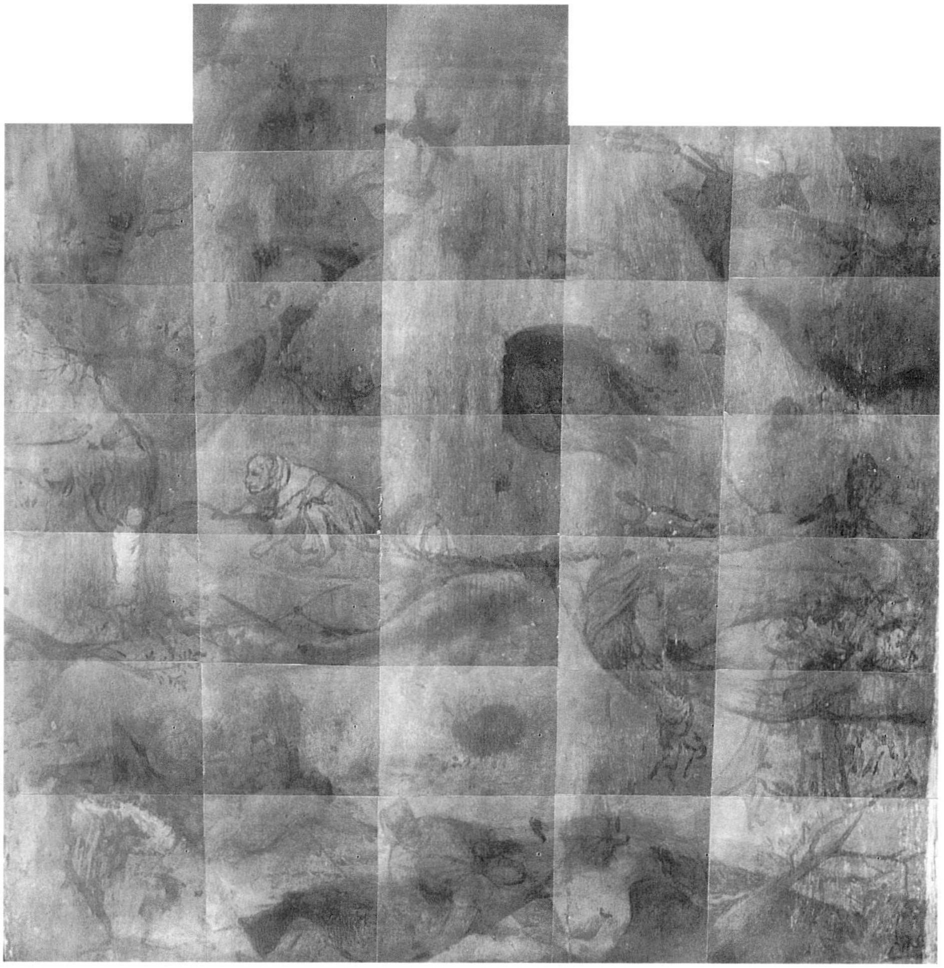

b. Infrared reflectogram assembly (Hell)

c. Infrared reflectogram assembly (The Flood)

can see three demons attacking the man, originally, at the back on the right, a fourth was drawn raising its staff. It had a pig's head and its tail stretched down to the bottom of the picture. In addition, the man being attacked was drawn about a centimetre lower and there was a large farm in the background which was not eventually painted. Finally, in the last scene (fig. g), Christ's right hand was drawn further forward and the kneeling figure being blessed was looking ahead in the direction of Christ and had his arms extended further. We can see how, in keeping with his lively and spirited imagination, Bosch continually changed his compositions throughout their creation.

Dendrochronological analysis was also carried out during the restoration, to obtain more information about dating.[7] It emerged first of all that one plank from each of the panels came from the same tree, and the two other planks from another tree. The panel would have been ready for painting by 1508, although it is more likely to have been painted after 1514. Bosch died, however, in 1516, so the panels must have been painted shortly before his death. Because Bosch presents considerable problems regarding chronology, such late paintings are important to characterise his later work.

The underdrawings and the dendrochronological dating provide clear confirmation that both panels were painted by Bosch himself. Although their condition leaves much to be desired, those parts which have remained intact bear ample witness to the painter's outstanding talent and brilliant artistry.
JG

1 The scientific examination was carried out alongside the restoration which began in 1981. Infrared reflectograms: AB 401-AB 402/33; AB 399/19-AB 400/36; AB 651-AB 653/12. Paint samples A 36/1-8 and A 37/1-3.

2 Fraenger (1950).

3 Wittrock (1979).

4 See the drawing of a reconstruction of this altar in exhib. cat. *Adriaen van Wesel*, Amsterdam, Rijksmuseum, 1980-81, p. 40, fig. 6.

5 The restoration was carried out by P.F.J.M. Hermesdorf. His article published in 1990 contains a short account of the work. A group of experts was set up to supervise the restoration: J. Giltaij, keeper of Old Masters, the physicist Dr J.R.J. van Asperen de Boer, and the art historian Dr J.P. Filedt Kok. The stereo x-radiographs made in 1975 were closely studied to determine the condition of both sides of the panels. The restoration lasted from the beginning of 1981 to the end of 1985. The painting of the *Flood* was the best preserved, whilst an extremely large portion of *Hell* was damaged down to the wood and extensively overpainted. Both reverse sides were also quite damaged. The *Hell* panel was, moreover, made out of two planks, between which a strip of plaster and twine had been secured with iron tacks. This strip was removed, along with later painting. It was decided to brighten up *Hell* a little, to make it a better match for the *Flood*, and not to retouch the bare patches on the reverse. The restorer completed the circles and made small retouches, particularly on the numerous patches of white ground that had become exposed. Cross-sections of paint samples had earlier shown that the original greyish purple around the circles was largely intact under grey overpainting.

6 Infrared reflectography had already been carried out by Van Asperen de Boer and Filedt Kok in 1972-3. However, Filedt Kok's article only reproduced two infrared photographs.

7 See the report made by Dr P. Klein, Hamburg, 23 December 1983.

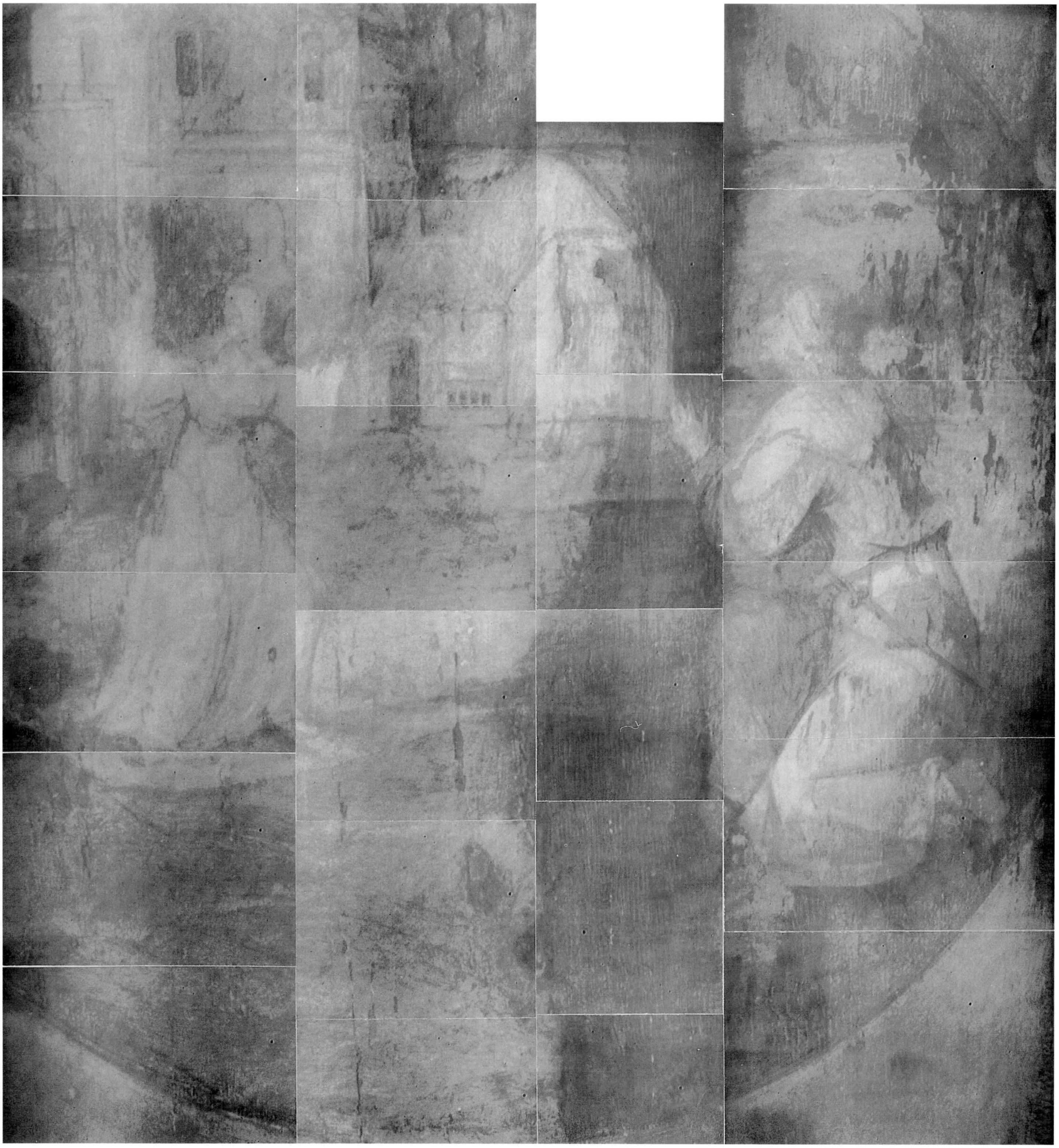

d. Infrared reflectogram assembly

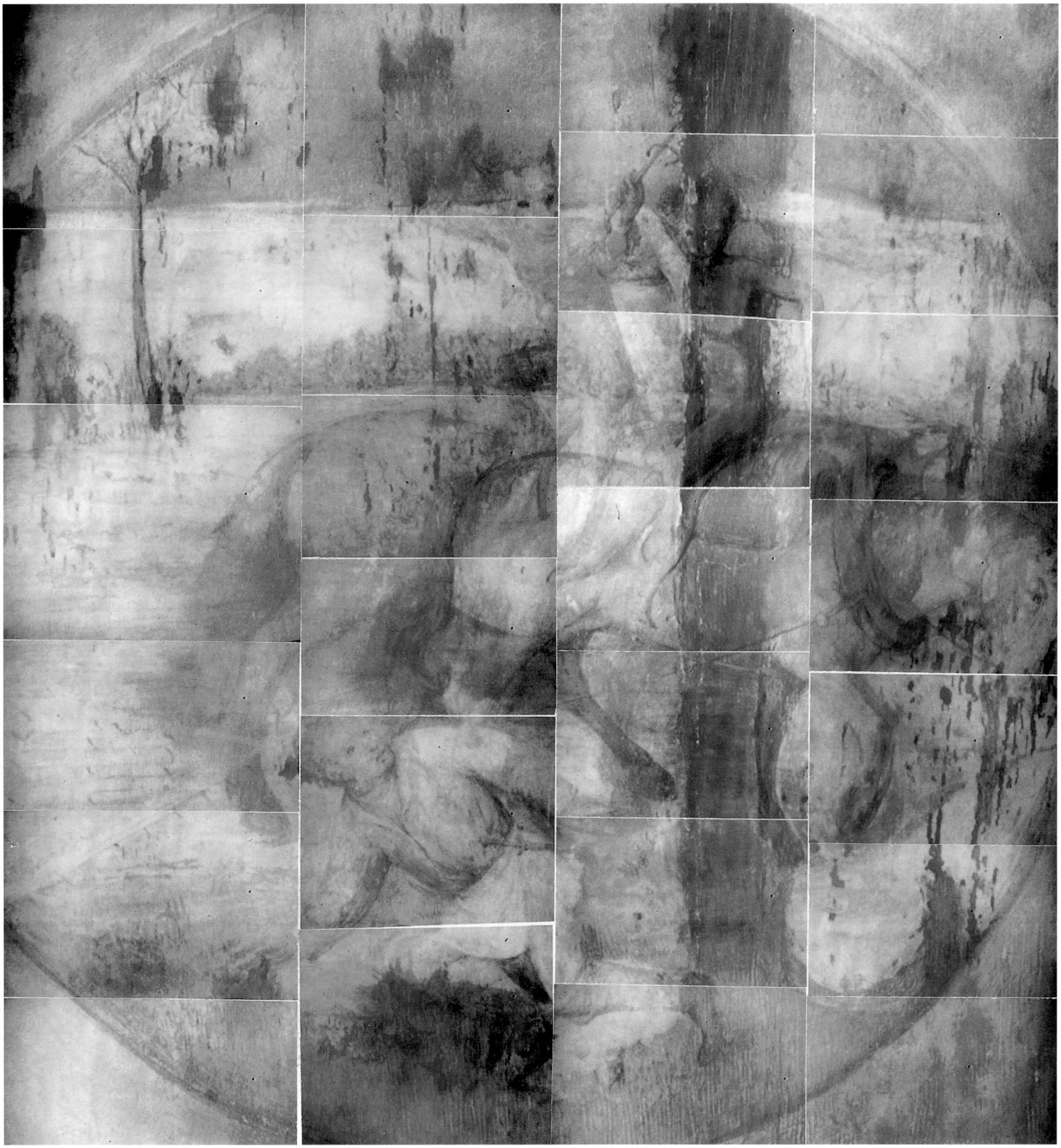
e Infrared reflectogram assembly

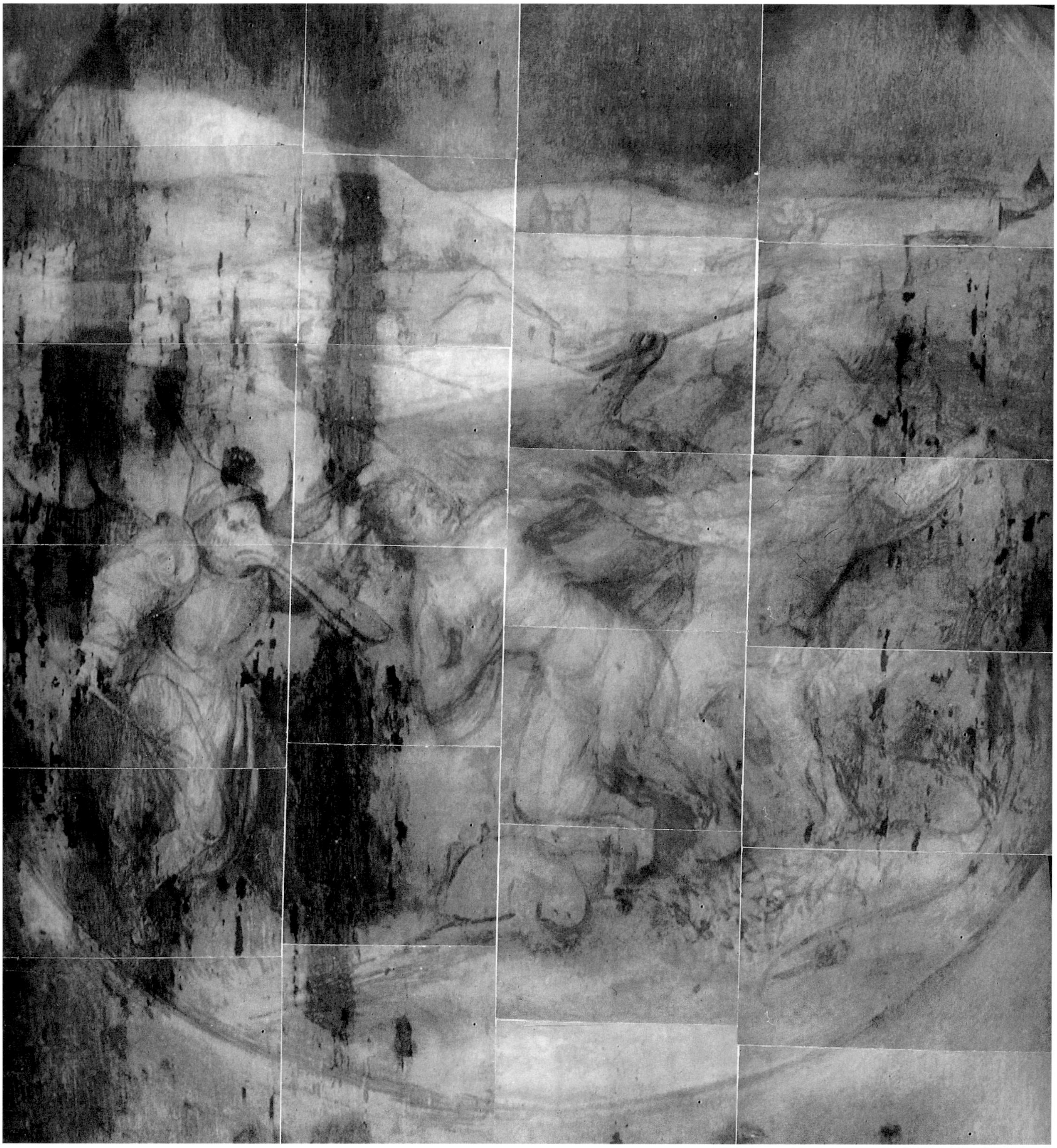

f. Infrared reflectogram assembly

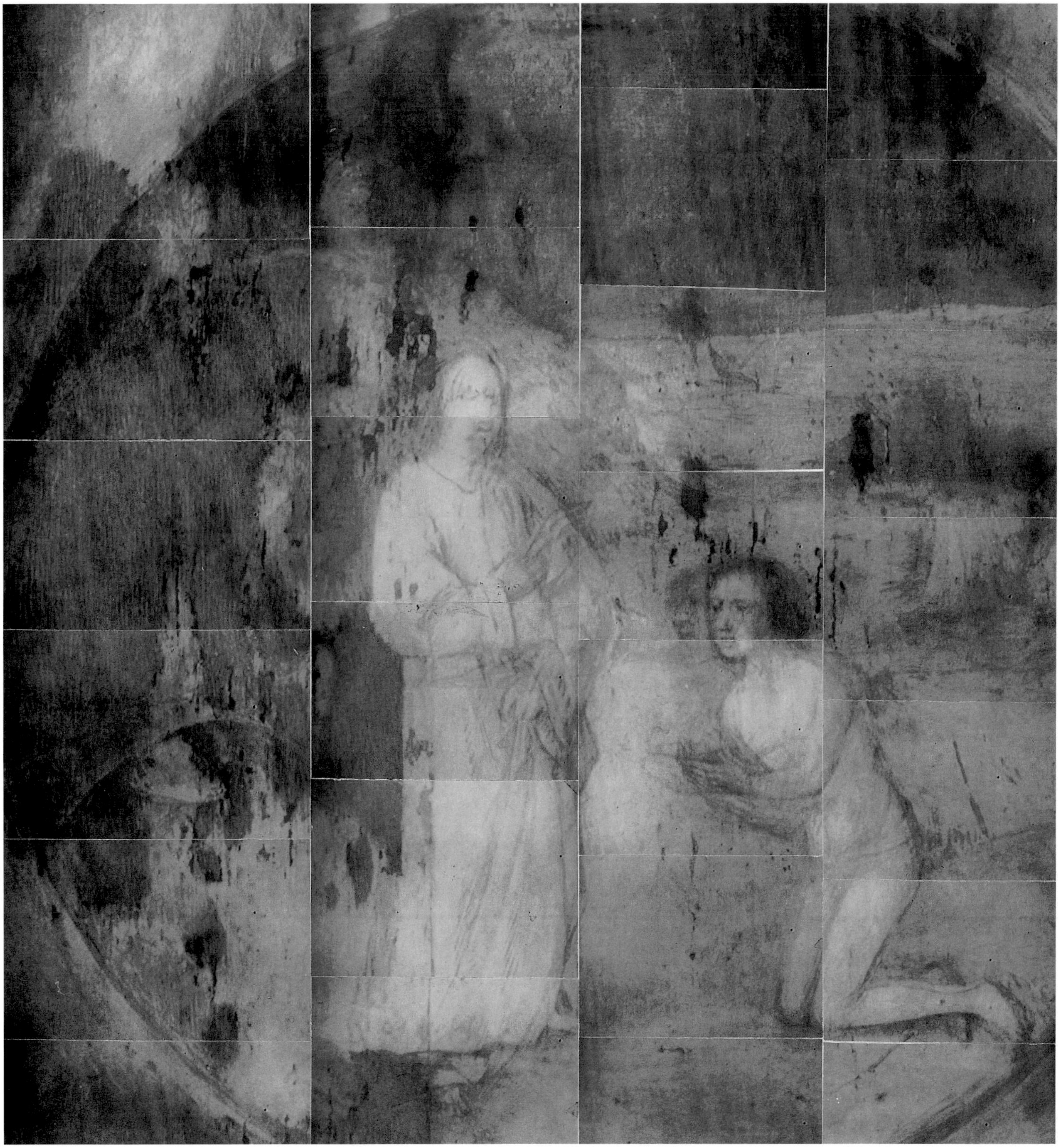

g. Infrared reflectogram assembly

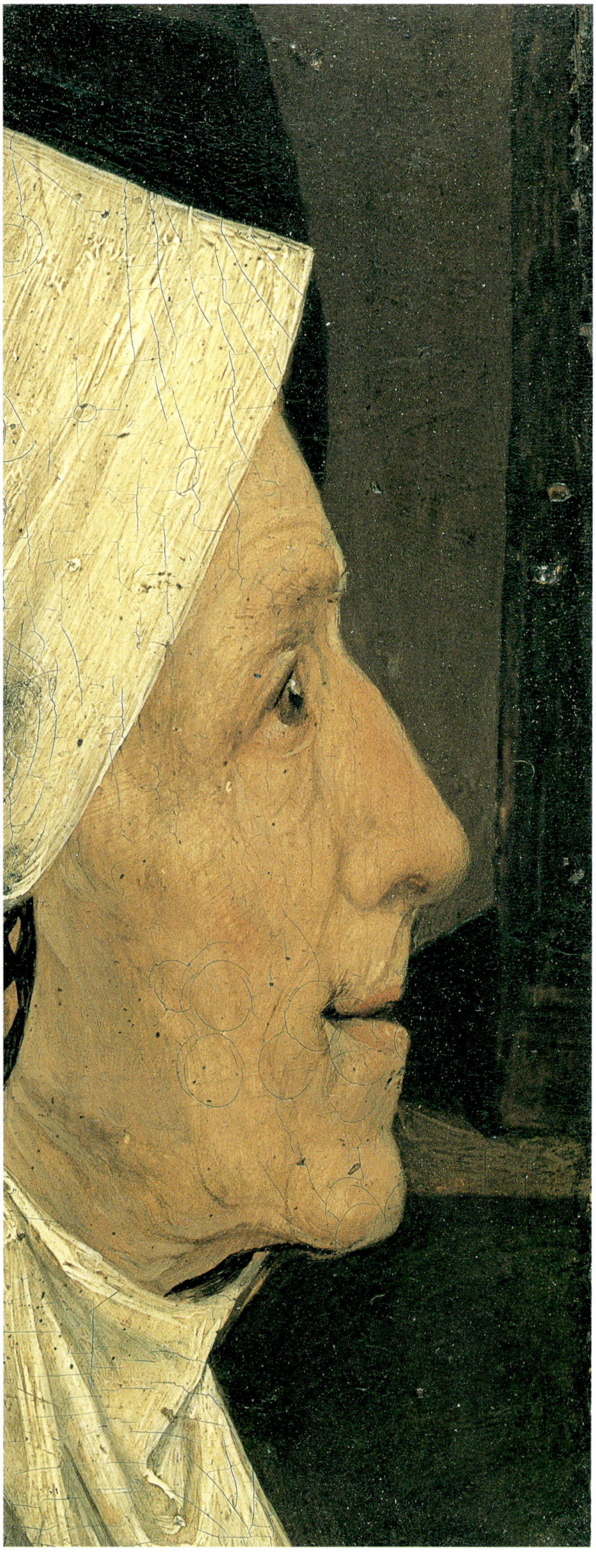

Head of an old woman

Jheronimus Bosch (?)
('s-Hertogenbosch c. 1450-
's-Hertogenbosch 1516)

Panel; 13 x 5 cm

This profile of an old woman is without doubt a fragment of a larger painting. Although a few architectural details can be seen in the background, it is impossible to ascertain the work's original subject.

The woman's profile was created with skilful, fluent brushwork. When Jacques Goudstikker offered the small panel to Van Beuningen in 1933, he wrote that "several art experts" considered it to be by Bosch or Pieter Bruegel. The art dealer himself thought Bruegel the more likely candidate.[2]

Bruegel was, however, usually more sparing in his use of paint. A number of authors in fact favour the attribution to Bosch. De Tolnay has drawn attention to certain stylistic similarities between the panel and the *Ship of fools* in the Louvre.[3] A comparison is nevertheless difficult to make, since the faces in the painting in Paris are so much smaller. The same applies to the triptych in Lisbon which also includes some fairly similar faces.[4] The style of the underdrawing does not provide a decisive answer either (fig. a).

The attribution to Bosch – albeit with a question mark – is retained here, on account of the painting's artistic excellence.
FL

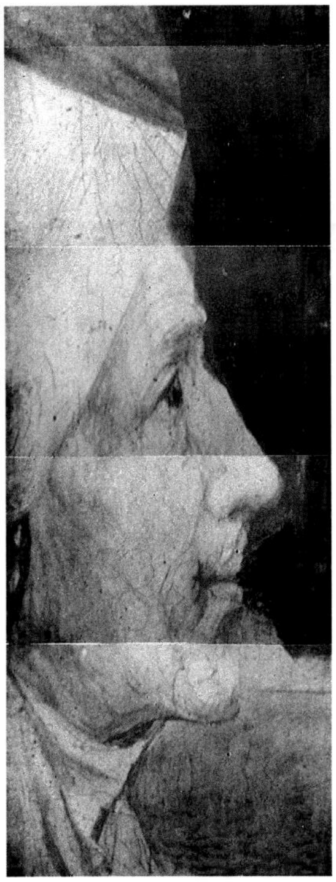

Physical characteristics: the panel consists of a single small plank.

Infrared reflectography[1]: brush underdrawing.

Provenance: Douwes Gallery, 1933; Goudstikker Gallery, Amsterdam, 1933; purchased from the gallery by D.G. van Beuningen, Rotterdam and Vierhouten, in 1933 for 7000 guilders; acquired by the Museum with the Van Beuningen Collection in 1958; inv. no. 2439.

Exhibitions: *Honderd jaar Museum Boymans Rotterdam. Meesterwerken uit de verzameling D.G. van Beuningen*, Rotterdam, Boymans Museum, 1949, no. 5.

Literature: Hannema, 1949, no. 5, fig. 48; cat. 1962, p. 29; D. Buzzati, M. Cinotti, *L'Opera completa di Bosch*, Milan 1966, no. 18, fig.; P. Reuterswärd, *Hieronymus Bosch*, Uppsala 1970, p. 269, no. 23, fig.; Ch. de Tolnay, *Hieronymus Bosch*, Baden Baden 1975 (1st edition 1937), p. 348, no. 9a, fig.; R. Schuder, *Hieronymus Bosch*, Berlin 1975, p. 71, fig. 79; J. Chailley, *Jérôme Bosch et ses symboles*, Brussels 1976 p. 113, no. 18; I. Bango Torviso, F. Marias, *Bosch. Reality, symbol and fantasy*, 1982, p. 172; W. Bosing, *Hieronymus Bosch um 1450-1516*, Cologne 1987, p. 8, fig.

1 Carried out by J.R.J. van Asperen de Boer on 24 September 1990. Infrared reflectograms: AB 1199/29-33A.
2 Letter dated 4 September 1933, from J. Goudstikker to D.G. van Beuningen, mentioning a price of 12,000 guilders for the painting. Accounts show that the painting was eventually sold for 7,000 guilders. The letter is in the Museum's file on D.G. van Beuningen.
3 De Tolnay (1975).
4 Von Reuterswärd (1970).

a. Infrared reflectogram assembly.

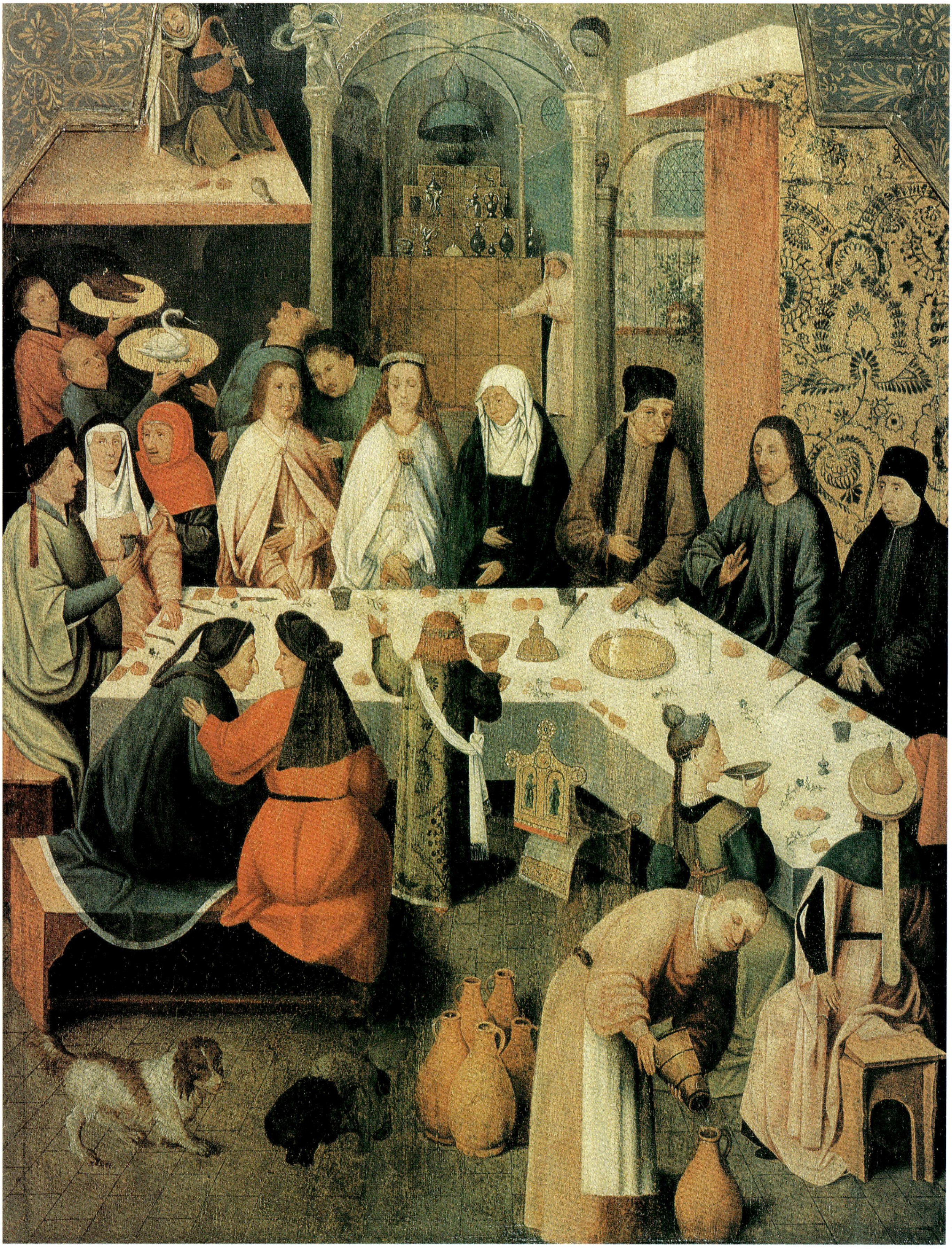

The marriage at Cana

Jheronimus Bosch, after
('s-Hertogenbosch c. 1450-
's-Hertogenbosch 1516)

Panel; 93 x 72 cm

Physical characteristics:[1] the panel consists of three vertical planks. Pieces of the panel have been sawn off from the upper left- and right-hand corners; it is not known when.

Infrared reflectography: no underdrawing could be discerned.

Dendrochronology: two of the three planks are from the same tree. The youngest heartwood growth ring dates from 1544. The panel could not have been painted before 1555; it was more probably painted in or after 1561. See article by P. Klein.

Paint samples: evidence of the pigment smalt. See text.

Provenance: possibly Hélène Fourment Collection, 1675, Antwerp;[2]private collection, Antwerp, 1873; Sir Frank Brangwyn, England; C. Thompson, London, May 1923; P. Cassirer, Berlin, 1923; F. Koenigs, Haarlem, 1923; on loan to Boymans Museum, Rotterdam from 1935 to 1940; purchased by D.G. van Beuningen in April 1940 with the Koenigs Collection; donated by him to the Boymans Museum Foundation, Rotterdam in 1941; inv. no. St. 25

Exhibitions: *Oude Kunst in particulier bezit te Haarlem*, Haarlem, Frans Halsmuseum, 1926-27, no. 1, fig.; *Exhibition of Dutch Art 1450-1900*, London, Royal Academy of Arts, 1929, no. 16, fig. 3; *Verzameling F. Koenigs, schilderijen*, Rotterdam, Boymans Museum, 1935, no. 3, fig. II; *Jeroen Bosch. Noord-nederlandsche primitieven*, Rotterdam, Boymans Museum, 1936, no. 48a, fig. 60; *Bijbelsche kunst*, Amsterdam, Rijksmuseum, 1939, no. 121a, fig. 5; *De Jerome Bosch à Rembrandt. Peintures et dessins de Musée Boymans de Rotterdam*, Dijon, Palais des États de Bourgogne, 1950, no. 4, fig.; *Het wonder. Miracula Christi*, Utrecht, Aartsbisschoppelijk Museum, 1962, no. 87, fig.; *Jheronimus Bosch*, 's-Hertogenbosch, Noordbrabants Museum, 1967, no. 17, fig.

Literature: K. Pfister, "Unbekannte Bilder des Hieronymus Bosch", *Belvedere* 4 (1923), p. 73-74, fig.; G. Ring, review of "W. Schürmeyer, Hieronymus Bosch, München 1923", *Jahrbuch für Kunstwissenschaft* 1923, p. 311, fig. 123; L. Baldass, "Betrachtungen zum Werke des Hieronymus Bosch", *Jahrbuch der Kunsthistorischen Sammlungen in Wien* N.F. I (1926), pp. 103-106, fig. 53; Friedländer, V, 1927, no. 73, fig. XLIX; T. Borenius, "Die Holländische Ausstellung in London", *Pantheon* III (1929), p. 134, fig.; L. Baldass, "Zur Entwicklungsgeschichte des Hieronymus Bosch", *Jaarboek der Koninklijke Museums voor Schoone kunsten van België* I (1938), p. 49; F.M. Huebner, *Hieronymus Bosch*, Berlin 1939, fig. 7; D. Hannema, *Jaarverslag Museum Boymans* 27 (1941), p. 4; D. Hannema, *Stichting Museum Boymans, Rotterdam. Verslag over de jaren 1939, 1940 en 1941*, p. 6; J. Combe, *Jérome Bosch*, Paris 1946, p. 12, no. 7, figs. 9, 10; E.R. Meijer, "Hieronymus Bosch en de Verloren Zoon", *Phoenix* 1, no. 7, (1946), p. 5, fig. 9; J. Mosmans, *Jheronimus Anthonis-zoon van Aken alias Hieronymus Bosch. Zijn leven en zijn werk*, 's-Hertogenbosch 1947, pp. 30, 50, 52-53, 71 (noot 36); D. Bax, *Ontcijfering van Jeroen Bosch*, The Hague, 1949, pp. 216-221; W. Fraenger, *Die Hochzeit zu Kana. Ein Dokument Semitischer Gnosis bei Hieronymus Bosch*, Berlin 1950, figs. 2, 3; L. van Puyvelde, "De bedoelingen van Bosch", *Mededelingen der Koninklijke Nederlandse Academie van Wetenschappen*, afd. Letterkunde, Nieuwe Reeks, vol. 19, no. 2 (1956), pp. 2, 8-9, 15; D. Bax, *Beschrijving en poging tot verklaring van het Tuin der Onkuisheiddrieluik van Jeroen Bosch, gevolgd door kritiek op Fraenger* (Verhandelingen der Koninklijke Akademie van Wetenschappen, Afdeling letterkunde, n.r. LXIII, 2), Amsterdam 1956, pp. 153-161; H. van de Waal, " W. Fraenger, *Die Hochzeit zu Kana. Ein Dokument Semitischer Gnosis bei Hieronymus Bosch*, Berlin 1950", *Bibliotheca Orientalis* XIV (1957), p. 110-112; L. Baldass, *Hieronymus Bosch*, Vienna-Munich 1959 (1943), pp. 54-55, 80, 243, fig. 109; C. Linfert, *Hieronymus Bosch. The paintings*, London 1959, pp. 8, 112, fig.; K.G. Boon, "The literature of art. Hieronymus Bosch", *The Burlington Magazine* CII (1960), p. 458; C.A. Wertheim Aymès, *Die Bildersprache des Hieronymus Bosch*, The Hague 1961, p. 30, fig. 47; H. Adhémar, *Le Musée national du Louvre, Paris* I, (Les Primitifs Flamands. I. Corpus de la peinture des anciens Pays-Bas méridionaux au quizième siècle) 5, Brussels 1962, p. 116; N. Beets, "De Nederlandse schilderkunst van de vijftiende eeuw", *Kunstgeschiedenis der Nederlanden*, II, Zeist-Antwerp 1963 (1st edition 1937), pp. 362-364, fig. 19; D. Buzzati, M. Cinotti, *L'Opera completa di Bosch*, Milan 1966, no. 3, fig.; P. Gerlach, "Studies Jheronimus van Aken (alias Bosch) II", *Spiegel der Historie* 1967, pp. 628, 637, 649-652; A.P. de Mirimonde, "La musique dans les allégories d'amours, II", *Gazette des Beaux-Arts* 69 (1967), p. 339, fig. 42. K. Arndt, "Zur Ausstellung 'Jheronimus Bosch'", *Kunstchronik* 21 (1968), p. 3-4; Friedländer, V, 1969 no. 73, fig. 54; P. Reuterswärd, *Hieronymus Bosch*, Uppsala, 1970, pp. 114, 170, no. 11, fig. 17; V. Wolff en M. Davies, *The National Gallery of Victoria, Melbourne* (Les primitifs flamands, I, Corpus de la peinture des anciens Pays-Bas méridionaux au quinzième siècle) 12, Brussels 1971, pp. 5-6; A.P. de Mirimonde, "Le symbolisme musical chez Jérôme Bosch", *Gazette des Beaux-Arts* 77 (1971), pp. 28-30, figs. 22-23; O. Benesch, "Hieronymus Bosch and the thinking of the late Middle Ages", in: *Collected Writings* II, London 1971, p. 14, fig.; W.S. Gibson, *Hieronymus Bosch*, London 1973, pp. 26, 28-31, fig. 17; A. Boczkowska, "Lunar and Christian symbolism of the painting "The marriage at Cana" by Hieronymus Bosch", *Studia Muzealne* 11 (1975), pp. 7-24; W. Fränger, *Hieronymus Bosch*, Dresden 1975, pp. 145-225, 293, 346-347, 394, 414, 444, 473, figs. 53-59; H. Holländer, *Hieronymus Bosch*, Cologne 1975, pp. 8, 110, 124, fig. 7; Ch. de

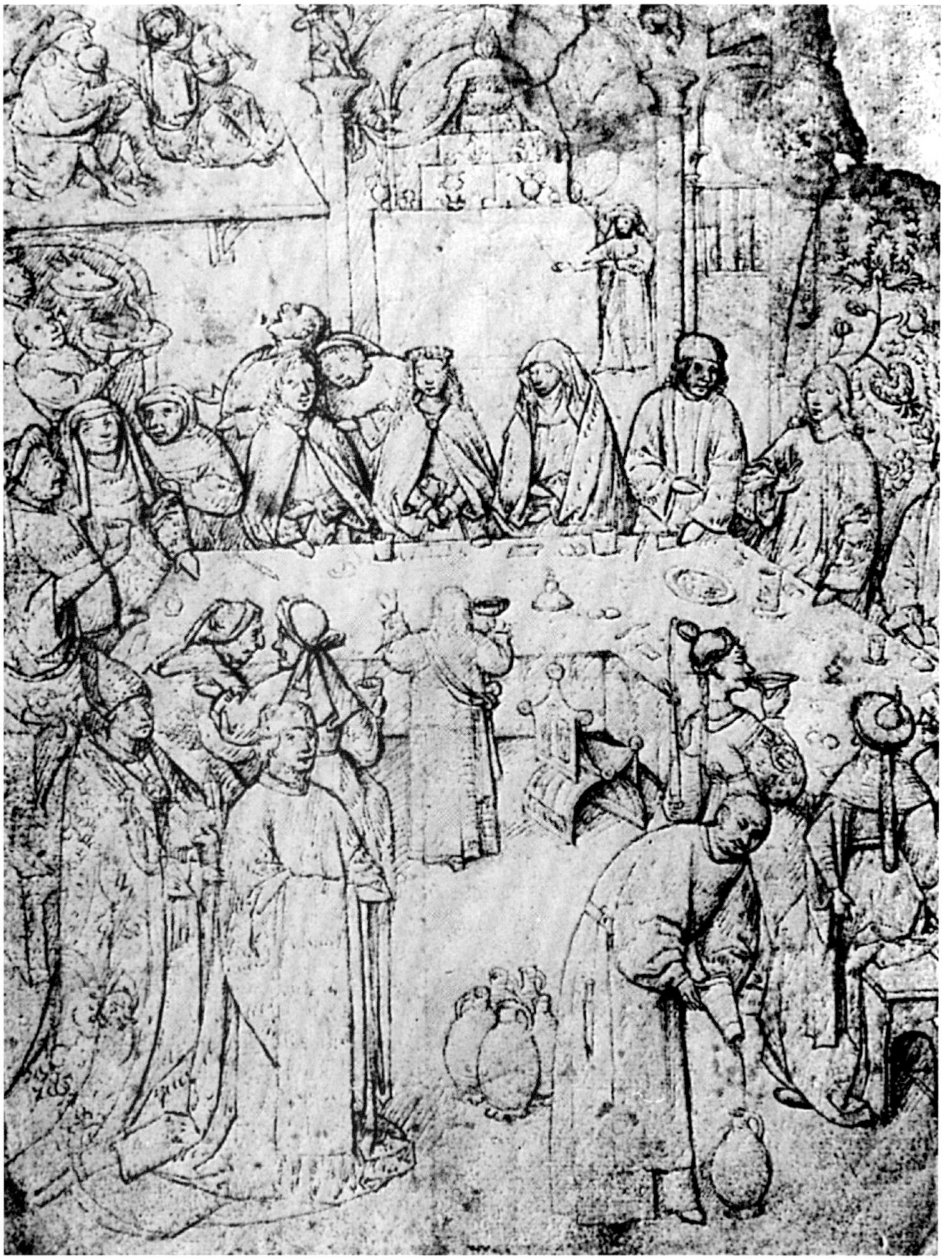

a. Anonymous follower of Jheronimus Bosch, *Marriage at Cana*
Pen
Paris, Musée du Louvre

The wedding guests are seated at an L-shaped table. Christ is on the right under a gold-brocaded canopy. A male guest, the Virgin Mary, the bride and the bridegroom are sitting to his right. A swan and a swine's head are being carried forward from the left on platters. A musician is playing on a platform. There is a piece of furniture with various unusual utensils in the background, whilst in the foreground a man is pouring water from a jug.

The painting depicts the Saviour's first miracle of turning water into wine, at a wedding in Cana (John 2:1-11). Although the Bible does not mention the couple's names, a medieval tradition identified the bridegroom as John the Evangelist. There are indeed similarities between the bridegroom in the painting and the Evangelist as portrayed by Bosch.[3]

Many art historians consider the panel to be more than a straightforward illustration of the biblical text. Ludwig Baldass, who in 1926 gave the first analysis of the painting's deeper significance, emphasised the dramatic tension between good and evil. Later authors agreed with his interpretation, including De Tolnay who believed that those present – with the exception of Christ, the man to his left and Mary – are all heretics.[4] For Bax the painting represents "the pure sullied by the impure",[5] whilst according to Gibson, the "chaste" wedding is taking place in the debauched setting of a tavern.[6]

Other commentators maintain that the painting contains astrological[7] and alchemical[8] references. Fraenger interpreted it as depicting the wedding of the converted Jew Jacob of Almaegiens.[9] Gerlach believed that the painting represented the wedding celebrations of a member of the Brotherhood of Our Lady in 's-Hertogenbosch.[10]

Most authors stress the sinful character of the feast. However, as Marijnissen (1987) has rightly pointed out, it is possible that not all the aspects they regard as pejorative were intended as such. The piece of furniture on which the utensils are displayed was, for example, quite commonly used at such festivities. The man standing next to it is the steward and certainly not a conjurer. Marijnissen thinks that the musicians, the figure with a bow and arrow and the fleeing monster could all be nothing more than witty embellishments.[11] Platters such as those carrying the swan and the swine's head were probably not unusual at banquets in Bosch's time.[12] The curious little chair next to the figure holding a chalice may in fact be a reference to the marriage.[13]

A donor was probably portrayed in the original painting (see below), and it seems highly unlikely that he would have had himself painted sitting with a group of sinful merrymakers.

Despite the extensive iconographic analysis carried out so far, many questions have yet to be answered convincingly. Why are there half-moon insignias on the musicians and on the platters with the swan and swine's head, who is the little figure holding a large chalice, and are some of the seated figures portraits?

Until recently this panel was generally regarded as an early work by Bosch himself. Doubts were first raised with the publication in 1960 of a drawing from the Rothschild Collection in the Louvre in Paris (fig. a).[14] It is exactly the same as the Boymans-van Beuningen panel except that, instead of two dogs in the bottom left-hand corner, there is a donor and a saint. This raised the possibility that the Paris sketch might show the original composition. The panel in Rotterdam would then be demoted to a good copy in which, for understandable reasons, the donor and his saint were omitted.[15]

In addition to the present work, three other paintings of *The marriage at Cana* are known to exist. The versions in Huis Bergh Castle in 's-Heerenberg (fig. b) and the Terninck Foundation in Antwerp (fig. c) are very similar to the panel in Rotterdam, although both are of lesser artistic merit. They are, however, of importance, since they provide numerous details which have disappeared from the Rotterdam panel.[16]

Tolnay, *Hieronymus Bosch*, Baden Baden 1975 (1st ed. 1937), pp. 13-14, no. 3, fig. p. 70-77; J. Chailley, *Jérôme Bosch et ses symboles. Essai de décryptage*, Brussels, 1976, pp. 86-90, no. 3, fig. XXVI; M. Bergman, *Hieronymus Bosch and alchemy. A study on the St. Anthony triptych*, Stockholm 1979, pp. 89-90; G. Martin, *Hieronymus Bosch*, London 1978, no. 4, fig.; G. Unverfehrt, *Hieronymus Bosch. Die Rezeption seiner Kunst im frühen 16. Jahrhundert*, Berlin 1980, pp. 24, 27, 90, 99-101, 121-122, 146, no. 19, fig. 34; D. Hammer-Tugendhat, *Hieronymus Bosch. Eine historische Interpretation seiner Gestaltsprinzipien*, Munich 1981, pp. 39-40, 74-75, 89, 98, fig. 37; L.S. Dixon, "Water, wine and blood – science and liturgy in the 'Marriage at Cana' by Hieronymus Bosch", *Oud Holland* 96 (1982), pp. 73-96; exhib. cat. *Tussen Heks en Heilige*, Nijmegen, Nijmeegs Museum 'Commanderie van St. Jan', 1985, p. 15, fig.; A. Cook, *Changing the signs. The fifteenth-century breakthrough*, Lincoln-London 1985, pp. 97, 105, 112, fig. 6; H.J. Raupp, *Bauernsatiren*, Niederzier 1986, p. 284; R.H. Marijnissen, *Hiëronymus Bosch. Het volledig oeuvre*, Antwerp 1987, pp. 420-431, fig.; exhib. cat. *Schatten uit de Schelde*, Bergen op Zoom, Markiezenhof, 1987, p. 54; P. Gerlach (compiled and edited by P.M. LeBlanc), *Jheronimus Bosch. Opstellen over leven en werk door drs. P. Gerlach O.F.M. cap*, The Hague 1988, pp. 8, 14-16, 20, 24, 26, 28, 64, 66, 101, 123-128, 161, fig.; (A.M. Koldeweij), exhib. cat. *In Buscoducis 1450-1629. Kunst uit de Bourgondische tijd te 's-Hertogenbosch. De cultuur van de late middeleeuwen en renaissance*, 's-Hertogenbosch, Noordbrabants Museum, 1990, with no. 149.

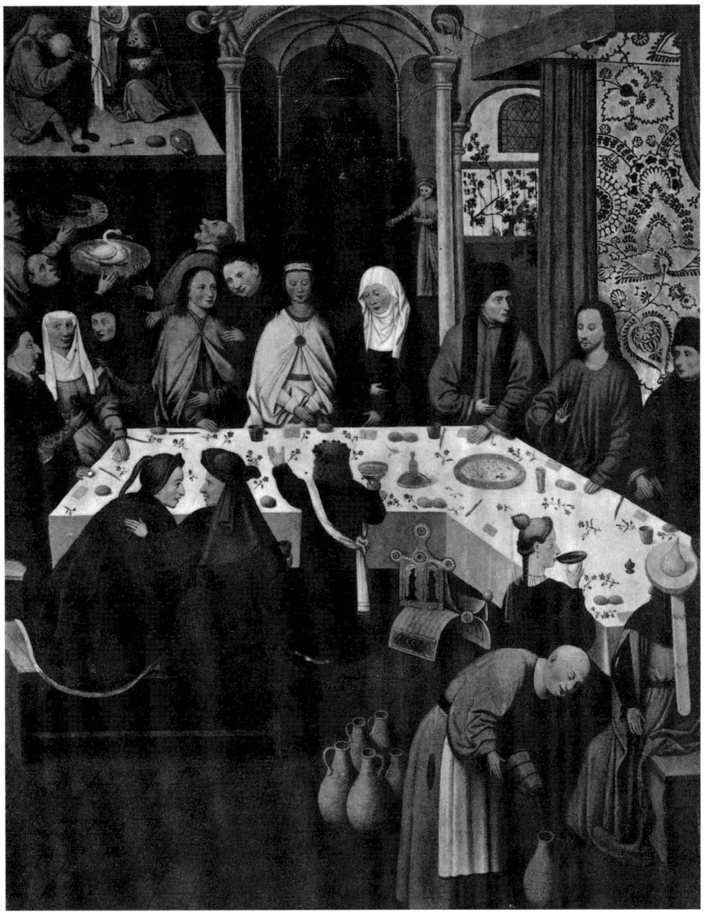

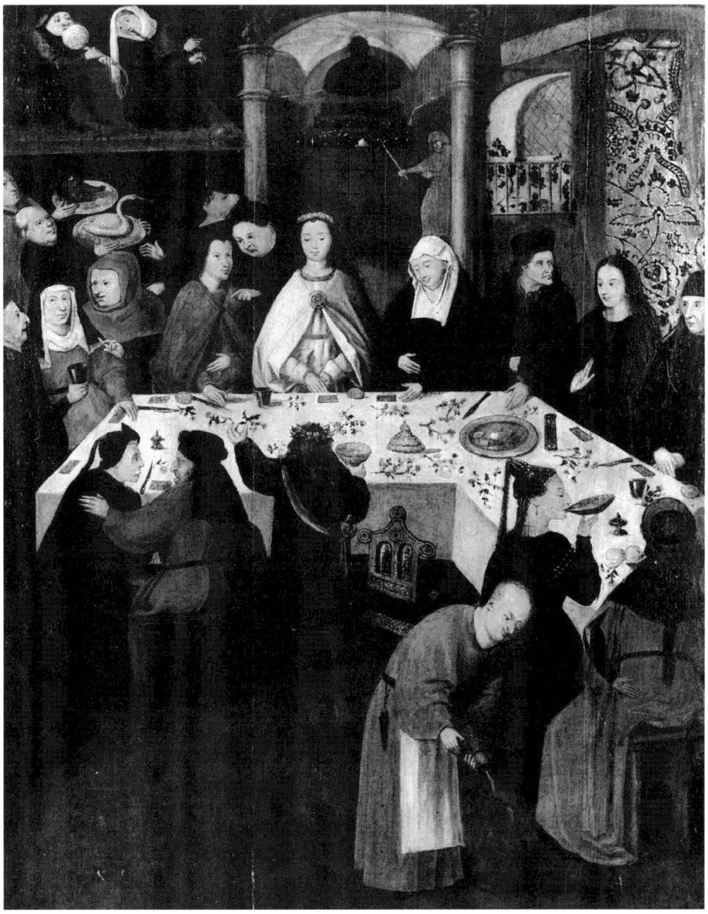

b. Anomymous follower of Jheronimus Bosch,
Marriage at Cana
Panel; 93.5 x 72 cm
'-s-Heerenbergh, Huis Bergh Castle

c. Anomymous follower of Jheronimus Bosch,
Marriage at Cana
Panel
Antwerp, Stichting Terninck

They also show what the upper right and left-hand corners were like originally. The painter of the third version, whose present location is unknown, changed the perpendicular format into a horizontal one.[17] With a number of alterations, he was able to add the portraits of three men and three women.

In the painted versions the donor and his saint in the lower left-hand corner are missing.[18] The portrayal of the two figures on the left, with their backs to the viewer, varies considerably amongst the different painted versions. Those in Rotterdam and 's-Heerenberg have the two men sitting together on a bench, whilst in the paintings in Antwerp, and in the one whose ownership is unknown, they are on separate stools. This can be accounted for if we assume that this part was concealed in the original by the donor and his saint. The copyists had to invent something themselves and provided different solutions.

The examination of the painting in Rotterdam provides conclusive evidence that it is not by Bosch himself. Unlike the other paintings of Bosch which have been investigated using infrared reflectography, no underdrawing could be discerned. Paint samples also show traces of smalt, a pigment which is absent in other paintings by Bosch and which only became widely used in the Low Countries between 1540 and 1560.[19] Finally, dendrochronological analysis has shown that the last heartwood growth ring dates from 1544, twenty-eight years after Bosch's death.

The Rotterdam panel is probably a copy, albeit a good one, of a lost original. It seems likely that the original was painted by Bosch, although this can not be stated with any certainty.
FL

1 Scientific examination conducted in 1989 by U.I. Nürnberger under the supervision of J.R.J. van Asperen de Boer. A copy of her minor thesis is in the Museum's file on the painting. Paint samples A 274/1-5.
2 It is frequently mentioned in the literature that the present painting may have come from the collection left by Rubens, although it was not included in the inventory made after his death; see J. Denucé, *De konstkamers van Antwerpen in de 16e en 17e eeuw*, Amsterdam 1932 and J.M. Muller, *Rubens. The artist as collector*, Princeton, New Jersey 1989. However, in the inventory made on 4 December 1675 of the estate of Hélène Fourment, who married Jan Baptist van Brouckhoven, Count of Bergeyck, after Rubens died, the following entry can be found: "Item une peinture representant ung bancquet de nopce a la façon de Jheronimus Bosch". This could refer to the present painting (see Gerlach (1967)).
3 See Gibson (1973), for details of analogies with the *John the Evangelist* in Berlin.
4 De Tolnay (1975).
5 Bax (1949).
6 Gibson (1973).
7 Boczkowska (1975).
8 Chailley (1978) and Dixon (1982).
9 Fraenger (1950 and 1975).
10 Gerlach (1988).
11 Marijnissen (1987).
12 Gerlach (1988).
13 See exhib. cat. *Schatten uit de Schelde*, 1987, in which reference is made to an insignia that is quite similar to the decoration on the chair. It is M-shaped with a man and a woman between the downstrokes of the letter. The "M" stands for Mary and the insignia itself is thought to be a marriage token. It is also worth noting here that the earthenware jugs into which water is being poured are of a type which was quite common in the fifteenth century. It should not, therefore, be assumed that the shape is based on a jug in Cologne which was regarded as a relic of the miracle (see e.g. Adhémar (1962)). Thanks are due to Alexandra van Dongen for this information.
14 Boon (1960).
15 Gibson (1973) states that the donor and the saint on the panel were painted over. X-radiographs show that this is not, however, the case.
16 Some areas have been painted over in the upper left- and right-hand corners of the Rotterdam panel, below the sawn-off pieces. In the upper left-hand corner, the part of the musician on the right which was not sawn off has been painted over. In the upper right-hand corner, a piece of the curtain has been painted over. The Rotterdam panel is in poor condition, perhaps due in part to the removal of an overpainting towards the end of the last century. Pfister (1923) writes that the panel's owner, Sir Frank Brangwyn, informed him that in 1873 it had been painted over with a portrait. The owner at the time was amazed to find the Marriage at Cana when he had the portrait removed.
17 In 1958 this painting was part of the collection of A. Koehler in Paris.
18 The lower left-hand corner was left empty in all the various versions, with the exception of the Rotterdam panel, where two dogs were painted. The dog on the right is generally dated in the 17th or 18th century. See, for example, exhib. cat. *Jheronimus Bosch*, 's-Hertogenbosch, 1967 and Arndt (1968).
19 See J.R.J van Asperen de Boer, M. Faries, J.P. Filedt Kok, "Schildertechniek en atelierpraktijk in de zestiende eeuwse Noordnederlandse kunst", exhib. cat. *Kunst voor de Beeldenstorm*, Amsterdam, Rijksmuseum, 1986, p. 91.

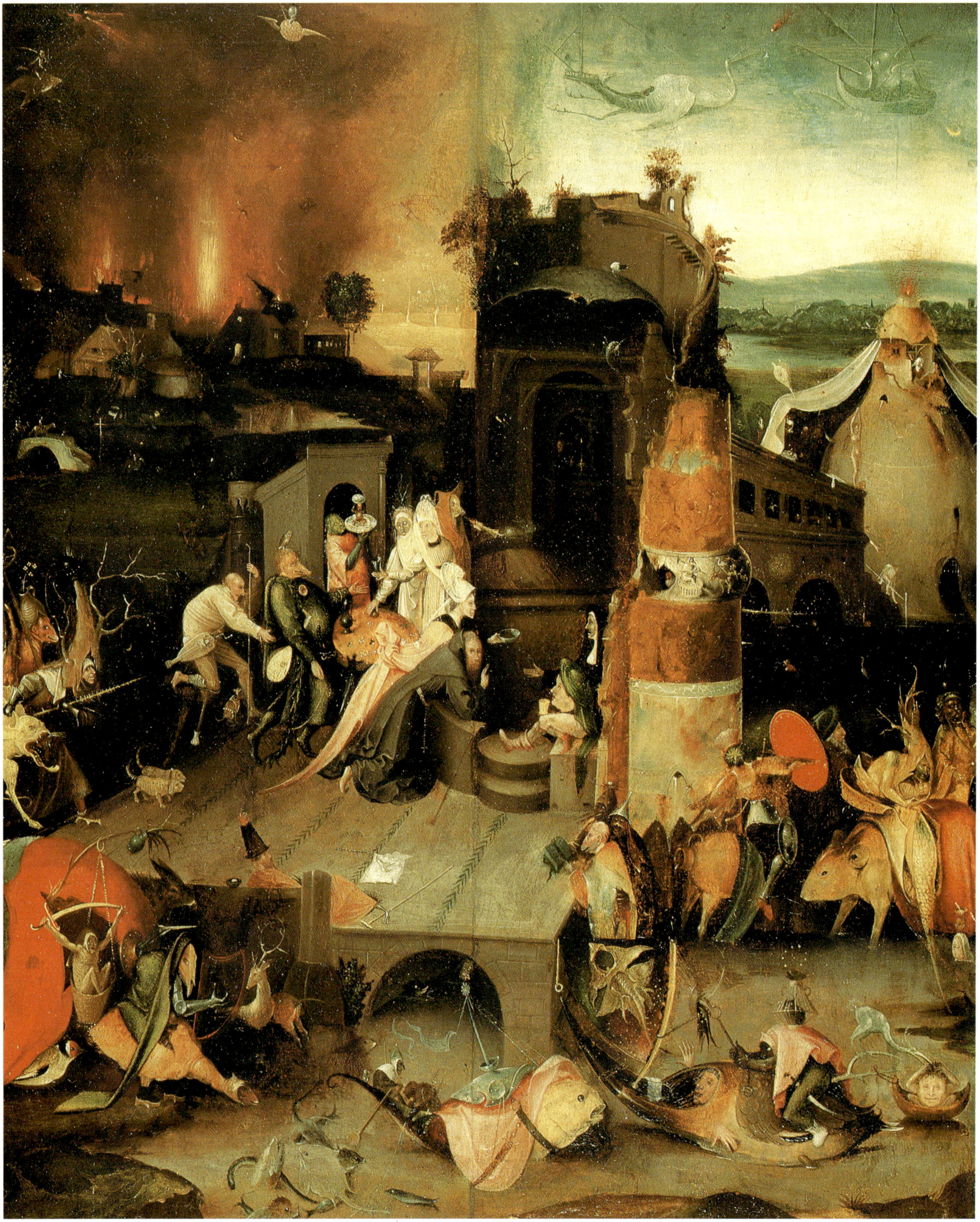

The temptation of St Anthony

Jheronimus Bosch, after
('s-Hertogenbosch c. 1450-
's-Hertogenbosch 1516)

Panel; 50 x 39.5 cm

Physical characteristics: the panel consists of two planks.

Infrared reflectography:[1] no underdrawing could be discerned.

Dendrochronology: the two planks come from the same tree. The youngest heartwood growth ring dates from 1522. The panel could not have been painted before 1533; it was more probably painted in or after 1539. Also see article by P. Klein.

Provenance: Augsburger Gemäldesammlung; sale Munich, Helbing Gallery, 1 October 1919, no. 9, fig. V; C.G. Boerner, Leipzig, 1925; J. Goudstikker Gallery, Amsterdam 1926-27; purchased from the gallery by D.G. van Beuningen, Rotterdam and Vierhouten, in 1928 for 47,000 guilders; acquired by the Museum with the D.G. van Beuningen Collection in 1958; inv. no. 2441.

Exhibitions: *Collection Goudstikker*, The Hague, Pulchri studio, 1926, no. 9, fig.; *Collection Goudstikker*, Rotterdam, Rotterdamsche kunststichting, 1926, no. 5; *Exhibition of Flemish and Belgian art 1300-1900*, London, Royal Academy of Arts, 1927, no. 111; *Honderd jaar Museum Boymans Rotterdam. Meesterwerken uit de verzameling D.G. van Beuningen*, Rotterdam, Boymans Museum, 1949, no. 7; *Chefs-d'œuvre de la collection D.G. van Beuningen*, Paris, Petit Palais, no. 41; *Tussen heks en heilige*, Nijmegen, Nijmeegs Museum "Commanderie van Sint-Jan", 1985, no. 63, fig.

Literatuur: Friedländer, V, 1927, no. 90a; Friedländer, XIV, 1937, p. 100; Hannema, 1949, no. 7, fig. 47; cat. 1962, p. 29; P. Gerlach, "De 'temptatie van St. Antonius' te Antwerpen afkomstig uit 's-Hertogenbosch", *Jaarboek van het Koninklijk Museum voor Schone Kunsten Antwerpen* 1968, p. 72; Friedländer, V, 1969, no. 90a, fig.; J. Chailley, *Jérôme Bosch et ses symboles*, Brussels 1976, p. 209, noot 2; J. de Vries, "Namaak op bestelling", *Openbaar Kunstbezit* 23 (1979), p. 102, fig. 2; G. Unverfehrt, *Hieronymus Bosch. Die Rezeption seiner Kunst im frühen 16. Jahrhundert*, Berlin 1980, p. 79-83, 98, no. 44, fig. 3.

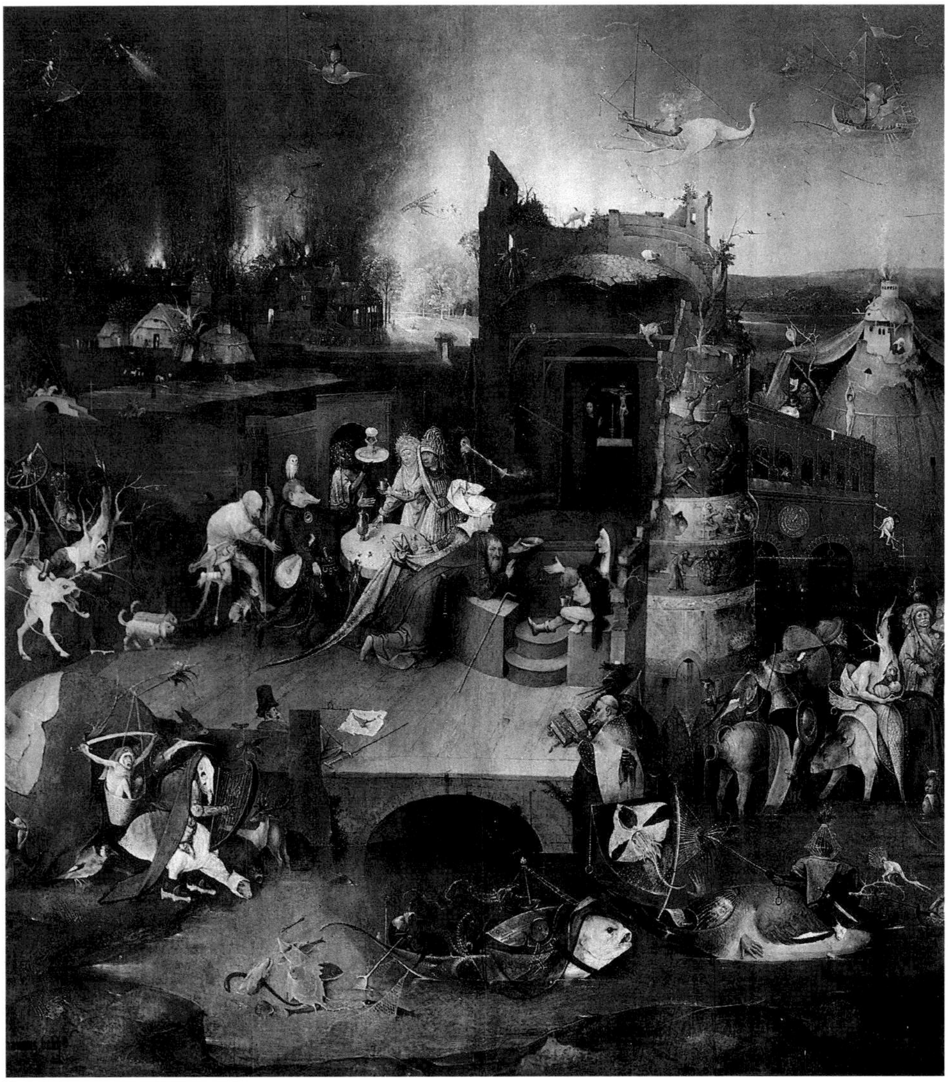

a. Jheronimus Bosch
The temptation of St Anthony
Centre panel; 131.5 x 119 cm
Museu Nacional de Arte Antiga, Lisbon

St Anthony spent much of his life in the Egyptian desert. Although haunted by the devil in a variety of ways, the saint remained steadfast and did not allow himself to be led astray.

The panel shows St Anthony on his knees before a wall, looking at the viewer. He is surrounded by a whole army of fantastic demons.

Friedländer examined the painting several times when the Boerner Gallery owned it. He was of the opinion that it was a reduced version by Bosch himself of the middle part of his famous triptych in Lisbon (fig. a). "Ich kann keinen Punkt in Ihrem Exemplar finden, wo sich Kopistenarbeit oder eine dem Meister fremde Handschrift erkenne liesse", he wrote in his certificate to the gallery.[2]

The panel is nowadays judged in a less positive light and is generally considered to be a copy. After a thorough investigation of the numerous versions based on the Lisbon triptych, Unverfehrt has concluded that the panel in Rotterdam should be dated around 1510-1520. He regards it as one of the earliest and most faithful known copies, and believes that it was in fact not based on the original but on another copy, now lost.[3]

Dendrochronological analysis shows that the painting should be dated considerably later than Unverfehrt has suggested. The panel was probably painted no earlier than about 1539.
FL

1 Scanned by J.R.J. van Asperen de Boer on 20 December 1993.
2 In the Museum's file on the painting.
3 Unverfehrt (1980).

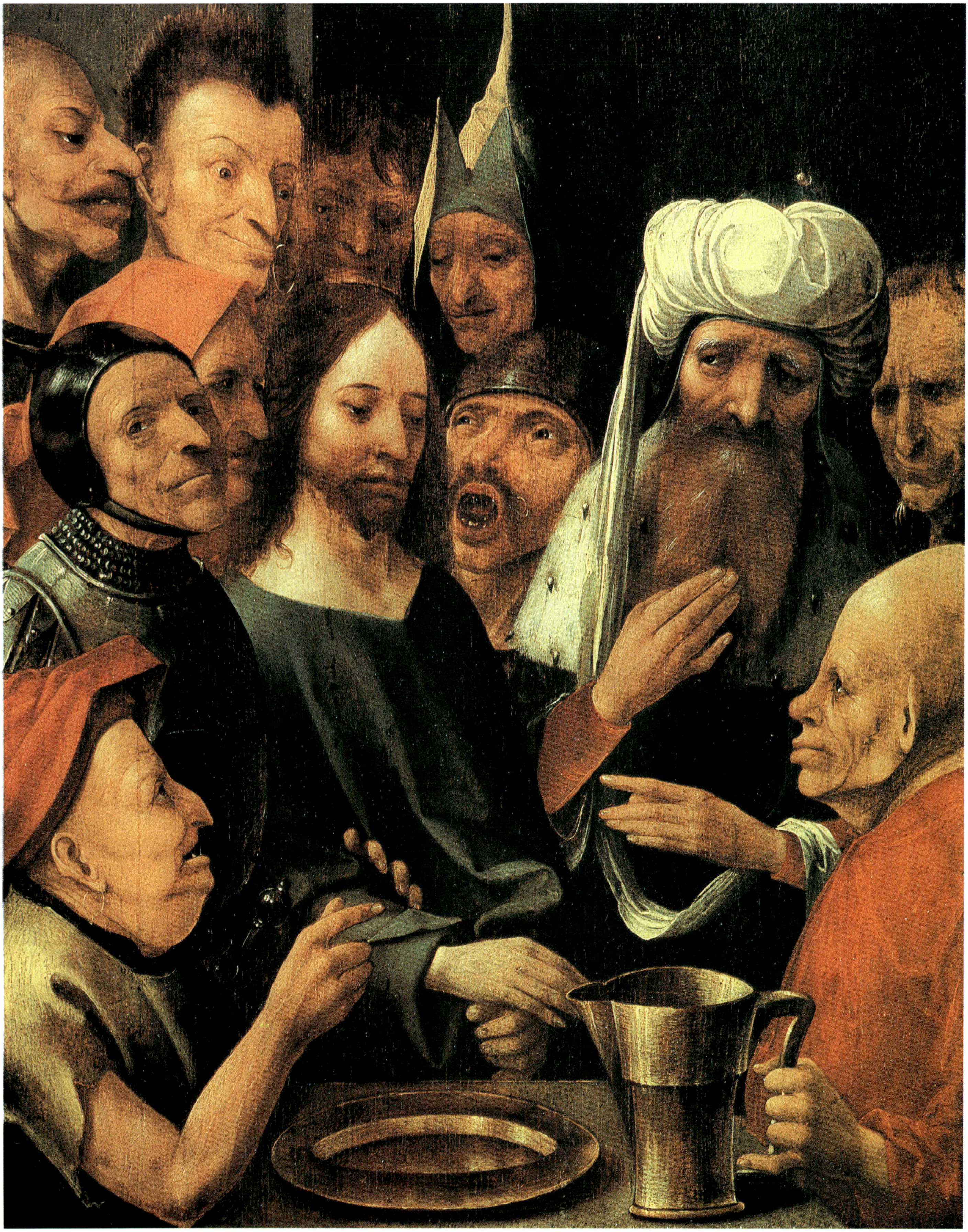

Christ before Pilate

Jheronimus Bosch, manner of
('s-Hertogenbosch c. 1450-
's-Hertogenbosch 1516)
Possibly Antwerp master, c. 1520

Panel; 46.5 x 36.5 cm

Physical characteristics: the panel consists of two planks. The *barbe* can be seen on the two side and lower edges. The upper edge may have been sawn off.

Infrared reflectography:[1] no underdrawing could be discerned.

Dendrochronology: the two planks come from the same tree. The youngest heartwood growth ring dates from 1497. The panel could not have been painted before 1508; it was more probably painted in or after 1514. Also see article by P. Klein.

Provenance: Kilmansegg Collection, Vienna; M. von Nemes Collection, Munich; Kleinberger Gallery, Paris; Goudstikker Gallery, Amsterdam, 1927; purchased from the gallery by D.G. van Beuningen, Rotterdam and Vierhouten, in 1928 for 40,000 guilders; acquired by the Museum in 1958 with the D.G. van Beuningen Collection; inv. no. 2438.

Exhibitions: *Collection Goudstikker*, Rotterdam, Rotterdamsche Kunststichting, 1927, no. 5; *Exhibition of Flemish and Belgian art 1300-1900*, London, Royal Academy of Arts, 1927, no. 106; *Kersttentoonstelling*, Rotterdam, Boymans Museum, 1927-28, no. 4, fig. 1; *Tentoonstelling van Oude kunst*, Amsterdam, Rijksmuseum, 1929, no. 9; *Trésor de l'art Flamand*, Antwerp, Koninklijk Museum voor Schone Kunsten, 1930, no. 21; *Jeroen Bosch. Noord-Nederlandsche primitieven*, Rotterdam, Boymans Museum, 1936, no. 61, fig.; *Oude kunst tentoonstelling*, Maastricht, Stedelijk Museum, 1939, no. 9; *Les Primitifs Flamands*, Paris, Musée de l'Orangerie, 1947, no. 4; *Honderd jaar Museum Boymans Rotterdam. Meesterwerken uit de verzameling D.G. van Beuningen*, Rotterdam, Boymans Museum, 1949, no. 4; *Chefs-d'œuvre de la collection D.G. van Beuningen*, Paris, Petit Palais, 1952, no. 39, fig. 19; *Kunstschatten uit Nederlandse verzamelingen*, Rotterdam, Boymans Museum, 1955, nr 3, fig. 10; *Jheronimus Bosch*, 's-Hertogenbosch, Noordbrabants Museum, no. 21, fig.

Literature: K. Pfister, "Unbekannte Bilder des Hieronymus Bosch", *Belvedere* IV (1923), p. 73, fig.; Friedländer, V, 1927, no. 75, fig. L; Friedländer, XIV, 1937, p. 100; F.M. Huebner, *Hieronymus Bosch*, Berlin 1939, fig. 2; L. von Baldass, *Hieronymus Bosch*, Vienna 1943, p. 43; Hannema, 1949, no. 4, figs. 44-45; L. Baldass, *Hieronymus Bosch*, Vienna-Munich 1959, p. 55; cat. 1962, p. 29; S. Ringbom, *Icon to narrative*, Abo 1965, p. 165, fig. 134; F.M. Huebner, *Le mystère Jérôme Bosch*, Brussels 1965, fig. on pp. 12-13; D. Buzzati, M. Cinotti, *L'Opera completa di Bosch*, Milan 1966, no. 68, fig.; Friedländer, V, 1967, no. 75, fig.; K. Arndt, "Zur Ausstellung 'Jheronimus Bosch' 's-Hertogenbosch 1967", *Kunstchronik* 21 (1968), pp. 18-19; W.S. Gibson, "Imitatio Christi: the Passion scenes of Hieronymus Bosch", *Simiolus* 6 (1972-73), p. 86, note 15; Ch. de Tolnay, *Hieronymus Bosch*, Baden Baden 1975 (1st ed. 1937), p. 381, no. 46, fig. 51; G. Unverfehrt, "Zu einigen Halbfigurenbildern Hieronymus Bosch und seines Kreis" *Jaarboek van het Koninklijk Museum voor Schone Kunsten, Antwerpen* 1975, pp. 122-123, fig. 10; J. Chailley, *Jérôme Bosch et ses symboles. Essai de décryptage*, Brussels 1976, pp. 289-90, no. 68; G. Unverfehrt, *Hieronymus Bosch. Die Rezeption seiner Kunst im frühen 16. Jahrhundert*, Berlin 1980, pp. 122, 129-130, 133, no. 32 a., fig. 75.

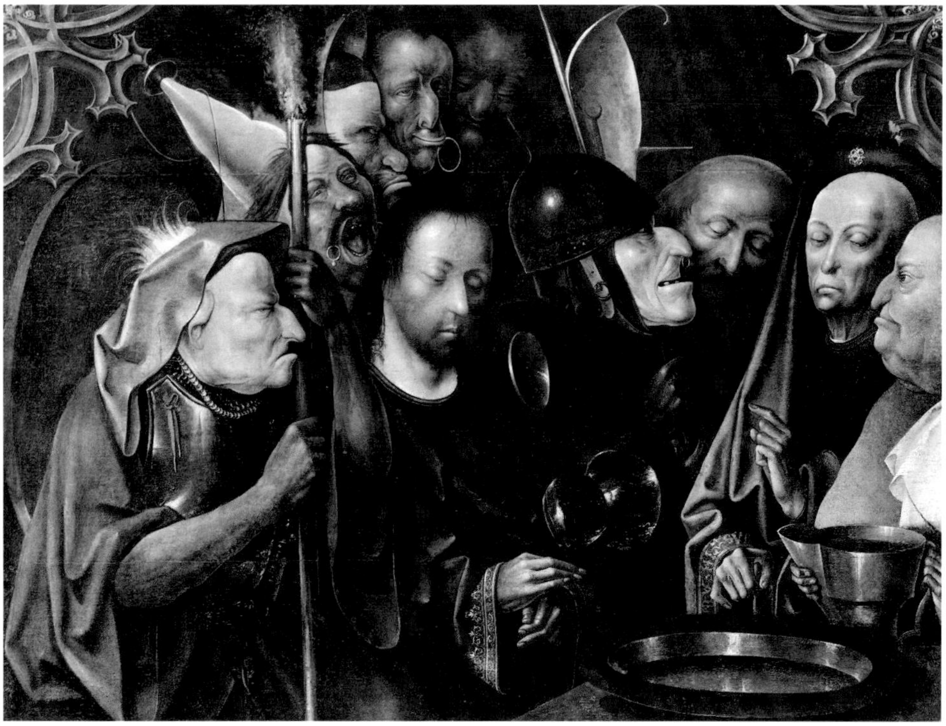

a. Follower of Jheronimus Bosch,
Christ before Pilate
Panel; 84.5 x 108 cm
Princeton, Art Museum

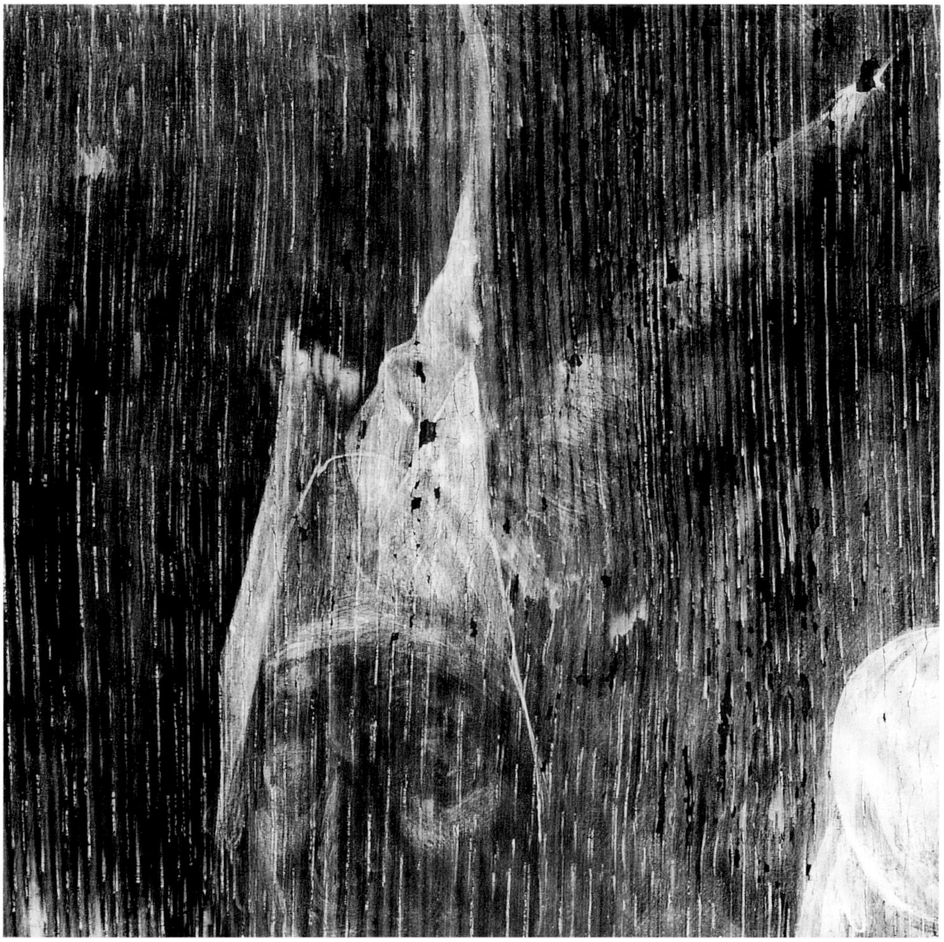

b. X-radiograph of a detail of the painting showing the changed hat.

After the people had called for Christ to be crucified, Pontius Pilate washed his hands and said, "I am innocent of the blood of this just person" (Matthew 27:24). The painting shows Christ and Pilate, who is wearing a turban, surrounded by a group of figures with highly caricatured faces. On a table in the foreground are a dish and water jug.

The painting was published for the first time in 1923 by Pfister who ascribed it, with some reservations, to Jheronimus Bosch. In 1927 Friedländer accepted it as an original work, but most later authors have regarded it as a copy or a work in the manner of Bosch.[2]

Almost all authors have stressed the painting's resemblance to Bosch's *Bearing of the cross* in Ghent, referring to the caricatured faces, the half-figures and the superimposed form of composition. The painting in the manner of Bosch in Princeton (fig. a), with the same subject as the present work, is also frequently mentioned.[3] Some particularly striking similarities include the profile of the lower-left figure, the position of Christ's hands and the dish and water jug.

Ringbom believed that the painting in Rotterdam came first and that the American panel was based on it.[4] Unverfehrt, however, has assumed – probably correctly – that the opposite was in fact the case. He is of the view that the painting in Princeton originated within Bosch's circle. He actually considers both paintings to be variations on Bosch's work rather than literal copies.

In addition to the panel in America already referred to, it is also worth mentioning a painting in the manner of Bosch in São Paulo showing *Christ before Annas.* The figure of the soldier with his mouth open closely resembles the one on the panel in Rotterdam.[5] The anonymous painter of the present panel was also probably influenced by the work of Albrecht Dürer, whose use of caricatured faces was particularly significant. The soldier with his mouth open and the gesture of the man on the left whose arm is linked with the Saviour's also correspond to Dürer's *Christ before Caiaphas* in his engraved Passion (Bartsch 6).

X-radiographs too suggest that the Rotterdam painting is not a literal copy. They show that a change was made to the striking pointed hat of the upper middle figure. The point was initially placed much further back (fig. b). Unverfehrt used the figure of Pilate to place the painting, as K. Arndt had done, in Antwerp around 1520.[6]
FL

1 Scanned by J.R.J. van Asperen de Boer on 10 January 1994.
2 Apart from Friedländer, only Van Puyvelde has ascribed it to Bosch himself, in exhib. cat. Paris, 1947. De Tolnay (1975) and Baldass (1943 and 1959) consider it to be a copy of a lost painting by Bosch. Arndt (1968), Gibson (1972, 1973) and Unverfehrt (1975 and 1980) believe it was inspired by Bosch's works.
3 *Christ before Pilate*, panel; 84.5 x 75 cm, Princeton, Art Museum. See Unverfehrt (1980) for details of this painting.
4 Ringbom (1965).
5 São Paulo, Museu de Arte. Panel; 61.5 x 75 cm. See Unverfehrt (1980), no. 86, fig. 76.
6 Unverfehrt (1975 and 1980), Arndt (1968).

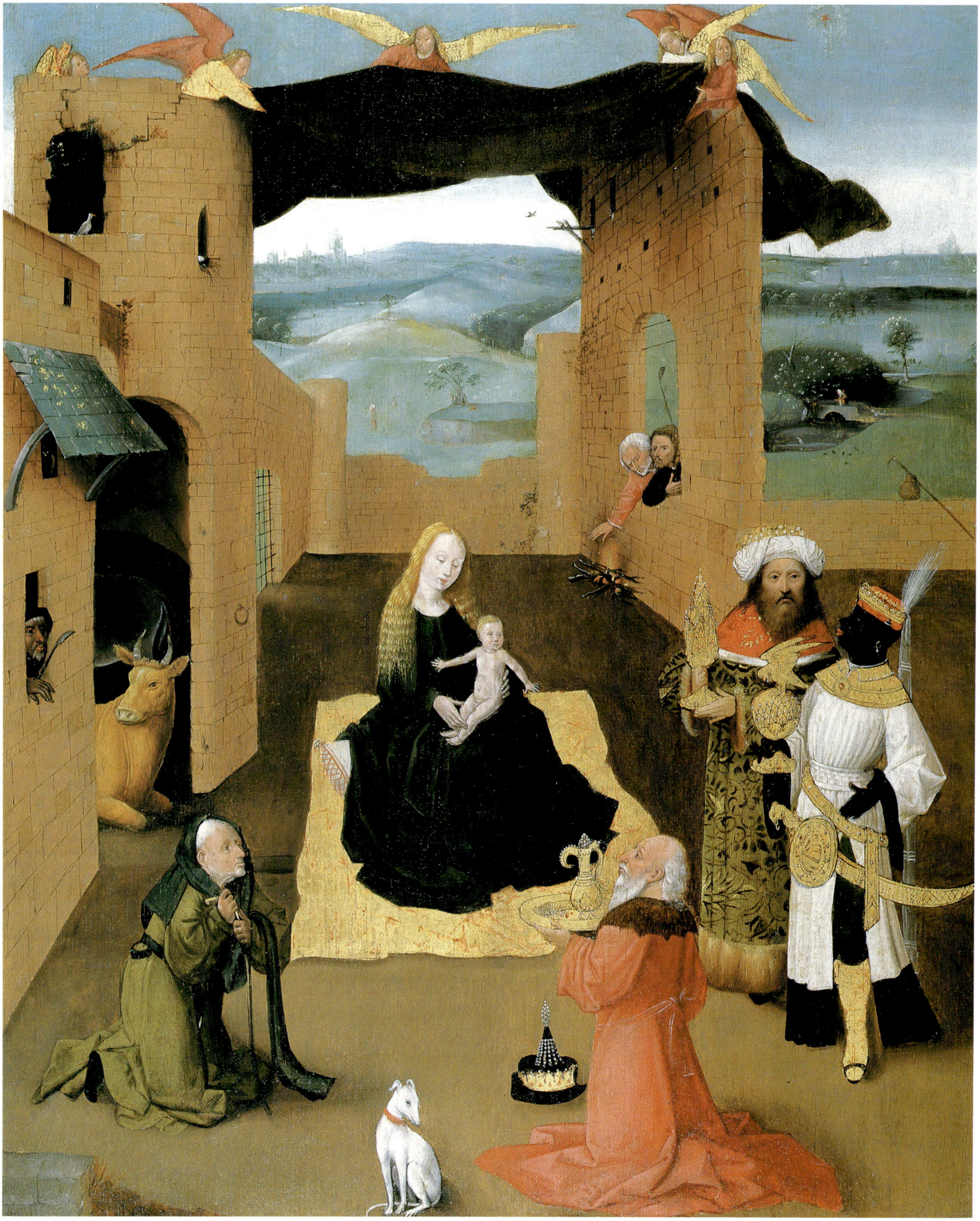

The adoration of the magi

Jheronimus Bosch, manner of
('s-Hertogenbosch c. 1450-
's-Hertogenbosch 1516)

Panel; *70* x *56.7* cm

Physical characteristics: the panel consists of two vertical planks.

Infrared reflectography:[1] small patches of underdrawing could be discerned, consisting of short, uncertain strokes.

Dendrochronology: the panel's two planks come from the same tree. The youngest heartwood growth ring dates from 1525. The panel could not have been painted before 1536; it was more probably painted in or after 1542. See article by P. Klein.

Provenance: private collection, Belgium; Goudstikker Gallery, Amsterdam; purchased from the gallery in 1934 by D.G. van Beuningen, Rotterdam and Vierhouten, for 6,500 guilders; acquired in 1958 with the D.G. van Beuningen Collection; inv. no. 2440.

Exhibitions: *Winter-tentoonstelling van oude kunst uit particulier bezit*, Haarlem, Frans Halsmuseum, 1940, no. 7; *Les primitifs Flamands*, Paris, Musée de l'Orangerie, 1947, no. 3; *Bourgondische pracht van Philips de Stoute tot Philips de Schone*, Amsterdam, Rijksmuseum, 1951, no. 296; *Chefs-d'œuvre de la collection D.G. van Beuningen*, Paris, Petit Palais, 1952, no. 40; *Jheronimus Bosch*, 's-Hertogenbosch, Noordbrabants Museum, 1967, no. 12, fig.; *The Boymans Masterpieces Exhibition*, Tokio, Sezon Museum of Art, Kochi, the Museum of Art, Osaka, Daimaru Museum, no. 1, fig.

Literature: F.M. Huebner, *Hieronymus Bosch*, Berlin 1939, fig. 27; (H.B. Wehle and M. Salinger), *The Metropolitan Museum of Art. A catalogue of early Flemish, Dutch and German paintings*, New York 1947, p. 121; Hannema, 1949, no. 6, fig.; Ch. de Tolnay, *Hieronymus Bosch*, Baden-Baden 1965, p. 383, cat. no. 47; D. Buzzati, M. Cinotti, *L'Opera completa di Bosch*, Milan 1966, no. 66, fig.; L. van Puyvelde, *Le renaissance Flamande de Bosch à Brueghel*, Brussels 1971, fig. on p. 17; J. Chailley, *Jerome Bosch et ses symboles. Essai de décryptage*, Brussels 1978, pp. 266-287; G. Unverfehrt, *Hieronymus Bosch. Die Rezeption seiner Kunst im frühen 16. Jahrhundert*, Berlin 1980, pp. 123-126, 146, 150, 234, no. 24; M.W. Ainsworth, "Implications of revised attributions in Netherlandish painting", *Metropolitan Museum Journal* 27 (1992), pp. 68-74, fig. 20.

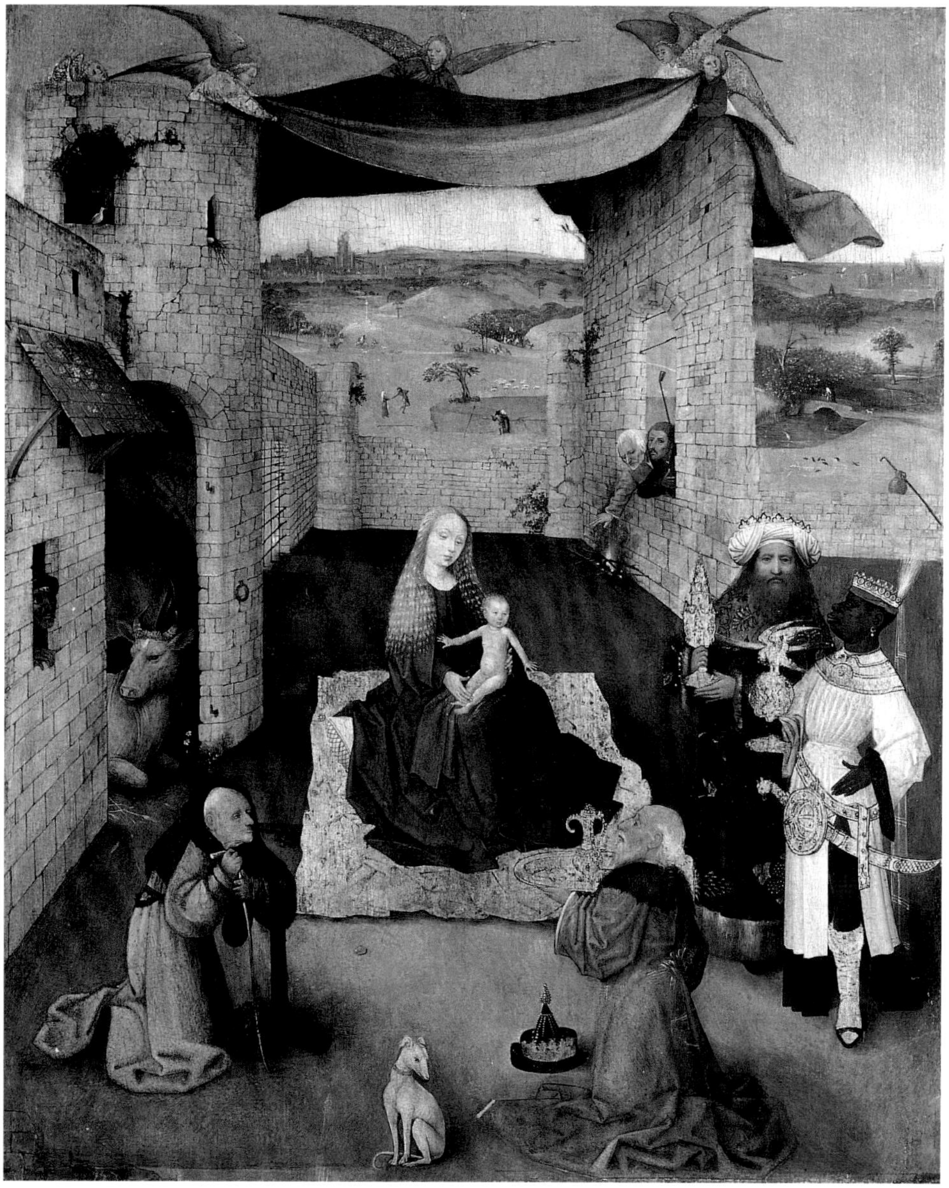

a. Jheronimus Bosch, manner of
The adoration of the magi
Panel; 71.1 x 56.6 cm
New York, The Metropolitan Museum of Art

The Virgin is seated in a ruin on a gold cloth. There are two kings standing on her left. Joseph and a third king are kneeling in front of her. Behind the remains of the building a broad landscape stretches into the distance. Most of the architectural lines meet in a central vanishing point. A series of lines scored into the uniformly painted floor all tend towards the same point.

There is second, extremely similar version of this painting in the Metropolitan Museum in New York (fig. a). In 1927, when the present work was still unknown, Friedländer published it as one of Bosch's early works.[2] De Tolnay, however, rejected the authenticity of both. Except for Puyvelde, who in 1971 still regarded the painting in Rotterdam as genuine, later authors have all concluded that neither of the panels is by Jheronimus Bosch himself. This view is supported by the figures' unusual spatial configuration. The way in which different features of Bosch's paintings have been combined also shows that the panel is more likely to be a pastiche in his style than a copy of a lost work.[3]

The group formed by Mary and the three kings bears a strong resemblance to a panel formerly ascribed to Bosch in Philadelphia which features the *Adoration of the magi*.[4] Similarities with Geertgen tot St Jans's *Adoration of the magi* in the Rijksmuseum have also been noted.

De Tolnay's claim that the architecture was inspired by a woodcut of the same subject made by Dürer around 1503 is not particularly convincing. It actually has a closer affinity with the ruin in Gerard David's *Adoration of the magi* in the National Gallery in London. There is, however, no clear evidence of any direct influence.

The dog in the foreground is almost identical to one in a painting by the Master of the Virgo inter Virgines (Milan, Pinacoteca di Brera).[5] In both paintings, angels hold a canopy over Mary and the infant Christ.

The landscape is very similar to Bosch's *Adoration of the magi* in the Prado, which is generally accepted to be a late work. There is, for example, an identical bridge and a tree with dead branches in both.

Most authors consider the painting in New York to be the earlier of the two versions. Unverfehrt was alone in thinking that the panel in Rotterdam was both better and older. The poor condition of the New York painting makes comparison between them difficult. It does, however, have a more extensive underdrawing than the painting in Rotterdam, as well as some contemporary alterations. For example, an angel in the upper left-hand window was painted over and replaced by a dove. The painting in Rotterdam has no such modifications.[6] These observations would appear to indicate that the panel in New York was painted first.

Dendrochronological examination has revealed a significant discrepancy in dating. Whilst the panel in New York could have been painted from around 1482, the one in Rotterdam could only have been painted in about 1536 at the earliest. It is difficult to reconcile the early date of the New York painting with the fact that it has, as mentioned above, the character of a pastiche. It seems likely that it was in fact produced after Bosch's death in 1516.
FL

1 The painting was scanned on 24 September 1990 by J.R.J. van Asperen de Boer.
2 Friedländer, V, 1927, pp. 88-89.
3 R.H. Wilenski, *Flemish Painters*, London 1960, pp. 85, 611, attributed the New York version to the "New York Adoration in a White Castle Painter".
4 The painting was previously regarded as one of Bosch's early works. Dendrochronological analysis has, however, shown that the painting should be dated at c. 1526. See Ainsworth (1992), p. 68.
5 Friedländer, V, 1969, fig. 48.
6 See Ainsworth (1992). Ainsworth does not consider the style of the underdrawing to be characteristic of Bosch. With the exception of one or two minor alterations, the artist followed the underdrawing closely.

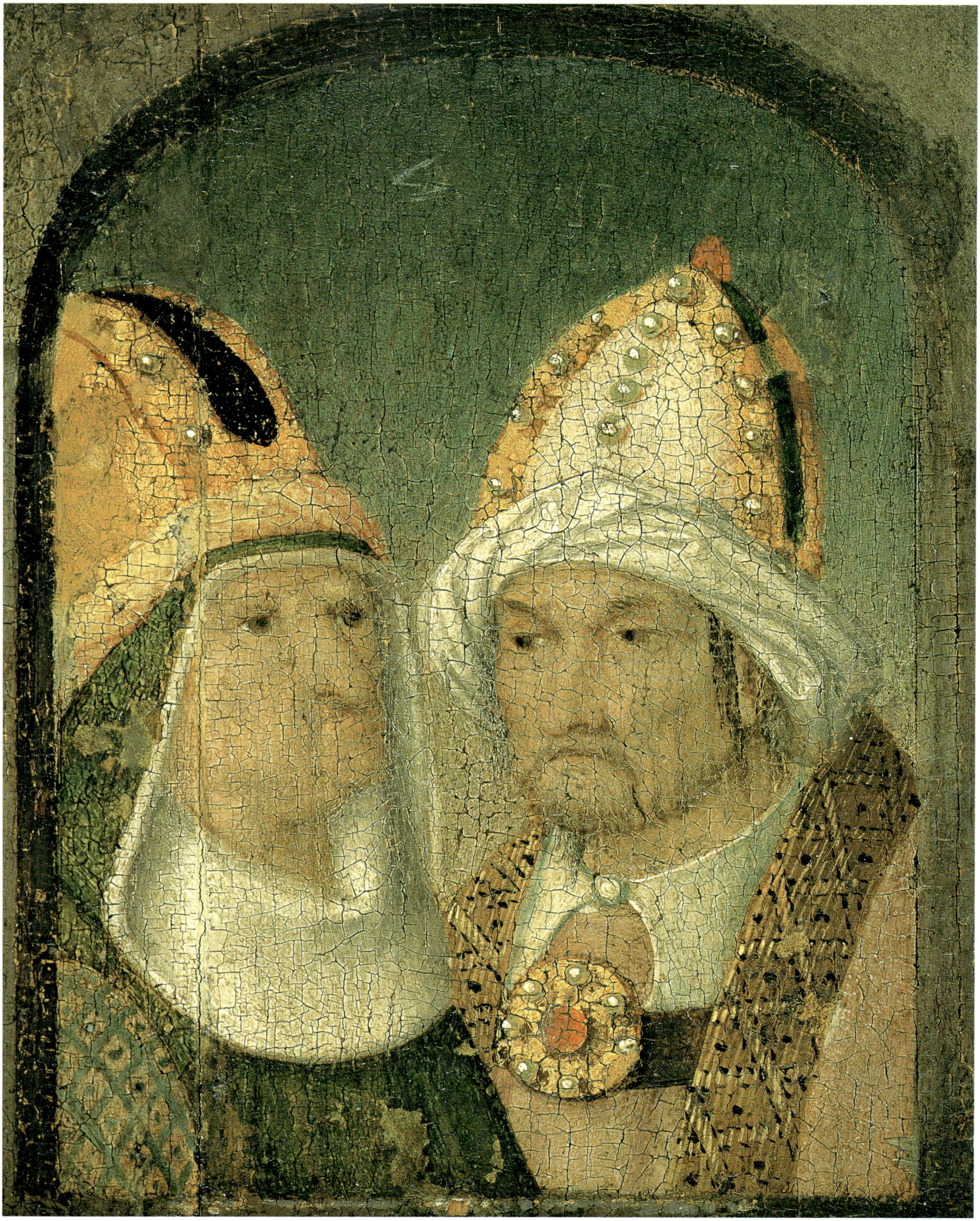

Two figures wearing mitres (fragment)

Anonymous
South Netherlandish (?) master
c. 1480 (?)

Panel; 14.5 x 12 cm

In the earliest catalogues of the Boymans Museum this panel was described as a fifteenth century work of the German or Dutch schools. Following a visit to the famous exhibition of Flemish Primitives in Bruges in 1902, the then director of the Boymans Museum, Haverkorn van Rijsewijk, attributed the painting to Jheronimus Bosch.

He regarded the panel, with its "loutish faces" as an early work. Several authors have since accepted his attribution and dating,[2] in some cases with certain reservations, since the painting's poor condition makes it difficult to judge.

Its condition makes the attribution almost impossible to verify. Since the painting seems to have little in common with Bosch's confirmed works, it has been attributed here to an anonymous southern Netherlandish artist.

The two figures looking through a window recess have been described as clerics, pharisees or high priests. Without, however, knowing of what this fragment was originally a part, we cannot identify them more precisely. Von Baldass's theory that it was part of the *Marriage at Cana* (cat. no. 20) is most unlikely.

In 1981 Hammer-Tugendhat made a connection with the interest shown in Eyckian motifs during the 1470s and 1480s, by drawing attention to similarities between the panel and a drawing in Berlin of two figures in the style of Van Eyck.
FL

Physical characteristics: the panel consists of two vertical planks.

Infrared reflectography[1]: no underdrawing could be discerned.

Dendrochronology: the youngest heartwood growth ring dates from 1366. The panel could not have been painted before 1377; it was more probably painted in or after 1391. See article by P. Klein.

Provenance: F.J.O. Boymans bequest, 1847; inv. no. 1177

Exhibitions: *Jheronimus Bosch*, 's-Hertogenbosch, Noordbrabants Museum, 1967, no. 16, fig.

Literature: *Beschrijving der schilderijen enz. in het Museum te Rotterdam, gesticht door mr. F.J.O. Boymans*, 1859, no. 432; P. Haverkorn van Rijsewijk, *Jaarverslag Museum Boijmans, Rotterdam* 1903, p. 9; L. Baldass, "Zur Entwicklungsgeschichte des Hieronymus Bosch", *Jaarboek der Koninklijke Museums voor Schoone kunsten van België* I (1938), p. 49, note 1; L. von Baldass, *Hieronymus Bosch*, Vienna 1943, pp. 42, 249, fig. 102; D. Bax, *Ontcijfering van Jeroen Bosch*, The Hague 1949, p. 219, note 72; L. von Baldass, *Hieronymus Bosch*, Vienna-Munich 1959, p. 55; cat. 1962, p. 27; D. Buzzati, M. Cinotti, *L'Opera completa di Bosch*, Milan 1966, no. 5, fig.; Ch. de Tolnay, *Hieronymus Bosch*, Baden Baden 1975 (1st ed. 1937), p. 339, no. 3a, fig. on p. 78; R. Schuder, *Hieronymus Bosch*, Berlin 1975, p. 71, fig. 80; J. Chailley, *Jérôme Bosch et ses symboles*, Brussels 1976, p. 90, no. 5; D. Hammer-Tugendhat, *Hieronymus Bosch. Eine historische Interpretation seiner Gestaltsprinzipien*, Munich 1981, p. 92, fig. 78; W. Bosing, *Hieronymus Bosch um 1450-1516*, Cologne 1987, p. 10, fig.; P. Gerlach (samenstelling en redactie P.M. Le Blanc), *Jheronimus Bosch. Opstellen over leven en werk door drs. P. Gerlach O.F.M. Cap.*, The Hague 1988, p. 117.

1 Scanned by J.R.J. van Asperen de Boer on 20 December 1993.
2 Von Baldass (1943 and 1959), De Tolnay (1975) and Schuder (1975).

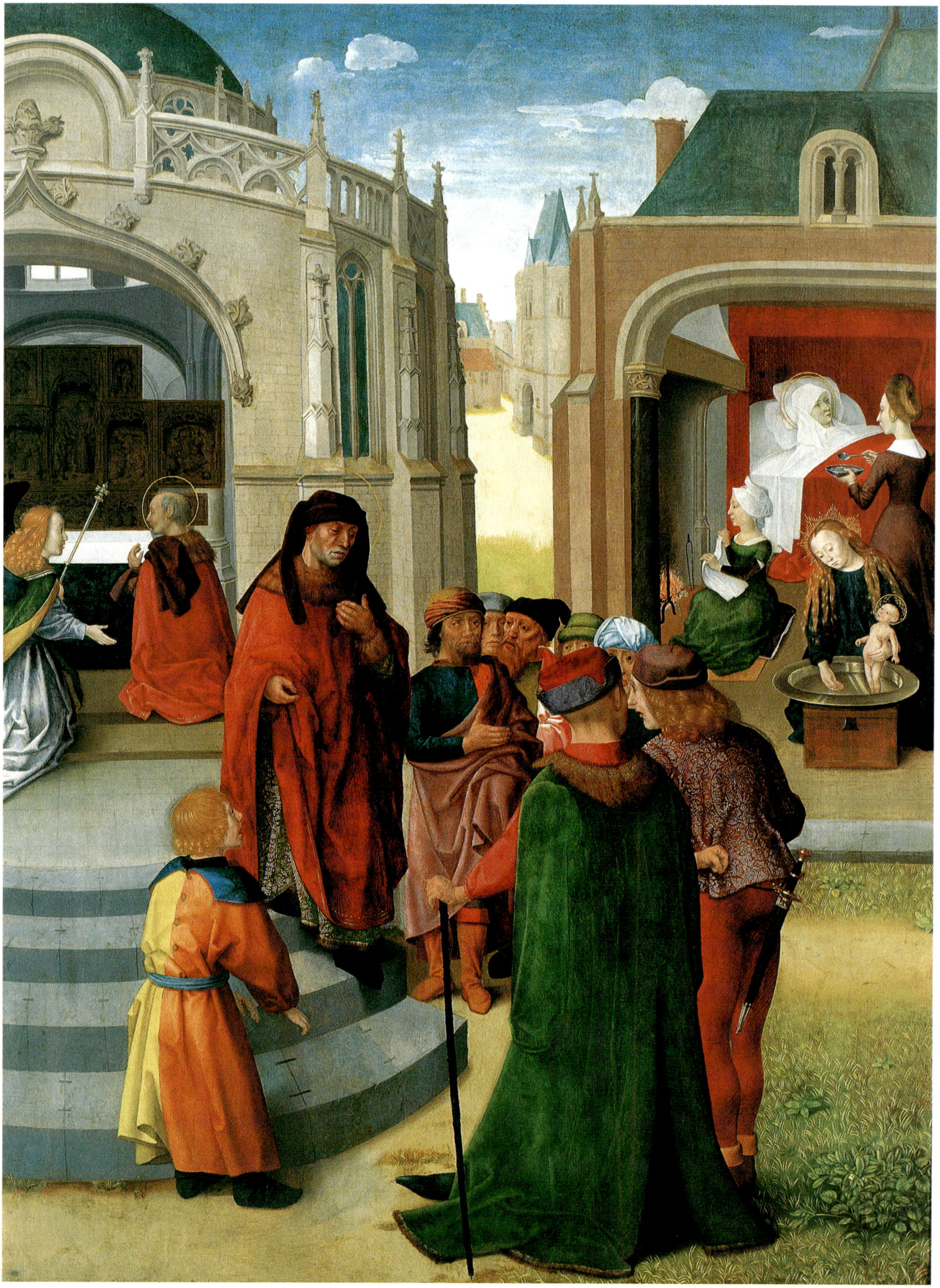

The birth of John the Baptist
Elizabeth fleeing with her son

Master of the St John Altarpiece
(Northern Netherlands,
active c. 1500)

Panels; 133 x 97 cm / 132 x 95 cm

Physical characteristics (cat. nos. 25[1] and 26[2]): the panels consist of three vertical planks.

Infrared reflectography: the paintings have a detailed underdrawing in brush. See entry.

Dendrochronology: the youngest heartwood growth ring dates to 1495. The panel could not have been painted before 1506; it was more probably painted in or after 1512. Cat. no. 25 and cat. no. 26 originally formed the back and front of a single panel. See entry and article by P. Klein.

Paint samples: the underdrawing was rendered directly on the chalk ground. The structure of the paint is simple, and the painting is built up of no more than two to three layers of paint. The pigments that have been identified are azurite, vermilion, copper resinate and lead white (cat. no. 25); azurite, copper resinate and lead white (cat. no. 26).

Provenance (cat. no. 25): Erhardt & Co., Berlin, Baden-Baden, 1928; A.L. Nicholson, London, 1936; acquired by the Boymans Museum in 1938 to commemorate the exhibition of *Meesterwerken uit vier eeuwen 1400-1800*, marking the fortieth jubilee of Queen Wilhelmina's reign; inv. no. 2118.

Provenance (cat. no. 26): Graham Collection; Mrs Margaret Post, London, until 1937; Vitale Bloch, London; acquired in 1937 to mark the exhibition of *Jeroen Bosch, Noord-Nederlandsche Primitieven*, Rotterdam 1936; inv. no. 2117.

Exhibitions: *Catalogue of a collection of pictures, furniture, Italian majolica and other objects of art*, London, Burlington Fine Arts Club, 1934-1935, no. 20; *Jeroen Bosch, Noord-Nederlandsche primitieven*, Rotterdam, Boymans Museum, 1936, no. 25, fig. 45; *Meesterwerken uit vier eeuwen 1400-1800*, Rotterdam, Boymans Museum, 1938, no. 15; *Middeleeuwse kunst der Noordelijke Nederlanden*, Amsterdam, Rijksmuseum, 1958, no. 62, fig. 33.

Literature: *Pantheon* 1 (1928) (advertisement Erhardt & Co., Berlin, Baden-Baden, fig. "The birth of John the Baptist"); L. Baldass, "Die Frühholländische Ausstellung in Rotterdam", *Pantheon* 18 (1936), p. 252, fig. on p. 253; Friedländer, XIV, 1937, p. 98; G.J. Hoogewerff, *De Noord-Nederlandsche schilderkunst*, II, The Hague 1937, pp. 285-286, fig. 138; *Museum Boymans. Beknopte catalogus schilderijen en beeldhouwwerken*, Rotterdam 1937, no. 275; D. Hannema, "De Meester van het Johannes-altaar", *Bulletin Museum Boymans Rotterdam* 1 (1937), pp. 3-4, figs. 1-2; W. Schöne, "Über einige Altniederländische Bilder, vor allem in Spanien", *Jahrbuch der Preussischen Kunstsammlungen* 58 (1937), p. 175; L. Baldass, "Die Zeichnung im Schaffen des Hieronymus Bosch und der Frühholländer", *Die Graphischen Künste* 2 (1937), p. 21; A.B. de Vries, "Vier Jahrhunderte Malerei 1400-1800 aus Holländischem Privatbesitz. Ausstellung im Museum Boymans, Rotterdam", *Pantheon* 22 (1938), p. 274, fig. on p. 276; *Catalogue of some early Flemish pictures in, or formerly in, the possession of Vitale Bloch*, London 1939, no. 8, fig. 8; J.Q. van Regteren Altena, "Nederlandsche schilderkunst. G.J.Hoogewerff, Noord-Nederlandsche schilderkunst. Deel I en II", *Tijdschrift voor Geschiedenis* 54 (1939), p. 63; G.J. Hoogewerff, *De Noord-Nederlandsche Schilderkunst*, V, The Hague 1947, p. 57, figs. 8, 9; K.G. Boon, "Een Hollands altaar van omstreeks 1470", *Oud Holland* 65 (1950), p. 213, note 1; H. Gerson, *Van Geertgen tot Frans Hals*, Amsterdam 1950, pp. 16, 67, fig. 19; *Museum Boymans Rotterdam. Gids schilderkunst & beeldhouwkunst*, Rotterdam 1951, pp. 6-7, figs. 2, 3; J.Q. van Regteren Altena, "Hugo Jacobsz", *Nederlands Kunsthistorisch Jaarboek* 6 (1955), pp. 110-111, figs. 2, 3; W. Wegner, "Mittelalterliche Kunst der Nördlichen Niederlande. Die Jubiläumsausstellung des Rijksmuseums in Amsterdam", *Kunstchronik* 12 (1959), p. 7; P. Wescher, "Drawings by the Gouda Master of the St John Altar", *The Art Quarterly* 22 (1959), p. 249, fig. 1; cat. 1962, pp. 85-86; B. Reith, "Uit de schatkamers van de beeldende kunst. Jacob Huyghsz. of Huygh Jacobsz.?", *Katholieke Illustratie* 99 (1965), p. 43, fig.; K.G. Boon, "Werk van een vroege Goudse of Leidse schilder in het Rijksmuseum", *Bulletin van het Rijksmuseum* 16 (1968), p. 5, figs. 3, 4; Friedländer, V, 1969, p. 90, suppl. no. 122, fig. 25; G. von der Osten, H. Vey, *Painting and sculpture in Germany and the Netherlands, 1500 to 1600*, Harmondsworth 1969, p. 165, fig. 149; S. Urbach, *Frühniederländische Tafelbilder, Museum der Bildenden Künste Budapest, Christliches Museum Esztergom*, Budapest 1971, with no. 27; B. Sweeney, *John G. Johnson Collection. Catalogue of Flemish and Dutch paintings*, Philadelphia 1972, p. 58; K.G. Boon, "De vroegste glaskartons uit de Sint Janskerk te Gouda", *Bulletin van het Rijksmuseum* 21 (1973), p. 165, fig. 11; G. von der Osten, *Deutsche und Niederländische Kunst der Reformationszeit*, Cologne 1973, p. 173, fig. 144; J. Schouten, "Goudse schilderkunst in de tweede helft van de zestiende en de eerste helft van de zeventiende eeuw", in: *Gouda zeven eeuwen stad. Hoofdstukken uit de geschiedenis van Gouda* 15 (1972), pp. 384, 386; J.P. Filedt Kok, "Underdrawing and other technical aspects in the paintings of Lucas van Leyden", *Nederlands Kunsthistorisch Jaarboek* 29 (1978), pp. 38, 40, fig. 37; Elisa Bermejo, *La Pintura de los Primitivos Flamencos en Espaia*, II, Madrid 1980, p. 74; K.G. Boon, "The life and work of Hugo Jacobsz before 1500", *Essays in Northern European art presented to Egbert Haverkamp-Begemann on his sixtieth birthday*, Doornspijk 1983, pp. 43, 47; A. de Bosque, *Mythologie en Maniërisme in de Nederlanden, 1570-1630. Schilderijen-tekeningen*, Amsterdam 1985, p. 77, fig.; A. Châtelet, *Early Dutch painting. Painting in the Northern Netherlands in the fifteenth century*, Lausanne 1988, pp. 145, 157-159, figs. 133-135, cat. no. 147; K.G. Boon, "A unique group of cartoons for glass reconsidered", *Festschrift to Erik Fischer. European drawings from six centuries*, Copenhagen 1990, pp. 301, 304, 305, figs. 4, 11; exhib. cat. *Le Maître de la Manne*, Douai, Musée de la Chartreuse, 1990, p. 9, fig. 4; exhib. cat. *Middeleeuwse kunst uit Hongarije*, Utrecht, Rijksmuseum Het Catharijneconvent, 1990, pp. 40-41; E. Lawton Smith, *The paintings of Lucas van Leyden. A new appraisal, with catalogue rasoinné*, Columbia-london 1992, pp. 10-12, fig. 66.

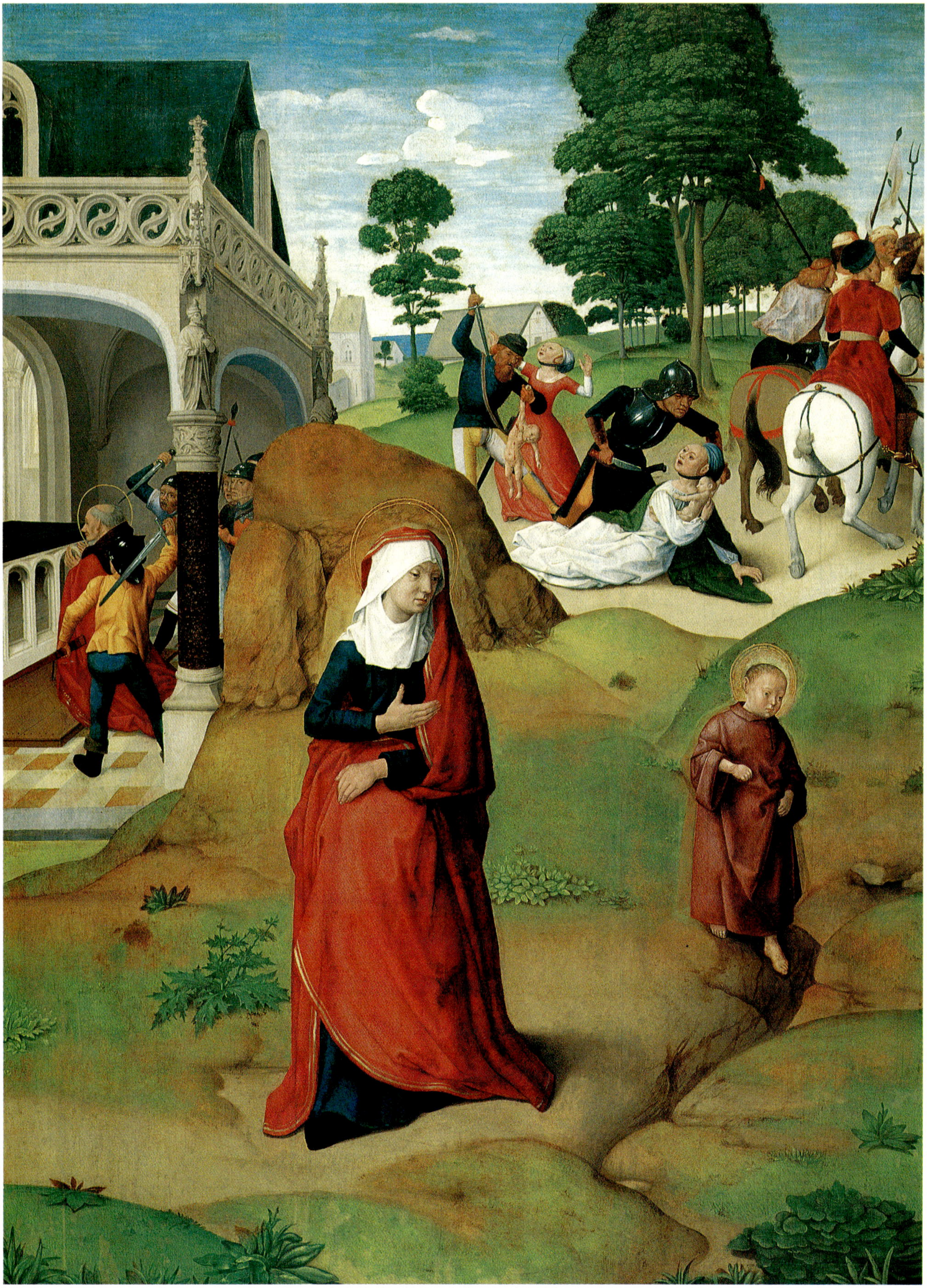

D. Hannema bought *Elizabeth fleeing with her son* in 1937 and *The birth of St John* in the following year. After his acquisition of *Elizabeth fleeing with her son* he wrote about the paintings, referring to the artist as the "Master of the St John Altarpiece". He also attributed to the same master a panel of *St John preaching to the multitude* (Philadelphia Museum of Art), which he regarded as belonging to the two Rotterdam panels (fig. a).

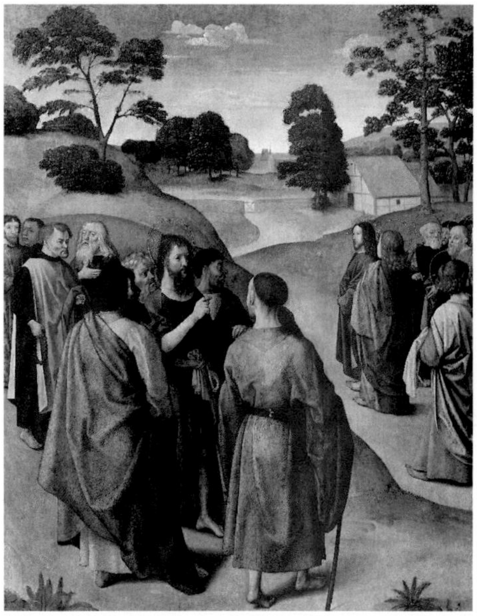

a. Master of the St John Altarpiece, St John preaching to the multitude
Panel; 123.5 x 94 cm
Philadelphia, Philadelphia Museum of Art.

The birth of St John illustrates three scenes. In the domed Gothic church in the left background is the scene of the angel Gabriel appearing to Zacharias, who kneels before an altar with a retable and predella (Luke 1:5-25). The angel prophesies the birth of John, but Zacharias receives the news with disbelief. He and his wife Elizabeth are advanced in years and he knows that Elizabeth is barren. The angel then announces that Zacharias will lose the power of speech until the child is born. The next episode is depicted in the centre foreground. The worshippers assembled at the temple during the incense-burning ceremony are bewildered by the priest's failure to emerge. When he finally reappears and is unable to speak, they understand that something momentous has happened. With his head covered, Zacharias descends from the temple to join the throng. The third scene is shown in the background on the right. Elizabeth is confined to her bed, where she is being fed with a spoon; a cloth is drying by the fire, and in the foreground, Mary, the mother of Christ, is washing the new-born John. Each of the protagonists has a distinctive halo to facilitate identification. Zacharias has been given a simple circle, Elizabeth a double circle, John a circle with three rays, and Mary a star-shaped crown. In the Philadelphia painting Christ has the star-shaped crown and the apostles have circles like Zacharias's.

A large altarpiece can be seen in the temple where the angel appears to Zacharias. It is an elaborately carved chest with two large and two small doors (fig. b). The scene portrayed in the middle shows Melchisedek offering Abraham bread and wine (Genesis 17-20). On the left is the celebration of the passover (Exodus 12), and on the right the gathering of manna (Exodus 16:13:37). These are all prefigurations of the eucharist. The illustration on the right panel is rather more difficult to interpret. Three people are gathered around a reclining figure, one of whom appears to be tugging at his robe. The scene is probably a representation of God's pledge to Abraham. According to the bible, Abraham was resting before his tent in the heat of the day, when the Lord appeared to him in the guise of three men. Abraham hastened to meet them, bowing himself to the ground. Then, after sharing a meal with their host, the men announced that a son was to be born to Abraham and his ageing wife Sarah (Genesis 18:1-15). This episode, too, is a typology for the Last Supper, while the prophesy that this elderly couple are to conceive a child has a parallel in the birth of John to Zacharias and Elizabeth. The painting on the small door on the left is a representation of the Fall, and that on the right the expulsion from Paradise. Both these events foreshadow the crucifixion of Christ. Two scenes are illustrated on the predella. On the left is the angel giving food to Elijah (1 Kings 19:1-8), and on the right are two seated men who appear to be prophets. The fact that Abraham and Melchisedek were chosen as the central theme attests to the artist's sense of history, since all his scenes are from the Old Testament. The Last Supper, which is normally the main representation in a sacramental retable, is an episode from the New Testament which only takes place once John, whose birth is merely predicted here, has reached adulthood.

Elizabeth fleeing with her son is also illustrated in three separate episodes. Her escape with the infant John is not a biblical theme but an episode described in the *Protevangelium of James* (22:2). Having heard Herod's command that all small children were to be slain, Elizabeth fled to the mountain. She implored the mountain to give refuge to her son, whereupon a crevice opened up and offered them shelter. Herod then dispatched messengers to Zacharias, ordering him to reveal his son's hiding place. But Zacharias remained silent. In retaliation Herod instructed his men to return to Zacharias and execute him at the first light of dawn. On the left of the painting is Zacharias in the temple, facing his death at the hands of the soldiers. He has a simple halo around his head. The scene in the middle shows the mountain opening up to shelter Elizabeth, who is portrayed with a double halo, and John, who has a halo with lines issuing from the centre. In the background are Herod's soldiers massacring the infants.

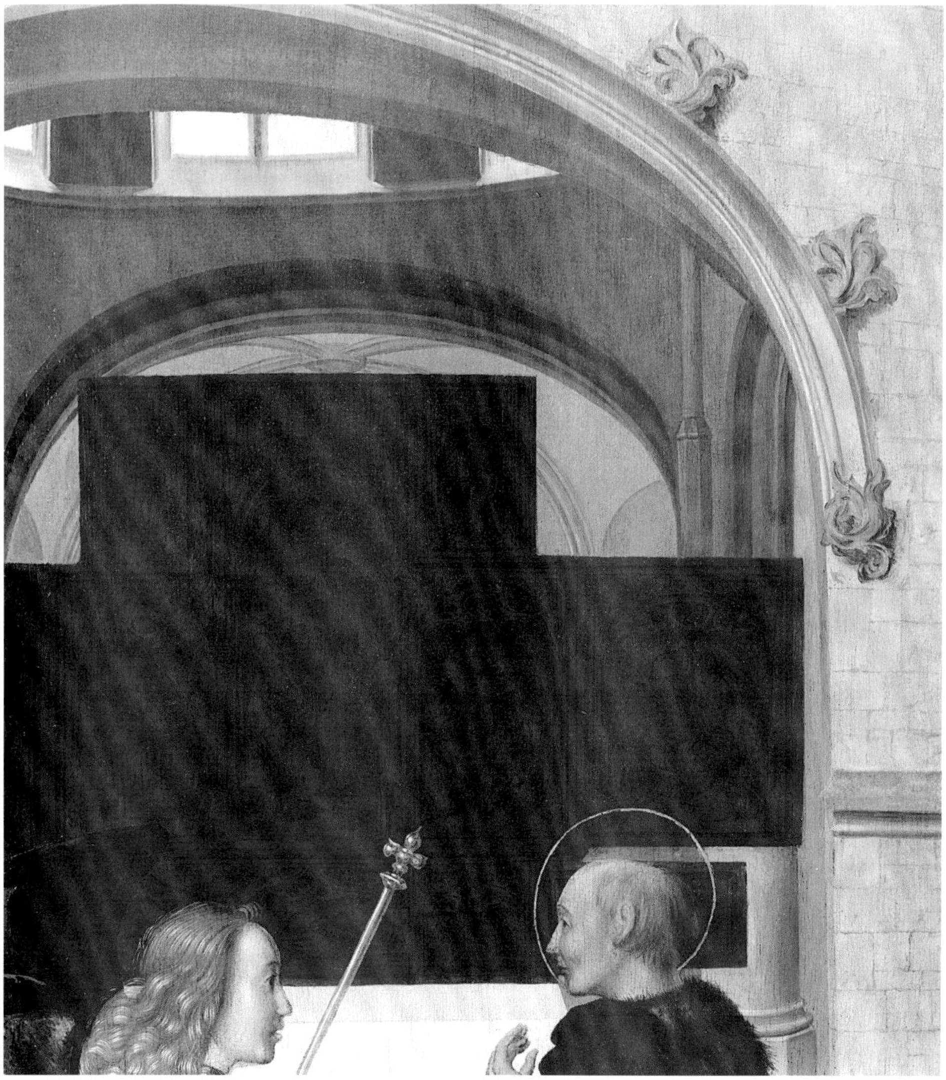

b. The birth of St John. Detail of the altarpiece.

The two Rotterdam panels together with the painting in Philadelphia illustrate all the important events of John the Baptist's youth. The three panels must originally have belonged to an altarpiece dedicated to St John. *The birth of John the Baptist* and *Elizabeth fleeing with her son* were initially painted back to back on the same panel. The panel was later sawn through the middle to separate the painting on the front from that on the reverse. Both were badly damaged in the process. They were beautifully restored by P.F.J.M. Hermesdorf between 1987 and 1990. The cradle on the backs were removed, and large areas of paint loss in Elizabeth's robe and other parts of the panels were filled in with outstanding success. These three paintings in Rotterdam and Philadelphia form the core of the oeuvre of the Master of the St John Altarpiece.[3] In 1927 Friedländer compared the Philadelphia painting to a series of woodcuts in the *Chevalier délibéré*, a book printed in Gouda in 1488. The similarities between them prompted him to suggest that the painting may have been made by an artist from Gouda.[4] Van Regteren Altena studied the life and work of Hugo Jacobsz, the father of Lucas van Leyden. The artist must have been born around 1470 and is believed to have died between 1534 and 1538. In Van Regteren Altena's view, the landscapes in the panels of the St John altar recall examples by Lucas van Leyden. He noted other similarities to Van Leyden's paintings, and consequently attributed the altar to Hugo Jacobsz. At the time the altar was dated around 1500.[5] A dendrochronological examination has since established that the two panels could not have been painted before about 1512, which is in fact far later than had hitherto been believed. Most scholars still supported the view that the altar was made in Gouda. Considering the subject of the paintings, Hoogewerff speculated that the retable may originally have belonged to the main altar of a church dedicated to St John, either in Gouda or Gorinchem. However no evidence has been found at the archives in Gouda to support this theory.

Infrared reflectography revealed an unusually detailed underdrawing (figs. c, d). The boy with the dangling hands in the left foreground of *The birth of St John* is an intriguing detail. In the underdrawing he is reaching out to what seems to be a dog, yet for some unknown reason the artist evidently changed his mind and decided not to paint the animal. The infrared reflectograms also show changes to the boy's face and to those of the group of onlookers. Though one might be tempted to conclude that the altar was made in Gouda and to attribute it to Hugo Jacobsz, too little evidence is available at present to draw any firm conclusions.
LH/JG

1 Scientific examination conducted by A. Wallert under the supervision of J.R.J. van Asperen de Boer. A copy of his minor thesis is in the Museum's file on the painting. Paint samples A 206/ 1-8. Infrared reflectograms: AB 551-AB 555/19; AB 371/30-AB 373.

2 Scientific examination conducted by A. Wallert and B. van Geffen under the supervision of J.R.J. van Asperen de Boer. The report is in the Museum's file on the painting. Infrared reflectograms: AB 555/21-AB 559; AB 560/1-27. Paint samples A 189/ 1-8.

3 Two more paintings are generally accepted as his work. They are *The Entombment* at the Museum in Budapest, and the *Virgin and Child with St Anne and John the Baptist* at the Rijksmuseum in Amsterdam (see Boon, 1990). The attribution of the former is especially convincing. The underdrawing, for instance, has much in common with the panels of the St John retable.

4 Friedländer, V, 1927, p. 62.

5 Van Regteren Altena (1955).

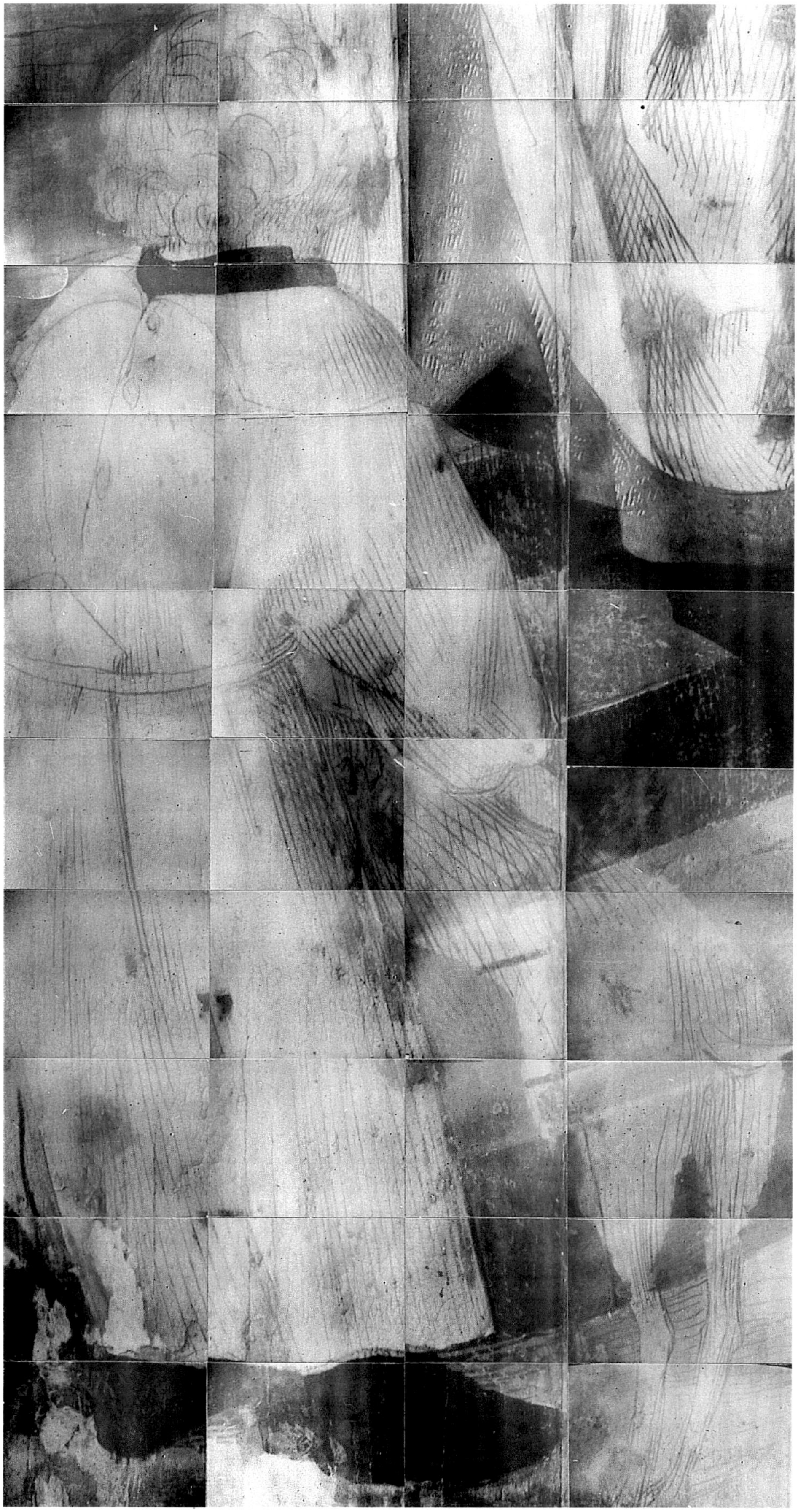

c. Infrared reflectogram assembly. Detail of The birth of John the Baptist. Detail showing the boy in the right foreground.

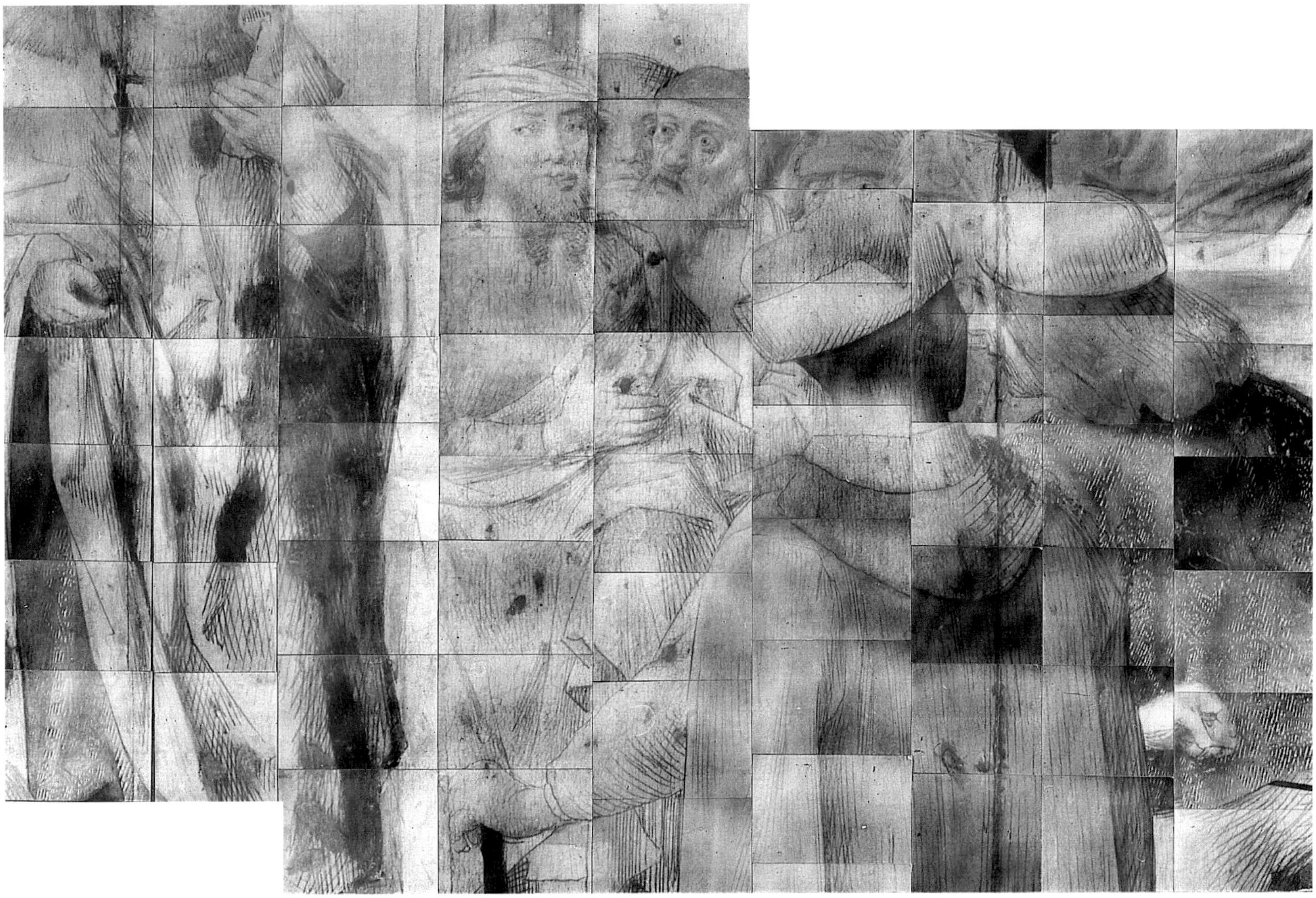

d. Infrared reflectogram assembly. Detail of The birth of John the Baptist. Detail of Zacharias and part of the crowd gathered at the temple.

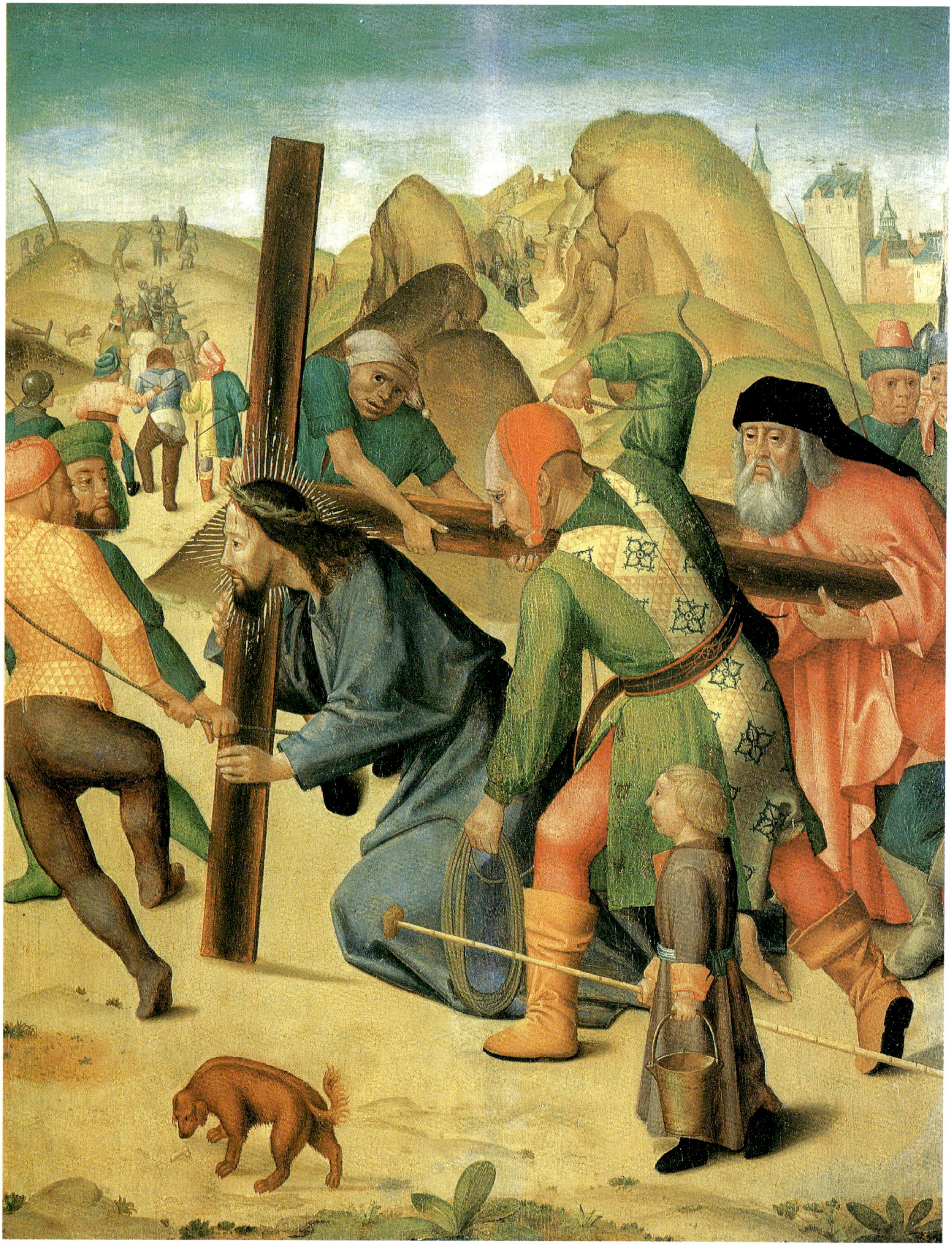

Christ bearing the cross

Master of the St John Altarpiece, circle
(Northern Netherlands,
active c. 1500)

Panel; 67.3 x 51 cm

Physical characteristics: the panel consists of two vertical planks.[1] The *barbe* can be seen along the upper and lower edges and on the left side.
Infrared reflectography: no underdrawing visible. The letter 'r' can be seen just above the left knee of the soldier with the rope (fig. a). This was a reminder to the artist that it should be painted red.[2] See entry.

Dendrochronology: the youngest heartwood growth ring dates from 1463. The panel could not have been painted before 1474; it was more probably painted after 1488. See entry and article by P. Klein.

Provenance: Lady Jekyll Collection, London, 1913; J.D. Klaasen Collection, Rotterdam, 1936; J.W. Frederiks Collection, The Hague, 1958; on loan to the Boymans-van Beuningen Museum from J.W. Frederiks since 1966; gift from the J.W. Frederiks Collection, 1994; inv. no. S 25.

Exhibitions: *Noord-Nederlandsche Schilder- en Beeldhouwkunst vòòr 1575*, Utrecht, Gebouw voor Kunsten en Wetenschappen, 1913, supplement, no. 174; *Jeroen Bosch, Noord-Nederlandsche Primitieven*, Rotterdam, Boymans Museum, 1936, no. 31, fig. 35; *Middeleeuwse kunst der Noordelijke Nederlanden*, Amsterdam, Rijksmuseum, 1958, no. 64; *Nederlandse Primitieven uit Nederlands particulier bezit*, Laren, Singer Museum, 1961, no. 95.

Literature: L. Baldass, "Die Frühholländische Ausstellung in Rotterdam", *Pantheon* 18 (1936), p. 254; L. Baldass, "Die Zeichnung im Schaffen des Hieronymus Bosch und der Frühholländer", *Die Graphischen Künste* 2 (1937), pp. 20-21; Friedländer, XIV, 1937, p. 97; J.Q. van Regteren Altena, "Hugo Jacobsz", *Nederlands Kunsthistorisch Jaarboek* 6 (1955), p. 114; W. Wegner, "Mittelalterliche Kunst der Nördlichen Niederlande. Die Jubiläumsausstellung des Rijksmuseums in Amsterdam", *Kunstchronik* 12 (1959), p. 7; P. Wescher, "Drawings by the Gouda Master of the St. John Altar", *The Art Quarterly* 22 (1959), p. 249; K.G. Boon, "Werk van een vroege Goudse of Leidse schilder in het Rijksmuseum", *Bulletin van het Rijksmuseum* 16 (1968), p. 6, fig. 7; Friedländer, V, 1969, p. 89, supp. 118 and fig. 108; K.G. Boon, "The life and work of Hugo Jacobsz before 1500", *Essays in Northern European art presented to Egbert Haverkamp Begemann on his sixtieth birthday*, Doornspijk 1983, p. 44; A. Châtelet, *Early Dutch painting. Painting in the Northern Netherlands in the fifteenth century*, Lausanne 1988, no. 146, p. 238.

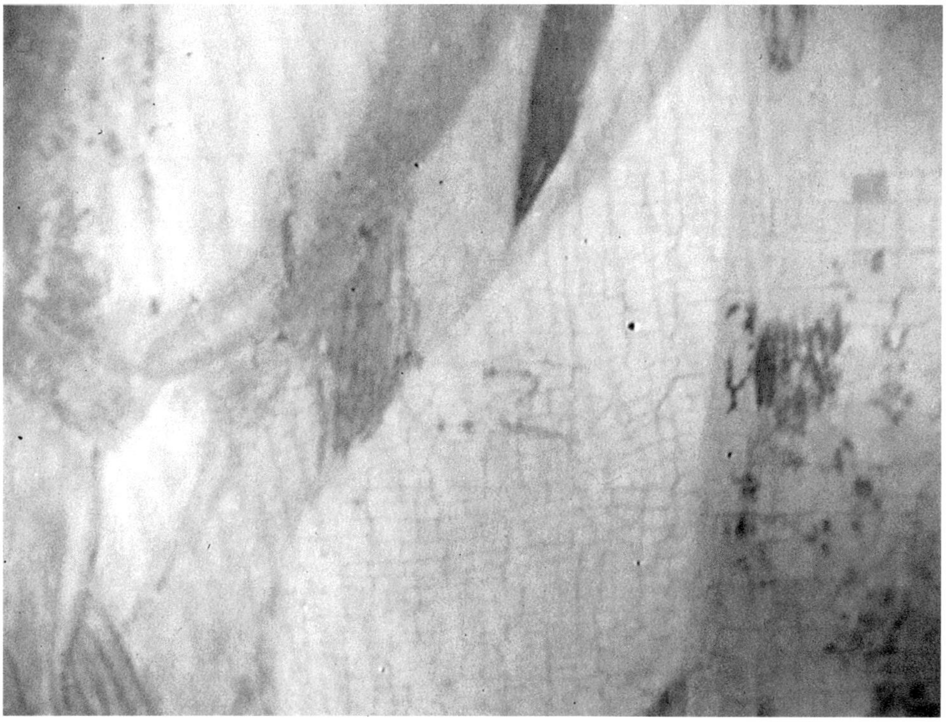

a. Infrared reflectogram showing the letter 'r' as a colour instruction.

Christ bearing the cross was a popular theme in North Netherlandish painting in the fifteenth and sixteenth centuries. Many artists were inspired by the Saviour's arduous procession to the hill of Golgotha, the place of his execution. The synoptic gospels give a different account of the event from that related by St John (19:17). John describes Christ carrying the cross single-handed, whereas in the synoptic version Simon the Cyrenian, a chance passer-by, is made to carry the cross.[3] This painting combines both accounts. Simon lends a helping hand to the Saviour, as indeed does a third man. Stumbling under the weight of the cross, Christ is drawn along by a rope held by one of the centurions. A second soldier brandishing a whip goads him on. Christ is still wearing the crown of thorns put on his head at the mocking, but he has been disencumbered of the purple cloak and is shown in his own clothing. A small boy walks beside the procession with a bucket of sour wine and myrrh in one hand and a sponge attached to a hyssop cane in the other. His name, according to legend, is Stephaton. The gospels mention that the centurions raised a sponge soaked in wine to Christ's lips shortly before he died. The men escorted by soldiers at the head of the procession are the two thieves who will be executed on either side of Christ. In the distance is Golgotha, the 'place of the skull', where preparations are being made for the crucifixion. The women can be seen on a hill as the drama unfolds below. The scene might refer to a later event of the three women at the tomb mourning the death of their master.

The subject of the painting has infinite dramatic potential, yet it is rendered without pathos. However, the figures have an air of solemn dignity that is often seen in work by other artists of this period. In 1958 the panel was attributed to the anonymous Master of the St John Altarpiece, so called after his altarpiece of John the Baptist.[4] Two panels of this altarpiece are now at the Boymans-van Beuningen Museum.[5] Dendrochronological analysis has established that the altarpiece was probably painted after 1512. *Christ bearing the cross* must have been made earlier. A scientific examination of the wood shows that it was probably painted after 1488.

Scholars have compared the artist's work to paintings attributed to the Master of the Virgo inter Virgines, who is believed to have been active in Delft. His style is characterised by large planes, and clothing rendered almost without folds. As a result, his work has a solid and rather monumental quality. Fine hatching is used to add shape and volume to the figures. The underdrawing, though not detailed, is painstaking and thorough.

In many respects *Christ bearing the cross* resembles the altar panels of the retable dedicated to John the Baptist. Both the colours and the broad modelling of the figures point to a related hand. Yet *Christ bearing the cross* lacks the monumentality that distinguishes work by the Master of the St John Altarpiece, while the technique is also different. The panels of the St John's retable have extensive underdrawings, whereas all that can be seen here is a single instruction to remind the artist what colour to use (fig. a). For lack of sufficient evidence at this stage, it would be more judicious to attribute the piece to an artist in the master's circle rather than to his studio.[6]
LH

1 No evidence has been found to show that the panel was originally larger. This theory was advanced by Châtelet, who suggested that Pilate and Caiaphas may also have been in the procession. See Châtelet (1988), p. 238.

2 In 1990 J.R.J. van Asperen de Boer examined the painting using infrared reflectography. Infrared reflectogram: AB 1201/6. Paint samples were also taken at the time, but the analysis has not yet been completed. They are numbered A 318/1-6.

3 Matthew 27:32, Mark 15:21 and Luke 23:26.

4 Van Regteren Altena (1955) ascribes the panel to the Master of the St John Altarpiece, whom he identifies as Hugo Jacobsz, the father of Lucas van Leyden. See cat. nos. 25-26. In 1959, however, both Wegner and Wescher questioned this attribution.

5 See cat. nos. 25-26.

6 Boon (1968 and 1983) considers it a studio work. Friedländer, V, 1969, describes it as Dutch and believes it was painted towards the end of the fifteenth century. Only Châtelet (1988) accepts the attribution without reservation. He has included it in his catalogue as a work by the Master of the St John Altarpiece, conceding however that there are substantial discrepancies between *Christ bearing the cross* and the panels of the retable of John the Baptist.

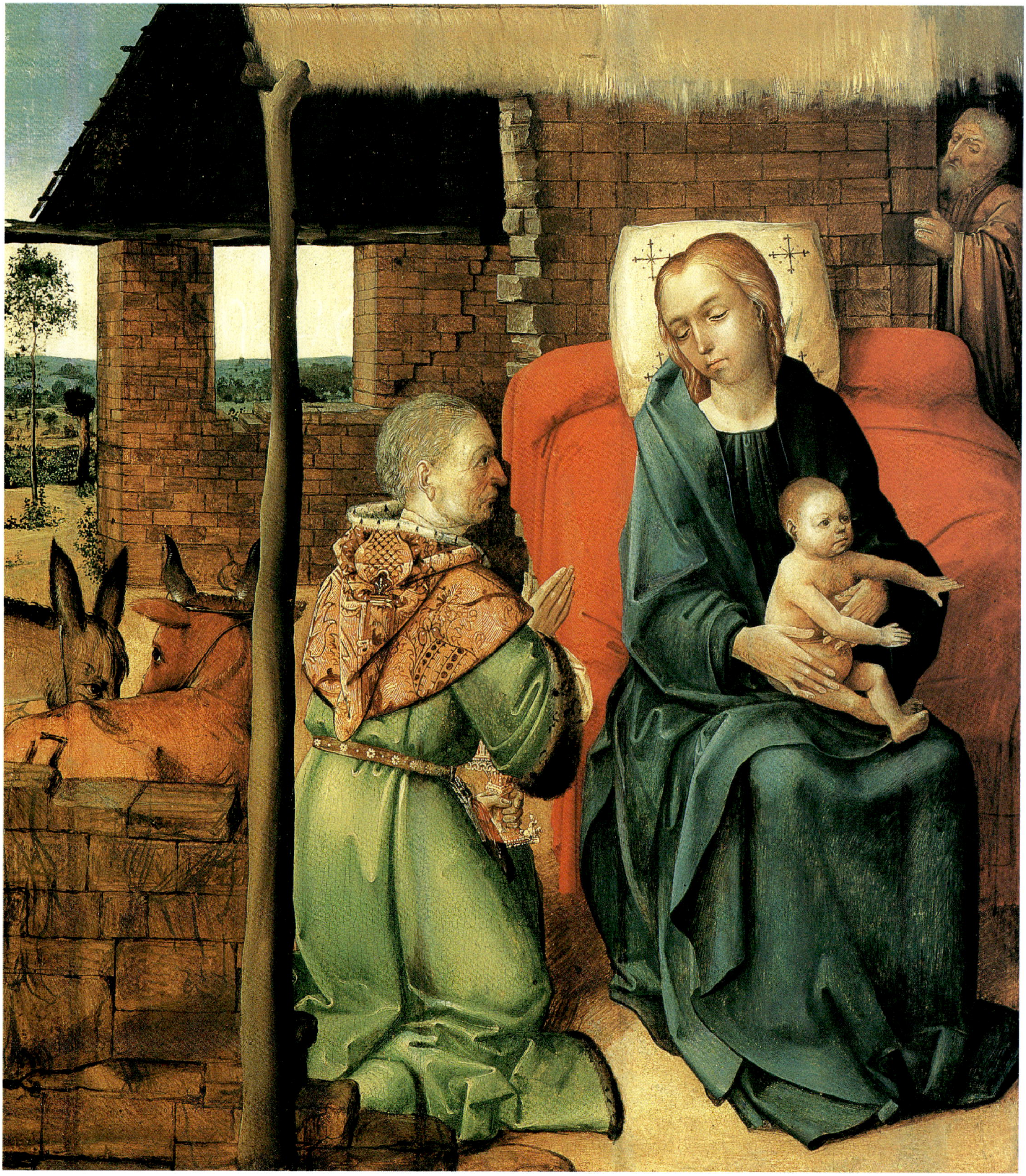

Adoration of the Christ Child
Ecce Homo

Anonymous
Netherlandish master
After 1480

Panels; 84 x 70.7 cm / 84 x 70.5 cm

The two paintings originally formed the left wing of a triptych of considerable dimensions (over 2.8 meters wide when opened). The exterior of the altarpiece displayed the *Adoration of the Magi*, presumably on two panels as only one Magus is depicted on the Boymans picture. The interior right wing possibly represented a scene from the Passion, preceding or following the *Ecce Homo* now in Rotterdam.

The Boymans panels have attracted little attention in scholarly literature. The paintings were first published in 1937 as "North Netherlandish, last decades of the fifteenth century" by Friedländer. In 1980 Châtelet agreed with Friedländer's attribution, drawing connections with late fifteenth-century paintings thought to be from Utrecht.[2] Ascribing the Rotterdam panels to any given school is exceedingly difficult in view of the lack of direct stylistic parallels and the heavy toll taken by sixteenth-century iconoclasm of art from the Northern Netherlands.

The *Ecce Homo,* Christ's presentation to the people after the flagellation, takes place in an open courtyard. Christ, flanked by two tormentors, stands on a platform facing a group of hostile, gesticulating onlookers. The Boymans *Ecce Homo* follows an iconographic scheme that was developed in the middle of the fifteenth century. A woodcut datable to that period and possibly made in Lorraine[3] already provides the basic framework for the Rotterdam composition, opposing an angry crowd to Christ raised on a platform (fig. a). This compositional scheme was taken over both in Germany and the Netherlands and is therefore not indicative of one particular region; examples include works by the Cologne Master of the St George Legend of c. 1460 and by Jheronimus Bosch of c. 1500.[4]

The *Adoration of the Christ Child* displays a borrowing of motifs from different sources, the most important being the works of Hugo van der Goes. The Rotterdam Magus, whose features verge on caricature, possibly reflects the same figure in Hugo's *Monforte Altarpiece* in reverse (fig. b). His body is seen more from the back, while his balding head is depicted in the same profile view. As in Hugo's more dignified Magus, the mouth is turned downwards and a long vertical wrinkle marks the cheek. In contrast to Hugo's figure, who lifts both hands before him in prayer, the Rotterdam Magus has only one hand raised, while the other holds a vessel. The broken wall with protruding stones may also derive from the same area of the *Monforte Altarpiece*. The bed behind the Virgin is found in another painting by Hugo, the Bruges *Death of the Virgin*, where the iconography of the scene requires this motif. In both the Rotterdam *Adoration* and Hugo's *Death of the Virgin*, the bed is positioned perpendicularly to the picture plane with its foot toward the observer, a white cushion resting on a bolster covered with the bedspread. For the lower part of Mary's drapery the artist drew inspiration from the Virgin's figure on the central panel of Van der Weyden's *Columba Altarpiece*. As in Rogier's painting the Virgin's knees are depicted frontally. Rogier's pattern of folds is reproduced in reverse, one broad diagonal fold running from one knee toward the foot of the other leg where the drapery gathers on the ground. The stable in the Rotterdam *Adoration*, with its thatched roof and a wooden post positioned vertically against the lower edge of the picture, is reminiscent of the architectural structure in Robert Campin's

Physical characteristics: the two panels (cat. nos. 28 and 29), which originally formed the front and reverse of an altarpiece wing, were separated between 1936 and 1939. The original support, made of three vertical planks, has been thinned down to a veneer and laminated with a new wooden backing, now cradled.

Infrared reflectography:[1] very free brush underdrawing. See text.

Dendrochronology: the youngest heartwood growth ring dates from 1462. The panels could not have been painted before 1473; they were more probably painted in or after 1487. See article by P. Klein.

Provenance: Arthur Cane, London; auctioned at Christie's on 20 November 1936, no. 14 (acquired by Rosenbaum); J. Goudstikker, Amsterdam, 1936-37; J.W. Frederiks, The Hague, acquired in 1939; since 1966 on loan to Museum Boymans-van Beuningen, Rotterdam; gift from the J.W. Frederiks Collection, 1994; (cat. no. 28) inv. no. BR.F. 2/S. 27; (cat. no. 29) inv. no. BR.F. 3/S. 28.

Exhibitions: *Rotterdamsche Kunstkring*, Rotterdam, 1936-37, no. 41; *Bijbelsche Kunst*, Rijksmuseum, Amsterdam, 1939, nos. 75a and 110a; *Nederlandse Primitieven uit Nederlands particulier bezit*, Singer Museum, Laren, 1961, nos. 96 and 97.

Literature: Friedländer, XIV, 1937, p. 98; Friedländer, V, 1969, p. 89, supp. 119; A. Châtelet, *Early Dutch Painting*, Fribourg 1980, no. 170, p. 245; Daniela Hammer-Tugendhat, *Hieronymus Bosch. Eine historische Interpretation seiner Gestaltungsprinzipien*, Munich 1981, p. 42; Jochen Sander, *Niederländische Gemälde im Städel 1400-1550*, Mainz 1993, p. 42 note 56.

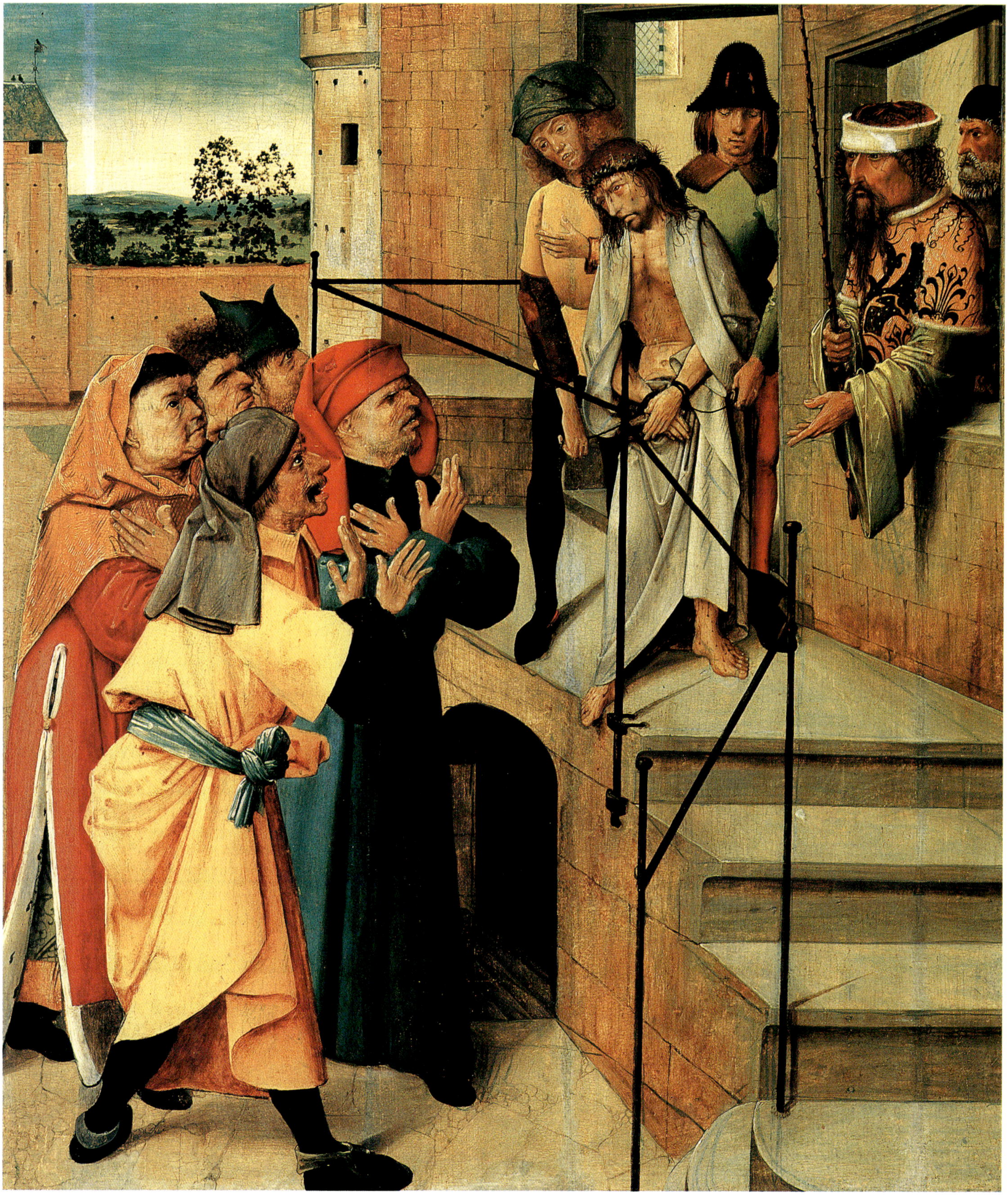

Dijon *Nativity*. The figure of Joseph in the doorway recalls the shepherd holding his hat in the Dijon painting. Like Campin's shepherd, Joseph wears mittens with three fingers, one of his shoulders is raised and his head is tilted in the direction of this shoulder.

The presence of motifs from Van der Goes, Van der Weyden and Campin in the Rotterdam *Adoration* does not qualify its artist as a follower of any of them. It does not even suffice to ascribe the panels to the South Netherlandish school, as the influence of the Flemings, Hugo in particular, was felt in the Northern provinces as well as in the South. The sometimes coarse style of the Rotterdam panels bears little resemblance to that of the great Flemish painters. The additive nature of the *Adoration* merely suggests that its creator had a wide-ranging repertoire of motifs at his disposal, possibly made available through drawings. The motifs from Hugo's works, though, provides external evidence for dating the paintings after 1480, a date which is supported by dendrochronology.

Infrared reflectography revealed very free brush underdrawing in both paintings (figs. c-e). The main drapery lines are positioned through rapid, angular strokes, which are sometimes reinforced by a second application of underdrawing material. The artist often draws a short, slanted stroke at the extremity of a fold line. Hatching is used sparingly to indicate general zones of shadow in the figures. Hands and faces are defined in an extremely summary fashion. Changes abound in many areas of the pictures, especially in draperies and hands, as the artist revised his compositions during the execution in paint. The most radical modification occurred in the lower-left portion of the *Adoration*, where a stone wall was painted on top of the underdrawn bodies of the ass and ox. Both paintings display the same rapid, cursory underdrawing style as well as numerous modifications of the initial composition, suggesting that the same hand was responsible for the lay-out of both panels. Although no direct parallel can be found for this underdrawing style, future infrared studies, especially of North Netherlandish works, may eventually allow more precise attribution of the Rotterdam panels.[5]
JC

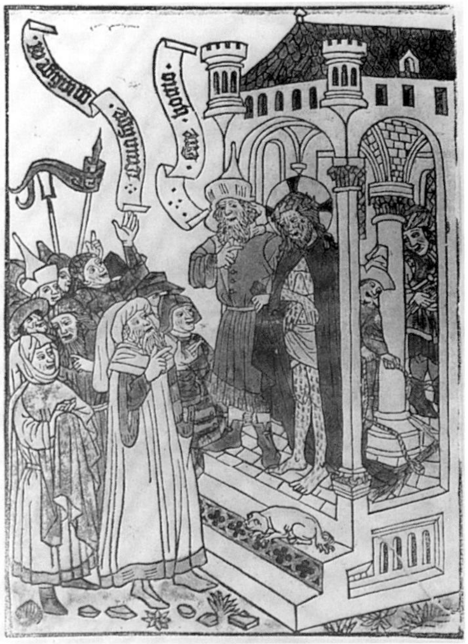

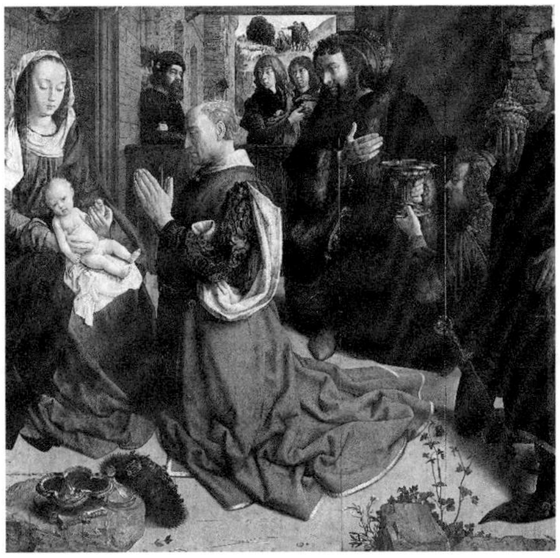

1 The paintings were examined with infrared reflectography on 16 September 1993 (Molly Faries, Julien Chapuis).

2 Châtelet (1980). As Châtelet observes, the Virgin's features in the *Adoration* bear resemblance to those of Mary in the *Mystic Marriage of Saint Agnes*, now at the Christian Museum, Esztergom (reproduced in Châtelet, plate 142). The attribution of the Esztergom painting to a Utrecht artist is in itself matter for debate.

3 Paris, Bibliothèque Nationale, reproduced in Sander (1993), fig. 5, p. 35.

4 On the Saint-George Master, see: Frank Günter Zehnder, *Katalog der Altkölner Malerei* (Kataloge des Wallraf-Richartz-Museums IX), Cologne 1990, pp. 252-258, fig. 172; on Bosch's Frankfurt painting, see: Sander (1993), pp. 28-45, fig. p. 29. This compositional scheme was in use well into the sixteenth century, as illustrated by the *Ecce Homo* on Pieter Claeissens I's *Triptych of the Passion* (auctioned at Christie's, Amsterdam, on 10 November 1992); Pieter Claeissens I became a master in Bruges in 1530.

5 The long, angular drapery lines found in the underdrawing of the Rotterdam panels is to a certain degree reminiscent of the lay-out of the *Annunciation* from the Vrancke van der Stockt group in Dijon, although there the use of hatching and cross-hatching is much more deliberate (J.R.J. van Asperen de Boer, Jellie Dijkstra, Roger van Schoute, *Underdrawing in Paintings of the Rogier van der Weyden and Master of Flémalle Groups, Nederlands Kunsthistorisch Jaarboek* 41 (1990), Zwolle, 1992, figs. 25-26, p. 39). The Boymans underdrawing differs markedly from the meticulous application of hatching found in the *Entombment* by the Master of the Virgo inter Virgines in Saint Louis (Maryan Ainsworth and Molly Faries, "Northern Renaissance Paintings. The Discovery of Invention", *Bulletin of the Saint Louis Art Museum* 18 (1986), p. 8-9). It is also executed in a more sketchy fashion than the underdrawing of Geertgen tot Sint Jans' Vienna panels, where, moreover, a combination of brush and chalk was discovered (Truus van Bueren and Molly Faries, "The 'Portraits' in Geertgen tot Sint Jans' Vienna Panels", in: H. Verougstraete-Marcq and R. van Schoute (eds.), *Dessins sous-jacent et copies* (Le dessin sous-jacent dans la peinture, colloque VIII), Louvain-la-Neuve, 1991, p. 141-150).

a. Lorraine (?), Ecce Homo, c. 1450
Woodcut
Paris, Bibliothèque Nationale

b. Hugo van der Goes, Monforte Altarpiece
Berlin, Staatliche Museen Preussischer Kulturbesitz, Gemäldegalerie

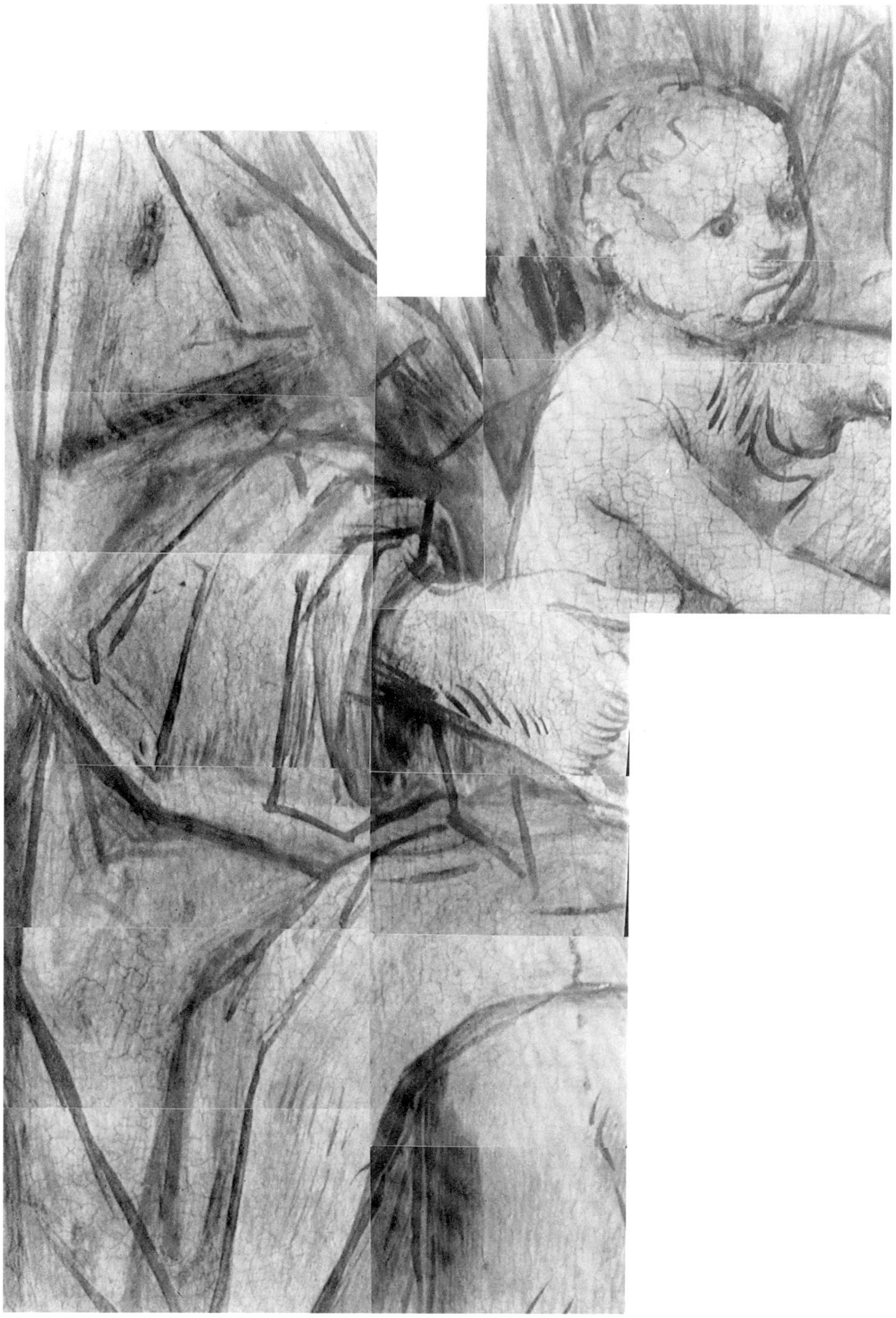

c. Infrared reflectogram assembly of a detail of the Adoration of the Christ Child, (infrared reflectography: Molly Faries)

d. Infrared reflectogram assembly of a detail of the Ecce Homo
(infrared reflectography: Molly Faries)

e. Infrared reflectogram assembly of a detail of the Ecce Homo
(infrared reflectography: Molly Faries)

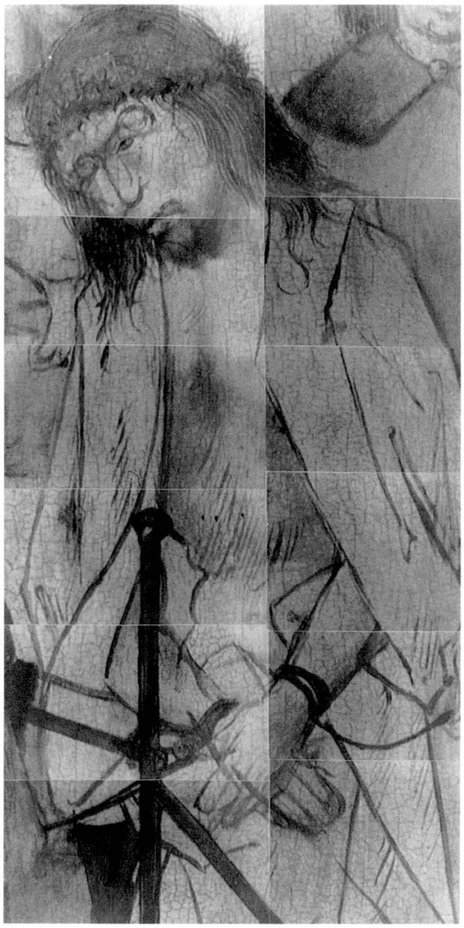

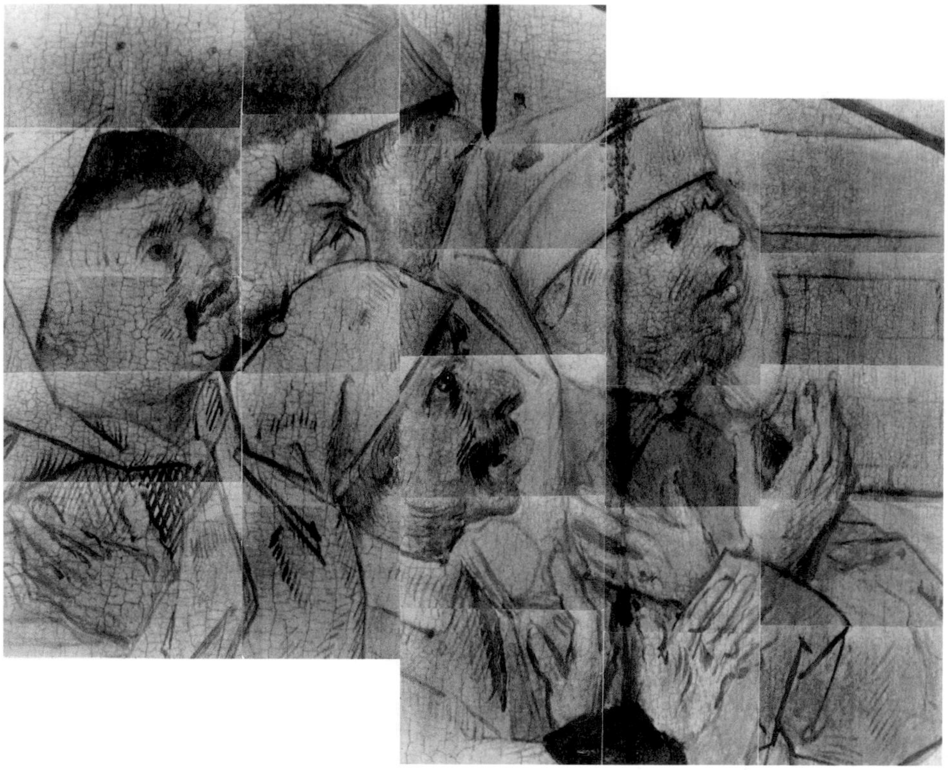

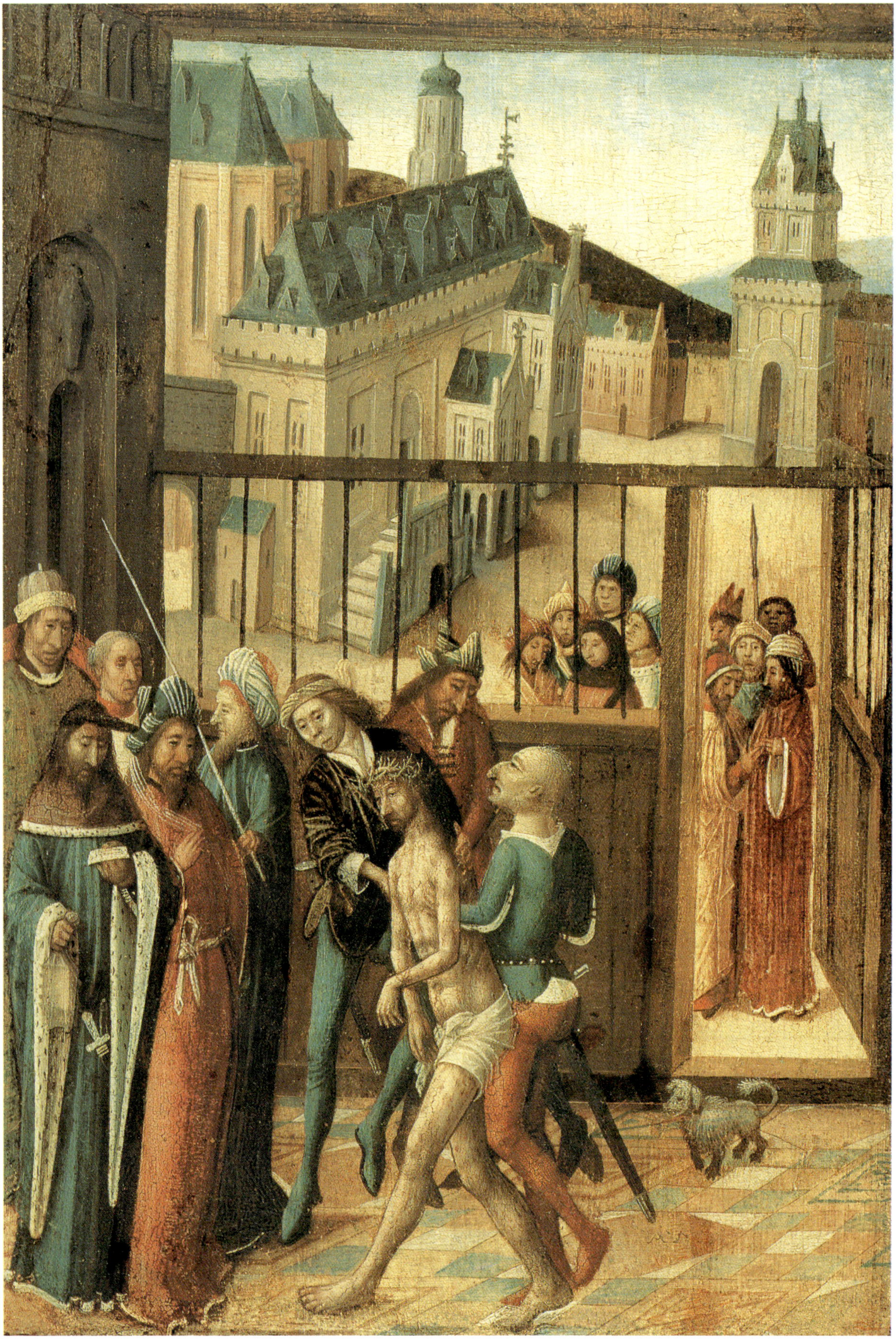

Christ before Pilate

Anonymous
North Netherlandish master
(active in Haarlem, second half of the fifteenth century)

Panel; 38.8 x 26.5 cm

Physical characteristics: the panel consists of a single plank. The *barbe* can be seen on all four sides.

Infrared reflectography: no underdrawing could be discerned.[1]

Dendrochronology: the youngest heartwood growth ring dates from 1449. The youngest sapwood growth ring dates from 1452. The panel could not have been painted before 1460; it was more probably painted in or after 1474. See article by P. Klein.

Provenance: private collection in Rome; Galleria Doria, Rome; Frederik Muller, Amsterdam, 8 April 1930, no. 179, fig.; M.J. Schretlen, Amsterdam; J.W. Frederiks, The Hague; on loan from J.W. Frederiks to the Boymans-van Beuningen Museum, Rotterdam, since 1968; inv. no. S. 32.

Exhibitions: *Jeroen Bosch, Noord-Nederlandsche Primitieven*, Rotterdam, Boymans Museum, 1936, no. 13, fig. 18; *Nederlandsche kunst van de XVde en XVIde eeuw*, The Hague, Mauritshuis, 1945, no. 18; *Nederlandse Primitieven uit Nederlands Particulier Bezit*, Laren, Singer Museum, 1961, no. 64; *Stedenspiegel*, The Hague, Gemeentemuseum, 1964, no. 168; *Opkomst en bloei van het Noordnederlandse stadsgezicht in de 17de eeuw* (*The Dutch Cityscape in the 17th Century and its Sources*), Amsterdam, Amsterdam Historical Museum, Ohio, Art Gallery of Ontario, Amsterdam-Toronto 1977, no. 1, fig.

Literature: G.J. Hoogewerff, "Zes onbekende oud-Nederlandsche schilderijen", *Onze Kunst* 46 (1929), pp. 60-61, fig.; M.J. Schretlen, "Een Haarlemsch stadsgezicht uit de 15de eeuw. "De Meester van Bellaert"", *Oud Holland* 47 (1930), pp. 122-129, fig.; Friedländer, XIV, 1937, p. 98; G.J. Hoogewerff, *De Noord-Nederlandsche Schilderkunst*, II, The Hague 1937, pp. 225-228, fig. 103; G.H. Kurtz, "De Dievenkelder in de Barteljorisstraat", in: *Haerlem Jaarboek 1962*, Haarlem 1963, pp. 43-52, fig. on p. 44; Friedländer, V, 1969, suppl. 120, plate 109, p. 89; H. Sarfatij, "Het klooster der Dominicanen te Haarlem'" in *Haarlems Bodemonderzoek 2*, Haarlem 1976, pp. 13-35, plate 1 (issued by the Municipal Commission for Archaeological Soil Research Haarlem); W. Kuyper, "Heemskercks bijbelse afbeelding van het Haarlemse stadhuis. Het stadhuis van 1564 in een Oud-Testamentische jas", in: *Haerlem Jaarboek 1985*, Haarlem 1986, pp. 65-73, fig. 3; A. Châtelet, *Early Dutch Painting. Painting in the Northern Netherlands in the Fifteenth Century*, Lausanne 1988, p. 143, no. 116, p. 230, fig. 220; J. Giltaij, "Perspectiven, Saenredam en de architectuurschilders van de 17e eeuw", in: exhib. cat. *Perspectiven: Saenredam en de architectuurschilders van de 17e eeuw*, Rotterdam, Boymans-van Beuningen Museum, 1991, p. 9, fig. 1.

This small panel shows Christ being led before Pilate, his hands bound and the crown of thorns on his head. Supported by two soldiers, he walks stiff-legged, his eyes cast down towards the governor who is also his judge. The latter is wearing a crimson gown trimmed with ermine. In his left hand is a piece of paper and in his right a small bag containing a book, possibly the penal code. He is surrounded by the elders and high priests who have brought the prisoner before him. Outside the closed room in which the trial is to take place stand the Jewish accusers. During the trial, which convinced him more and more of Jesus's innocence, Pilate received a message from his wife. The moment at which Pilate reads the note is portrayed here. According to Matthew 27:19, the only evangelist who reports this incident, her warning was "Have thou nothing to do with this just man: for I have suffered many things this day in a dream because of him". In an attempt to save Christ from being condemned, and to calm the angry crowd, Pilate then turned to the people and asked them which prisoner he should set free on the occasion of the Passover feast: Barrabus, the infamous murderer, or Christ. When, to his surprise, the crowd demanded the release of Barrabus, he realised that there was no way back. He washed his hands and declared himself innocent of the blood of the condemned. He then set Barrabus free and handed Christ over to the Jewish people to be crucified.

The tribunal where the scene is set lies beside a city square, whose buildings have been reproduced with topographical accuracy. It was Schretlen who discovered that one of the buildings shown is Haarlem city hall as it must have looked before the great re-building work of the fifteenth century.[2] It is the oldest picture showing the city hall and also a rare early example of a topographically faithful reproduction of an existing city view in the northern Netherlands. To the left of the city hall is the *Pandpoort* gate, which commanded the entrance to the church and the Dominican abbey.[3] According to Kurtz, the big gate on the right-hand side of the painting belongs to the house of the Van Berckenrode family, next to which stood the old prison (*Dievenkelder*) in the Barteljorisstraat.[4]

As shown in the painting, medieval tribunals were fenced off with bars, which allowed the public to follow the proceedings. The tribunal here is covered and forms part of an indistinct building of which one wall is visible to the left. The real tribunal of Haarlem where trials were held in the fifteenth century was inside the city hall. It may be that this example of a miscarriage of justice is intended to denote a link with the tribunal in the background. It has been suggested that the panel was part of the decoration of the Haarlem tribunal.[5] If so, this portrayal of the sentence passed by Pilate would have been held up to the Haarlem judges as a negative example. In this context, the painting in fact has an underlying meaning as a warning to judges not to convict the innocent. There are many paintings showing examples of just and unjust administration of law, which were intended to guide sheriffs and aldermen. In the fifteenth and sixteenth centuries, paintings showing, for example, the judgements of Solomon and Cambyses often hung in tribunals and sheriffs' courtrooms.

The size of this painting makes such a function seem unlikely.[6] Moreover, examples of Pilate's verdict are unknown in this context and it would therefore be a unique case. The theme is, in any case, very rare in the visual arts. The moment immediately after this one is depicted much more often, when Pilate shows Jesus to the people after his flogging, with the words "Behold the man" (John 19:4-5). The scene is usually shown taking place on the steps of a city hall. In these so-called "Ecce Homo" representations, Jesus is shown with a purple robe around his shoulders as well as the crown of thorns on his head. Both the crowning and the enrobement are part of the ridiculing of Jesus as the king of the Jews. It is possible that the painting was part of a Passion series.[7] Unfortunately, nothing is known about the painting's provenance. We can therefore only guess who commissioned the painting, or for what reason.

The identity of the painter is unknown. It is difficult to compare with the work of other masters from the final quarter of the fifteenth century. The figures are painted with rough brushstrokes, leaving brush marks which can still be clearly seen, despite the detail with which they are rendered. Their faces are peasant-like and in some cases almost caricatural. The proportions of the bodies are striking. The Jewish accusers outside the fence in particular are relatively tall and narrow, but the figures of Pilate and his consorts are also noticeably tall. Unlike the figures, the architecture is finely rendered and detailed.

Due to the presence of Haarlem city hall, the author of this work has always been sought in this city or its environs. According to Schretlen, the similarities with the woodcuts in books by the Haarlem printer Jacob Bellaert are so great that the panel was probably made by the same person as the woodcuts.[8] Woodcuts from the hand of this Master of Bellaert, so called after the printer, were published in *Der Sonderen Troest* in 1484 and in *De Historie van Jason* in 1485. Schretlen cites the endless variation in headgear, the ugly people with prominent noses, large eyes and dilated pupils in several of these illustrations. The woodcuts are also characterised by the primitive rendering of anatomy. The figures remain wooden despite the artist's efforts to introduce movement and life into his work.[9]

The panel certainly bears some resemblance to the woodcuts. However, there are also important differences which argue against an attribution to the Master of Bellaert. The woodcuts are characterised by an elegance which is completely absent in the painting. The movement of the figures and the contact between them is also lacking. Although the figures have been placed together in groups, they do not communicate.

In his book on Dutch painting, Châtelet also rejects this attribution. Due to the presence of the city hall, the author does retain the attribution to a Haarlem master. He even identifies the painting as the starting point for the so-called 'rustic tendency' in late-fifteenth century painting in Haarlem.[10] However, the fact that the artist painted the city hall of Haarlem does not make him a Haarlem painter. He may have come from elsewhere and only worked in Haarlem for a short time. It therefore seems better to retain faith for now in Friedländer's certificate which accompanied the painting when it came onto the market in the Netherlands in the 1920s. He described it as a work by a north Netherlandish master and dated it around 1480.[11]
LH

1 Scanned by J.R.J. van Asperen de Boer on 20 December 1993.
2 Schretlen (1930); Kuyper (1986).
3 Kuyper (1986), p.70.
4 Kurtz (1963), p.44; Kuyper (1986), p.71 believes this represents an ideal city gaol.
5 Schretlen (1930), p. 127, suggests that it may have hung in the courtroom of Haarlem city hall.
6 The small size is the main reason for Hoogewerff (1937), p. 227, to reject the idea that the painting hung in the courtroom. He suggests that it may have hung in the sheriff's room or above the *prie-dieu* in his bedroom.
7 See also Châtelet (1988), p. 230.
8 Schretlen (1930), pp. 127-128.
9 Schretlen (1930), pp. 127-128 and M.J.A.M. Schretlen, *Dutch and Flemish woodcuts of the fifteenth century*, London 1925, pp. 22-29.
10 Châtelet calls the movement 'la tendance "rustre"'. A. Châtelet, *Les primitifs hollandais: la peinture dans les Pays-Bas du Nord au XVe siècle*, Fribourg 1980, p. 141. The English translation is 'the "rustic" tendency'. Châtelet (1988), p. 143.
11 Schretlen (1930), p. 122.

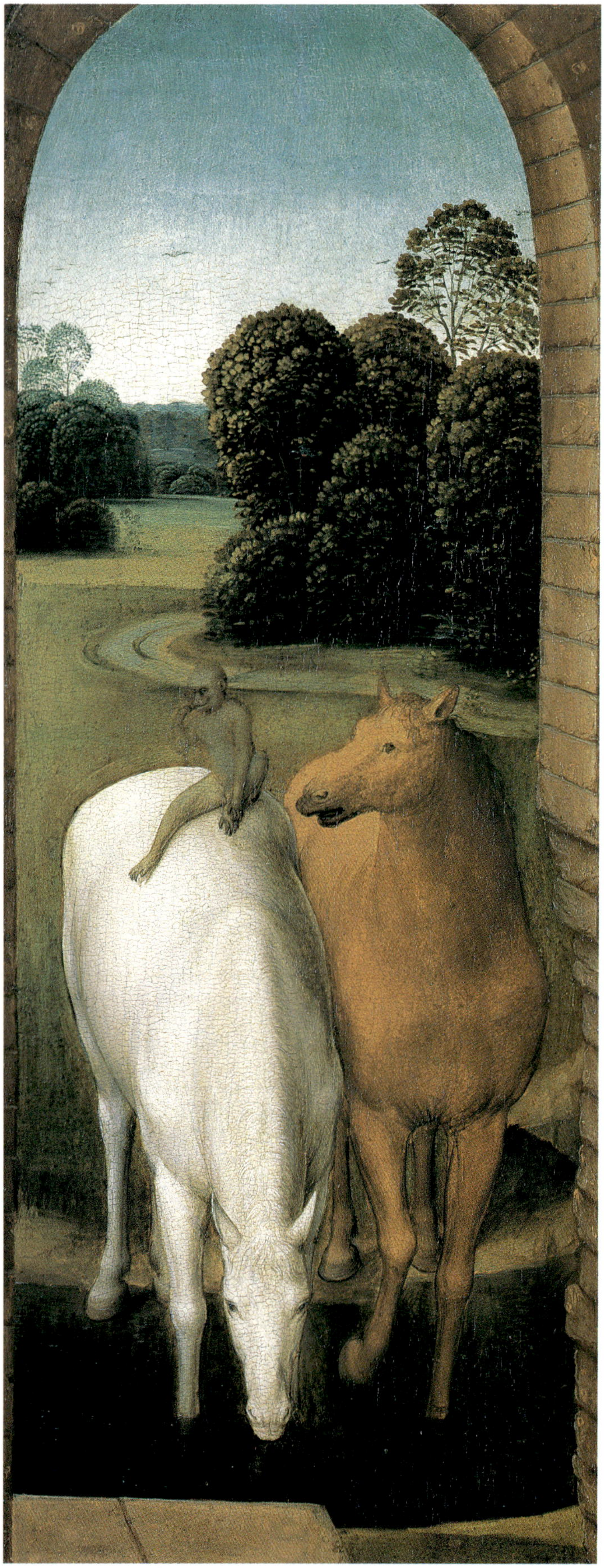

Two horses in a landscape

Hans Memling
(Seligenstadt, active c. 1465-
Bruges 1494)

Panel; 43.4 x 18 cm

Physical characteristics: the panel consists of a single plank. The *barbe* can be seen on the two sides, but not on the upper and lower edges.

Infrared reflectography: no underdrawing could be discerned.

Dendrochronology: the youngest heartwood growth ring dates from 1446. The panel could not have been painted before 1476; it was more probably painted in or after 1490. See description and article by P. Klein.

Provenance: F. Kleinberger, acquired in Spain, 1907; Charles-Léon Cardon, Brussels; K.W. Bachstitz Gallery, The Hague; purchased in 1928 by D.G. van Beuningen, Rotterdam and Vierhouten, for 139,150 guilders; acquired by the Museum with the Van Beuningen Collection, 1958; inv. no. 2470.

Exhibitions: *Exposition de la Toison d'Or à Bruges*, Brussels, 1907, no. 194; *Les chefs-d'œuvre d'art ancien à l'exposition de la Toison d'Or à Bruges en 1907*, Brussels, 1908, no. IX (194), pl. 46 IX; *Meesterwerken uit vier eeuwen 1400-1800*, Rotterdam, Boymans Museum, 1938, no. 14, fig. 35; *Memling tentoonstelling*, Bruges, Stedelijk Museum, 1939, no. 45, fig. 40; *Nederlandsche kunst van de XVde en XVIde eeuw*, The Hague, Mauritshuis, 1945, no. 70; *Les Primitifs Flamands*, Paris, Musée de l'Orangerie, 1947, no. 73; *Honderd jaar Museum Boymans Rotterdam. Meesterwerken uit de verzameling D.G. van Beuningen*, Rotterdam, Boymans Museum, 1949, no. 24; *Chefs-d'œuvre de la collection D.G. van Beuningen*, Paris, Petit Palais, 1952, no. 61, fig. 15.

Literature: K. Voll, *Memling, des Meisters Gemälde*, Stuttgart-Leipzig 1909, fig. p. 40, pp. 172, 177; M.J. Friedländer, *Von Eyck bis Bruegel*, Berlin 1921, p. 188; K. Voll, *Die Altniederländische Malerei von Jan van Eyck bis Memling*, Leizpig 1923, p. 194; F. Winkler, "An unknown portrait of a woman by Memling", *Apollo* 7 (1928), p. 9, fig. II; Friedländer, VI, 1928, no. 16A, fig. XIX; Friedländer, XIV, 1937, p. 103; H. Vollmer, *Thieme-Becker*, XXIV, Leipzig 1930, p. 376; A.M. Frankfurter, "European Postscript 1939", *The Art News* 38 (1939), p. 8, fig.; A. Glavimans, "Notities bij de primitieven in het Mauritshuis", *Phoenix* I (1946), p. 51, fig.; H.B. Wehle, M. Salinger, *The Metropolitan Museum of Art, A Catalogue of Early Flemish, Dutch and German Painters*, New York 1947, pp. 64, 65; M.J. Friedländer, *H. Memling*, Amsterdam 1949, fig. p. 58; Hannema, 1949, no. 24, fig. 25; E. Panofsky, *Early Netherlandish Painting, its origins and character*, Cambridge Mass. 1953, p. 506, note 7; M.J. Friedländer, *From Van Eyck to Breugel*, London 1956, p. 188; L. Rosten, *The story behind the painting*, New York 1962, p. 76, fig.; cat. 1962, pp. 88, 89; A. Dohmann, *Die Altniederländische Malerei des fünfzehnten Jahrhunderts von Van Eyck bis Bosch*, Leipzig 1964, p. 82, fig. 208; M.J. Friedländer, *Von Van Eyck bis Bruegel*, Cologne 1965, fig. 123; G.H. Dumont, *Hans Memling*, Utrecht 1966, fig. 46; M. Corti, G.T. Faggin, *L'Opera completa di Memling*, Milan 1969, no. 86B, fig. LXVIII; Friedländer, VI, 1971, p. 48, no. 16A, fig. 55; K.B. MacFarlane, *Hans Memling*, Oxford 1971, p. 41, note 51, fig. 138; J. Foucart, G.T. Faggin, *Tout l'œuvre peint de Memling*, Paris 1973, no. 86B, fig. pl. LXIII; P. Trceziak, *Hans Memling*, Berlin 1977, no. 23, fig.

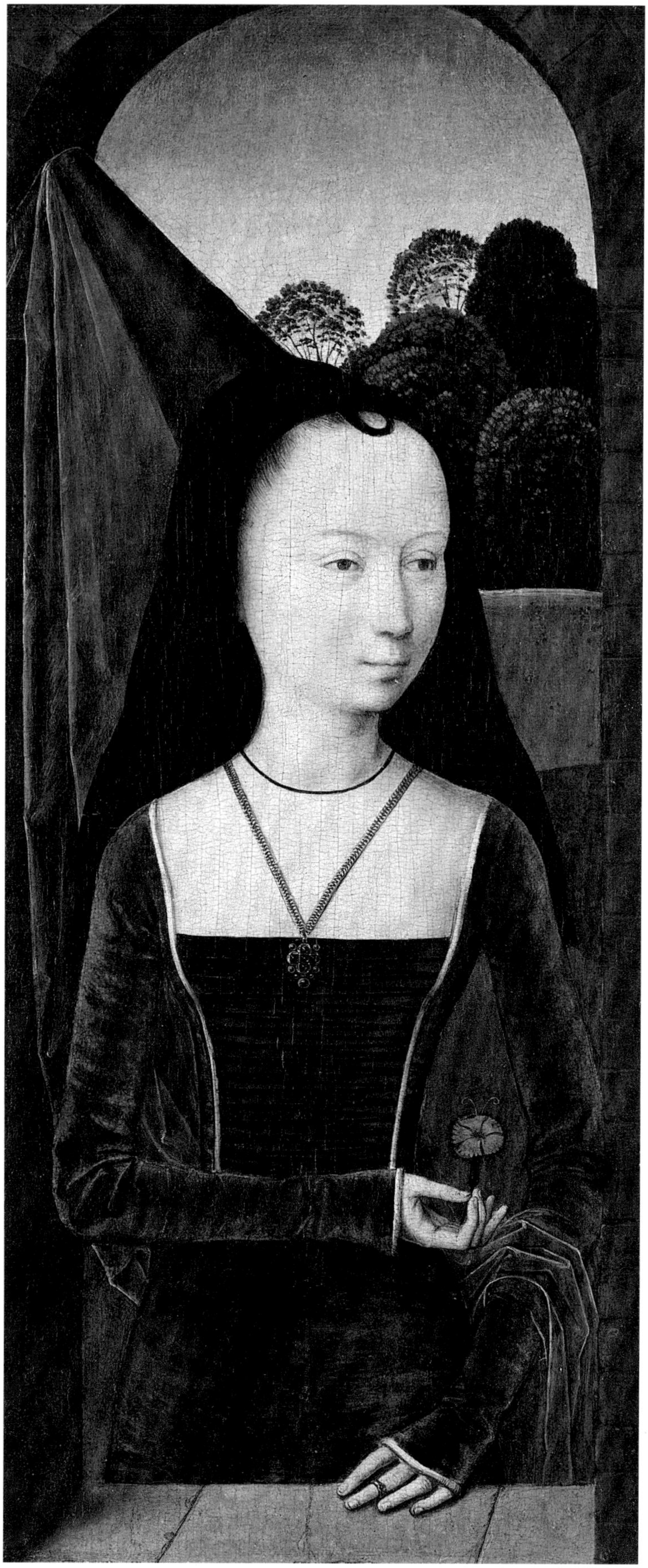

a. Hans Memling, Woman with a carnation
Panel: 43.2 x 18.4 cm
New York, Metropolitan Museum of Art

This unusual painting shows two horses behind an archway in a landscape. The white horse on the left drinks from the water in the foreground and carries a monkey on its back. The brown horse beside it looks at the monkey. The wall on the right is painted to fit the contours of the brown horse.

Since it was thought that the painting would be unusual as a work on its own, Winkler (?) suggested in 1928, the year in which it was purchased by D.G. van Beuningen, that it was the front of a panel painted on both sides, and that the *Woman with a carnation* in the Metropolitan Museum, New York, was originally the reverse (fig. a).

In Panofsky's view, the two works formed a diptych in which the white horse ridden by the monkey symbolised the self-seeking, base elements in man's nature. The monkey takes no notice of the young woman in the other painting. The brown horse is looking not at the monkey, but in devotion at the young woman in the other panel, which must have been on the left of this panel. The white horse therefore represents the deficient, uninterested lover, and the brown horse the good lover.[1]

MacFarlane dismisses the diptych theory, and believes the panels formed part of a lost polyptych.[2] He notes a close resemblance between these horses and those in Memling's *Seven joys of the Virgin* in the Alte Pinakothek, Munich and suggests the same period, around 1480. The dendrochronological research conducted by P. Klein in August 1988 shows that the earliest date for the felling of the tree from which the panel was made may be taken as 1474, but more probably as around 1480. It could then have been painted some time after 1490. After investigating the New York panel, Klein concluded that the panels could not have comprised a front and back as they contain sapwood on their left sides. At most, they could have hung one above the other, which of course in practical terms is inconceivable. The fact that they originate from the same tree warrants the supposition of a relationship between the two, and the possibility of a diptych, with the woman on the left and the horses on the right, is not ruled out by the dendrochronological investigation. The New York panel does not appear to be a portrait. It may well be the case that the two panels were indeed a diptych with an amorous significance.

That the Rotterdam painting is by Memling was never doubted in the past. But comparison with his other works is difficult because no similar paintings by him are known. The detailed rendering of the horses and the manner in which the trees are executed would not be unusual for Memling. On the other hand, the trees in the New York panel are much more schematic, and some details of the figure are not characteristic of Memling. The arms, for instance, are long and thin, and the face does not have his typical heavy-lidded eyes. If the attribution of this painting is in doubt, there will probably be some corresponding uncertainty about the Rotterdam panel. It is a question that will be very difficult to resolve.
JG

1 Panofsky (1953).
2 MacFarlane (1971).

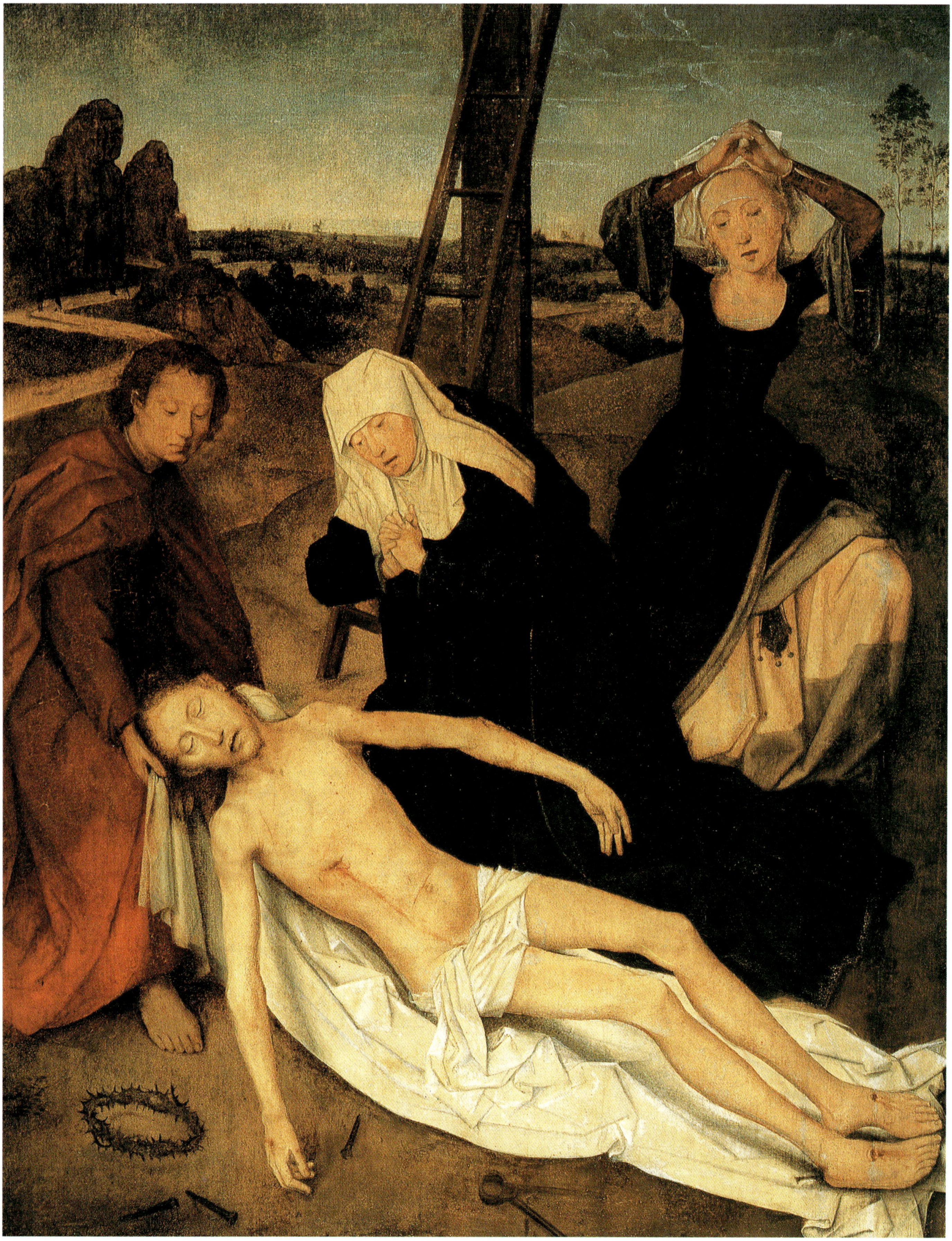

The Lamentation

Hans Memling
(Seligenstadt, active c. 1465-
Bruges 1494)

Panel; 57 x 48 cm

Physical characteristics: the panel was seriously damaged by fire and has been heavily retouched.

Infrared reflectography:[1] there is a comprehensive underdrawing in brush and black chalk.

Provenance: Rev. J. Heath, Vicar of Enfield, Liphook, 1857; Richard von Kaufmann, Berlin; sale at Christie's, 1937;[2] D.G. van Beuningen, Rotterdam and Vierhouten; acquired in 1958 with the D.G. van Beuningen Collection; inv. no. 2471.

Exhibitions: *National exhibition of works of art at Leeds*, 1868, no. 515; *Ausstellung von Kunst Werken des Mittelalters und der Renaissance aus Berliner Privatbesitz Veranstaltet von der Kunstgeschichtlichen Gesellschaft*, Berlin, 1898, pp. 8-9; *Exposition des primitifs flamands et d'art ancien*, Bruges, 1902, no. 92; *Memling tentoonstelling*, Bruges, Stedelijk Museum, 1939, no. 4; *Honderd jaar Museum Boymans. Meesterwerken uit de verzameling D.G. van Beuningen*, Rotterdam, Boymans Museum, 1949, no. 25; *Chefs-d'œuvre de la collection D.G. van Beuningen*, Paris, Petit Palais, 1952, no. 62.

Literature: Dr. Waagen, *Galleries and Cabinets of Art in Great Britain*, 4, London, 1857, pp. 313-314; L. Kaemmerer, *Memling*, Bielefeld-Leipzig 1899, pp. 102-105, fig. 61; *Gemälde des XIV-XVI. Jahrhunderts aus der Sammlung von Richard von Kaufmann*, Berlin 1901, no. 7, fig. VI; M.J. Friedländer, "Die Brügger Leihausstellung von 1902", *Repertorium für Kunstwissenschaft* 26 (1903), p. 84 (c. 1470); K. Voll, *Memling, des Meisters Gemälde*, Stuttgart-Leipzig 1909, pp. 54-55, fig. p. 173; K. Voll, *Die Altniederländische Malerei von Jan van Eyck bis Memling*, Leipzig 1923, p. 197; Friedländer, VI, 1928, p. 34, p. 115, no. 6; Hannema, 1949, no. 25; cat. 1962, p. 89; M.J. Friedländer, *Von Van Eyck bis Bruegel*, Cologne 1965, p. 51; exh. cat. *Dipinti fiamminghi di collezioni Romane*, Rome, Palazzo Barberini, 1966, p. 31; M. Corti, G.T. Faggin, *L'opera completa di Memling*, Milan 1969, no. 22B, fig.; Friedländer, VI, 1971, no. 6, fig. 23; J. Foucart, G.T. Faggin, *Tout l'œuvre peint de Memling*, Paris 1973, no. 22B, fig.; P. Trceziak, *Hans Memling*, Berlin 1977, with no. 24; Didier Martens, "Le triptyque de Bientina: motifs et sources", *Gazette des Beaux-Arts* 120 (1992), p. 160, fig. 13.

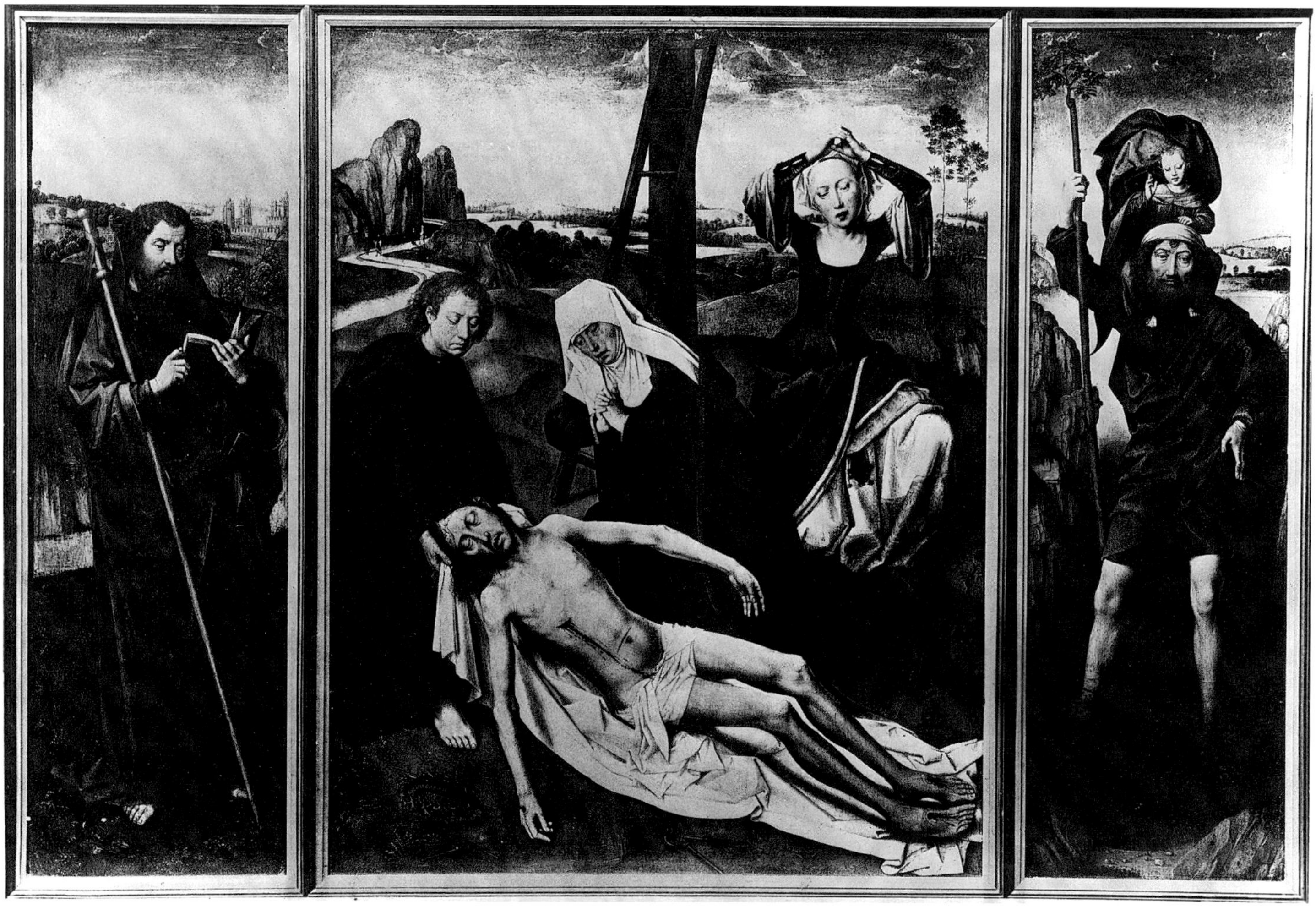

a. Hans Memling, Triptych with The Lamentation (centre panel) and James the Greater and St Christopher (side panels). Photograph of the triptych before the fire.

This painting of the *Lamentation* was originally the centre panel of a triptych (fig. a). The left wing depicts James the Greater and the right wing St Christopher. Around 1900 the triptych formed part of the collection of Richard von Kaufmann in Berlin. Despite being seriously damaged by fire, it was nevertheless bought by Van Beuningen. According to the 1939 Memling exhibition catalogue it was sold at Christie's in 1937, and this is probably where he purchased it. There are, however, no records of the sale and, since the painting cannot be found in Van Beuningen's purchase journal either, nothing of this whole episode can be stated with any certainty. Both wings were still in the Van Beuningen Collection in 1949. He sold them sometime before 1957, by which time they had found their way into a private collection in Bruges.[3] In 1988 the wings formed part of a private collection in Brussels,[4] and were sold by auction in New York in 1994.[5]

It is difficult to provide an adequate criticism of the centre panel and the two wings as a result of the fire in 1904 or 1917.[6] The paint was so severely damaged that the surface was reduced to the scorched and shrunken state it is now in. Nevertheless, only Voll has expressed any doubts about the painting's attribution to Memling. In 1903 Friedländer dated the Rotterdam work at around 1470, but in 1928 revised his estimate to 1475. Two other pictures by Hans Memling are also closely related, in particular the triptych of the *Lamentation* in the St Jans Hospital in Bruges,[7] made in 1480 and donated by Adriaen Reins. Another comparable work is the *Lamentation* in the Palazzo Doria Pamphilj in Rome.[8]

To judge from old photographs taken before the fire, the painting in Rotterdam must have formed an excellent example of Memling's triptychs.
JG

1 The panel was examined by J.R.J. van Asperen de Boer in 1971. The underdrawing stylistically is not clearly associated with Memling.
2 Exhib. cat. Bruges, 1939.
3 Note by J.C. Ebbinge Wubben on the back of a photograph: "These wings are now (1957) owned by the sisters De Wijnter, St Maartensplein 2, Bruges. The panels have been comprehensively restored, after suffering serious damage in the fire which struck the v. Kaufmann collection."
4 Information kindly supplied by Mrs Nicole Veronee-Verhaegen, 27 May 1988: the author of the text saw the panels in Brussels where the then owner (since deceased) was Monsieur Jean de Maleingreau d'Hembise.
5 Sale at Christie's, New York, 12 January 1994, no. 61, fig.
6 In 1904 according to Corti and Faggin, 1969, and in 1917 according to M.J. Friedländer, 1971, caption to fig. 6.
7 Friedländer, VI a, 1971, no. 5, fig.
8 Friedländer, VI a, 1971, no. 36, fig.

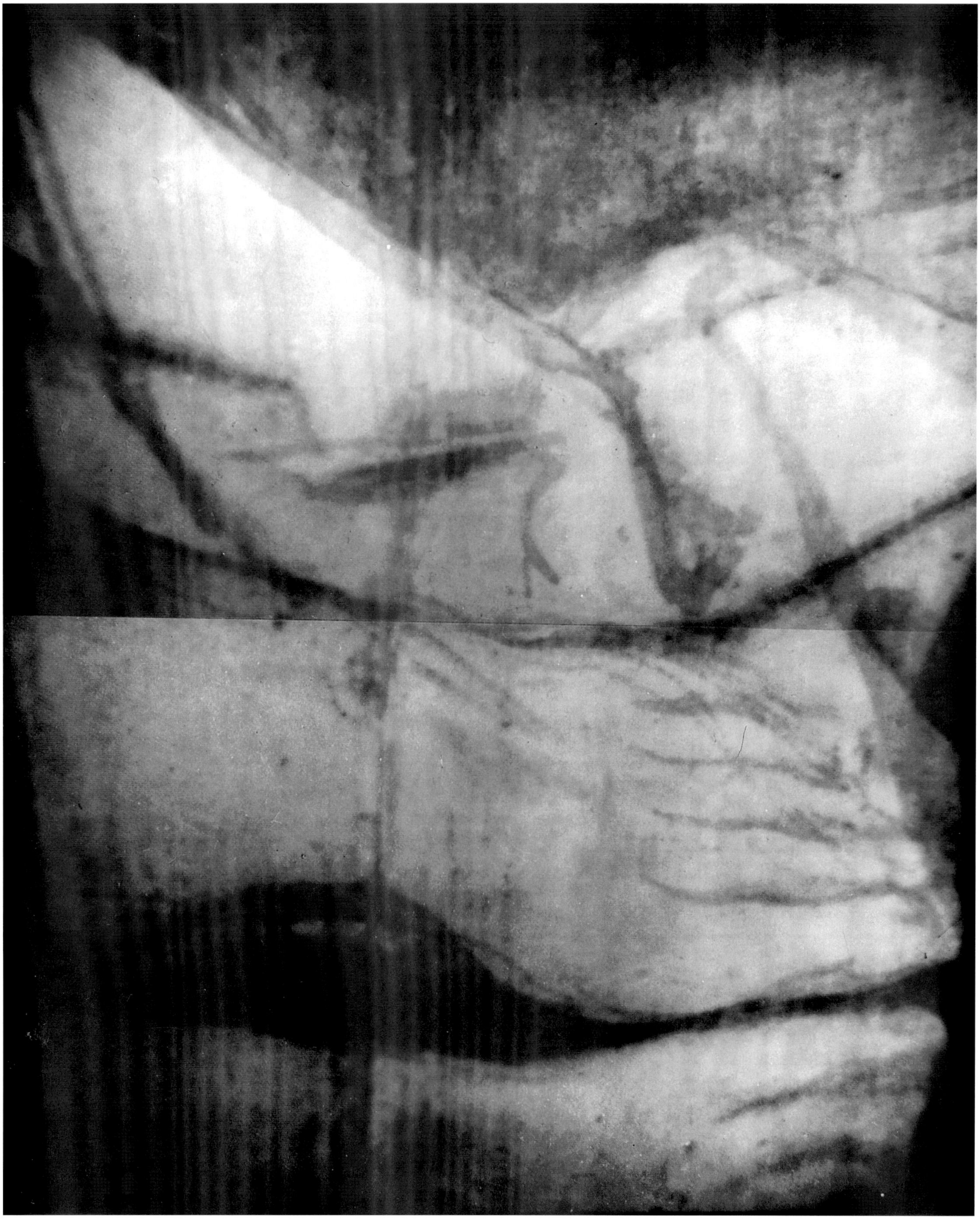

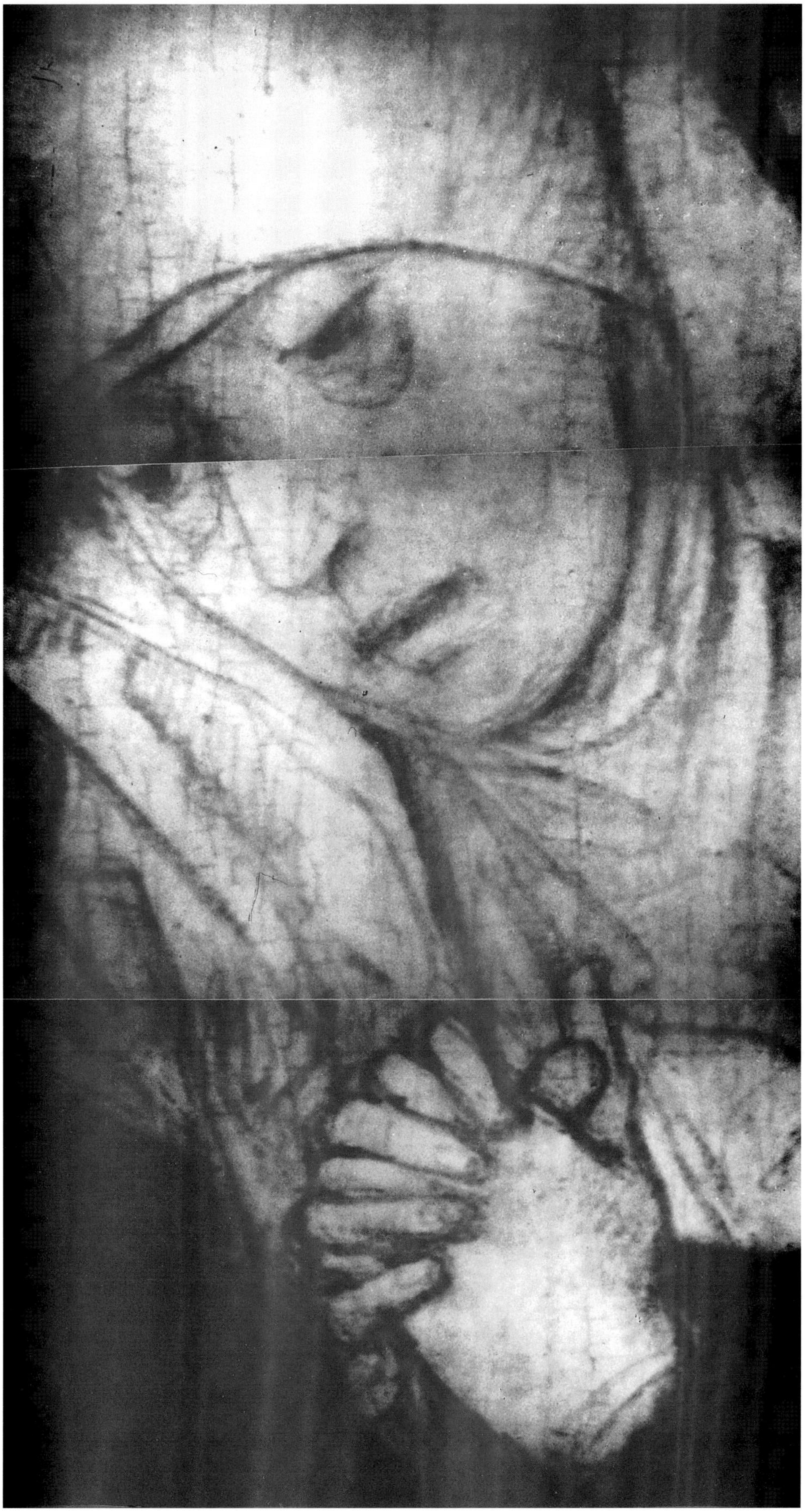

b. Infrared reflectogram assembly. Detail of Christ's feet.

c. Infrared reflectogram assembly. Detail of the Virgin's head.

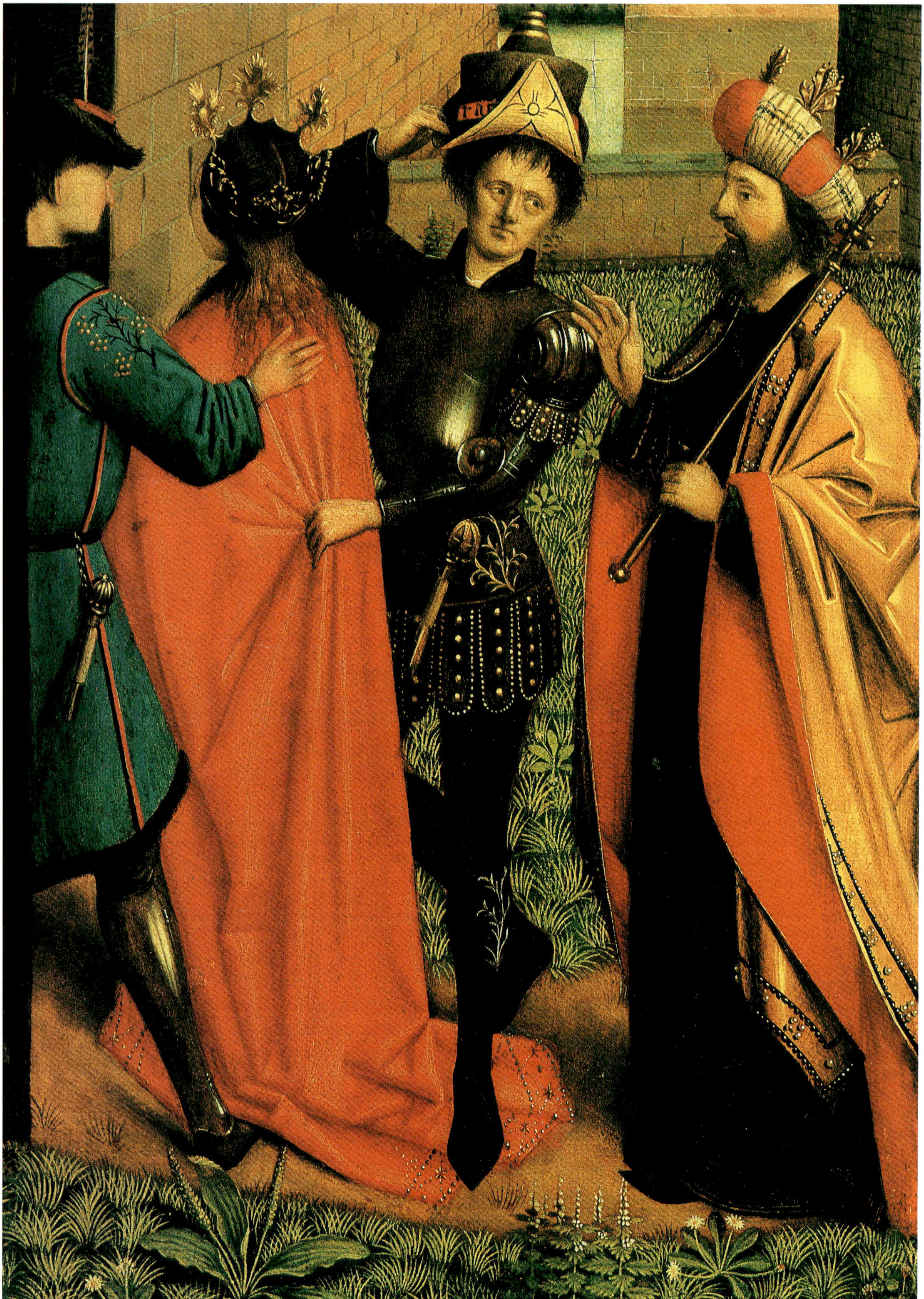

St Catherine being led away

Anonymous
South Netherlandish master, Bruges?
c. 1460-1470

Panel; 26.5 x 37.3 cm

Physical characteristics:[1] the panel consists of a single plank. The paint extends to the edges. The back is now cradled but was marbled in red and black; this is evident from a fragment which was not planed off.

Infrared reflectography: elaborate underdrawing in fine brush strokes. See description.

Dendrochronology: the youngest heartwood growth ring dates from 1415. The panel could not have been painted before 1426; it was more probably painted in or after 1440. See article by P. Klein.

Paint samples: the underdrawing was executed on a white ground and covered by a slightly greyish intermediate layer. The paint was applied in one to four layers on the intermediate layer.

Provenance: N. Beets Gallery, Amsterdam; Agnew Gallery, London; Von Auspitz Collection, Vienna; bought through K.W. Bachstitz, The Hague, in 1934 by D.G. van Beuningen, Rotterdam and Vierhouten, for 3,500 guilders; acquired by the Museum in 1958 with the Van Beuningen Collection; inv. no. 2468.

Exhibitions: *Schilderijen, teekeningen en beeldhouwwerken uit particuliere Nederlandsche verzamelingen*, Rotterdam, Boymans Museum, 1938-39, no. 7, fig. IX; *Oude kunst tentoonstelling*, Maastricht, Stedelijk Museum, 1939, no. 5, fig.; *Nederlandsche kunst van de XVde en XVIde eeuw*, The Hague, Mauritshuis, 1945, no. 8; *Les Primitifs Flamand*, Paris, Musée de L'Orangerie, 1947, p. 30, no. 56; *Honderd jaar Museum Boymans Rotterdam. Meesterwerken uit de verzameling D.G. van Beuningen*, Rotterdam, Boymans Museum, 1949, no. 34, fig. 22; *Chefs-d'œuvre de la collection D.G. van Beuningen*, Paris, Petit Palais, 1952, no. 47.

Literature: W.R. Valentiner, *Catalogue of a collection of paintings and some art objects - Flemish and Dutch paintings*, II, John G. Johnson, Philadelphia 1913, p. 6, fig. 197; *Catalogue of the John G. Johnson Collection*, Philadelphia 1941, p. 22; Hannema, 1949, no. 34, fig. 22; J. Q. van Regteren Altena, "D. Hannema, Catalogue of the D.G. van Beuningen Collection. Foreword by Dr. Max J. Friedländer. Ad. Donker, Rotterdam, 1949. 2 vols. fol." (book review), *Oud Holland* 68 (1953), pp. 226-227, 229, fig. 6; cat. 1962, p. 159; H. Wagner, *Gemälde des 15. und 16. Jahrhunderts, Kunstmuseum Bern*, Berne 1977, p. 57.

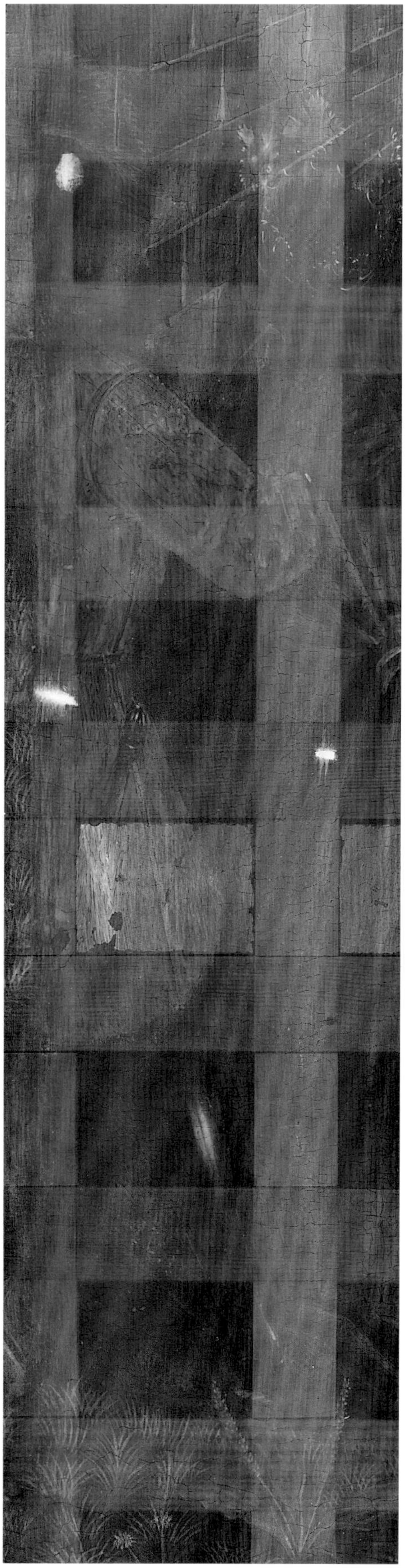

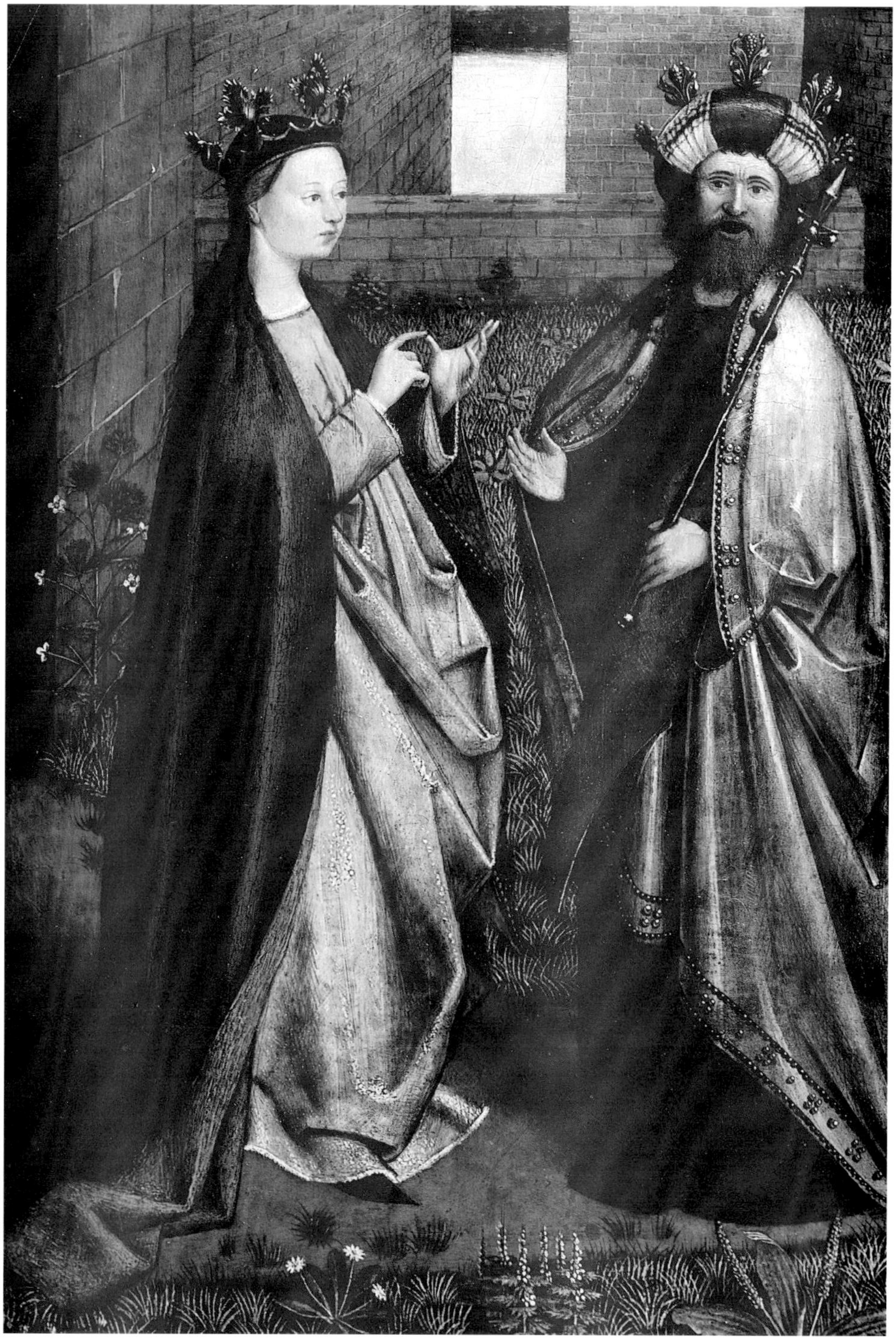

Very probably this is an episode in the life of St Catherine, daughter of King Costus. According to the legend,[2] Emperor Maxentius or Maximinus[3] ordered his subjects to sacrifice to the gods in the temple at Alexandria. For fear of punishment, most Christians obeyed, but Catherine went directly to the temple to condemn the idolatry of the emperor. Charmed by her beauty, the emperor called her to his palace, where she tried to convince him that there was only one God. Unable to refute her arguments, he brought in fifty philosophers to dispute with her. Not one of them, however, succeeded in countering her arguments, and they allowed themselves to be converted. Enraged by this defeat, the emperor ordered them to be burnt, and renewed his efforts to make Catherine deny her faith. Failing again, the emperor had her whipped and thrown into a dungeon in the hope that she would change her mind. When, some time later, she proved to be still firm in her faith, he had a torture instrument made of four spiked wheels. Seeing this, Catherine prayed to God, who sent an angel to destroy it. The emperor then ordered her to be beheaded.

In the painting two guards lead Catherine out of a walled garden on the orders of the emperor. The precise moment of the story which is depicted here is uncertain. In the legend, she is led away several times to be tortured. Maxentius (or Maximinus) wears a turban with metal ornaments which characterises him as an eastern ruler.[4] The guards wear typically fifteenth-century dress. The one on the left is clad in a blue doublet, greaves and a tall, plumed fur hat. The other wears a cuirass and black hose, and a hat with a triangular flap at the front and back. An interesting detail is the unmatching sleeves of the cuirass. Another interesting detail is that his left foot is on the train of St Catherine's mantle.

The saint is portrayed without her attributes of the wheel and the sword, while moreover she is seen from the back. It may thus be assumed that the panel was part of a larger work showing different scenes from her life. It may have been a triptych, but may equally well have been a retable with a carved central panel and painted wings. Another indication is the brown paint along the left edge, under which X-radiographs show tufts of grass and part of a wall corresponding to the rest of the painting (fig. a). This is corroborated by paint cross-sections. Furthermore, only half of the guard on the left is visible, his figure ending where the brown edge begins. The grass tufts and wall fragment must have been part of something, presumably a scene preceding that which we see here, such as an earlier episode in the saint's life. An example of such illustrations of a saint's life is provided by two wings with eight "cartoon"-style scenes from the life of St Ursula.[5] The central panel has been lost.[6]

The hypothesis of an originally larger work is further reinforced by a panel in Philadelphia (fig. b).[7] It shows St Catherine in dispute with the emperor. Roughly the same size as the Rotterdam panel, it has the same walled garden with the same plants and tufts of grass. Maxentius (or Maximinus), now seen *en face*, wears the same yellow jewelled mantle, blue robe, and red and white turban. The counting gesture St Catherine makes with her hands was a convention used to indicate a dispute.[8] The similarities between the two panels are so evident as to make it virtually certain that they originally belonged together.

a. X-radiograph of the left section

b. South Netherlandish Master, St Catherine disputing with the emperor Maxentius
Panel; 24 x 37.5 cm
Philadelphia, Philadelphia Museum of Arts, John G. Johnson Collection

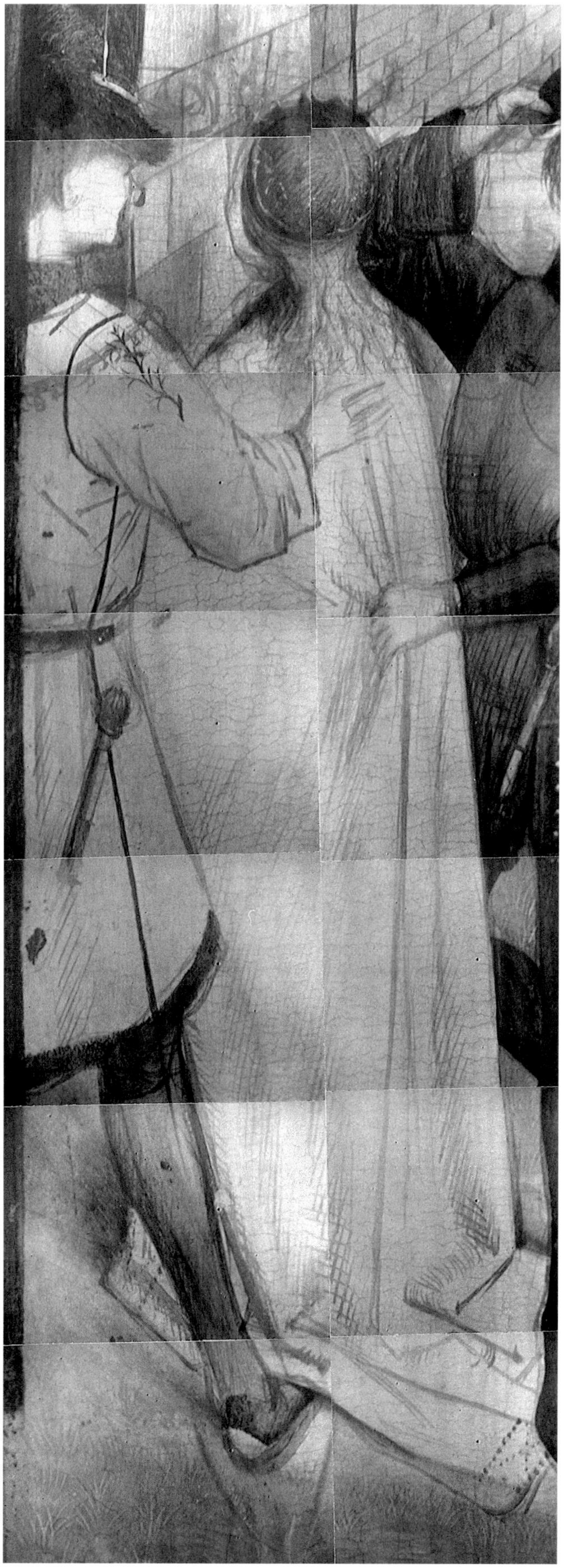

c. Infrared reflectogram assembly of the left section

The Rotterdam panel has an elaborate underdrawing. In parts, for instance in the garment and hat of the guard on the left, the artist deviated from the underdrawing in applying the paint (fig. c).

Opinions differ on the provenance of the work. Van Beuningen bought it in 1934 as the work of a Bruges master, dating from around 1460. In 1949 Hannema attributed it to a painter in the circle of Jan van Eyck. In 1953 Van Regteren Altena postulated that it was from the hand of a German master. In view of its affinity with South Netherlandish art, it is more likely to have originated in that region. Indeed, the figure holding his hat with his right hand is a direct borrowing from the figure of St George in Jan van Eyck's celebrated *Madonna of Canon van der Paele* dated 1436.[9] The panels in Rotterdam and Philadelphia probably date from 1460-1470.
SL

1 Scientific examination conducted by Suzanne Laemers under the supervision of J.R.J. van Asperen de Boer in 1994. The report is in the Museum's file on the painting. Paint samples A 358/1-7. Infrared reflectograms: AB 1122/23-36; AB 1223/21-28; AB 1484/1-17.

2 Jacobus de Voragine, *Legenda Aurea - Das Leben der Heiligen*, E. Weidinger, Aschaffenburg 1986, pp. 502-507.

3 Jacobus de Voragine states at the end of his account of the saint's life that there is some doubt about the identity of the emperor, Maxentius or Maximinus. "At that time," he writes, "there were three emperors: Constantine, who succeeded his father; Maxentius, son of Maximianus, proclaimed emperor at Rome by the Praetorian Guard; and Maximinus, emperor in the East. Maxentius and Maximinus are sometimes mistaken for each other." *op. cit.* (note 2), p. 507.

4 In a miniature based on *Gillion de Trazegnies* (a 1464 copy of an anonymous French text thought to be by David Aubert and illuminated by Lieven van Lathem for Louis of Gruuthuse, now in Chatsworth, Duke of Devonshire Collection and the Chatsworth Settlement Trustees, ms. 7535, fol. 158V) depicting a debate at the sultan's court, the sultan is wearing a similar turban (fig.: M.P.J. Martens, *Lodewijk van Gruuthuse*, Bruges 1992, p. 170). In another miniature in the same manuscript, depicting Gillion and Hertan fighting the Saracens at Babylon, the Saracens wear turbans and the knights from the west are clad in armour (fig: *ibid.*, p. 168).

5 Bruges, Groeninge Museum, c. 1480.

6 The fact that saints' legends were depicted not only on altarpieces but also on single panels is evidenced by a panel with scenes from the life of St Lucy (Bruges, St Jacobskerk). Hans Memling's St Ursula shrine (Bruges, Memling Museum) which illustrates her life in three scenes on each of the longitudinal sides, is another such example.

7 Philadelphia Museum of Arts, John G. Johnson Collection.

8 See cat. no. 43.

9 Groeninge Museum, Bruges, inv. no. 0.161.

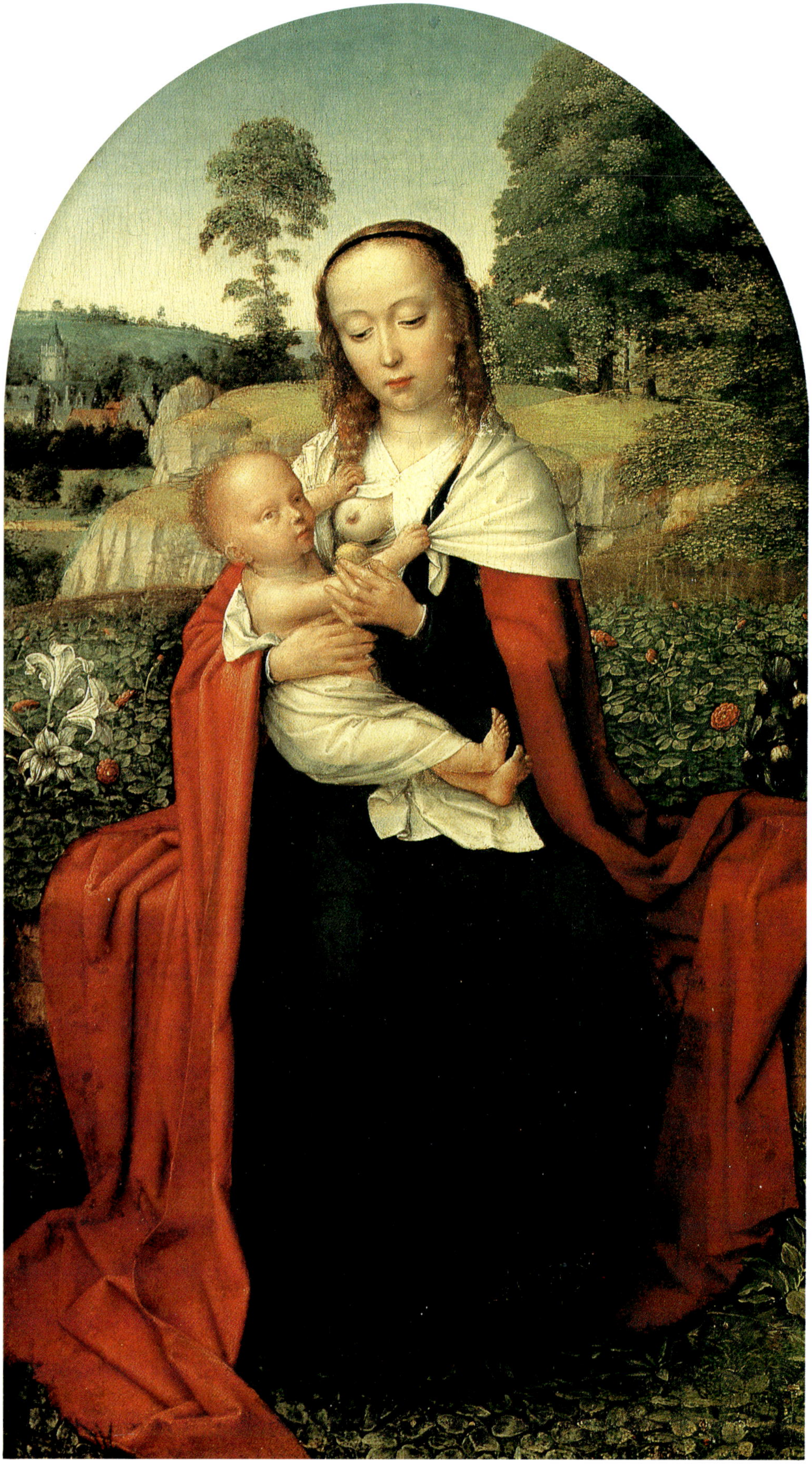

The Virgin and Child in a landscape

Gerard David
(Oudewater c. 1460-Bruges 1523)

Panel; 42.6 x 24.7 cm

Physical characteristics:[1] the panel consists of a single plank, arched at the top.
The *barbe* can be seen along the full length of the lower edge, but patches are missing from the left and right sides. The panel was sawn along the *barbe* on the sides, after which narrow strips of wood were glued to the edges. The back of the panel is painted black.

Infrared reflectography: the underdrawing is only visible in parts (fig. a); the red cloak, the child's eyes and feet and the Virgin's hands can be seen quite clearly. The underdrawing was executed with a fine brush. Some corrections can be seen in the drawing of Mary's hands.

Dendrochronological examination: the youngest heartwood growth ring dates from 1475. The panel could not have been painted before 1486; it was more probably painted after 1500. See article by P. Klein.

Paint samples: chalk was used for the ground. There is no trace of an intermediate layer containing lead white. The paint structure is complex, consisting of six or seven layers in parts. A sample taken from the red cloak contains three thin layers of two different values of red. The artist was evidently dissatisfied with the first colour, and applied another three layers to obtain a slightly different colour.[2] The following pigments were found: lead white, azurite, copper resinate green and malachite.

Provenance: believed to have been presented to the Carmelite monastery in Salamanca in 1630 by Maria van Mol of Antwerp;[3] Marczell von Nemes Collection, Budapest; sale Paris, 17 June 1913, no. 16, fig.; Ducrey Collection, Paris; Comte de Chavagnac Collection, Paris; Kleinberger Gallery, New York;[4] G. Wildenstein Gallery, New York; purchased in 1953 by D.G. van Beuningen, Rotterdam and Vierhouten, for 375,000 guilders; acquired by the Museum in 1958 with the Van Beuningen Collection; inv. no. 2446.

Exhibitions: *Sammlung Marczell von Nemes-Budapest*, Dusseldorf, Städtische Kunsthalle, 1912, no. 23, fig.; *Kunstschatten uit Nederlandse verzamelingen*, Rotterdam, Boymans Museum, 1955, no. 8, fig. 8.

Literature: Friedländer, VI, 1928, p. 154, no. 213; cat. 1962, p. 44; F. Grossmann, "Notes on some Dutch and Flemish paintings at Rotterdam", *The Burlington Magazine* 97 (1955), p. 336, fig. 4; Friedländer, VIb, 1971, pp. 107-108, no. 213, fig. 216; D.G. Scillia, *Gerard David and manuscript illumination in the Lowlands* (diss.), Cape Western Reserve University 1975, p. 297; R.L. Falkenburg, *Landscape as an image of the pilgrimage of life*, Amsterdam-Philadelphia 1988, p. 26, fig. 19; exhib. cat. *The age of Bruegel*, Washington, National Gallery of Art, 1986, with no. 45, note 1; Hans J. van Miegroet, *Gerard David*, Antwerp 1989, pp. 254, 307, no. 39, fig. on p. 253.

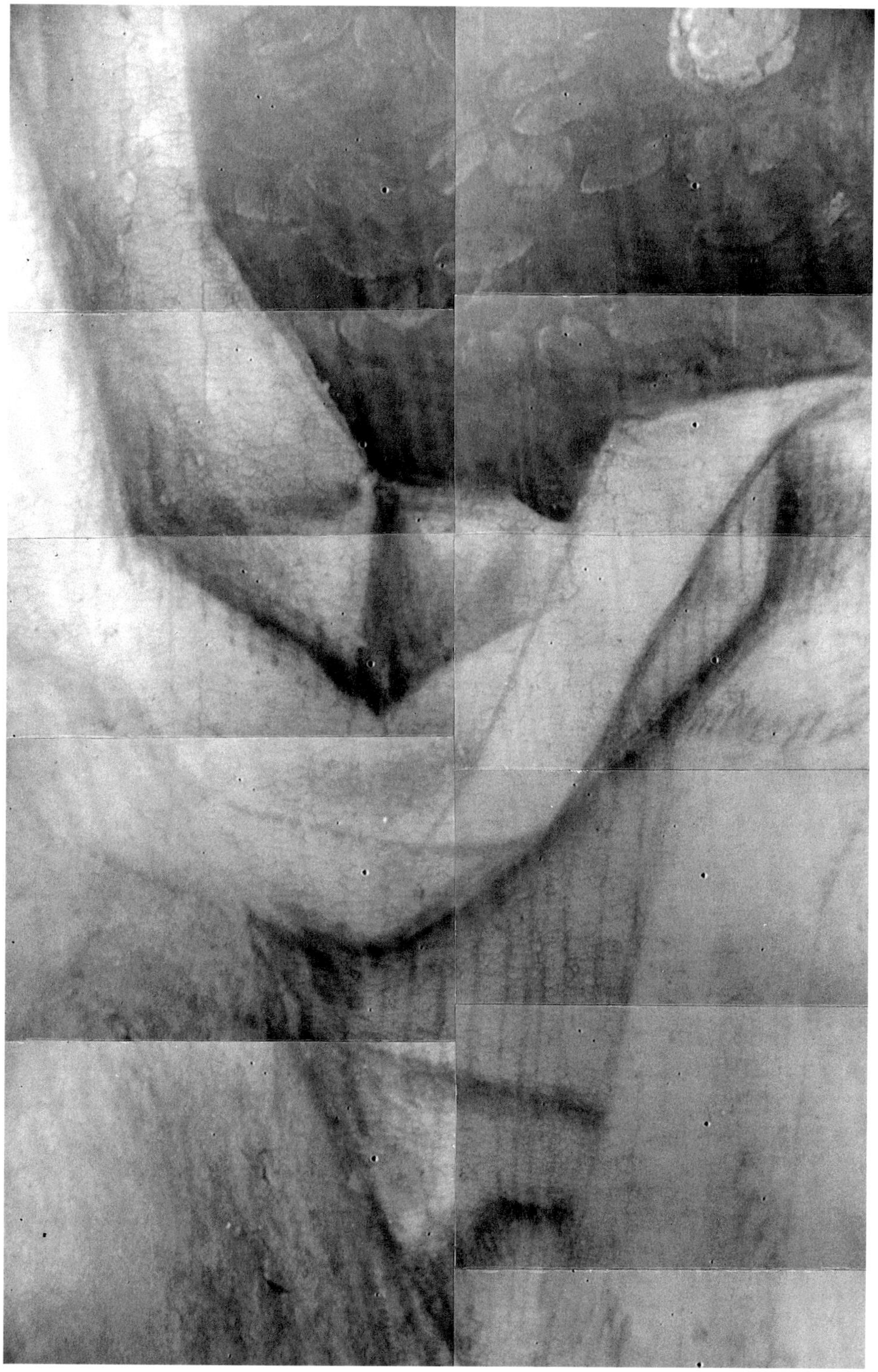

a. Infrared reflectogram assembly showing a detail of the Virgin's cloak.

The Virgin is seated on a low wall covered with flowers and plants, holding the child on her lap. The scene is set in a hilly landscape with a church and a cluster of houses in the left-hand background. Mary is portrayed in a dark blue outer garment and a voluminous red cloak over a white tunic. She has a white shawl draped over her shoulders and a simple diadem on her head. The child is swaddled in a white cloth. He gazes intently at the observer, indifferent to his mother's breast or the piece of fruit she holds out. The painting is a typical example of a devotional panel made for the personal use of its owner. Such objects were used for prayer and meditation, as they were intended to inspire reflection and generosity of spirit. Like most paintings of its kind, the *Virgin and Child* contains a wealth of symbolic reference. The image of the Virgin suckling her child (the Virgo lactans) not only arouses tenderness, but it also had a wide range of theological connotations.[5] The flowers could allude either to Mary's virtues or to Christ's future mission as the Redeemer and the agony he is destined to suffer. The white lilies on the left, for instance, refer to the Virgin's chastity, the purple iris on the right to her grief and compassion at Christ's agony, while the abundance of red roses could represent Mary's love, Christ's suffering or even the Mother of God – the "rose without thorns". The fruit she is holding might be a lemon,[6] but it seems to have been overpainted and is therefore difficult to identify. It could also be an apple, which is more often shown in this context as the fruit of the Tree of Knowledge and evil which Mary (a postfiguration of Eve) offers to Christ (Adam) who will redeem the world from mortal sin.

Since 1928, when the painting was published in Friedländer's catalogue of David's oeuvre, the attribution has seldom been questioned.[7] The style, composition and figures are distinctive of Gerard David's work. The underdrawing (fig. a) bears a certain similarity to that in other paintings attributed to David. Folds of drapery, for instance, are sometimes suggested by a series of ascending, short hatchings or by an outline intersected by similar hatching.

The panel is closely related to David's versions of the *Rest on the flight into Egypt.* These were all made after 1509, the year in which David completed his only fully documented painting, the *Virgo inter Virgines*, which is now at the Musée des Beaux-Arts in Rouen. *The Virgin and Child in a landscape* was probably made around the same time. Van Miegroet, one of the few authors to propose a more specific dating, places it after 1515, and describes it as one of the finest examples of David's late style. The relatively summary underdrawing, which has been faithfully followed in the painting, suggests that the artist had probably practised the composition in the studio.[8] This of course would in some degree support Van Miegroet's dating.
JD

1 Scientific examination conducted by T.D.W. Dibbits under the supervision of J.R.J. van Asperen de Boer. A copy of his minor thesis dated 1991 is in the Museum's file on the painting. Paint samples: A 299/1-6. Infrared reflectograms: AB 1148/3-AB 1151/23.

2 For comparison see M. Wyld, A. Roy, A. Smith, "Gerard David's *The Virgin and child with saints and a donor*", *National Gallery Technical Bulletin* 3 (1979), pp. 51-56.

3According to exhib. cat. Dusseldorf, 1912.

4 On the provenance, see Miegroet (1989).

5 On the interpretation of this symbolism, see Falkenburg (1988).

6 See Falkenburg (1988).

7 Scillia (1975) p. 297 attributes the piece to a painter she refers to as the Master of the Baptism of Christ. He was probably one of David's assistants.

8 Suggested by Dibbits (see note 1).

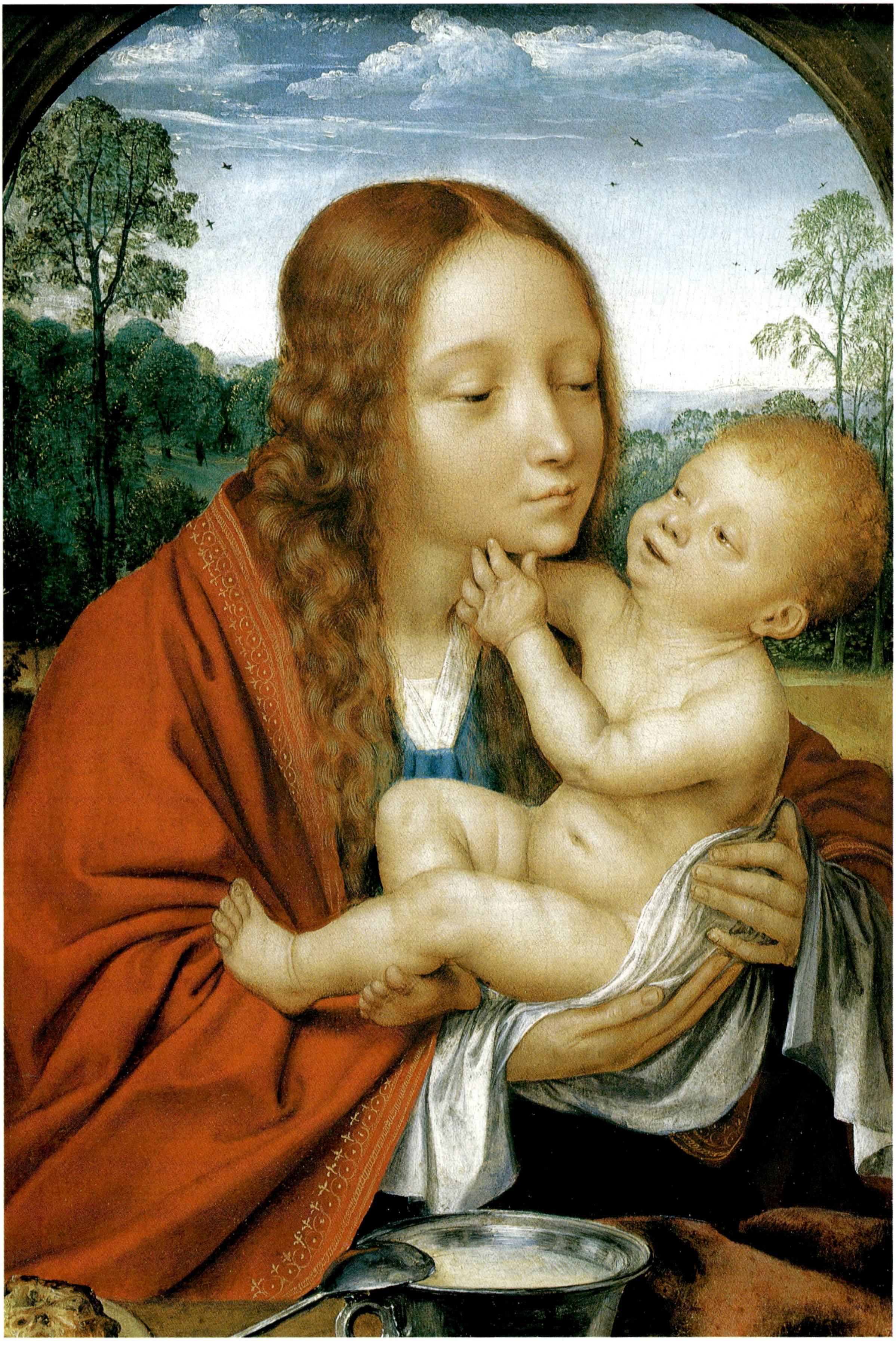

Virgin and Child in a landscape

Quinten Massys
(Louvain 1466-Antwerp 1530)

Panel; 41 x 28 cm

Physical characteristics: the panel consists of a single plank. The *barbe* can be seen on the top and sides but is missing on the lower edge, which was probably shortened. On the back are traces of a blue floral motif which was added later. See also the article by Annetje Boersma in the catalogue.

Dendrochronological examination: the youngest heartwood growth ring dates from 1500. The panel could not have been painted before 1511, it was more probably painted in or after 1517. See article by P. Klein.

Provenance: private collection, Paris; Beets Gallery, Amsterdam; purchased by D.G. van Beuningen, Rotterdam and Vierhouten, for 30,000 guilders; acquired by the Museum in 1958 with the Van Beuningen Collection; inv. no. 2460.

Exhibitions: *Meesterwerken uit vier eeuwen 1400-1800*, Rotterdam, Boymans Museum, 1938, no. 13, fig. 36; *Nederlandsche kunst van de XVde en XVIde eeuw*, The Hague, Mauritshuis, 1945, no. 67; *Les primitifs Flamands*, Paris, Musée de l'Orangerie, 1947, no. 79, fig. LIV; *Honderd jaar Museum Boymans Rotterdam. Meesterwerken uit de verzameling D.G. van Beuningen*, Rotterdam, Boymans Museum, 1949, no. 26; *Chefs-d'œuvre de la collection D.G. van Beuningen*, Paris, Petit Palais, 1952, no. 63, fig. 16; *Kunstschatten uit Nederlandse verzamelingen*, Rotterdam, Boymans Museum, 1955, no. 15, fig. 17.

Literature: Friedländer, XIV, 1937, p. 108, fig. XXV; C. Veth, "Meesterwerken uit vier eeuwen", *Maandblad voor Beeldende Kunsten* XV (1938), p. 203, fig. p. 198; K.G. Boon, *Quinten Massys*, Amsterdam 1942, pp. 58-59; L. van Puyvelde, *Les primitifs Flamands*, Brussels 1947, p. 27, fig. 118; Hannema, 1949, no. 26, fig. 34; M. Davies, "Catalogue of the D.G. van Beuningen Collection", *The Burlington Magazine* XCIII (1951), p. 242; J.Q. van Regteren Altena, review of D. Hannema, "Catalogue of the D.G. van Beuningen collection, Rotterdam 1949", *Oud Holland* LXVIII (1953), p. 229; F.M. Godfrey, "The Van Beuningen collection at Vierhouten", *The Connoisseur*, 1954, p. 96, fig. III; cat. 1962, p. 83; J.G. van Gelder, "Quinten Massys (1466-1530), Madonna met kind", *Openbaar Kunstbezit* 8 (1964), no. 40, fig.; Friedländer, VII, 1971, p. 81, no. 168, fig. 120; A. de Bosque, *Quinten Metsys*, Brussels 1974, p. 218, fig. 253; L. Silver, *The paintings of Quinten Massys*, Oxford 1984, pp. 80, 177, 221, no. 27, fig. 65; H.J. van Miegroet, *Gerard David*, Antwerp 1989, pp. 271, 302, fig. 258.

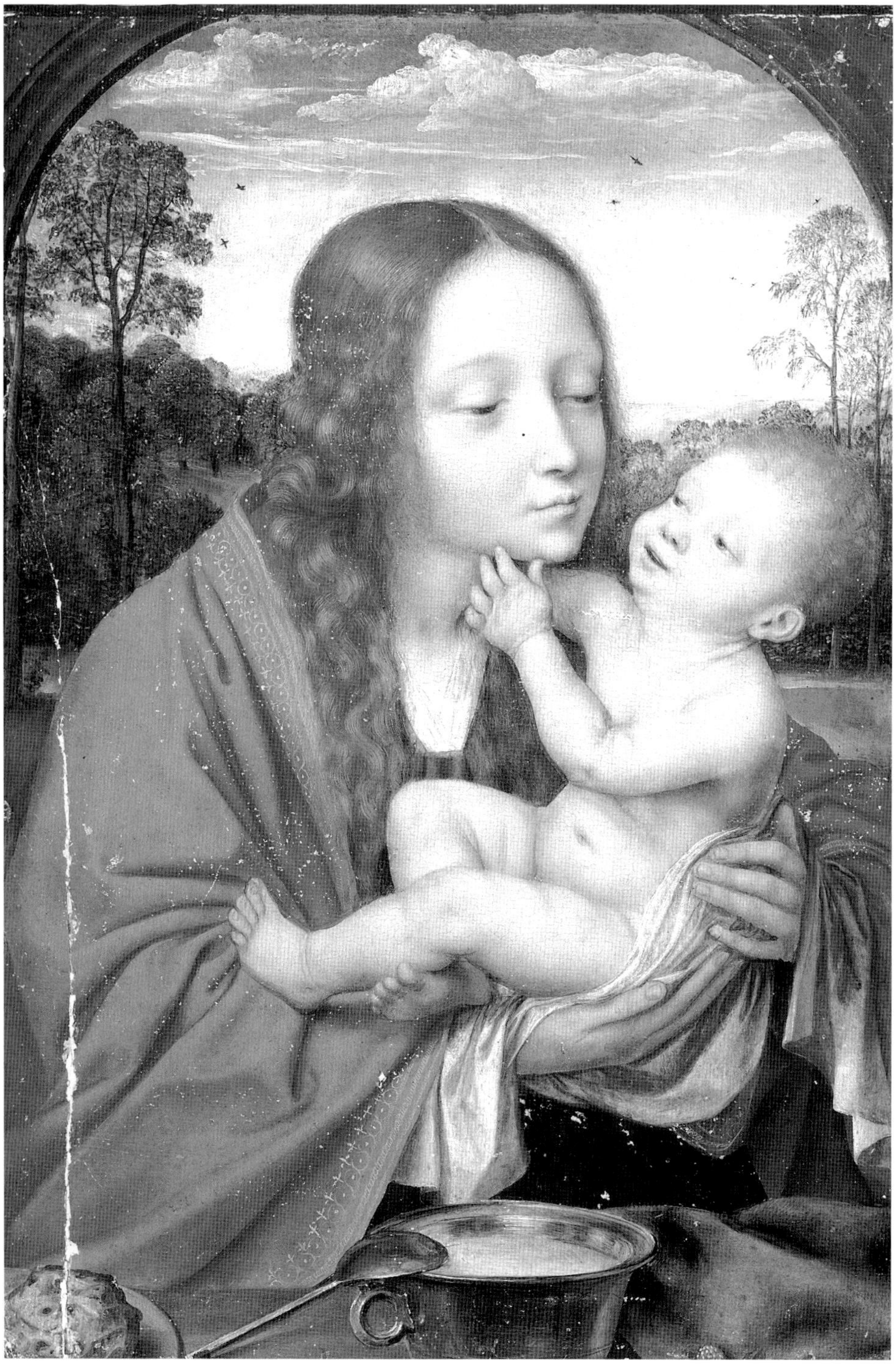

a. Quinten Massys, *Virgin and Child in a landscape*. Condition after cleaning and before restoration. See Annetje Boersma's article for information on the restoration.

The Virgin holds the Child in her arms. She is seated at a balustrade with a wooded landscape in the background, in which a figure holding a stick is discernible at the left. Before her on the stone ledge lies a piece of bread on a plate, a pewter bowl and spoon, and a cushion.

The panel is celebrated for its special charm. The close bond between mother and son is sensitively conveyed in the Virgin's tender gaze and the Child's chubby hand reaching up to caress her chin. The gentle mood is accentuated by the subtle use of colour, particularly in the softly rounded contours of the Child and of the Madonna's head, possibly influenced, as observed by some authorities, by Leonardo da Vinci.[1] The figure of the Child, with his blonde curls, is also thought to derive from the Italian master.[2] Leonardo's influence on Massys is however not nearly so evident as his influence on Massys's contemporary and fellow citizen Joos van Cleve. Massys's rendering of form is substantially different from Leonardo's. Moreover, *sfumato* was also employed by other artists such as Gerard David. The Virgin's face is consistent with Massys's earlier works and does not necessarily indicate Italian influences.[3]

The theme of the painting is clearly in the Flemish tradition. Memling painted a Virgin and Child behind a balustrade against a landscape background in about 1487. This panel also features an arch above the figures which is virtually identical to that in the present painting.[4] The combination of the Virgin, the Child and a bowl of pap was probably introduced by Gerard David around 1510-1515 in a painting that was frequently copied.[5] The pap is interpreted as a reference to the merciful intercession of the Virgin Mary, and the bread as representing the grace of Christ.[6] Mundy sees the figure of David's Virgin feeding the Child as symbolising the Church providing the spiritual sustenance that is just as vital as real food.[7]

Van Gelder perceives a correlation with medieval songs, such as one about the Virgin feeding pap to the Child while Joseph gathers firewood. Whether the figure in the background is Joseph is a moot point. The author is of the opinion that the seven birds in flight symbolise the Seven Joys of the Virgin. He is in any event convinced that they are symbolic.[8] Massys's panel was formerly regarded as a late work.[9] Silver, however, makes a good case for dating it to 1518-1520. It displays many similarities with the triptych by Lucas Rem, which has been dated to the same period on the basis of data on the patron (Munich, Alte Pinakothek).[10]
FL

1 Van Gelder (1964), De Bosque (1974).
2 The figure is very similar to that of the Child embracing the infant John the Baptist in another painting attributed to Massys (Chatsworth, Devonshire Collection, see Silver (1984), no. 34). The composition of the panel is thought to be modelled on a drawing by Leonardo of the same subject in Windsor Castle. Leonardo's composition was also emulated several times by Joos van Cleve (see Friedländer, IX, 1972, no. 37). Silver (1984) believes that the Leonardo-inspired Child was first painted in Antwerp by Joos van Cleve, whose work influenced Massys.
3 See Silver (1984), e.g. p. 219.
4 The panel is at present in Lisbon (inv. no. 1065). Measuring 45.5 x 31.5 cm, it is only slightly larger than Massys' painting. See M.L. Lievens-De Waegh, *Le Musée National d'Art Ancien et le Musée National des carreaux de faïnce de Lisbone* (Les Primitifs Flamands, I. Corpus de la peinture des anciens Pays-Bas Méridionaux au quinzième siècle, 16), no. 169.
5 The best-known version of this painting is in the Koninklijke Musea voor Schone Kunsten, Brussels (inv. no. 3559). On the various versions, see Van Miegroet (1989) no. 33; see also cat. no. 42.
6 Silver (1984), p. 218.
7 E.J. Mundy, "Gerard David's Rest on the flight into Egypt: further additions to grape symbolism," *Simiolus* 12 (1981-82), p. 220.
8 Van Gelder (1964).
9 Van Puyvelde in exhib. cat. Paris 1947, and Hannema (1949).
10 Silver (1984). A date shortly before 1520 was suggested earlier by De Bosque (1974).

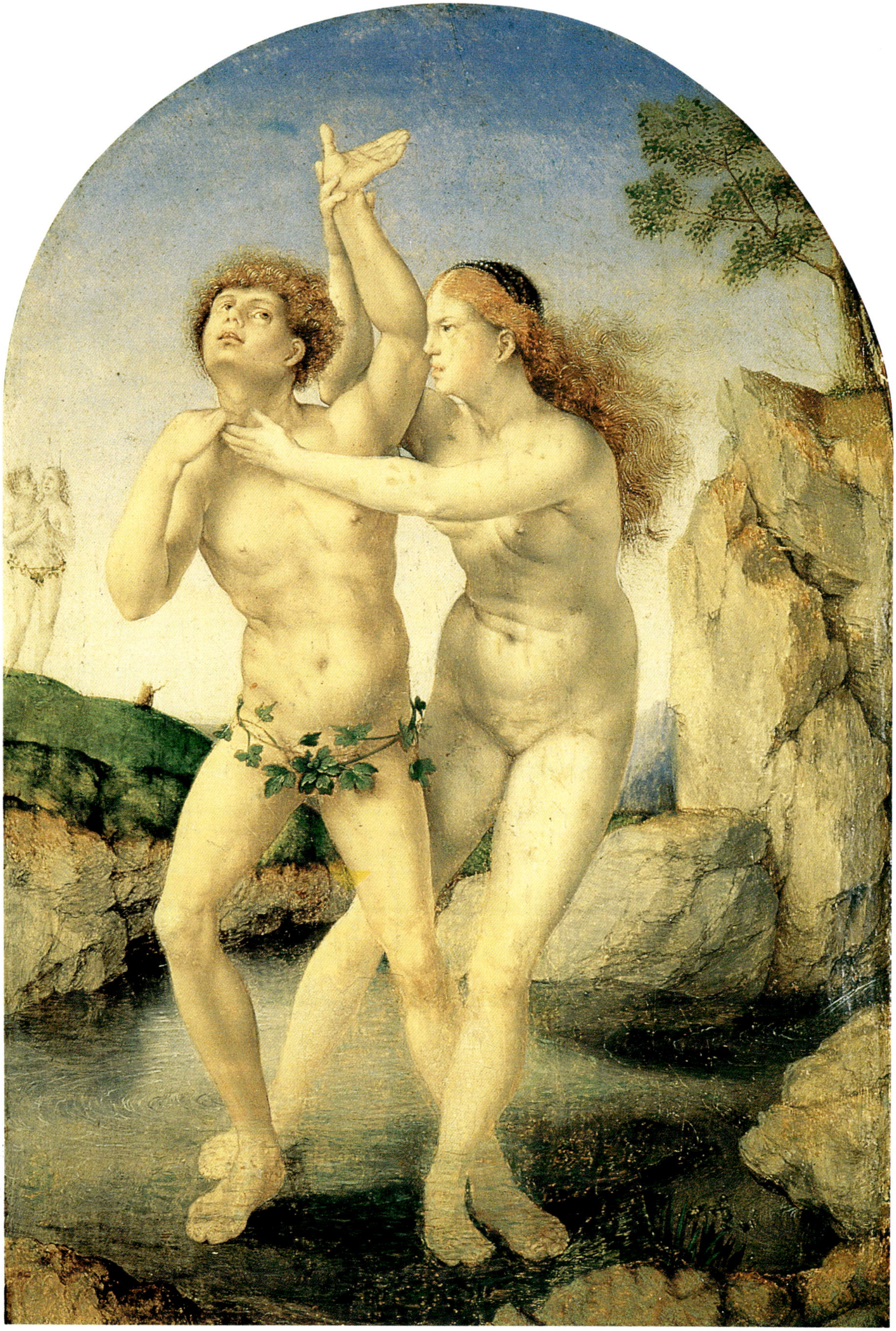

The metamorphosis of Hermaphrodite and the nymph Salmacis

Jan Gossaert, called Mabuse
(Maubeuge 1478-Middelburg 1533/36)

Panel; 32.8 x 21.5 cm

Physical characteristics:[1] the panel and frame consist of a single arched plank.

Infrared reflectography: black chalk underdrawing. See description.

Dendrochronological examination: the youngest heartwood growth ring dates from 1480. The panel could not have been painted before 1491; it was more probably painted in or after 1505. See article by P. Klein.

Paint samples: the underdrawing was probably executed directly on the ground. Natural ultramarine (lapis lazuli) was found in the paint of the sky.

Provenance: Margaret of Austria, Mechelen (inventory 1523: "Item, ung beau tableau auquel est painct ung homme et une femme nuz, estant les pieds en l'eaue, le premier bort de mabre, le second doré et en bas ung escripteau, donné par. Monsgr. d'Utrecht);[2] private collection northern France; Goudstikker Gallery, Amsterdam; purchased from the gallery in 1934 by D.G. van Beuningen, Rotterdam and Vierhouten, for 12,500 guilders; acquired by the Museum in 1958 with the Van Beuningen Collection; inv. no. 2451.

Exhibitions: *Jeroen Bosch. Noord-Nederlandsche primitieven*, Rotterdam, Boymans Museum, 1936, no. 108, fig. 126; *Meesterwerken uit vier eeuwen 1400-1800*, Rotterdam, Boymans Museum, 1938, no. 6, fig. 38; *Nederlandsche kunst van de XVde en XVIde eeuw*, The Hague, Mauritshuis, 1945, no. 56; *Honderd jaar Museum Boymans Rotterdam. Meesterwerken uit de verzameling D.G. van Beuningen*, Rotterdam, Boymans Museum, 1949, no. 13; *Chefs-d'œuvre de la collection D.G. van Beuningen*, Paris, Petit Palais, 1952, no. 50; *Kunstschatten uit Nederlandse verzamelingen*, Rotterdam, Boymans Museum, 1955, no. 12, fig. 19; *De eeuw van Bruegel*, Brussels, Koninklijke Musea voor Schone Kunsten van België, 1963, no. 109, fig. 70; *Jan Gossaert genaamd Mabuse*, Rotterdam, Boymans Museum, Bruges, Groeningemuseum, 1965, no.16, fig.; *Kunst voor de Beeldenstorm*, Amsterdam, Rijksmuseum 1986, no. 2, fig.

Literature: N. Beets, "Een geschilderde naaktfiguur van Lucas van Leyden", *Maandblad voor Beeldende Kunsten* XII (1935), p. 201, fig. 7; F. Schmidt-Degener, "La Belgique et la Hollande, divergences artistiques", *Gazette des Beaux-Arts* XIV (1935), p. 4, fig. 4; H.P. Bremmer, *Beeldende Kunst* XXII (1935-36), p. 3, no. 3, fig.; L. Baldass, "Die Frühholländische Ausstellung in Rotterdam", *Pantheon* XVIII (1936), pp. 256-257, fig.; Friedländer, XIV, 1937, p. 112; J.G. van Gelder, "Jan Gossaert in Rome, 1508-1509", *Oud Holland* LIX (1942), p. 8; G. Glück, "Mabuse and the development of the Flemish renaissance", *The Art Quarterly* VIII (1945), pp. 131-132; Hannema, 1949, no. 13, fig. 41; G. Marlier, *Erasme et la peinture Flamande de son temps*, Damme 1954, p. 36; J. Folie, "Un tableau mythologique de Gossart dans les collections de Marguerite d'Autriche", *Bulletin de l'Institut Royal du Patrimoine Artistique* III (1960), pp. 195-201, figs. 1, 2; G. von der Osten, "Studien zu Jan Gossaert", *De Artibus Opuscula XL, Essays in honor of Erwin Panofsky*, 1961, pp. 465, 467; cat. 1962, pp. 56-57; B. Herzog, *Jan Gossaert, called Mabuse*, (diss.), Bryn Mawr, Pennsylvania 1963, no. 62; J. Bruyn, "Jan Gossaert (ca. 1475-1533/36), De gedaanteverwisseling van Hermaphroditus en de nimf Salmacis", *Openbaar Kunstbezit* 9 (1965), no. 17, fig; A. Misiag-Bochenska, "Un Gossart inconnu?", *Bulletin Koninklijke Musea voor Schone Kunsten van België* 14 (1965), p. 42; G. von der Osten, H. Vey, *Painting and sculpture in Germany and the Netherlands 1500-1600*, Harmondsworth 1969, p. 157; Friedländer, VIII, 1972, p. 112, fig. 139; J. Sterk, *Philips van Bourgondië (1465-1524), bisschop van Utrecht als protagonist van de renaissance, zijn leven en maecenaat* (diss.), Zutphen 1980, pp. 126, 127, 133, 146, fig. 33; L.S. Dixon, "Water, wine and blood - science and liturgy in the *Marriage at Cana* by Hieronymus Bosch", *Oud Holland* 96 (1982), p. 86, fig. 12; A. de Bosque, *Mythologie en Manierisme in de Nederlanden*, Antwerp 1985, fig. 270; L. Silver, "Figure nude, historie e poesie: Jan Gossaert and the renaissance nude in the Netherlands", *Nederlands Kunsthistorisch Jaarboek* 37 (1986), pp. 16-18, fig. 31; exhib. cat. *Zauber der Medusa*, Vienna, Wiener Künstlerhaus, 1987, p. 255, fig.; L. Silver, "The 'Gothic Gossaert'. Native and traditional elements in a Mabuse madonna", *Pantheon* XLV (1987), p. 64, fig. 17.

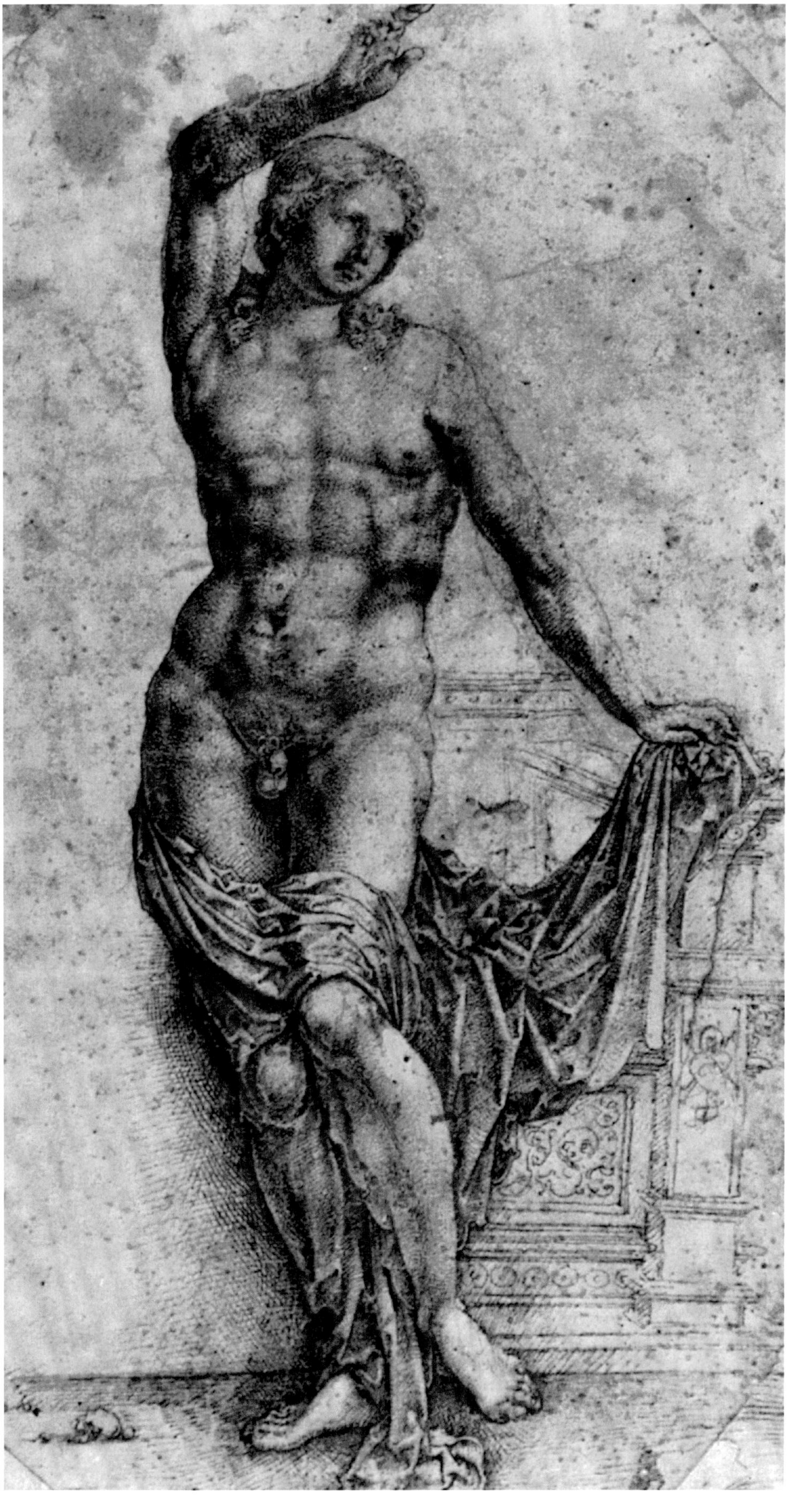

a. Jan Gossaert, Apollo Citharoedus
Ink; 305 x 178 mm
Venice, Gallerie dell'Accademia

Jan Gossaert spent some years in the service of Philip of Burgundy (1465-1524), the youngest illegitimate son of Philip the Good. On his return with Gossaert from a journey to Rome in 1509, Philip surrounded himself with an Italianate court of scholars and artists. First at his castle in Souburg, Zeeland, and later, after his appointment as bishop of Utrecht in 1517, at Wijk Castle, Duurstede, he sought to re-create the spirit of the Italian Renaissance. Between about 1515 and 1524 Gossaert painted a series of mythological scenes, large and small, depicting nude figures drawn from classical Latin and Greek authors. The only large work surviving from this period dates from 1516, and was probably painted for the Souburg castle.[3] Several of his smaller works have survived. Some of his smaller panels, of an unmistakably erotic nature, adorned a house in Wijk where the bishop entertained young women.[4] The Rotterdam panel is a finely detailed work of this kind. According to Margaret of Austria's inventory of 1523, it was a gift from Philip (see provenance). The subject was borrowed from Ovid's *Metamorphoses*, IV, 285-388. The nymph Salmacis fell in love with the handsome Hermaphrodite, bathing in the limpid waters of a pool. When he failed to respond to her passion, she prayed to the gods to unite their bodies for ever. In the foreground Hermaphrodite struggles to break free of her embrace; in the background we see the beginning of the metamorphosis of their two bodies into a being combining both sexes. The figures are believed to be based on classical writings, the representation of the two bodies being thought to accord with Vitruvius's canon of proportion, and the slightly parted lips, affording a glimpse of the teeth, to have been inspired by Pliny's description of the work of the Greek painter, Polygnotus of Thasos.[5] Various commentators have observed that Hermaphrodite's stance is modelled on the Apollo Citharoedus, a classical sculpture of which Gossaert made a drawing (fig. a), and which at that time was thought to portray Hermaphrodite.[6]

In the underdrawing (figs. b, c), Gossaert delineated the figures in some detail by means of thin lines, but sketched in the landscape only roughly. He made a few corrections at this point, including slightly reducing the contours of Salmacis and changing the feet of Hermaphrodite. He seems first to have painted the sky, leaving blank spaces for the two figures, the hill and the rocks. At a later stage he heightened the hill and the rocks, and changed the outlines of the figures. The tree on the rocks and the figure in the background were painted over the blue of the sky. Neither formed part of the underdrawing, from which he deviated in parts, for instance altering the leaves covering Hermaphrodite's loins and omitting a small bush on the left.

In its present state the frame is partly gilded and partly ornamented with carved leaves. Though forming part of the panel, it does not appear to have retained its original form. An entry in Margaret of Austria's inventory which almost certainly relates to this painting describes the frame thus: "le premier bort de marbre, le second doré et en bas un escripteau" (the first frame of marble, the second gilded, bearing an inscription underneath). The original first frame of marble was probably later partially gilded and partially removed, and embellished with a motif of ivy leaves. The second frame was probably removable and has since been lost.[7] The inscription it bore is likely to have been of a moralistic nature. The only comparable Gossaert painting whose frame is still intact bears an inscription warning of the dangers of love.[8] The lost inscription will have been in a similar vein, perhaps emphasising the negative role of women, for in other paintings, of Adam and Eve and Hercules and Deianira, for example, the artist seems to have alluded to the wiles and jealous nature of women.[9]

Herzog queries the attribution of the Rotterdam panel to Gossaert, suggesting instead that it is a studio piece. However its superior quality contradicts this view.[10] Although it has been described as a smaller version of a lost painting by Gossaert for the castle at Souburg,[11] the changes in the underdrawing and during the painting process refute this hypothesis. It closely resembles the Birmingham panel of *Hercules and Deianira* which is dated 1517. It must therefore have been made around the same time.
FL

1 Scientific examination conducted by Sanne R. Wellen under the supervision of J.R.J. van Asperen de Boer. A copy of her minor thesis is in the Museum's file on the painting. Infrared reflectograms: AB 1142/8-AB 1144. Paint samples A297/1-5.
2 Quoted from Folie (1960). Gluck (1945) was the first to relate the painting to this inventory.
3 *Neptune and Amphitrite*, Staatliche Museen zu Berlin, Berlin. Panel: 188 x 124 cm.
4 See Sterk (1980), p. 126.
5 Sterk (1980), p. 126.
6 The drawing is now in the Gallerie dell'Accademia, Venice. Bruyn (1965) and Sterk (1980, p. 126) are amongst the commentators who have pointed out the similarity.
7 Contemporary descriptions of other Gossaert paintings indicate that this frame was removable. See Sterk (1980), p. 126.
8 *Venus and Amor*, Koninklijke Musea voor Schone Kunsten van België, Brussels. Panel; 41.5 x 30.7 cm. See Sterk (1980), pp. 133-136.
9 On this theme and Gossaert's various versions of *Adam and Eve*, see Silver (1986 and 1987). *Hercules and Deianira* is at present in The Barber Institute of Fine Arts, University of Birmingham, Birmingham. Sterk (1980), pp. 126-127, suggests that the inscription on the missing *Metamorphosis* frame will have warned against the luxurious nature of court life, a view based on Boccaccio's comparison of Hermaphrodite and the opulence of courts. In the absence of other comparable examples, this interpretation must remain highly speculative.
10 Herzog (1963), no. 62.
11 See, for example, exhib. cat. *De eeuw van Bruegel*, Brussels, 1963.

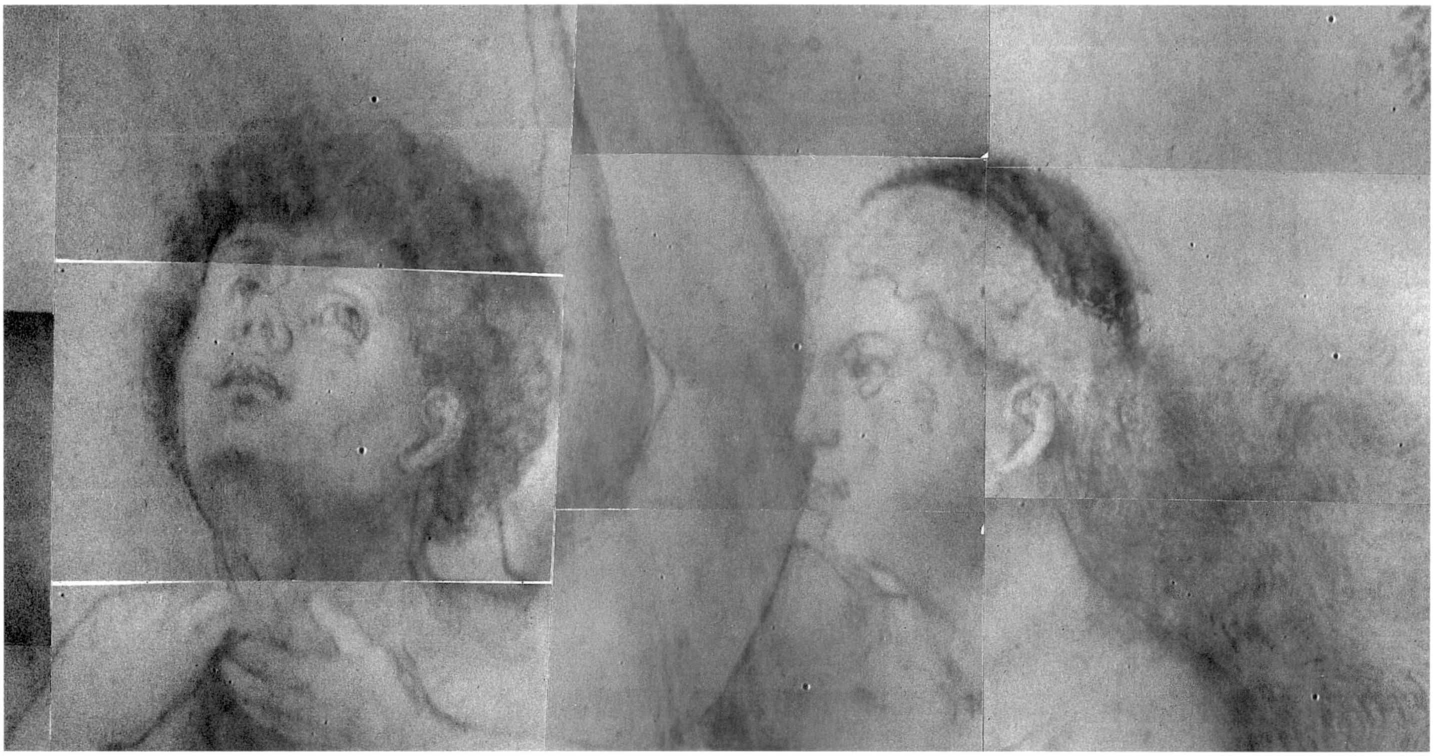

b. Infrared reflectogram assembly showing a detail of the heads of Hermaphrodite and Salmacis

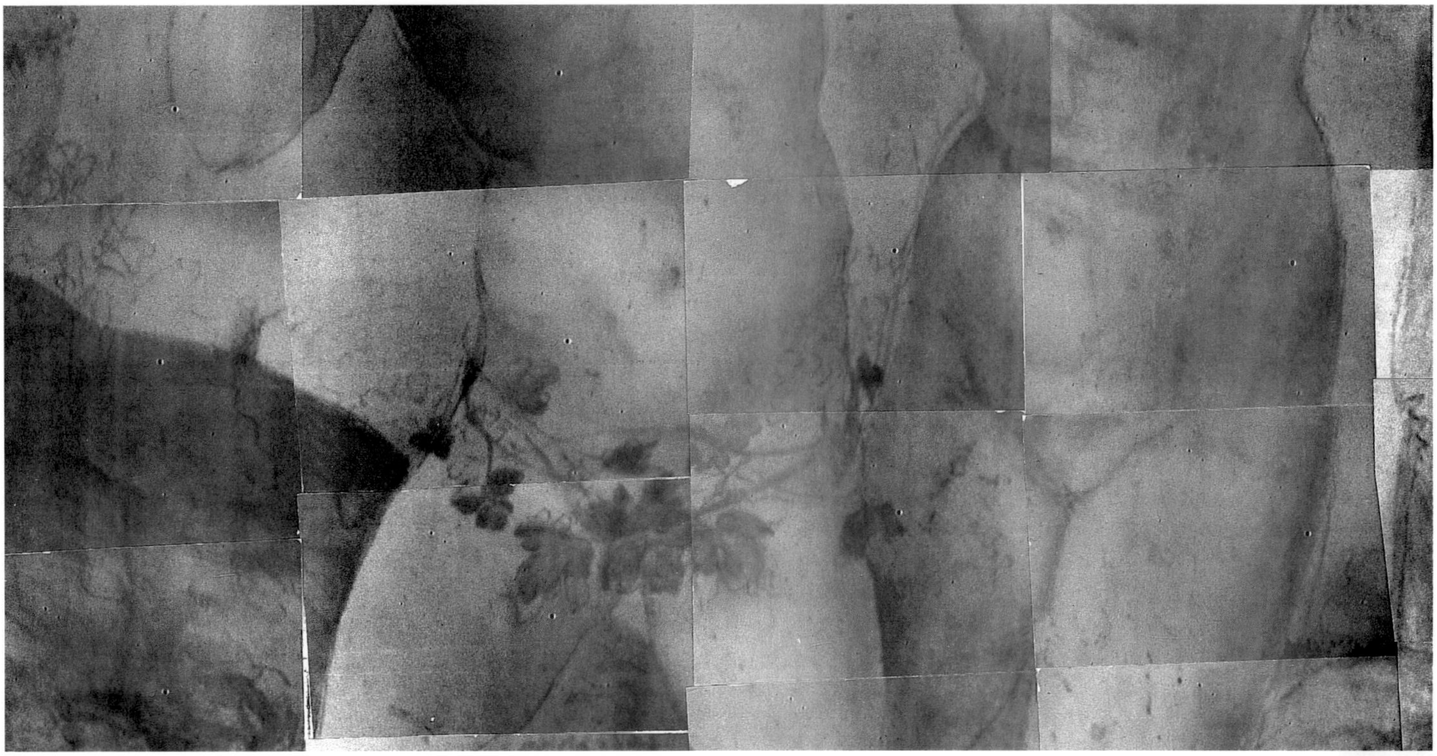

c. Infrared reflectogram assembly showing a detail of the figures and the bush on the left which does not appear in the painting

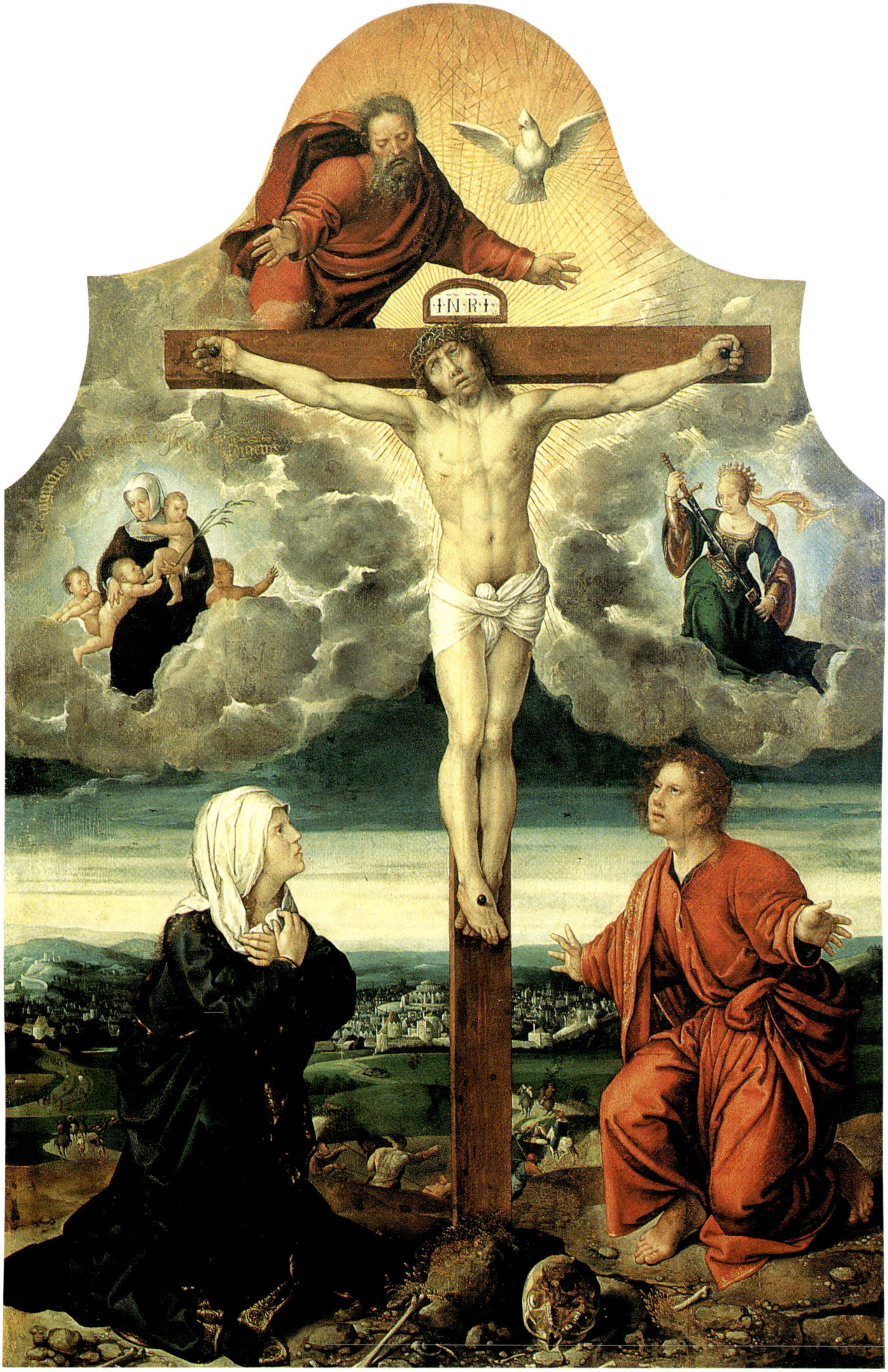
·I·N·R·I·

Crucifixion, with the Virgin and St John

Bernard van Orley
(Brussels c. 1488-Brussels 1541)

Panel; 140 x 90.5 cm
Inscription under the left bar of the Cross:
sanguinis hoc preciū distribuā indigenis

Physical characteristics:[1] the panel originally consisted of four vertical planks. The painting was transferred to a new rigid support in 1840.[2]

Infrared reflectography: elaborate underdrawing in black chalk. See description.

Paint samples: the underdrawing was executed on an intermediate layer containing lead white. The pigments ultramarine and azurite were identified.

Provenance: Dominican convent, Bruges (probably up to 1796); Himbert Collection, Bruges;[3] L.J. Nieuwenhuys, art dealer, Brussels, 1818; King Willem II Collection, 1823; purchased by Mr Viruly for 200 guilders at the auction of the King Willem II Collection, The Hague, 1850-1851; donated to the Museum in 1867 by Mrs M. Viruly-van Vuren van Dalem; inv.no. 1629.

Exhibitions: *Cinq siècles d'art, Exposition Universelle et Internationale de Bruxelles*, Brussels 1935, vol. I, no. 114; *Nederlandsche kunst van de XVde en XVIde eeuw*, The Hague, Mauritshuis 1945, no. 73; *Maria van Hongarije, Koningin tussen keizers en kunstenaars, 1505-1558*, 's-Hertogenbosch, Noordbrabants Museum, Utrecht, Rijksmuseum Het Catharijneconvent 1993, no. 218, fig.

Literature: L.J. Nieuwenhuys, list of 23 works sold to King Willem II, 1823, (Koninklijk Huisarchief A40-VIII-126, The Hague); C.J. Nieuwenhuys, *Description de la galerie des tableaux de S.M. le Roi des Pays-Bas, avec quelques remarques sur l'histoire des peintres et sur les progrès de l'art*, Brussels 1843, pp. 83-84; *Gravures aux Traits, d'après les tableaux, de la galerie de Sa Majesté le Roi des Pays-Bas. Dessinées et gravées par A.L. Zeelander*, The Hague, no date, no. 31; auction cat., *Catalogue des tableaux anciens et modernes de diverses écoles, dessins et estampes encadrés, formant la seconde partie de la galerie de feu Sa Majesté Guillaume II*, Amsterdam 1851, p. 7, no. 17; *Beschrijving der schilderijen van het Museum te Rotterdam gesticht door Mr. F.J.O. Boymans*, 1867, no. 162; M.J. Friedländer, "Bernaert van Orley", *Jahrbuch der Königlich Preuszischen Kunstsammlungen* 30 (1909), pp. 99-102; A. Oberheide, *Der Einfluss Marcantonio Raimondis auf die nordische Kunst des 16. Jahrhunderts*, Hamburg 1933, pp. 30-31, 146, 167; G. Glück, "Bildnisse aus dem Hause Habsburg: II. Königin Maria von Ungarn", *Jahrbuch der Kunsthistorischen Sammlungen in Wien* N.F. 8 (1934), pp. 182-183; Friedländer, VIII, 1934, pp. 118, 171, no. 113; E. Wind, "Charity. The Case History of a Pattern", *Journal of the Warburg Institute* 1 (1937-1938), p. 326.; Ch. Dessart (ed.), *Bernard van Orley 1488-1541*, Brussels 1943, pp. 47, 57, 109; L. Baldass, "Die Entwicklung des Bernart van Orley", *Jahrbuch der kunsthistorischen Sammlungen in Wien* N.F. 13 (1944), p. 178; H.E. van Gelder, "De Kunstverzameling van Koning Willem II", *Maandblad voor beeldende kunsten*, 24 (1948), fig. p. 144; cat. 1962, pp. 99-100; Friedländer, VIII, 1972, pp. 72, 106, no. 113, Pl. 105; J.D. Farmer, *Bernard van Orley of Brussels*, Princeton 1981, p. 339; E. Hinterding, F. Horsch, "'A small but choice collection': the art gallery of King Willem II of the Netherlands (1792-1849)", *Simiolus* 19 (1989), p. 64; D. Martens, "Une 'Crucifixion' Flamande et sa descendance au XVIe siècle. Lecture d'une séquence de copies", *Jaarboek Koninklijk Museum voor Schone Kunsten Antwerpen* 1990, p. 256, fig. 19; G. Delmarcel, "De Passietapijten van Margareta van Oostenrijk (ca. 1518-1524) nieuwe gegevens en documenten", *Revue Belge d'Archéologie et d'Histoire de l'Art* LXI (1992), p. 145.

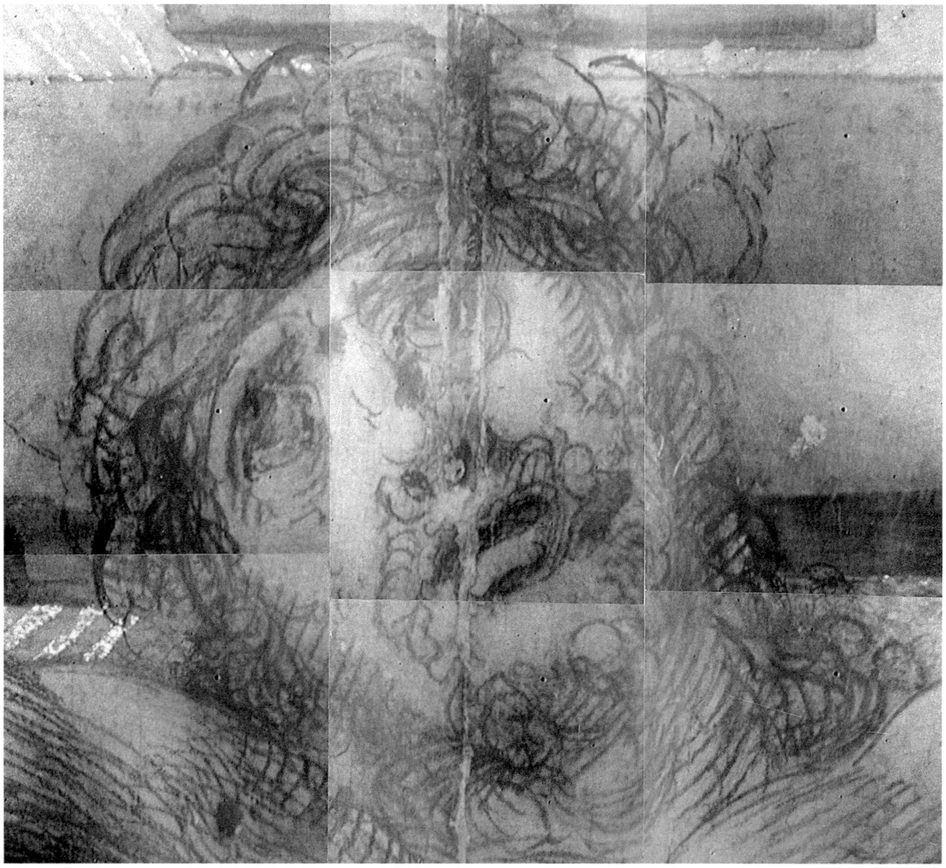

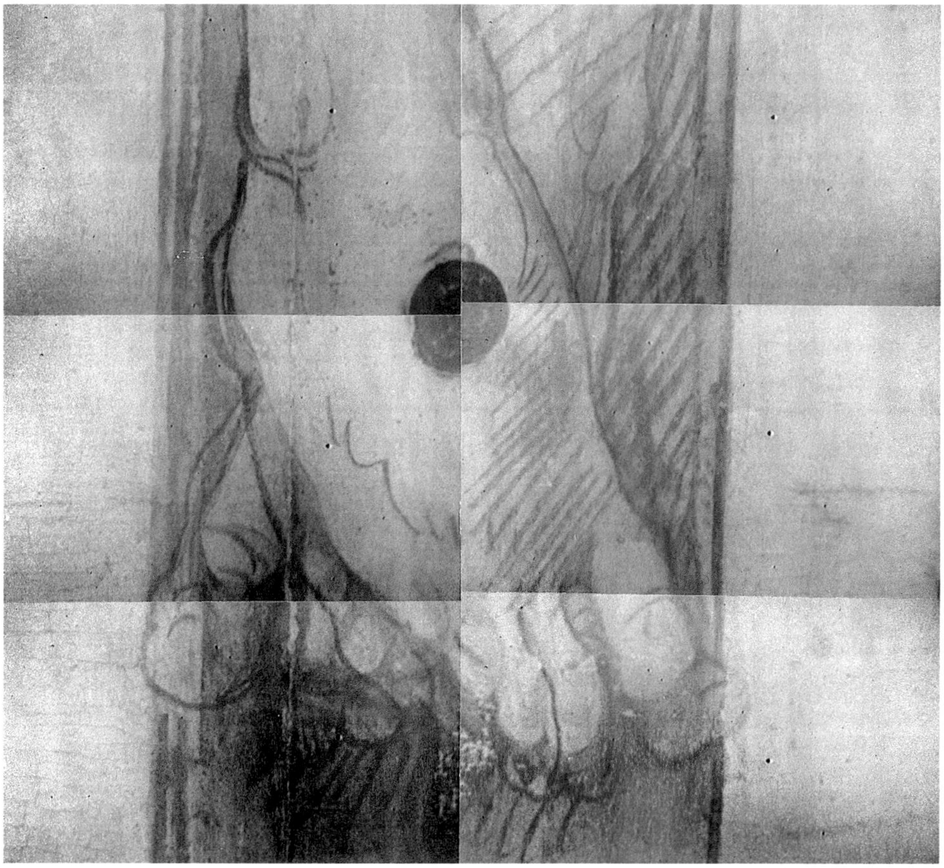

a. Infrared reflectogram assembly of the head of Christ.

b. Infrared reflectogram assembly of Christ's feet.

When King Willem II bought this painting in 1823 it was thought to be by Jan Gossaert. In 1843, it was attributed to Bernard van Orley and is now unanimously accepted as his work. Given the stylistic similarities to Van Orley's *Last Judgement and the Seven Works of Mercy* in the Koninklijk Museum voor Schone Kunsten, Antwerp, which he completed in 1525, it is dated to about that year.

The panel, whose wings have not survived, depicts the Virgin to the left of the Christ figure, and John to the right, both in a kneeling position. Above the Cross are God the Father and the Holy Spirit in the form of a dove. Jerusalem is seen in the background. Two figures on the dark clouds represent Charity and Justice. As was customary, Charity is surrounded by nude children. This is known to be a portrait of Margaret of Austria, the Governess of the Netherlands to whom Van Orley was court painter. The dress and face accord with other portraits of her.[4] Charity is not facing Christ as might be expected in the interests of symmetry, but is in fact turned away from Him,[5] thus constituting a more separate element in the composition. Justice is probably a portrait of Isabella of Austria, the consort of Christian II of Denmark, at that time residing at the court in Mechelen.[6]

The appearance of Charity and Justice in a Crucifixion scene may be related to interpretations of Psalm 84 (85):11:[7] "Mercy and Truth are met together; Justice and Peace have kissed each other". This was interpreted as implying that these virtues had previously been in conflict as a result of the Fall. The virtues are brought together by the sacrifice of the innocent Christ, turning the Divine wrath away from man. Here their reconciliation takes place by the sacrifice of the Cross.[8] Justice signifies the end of the conflict by sheathing her sword. The fact that Charity is depicted but not the Misericordia in the Psalm, also stems from literary sources. The inscription above Charity, *sanguinis hoc preciu[m]* - or preciosum - *distribua[m] indigenis*, meaning "I shall divide this ransom of blood (or 'this redeeming/precious blood') amongst the needy", refers in this context to redemption through the blood of Christ. Van Orley also used this theme in his design for the tapestries woven in 1523-1524 as a throne canopy for Margaret of Austria (Madrid, Patrimonio Nacional).[9] The Crucifixion scene on the back panel shows Mercy and Justice, again sheathing her sword, on the lower left of the Cross. The text beside Mercy is practically identical to that in the Rotterdam painting. The iconography of the canopy is in distinct concordance with the panel, which dates from about the same time.

A later work in Van Orley's oeuvre displays an even closer affinity with this painting. It is the large triptych which he was commissioned to paint for Margaret of Austria's burial church at Brou (now in the Onze Lieve Vrouwekerk, Bruges).[10] The representation of the crucified Christ, God the Father and the Holy Spirit in the centre panel follows a comparable scheme, while in the clouds under the arms of the cross are Charity – likewise with Margaret of Austria's features – and Justice. Scenes from the Passion are depicted on the wings. Given the similarity of the two works, it is not inconceivable that the lost wings of this painting also portrayed Passion scenes.

Though it might be surmised from the use of the same composition for the Bruges triptych that Van Orley's studio worked from models, the scientific examination of the present painting yielded no data to substantiate such a hypothesis. The infrared reflectograms reveal a highly detailed black chalk underdrawing, whose vigorous style suggests an experienced hand (fig. a).[11] Hatching and cross-hatching are used to model the figures and indicate shading. All the elements in the painting appear in the underdrawing, except for the city in the background.

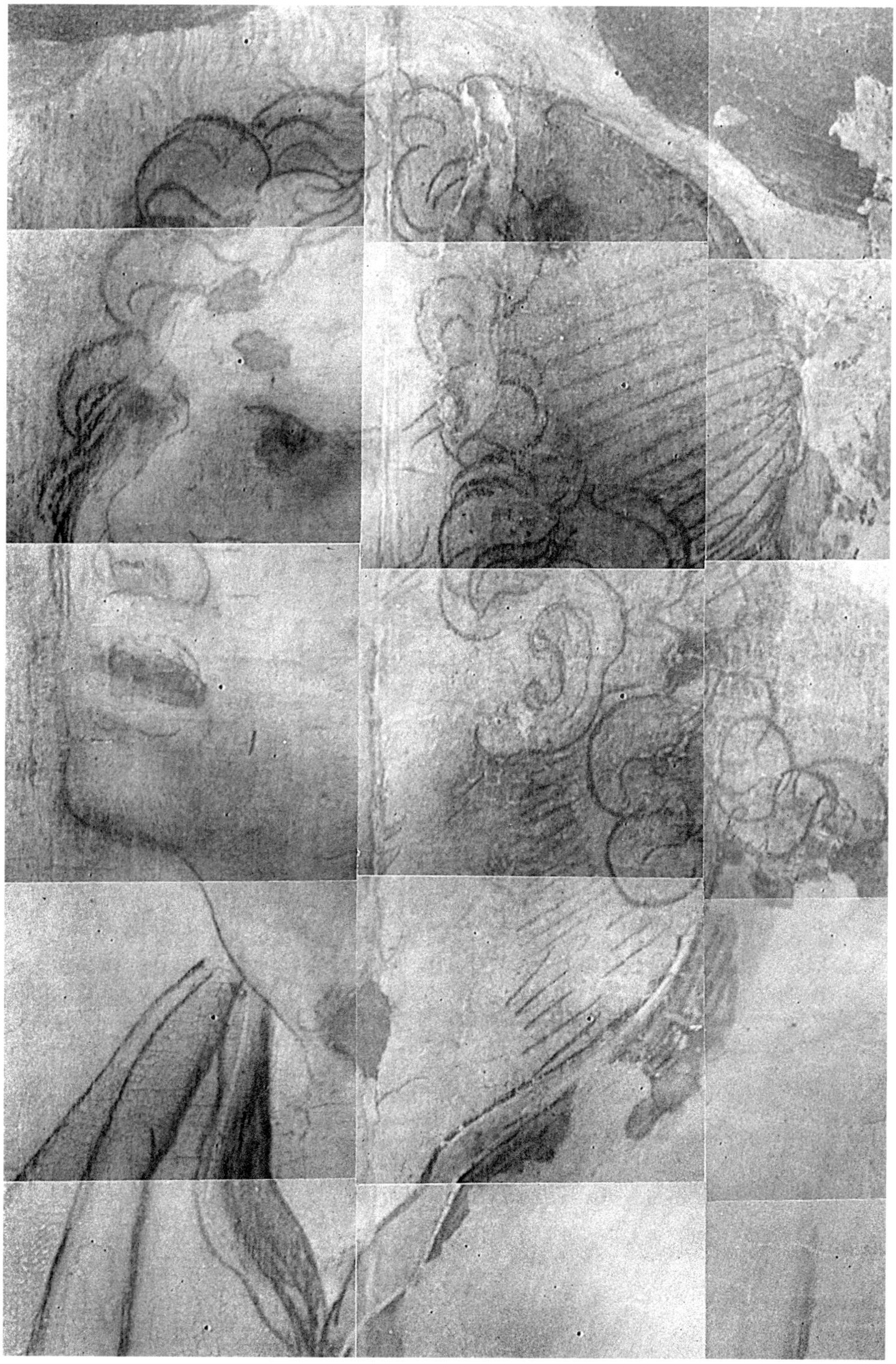

c. Infrared reflectogram assembly of John's head.

X-radiographs show the contours of the underdrawing to have been fairly closely followed in the application of the first paint layer. Corrections made in the final elaboration of the work left the composition unchanged. They are evident in such details as the faces of Charity and Justice, the feet of Christ (fig. b) and the hair of St John (fig. c). The changes in the heads and other parts of the body were probably made by the artist himself in a final creative touch. Except for these changes, it is probable that the master was aided by studio assistants. Though Friedländer views it as one of the few paintings executed entirely by Van Orley himself, the above points support Farmer's belief that much of the work was done by assistants. A copy of the painting was auctioned in 1966.[12]
MW

1 Scientific examination conducted by Margreet Wolters under the supervision of J.R.J. van Asperen de Boer. A copy of her minor thesis dated 1990 is in the Museum's file. Infrared reflectograms: AB 1094-AB 1100; AB 1119/19-1122/22. Paint samples A 275/1-7.

2 The transfer was carried out by Emile Mostemarte of the Musée Royale de France. His notes are in the Koninklijk Huisarchief, The Hague, A 40-VIII-126.

3 Nieuwenhuys (1823) and Nieuwenhuys (1843) mention the Dominican convent and the Himbert Collection.

4 See a copy of Van Orley's work in the Koninklijk Musea voor Schone Kunsten, Brussels, inv. no. 4059.

5 In his engraving of the painting, Zeelander changed the composition to allow Charity's gaze to be fixed on the Cross. Zeelander, undated, no. 31.

6 Justitia's hair ornamentation is similar to that of Isabella in a preliminary drawing by Jan Gossaert. See exhib. cat. Utrecht/'s-Hertogenbosch 1993, no. 178, p. 241.

7 Such as Bernardus van Clairvaux's sermon on the Annunciation.

8 See H. Kraft, *Die Bildallegorie der Kreuzigung Christi durch die Tugenden*, Frankfurt 1976, pp. 65-94.

9 See Delmarcel (1992), pp. 143-147.

10 The triptych was completed after Van Orley's death by Marcus Geeraerts. See Farmer (1981).

11 Other Van Orley underdrawings revealed through infrared reflectography are stylistically comparable. See, P.B.R. van den Brink, "Underdrawing in the workshop-production of Bernard van Orley. A first impression", *Colloque X pour l'étude du dessin sous-jacent dans la peinture*, Louvain-la-Neuve 1995 (to be published).

12 Kunsthaus Lempertz, 5-7 May 1966, No. 58, fig. 7.

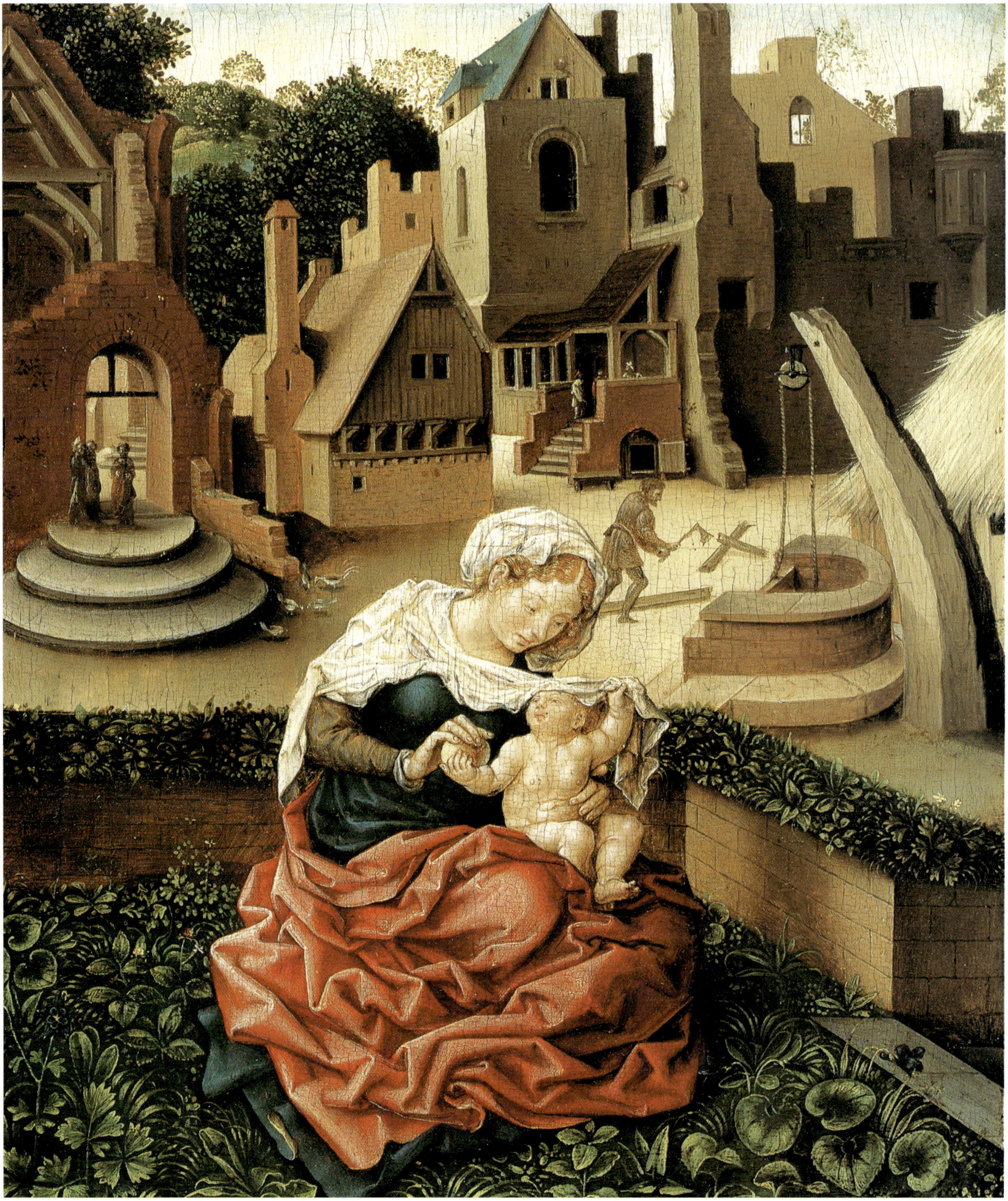

Virgin and Child seated in a garden

Anonymous
South Netherlandish master
c. 1520-1530

Panel; 25 x 21 cm

The Virgin is seated with the Child on her lap in a walled garden. The Child's left hand holds her veil. Joseph, axe in hand, is chopping wood near the buildings and ruins in the square behind them. The walled garden, or "hortus conclusus," symbolises the Virgin's purity. Similarly, the well to her left may signify the Immaculate Conception.[2] Van Beuningen bought the panel in 1951 as a work by Bernard van Orley, an attribution which would now seem to be erroneous. It bears little resemblance to the known works of the artist, while the composition has been designed fairly literally with help from other artists' work.

The Virgin and Child are copied from an engraving by Jan Gossaert dated ca. 1520-22 (fig. a).[3] There is an identical Madonna in a painting in Bourg en Bresse which is attributed to Van Orley (fig. b). The buildings in the background are the same in almost all respects as those on a panel attributed to a follower of Joachim Patinir (fig. c).[4] Except for a few alterations, the houses are also identical to those in a painting by an anonymous Flemish artist in Copenhagen (fig. d),[5] in which the architecture is somewhat more elaborate. It may be an earlier work. The architecture appears to have been inspired by Dürer prints, although no literal similarities can be indicated. The figure of Joseph chopping wood may also be taken from a woodcut by the German master.[6]

Attribution of the Rotterdam panel is complicated by its composite nature. It was probably painted in the southern Netherlands in about 1520-1530.
FL

Physical characteristics: the panel consists of a single plank.

Infrared reflectography: no underdrawing could be discerned.[1]

Provenance: Borghouts Gallery; purchased from the gallery in 1951 by D.G. van Beuningen, Rotterdam and Vierhouten, for 10,000 guilders; acquired by the Museum in 1958 with the Van Beuningen Collection; inv. no. 2472.

Exhibitions: *Chefs-d'œuvre de la collection D.G. van Beuningen*, Paris, Petit Palais, 1952, no. 65.

Literature: Cat. 1962, p. 100; exhib.cat. *Jan Gossaert genaamd Mabuse*, Rotterdam, Boymans Museum, Bruges, Groeninge Museum, 1965, p. 349; B. Broos, exhib.cat. *Liefde, Lust & Lijden. Historiestukken in het Mauritshuis Den Haag*, The Hague, Mauritshuis, 1993-94, p. 135, note 15.

1 Scanned in September 1993 by Molly Faries.
2 See inter alia R.L. Falkenburg, *The Fruit of Devotion. Mysticism and the imagery of love in Flemish paintings of the Virgin and Child, 1450-1550*, Amsterdam-Philadelphia 1994, pp. 9-11, and the literature discussed in this work.
3 See exhib.cat. Rotterdam and Bruges, 1965, no. 71.
4 Auctioned at Christie's, Amsterdam, on 20 June 1989, no. 36.
5 See *Royal Museum of Fine Arts. Catalogue of old foreign paintings*, 1951, no. 867, p. 381. With thanks to Gijsbert van Nifterik for the reference.
6 See the woodcut, *Rest on the Flight into Egypt*, in the series on the life of the Virgin (Meder 202), ca. 1501-1502.

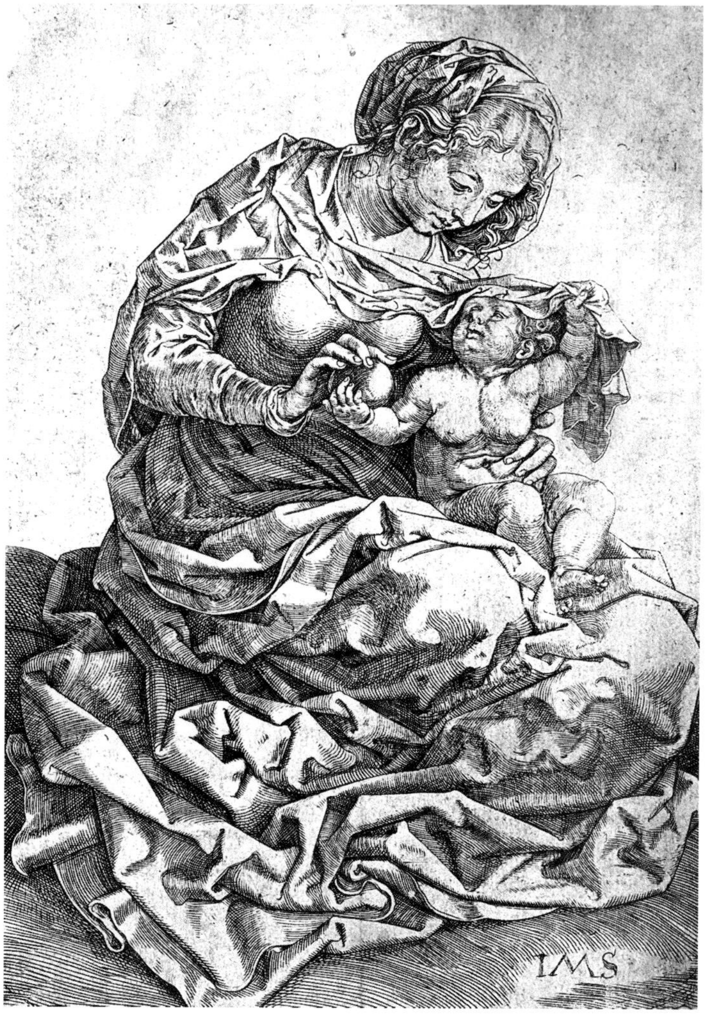

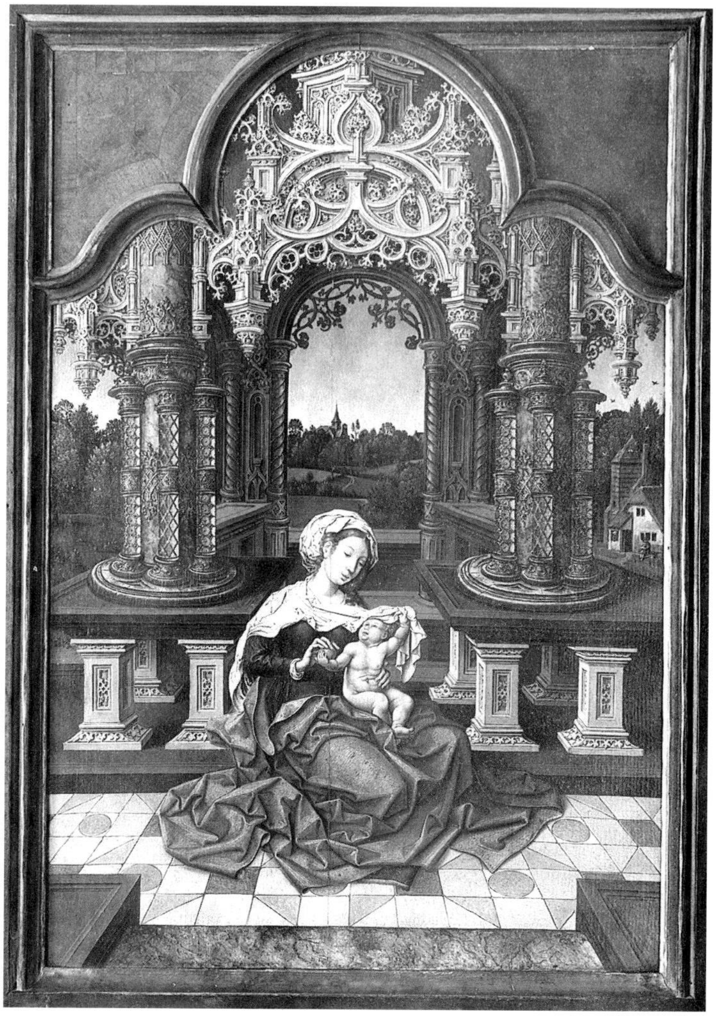

a. Jan Gossaert, Virgin and Child
Engraving; 147 x 103 mm
Boymans-van Beuningen Museum, Rotterdam

b. Attributed to Bernard van Orley
Virgin and Child
Panel; 75 x 50 cm
Musée de Brou, Bourg en Bresse

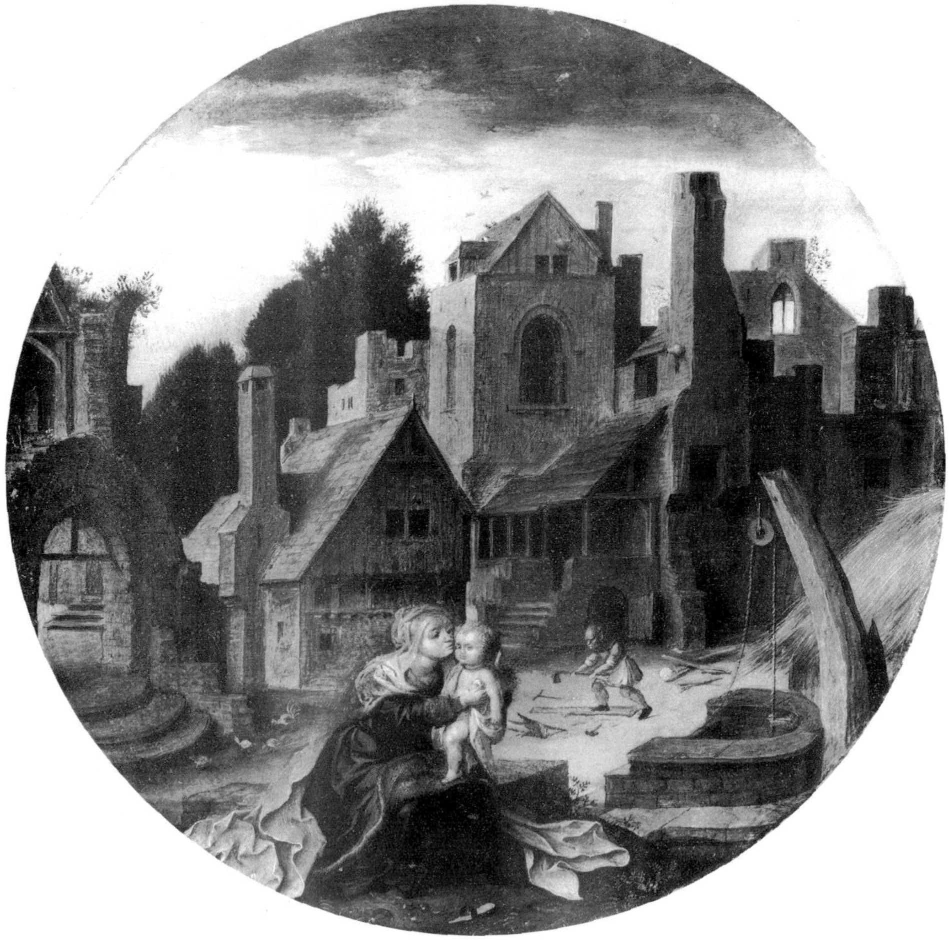

c. Joachim Patinir, follower of
Virgin and Child
Panel; diameter 20 cm
Whereabouts unknown

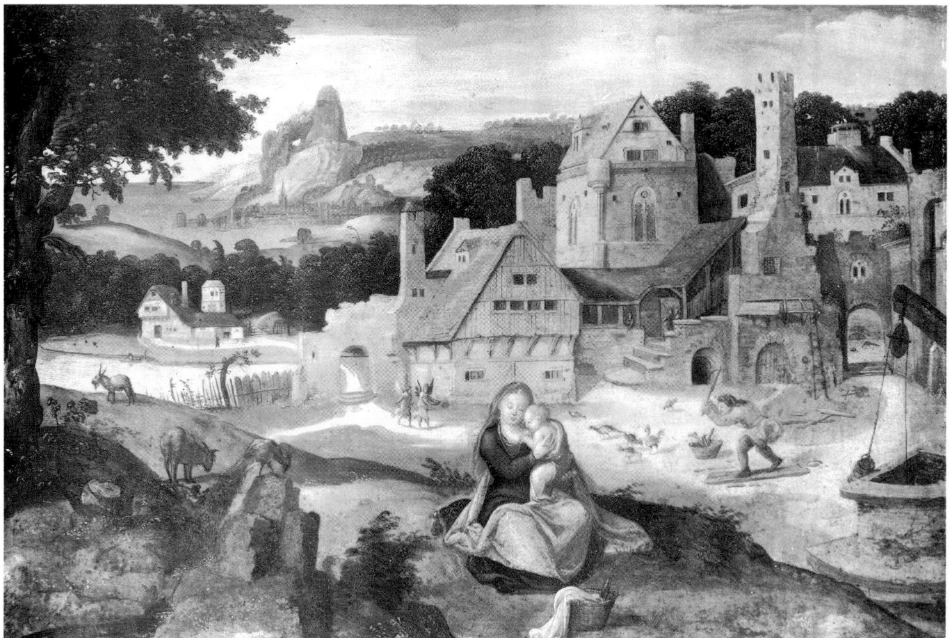

d. Anonymous Flemish, 16th century
The Holy Family
Panel; 31.5 x 43.5 cm
Statens Museum for Kunst, Copenhagen

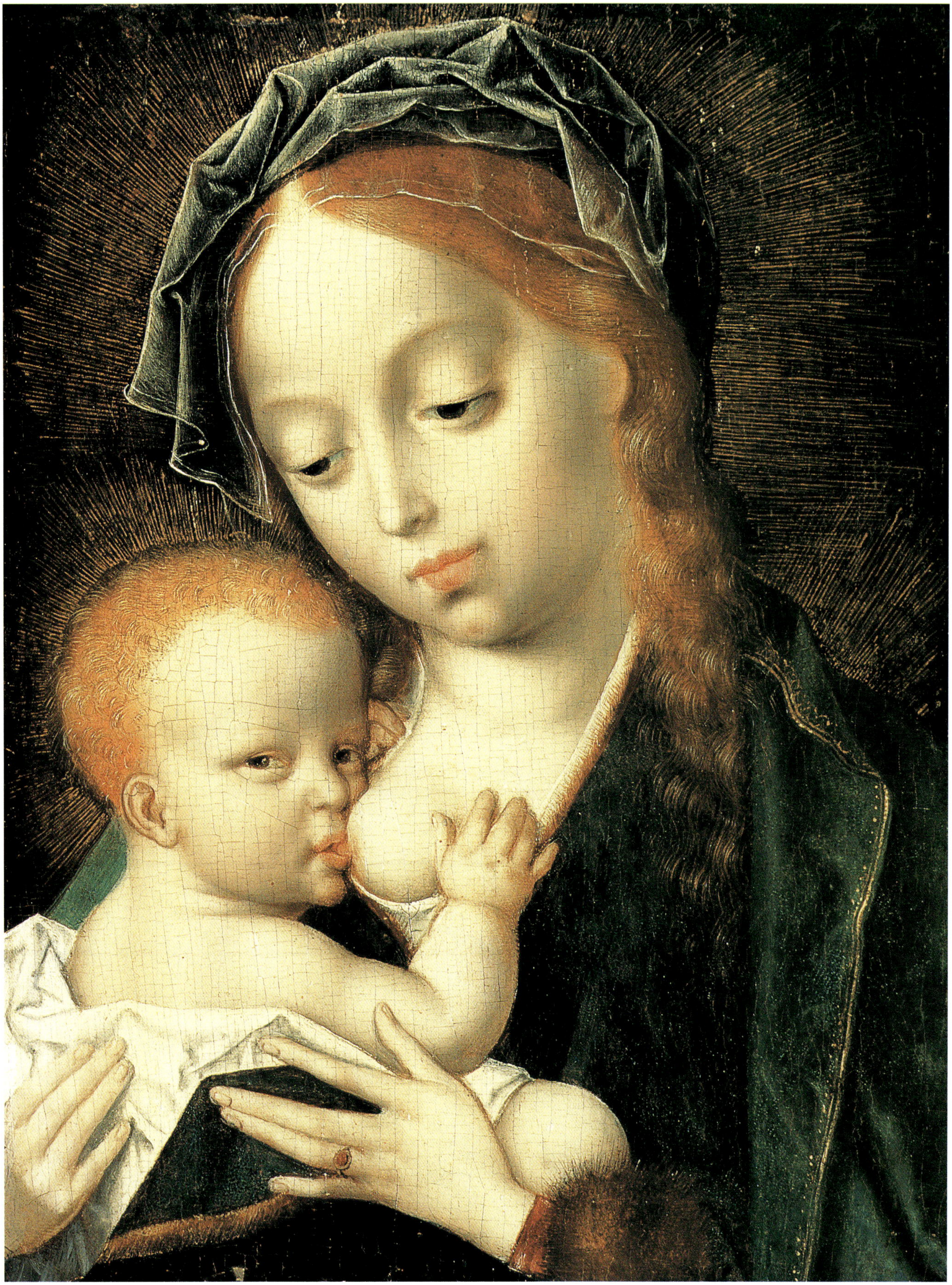

The Virgin suckling the infant Christ

Joos van Cleve, after
(c. 1485-Antwerp 1540/1541)

Panel; 25 x 18 cm

This small painting of *The Virgin suckling the infant Christ* was acquired by Van Beuningen in the same year as the panel with the *Rest on the Flight into Egypt* by a follower of Patinir.[2] Both works originally came from the collection of Sir Hugh Cholmeley.

Van Beuningen bought the piece in 1951 as an original work by Joos van Cleve. At that time it was already known that a great many versions of this composition existed. Baldass and Friedländer had published a painting in the former Rathenau collection as the original (fig. a).[3] The latter writer mentioned twelve other versions in 1931.

The Rotterdam painting lacks the fine execution which is characteristic of Van Cleve. It must therefore be regarded as a copy. Van Cleve copied the postures of the Virgin and the infant Christ from a painting by Gerard David of the *Rest on the Flight into Egypt*, the most famous version of which is at the Prado in Madrid.[4] The original by Van Cleve is generally dated early, around 1510-1514.[5]
FL

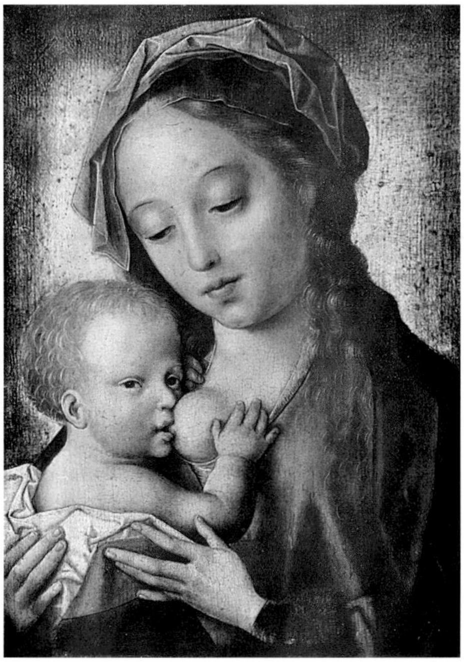

Physical characteristics: the panel consists of a single plank.

Infrared reflectography: no underdrawing could be discerned.[1]

Provenance: Sir Hugh Cholmeley, Easton Hall, Grantham; auction London, Christie's, 1 June 1951, no. 145; Borghouts Gallery; bought there by D.G. van Beuningen, Rotterdam and Vierhouten, in 1951 for 20,000 guilders; acquired in 1958 with the D.G. van Beuningen Collection; inv. no. 2444.

Exhibitions: *Chefs-d'œuvre de la collection D.G. van Beuningen*, Paris, Petit Palais, 1952, no. 44.

Literature: Cat. 1962, p. 38.

1 Scanned on 20 December 1993 by J.R.J. van Asperen de Boer.
2 See cat. no. 49.
3 L. Baldass, *Joos van Cleve. Der Meister des Todes Mariä*, Vienna 1925, no. 5, fig. 10 (the painting was then in the Kappel Collection); Friedländer, IX, 1931, no. 55, fig. XXXII. To judge by the photograph, this painting does indeed appear to be of a higher quality than the Rotterdam panel. Whether it really is an original work is difficult to establish.
4 J.O. Hand, *Joos van Cleve: the early and mature paintings*, (diss. Princeton University 1978), pp. 74-75.
5 Baldass, *op. cit.* (note 3), dates it around 1510; Friedländer, *op. cit.* (note 3), around 1512 and Hand, *op. cit.* (note 4) around 1511-1513/14.

a. Joos van Cleve (?), The Virgin suckling the infant Christ
Panel; 25 X 20 cm.
Whereabouts unknown (formerly in the Rathenau Collection, Berlin).

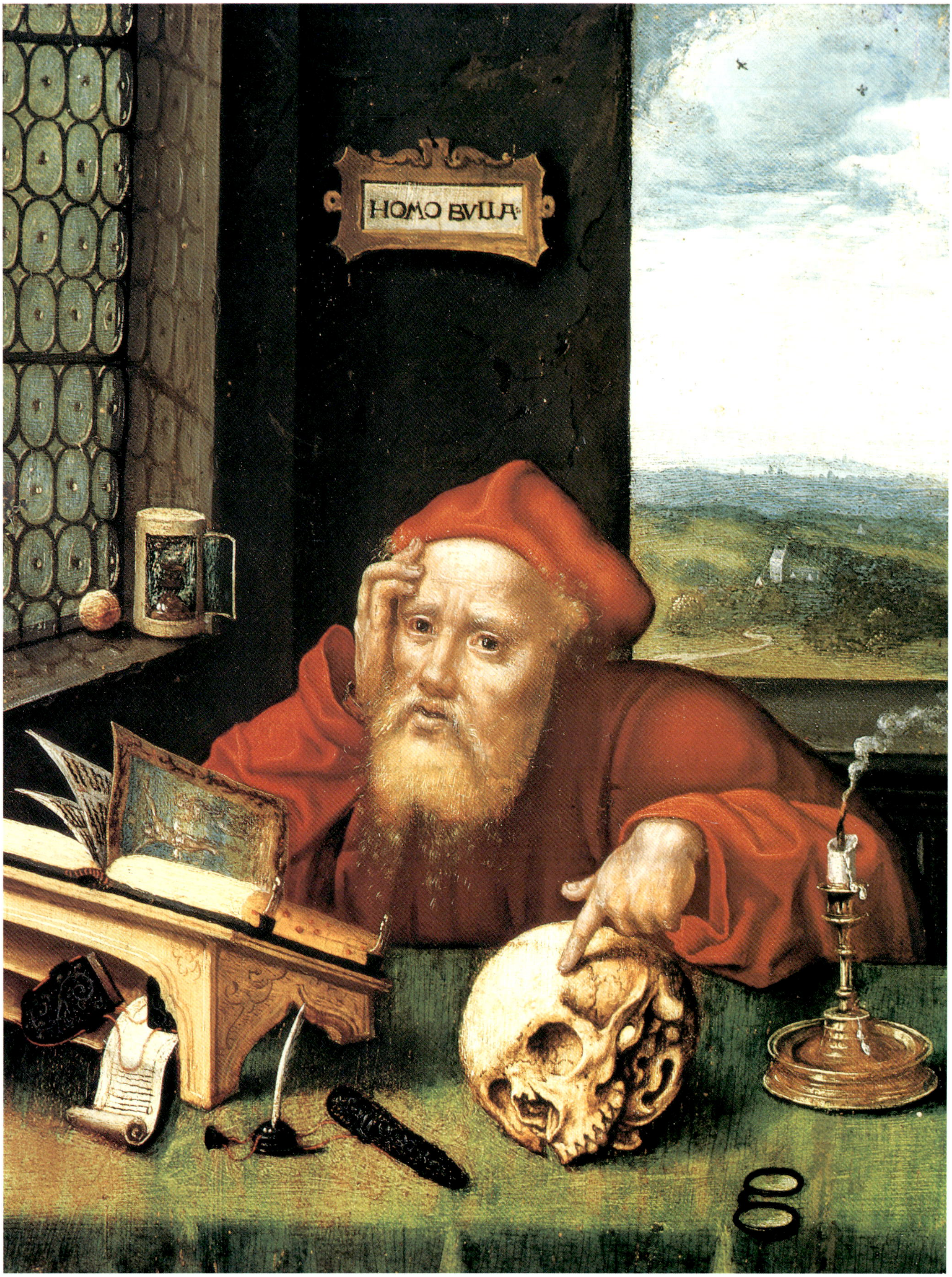
HOMO BVLLA

St Jerome in his study

Joos van Cleve, after
(c. 1485-Antwerp 1540/1541)

Panel; 31 x 22.5 cm
Inscription on the rear wall in a cartouche: homo bulla

St Jerome is seated behind a table, resting his head on his right hand. His left forefinger is pointing to a skull. In front of him is an open book with an illustration of the *Crucifixion*. On the table stands a candlestick with a snuffed-out candle and a pen in a holder. To the left, on the window sill, are an apple and an hourglass. Against the rear wall hangs a sign bearing the inscription "homo bulla" (man is a bubble of air).[2] The inscription and the details such as the hourglass, the candle and the skull, make it clear that this is a reference to the temporary nature of human existence on earth.[3]

The painting is a copy after a work by Joos van Cleve which has presumably been lost (fig. a).[4] Many versions of this composition are known, varying greatly in quality. The composition seems to have been especially popular in the first half of the sixteenth century. Most of these paintings were probably made in Antwerp.[5]

Van Cleve based this composition on Albrecht Dürer's *St Jerome* (Lisbon, Museu Nacional de Arte Antiga). The German artist painted this work during a visit to Antwerp in 1521.[6] The Rotterdam painting covers a freely-rendered underdrawing in black chalk. Shadow is indicated with hatching. In some places, the painting differs from the contours of the underdrawing (figs. b, c).

The panel was described in the Museum's first catalogue in 1849 as "George Pentz or Pens. A scholar in his study". In the Museum's annual report of 1887, the painting was first linked to the Master of the Death of the Virgin, who was later identified as Joos van Cleve.[7] The rather clumsily painted panel is quite far removed from the original work of Van Cleve. It can probably be dated around 1530-1540.
FL

Physical characteristics: the panel consists of a single plank.

Infrared reflectography: extensive underdrawing in black chalk.[1] See text.

Provenance: estate of F.J.O. Boymans, Utrecht, 1847; inv. no. 1918.

Not exhibited

Literature: *Catalogus van schilderijen enz. in het museum te Rotterdam gesticht door mr. F.J.O. Boymans*, 1849, no. 212; J. Held, *Dürers Wirkung auf die Niederländische Kunst seiner Zeit*, The Hague 1931, p. 139; cat. 1962, p. 160.

1 Scanned and partially recorded on 10 and 17 January 1994 by J.R.J. van Asperen de Boer. The infrared reflectogram assemblies were made by Cunera Vergeer. Infrared reflectograms: AB 1559/15A-25A.

2 This motto first appears in the paintings of Joos van Cleve. Stechow pointed out that the appearance of this saying, which was already known in classical antiquity, is linked to its publication by Erasmus in his *Adagia* in 1500. See W. Stechow, "Homo Bulla", *The Art Bulletin* XX (1938-1939), pp. 227-228. See further H.W. Janson, "The putto with the death's head", *The Art Bulletin* XIX (1937), p. 431-432.

3 See for the iconography, J.O. Hand, *Joos van Cleve and the Saint Jerome in the Norton Gallery and School of Art (Norton Gallery studies I)* West Palm Beach (1972).

4 L. Baldass, *Joos van Cleve. Der Meister des Todes Mariä*, Vienna 1925, no. 92, regards the examples which were formerly in the collections of the Provinzialmuseum, Hannover and of the Duke of Fife as copies after a lost work by Van Cleve. These two paintings are also regarded by Friedländer as the two best replicas (Friedländer, IX, 1931, no. 39). Hand endorses this view (J.O. Hand, *Joos van Cleve: the early and mature paintings* (diss. Princeton University 1978), p. 182).

5 Held (1931) gives a list of 24 copies. He writes that Friedländer had identified no fewer than 40 copies in 1912.

6 See for example E. Panofsky, *Albrecht Dürer*, Princeton, New Jersey, 1945, pp. 211-213.

7 *Verslag omtrent den toestand en de aanwinsten van het Museum Boymans over het jaar 1887*, p. 16.

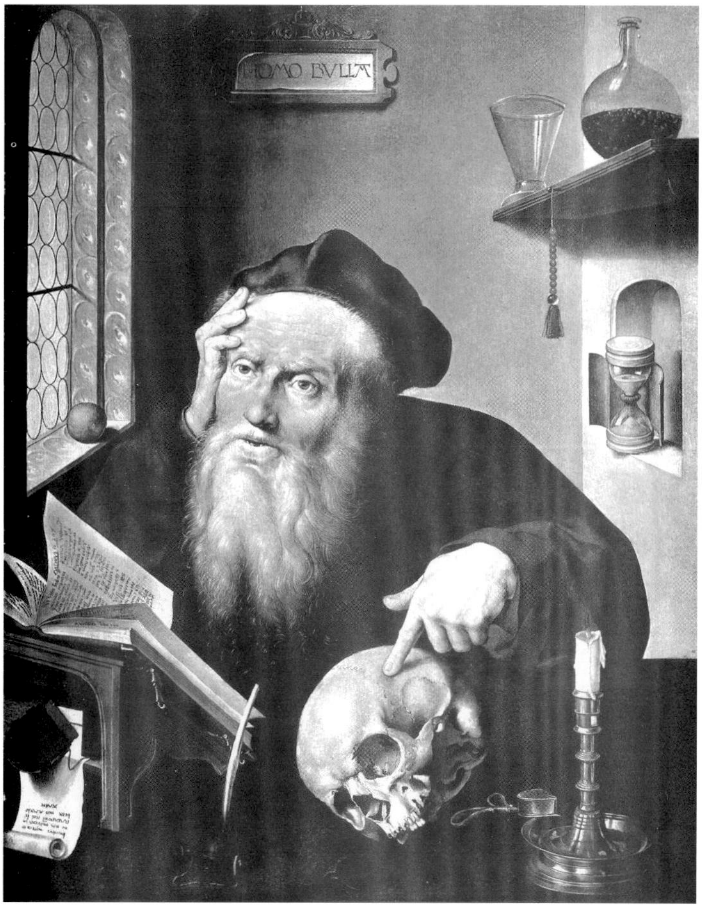

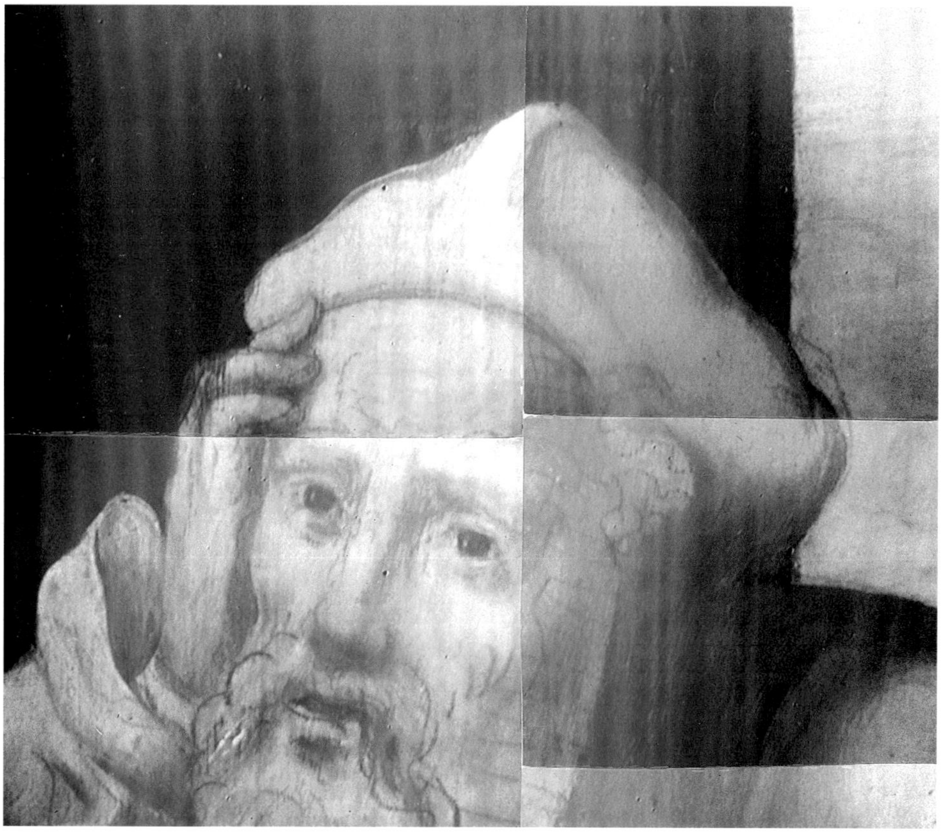

a. After Joos van Cleve, St Jerome in his study
Formerly in the collection of the Provinzialmuseum, Hannover

b. Infrared reflectogram assembly showing a detail of the head.

c. Infrared reflectogram assembly showing a detail of the table.

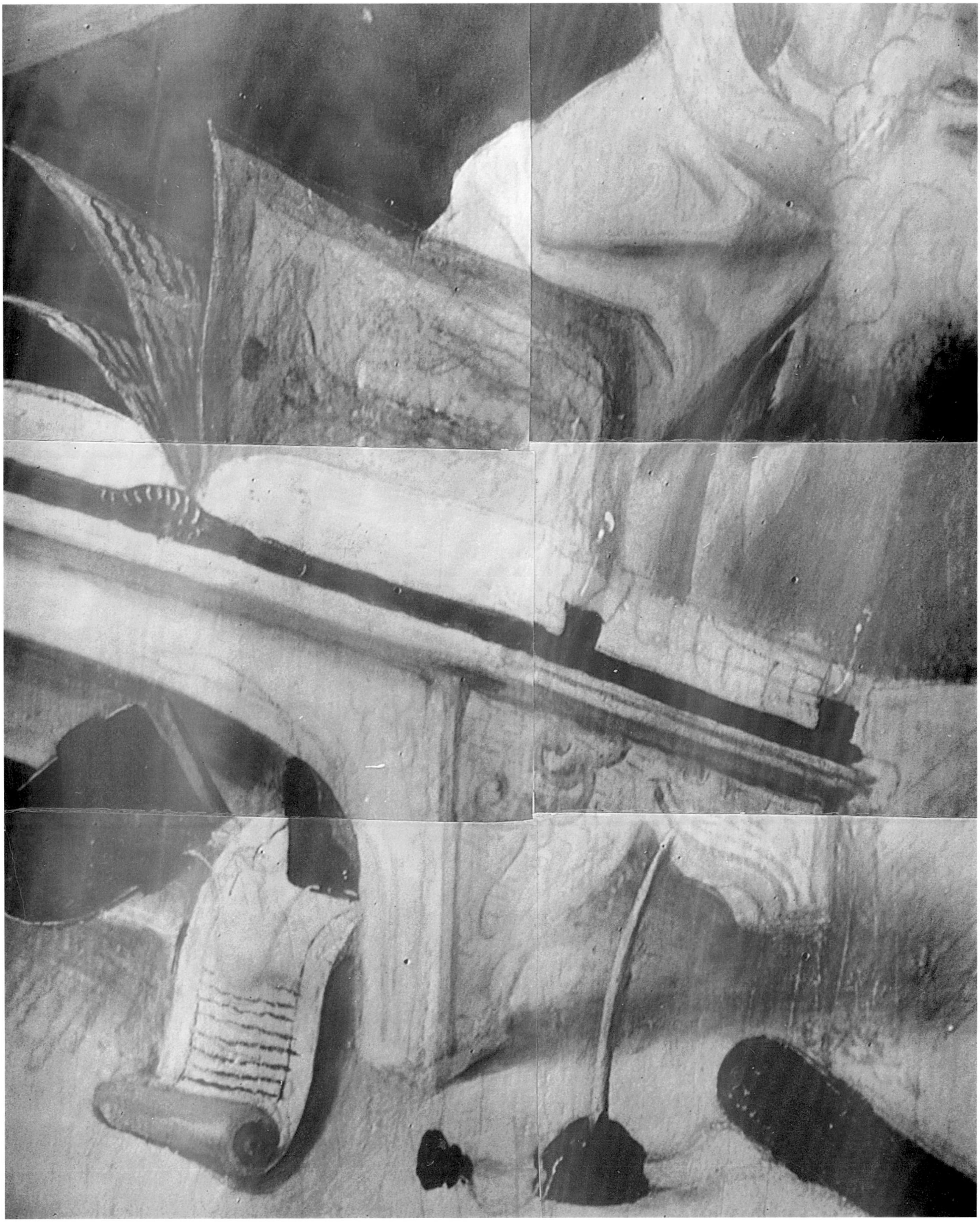

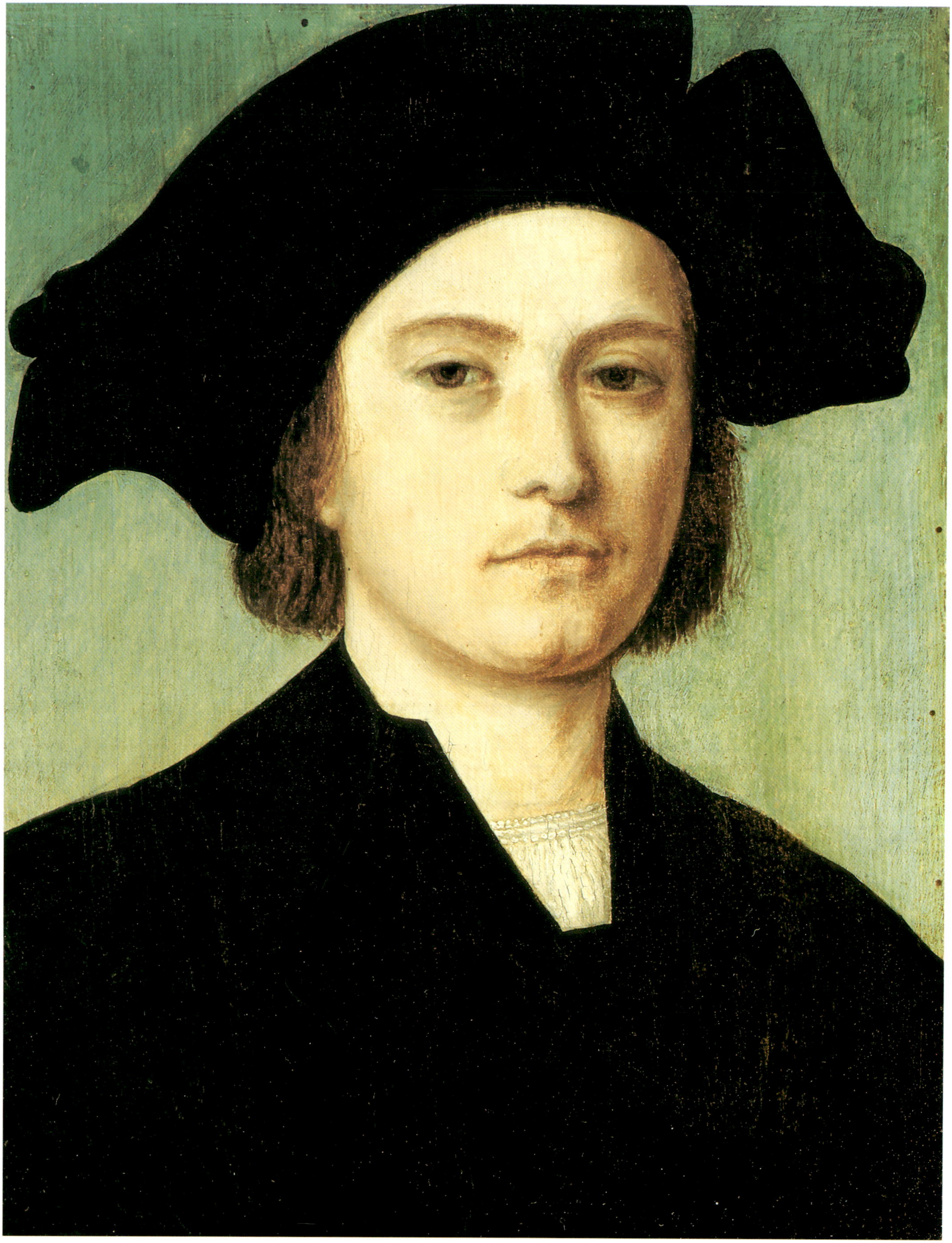

Portrait of a young man wearing a dark beret

Anonymous
South Netherlandish master
c. 1520-1530

Panel; 28.5 x 22 cm

On 12 October 1951, eight days before Van Beuningen bought this portrait, Max Friedländer wrote on the back of a photograph of the painting:[2] "This photograph shows a good, characteristic work by Joos van Cleve dating from around 1525."

In the Museum's catalogue of 1962 the panel was described as circle of Joos van Cleve. It is obvious from the relatively rough style of painting that the work is not by Van Cleve. Any resemblance to Van Cleve's portraits of men is confined to the subject's clothing. The painting was probably made by a South Netherlandish master around 1520-1530.[3]

A notable aspect of this work is the fine, fluid, underdrawing in brush (fig. a). In some parts the painting differs from the underdrawing. For example, the sitter's left eye and eyebrow were originally drawn higher, and the iris of his right eye was further to the left.
FL

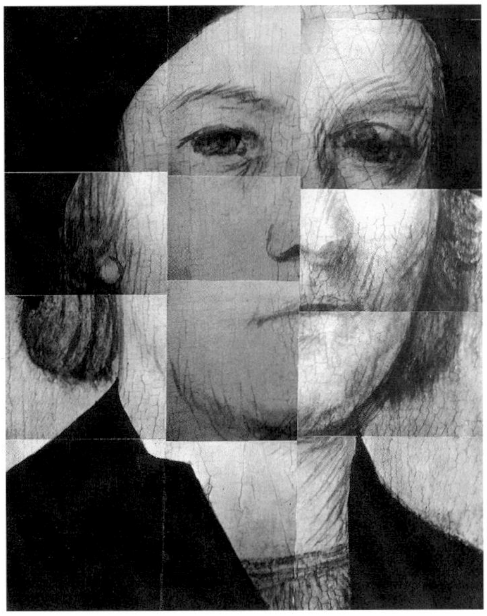

Physical characteristics: the panel consists of a single plank.

Infrared reflectography:[1] underdrawing in brush. See text.

Provenance: private collection, Paris; Borghouts Gallery; purchased from the gallery by D.G. van Beuningen, Rotterdam and Vierhouten, for 10,000 guilders in 1951; acquired by the Museum with the Van Beuningen collection in 1958; inv. no. 2445.

Exhibitions: *Chefs-d'œuvre de la collection D.G. van Beuningen*, Paris, Petit Palais, 1952, no. 45

Literature: Cat. 1962, p. 39.

1 The panel was scanned and recorded on 12 December 1993 and 17 January 1994 by J.R.J. van Asperen de Boer. The infrared reflectogram assembly was made by Joris Dik. Infrared reflectograms: AB 1555/14A-26A.
2 "Umstehend photographiertes Bild ist ein gutes charakteristisches Werk von Joos van Cleve aus der Zeit um 1525". The photograph is in the Museum's file on the painting.
3 A *Portrait of a young man* in the John G. Johnson Collection, Philadelphia, cat. no. 375, bears some resemblance to the Boymans-van Beuningen portrait. Letter from S. Elliston Weiner to the Museum, 9 December 1985.

a. Infrared reflectogram assembly

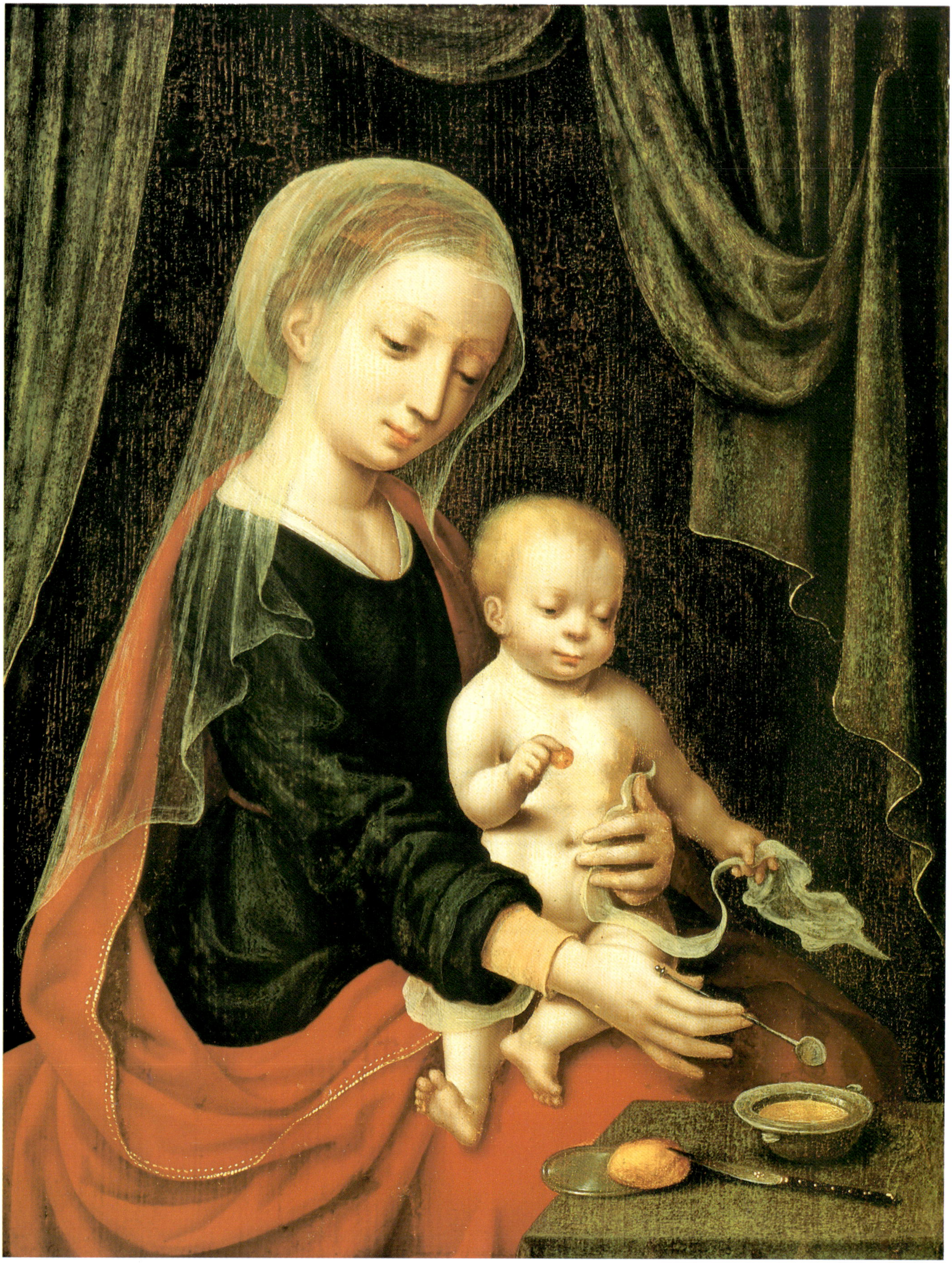

The Virgin feeding the Child from a pewter dish

Anonymous
South Netherlandish master, Bruges?
c. 1520-1530

Panel; 43 x 32.5 cm

Physical characteristics:[1]
the panel consists of a single plank.

Infrared reflectography: detailed black chalk underdrawing of the entire composition. See entry.

Paint samples: the original colour of the curtain was green. Its present brown tone results from discoloration of the pigment, copper resinate.

Provenance: estate of F.J.O. Boymans, Utrecht, 1847; inv.no. 1504.

Not previously exhibited.

Literature: *Catalogue d'un magnifique cabinet de tableaux [...] Le tout depuis nombre d'années rassemblé par monsieur F.J.O. Boymans*, 1811, no. 72 (catalogue for an auction which was cancelled); *Catalogus van schilderijen enz. in het Museum te Rotterdam*, 1849, no. 365; *Verslag omtrent den toestand en de aanwinsten van het Museum Boymans over het jaar 1887*, p. 6; *Verslag omtrent den toestand en de aanwinsten van het Museum Boijmans over het jaar 1906*, p. 21; Friedländer, IX, 1931, pp. 67, 68; cat. 1962, p. 160; Friedländer, IX, 1972, p. 44, fig. 78 B.

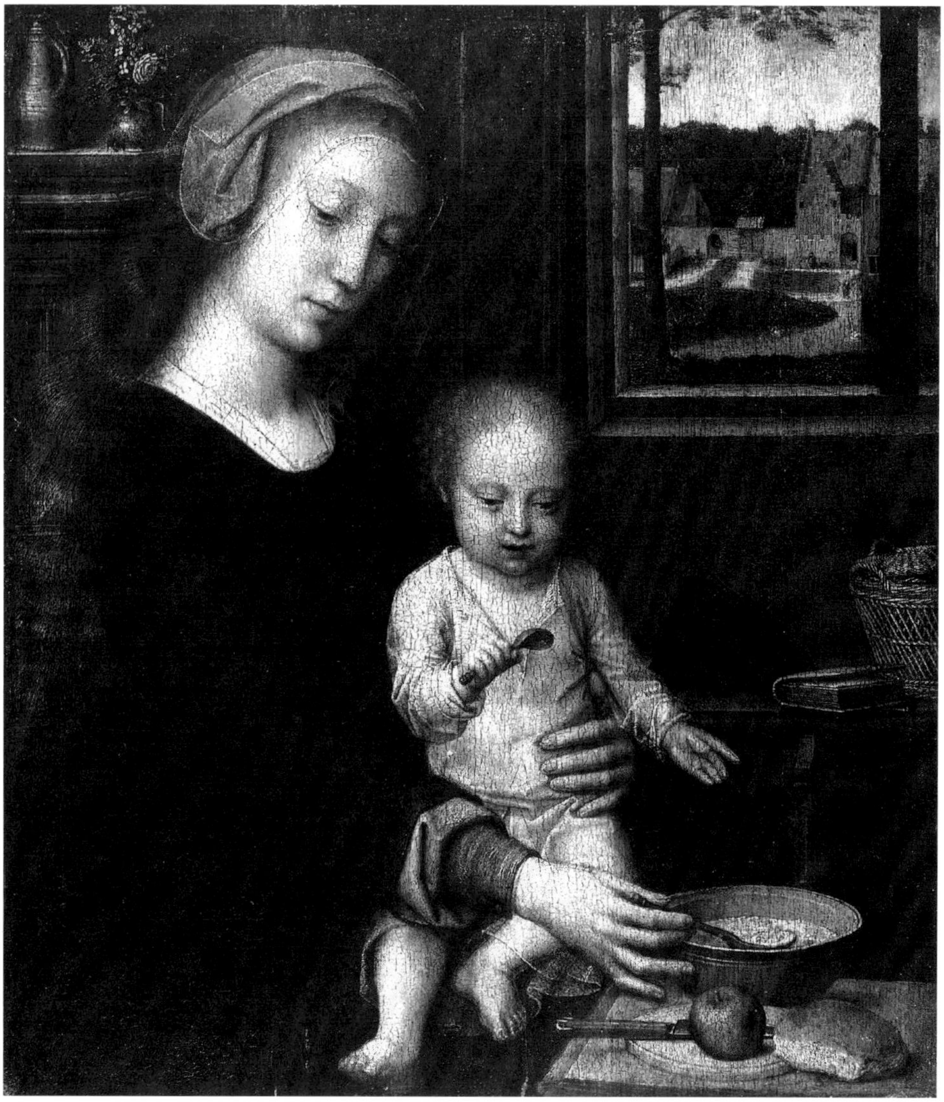

a. Gerard David, *Virgin with pap spoon*. Panel; 35 x 29 cm., Brussels, Koninklijke Musea voor Schone Kunsten, inv. no. 3559

"Raphael (d'Urbino) [...] La Madonne, tenant l'enfant nud sur son giron; ce tableau est admirable sous tous les rapports; l'on sait, a quel point sont rares les productions de ce célèbre auteur, qui a rallié un stile nöble, un port gracieux; une belle couleur, et un dessin correct." (Raphael (of Urbino)..... The Madonna holds the nude child on her lap; this painting is admirable in every way; we know how few are now the works of this celebrated artist, combining a noble style, graceful composition, beautiful colour and sound execution). This is the description of the panel in the catalogue for the auction of the Boymans Collection in 1811. By 1849, when the Museum issued its first catalogue, the painting had been down-graded to the level of an anonymous Italian master. In the 1887 annual report it was associated with the Master of the Death of the Virgin, who was later identified as Joos van Cleve. In 1906 Haverkorn van Rijsewijk observed that the subject was similar to the work of Gerard David, and in point of colour to that of Adriaen Ysenbrant.[2]

The panel can in fact be traced back to Gerard David's *Virgin with pap spoon* (fig. a). The best-known example of this composition, probably dating from 1510-1515,[3] is in the Koninklijke Musea voor Schone Kunsten, Brussels.

The painter of the Rotterdam panel made an almost identical copy of the two figures, but replaced David's handsome interior with a background landscape vista by a plain background adorned only with a curtain. The still life on the table with the pap dish, knife, bread and plate was arranged differently by the anonymous master.

The underdrawing is highly detailed, and was generally adhered to in the painting, though with a few minor exceptions. The spoon was originally longer, the Virgin's ear was more to the right, and the knife, bread and plate were all painted slightly differently (fig. b). Nor was the curtain on the left in the underdrawing.

After David's death many works painted in Bruges were directly influenced by his compositions. Examples are the paintings known collectively by the name of Ysenbrant. The quality of the present work is however not such as to be associated with this group. It was probably painted in Bruges around 1520-1530, but it could also have been painted in Antwerp, where David's work was equally popular. For instance, Quinten Massys was influenced about that time by David's theme of the Virgin with a pap bowl.[4] In Friedländer's view, the work should be attributed to an imitator of Joos van Cleve, whose influence is clearly perceptible in the Virgin's face.[5] A virtual replica of the Rotterdam panel, possibly painted by the same artist, was in the Cassirer Gallery, Amsterdam, in 1938 (fig. c).[6]
FL

1 Scientific examination conducted by Liesbeth Meilink under the supervision of J.R.J. van Asperen de Boer. Paint samples A 378/1-5. Infrared reflectograms: AB 1550/22-1555/22.

2 *Verslag omtrent den toestand [...] over het jaar 1906*. It is likely that the author reached these conclusions through Friedländer. In any case reference is made to this great art historian in the Museum's 1907 catalogue, *Beknopte catalogus der Schilderijen en beeldhouwwerken van het Museum te Rotterdam*, 1907, no. 315.

3 On the various versions of the painting, see H.J. van Miegroet, *Gerard David*, Antwerp 1989, no. 33. That in the former Von Panwitz Collection bears the closest resemblance to the Rotterdam panel. In contrast to the others, the Child is holding not a spoon but a bunch of cherries.

4 See cat. no. 35.

5 Friedländer (1931 and 1972).

6 It was auctioned in Cologne by J.M. Heberle on 23 November 1903 as a work of Barend van Orley (no. 101). In 1907 it was auctioned in Paris by Sedelmeyer as "école Flamande, XVIe siècle" (3-5 June 1907, no. 218, C.H. Sedelmeyer Collection). In 1903 the dimensions were listed as 44 x 30 cm; in 1907 as 40 x 28 cm. A photograph in the Museum's file shows the painting to have been in the possession of the Cassirer Gallery in 1938.

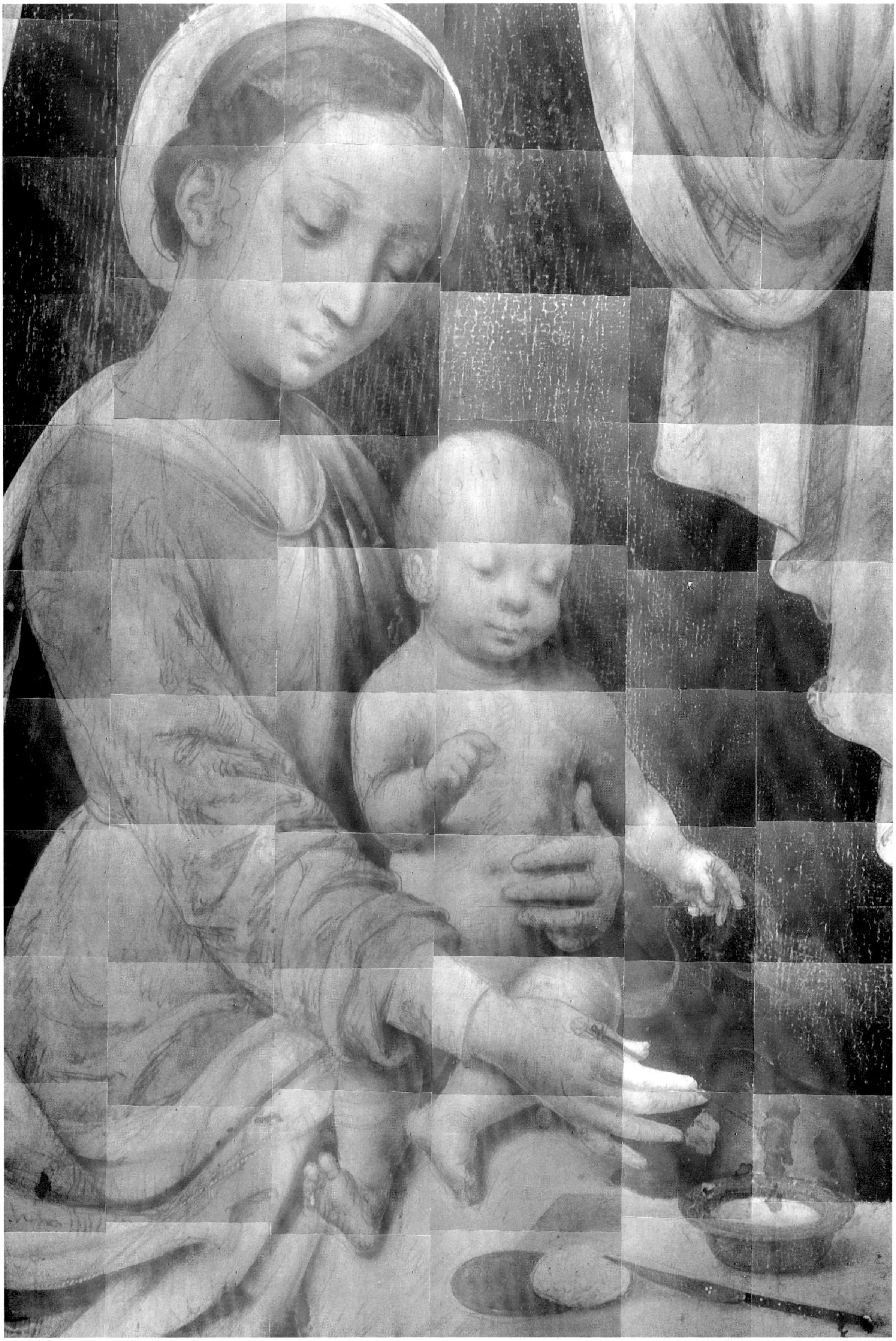

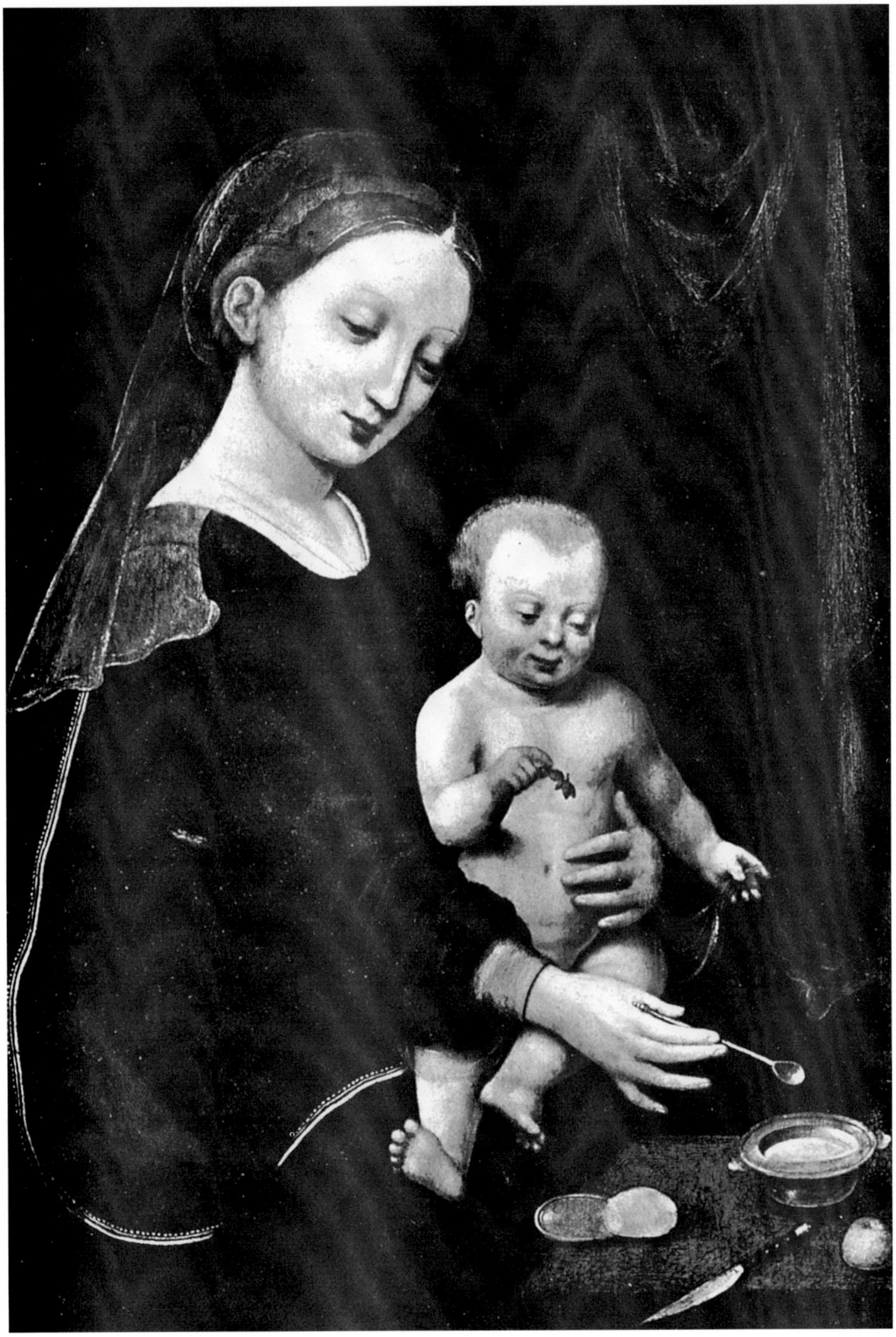

b. Infrared reflectogram assembly

c. Anonymous master, *The Virgin feeding the Child from a pewter dish*. Panel. Formerly at the Cassirer Gallery, Amsterdam (1938)

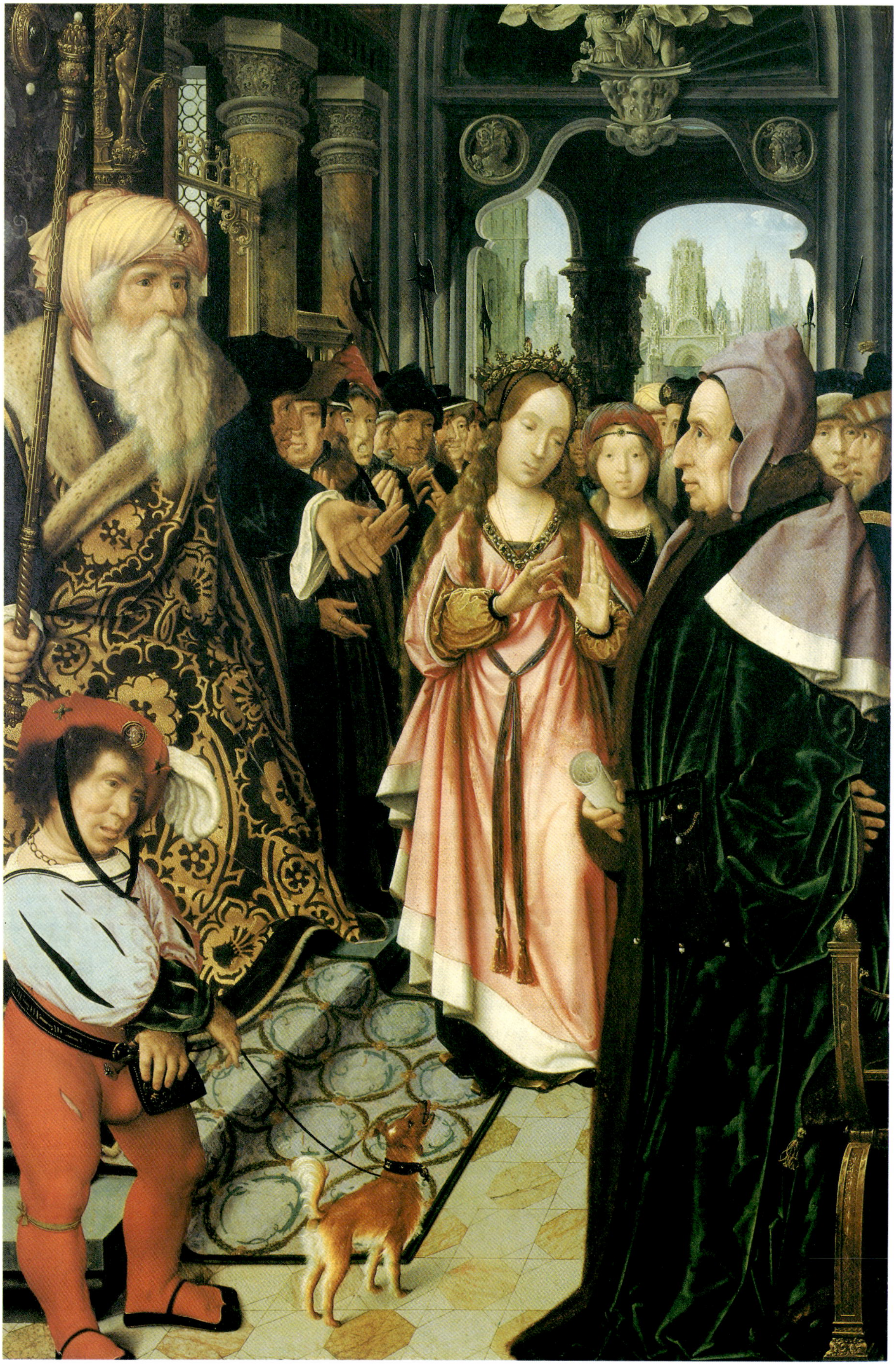

The dispute of St Catherine of Alexandria
Reverse: St Catherine of Alexandria (in grisaille)

Jan Provoost
(Bergen, Henegouwen c. 1465-Bruges 1529)

Panel; 105.2 x 70.2 cm

Physical characteristics:[1] the panel consists of three vertical planks joined with dowel pins. The raised *barbe* can be seen along the lower edge and sides. The upper edge must have been trimmed by 10-20 cm. The reverse, with a grisaille of St Catherine, is badly damaged. The paint is missing down to the ground in various places, exposing the underdrawing.

Infrared reflectography (figs. a, b): the entire picture has an extensive underdrawing in a dry medium, probably black chalk (see entry).

Paint samples: the underdrawing was made directly on the ground. A white intermediate layer was painted over the underdrawing, and layers of paint then applied to it were built up from light to dark. Analysis of the paint samples has identified the pigments azurite, copper resinate green and lapis lazuli.

X-radiographs: rather than being included in the underdrawing, the horizontal lines in the floor were prepared by means of incisions.

Provenance: Brunner Gallery, Paris 1911; J.J.L. Laverge Collection, Rotterdam 1917; acquired by the Museum in 1918, with the personal support of 22 Rotterdam citizens; inv. no. 1682.

Exhibitions: *Nederlandsche kunst van de XVde en XVIde eeuw*, The Hague, Koninklijk Kabinet van Schilderijen Mauritshuis, 1945, no. 80; *De Jerome Bosch à Rembrandt, Peintures et dessins du Musée Boymans de Rotterdam*, Dijon, Musée de Dijon, 1950, no. 13; *Keizer Karel en zijn tijd*, Ghent, Museum voor Schone Kunsten, 1955, no. 108; *De eeuw van Bruegel, De schilderkunst in België in de 16de eeuw*, Brussels, Koninklijke Musea voor Schone Kunsten, 1963, no. 208, fig. 19.

Literatuur: F. Schmidt-Degener, *Nieuwe Rotterdamse Courant*, 14 July 1918; "Het Dispuut der Heilige Katharina", *De Amsterdammer*, 27 July 1918; Plasschaert, "In het Boymans-Museum te Rotterdam; Het Dispuut van Sinte Catharina, door Jan Provoost", *De Amsterdammer*, 3 August 1918; F. Schmidt-Degener, *Verslag omtrent den toestand en de aanwinsten van het Museum Boijmans over het jaar 1918*, pp. 2-8; Idem, *Oude Kunst* IV (1919) (1), pp. 285-289, fig.; Idem, "Jan Provost und seine Disputation der Hl. Catharina", *Zeitschrift für Bildende Kunst* LIV (1919) (2), pp. 68-72, fig.; M.J. Friedländer, *Von Eyck bis Bruegel*, Berlin 1921, p. 121; J. Held, *Dürers Wirkung auf die niederländische Kunst seiner Zeit*, 1931, pp. 78-79; Friedländer IX, 1931, pp. 81-82; K. Smits, *Iconografie van de Nederlandse primitieven*, Amsterdam 1933, p. 194; G. Knuttel, *De Nederlandse schilderkunst*, Amsterdam 1938, pp. 123-124, fig. 115; M.H. Gans, *Juwelen en mensen*, Amsterdam 1961, pp. 33-34; cat. 1962, p. 107; S. Speth-Holterhoff, "Trois panneaux de Jean Provost", *Bulletin Musées Royaux de Belgique* XIV (1965), pp. 15-26; L. van Puyvelde, *La Peinture Flamande des Van Eyck à Metsys*, Brussels 1968, p. 222; G. von der Osten en H. Vey, *Painting and Sculpture in Germany and the Netherlands: 1500-1600*, Harmondsworth 1969, pp. 142-143; Friedländer IXb, 1973, pp. 87-88, fig. 156; G. von der Osten, *Deutsche und Niederländische Kunst der Reformationszeit*, Cologne 1973, p. 140, fig. p. 12.

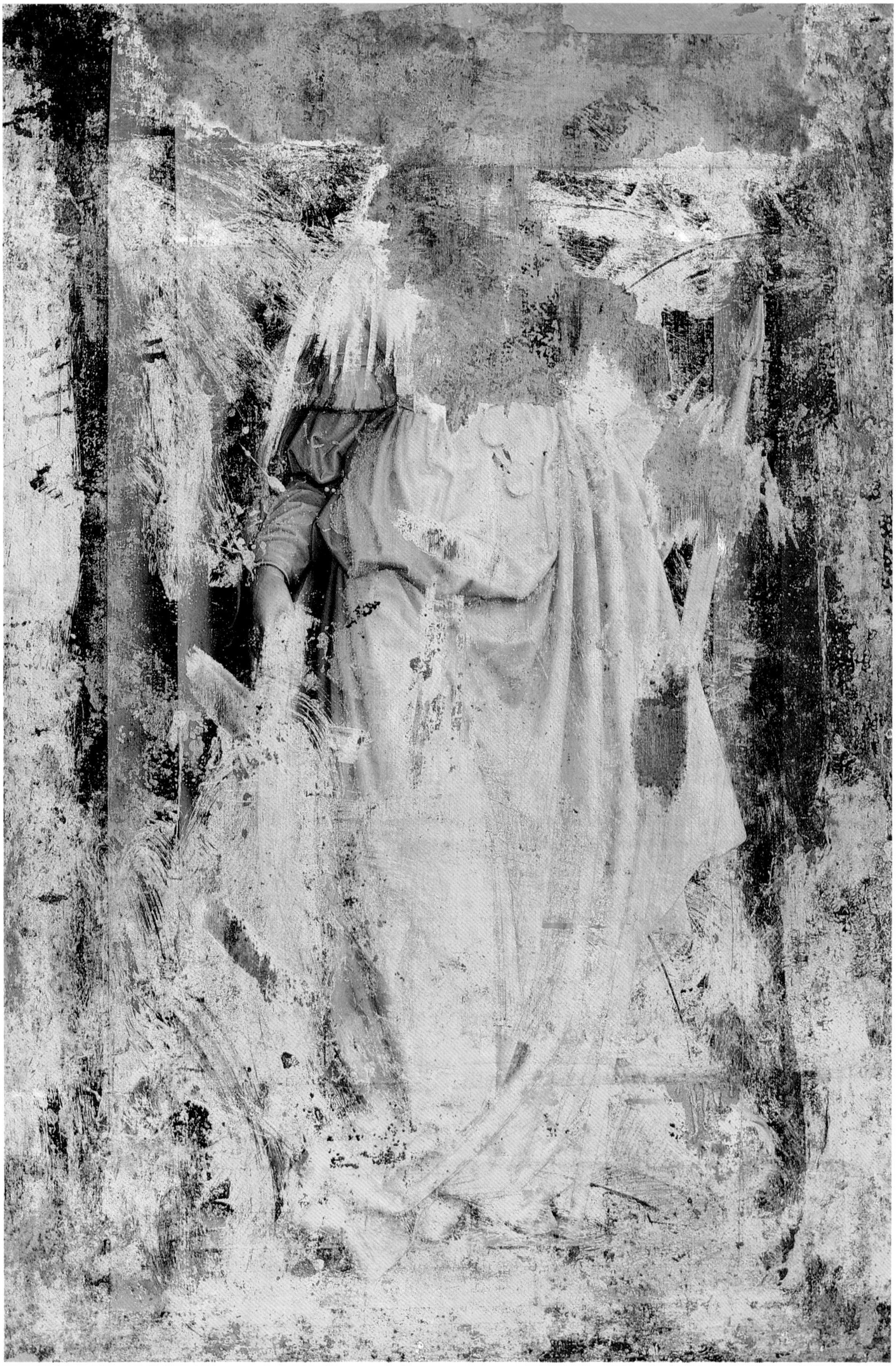

Jan Provoost's portrayal of *The dispute of St Catherine of Alexandria* is faithful to the text of the *Legenda Aurea.*[2] Princess Catherine, who lived at the beginning of the fourth century, tried to convert the heathen Emperor Maximinus to the Christian faith.[3] The Emperor could not match the skilful reasoning presented by Catherine, who had been educated in the liberal arts since early childhood, and enlisted the help of fifty philosophers. Catherine was assisted in the ensuing debate by the archangel Michael, standing behind her disguised as a girl, and had a suitable response to every argument that was put to her. She was, in fact, so convincing that the philosophers converted to Christianity. Despite Catherine's religious fervour, the Emperor fell in love with her. But she refused him, because she had regarded herself as the bride of Christ ever since beholding her own marriage to the Christ Child in a vision.

The Emperor eventually condemned Catherine to death by torture on a wheel studded with sharp blades. The fifty philosophers, for their part, were sentenced to die at the stake.

In the Rotterdam painting, Provoost shows St Catherine and a number of philosophers in debate, counting off the arguments on their fingers. The artist seems to have depicted the moment at which the Emperor puts an end to the debate and delivers his verdict.

The dispute of St Catherine of Alexandria, with the *St Catherine* in grisaille on the reverse, was originally the left wing of a triptych. The right wing of the altarpiece was formed by *The beheading of St Catherine of Alexandria*, with *St Barbara* in grisaille on the reverse, which is now in Antwerp (fig. c).[4]

The panels are exactly the same breadth and are unmistakeably by the same artist. Although St Catherine's clothing is identical, a large part of her face on the Rotterdam panel is not original. It must have been reconstructed in 1912 and, as a result, differs significantly from the face on the Antwerp panel. They would originally have corresponded.

A problem in attempting to reconstruct the triptych is that there are few examples of panels depicting the dispute of St Catherine.[5] Iconographically, the most obvious subject for the centre panel would appear to be the mystic marriage of St Catherine of Alexandria. Such a work is not, however, known within Provoost's circle.[6] Since the dispute is such a rare theme, Provoost could not have referred to earlier examples of it, but would have made use of imagery based on other subjects.

The artist seems to have found inspiration for the overall composition in a woodcut by Albrecht Dürer, *The torture of John the Evangelist* (fig. d).[7] Another possible source for Provoost was Quinten Massys's *Salome presenting the head of John the Baptist to her Father.*[8]

The Rotterdam painting has a comprehensive and accurate underdrawing (figs. a, b), which was, on the whole, closely followed during painting. A significant change to the philosopher on the right is, however, apparent (fig. b). In the underdrawing, his cloak is open and two legs have been sketched. It is not clear whether a single leg was drawn and then redrawn in a new position, or whether both legs were drawn separately.

The style of the underdrawing is characterised by extensive use of double lines and tube-shaped folds, and by carefully sketched shadows, volumes and materials, as is the case with the Antwerp panel. Although the underdrawing on the *Entombment* in Frankfurt is also very similar, its attribution to Provoost has recently been rejected, in favour of an anonymous artist from Antwerp.[9] Nevertheless, in view of the similarities between the

1 The scientific examination was carried out by R. Spronk under the supervision of J.R.J. van Asperen de Boer. For a full account, see R. Spronk, *Jan Provoost. Art Historical and Technical Examinations*, Groningen 1993 (unpublished master's thesis, Groningen University), pp. 65-132, cat. no. 1. A copy of this thesis is in the Museum's files. Paint samples A 328/1-8. Infrared reflectograms: AB 1205/1-AB 1212/37, AB 1215/0-5A.

2 More than a hundred different editions of F. de Voragine's popular 13th century work appeared between 1470 and 1500, in addition to many translations. See Teodor de Wyzewa's introduction to the 1939 Paris edition, p. XVIII. Around 1500 an elaborated version of the legend of St Catherine appeared, in which the saint was described as an Armenian princess. This provided Provoost with the motive for portraying St Catherine with a crown and purple robes, according to Schmidt-Degener. See F. Schmidt-Degener, "Jan Provost und seine Disputation der Hl. Catharina", in: *Zeitschrift für Bildende Kunst* LIV (1919), pp. 68-72. Schmidt-Degener states that Provoost used the 1505 or 1516 Dutch edition of the Golden Legend (the *Passionael*) printed in Antwerp. Provoost was, however, most probably French speaking; see J.M.W.H. Weale, "Jean Prévost, Peintre", *Le Beffroi* 4 (1875). Faries has found colour indications in French in the underdrawing of the *Last Judgement* in Bruges. See Molly Faries, "The Underdrawing of Jan Provoost's *Last Judgment* and Related Paintings", *Le dessin sous-jacent dans la peinture*, Colloque VII (1987), eds. Van Schoute and Verougstraete-Marcq, Louvain-la-Neuve 1989, pp. 138-144, figs. 88-91.

3 Also see cat. no. 33.

4 Jan Provoost, *The beheading of St Catherine of Alexandria* with *St Barbara* in grisaille on the reverse. Panel; 94 x 72.2 cm, trimmed at the top and bottom. Antwerp, Koninklijk Museum voor Schone Kunsten, no. 838. Schmidt-Degener described the panels as wings of the same altar piece in an article in the *Nieuwe Rotterdamse Courant*, 14 July 1918.

5 I know of only two other versions of the dispute on panel. One is a triptych by Goswyn van der Weyden, whose current ownership is unknown (see Friedländer, XI, 1974, fig. 25). The second is a small panel, without the philosophers, by an anonymous South Netherlandish master in the Philadelphia Museum, which probably forms part of an altarpiece depicting a Catherine cycle. The only other panel from this retable to have survived is in the Boymans-van Beuningen Museum (see cat. no. 33). The debate is missing from the only other Catherine cycle (for further details of this painting by the Master of the Catherine legend, see Friedländer, IV, 1926, no. 47, pl. XLV.)

6 As far as measurements are concerned, there is an *Entombment* in Frankfurt which could have formed the centre panel (transferred from panel to canvas; 114 x 157.9 cm, Frankfurt am Main, Städelsches Kunstinstitut, no. 751). The style of the underdrawing is extremely similar to those of both the Antwerp and Rotterdam panels (see below). This would, however, be unique from an iconographical point of view. Moreover, the figures in the Frankfurt painting are only shown in half length, compared to the full-length figures of the Rotterdam and Antwerp panels.

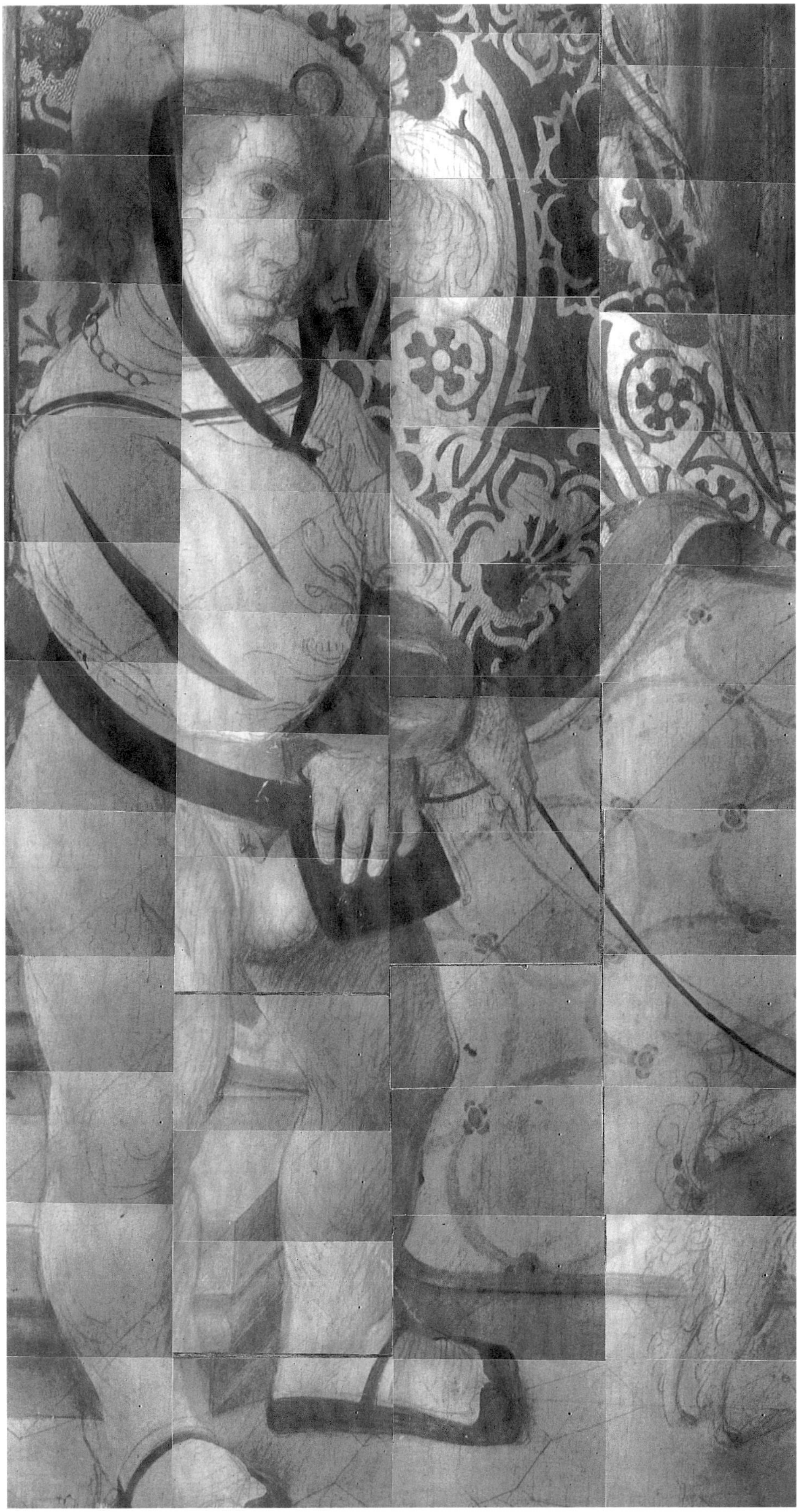

a. Infrared reflectogram assembly showing the dwarf.

underdrawings, it would seem reasonable to maintain the earlier attribution to Provoost. The underdrawing in his *Last Judgement* in Bruges has similar features to those in the paintings in Rotterdam, Antwerp and Frankfurt, both in terms of style and method,[10] and the panel in Bruges is the one painting that is, without any doubt, by the master himself.[11]

The Boymans-van Beuningen panel was probably made a few years earlier than the *Last Judgement*, which dates from 1525.
RS

[7] Albrecht Dürer, *The torture of John the Evangelist*, 1498. Woodcut from the *Apocalypse* series. 395 x 282 mm, B. 61. The possible relationship between Dürer's woodcut and *The dispute of St. Catherine of Alexandria* has been discussed by a number of authors. See Schmidt-Degener (1919) (1), Held (1931), and Friedländer (1931 and 1973).

[8] Quinten Massys, *Salome presenting the head of John the Baptist to her Father*, 1508-1511. Panel; 260 x 120 cm. Left wing of the *St John Altarpiece*, with the *Lamentation* as the centre panel, and the *Torture of John the Baptist* on the right wing. Antwerp, Museum voor Schone Kunsten, no. 246. The similarities between the compositions of Massys and Provoost are given in Friedländer (1931 and 1979). In any event, Massys himself must also have been influenced by Dürer's *Torture of John the Baptist.*

[9] J. Sander, *Niederländische Gemälde im Städel 1400-1550*, Frankfurt 1993, pp. 434-440. Any stylistic comparison with other work by Provoost is impeded by the fact that the picture was heavily overpainted in 1824.

[10] One of the features of this method of underdrawing is an extensive use of double outlines and tube-shaped folds. There is also agreement in the use of semicircles for drawing hair. The virtual absence of any form of shading in the *Last Judgement* in Bruges is no reason to suspect a different artist. It more likely indicates that the underdrawing played a different role in the painting process, perhaps providing information about the division of labour within the studio. See Faries, *op. cit.* (note 2); Spronk, *op. cit.* (note 1), pp. 44-64, 124-125.

[11] Jan Provoost, *The Last Judgement*, 1525. Panel, 145 x 169 cm. Groeningemuseum, Bruges, no. 117. Receipts from 1525 and 1526 made out to Jan Provoost have been preserved. See James Weale, "Jean Prévost, Peintre", *Le Beffroi* 4 (1875), pp. 209-211; G. Hulin de Loo, "Geschiedenis der Kunst in de Nederlanden (België en Holland), eenige Brugsche schilders van de eerste helft der XVIe eeuw", *Kunst en Leven* 1, no. 5 (1902), pp. 8-9.

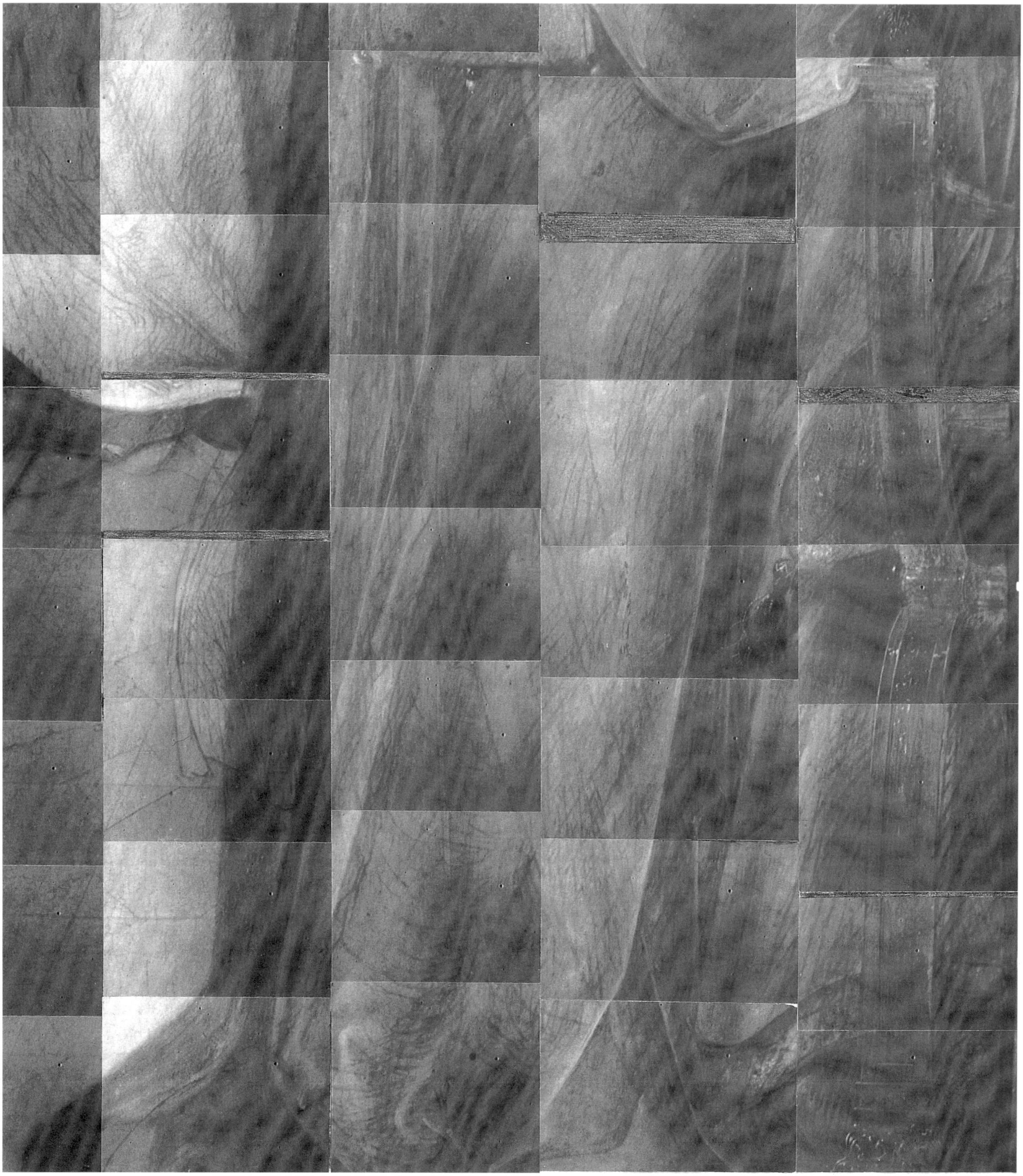

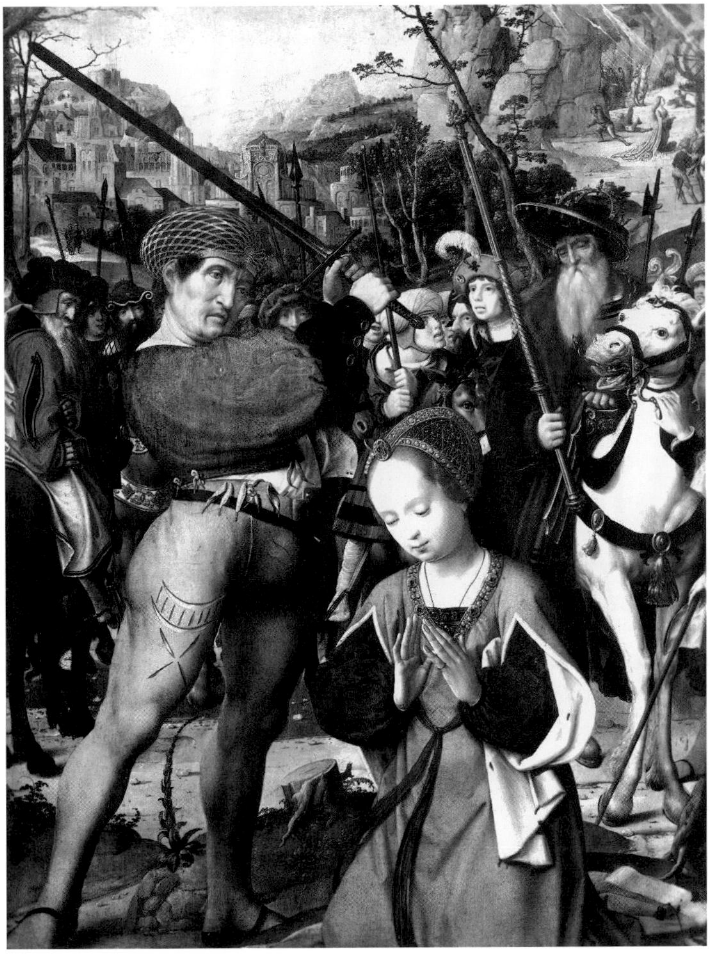

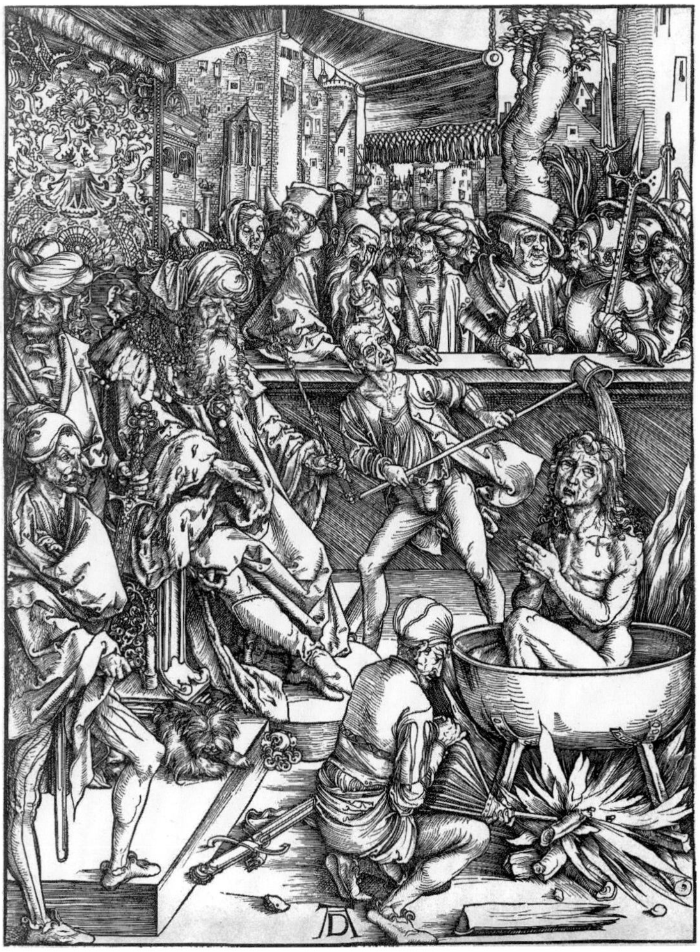

b. Infrared reflectogram assembly showing the legs of the philospher on the right.

c. Jan Provoost, The beheading of St Catherine of Alexandria
Panel; 94 x 72.2 cm
Antwerp, Koninklijk Museum voor Schone Kunsten

d. Albrecht Dürer, *The torture of John the Evangelist*
Woodcut
Amsterdam, Rijksprentenkabinet

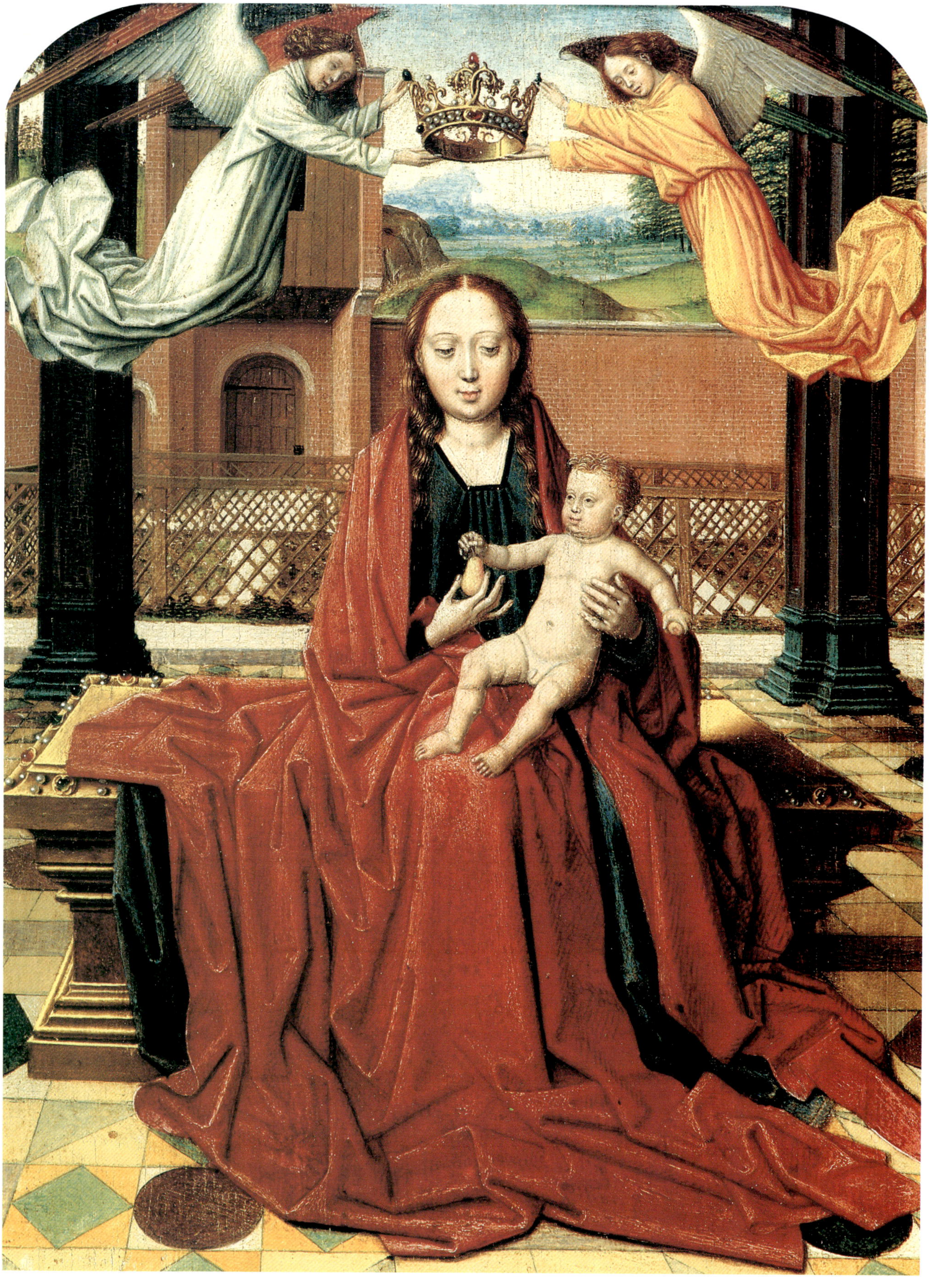

Virgin and Child in a courtyard

Anonymous
South Netherlandish master
c. 1500

Panel; 30.2 x 22.7 cm

Physical characteristics:[1] the panel consists of a single plank. The *barbe* can be seen on all four sides. The back of the panel is marbled.

Infrared reflectography: extensive underdrawing in black chalk. See entry.

Dendrochronology: the youngest heartwood growth ring dates from 1462. The panel could not have been painted before 1473; it was more probably painted in or after 1487. See articly by P. Klein.

Provenance: Convento de Serradella, Laceres/ Estramadure; bought in Spain in 1932 by D.G. van Beuningen, Rotterdam and Vierhouten, for 2,700 guilders; acquired by the Museum with the Van Beuningen Collection in 1958; inv. no. 2478.

Exhibitions: *Kersttentoonstelling*, Rotterdam, Boymans Museum, 1932, no. 12, fig. III; *Honderd jaar Museum Boymans Rotterdam. Meesterwerken uit de verzameling D.G. van Beuningen*, Rotterdam, Boymans Museum, 1949, no. 31; *Chefs-d'œuvre de la collection D.G. van Beuningen*, Paris, Petit Palais, 1952, no. 71.

Literature: Hannema, 1949, no. 31, fig. 36; cat. 1962, p. 107.

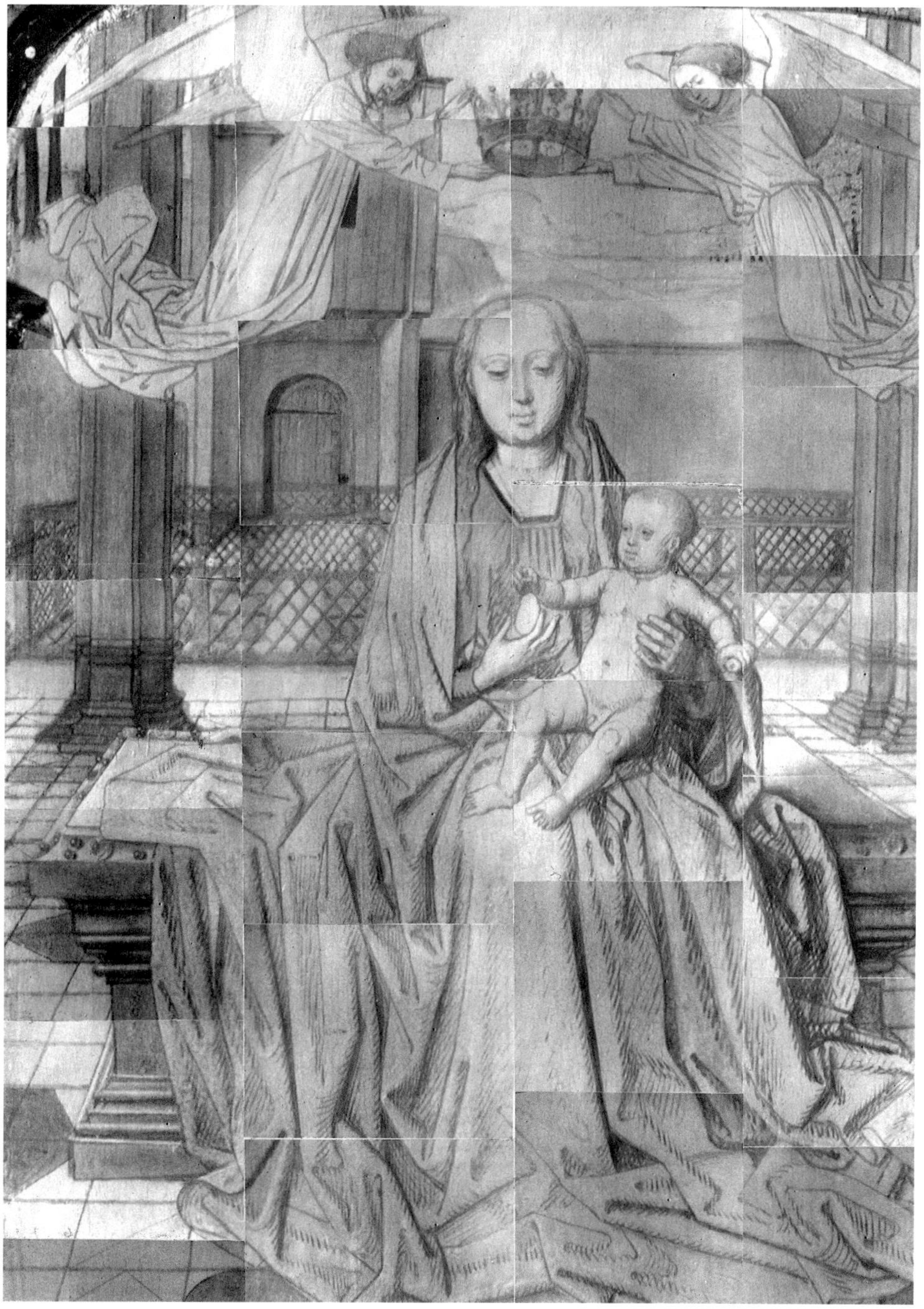

a. Infrared reflectogram assembly.

The Virgin is seated on a stone bench inlaid with precious gems in the middle of a courtyard. She is holding the infant Christ on her lap. Two angels hovering above her are about to place a crown on her head. At the far end of the courtyard is a fenced-off garden with a stone wall behind it. Beyond the wall is a stretch of open countryside. The child holds an apple in his left hand and accepts a pear from his mother with his right. The apple is the fruit of good and evil from Paradise. When held by the infant Christ it alludes to his mission as the Redeemer.[2] The reverse of the panel is painted in a marble-like pattern of black and green. It was common practice to apply a layer of paint to the back of a panel to stop the wood from working, but an alternative explanation in this case is that panel may have been part of a triptych intended as a travelling altar, or of a diptych with a private portrait as a pendant. Objects of this kind were often painted on the outside. The marbled effect would have been intended to suggest the luxury of this costly material.[3]

D.G. van Beuningen bought the panel in 1932 as a work by the painter Jan Provoost, whose oeuvre has been reconstructed on the basis of a painting in Bruges which is known from documents to have been made by the master.[4] The Rotterdam panel, however, bears no resemblance to this work, and the attribution to Provoost seems untenable. The underdrawing is stiffer and more laboured than that in other works by Provoost, where it tends to be relatively sketchy.[5] Another consideration is that the painting closely follows the drawing, although it should also be said that it is finely rendered and shows a keen eye for detail. The unfaltering underdrawing suggests that the artist may have been working after an existing composition. The painting as such is a superior work from an unidenitifed South Netherlandish studio. On the basis of its style and the findings of a dendrochronological examination it can be dated to the late fifteenth or early sixteenth century.
ED

1 Scientific examination conducted by Esther Darley in 1991 under the supervision of J.R.J. van Asperen de Boer. Paint samples A 316/1-4. Infrared reflectograms: AB 1201/7-AB 1202/15.

2 For a comprehensive study of the symbolic meaning of fruit in representations of the Virgin in early Netherlandish painting, see R.L. Falkenburg, *The fruit of devotion, mysticism and the imagery of love in Flemish paintings of the Virgin and child 1450-1550*, Amsterdam 1994.

3 A. Dülberg, *Privatporträts, Geschichte und Ikonologie einer Gattung im 15. und 16. Jahrhundert*, Berlin 1990, pp. 116-126.

4 *The Last Judgement*, Groeninge Museum, Bruges. See cat. no. 43.

5 M. Faries, "The underdrawing of Jan Provoost's *Last Judgement* and related paintings", *Le dessin sous-jacent dans la peinture. Colloque VII* (1987), eds. Van Schoute and Verougstraete-Marcq, Louvain-la-Neuve 1989, pp. 137-144; see also cat. no. 43.

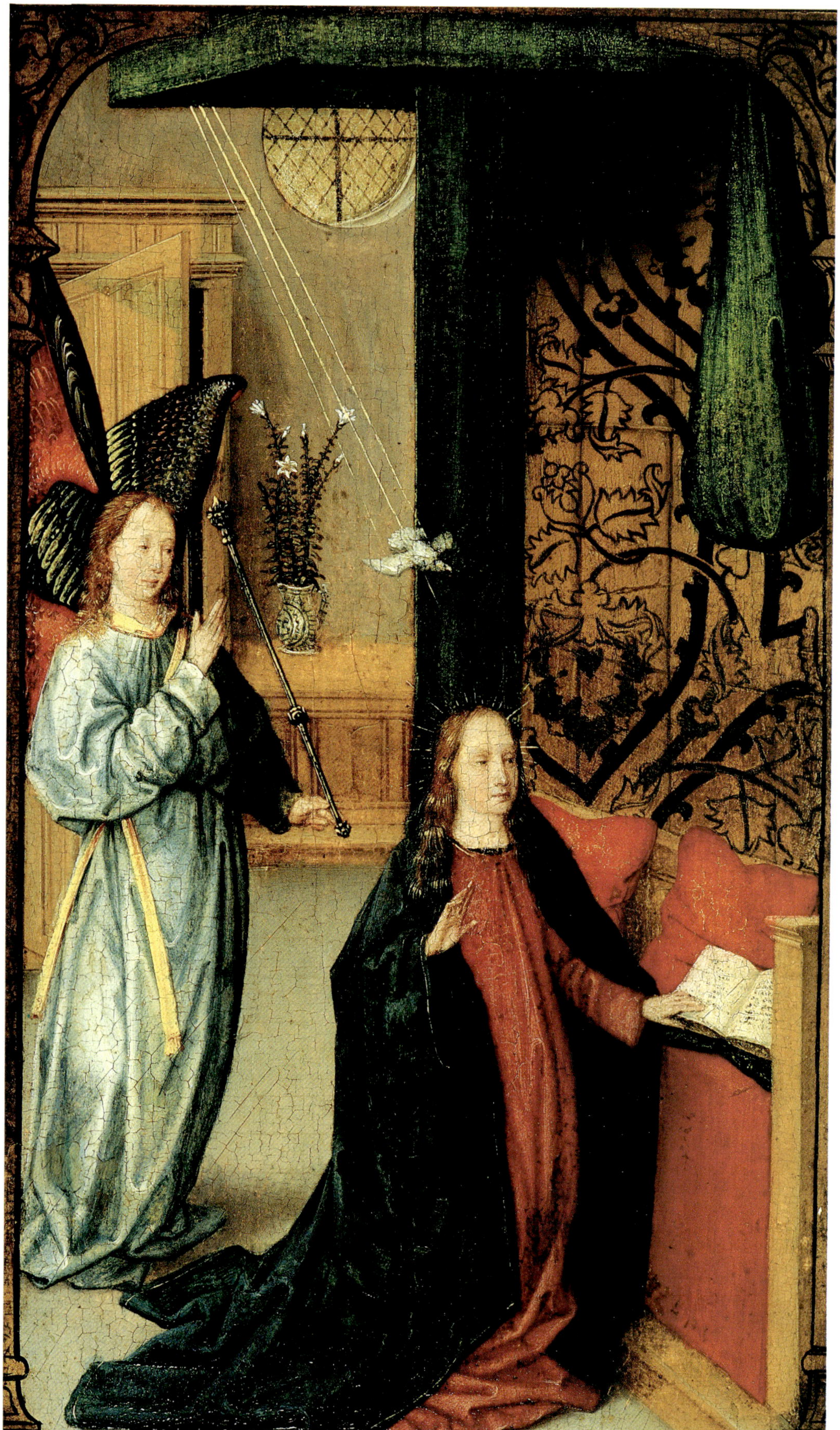

The Annunciation

Anonymous
South Netherlandish master
Late fifteenth century

Panel; 33.7 x 19.3 cm

The Virgin kneels modestly on the floor and behind her the archangel Gabriel announces that she is to give birth to the Christ Child. The moment just before the conception is depicted as the Holy Spirit in the form of a dove descends above her. The white lilies in the background symbolise her purity. The Annunciation is described in Luke (1:26-38), which tells of Gabriel's salutation and her response, but makes no mention of where this took place. This allowed artists a considerable amount of freedom in their representation of the Annunciation.[3] The Rotterdam panel shows a room midway between a living room and a bedroom. The artist has adopted Dirk Bouts' innovation of a canopied bench rather than a bed.[4]

Partly visible on each side is a black and gold column with a capital and plinth, supporting an architrave closing off the top of the painting. This framework is an important clue in reconstructing the altarpiece to which the panel originally belonged. Three other panels with such a painted framework are known, all of which portray episodes in the life of the Virgin. They are the *Birth of the Virgin* (fig. a), the *Presentation in the temple* (fig. b), and *Christ's appearance to the Virgin* (fig. c).[5]

The original form of the altarpiece to which they belonged is uncertain.[6] A possible indication is an altarpiece depicted in the *Adoration of the Sacrament* in Antwerp (fig. d).[7] It shows four painted scenes from the life of Christ, two on each side as the wings of a carved altar shrine. The frames around them are painted in gold and black. The four panels of the Virgin may have been the wings of a similar work. An argument against this hypothesis is the fact that the reverse side of the Rotterdam panel is not painted or planed down.[8]

The *Annunciation* was attributed by Friedländer in 1931 to Jan Provoost (Bergen, Henegouwen, c. 1465-Bruges 1529) on stylistic grounds. Grete Ring, who shares this view, dates the panel to between 1485 and 1495. As she perceives no Bruges influence, she believes it was painted before 1494, when Provoost took up residence in the city.[9] She discerns in the Virgin panels the influence of both illuminated manuscripts and French art, which she uses as an argument for attributing them to Jan Provoost, who studied with Simon Marmion in Valenciennes.[10] There is however insufficient reason to maintain the attribution to Provoost. There is no signed work by Provoost, and only one painting can be attributed to him with certainty.[11] A panel dating from 1525, it provides insufficient evidence for attributing earlier and stylistically different works to the same hand. Furthermore, infrared reflectograms have revealed underdrawings in 23 of the 24 works in the Provoost group examined so far.[12] This makes the Rotterdam panel the only one of the group in which no underdrawing has been found to date. Its absence complicates all further efforts to establish the identity of the artist.
RS

Physical characteristics: the panel consists of a single plank. The *barbe* can be partly seen on the lower edge.

Infrared reflectography: no underdrawing could be discerned.[1]

X-radiography: the X-radiograph shows an earlier composition with the dove more to the right. The rays on which the dove is descending and the door lintel were first incised.

Provenance: Henry Wagner Collection; auctioned at Christie's, London, 16 January 1925, no. 59; T.D. Barlow Collection, 1925; auctioned at Sotheby's, London, 20 July 1955, no. 57, sold for 850 pounds to J.L. Leverton; private collection, London, 1958; Drey Gallery, London; P. de Boer Gallery, Amsterdam; lent by the Gallery to the Boymans-van Beuningen Museum in 1960; acquired by the Museum in 1962 for 47,800 Swiss francs; inv. no. 2642.

Exhibitions: Manchester, Whitworth Art Gallery, 1947, no. 5; *Flemish Art 1300-1700*, London, Royal Academy of Arts, 1953-54, no. 49; *Meisterwerke Flämische Malerei*, Schaffhausen, Museum zu Allerheiligen, 1955, no. 76.[2]

Literature: Friedländer IX, 1931, no. 127, p. 145; D. Robb, "The Iconography of the Annunciation in the Fourteenth and Fifteenth Centuries", *Art Bulletin* 18 (1936), p. 513, note 91; Grete Ring, "Additions to the Work of Jan Provost and Quintin Massys-I", *The Burlington Magazine* 79 (1941), pp. 156-160; cat. P. de Boer Gallery, Amsterdam, summer 1961, no. 60, fig.; cat. 1962, pp. 106-107; Friedländer IXb, 1973, no. 127, p. 111, fig. 148; Robert Koch, "The Getty 'Annunciation' by Dieric Bouts", *The Burlington Magazine* 130 (1988), p. 512.

1 Scanned by M. Faries in September 1993.
2 Up to 1955 the *Annunciation* was framed together with a *Presentation in the temple* (see note 5). The two were always exhibited together. They were separated and sold separately in 1955.
3 See Robb (1936), p. 480.
4 See Koch (1988).

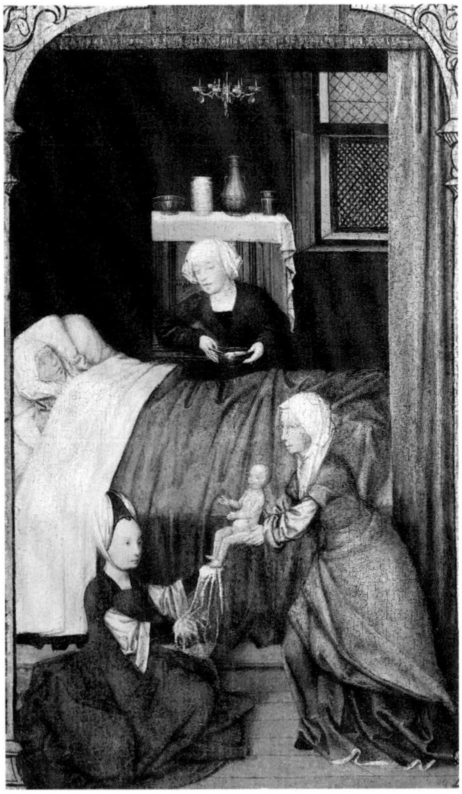

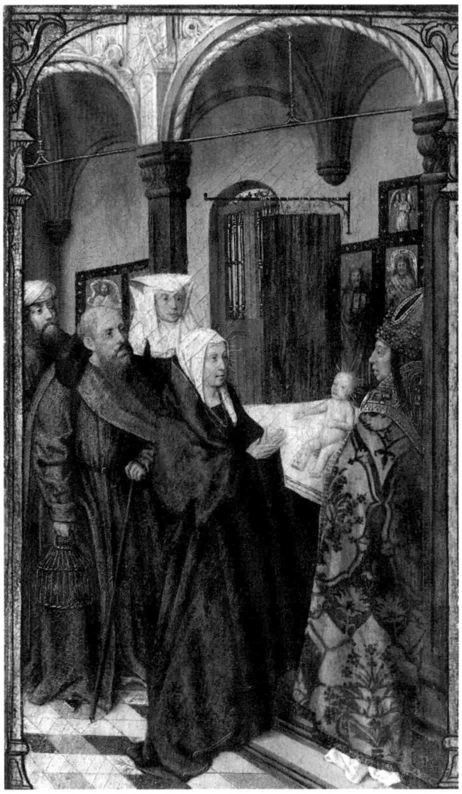

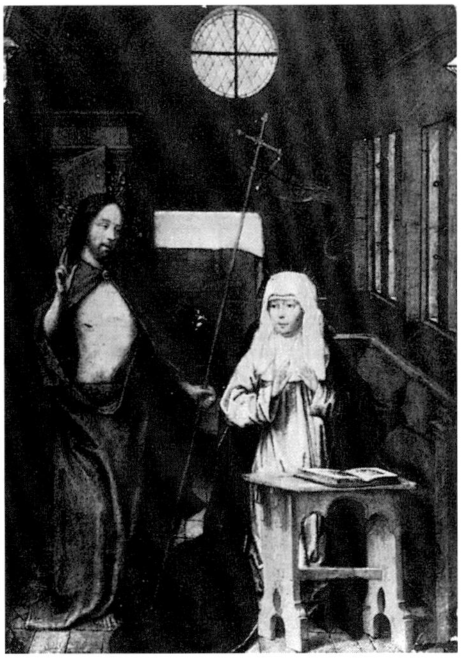

a. South Netherlandish master, Birth of the Virgin
Panel; 33 x 19 cm
Whereabouts unknown

b. South Netherlandish master, Presentation in the temple
Panel; 34 x 19 cm
Whereabouts unknown

c. South Netherlandish master, Christ's appearance to the Virgin
Panel
Whereabouts unknown

[5] *Birth of the Virgin*. Panel, 33 x 19 cm. Stolen from Boymans-van Beuningen Museum, Rotterdam, on 17 December 1960, inv. no. 2479. Its present location is unknown. *Presentation in the temple*. Panel, 34 x 19 cm. Auctioned from a private collection in Laren by Sotheby Mak van Waay, Amsterdam, on 14 March 1983. Present location unknown. *Christ's appearance to the Virgin*. Location unknown. See Friedländer IXb (1973), supp. 262, p. 125, fig. 148; add. 273a, pp. 126, 130, fig. 149; no. 127, fig. 149.

[6] According to Friedländer, there was a fourth panel, the *Birth of Christ*. See Friedländer IXb (1973), no. 127, p. 111, fig. 148. In view of its different measurements, however, and its lack of a painted framework, this is not very likely. According to Grete Ring, who first rightly associated the *Birth of the Virgin* with the series, it also included *Tobias and the angel and the adoration of Christ*. This too may be queried, given the different measurements, the absence of a painted framework and the different iconography of the representation. See Ring (1941).

[7] South Netherlandish School, *Adoration of the Sacrament*. Panel, 69 x 59 cm. Museum voor Schone Kunsten, Antwerp, inv. no. 224. See P. Vandenbroeck, *Catalogus Schilderkunst 14e-15e eeuw*, Antwerp 1985, pp. 35-38, fig. 19; Koninklijk Museum voor Schone Kunsten, *Catalogus Schilderkunst Oude Meesters*, Antwerp 1988, p. 467, fig.

[8] It is not known whether the other scenes from the life of the Virgin are painted on the reverse.

[9] Provoost became a citizen of Bruges in 1494, and probably joined the guild there between 1493 and 1498. See J.M.W.H. Weale, "Jean Prévost, Peintre," *Le Beffroi* 4 (1875), p. 205, notes 1, 2; G. Hulin de Loo, "Geschiedenis der Kunst in de Nederlanden (België en Holland), eenige Brugsche schilders van de eerste helft der XVIe eeuw," *Kunst en Leven* 1, no. 5 (1902), p. 7.

[10] Provoost married Marmion's widow, Johanna de Quarouble. See James Weale, "Early Painters of the Netherlands as illustrated by the Bruges Exhibition of 1902, Article V," *The Burlington Magazine* 2 (1903); Ring (1941), p. 159. There is no evidence of the influence of Simon Marmion in this *Annunciation*. Marmion's figures were of a different type, and in accordance with French tradition, he situated his Annunciations in a church or chapel. Moreover, Gabriel and the Virgin are always facing each other. See, for instance, the following versions of the *Annunciation* by Marmion: a Book of Hours in Turin, Museo Civico (Ms. 558, fol. 37); the Jean Rolin II Book of Hours in Madrid, Biblioteca Nacional (Ms. Res. 149, fol. 34v); the Berleymont Book of Hours in San Marino, Huntington Library; the Jean Gros Book of Hours, Chantilly, Musée Condé (Ms. 85, fol. 92v); the Book of Hours of Henry VIII in Tournai, Bibliothèque de la Ville; the Louthe Book of Hours in Louvain-la-Neuve, Université Catholique de Louvain.

[11] Proof of payments made to Jan Provoost in 1525 and 1526 for the *Last Judgement* in the Groeninge Museum, Bruges, has survived. See Weale, *op.cit.* (note 9), pp. 209-211; Hulin de Loo, *op.cit.* (note 9), pp. 8-9.

[12] An underdrawing has also been found in panels of a comparably small size. See R. Spronk, *Jan Provoost, Art Historical and Technical Examinations.* Groningen 1993 (unpublished master's thesis, Groningen University), pp. 191-196.

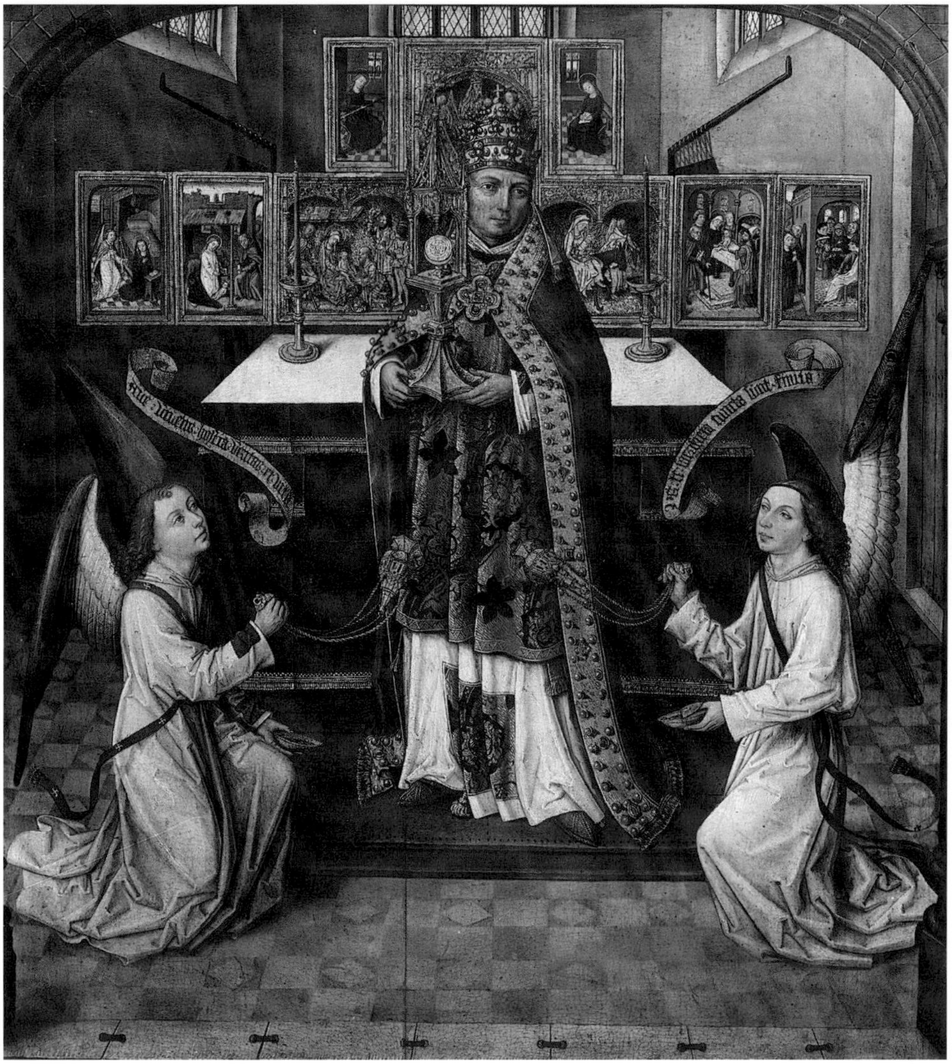

d. South Netherlandish School, Adoration of the Sacrament
Panel; 69 x 59 cm
Antwerp, Museum voor Schone Kunsten

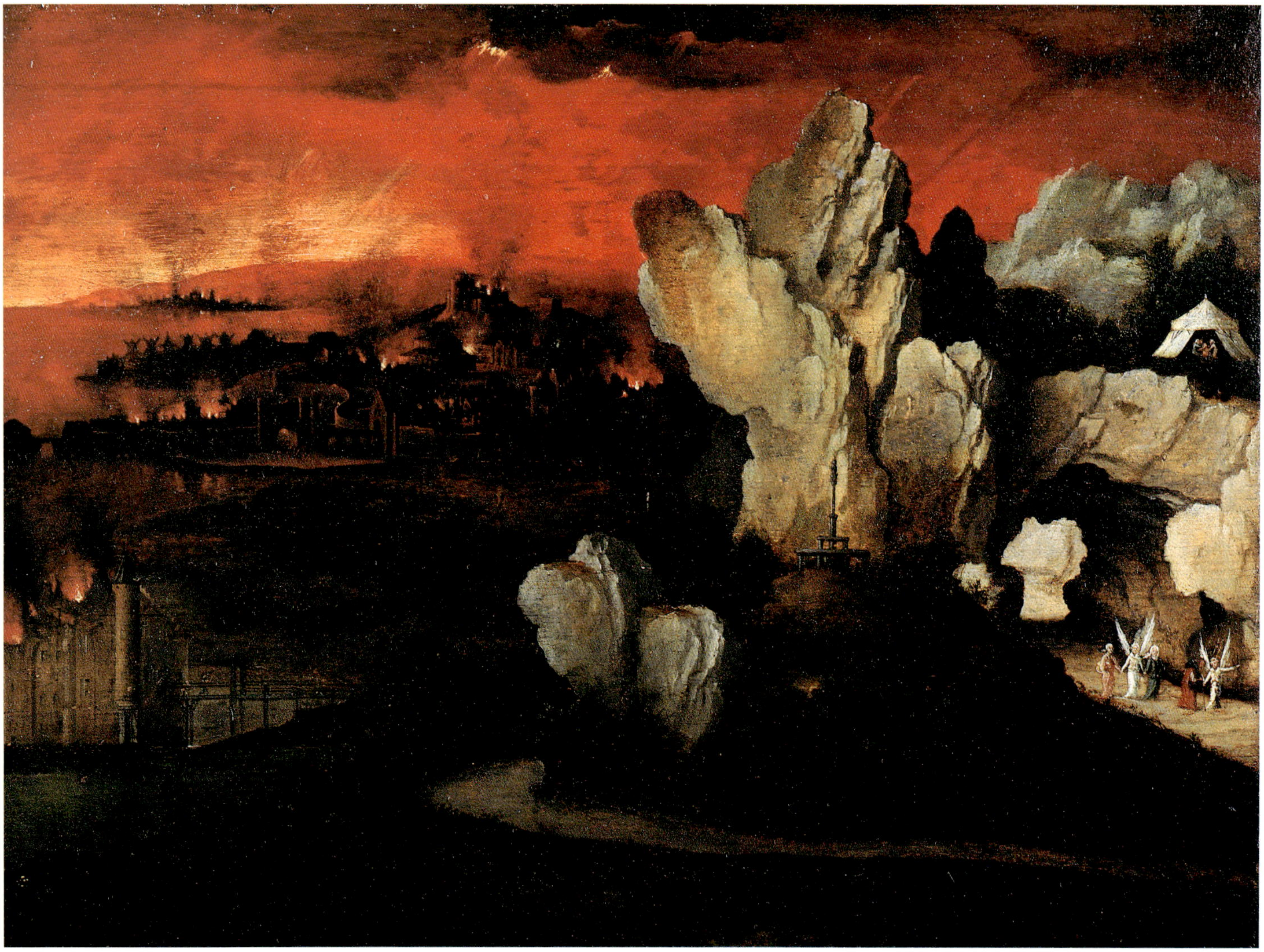

Landscape with the destruction of Sodom and Gomorrah

Joachim Patinir
(Bouvignes or Dinant c. 1480-Antwerp 1524)

Panel; 22.5 x 30 cm

Physical characteristics:[1] the panel consists of a single plank; no *barbe* along the edges.

Infrared reflectography: the partly visible underdrawing is schematic, and appears to have been executed with a fine brush. See description.

Dendrochronology: the youngest heartwood growth ring dates from 1504. The panel could not have been painted before 1515; it was more probably painted in or after 1521. See article by P. Klein.

Paint samples: the ground is probably white chalk. In the two samples taken from the upper part of the painting a black layer covers the ground, which could indicate that the sky was underpainted with black. It could also indicate a black underdrawing. The pigments identified are azurite and, possibly, vermilion and lead-tin yellow.

Provenance: for the possible early provenance, see description; P. de Boer Gallery, Amsterdam; bought as anonymous for 800 guilders by D.A. Hoogendijk Gallery, Amsterdam, in 1925; Ch. A. Burlet Gallery, Berlin, 1927; F. Koenigs, Haarlem; on loan to Boymans Museum, Rotterdam, from 1935 to 1940; Netherlands Office for Fine Arts, The Hague, inv. no. N.K. 2670; on loan to the Museum since 1948; inv. no. 2312.

Exhibitions: *Verzameling F. Koenigs, schilderijen*, Rotterdam, Boymans Museum, 1935, no. 16, fig. X; *Herwonnen Kunstbezit*, The Hague, Mauritshuis, 1946, no. 8; *Herwonnen Kunstbezit*, Utrecht, Centraal Museum, 1946, no. 22; *De Jerome Bosch à Rembrandt*, Dijon, Musée de Dijon, 1950, no. 11; *Europees Humanisme*, Brussels, Paleis voor Schone Kunsten, 1954-55, no. 55; *Scaldis*, Antwerp, Stedelijke Feestzaal en Provinciaal Veiligheidsinstituut, 1956, no. 545; *De eeuw van Bruegel. De schilderkunst in België in de 16de eeuw*, Brussels, Koninklijke Musea voor Schone Kunsten van België, 1963, no. 188, fig. 48; *Albrecht Dürer in de Nederlanden*, Brussels, Paleis voor Schone Kunsten, 1977, no. 192, fig.

Literature: L. Baldass, "Ein Landschaftsbild von Matthys Cock", *Zeitschrift für Bildende Kunst* 61 (1927-28), pp. 92, 94, fig.; Friedländer, IX, 1931, p. 156, no. 219; G.J. Hoogewerff, "Matthijs Wellens de Cock en Hans Dooven Keynoogh", *Mededeelingen van het Nederlandsch Historisch Instituut te Rome*, 2nd series V (1935), p. 52, note 1; Friedländer, XIV, 1937, p. 119; *Verslag omtrent de toestand en de aanwinsten van het Museum Boijmans over het jaar 1948*, p. 5; A.B. de Vries, "Joachim Patinier (ca. 1480 - 1524), Landschap met de brand van Sodom en Gomorrha", *Openbaar Kunstbezit* 2 (1958), no. 5, fig.; cat. 1962, p. 101; *Paintings in the Ashmolean Museum. Illustrated catalogue*, 1962, with no. 320; P. Philippot, "Réflexions sur l'exposition, 'Le siècle de Brueghel, la peinture en Belgique au XVIe siècle'", *Gazette des Beaux-Arts* 63 (1964), p. 55; A. Barret, "Patinir", *Connaissance des Arts* 190 (1967), p. 102, fig.; G.T. Faggin, *La pittura ad Anversa nel cinquecento*, Florence 1968, p. 28, fig. 30; R.A. Koch, *Joachim Patinir*, Princeton, New Jersey 1968, pp. 12, 15, 16, 18, 22, 23, 24, 45, no. 3, fig. 2; H.G. Franz, *Niederländische Landschaftsmalerei im Zeitalter des Manierismus*, Graz 1969, pp. 33, 34, fig. 8; Friedländer, IX, 1973, no. 219, fig. 221; M. Pons en A. Barret, *Patinir ou l'Harmonie du Monde*, Paris 1980, pp. 53, 121, fig.; G. Unverfehrt, *Hieronymus Bosch. Die Rezeption seiner kunst im frühen 16. Jahrhundert*, Berlin 1980, pp. 178, 179; O. Bätschmann, "Lot und seine Töchter im Louvre", *Städel-Jahrbuch* 8 (1981), pp. 164, 174, fig. 3; R.L. Falkenburg, *Joachim Patinir. Landscape as an image of the pilgrimage of life*, Amsterdam-Philadelphia 1988, pp. 6, 55, 65, 106, fig. 4; W.S. Gibson, *'Mirror of the earth'. The world landscape in sixteenth-century Flemish painting*, Princeton, New Jersey 1989, pp. 5, 6, 7; J.C. Smith, "Netherlandish artists and art in Renaissance Nuremberg", *Simiolus* 20 (1990-91), p. 165, fig. 22; H. Stangerup, *Joachim Patinir*, Paris 1992, pp. 72, 75.; *Old Master Paintings. An illustrated summary catalogue. Rijksdienst Beeldende Kunst*, Zwolle - The Hague, no. 2045, p. 237, fig.

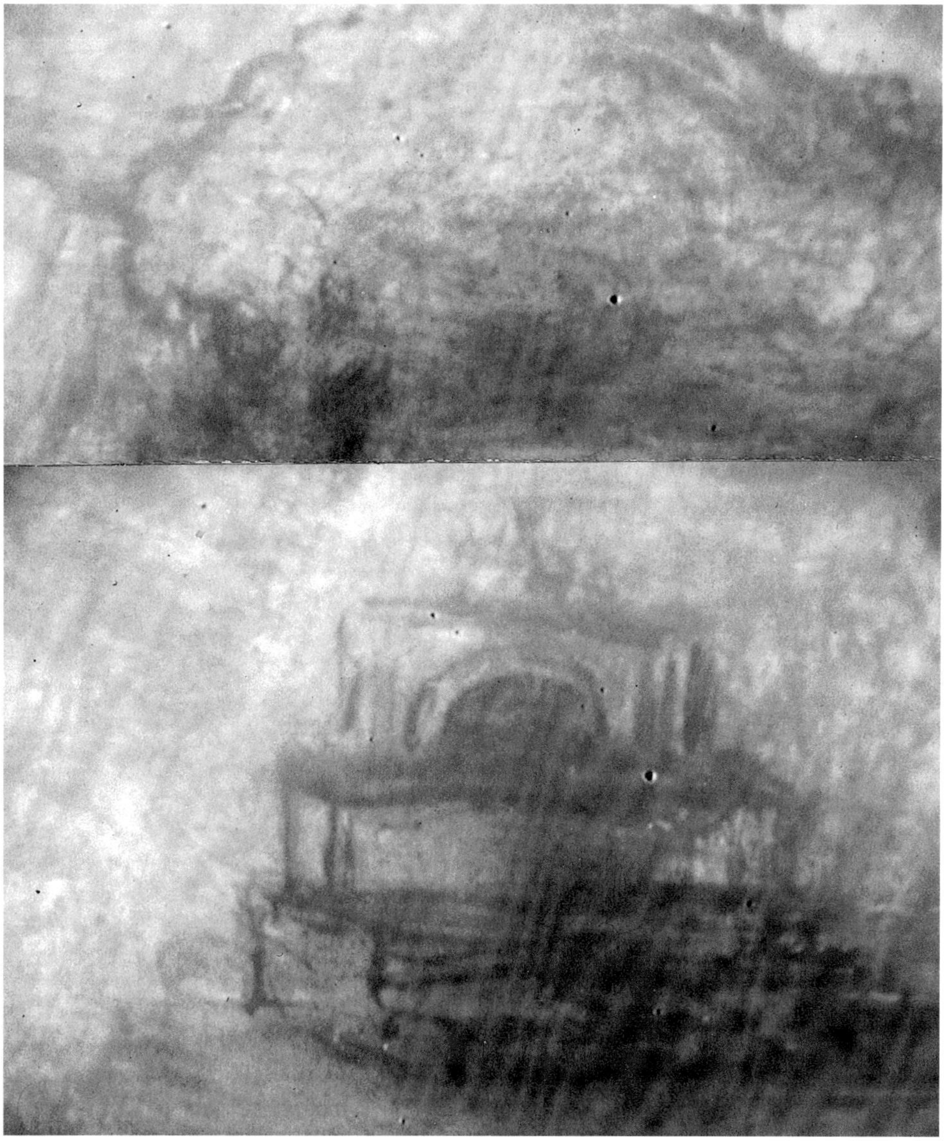

a. Infrared reflectogram assembly showing a detail of the structure which does not appear in the painting.

God punished the inhabitants of Sodom and Gomorrah for their wickedness by raining down fire and brimstone. Aided by two angels, Lot and his wife and two daughters escaped in time. Disobeying the angels' command, Lot's wife looked back as they fled and was changed into a pillar of salt (Genesis 19:1-29). The painter of the Rotterdam panel rendered them as small figures in a vast landscape. The pillar of salt can be dimly perceived to the left of the jagged rocks. Sky and water are in tones of fiery red.

The sequel to these events can be seen in the upper right corner, where Lot, made drunk by his daughters, is seduced by them in a tent (Genesis 19:30-38). The Bible makes no mention of a tent; it states instead that they dwelt in a cave. A tent also features in other representations of the story of Lot and his daughters that were painted in Antwerp around 1520.[2]

In front of the rock formation stands a strange building with a slender column surmounted by a statue, the significance of which is unknown. It may represent a pagan image, emphasising the wickedness of the inhabitants of Sodom and Gomorrah. Analysis showed that the artist changed his mind as he was painting the panel, the infrared reflectograms revealing under the strange building the drawing of a different structure with steps leading to a kind of altar which supports an arch with a rectangular shape on top (fig. a). This is no doubt a first version of the supposed pagan image, which the artist later painted a bit higher on the panel. A second change is clearly visible on an infrared reflectogram: the tent was initially much larger (fig. b).

The alterations and the superior quality of the painting make it amply clear that the Rotterdam panel is an original work. It is generally regarded as an early work by Joachim Patinir, probably painted before 1514.[3] However, dendrochronological evidence argues in favour of a later dating, around 1520. A very similar later version in *tondo* form is at the Ashmolean Museum, Oxford (fig. c).[4] Another, privately owned, panel is a variation of the Rotterdam panel (fig. d).[5] All three works are related to an entry in Albrecht Dürer's journal of his visit to the Netherlands: "I dined with Master Arion, secretary of the city of Antwerp, who presented me with a small panel painting by Master Joachim, portraying Lot and his daughters".[6] An eighteenth-century inscription on the back of the privately-owned panel reads: "Aus Albrecht Dürers Nachlass, Er bekam dieses Bild vom Stadtsekretär zu Antwerpen zum Geschenk". This suggests that it is the panel mentioned by Dürer, a conclusion reinforced by the fact that it is thought to have come from the Praun collection, which included works from Dürer's collection.[7] But it is clear from the poor quality of the work that it was not painted by Patinir, and it is very unlikely that the secretary would have dared to present such a work to Dürer, who frequently saw Patinir during his visit to Antwerp. The question remains undecided.
FL

1 Scientific examination conducted in 1991-1992 by M.C. Janselijn under the supervision of J.R.J. van Asperen de Boer. A copy of his minor thesis is in the Museum's file on the painting. Paint samples A 317/ 1-3. Infrared reflectograms: AB 1201/7-AB 1202/ 15.

2 See cat. no 51.

3 See Koch (1968).

4 Panel; 34 x 33 cm. See *Paintings in the Ashmolean Museum. Illustrated catalogue*, 1962, no. 320.

5 Panel; 27.5 x 32.5 cm. See Friedländer (1973), supp. 268. He erroneously describes it as a *tondo* painting, whereas it is a rectangular panel on which a *tondo* is painted and the corners are marbled. See also note 7.

6 "Ich hab gessen mit dem maister Arion [i.e. Adrian Herbouts], der von Antorff secretarij; den hat mir geschenckt das klein gemahlt täffelein, das maister Joachim gemacht hat, ist S. Loth mit den töchtern". See Hans Rupprich (2nd ed.), *Duerer. Schriftlicher Nachlass*, Berlin 1956, p. 156.

7 The information concerning the inscription and the provenance of the privately-owned panel is cited from the catalogue, *Tafelbilder des 15. und 16. Jahrhunderts*, Zurich, Kunsthaus, 1934, no. 110, p. 35, fig. XXXIX. See also K. Achilles-Syndram, "'...und sonderlich von grossen stuckhen nichts bey mihr vorhanden ist.' Die Sammlung Praun als kunst- und kulturgeschichtliches Dokument," in exhib. cat., *Das Praunsche Kabinett. Meisterwerke von Dürer bis Carracci*, Nuremberg, Germanisches National Museum, 1994, p. 41. The panel and its provenance are referred to in the catalogue of the Praun Collection, compiled in 1797 by C.T. de Murr. Another panel attributed to Patinir has also been linked to Dürer's journal entry (catalogue, *Jeroen Bosch. Noord-Nederlandsche primitieven*, Rotterdam, Boymans Museum, 1936, no. 64, fig. 79). It depicts a landscape with a burning city. But there is no trace of Lot and his daughters. On a label attached to the back is written: "Aus Albrecht Dürers Nachlass". A second label bears the name of Imhoff, while the name "Jerome Bosch" is written on the panel. This could well be the Bosch "incendie" listed in the 1797 catalogue of the Praun collection, which notes that the panel came from Dürer's heirs. But it is neither a Bosch nor a Patinir. Photographs of the painting and the back of the panel are in the Museum's file. In 1968 it was in the Bliss collection, Dumbarton Oaks, Washington D.C. (see Koch, 1968). On the Praun collection, see Smith (1990-91) and the above-mentioned catalogue of the exhibition in Nuremberg.

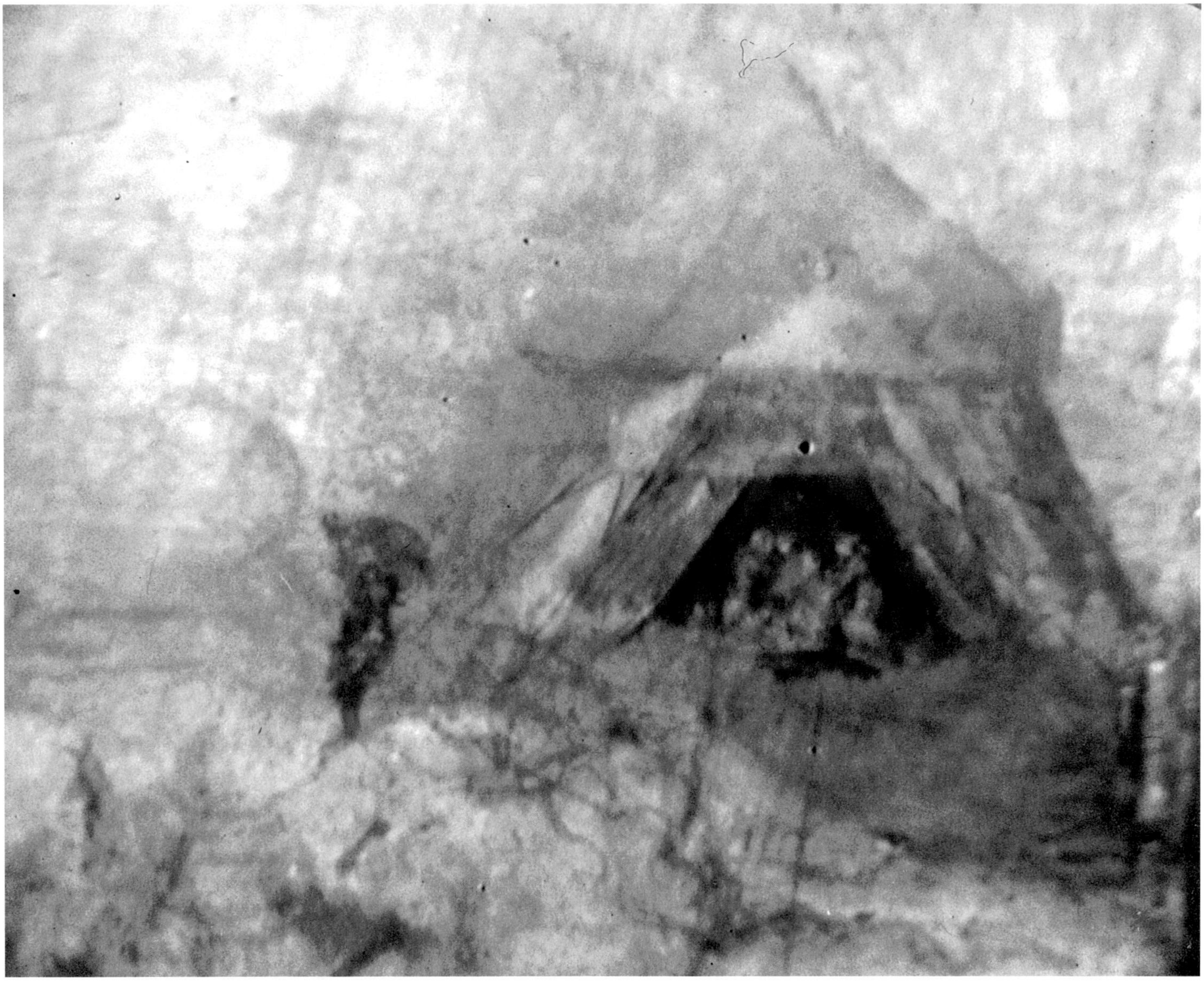

b. Infrared reflectogram showing the tent.

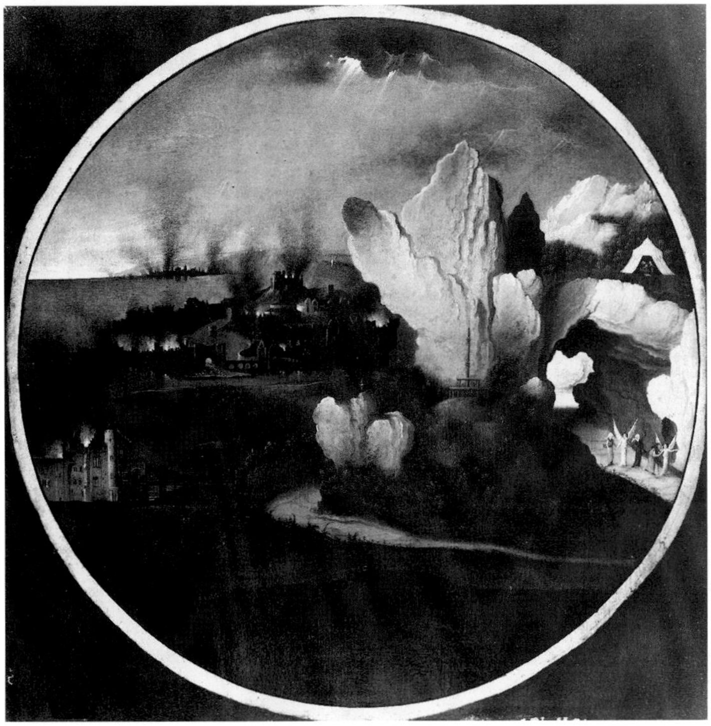

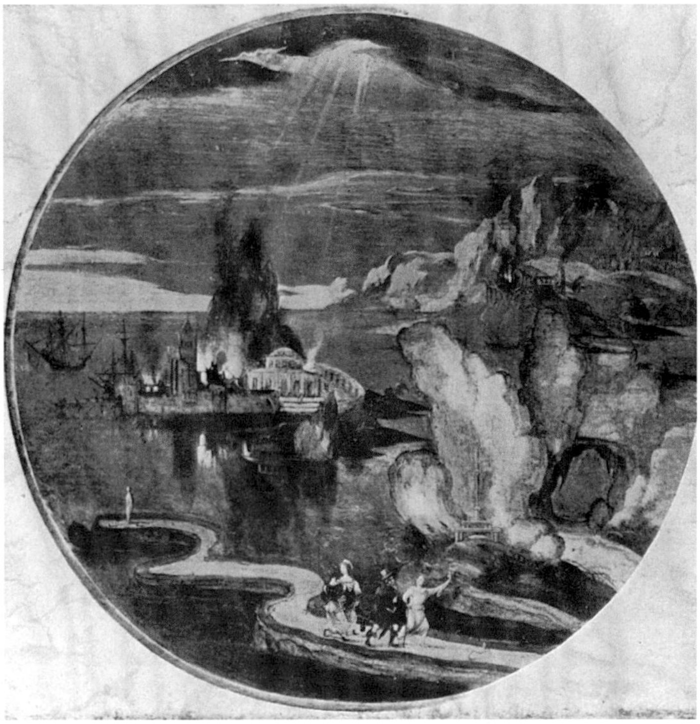

c. Joachim Patinir (?), Landscape with the destruction of Sodom and Gomorrah
Panel; 34 x 33 cm
Ashmolean Museum, Oxford.

d. Manner of Joachim Patinir, Landscape with the destruction of Sodom and Gomorrah
Panel; 27.5 x 32.5 cm
Whereabouts unknown.

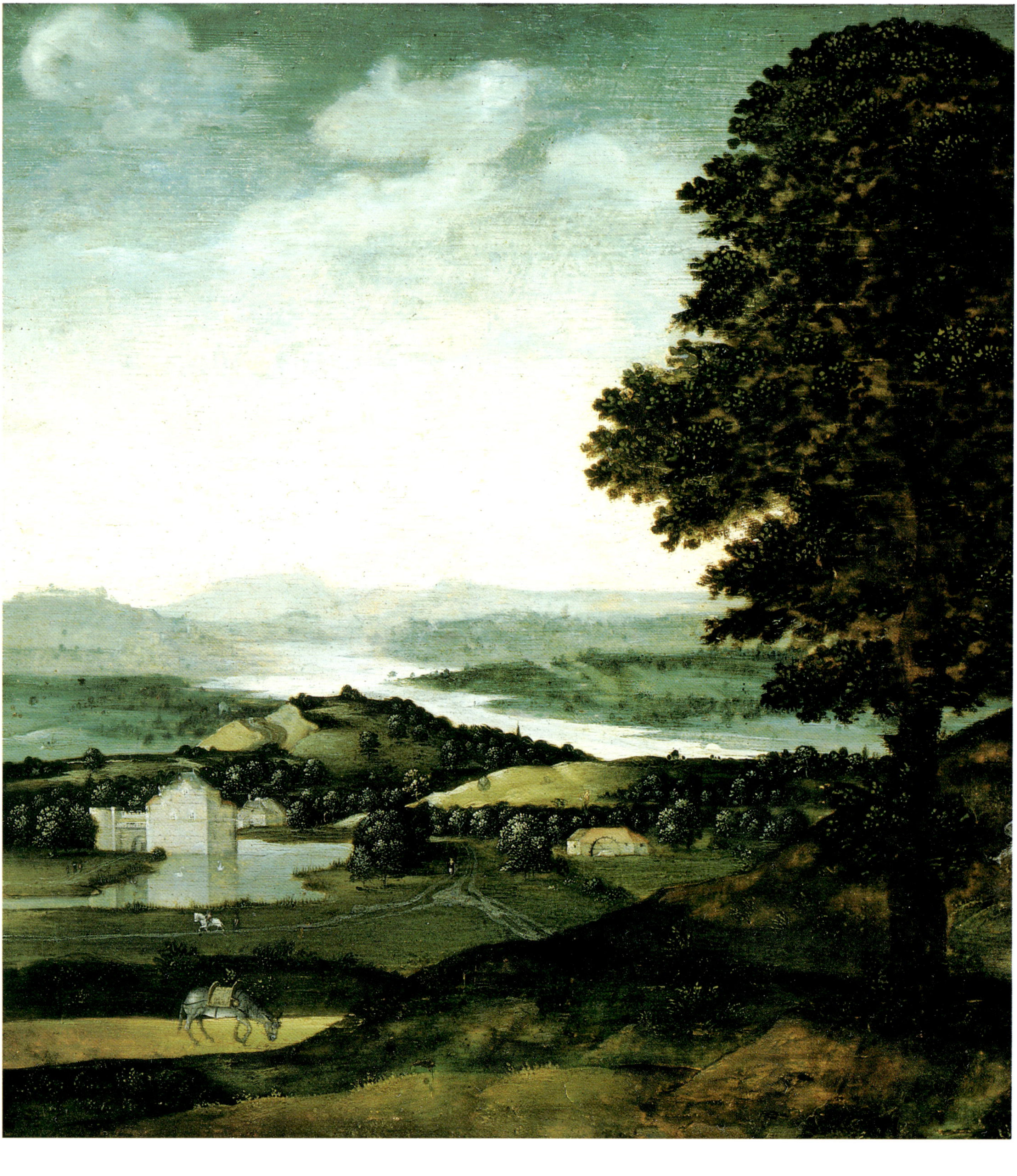

Landscape with grazing donkey

Joachim Patinir
(Bouvignes or Dinant c. 1480-Antwerp 1524)

Fragment of Rest on the Flight into Egypt
Panel; 27 x 23 cm

Physical characteristics:[1] the panel consists of a single plank. No *barbe* remains. It appears to have been sawn along the four edges.

Infrared reflectography: the underdrawing is limited to contours. No changes were made at the time of painting. See description.

Dendrochronology: the youngest heartwood growth ring dates from 1471. The panel could not have been painted before 1482; it was more probably painted in or after 1496. See article by P. Klein.

Paint samples: an intermediate layer was applied onto the ground. Three paint samples show it to be coloured and to contain orange particles; the other three samples show no colour. The pigments in the top layers are azurite and possibly copper resinate green. The number of layers varies from two to four.

Provenance: Josef Cremer Collection, Dortmund; auctioned by Wertheim, Berlin, 29 May 1929, no. 29, fig.; Goudstikker Gallery, Amsterdam, 1929; purchased there in 1931 by D.G. van Beuningen, Rotterdam and Vierhouten, for 11,000 guilders; acquired by the Museum in 1958 with the Van Beuningen Collection; inv. no. 2474.

Exhibitions: *Nouvelles acquisitions de la collection Goudstikker*, Amsterdam, 458 Heerengracht, 1929, no. 29, fig.; *Tentoonstelling van Oude Kunst*, Amsterdam, Rijksmuseum, 1929, no. 110, fig.; *Kersttentoonstelling*, Rotterdam, Boymans Museum, 1932-33, no. 11; *Winter-tentoonstelling van oude kunst uit particulier bezit*, Haarlem, Frans Halsmuseum, 1940, no. 53; *Honderd jaar Museum Boymans Rotterdam. Meesterwerken uit de collectie D.G. van Beuningen*, Rotterdam, Boymans Museum, 1949, no. 28; *Chefs-d'œuvre de la collection D.G. van Beuningen*, Paris, Petit Palais, 1952, no. 67.

Literature: A. Heppner, "Particulier kunstbezit in het Frans Halsmuseum", *Maandblad voor Beeldende Kunsten* 17 (1940), p. 244, fig.; Hannema, 1949, no. 28, fig. 31; cat. 1962, p. 102; R.A. Koch, *Joachim Patinir*, Princeton, New Jersey 1968, p. 74, no. 7a, fig. 13; J.C. Ebbinge Wubben in: *The Thyssen-Bornemisza collection*, Castagnola 1969, p. 264; C. Eisler (ed), *The Thyssen-Bornemisza Collection. Early Netherlandish Painting*, London 1989, p. 182.

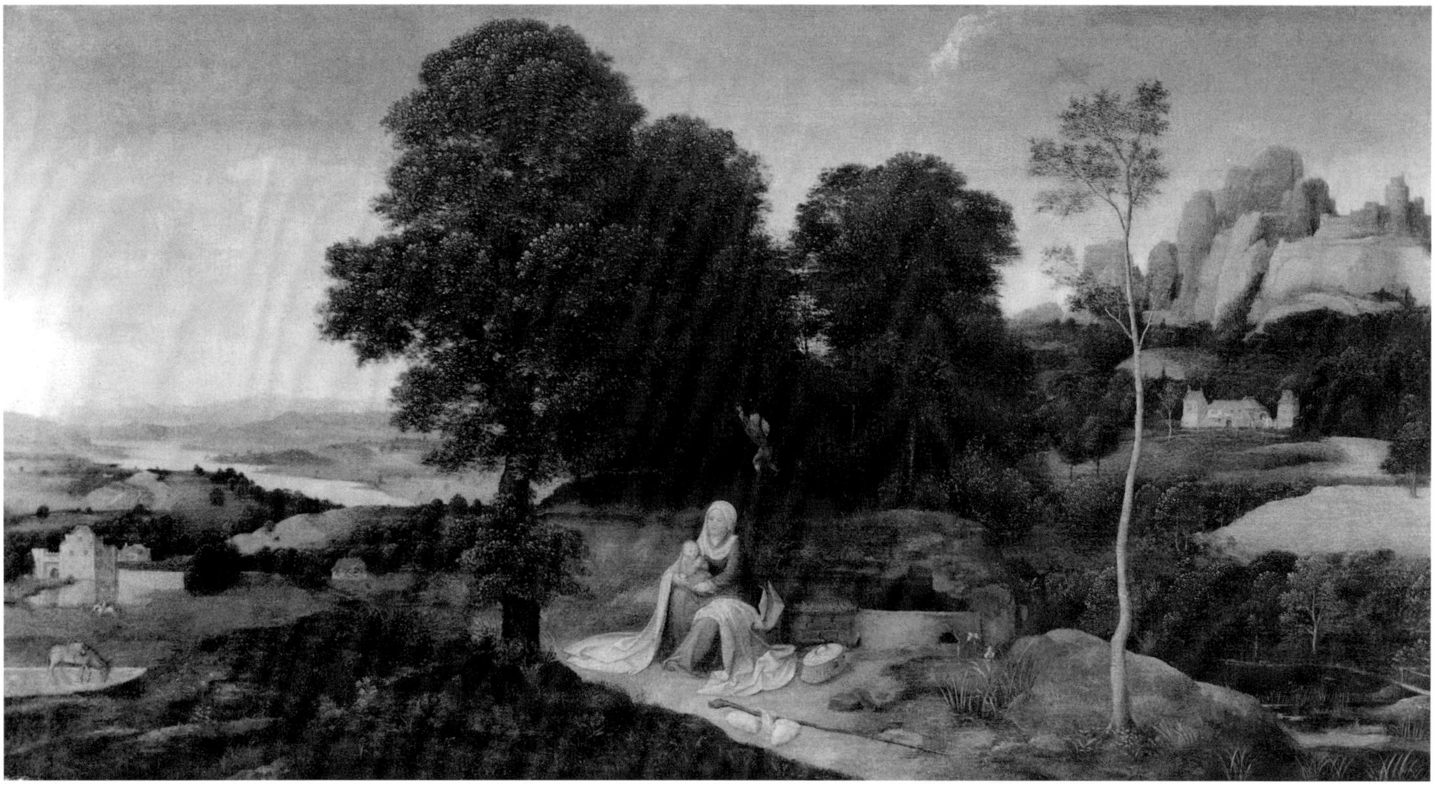

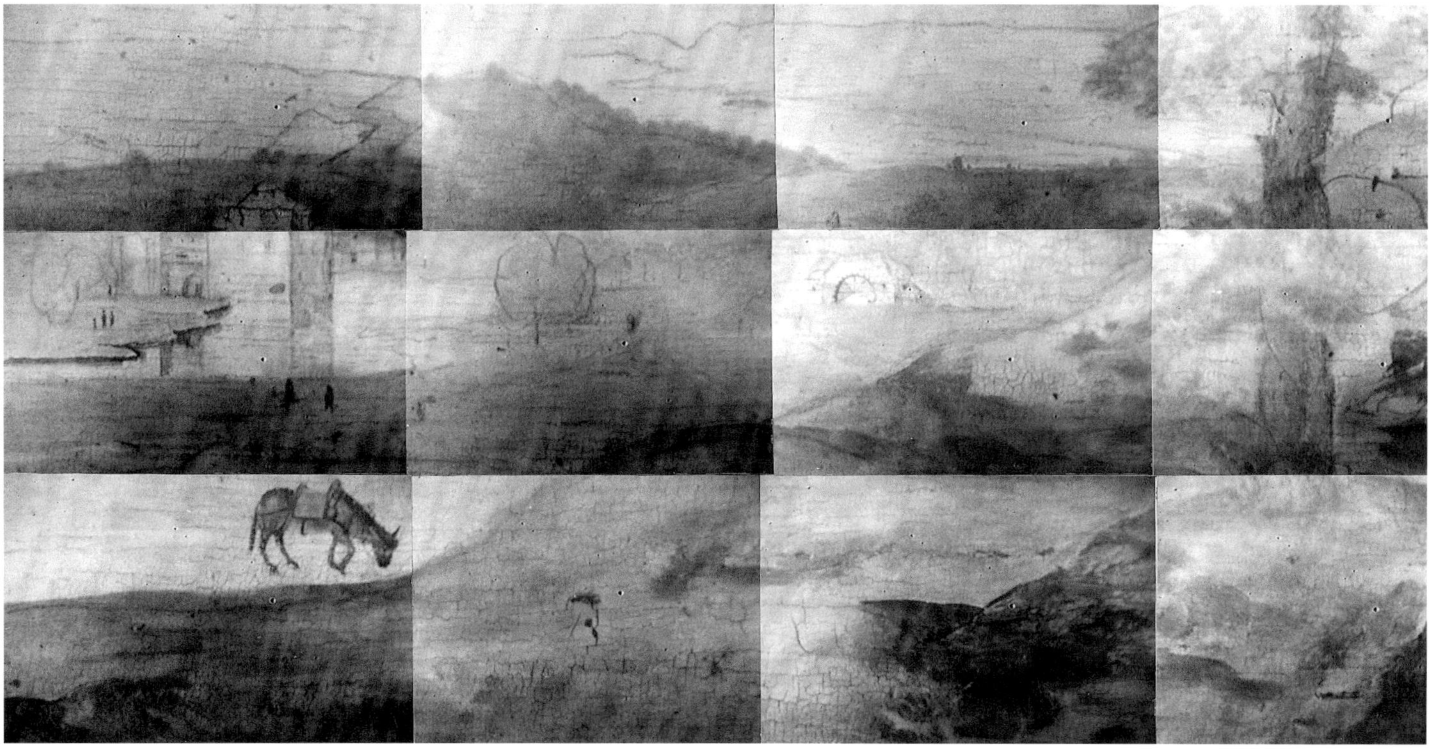

a. Joachim Patinir, *Rest on the Flight into Egypt*
Panel; 31.5 x 57.5 cm
Madrid, Thyssen-Bornemisza Collection.

b. Infrared reflectogram assembly showing the lower section of the painting.

This small landscape is part of a larger work. The original composition is known from the artist's *Rest on the Flight into Egypt* in the Thyssen Collection in Madrid (fig. a), which shows the Rotterdam panel to be the left part of a rectangular painting with the Virgin and Child in the centre. A small part of the Virgin's garment is visible on the right.[2] The painting in the Thyssen Collection has always been regarded as an original work by Patinir. A recent examination has shown that the underdrawing was executed with fine brush strokes. In painting the work the artist changed a few details, such as a house and the position of the basket.[3]

There are two different styles in the underdrawing of the Rotterdam fragment (fig. b): the freely sketched small trees and castle, possibly rendered with a fine brush, resembling the Madrid work; and another section composed of fine, linked dots delineating the mountains and water in the background. A combination of both techniques was used for the large tree on the right. The small dots indicate an initial drawing or cartoon consisting of small pricked holes along the contour lines through which were subsequently dusted black chalk or powdered charcoal for transference to the prepared panel. The technique of pouncing was widely used in the sixteenth century.[4] The artist would have completed the underdrawing with a fine brush.

In view of the corrections and the absence of any trace of pouncing, the Madrid painting is probably the first version. The Rotterdam work, with no corrections, would have been executed later.

From the technical data and the superior quality of the painting it may be assumed that the Rotterdam fragment is from the hand of Patinir himself, or was in any event painted under his direct supervision.

Besides the Rotterdam fragment, many other versions of the Madrid panel are ascribed to Patinir and his followers.[5] In addition, the landscape was copied by Joos van Cleve in a number of paintings.[6] Further examination is needed to determine whether pouncing was used in some of these works or, in other words, whether the cartoon used for the Rotterdam panel was also used for other works or even lent to another artist.

Koch puts the date of the Madrid panel at around 1515-1516, the middle period of the master. It is difficult to give such an exact date for the Rotterdam panel, which may have been painted shortly afterwards, though this is uncertain. It seems to be the case that certain compositions were obtainable from an artist's studio for some considerable time.
FL

1 Scientific examination conducted by Saskia G. Willner under the supervision of J.R.J. van Asperen de Boer. A copy of her minor thesis, dated 1993, is in the Museum's file on the painting. Paint samples A 315/1-6. Infrared reflectograms: AB 1199/34-AB 1200/30.

2 It is covered at the present time by the frame.

3 The painting was examined by Saskia G. Willner and G. Hoephner on 20 June 1991. The report is in the Museum's file on the painting. On the painting in the Thyssen Collection, see Eisler (1989) and the literature he lists.

4 See also cat. no. 61.

5 1. *Rest on the Flight into Egypt*, Stockholm, National Museum (see Friedländer, IXb, 1973, no. 238, fig.). 2. *Rest on the Flight into Egypt*, Philadelphia, John G. Johnson Collection (see Friedländer, IXb, 1973, no. 234, fig.); 3. *Rest on the Flight into Egypt*, auctioned at Sotheby's, London, on 6 April 1977; 4. *Rest on the Flight into Egypt*, formerly in Stephens Gallery, Paris (photograph R.K.D.); 5. *Rest on the Flight into Egypt*, formerly L. Moreno Collection, Paris. With acknowledgements to Saskia Willner.

6 1. Joos van Cleve, *Rest on the Flight into Egypt*, Brussels, Musea voor Schone Kunsten in België (see Friedländer, IXa, 1972, no. 49, fig.); 2. Joos van Cleve, *Virgin with Child and angels*, Liverpool Walker Art Gallery (see Friedländer, IXa, 1972, no. 67, fig.); Joos van Cleve (?), *The Holy Family*, Lugano, Thyssen-Bornemisza Collection (?) (see Friedländer, IXa, 1972, no. 64a, fig.). Another version is in Rome, Palazzo Odescalchi: 4. Style of Joos van Cleve, *Virgin with cherries*, location unknown (see Friedländer, IXa, 1972, no. 63K, fig.).

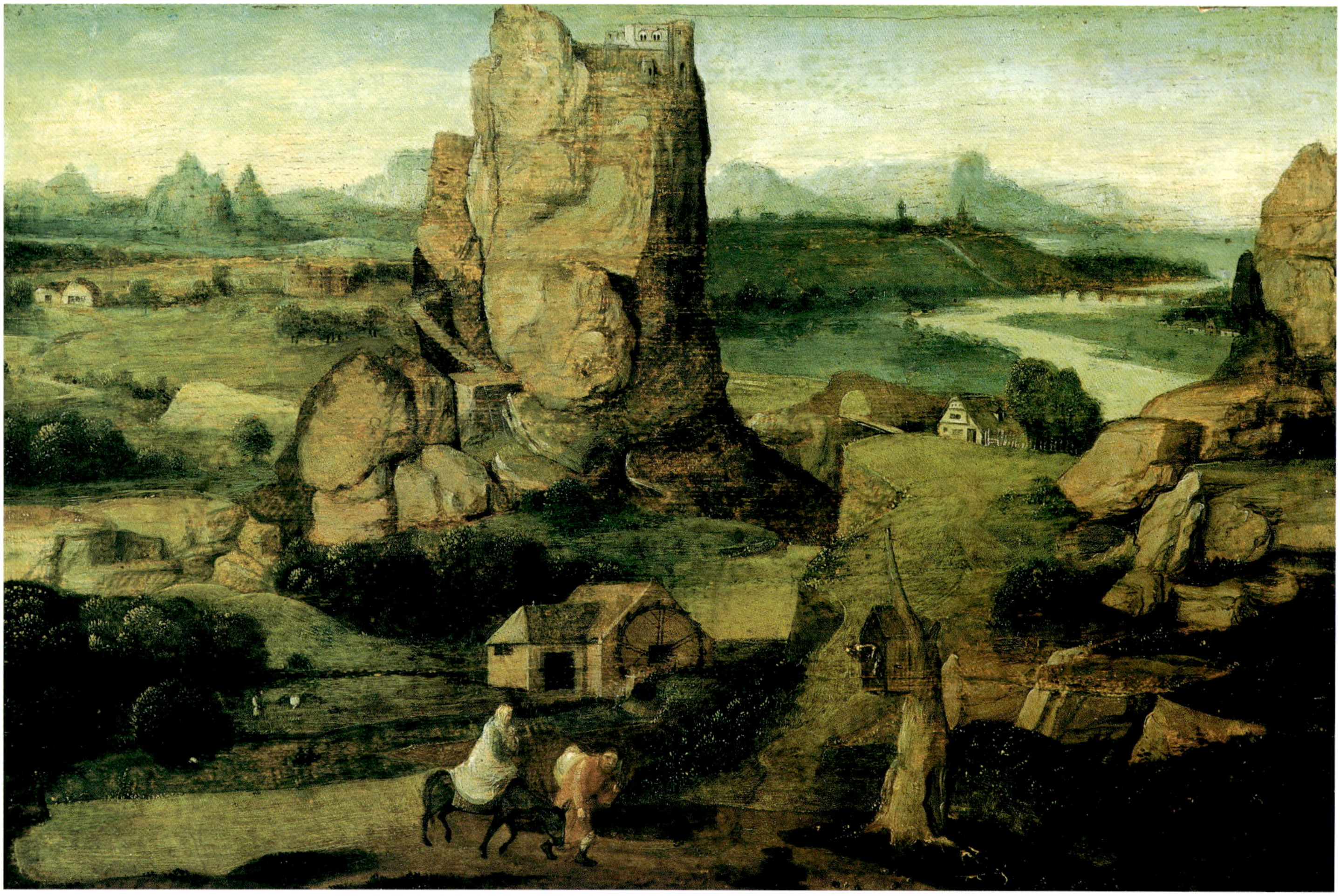

Landscape with the Flight into Egypt

Joachim Patinir, circle of
(Bouvignes or Dinant c. 1480-Antwerp 1524)

Panel; 24 x 37 cm

Physical characteristics: the panel consists of a single plank. The *barbe* can be seen on the sides, but not on the upper and lower edges.

Infrared reflectography:[1] no underdrawing could be discerned.

Dendrochronology: the youngest heartwood growth ring dates from 1481. The panel could not have been painted before 1492; it was more probably painted in or after 1506. See article by P. Klein.

Provenance: A. von Kolasinski Collection, Warsaw; auctioned in Berlin, R. Lepke, 5 June 1917, no. 142, fig. 10; Cassirer Gallery, Berlin, 1921; Böhler and Steinmayer Gallery, Munich; Antoon van Welie Collection; auctioned by Mak van Waay, Amsterdam, 7 April 1936, no. 64, fig.; J. Gans Gallery, The Hague, 1938; purchased by D.G. van Beuningen, Rotterdam and Vierhouten, on 31 August 1939 for 12,000 guilders; acquired by the Museum in 1958 with the Van Beuningen Collection; inv.no. 2473.

Exhibitions: *Les primitifs Flamands*, Paris, Musée de l'Orangerie, 1947, no. 90, fig. LXIII; *Honderd jaar Museum Boymans Rotterdam. Meesterwerken uit de verzameling D.G. van Beuningen*, Rotterdam, Boymans Museum, 1949, no. 66; *Chefs-d'œuvre de la collection D.G. van Beuningen*, Paris, Petit Palais, 1952, no. 66.

Literature: Hannema, 1949, no. 27, fig. 32; cat. 1962, p. 102; exhib.cat. *Oude tekeningen. Een keuze uit de verzameling P. en N. de Boer*, Laren, Singer Museum, 1966, no. 130; R.A. Koch, *Joachim Patinir*, Princeton, New Jersey, 1968, p. 65, note 29.

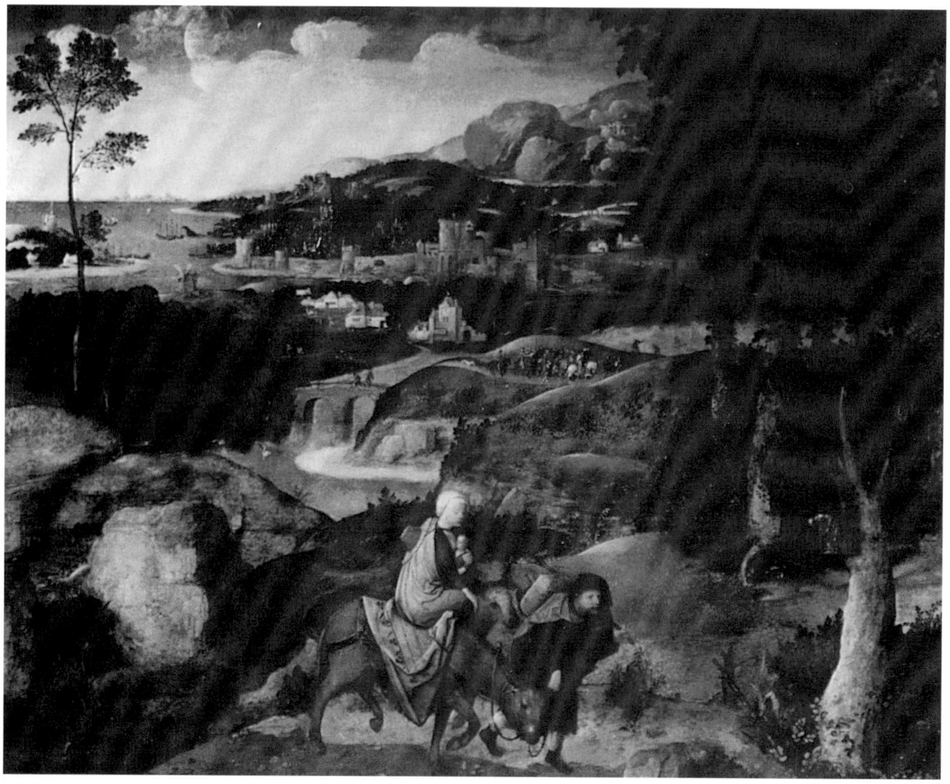

a. Adriaen Ysenbrant (?), Landscape with the Flight into Egypt
Panel
Pittsfield (Mass.), Berkshire Museum

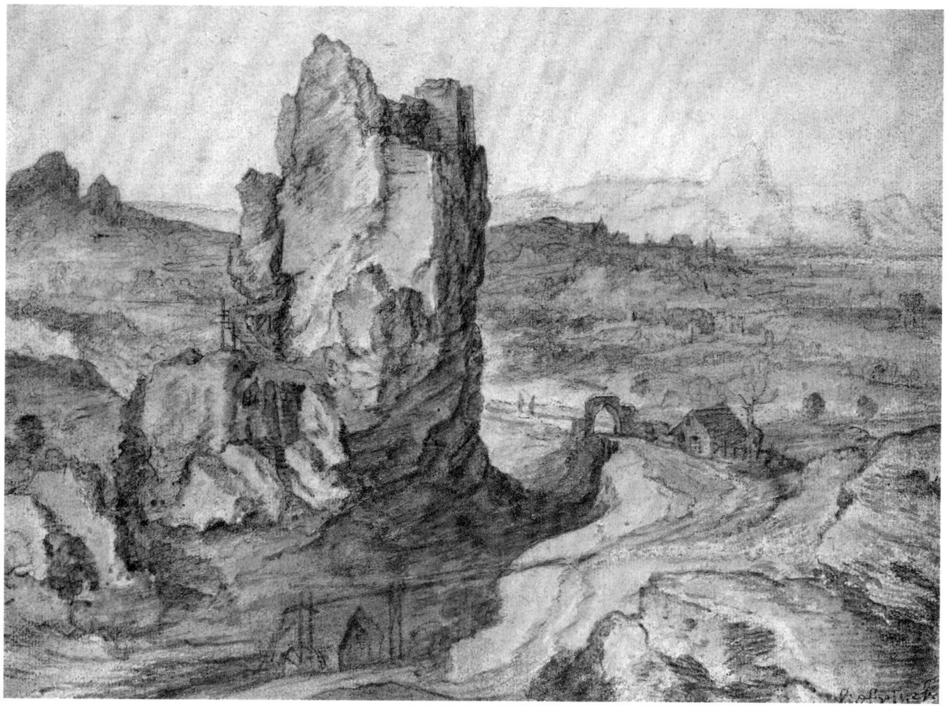

b. Cornelis (?) Liefrinck, Landscape with rock formation
Black chalk, washed; 19 x 25.9 cm
Stichting P. en N. de Boer, Amsterdam

Against a wide mountainous landscape Joseph walks before the donkey carrying the Virgin and Child. A pagan image falls from a small shrine affixed to a tree trunk in front of him.

Two weeks before Van Beuningen bought the panel, Max Friedländer wrote on the back of a photograph that it was "a work characteristic of Joachim Patinir".[2] The Museum adopted this attribution in its 1962 catalogue.

Koch attributes the painting to the school of Ysenbrant[3] by analogy with a painting in Pittsfield attributed by him to the Bruges master (fig. a).[4] In his view the two works are "vaguely related", but the similarities are rather more than vague, the figures of the Virgin and Child on the donkey and of Joseph being virtually identical. The composition of the figures is based on a woodcut by Dürer.[5] However, the tree with the shrine and falling image is not in the woodcut, while these details are the same in the Pittsfield and Rotterdam paintings. The landscapes in the two panels are entirely unrelated. The quality of the Pittsfield painting is greatly superior to that in Rotterdam.

The Rotterdam panel bears little resemblance to the work generally attributed to Ysenbrant, and while it displays marked similarities to the work of Patinir, such as the archway spanning the road,[6] its quality is not such as to justify its attribution to the artist himself. It was probably painted in the circle of Patinir in the early years of the sixteenth century. Owing to the poor condition of the work, it is impossible to reach any definite conclusion.

Remarkably enough, the rock formation so prominent in the Rotterdam panel is a feature of a drawing signed "Liefrinck" (fig. b), which also depicts the same river landscape and the house beside a large gateway. The drawing is attributed both to Hans Liefrinck (Augsburg? 1518 - Antwerp 1573) and to Cornelis Liefrinck (Leiden c. 1581 - after 1640).[7] Hans Liefrinck is known only from a few engravings; Cornelis is also known from a small number of paintings. Samuel van Hoogstraeten was probably referring to Cornelis when he wrote about "a Lijfring who painted attractive rock formations".[8]

Quite possibly, both the panel and the drawing are based on a painting by Patinir himself which is now unknown.
FL

1 Scanned on 17 January 1994 by J.R.J. van Asperen de Boer.
2 The photograph is in the Museum's file. The text reads: "Das umstehend photographierte Bild ist meiner Ansicht nach ein charakteristisches Werk von Joachim Patinir," and is signed, "M.J. Friedländer, Den Haag, 12.VIII.39".
3 Koch (1968).
4 On the painting in Pittsfield, see also H.G. Franz, *Niederländische Landschaftsmalerei*, Graz 1969, pp. 36, 38, fig. 18. He assumes the landscape to be by Patinir, and believes the figures may have been added later. A replica is in the Palazzo Borghese, Rome.
5 The woodcut is one of the series on the life of the Virgin and dates from around 1504-1505. See W.S. Strauss, *Albrecht Dürer woodcuts and woodblocks*, New York 1980, no. 92. In the woodcut and the Pittsfield painting there is an ox behind the donkey, but not in the Rotterdam painting.
6 A similar archway appears in an early work by Patinir, *St Jerome*, Staatliche Kunsthalle, Karlsruhe. See Friedländer, IX, 1973, no. 239.
7 See exhib. cat., *Oude tekeningen. Een keuze uit de verzameling P. en N. de Boer*, Laren, Singer Museum, 1966, no. 130.
8 "[...] eenen Lijfring koloreerde geestige steenrotsen". S. van Hoogstraeten, *Inleyding tot de Hooge Schoole der Schilderkonst*, Rotterdam 1678, p. 232.

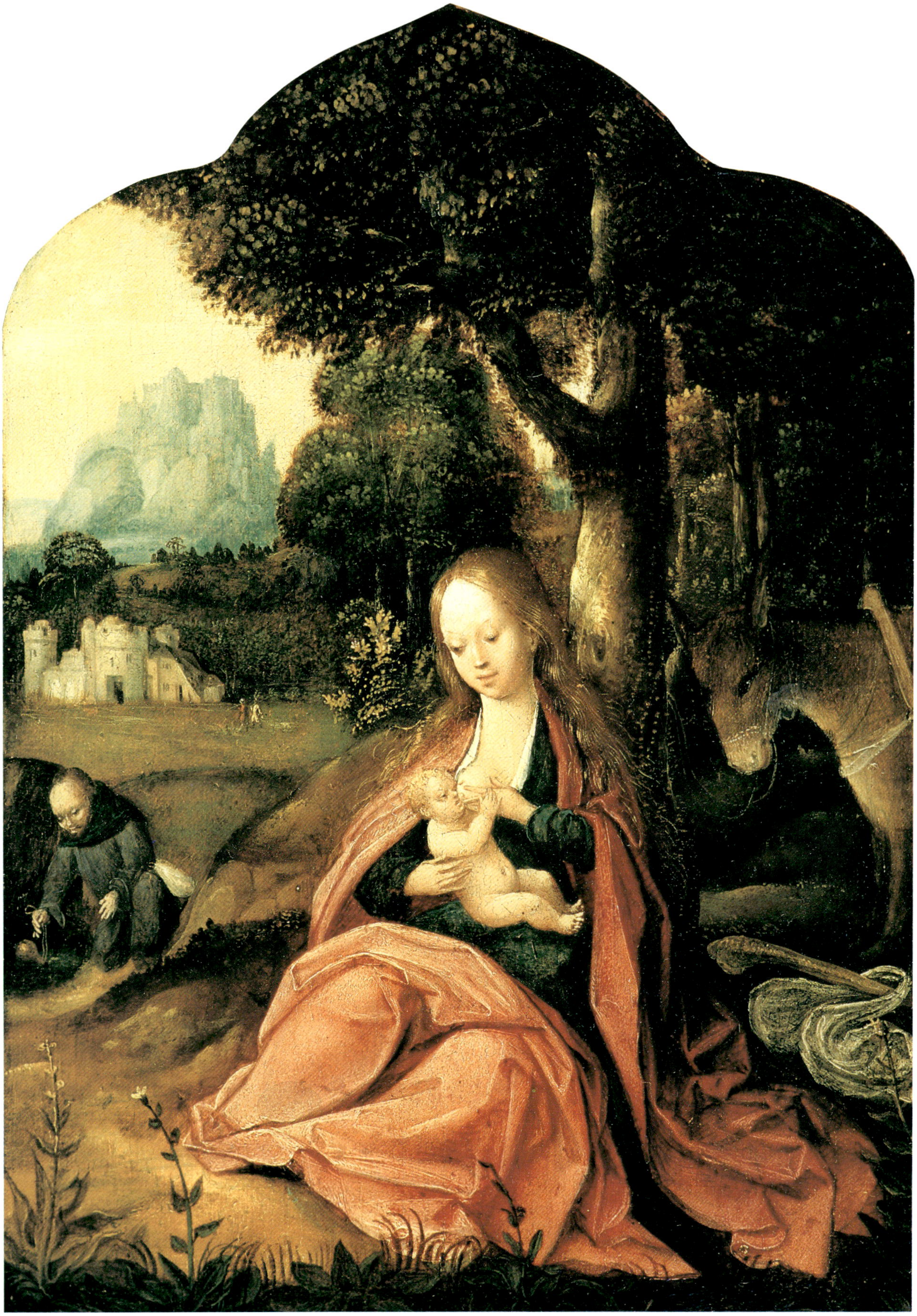

Rest on the Flight into Egypt

Joachim Patinir, follower of
c. 1520-1530

Panel; 31 x 21 cm

Physical characteristics: the panel consists of a single plank, the top of which forms a pointed arch. The frame is part of the panel.

Infrared reflectography:[1] black chalk underdrawing of the entire composition, freely executed. See description.

Dendrochronology: the youngest heartwood growth ring dates from 1496. The panel could not have been painted before 1507; it was more probably painted in or after 1513. See also article by P. Klein.

Provenance: Sir Hugh Cholmeley, Easton Hall, Gratham; Koetser Gallery, London; Borghouts Gallery; purchased from the Gallery in June 1951 by D.G. van Beuningen, Rotterdam and Vierhouten, for 20,000 guilders; acquired by the Museum in 1958 with the Van Beuningen Collection; inv. no. 2476.

Exhibitions: *Chefs-d'œuvre de la collection D.G. van Beuningen*, Paris, Petit Palais, 1952, nr. 68.

Literature: cat. 1962, p. 102.

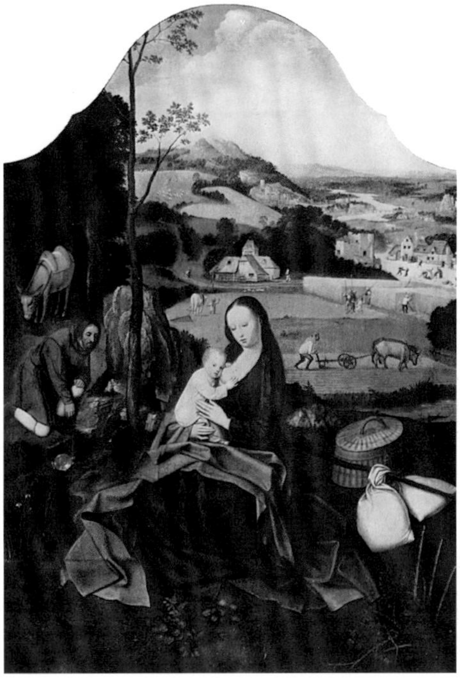

a. Joachim Patinir, Triptych, Rest on the Flight into Egypt
Panel; central panel; 72 x 110 cm
(formerly) Willy Kaus Collection, Frankfurt

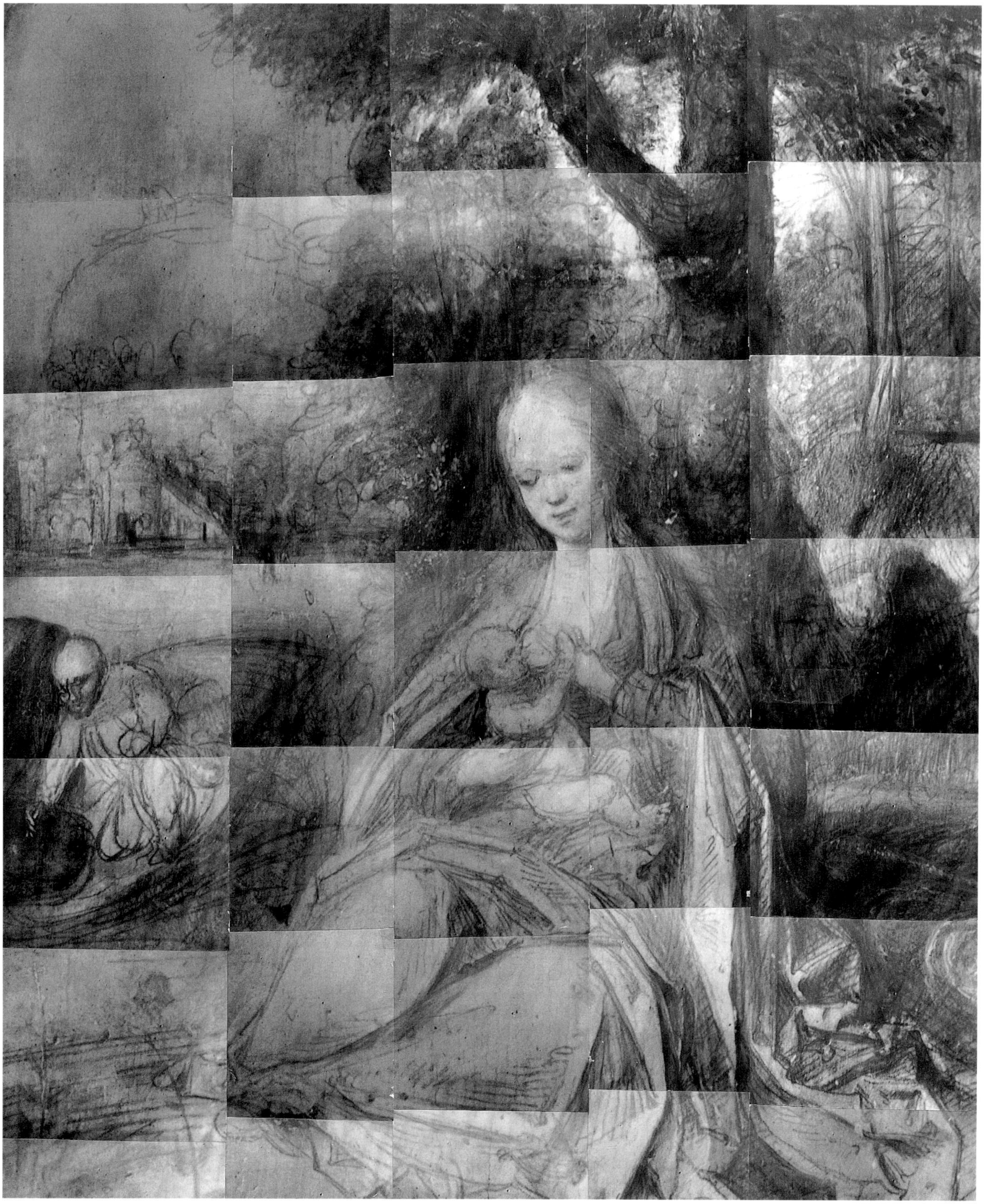

b. Infrared reflectogram assembly

This small panel was bought by Van Beuningen in 1951 as an original work by Patinir. However, it lacks the fine detail so characteristic of Patinir's work.

The anonymous artist seems to have modelled the work on the central panel of Patinir's triptych devoted to the same theme. But it is doubtful whether he actually saw the original or any of the many variations based on it. Patinir's triptych, badly damaged by fire, was in the Kaus Collection, Frankfurt (fig. a).[2] In the foreground the Virgin is suckling the Child. As in this panel, a travel bag wrapped around a stick lies to her left, while to her right Joseph is kneeling to fill a water jar.

The Virgin's face in the Rotterdam panel appears to be inspired by paintings by Joos van Cleve.[3] Although many details have clearly been borrowed, none can be termed a direct copy of work by other artists. The underdrawing is remarkable in that it is freely drawn (fig. b). It is clear from this free style that it can only be an original composition. It probably dates from around 1520-1530.

The stick with the travel bag, known as a "scaerpe," and the jar in Joseph's hand are often found in representations of *Rest on the Flight into Egypt* painted in this period. These attributes are thought to signify the Holy Family as pilgrims, endowing the story of the flight into Egypt with the added significance of man's journey or pilgrimage through life.[4]
FL

1 The panel was scanned and recorded on 20 December 1993 and 17 January 1994 by J.R.J. van Asperen de Boer. The infrared reflectogram assembly was made by Cunera Vergeer. Infrared reflectograms: AB 1556/19A-AB 1557/36A.

2 On this painting and some of the variations, see R.A. Koch, *Joachim Patinir*, Princeton, New Jersey 1968, no. 8, figs. 16, 17, 18, and nos. 20, 24, 32. Another variation was painted by the Master of the Female Half-Lengths. See idem, no. M.H.L.2, fig. 91.

3 See cat. no. 39.

4 R.L. Falkenburg, *Joachim Patinir. Landscape as an image of the pilgrimage of life*, Amsterdam-Philadelphia 1988, p. 97.

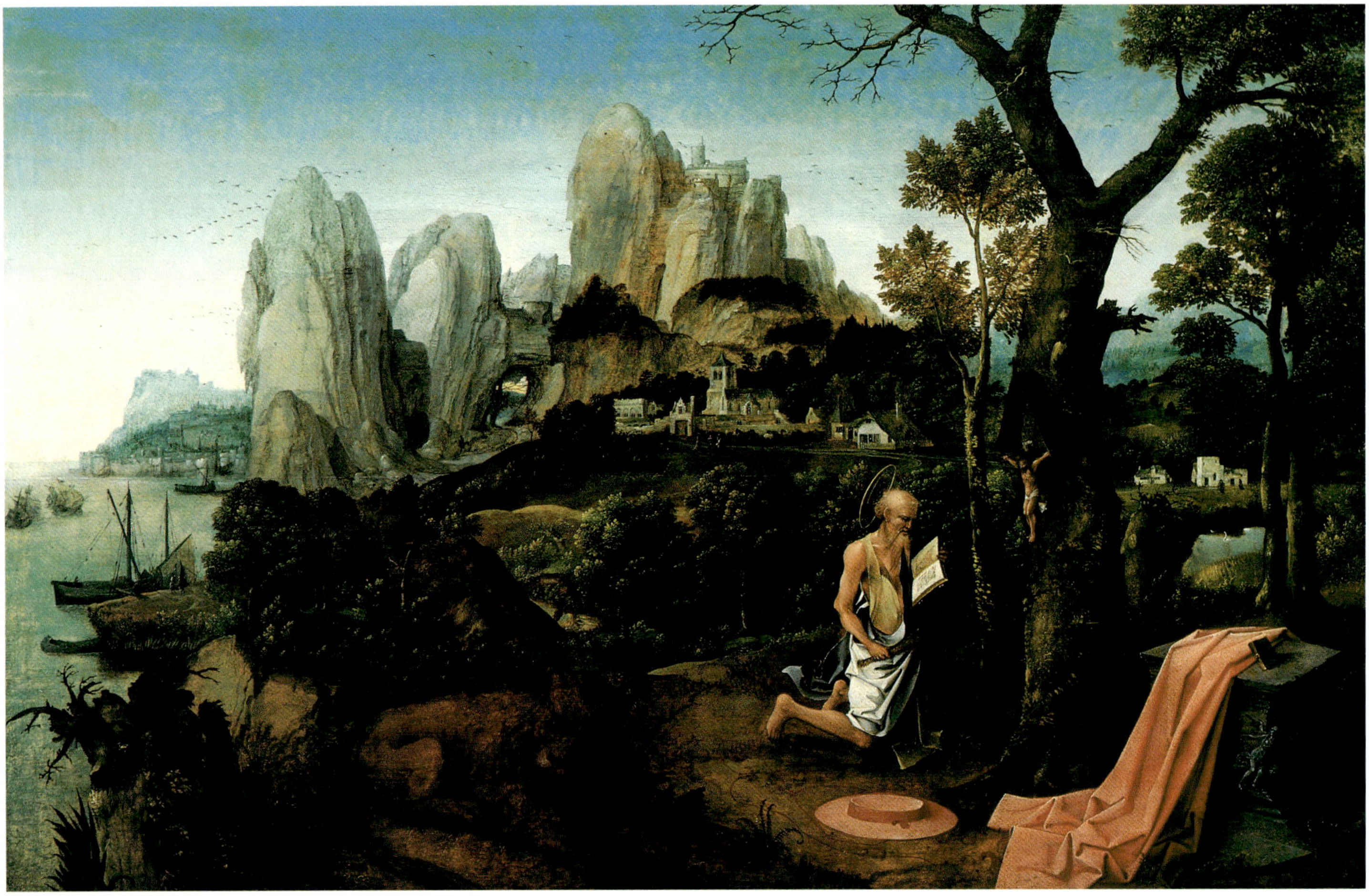

St Jerome in a landscape

Anonymous
South Netherlandish master, Antwerp
c. 1525

Panel; 56 x 83.6 cm
Signed on altar plinth, lower right: L

Physical characteristics:[1] the panel consists of two horizontal planks.

Infrared reflectography: detailed underdrawing (figs. a and b).

Provenance: Bonti Bernetti Collection (?), Fervio, 1897; Ernesto delle Fratte Collection, Rome; collection auctioned at Rome, Galleria Mario Giacomini, 22 April 1924, no. 263, fig.; private collection, Italy, 1937; donated to the Museum by W. van der Vorm, Rotterdam, in 1938; inv.no. 2120.

Literature: *Verslag omtrent den toestand en de aanwinsten van het Museum Boymans over het jaar 1938*, p. 2, fig. IV; G.J. Hoogewerff, *De Noord-Nederlandsche schilderkunst*, III, The Hague 1939, pp. 252-257, 366, figs. 131, 132, 194; N. Beets, "Nog eens 'Jan Wellens de Cock' en de zonen van Cornelis Engelbrechtsz: Pieter Cornelisz Kunst, Cornelis Cornelisz Kunst, Lucas Cornelisz de Kock," *Oud Holland* LXVII (1952), pp. 17-18, note 6; J. de Coo, *Museum Mayer van den Bergh. Catalogus I*, Antwerp 1960, p. 125 (2nd ed. 1966, p. 128); cat. 1962, p. 18; H.G. Franz, *Niederländische Landschaftsmalerei im Zeitalter des Manierismus*, Graz 1969, p. 50, fig. 29; J.R. Judson, *Dirck Barendsz.*, Amsterdam 1970, p. 68, note 1; S. Donahue Kuretsky, "Rembrandt's Tree Stump: An Iconographic Attribute of St Jerome", *The Art Bulletin* 56 (1974), p. 576, note 23.

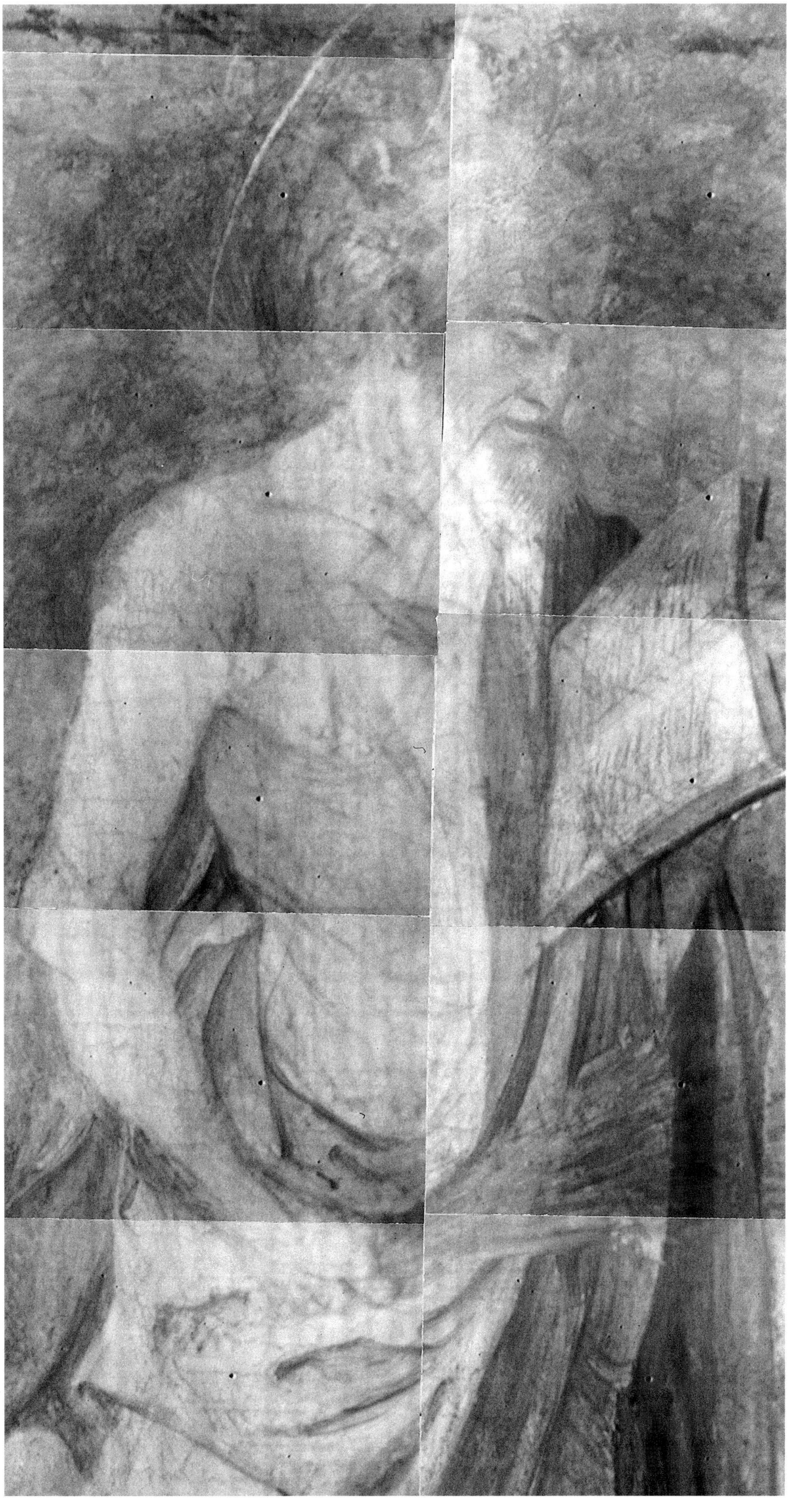

a. Infrared reflectogram assembly showing a detail of St Jerome.

In a vast landscape St Jerome kneels before a crucifix. In his left hand he holds a book, in his right hand a rod for self-flagellation. Beside him lies a rather surly-looking lion. The saint's red mantle is draped over an altar in the lower right corner. The altar bears a relief of a monster ridden by a bare-breasted winged female figure. Behind the saint, the idyllic landscape ends abruptly in jagged rocks, behind which a walled port city can be seen in the distance.

St Jerome, one of the four Church Fathers, withdrew from the sinfulness of worldly life to spend some time in the wilderness. His penance in the wilderness was the subject of numerous early sixteenth-century paintings.[2] As in this painting, there was usually a lion, with camels and various figures in the background. They probably referred to a story in the *Legenda Aurea*.[3] A lion with a thorn in its foot once came to St Jerome's monastery. The saint removed the thorn and bade the lion protect a donkey. One day, while the lion slept, the donkey was stolen by a passing caravan. It then had to assume the donkey's role as a beast of burden. Some time later the caravan again passed by. Through its savage roars the lion drove off the thieves and returned the donkey to the monastery. St Jerome's subsequent forgiveness of the thieves has been interpreted as symbolising the forgiveness of the sins of those who choose to lead a Christian life.[4]

The tree to which the crucifix is attached is of particular interest. The branches on the left are dead, while those on the right are in leaf. A dead tree trunk bearing a crucifix is a frequent feature of paintings of St Jerome. It is interpreted as signifying the rejection of sensual appetites or else death itself. In the latter case the crucifix symbolises eternal life.[5] The classical-type altar with a book, most probably the Bible, and the saint's mantle could represent the triumph of Christianity over the sinful pagan life.[6]

The work was probably painted in Antwerp around 1520-1530, though the artist must for the moment remain anonymous. Partly on the basis of the letter L on the altar, Hoogewerff attributes the painting to Lucas van Leyden, a conclusion that is rightly rejected by Beets.[7] Franz groups around the Rotterdam panel a number of works which he attributes to a follower of Joachim Patinir.[8] One, in the Mayer van den Bergh Museum, Antwerp (fig. c), is a freely executed copy of the panel which does not appear to be from the same hand. A St Jerome which was formerly in the collection of the princes of Liechtenstein does however appear to be by the master who painted the panel (fig. d).[9] A painting in Vienna which is tentatively attributed to Jan de Beer could also be by the same artist (fig.e).[10]
FL

1 Scientific examination conducted by J.R.J. van Asperen de Boer. Paint samples: A 332/1-3. Infrared reflectograms: AB 1233/1-AB 1234/18. The infrared reflectogram assemblies were made by J.R.J. van Asperen de Boer.

2 See, for example, W.S. Gibson, *'Mirror of the earth.' The world landscape in sixteenth-century Flemish painting*, Princeton, New Jersey 1989, p. 29. Patinir's landscapes with St Jerome made a tremendous impression on his contemporaries. His compositions were copied in countless variations by anonymous artists in the first decades of the sixteenth century.

3 R.L. Falkenburg, *Joachim Patinir. Landscape as an image of the pilgrimage of life*, Amsterdam-Philadelphia 1988, pp. 54, 91-92, 94-95.

4 Falkenburg, *op. cit.* (note 3) The author invests this interpretation with a far-reaching application to Patinir's landscapes, which would certainly not seem to be valid in the case of this particular painting. Falkenburg's interpretations also seem too extreme in regard to paintings produced in Patinir's workshop. See, for example, Edwin Buijsen's review of Falkenburg's book in *Simiolus* 19 (1989), pp. 209-215.

5 Falkenburg, *op. cit.* (note 3). A less likely interpretation is that of Kuretsky (1974), who associates the dead branches with the crucifix and the leaved branches with the altar. In her view, the artist's purpose was "to emphasize the contrast between the ascetic trials of Christian piety and the voluptuous life of the senses".

6 A painting of St Jerome perhaps by the same master that was formerly in the collection of the princes of Liechtenstein can probably be interpreted in the same way. It depicts a crucifix against an altar decorated with a relief of imps and a half nude woman (fig. d). Kuretsky (1974) posits that the relief on the altar of the Rotterdam panel represents Aristotle and Phyllis. But this cannot be so as the female figure is winged and is seated on a monster.

7 Hoogewerff (1939), Beets (1952).

8 Franz (1969).

9 Its present whereabouts are unknown. Franz (1969) erroneously names the Kunsthistorisches Museum, Vienna, as the owner. With acknowledgements to Dr Karl Schütz, Kunsthistorisches Museum, Vienna.

10 See *Katalog der Gemäldegalerie. Flämische Malerie von Jan van Eyck bis Pieter Bruegel d. Ä Wien, Kunsthistorisches Museum*, 1981, pp. 47, 48. The Houston museum possesses a second version of this painting. See *The Museum of Fine Arts, Houston. A guide to the collection*, 1981, p. 34, no. 63.

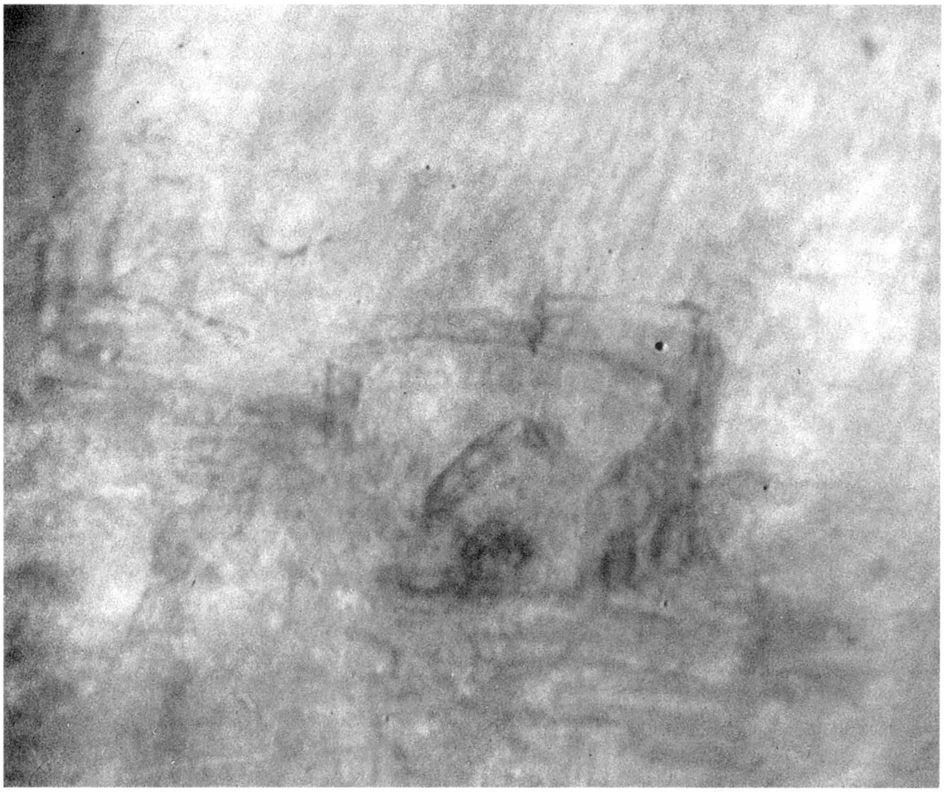

b. Infrared reflectogram showing a detail of the building above a pass in the rocks.

c. Antwerp master, c. 1525, St Jerome in a landscape
Panel; 47.2 x 37.3 cm
Mayer van den Bergh Museum, Antwerp
(inv. no. 375).

d. Antwerp master, c. 1525, St Jerome in a landscape
Panel
Whereabouts unknown.

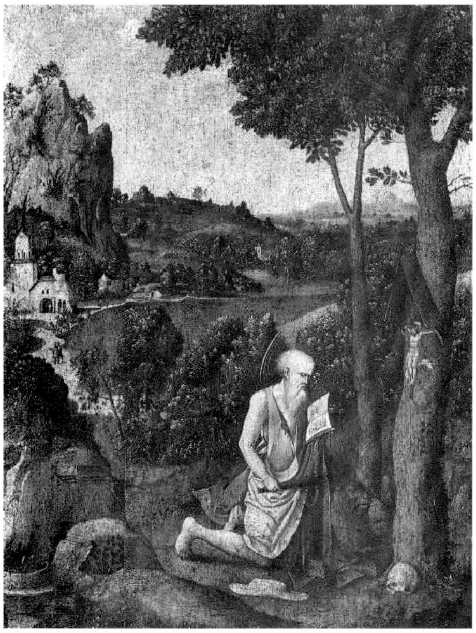

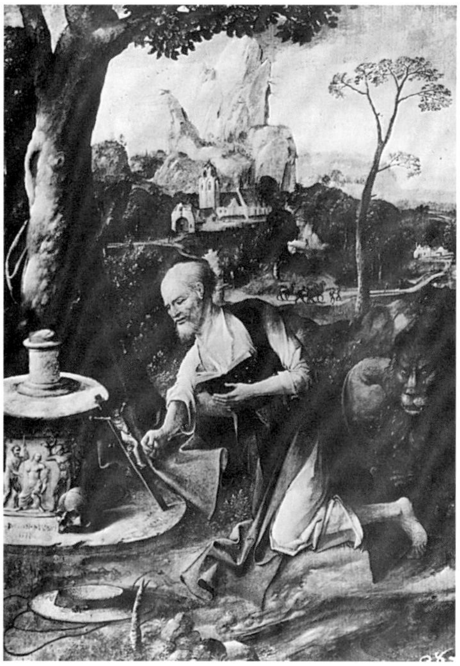

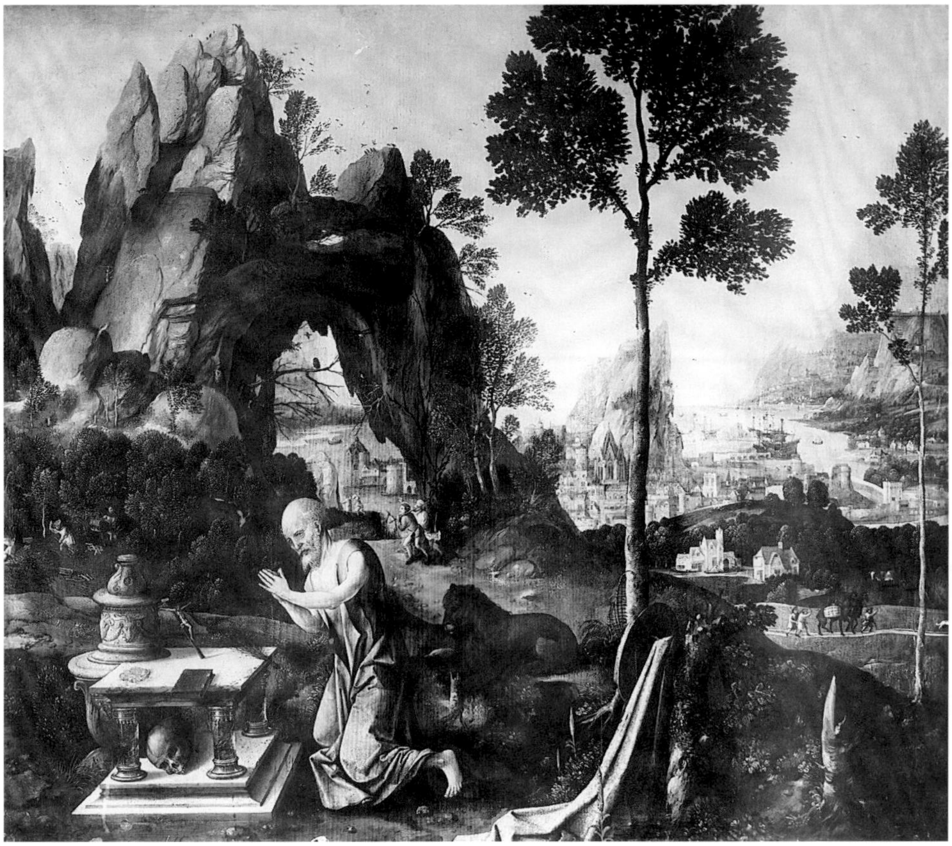

e. Antwerp master, c. 1525, St Jerome in a landscape
Panel; 68.5 x 76 cm
Kunsthistorisches Museum, Vienna (inv. no. 978).

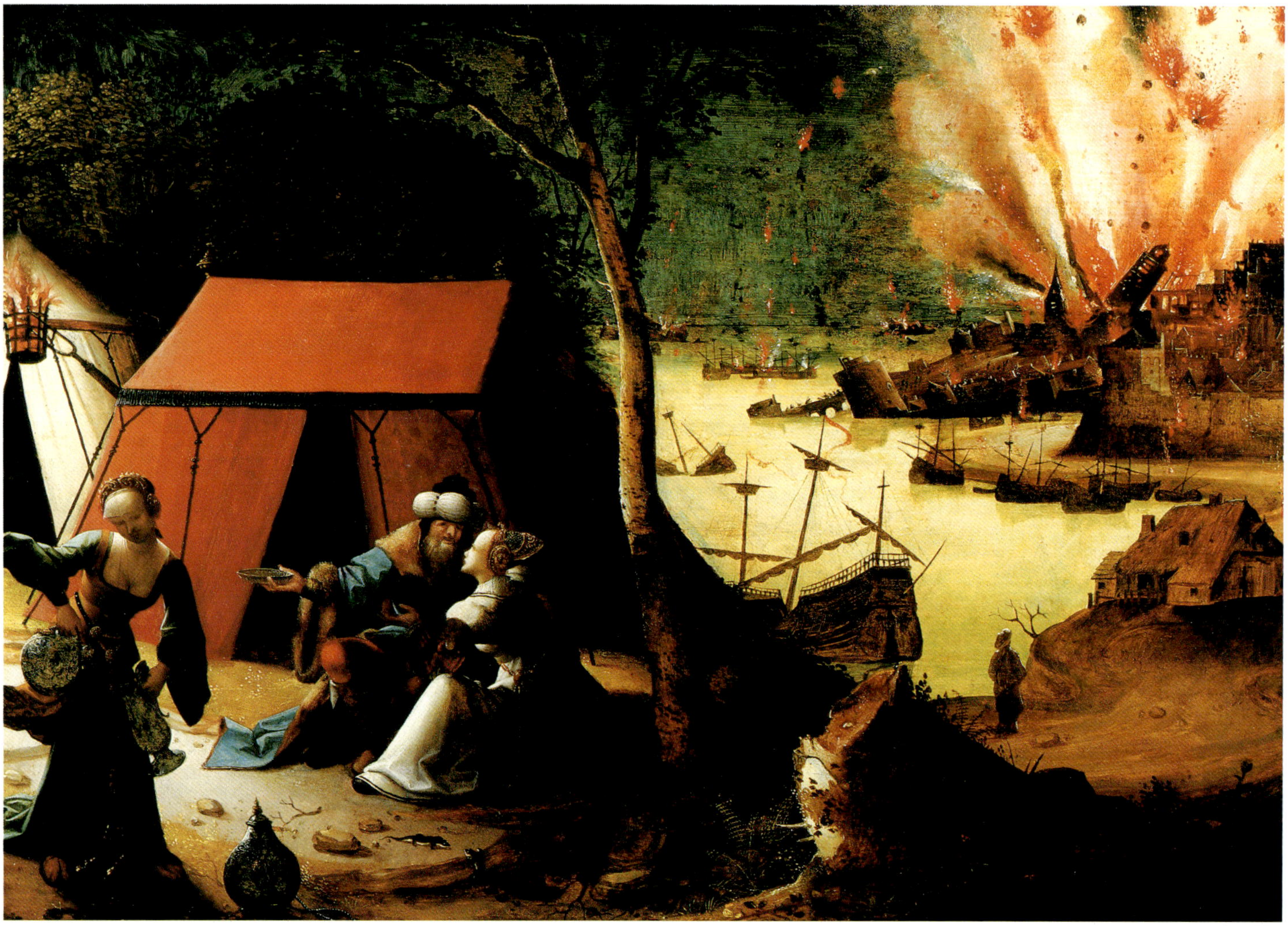

Lot and his daughters

Anonymous
South Netherlandish master, Antwerp?
c. 1520

Panel; 32.5 x 45 cm

Physical characteristics: the panel consists of a single plank.

Infrared reflectography:[1] no underdrawing could be discerned.

Provenance: estate of Francesco Crispi, died 1901;[2] purchased in Rome by G.J. Hoogewerff from an unnamed princess;[3] Beets Gallery, Amsterdam, 1933; purchased from the Gallery in 1934 by D.G. van Beuningen, Rotterdam and Vierhouten, for 8000 guilders; sold by Van Beuningen in the second world war to the German authorities together with seventeen other works from his collection;[4] in or shortly after 1950 all eighteen works were repurchased by him from the State, which had meanwhile recovered them from Germany;[5] acquired by the Museum in 1958 with the Van Beuningen Collection; inv. no. 2456.

Exhibitions: *Jeroen Bosch, Noord-Nederlandsche Primitieven*, Rotterdam, Boymans Museum, 1936, no. 78, fig. 114; *Chefs-d'œuvre de la collection D.G. van Beuningen*, Paris, Petit Palais, 1952, no. 56.

Literature: N. Beets, "Zestiende-eeuwsche kunstenaars - III Lucas van Leyden", *Oud Holland* 51 (1934), pp. 53-57, 59, fig. 2; N. Beets, "Een geschilderde naaktfiguur van Lucas van Leyden", *Maandblad voor Beeldende Kunsten* 12 (1935), pp. 198-199; C. Veth, "Rotterdam. De tentoonstelling in Boymans: Jeroen Bosch, van Geertgen tot Scorel, Noord-Nederlandsche Primitieven", *Maandblad voor Beeldende Kunsten* 13 (1936), p. 290; L. Baldass, "Die Niederländischen Maler des spätgotischen Stiles", *Jahrbuch der kunsthistorisches Sammlungen in Wien* XI (1937), p. 128, fig. 140; G.J. Hoogewerff, *De Noord-Nederlandsche schilderkunst*, III, The Hague 1939, pp. 235, 237, fig. 121; N. Beets, *Lucas van Leyden*, Amsterdam 1940, pp. 40, 43, fig. p. 29; G.J. Hoogewerff, *Het landschap van Bosch tot Rubens*, Antwerp 1954, pp. 58-59, fig. 40; J. Leymarie, *La peinture Hollandaise*, Geneva-Paris-New York 1956, p. 51; cat. 1962, pp. 77-78; M.J. Friedländer, *Lucas van Leyden*, Berlin 1963, pp. 49-50; Friedländer, X, 1973, p. 87, supp. 168, fig. 93; L. Silver, S. Smith, "Carnal knowledge: the late engravings of Lucas van Leyden", *Lucas van Leyden studies (Nederlands Kunsthistorisch Jaarboek) 29 (1978)*, p. 288 (note 56); O. Bätschmann, "Lot und seine Töchter im Louvre - Metaphorik, Antithetik und Ambiguität in einem Niederländischen Gemälde des frühen 16. Jahrhunderts", *Städel-Jahrbuch* 8 (1981), p. 164, fig. 6; J.D. Bangs, "The Leiden Pieterskerk west end, 1512-1637 - aspects of rebuilding and change", *Bulletin KNOB* 84 (1985), p. 2; E. Lawton Smith, *The paintings of Lucas van Leyden, a new appraisal, with catalogue raisonné*, Columbia-London 1992, pp. 182-184.

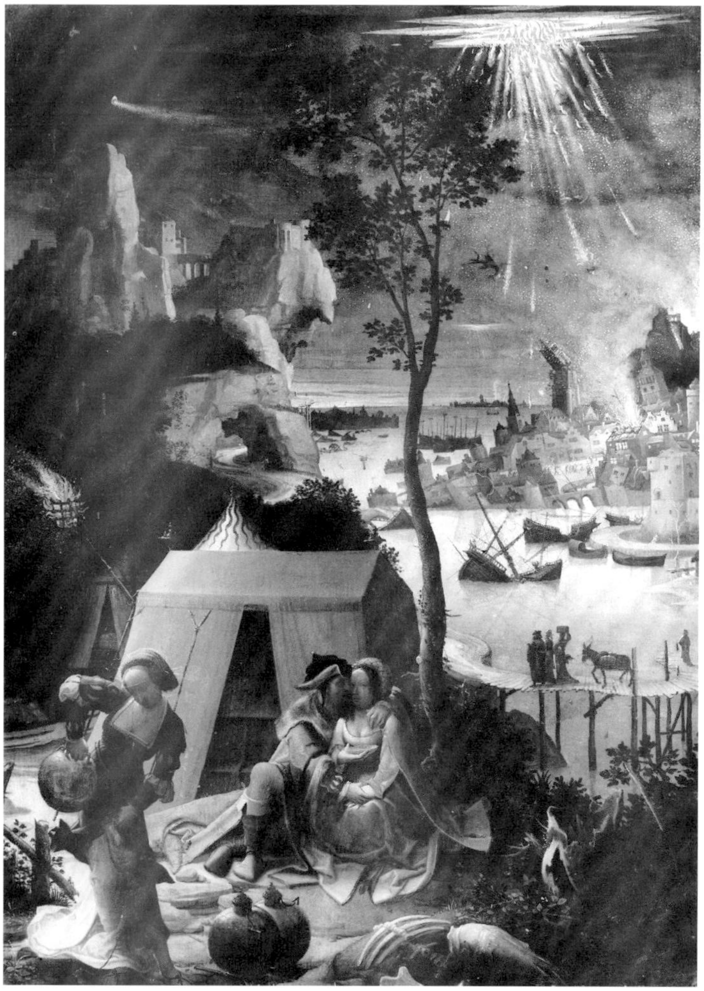

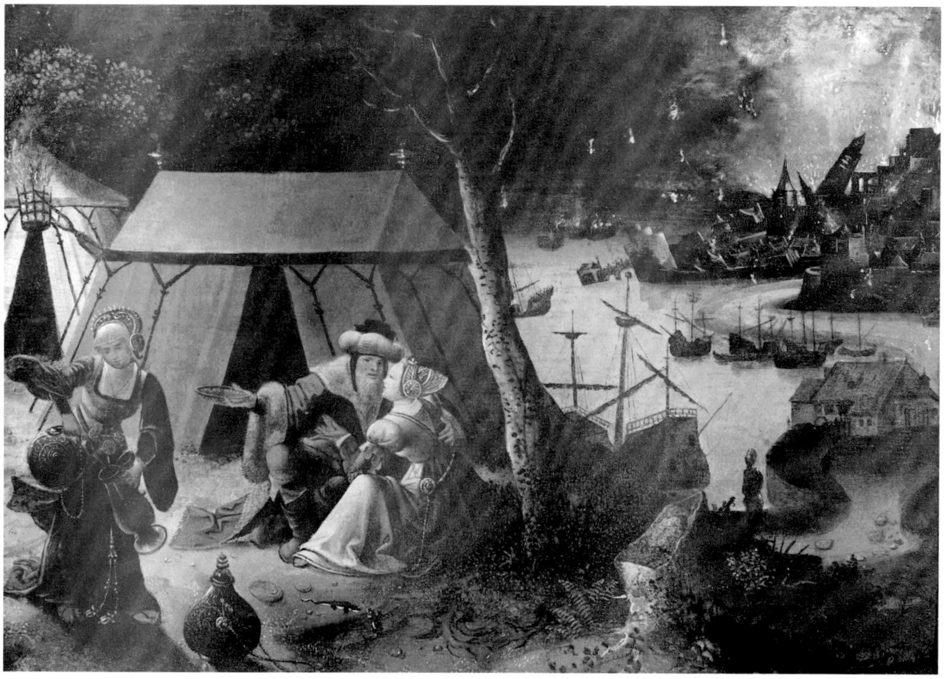

a. South Netherlandish master, Lot and his daughters
Panel; 58 x 34 cm
Paris, Musée du Louvre

b. South Netherlandish master, Lot and his daughters
Panel; 30.5 x 41.5 cm
Tellander Collection, Monnaz s/Morges, Switzerland

Before punishing the wicked inhabitants of Sodom and Gomorrah by destroying their cities, God allowed Lot and his wife and two daughters to escape, warning them not to look back as they fled. Lot's wife disobeyed God's command and was changed into a pillar of salt. Fearing he would have no heirs, Lot's daughters made him drunk and seduced him. In the left foreground Lot is seated with one daughter while the other pours wine. In the right background is the destruction of Sodom, and before it the pillar of salt that was Lot's wife (Genesis 19).

The Old Testament story of Lot, and notably the episode with his daughters, was a widely used theme in the visual arts during the early decades of the sixteenth century. It is the subject, for instance, of an engraving executed in 1530 by Lucas van Leyden, to whom this panel was long attributed (B 16). Many representations of Lot and his daughters were a warning against the wiles used by women to entice men into sin.[6]

The background of the Rotterdam panel shows Sodom in flames, and a tower crashing to the ground. The tower is believed to signify the collapse of the west tower of Leiden's Pieterskerk in 1512.[7] Just as God warned the inhabitants of Leiden ten days before by falling stones, so was Lot warned to flee from Sodom. It is a fanciful interpretation, and in any case unlikely because the panel was probably painted in Antwerp. As noted above, Beets attributed it to Lucas van Leyden in 1934, and Hoogewerff accepted this view. Both authors point to compositional similarities with Lucas's engravings,[8] but the correspondence is minimal. Moreover, any comparison with prints gives rise to problems because Lucas's engravings were a source of inspiration for numerous other artists.

Besides this particular painting, there are five more known versions of the same composition.[9] A panel in Paris is the most divergent of the six. Unlike the others, it is vertical, and the details are different, such as the rocks and the bridge in the background (fig. a). None of them is now attributed to Lucas van Leyden.

Both this work and the Paris painting have also been attributed to the Patinir school.[10] Beets had earlier perceived similarities to the landscapes painted by this Antwerp master.[11] But apart from the rocks, which occur only in the Paris version, the paintings are hardly reminiscent of Patinir's landscapes.

Of the six versions, those in Paris and Rotterdam may be regarded as the best. The Paris version, probably the original, was used as a model by the anonymous painter of the Rotterdam work. Given the style of the two works, they were probably painted in Antwerp about 1520. The others may be regarded as copies of the Rotterdam panel. A seventh panel in Detroit closely resembles them in composition and the attitudes of the figures.[12]
SL

1 Scanned 10 January 1994 by J.R.J. van Asperen de Boer.
2 Letter from N. Beets to D.G. van Beuningen dated 3 July 1934, Boymans-van Beuningen Museum file.
3 See Note 2; Beets (1934), p. 53 (note 2).
4 Letter to Van Beuningen from J. Jolles, director, Stichting Nederlands Kunstbezit, dated 13 April 1950, Boymans-van Beuningen Museum file.
5 Letters from Jolles to Van Beuningen dated 13 April and 3 June 1950, Boymans-van Beuningen Museum file.
6 See Silver and Smith (1978).
7 Bangs (1985).
8 Beets (1934) cites inter alia Lucas' print, *The milkmaid* (B 158), his two woodcuts of *Salome with the head of John the Baptist* (B 12 and 13) and, for the composition as a whole, the engraving, *The Prodigal Son* (B 78), showing a similar landscape with the narrative scene in the left foreground and a vista on the right. Hoogewerff (1939) adds to the examples Beets gives for the standing daughter the figure of Hagar in the engraving *The Casting Forth of Hagar* (B 17), and also remarks on the likeness of the figure of Abraham in this engraving to that of Lot.
9 1. Paris, Musée du Louvre. This version is attributed by most authors to Lucas van Leyden or his circle (for a survey, see Lawton Smith (1992), pp. 181-18; 2. Monnaz s/Morges (Switzerland), Tellander Collection, 1970. First published in 1927 by Vogelsang ("An unknown painting by Lucas van Leyden," *Maandblad voor Beeldende Kunsten* 4, pp. 3-5); 3. Vienna, private collection, 1923. Referred to by Ehrenstein (*Das alte Testament im Bilde*, Vienna 1923, no. 15) and attributed by him to the Brunswick Monogrammist; 4. Present location unknown. First mentioned by Friedländer (1963) (last seen at an auction on Friday, 14 April 1989, where it was described as attributed to Lucas van Leyden by Ader Picard Tajan, Paris); 5. Brussels, Finck Collection, listed in Collection catalogue in 1968, 1972 and 1983.
10 Smith (1992) and J. Held, "Max J. Friedländer, Lucas van Leyden, F. Winkler, ed., Berlin, Walter de Gruyter & Co., 1963" (book review), *The Art Bulletin* 48 (1966), p. 447.
11 Beets (1934).
12 Attributed to Jan de Cock, *Lot and his daughters*; panel; 35.5 x 48 cm, *Treasures from the Detroit Institute of Arts*, Detroit 1966, p. 133.

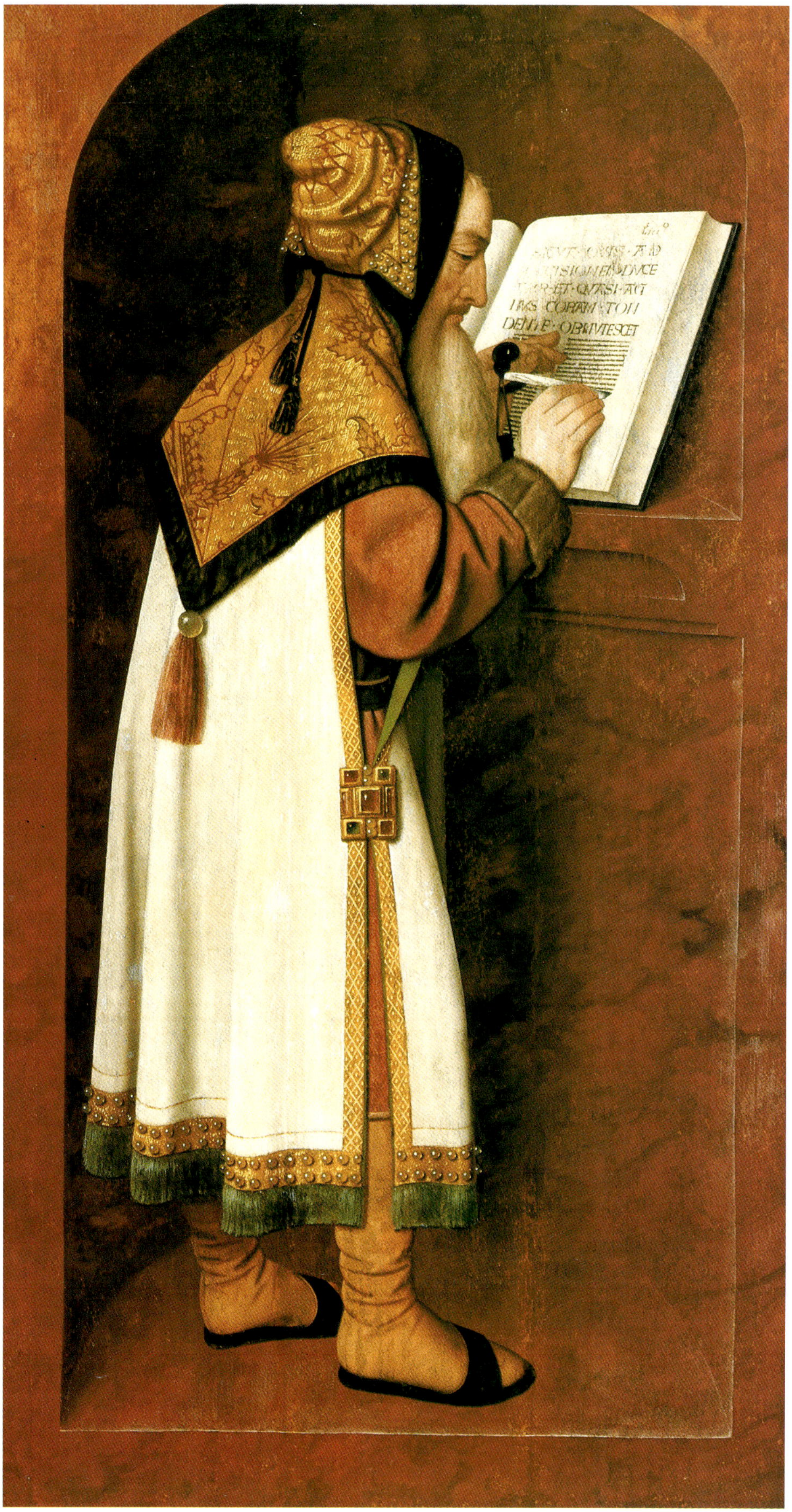
DVCE
ET · QVASI
CORAM
OBMVTESCET

The prophet Isaiah
The prophet Jeremiah

Jan Mostaert
(Haarlem c. 1475-Haarlem 1555/56)

Panels; 100 x 53 cm
The text on the book reads:
(cat. 52) LIIlo/sicut.ovis ad/occisionem.duce/tur.et.quasi.ag/nus.coram.ton/dente.obmvtescet
(cat. 53) frenorum IIlo/memoria. memor/ ero.et.tabescet/in.me.anima.mea.

In the first painting we see the prophet Isaiah, who is busy writing the 53rd chapter of his prophecy. The text means: "He is brought as a lamb to the slaughter, and as a sheep before her shearers is dumb, so he openeth not his mouth." (Isaiah 53:7).

The prophet Jeremiah is standing in an alcove with his back to the text. In his right hand he is holding a goose quill pen, whose sharpness he is testing with his left thumb. The text on his book means: "My soul hath them still in remembrance, and is humbled in me" (Lamentations of Jeremiah 3:20). Both paintings were very likely once parts of a larger work, possibly an altarpiece. It is less certain that they form the wings of a triptych, as Snyder believes, because the reverse of the panels are not painted.[3]

The top right-hand corner of the Isaiah panel and the top left-hand corner of the Jeremiah panel were originally bevelled, which appears to suggest a different original function than two separate panels.

Whilst both paintings were still listed as "Dutch school" at the auction of 1937, Hannema, after donating them to the Boymans Museum Foundation in 1940, ascribed them to Jan Mostaert, an attribution which has been accepted by later authors. The figure of the prophet Jeremiah bears a close resemblance to the figure of Abraham in Mostaert's painting of *The banishment of Hagar* in the Thyssen-Bornemisza collection.[4]

Winkler was the first to publish a comprehensive study of the paintings.[5]He refers to the unconventional posture of the prophet Isaiah, who is standing with his back to the viewer, which demonstrates the narrative qualities of the painter. This contrasts with the prophet Jeremiah, who is shown *en face* and is looking the viewer straight in the eye.

Hannema dated the two panels around 1490-1500. Winkler, however, commented on the dull colours and matt modelling, which suggested to him a fairly late dating in Mostaert's oeuvre. Snyder, by contrast, believed that these pieces show Mostaert at work as a young artist.[6]Until we know more about Mostaert's oeuvre, it will be difficult to clarify this further.

The state of the paintings is regrettable. The paint has flaked heavily in many places in the past and the original quality has been considerably reduced.
JG

Physical characteristics: both panels consist of three vertical planks.

Infrared reflectography: (cat. 52)[1] underdrawing is only visible in parts. The pen was originally longer, extending over the beard (fig. a); small lines in the shade of the drapery folds; (cat. 53) no underdrawing could be discerned.[2]

Provenance: Hidde Nijland, auction The Hague, Venduhuis, 5 and 6 October 1937, nos. 371 and 372 (700 guilders); D. Hannema, Rotterdam; donated to the Boymans Museum Foundation in memory of Mr and Mrs Hannema-de Stuers of The Hague by their children, 1940; (cat. 52) inv. no. St. 13; (cat. 53) inv. no. St. 14.

Exhibitions: *Catalogus schilderijen, teekeningen en beeldhouwwerken uit particuliere Nederlandsche verzamelingen*, Rotterdam, Boymans Museum, 1938-1939, no. 25, fig. X.

Literature: *Stichting Museum Boymans Rotterdam, Verslag over de jaren 1939, 1940 en 1941*, p. 5, fig.; F. Winkler, "Zur Kenntnis und Würdigung des Jan Mostaert", *Zeitschrift für Kunstwissenschaft* 13 (1959), pp. 212-213, figs. 23, 24; cat. 1962, p. 93; J. Snyder, "The Early Haarlem School of Painting, Part III: The Problem of Geertgen tot Sint Jans and Jan Mostaert", *The Art Bulletin* 53 (1971), p. 455, figs. 12, 13; Friedländer, X, 1973, p. 88, Add. 176, p. 90, fig. 120.

1 Scanned and recorded by J.R.J. van Asperen de Boer on 10 and 17 January 1994. The assemblies were made by Cunera Vergeer. Infrared reflectograms: 1558/23A-27A.
2 Scanned on 10 January 1994 by J.R.J. van Asperen de Boer.
3 Snyder (1971).
4 See Friedländer, X, 1973, p. 69, no. 7, pl. 9.
5 Winkler (1959).
6 Winkler (1959); Snyder (1971).

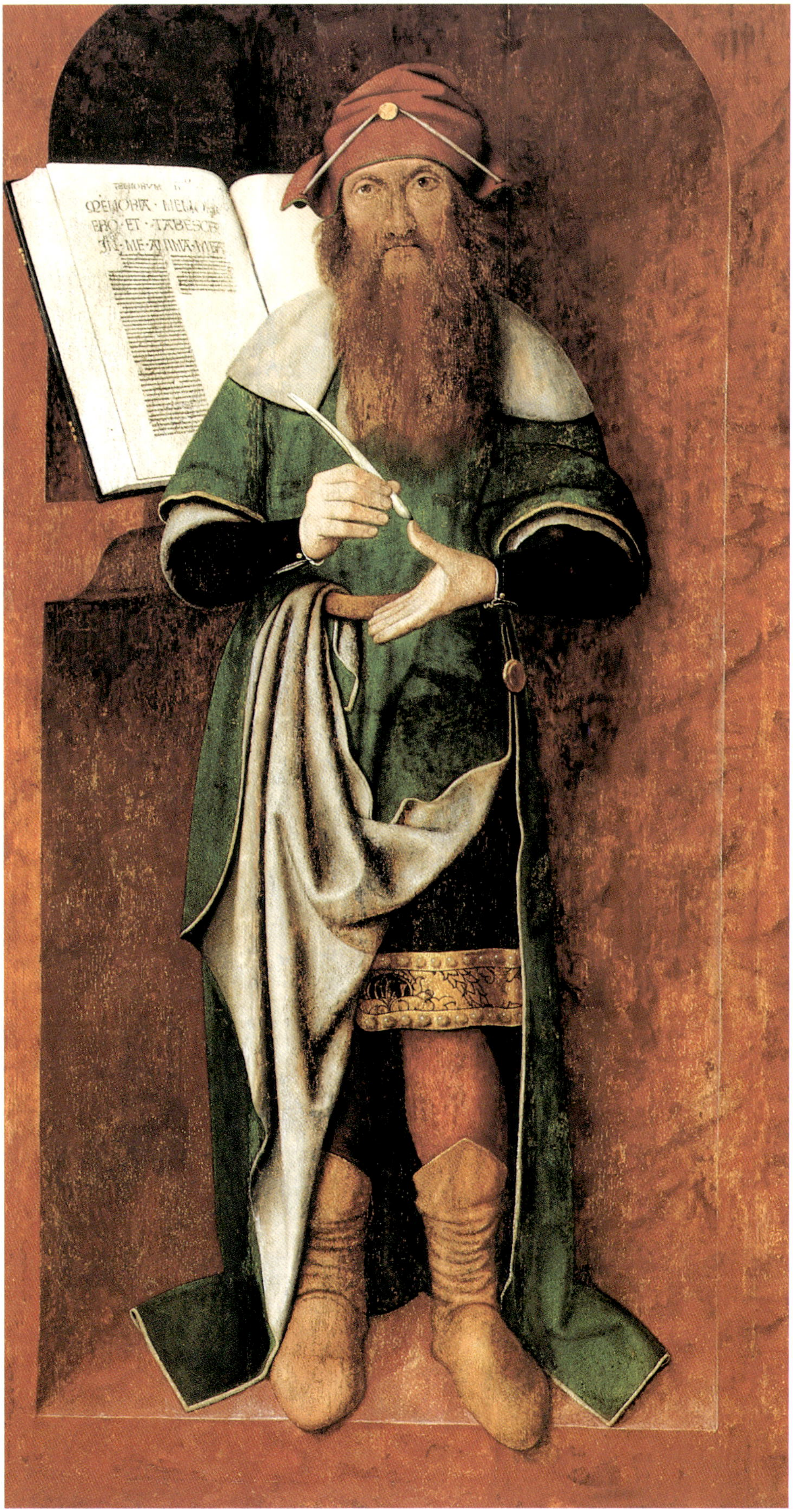

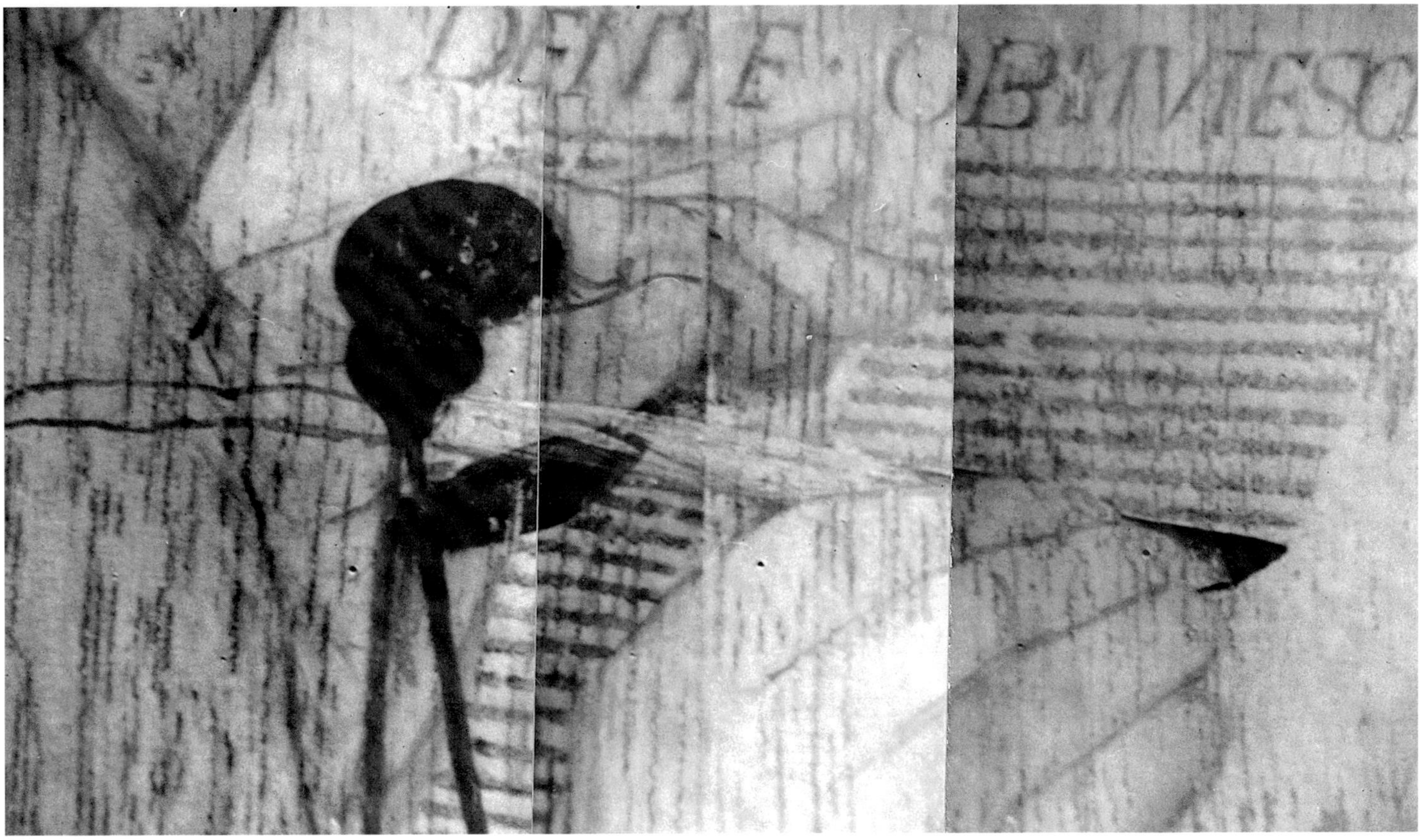

a. Infrared reflectogram assembly. Detail of the prophet Isaiah's right hand.

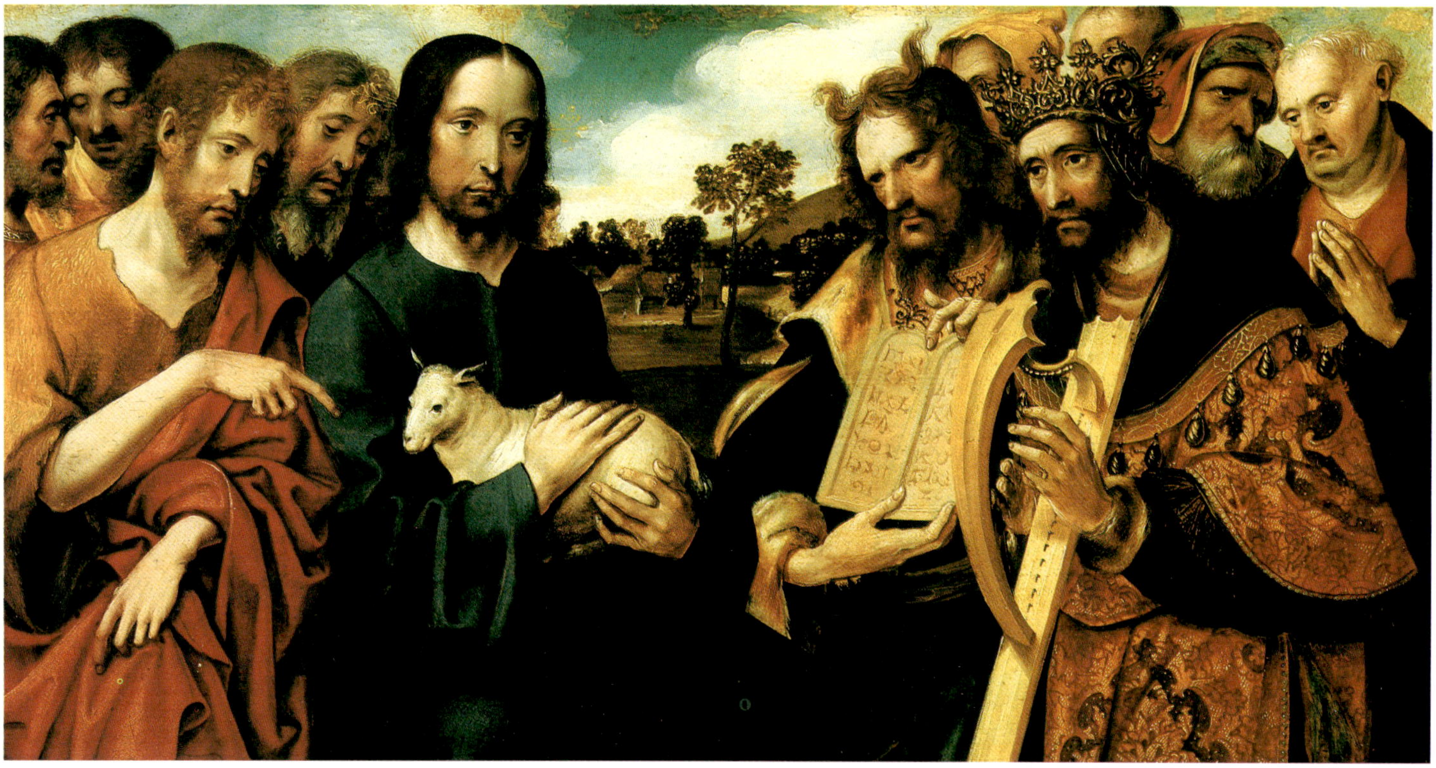

Christ as the Good Shepherd with John the Baptist opposite Moses and David

Cornelis Engebrechtsz (group)
(Leiden 1468-Leiden 1527)

Panel; 23.5 x 42.5 cm

Most of the picture space is occupied by the figures of eleven men. They are divided into two groups, separated from one another by a view of a landscape with trees and farmhouses. It is just possible to discern a shepherd and his flock under the trees in the distance. The figures are depicted in three-quarter length, their heads almost reaching the top of the panel. One of them in fact extends all the way up. Small as it is (23.5 x 42.5 cm), the painting has a surprising monumentality.

The four figures in the foreground are the most prominent. Their clothing and attributes identify them as Christ, John the Baptist, Moses and David. The first figure left of centre, and the only seated figure in the picture, is Christ. He wears a blue robe and has a cruciform halo. On his lap is the lamb that symbolises him. The association of the lamb with Christ harks back to John the Baptist's exclamation to two of his disciples when they noticed Christ coming towards them: "There is the Lamb of God" (*Ecce Agnus Dei*). Christ with the lamb is also a representation of the Good Shepherd who watches over his flock.[2] In the words of Isaiah (40:11), Christ "shall feed his flock like a shepherd: he shall gather the lambs with his arms, and carry them in his bosom". The lamb is also the attribute of John the Baptist, who is standing beside Christ and pointing to the animal. John's camelskin tunic can be seen under his red cloak.

The principal figures of the group on the right side of the painting are Moses and David. Moses, in a blue-green fur-lined robe, is holding the stone tablets inscribed with the ten commandments that he received from God at Mount Sinai (Exodus 24:12-18 and Exodus 34). He can also be recognised by the 'horns' sprouting from either side of his head, rendered here as protruding locks of hair.[3] The man wearing a crown next to Moses is King David, resplendent in a brocade robe and luxurious cape. The harp he is playing is his customary attribute. The identity of the seven figures in the background is unclear. Since 1913, when the painting was first exhibited in public, the three men behind Christ and St John have been regarded as *partes pro toto* for the twelve disciples.[4] Yet if they were indeed meant to be apostles, it is odd that the artist has not indicated exactly who they were. Some scholars have also identified the three men behind Moses and David as sages and heroes, in this case of the Old Testament, but this hypothesis has not been substantiated. Two of the faces are partly obscured, adding to the difficulty of identifying them. We can only speculate as to who they might be, or whether the painter had anyone particular in mind. The distinctive-looking figure on the far right in an attitude of prayer was probably the donor.[5] He bears a strong resemblance to the donor in the painting of *The descent from the cross* in the J. Böhler Collection in Munich (fig. 55. b). The iconography of the painting is highly unusual. John the Baptist, the forerunner of Christ and the first saint of the New Testament, is portrayed together with the Saviour opposite Moses and David. David, the prototype and ancestor of Christ, represents together with Moses, the Old Law. Moses, even more than David, is seen as a prefiguration of Christ. The painting depicts both the Old and New Covenants, with Christ, the fulfilment of the Old Testament prophecy, as the central figure.

Physical characteristics: the panel consists of a single plank.

Infrared reflectography: black chalk underdrawing of a landscape which appears to be unrelated to the present painting. See entry.

Paint samples: the structure of the paint is simple, generally consisting of a single layer.[1]

Provenance: M. Flersheim, Paris; Ivar Kreuger, Stockholm and New York; sale Stockholm, 14-16 September 1932, no. 46, fig.; Warnenck, Stockholm; sale Bukowksi, Stockholm, 5-8 November 1975, no. 19, fig.; S. Nystad, The Hague; bought by the Museum in 1976 for 301,600 guilders; inv. no. 2885.

Exhibitions: *Noord-Nederlandsche schilder- en beeldhouwkunst vóór 1575*, Utrecht, Gebouw voor Kunsten en Wetenschappen, 1913, supplement to the catalogue, no. 165.

Literature: N. Beets, "De tentoonstelling van Noord-Nederlandsche schilder- en beeldhouwkunst vóór 1575 (Utrecht, 3 September-3 October 1913)", *Onze Kunst* 25 (1914), pp. 53-54, fig. 8; W. Cohen, "Die Ausstellung Frühholländischer Malerei und Plastik in Utrecht", *Zeitschrift für Bildende Kunst* 25 (1914), p. 30, fig. 1; M. Conway, *The Van Eyck and their followers*, London 1921, fig. XXIII, 4; P. Wescher, "Zur Chronologie der Gemälde des Cornelis Engebrechtsen", *Zeitschrift für Bildende Kunst* 58 (1924-25), pp. 98, 103; Friedländer, X, 1932, pp. 54, 132, 141, fig. 99; Friedländer, XIV, 1937, p. 121; G.J. Hoogewerff, *De Noord-Nederlandsche Schilderkunst*, III, The Hague 1939, pp. 198-199, fig. 105; E. Pelinck, "Cornelis Engebrechtsz, de herkomst van zijn kunst", *Nederlandsch Kunsthistorisch Jaarboek* 2 (1948-49), p. 55, fig. 12; J. Giltay, "De Goede Herder met Johannes de Doper, apostelen en figuren uit het Oude Testament, *Cornelis Engebrechtsz, Leiden (ca. 1468-1533)*", *Vereniging Rembrandt Verslag over 1976*, pp. 31-33, fig.; W.S. Gibson, *The paintings of Cornelis Engebrechtsz*, New York-London 1977, p. 111, no. 19, fig. 29; Susanne Urbach, "Eine unbekannte Darstellung von *Sündenfall und Erlösung* in Budapest und das Weiterleben des Cranachschen Rechtfertigungsbildes", *Niederdeutsche Beiträge zur Kunstgeschichte* 28 (1989), p. 40, fig. 12.

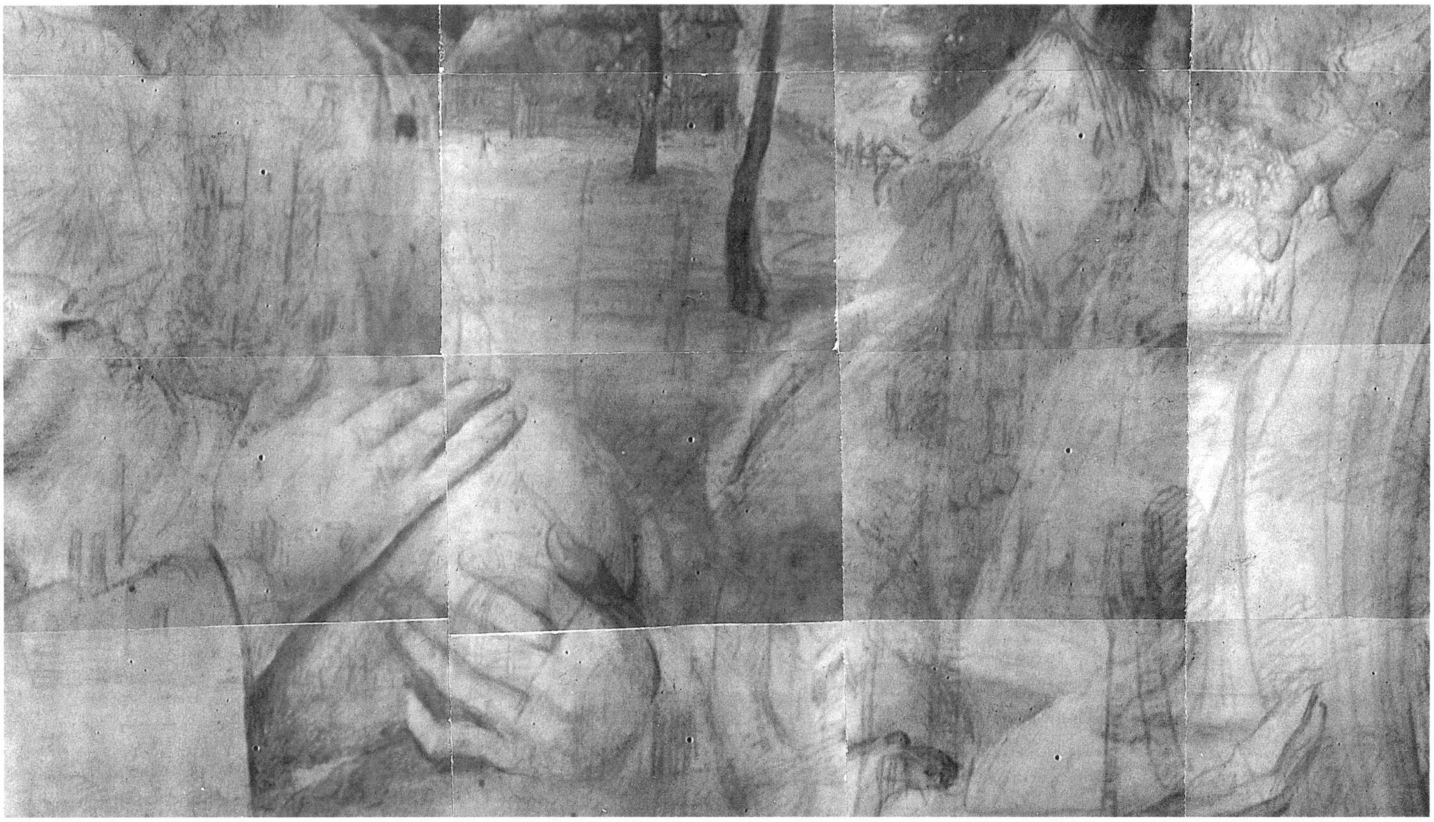

a. Infrared reflectogram assembly. Detail of the middle section showing the tower with battlements.

Art historians have generally ranked the panel among Cornelis Engebrechtsz's best works. It is a colourful and well balanced composition with strong details. The hands, for instance, are worth noting in this respect. The pioneer of panel painting in Leiden, Engebrechtsz managed a large workshop. His assistants and pupils included not only his three sons, but also Lucas van Leyden and Aert Claesz. Because of his far-reaching influence and numerous assistants it is difficult to distinguish his oeuvre. Only three paintings can be considered to be predominantly the master's own work. All three are mentioned in Van Mander's *Schilderboeck* of 1604.[6] Two of them are the altarpieces of *The Crucifixion* and *The Lamentation*, now at De Lakenhal in Leiden. Gibson's monograph of 1977 attributes twenty paintings and two drawings to Cornelis Engebrechtsz, and names four other artists as the authors of the remaining works associated with the master or his studio. Gibson accepts *Christ as the Good Shepherd* as an autograph work, and dates it after 1510. Even before this, however, its authorship had never been questioned.

In the 1970s, investigations were carried out on the three paintings documented by Van Mander as well as two panels at the Rijksmuseum which are attributed to Engebrechtsz.[7] All were found to have extensive underdrawings, and the similarities in style confirmed the attribution of the two Amsterdam paintings. *Christ as the Good Shepherd* has now been examined as well. The study revealed traces of a black chalk underdrawing that bears no relation whatsoever to the picture. With some difficulty it is possible to discern a scene of buildings in a landscape. A tower with battlements, for instance, can be seen under the stone tablets in Moses's hands (fig. a.). The panel may originally have been the top section of a far larger painting in which the landscape served as a background to a biblical scene. The fragments of landscape that can be seen in the drawing are quite different from the extensive underdrawings in the five paintings mentioned above. No drawing is visible under the actual representation of *Christ as the Good Shepherd*. These considerations argue against an attribution to Engebrechtsz. Although the style of the work places it firmly in the circle around the master, more needs to be known about how work was distributed in his studio, who actually worked there, and exactly how much of the work was done by the master and how much by his assistants.
LH

1 The examination with infrared reflectography was carried out on 22 January 1990 by J.R.J. van Asperen de Boer. Infrared reflectograms: AB 1145-AB 1147. The assembly was made by G. Hamming. Paint samples: AB 300/1-8.
2 See Hoogewerff (1939).
3 J. Hall, *Dictionary of subjects & symbols in art*, London 1974, p. 213. The legend that Moses had horns on his head derived from a mistranslation of the word *cornutam*, which was used in the Vulgate to describe Moses's face when he descended from Mount Sinai. The translation should read: "When Moses came down from mount Sinai... he wist not that the skin of his face shone while he talked with him" (Exodus 34:29). In the Latin of this period the word meant "horns" as well as "rays of light".
4 Exhib. cat. Utrecht, 1913.
5 Giltay (1976).
6 Karel van Mander, *Het Schilderboeck*, Haarlem 1604, fol. 210 verso.
7 J.R.J. van Asperen de Boer and A.K. Wheelock, "Underdrawings in some paintings by Cornelis Engebrechtsz", *Oud Holland* 87 (1973), pp. 61-94.

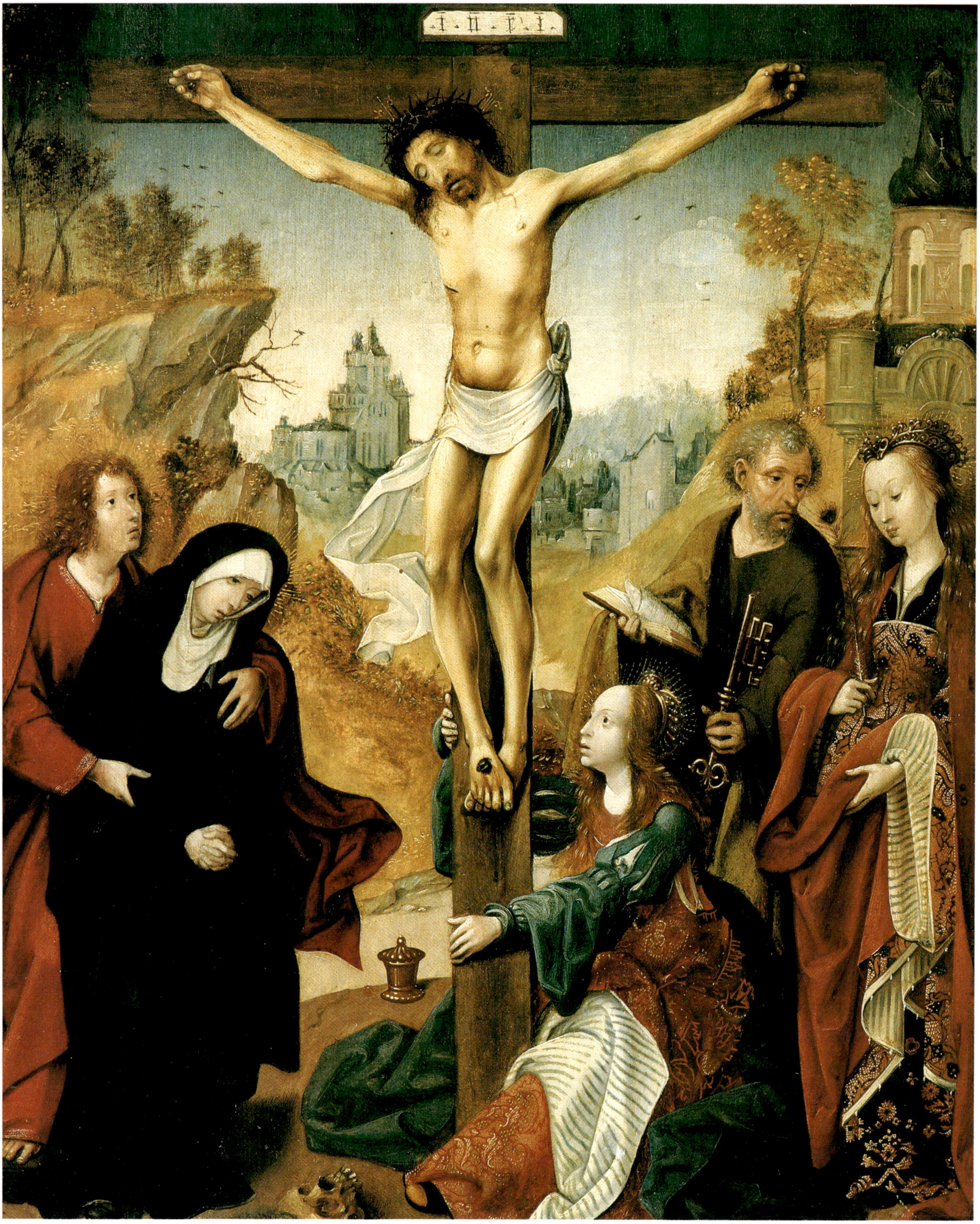
I.N.R.I

The Crucifixion

Cornelis Engebrechtsz (group)
(Leiden 1468-Leiden 1527)

Panel; 44 x 34.5 cm

A grieving Virgin Mary stands at the foot of the cross on which Christ has been crucified. Her hands are folded and her eyes cast down. She is supported by St John, who gazes up at the body of the dead Saviour. St Peter, Mary Magdalene and St Barbara, recognisable by their clothing and attributes, are on the opposite side of the cross. The positions in which they are shown at the scene of the execution follow an established pattern. The Virgin and St John are on the right of the Saviour, the 'good' side, while Mary Magdalene is shown in her customary place at the foot of the cross. She is conventionally portrayed with flowing blonde hair, and is wearing a beautiful red, embroidered cloak over a blue robe. A pot of salve, her traditional attribute, stands beside her. Peter, too, can be identified by his usual symbol, the key to the kingdom of Heaven, and St Barbara by the tower behind her. The tower in this picture has not always been associated with St Barbara, as it is only one of several castle-like structures in the landscape.[2] Nevertheless the peacock feather she holds is also one of her attributes. It is a symbol of immortality alluding to her frequent escapes from death.[3] The daughter of a heathen nobleman, Barbara too is elegantly dressed. The scene is set in a hilly, wooded landscape with a town in the distance.

Gibson published a monograph on Engebrechtsz in 1977, in which *The crucifixion* was accepted as an autograph work. Yet other scholars have questioned the attribution of this colourful and well-preserved panel. Hoogewerff describes it as a typical studio piece from the second quarter of the sixteenth century, adding, however, that this "profoundly moving, beautiful and well-considered panel, notwithstanding the conventional presentation of the protagonists [...] would not be unworthy of the venerable master of the studio".[4] Pelinck also ascribes it to the circle around Engebrechtsz, but dates it earlier, around 1495-1500.[5] Gibson, on the other hand, believes it was made after 1510. While it is true that the women's faces, costumes and hairstyles are similar to those in Engebrechtsz's work from the period before 1510, the actual style of the painting is closer to work from his later period. In view of the slightly outdated composition and landscape features, Gibson concludes that the painting must have been a later version of an early design.[6]

Gibson attributes to four different artists a group of paintings which are associated with the studio, but which were not made by Engebrechtsz himself. He refers to these painters as Hand A, Hand B, the Hagar Master and the Master of the Viennese Lamentation. In his view, one of the paintings he ascribes to Hand A bears such a close resemblance to *The Crucifixion* that the two works were probably part of the same altarpiece. The work in question, a *Descent from the cross* (J. Böhler Collection, Munich) was formerly in the H. Petri Collection in Antwerp (fig. b).[7] The paintings Gibson ascribes to Hand A are studio pieces that clearly reflect Engebrechtsz's style, but are not quite up to his standard.

Not only is there a strong resemblance between the figures in *The crucifixion* and *The descent from the cross*, but the panels themselves are almost exactly the same size.[8]

Physical characteristics: the panel consists of three vertical planks.

Infrared reflectography: extensive underdrawing in black chalk (fig. a).[1] See entry.

Provenance: M.J. Schretlen Collection, Amsterdam; Netherlands Office for Fine Arts, The Hague, inv. nr. NK 2666; on loan to the Boymans-van Beuningen Museum from the Netherlands Office for Fine Arts since 1948; inv. no. 2315.

Exhibitions: *Noord-Nederlandsche Schilder- en Beeldhouwkunst vòòr 1575*, Utrecht, Gebouw voor Kunsten en Wetenschappen, 1913, supplement, no. 166; *Jeroen Bosch Noord-Nederlandsche Primitieven*, Rotterdam, Boymans Museum, 1936, no. 69, fig. 104; *Herwonnen Kunstbezit*, Utrecht, Centraal Museum, 1946, no. 47, fig. 6.

Literature: Friedländer, XIV, 1937, p. 121; Mtr., "Meisterwerke im Amsterdamer Handel", *Die Weltkunst* 12 (1938), no. 8, pp. 1-2, fig. on p. 2; G.J. Hoogewerff, *De Noord-Nederlandsche Schilderkunst*, III, The Hague 1939, p. 202, fig. 107; E. Pelinck, "Cornelis Engebrechtsz, de herkomst van zijn kunst", *Nederlandsch Kunsthistorisch Jaarboek* 2 (1948-49), pp. 53, 55; *Jaarverslag Museum Boymans* 27 (1948), p. 5; cat. 1962, p. 48; W.S. Gibson, *The paintings of Cornelis Engebrechtsz*, New York-London 1977, pp. 35, 111-113, 168, cat. no. 14, p. 240, fig. 30.

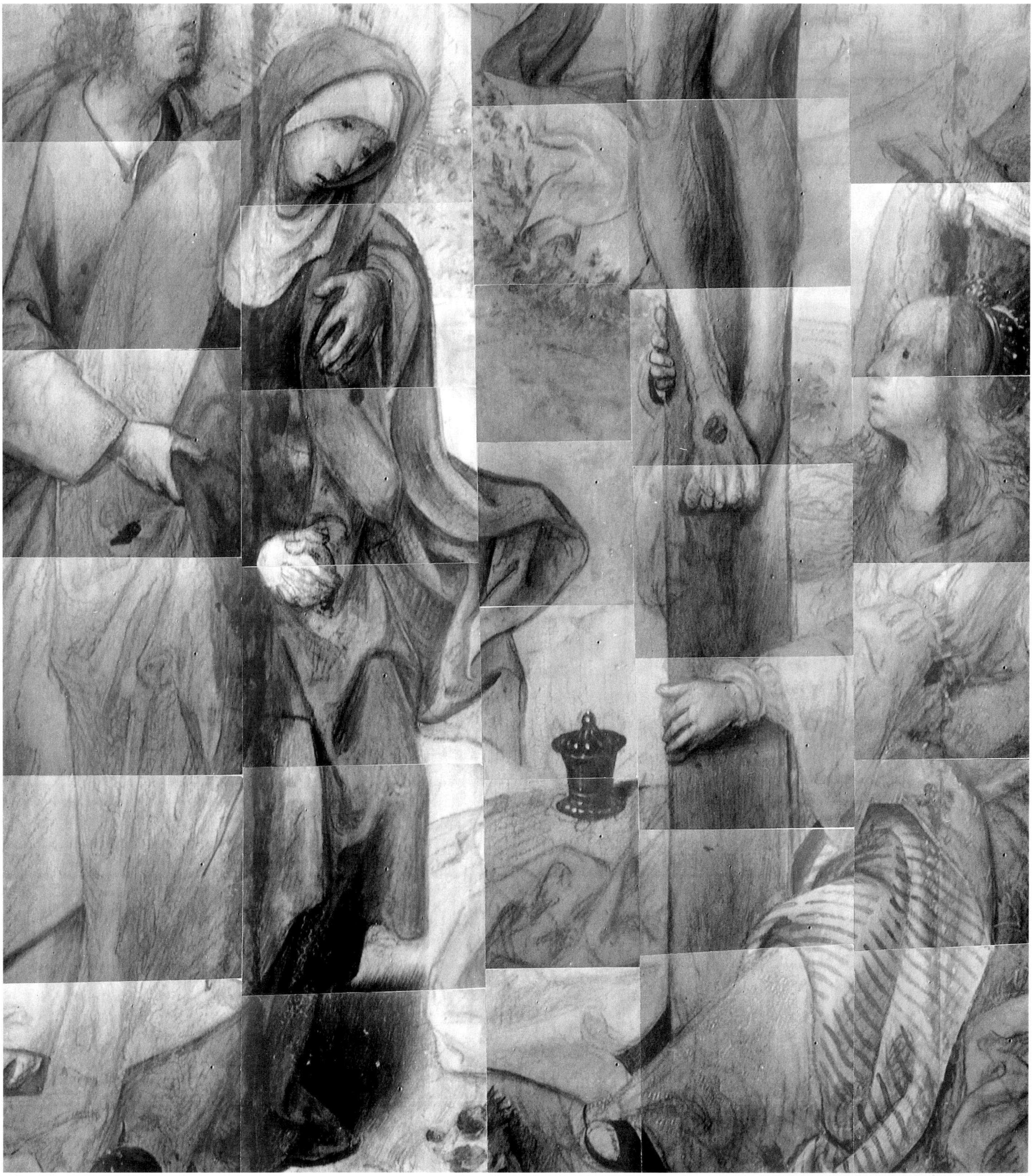

a. Infrared reflectogram assembly. Detail of St John, the Virgin Mary and Mary Magdalene.

Yet there are important differences as well, such as the fact that Mary Magdalene and St Barbara are depicted in different costumes in the two paintings. This undermines Gibson's proposal that the panels were made for the same altarpiece, since it is unlikely that the figures on a retable illustrating a series of chronological events would be depicted in different clothing. Another argument against this suggestion is that the Virgin and St John would be repeated almost literally on the same retable.

The Rotterdam painting has an extensive but rather scratchy underdrawing in black chalk (fig. a), quite unlike the drawings in works that are firmly attributed to Engebrechtsz.[9] The fact that few changes have been made in the drawing suggests that it may have been copied from a preliminary study. The painting itself faithfully follows the underdrawing. In view of the stylistic differences between the underdrawing here and that in paintings securely attributed to Engebrechtsz, the attribution of *The crucifixion* as an entirely autograph work is probably untenable. More information is needed to establish whether it was made in Engebrechtsz's studio, and what role the master himself played in its production.
LH

1 The painting was scanned and recorded on 20 December 1993 and 17 January 1994 by J.R.J. van Asperen de Boer. The assembly was made by Liesbeth M. Helmus. Infrared reflectograms: AB 1552/26-1557/29A.
2 Exhib. cat. Rotterdam, 1936, misidentifies the woman as St Catherine.
3 J. Hall, *Hall's dictionary of subjects & symbols in art*, London 1974, p. 41.
4 " [...] bijzonder treffende en, ondanks conventioneele inkleeding der begeleidende figuren, gave en bezonken paneel [...] den bedaagden leider van het atelier zeker niet onwaardig [zou zijn]". Hoogewerff (1939).
5 Pelinck (1948-49), p. 53.
6 Gibson (1977), p. 111.
7 Cat. 1962 and Gibson (1977), p. 168.
8 See Gibson (1977), no. 34, p. 247.
9 See cat. no. 54. On Engebrechtsz's underdrawing, see J.R.J. van Asperen de Boer, A.K. Wheelock, "Underdrawing in some paintings by Cornelis Engebrechtsz", *Oud Holland* 87 (1973), pp. 61-94.

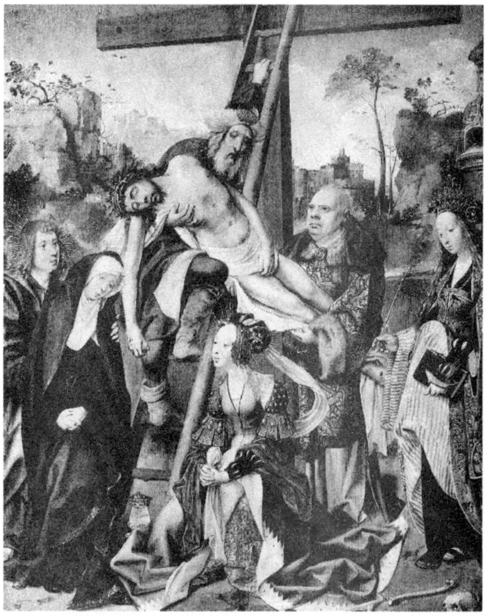

b. Cornelis Engebrechtsz (group), Descent from the cross
Panel; 42.5 x 33.5 cm
Munich, J. Böhler Collection.

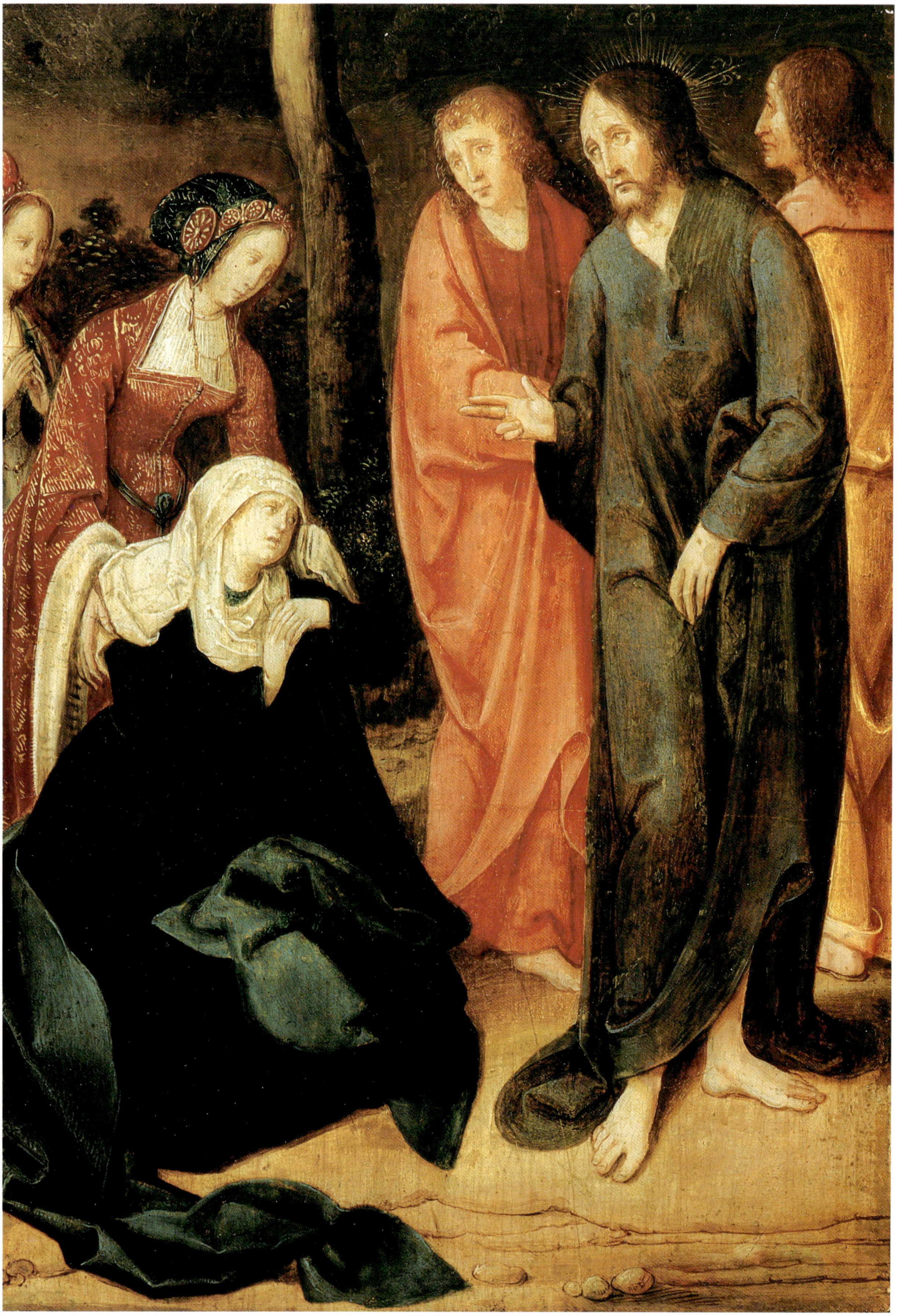

Christ taking leave of his mother

Cornelis Engebrechtsz (group)
(Leiden 1468-Leiden 1527)

Panel; 23.5 x 16 cm

The *Meditations on the life of Christ* by Pseudo-Bonaventura describes how the Saviour parted from his mother at the village of Bethany before entering Jerusalem for the last time. The theme was especially popular in sixteenth-century German painting. The scene shown here is based to a large extent on a woodcut by the German artist Albrecht Dürer.[3] The Virgin Mary kneels before Christ with her hands folded in anguish. Her gaze is fixed on her son's hand, which is raised in benediction. Directly behind her is the resplendent Mary Magdalene. The woman known as the third Mary can be seen on the left of the painting. She later appears at Christ's tomb as well, in the company of her two namesakes. At Christ's side are St John, recognisable by his golden curls and red robe, and an unidentified man in a yellow cloak.

The composition was copied from a woodcut made by Dürer in about 1504-1505, the last in a series on the life of the Virgin Mary (fig. a).[4] Christ, the Virgin and Mary Magdalene are portrayed in almost exactly the same attitudes and positions as in the example. The details too are essentially the same. Mary's cloak, for example, and the finely drawn pebbles in the foreground have been copied exactly. In Dürer's version, however, the tree is on the right, behind Christ. The main differences between the woodcut and the painting are in the number of figures and the background. The painter has added two men to Dürer's composition, and omitted the walled city. The black chalk underdrawing has a rather wooden quality and looks like the work of an unpractised hand (fig. b).

The panel has been attributed to various artists, mostly in the circle around Cornelis Engebrechtsz. They include Engebrechtsz's sons Cornelis Cornelisz Kunst and Lucas Cornelisz de Cock, both of whom were employed at their father's large studio. It has also been ascribed to the painter Jan de Cock, who worked in Antwerp in the early decades of the sixteenth century. Gibson's monograph on Cornelisz Engebrechtsz associates Jan de Cock's work with the oeuvre of the Master of the Viennese Lamentation, a painter who was active from about 1512/14 to 1530. Gibson draws attention to the distinctive features of his style, notably the relatively large figures and rather weakly drawn faces and hands. He also accepts *Christ taking leave of his mother* as a work by the same master. In doing so, however, he disregards the fact that it is not an original composition.[5]

It is not yet possible to conclude whether the painting was made by an apprentice at Cornelis Engebrechtsz's studio, or by an artist who was influenced by the master's work. Its style in any event links it to Cornelis Engebrechtsz and his studio, but further research is needed in order to distinguish between the oeuvres of the different artists who formed this group.[6]
LH

Physical characteristics: the panel consists of a single plank with bevelled edges on all four sides.[1]

Infrared reflectography: underdrawing in black chalk.[2] See description.

Provenance: Colnaghi Gallery, London; bought there in 1935 by D.G. van Beuningen, Rotterdam and Vierhouten, for 1,500 guilders; acquired with the D.G. van Beuningen Collection in 1958; inv. no. 2448.

Exhibitions: *Nederlandse Primitieven uit Nederlands particulier bezit*, Laren, Singer Museum, 1961, no. 34.

Literature: N. Beets, "Zestiende-eeuwse kunstenaars IV. Lucas Cornelisz de Kock (slot)", *Oud Holland* 53 (1936), p. 73; L. Baldass, "Die Niederländischen Maler des spätgotischen Stiles", *Jahrbuch der Kunsthistorischen Sammlungen in Wien* 11 (1937), p. 125, fig. 133; G.J. Hoogewerff, *De Noord-Nederlandsche Schilderkunst*, III, The Hague 1939, p. 373; E. Pelinck, "Cornelis Engebrechtsz. De herkomst van zijn kunst", *Nederlandsch Kunsthistorisch Jaarboek* 2 (1948-49), p. 62; cat. 1962, p. 48; W.S. Gibson, *The paintings of Cornelis Engebrechtsz*, New York-London 1977, pp. 186-187, 195, cat. no. 69, p. 257 and fig. 63.

1 The left and upper sides of the panel were not sawn off as Baldass (1937) suggests.
2 Scanned and recorded by J.R.J. van Asperen de Boer on 20 December 1993 and on 17 and 24 January 1994. The assembly was made by Cunera Vergeer. Infrared reflectograms: AB 1555/28-AB 1556/19, AB 1562/11A-15A.
3 Baldass (1937), p. 125.
4 W.L. Strauss, *Albrecht Dürer. Woodcuts and wood blocks*, New York 1980, no. 93, pp. 310-311, 318.
5 W.S. Gibson (1977), pp. 185-186.
6 See cat. nos. 54 and 55.

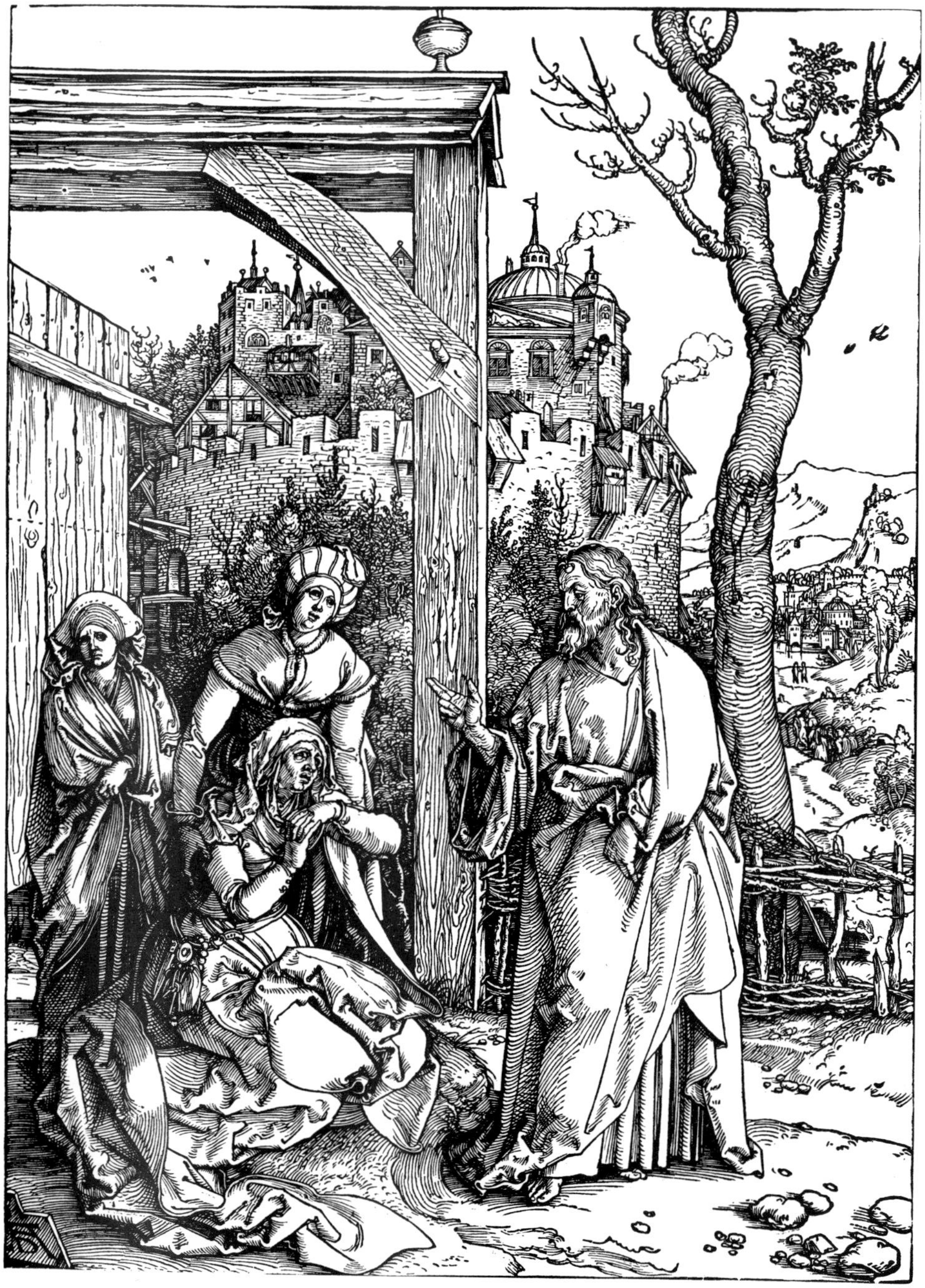

a. Albrecht Dürer, Christ taking leave of his mother
Woodcut
Amsterdam, Rijksprentenkabinet

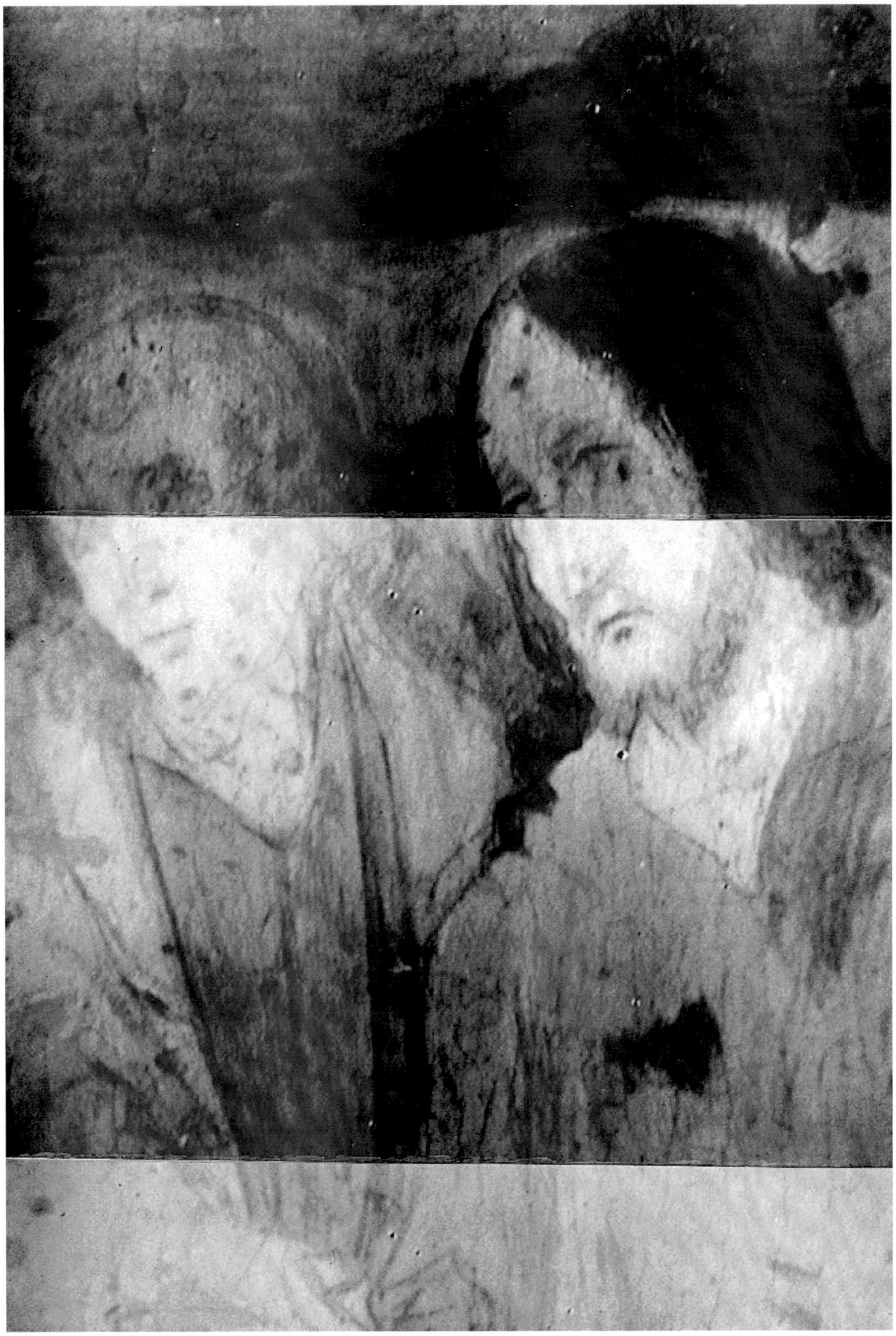

b. Infrared reflectogram assembly. Detail of Christ.

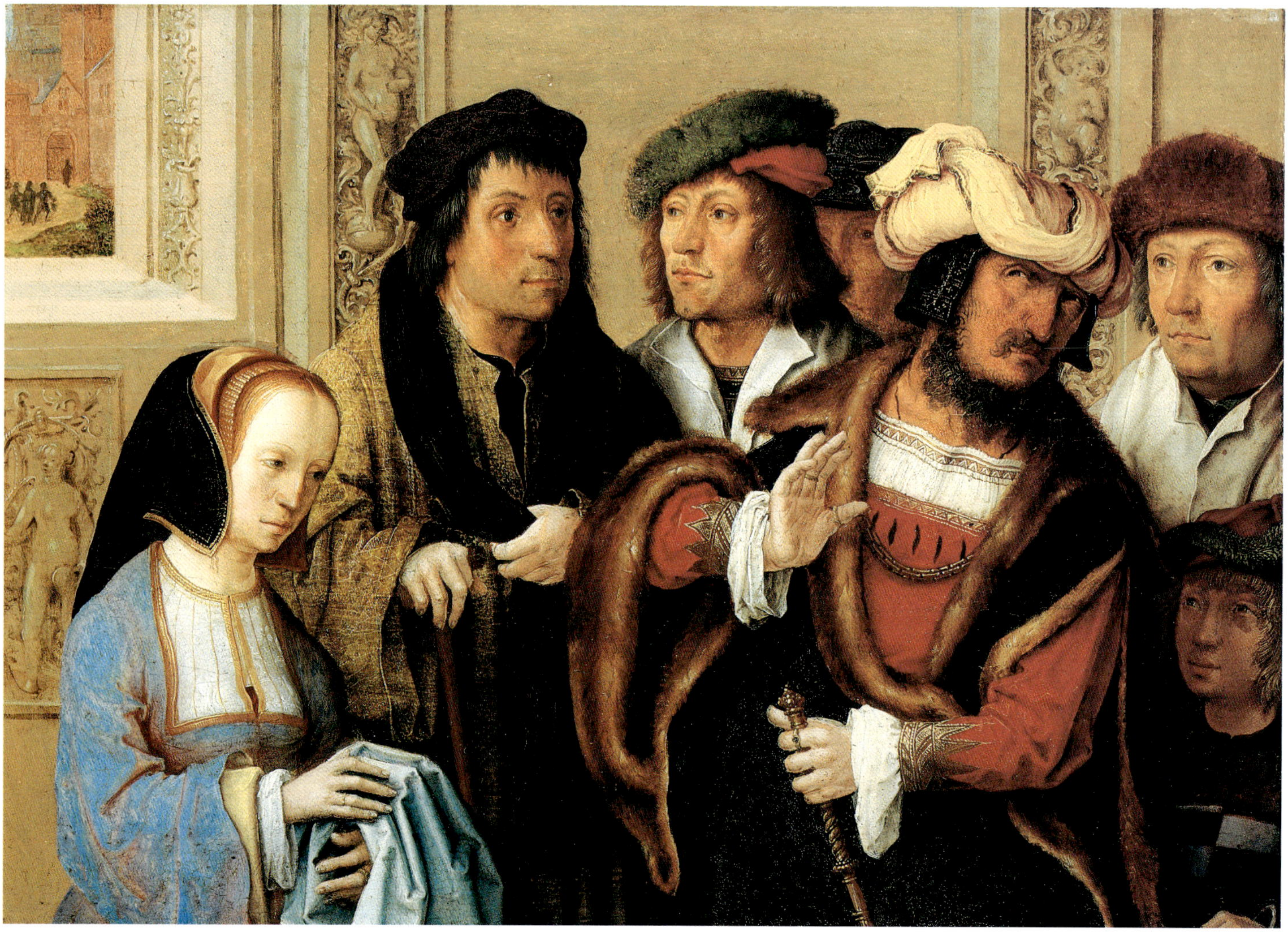

Potiphar's wife displays Joseph's garment

Lucas van Leyden
(Leiden 1489 or 1494-Leiden 1533)

Panel; 26.2 x 36 cm

Physical characteristics: the panel consists of a single plank.

Infrared reflectography: the underdrawing was executed with fine brush strokes. One of the few changes made in the painting was to omit the cap worn by Potiphar's wife which appears in the underdrawing. The gaze of the boy behind and to the right of Potiphar was more upward, and his hand was slightly different.[1]

Dendrochronology: the youngest heartwood growth ring dates from 1426. The panel could not have been painted before 1437; it was more probably painted in or after 1451. See article by P. Klein.

Provenance: F.G. Baumgärtner Collection, Neurenberg, sold in 1820;[2] Count Silva Taroncca Collection;[3] bequeathed to Count Sternberg, Prague;[4] purchased in 1930 by the Goudstikker Gallery, Amsterdam; purchased from the Gallery in 1930 by D.G. van Beuningen, Rotterdam and Vierhouten, for 140,000 guilders; acquired by the Museum in 1958 with the Van Beuningen Collection; inv. no. 2455.

Exhibitions: *Nouvelles acquisitions de la collection Goudstikker*, Amsterdam, 458 Heerengracht, Rotterdam, Rotterdamsche Kunstkring, 1930-1931, no. 33, fig.; *Kersttentoonstelling*, Rotterdam, Boymans Museum, 1930-1931, no. 11, fig. III; *Jeroen Bosch, Noord-Nederlandsche Primitieven*, Rotterdam, Boymans Museum, 1936, no. 80, fig. 115; *Meesterwerken uit vier eeuwen 1400-1800*, Rotterdam, Boymans Museum, 1938, no. 10, fig. 42; *Schilderijen, tekeningen en beeldhouwwerken uit particuliere Nederlandsche verzamelingen*, Rotterdam, Boymans Museum, 1938-1939, no. 7, fig. IX; *Tentoonstelling bijbelsche kunst*, Amsterdam, Rijksmuseum, 1939, no. 70a; *Nederlandsche kunst van de XVde en XVIde eeuw*, The Hague, Mauritshuis, 1945, no. 63, fig. 63; *Honderd jaar Museum Boymans Rotterdam. Meesterwerken uit de verzameling D.G. van Beuningen*, Rotterdam, Boymans Museum, 1949, no. 16, fig. 42; *Chefs-d'œuvres de la collection D.G. van Beuningen*, Paris, Petit Palais, 1952, no. 54; *Kunstschatten uit Nederlandse verzamelingen*, Rotterdam, Boymans Museum, 1955, no. 14, fig. 12; *Middeleeuwse kunst der Noordelijke Nederlanden*, Amsterdam, Rijksmuseum, 1958, no. 127, fig. 64; *Het Laatste Oordeel*, Leiden, Stedelijk Museum De Lakenhal, 1978, no. 2.

Literature: M.J. Friedländer, "Über die Anfänge des Malers Lucas van Leyden", *Der Cicerone* XXII (1930), pp. 498-499, fig.; F. Dülberg, "Lucas van Leyden", *Elsevier's Geïllustreerd Maandschrift* 43 (1933), p. 7; N. Beets, "Zestiende-eeuwse kunstenaars - III Lucas van Leyden", *Oud Holland* 51 (1934), p. 50; H. Gerson, "Jerome Bosch and the North-Netherlandish Primitives", *The Burlington Magazine* 69 (1936), p. 137; G.J. Hoogewerff, *De Noordnederlandsche schilderkunst*, III, The Hague, 1939, pp. 230-231, fig. 119; N. Beets, *Lucas van Leyden*, Amsterdam 1940, pp. 47-51, fig. p. 33; Hannema, 1949, no. 16, fig. 42; N. Beets, "De Noordnederlandse schilderkunst in de zestiende eeuw (1)", *Kunstgeschiedenis der Nederlanden*, I, Utrecht 1954 (3rd ed.), p. 445; J. Leymarie, *La peinture Hollandaise*, Geneva-Paris-New York 1956, p. 48; Cat. 1962, p. 77; M.J. Friedländer, *Lucas van Leyden*, Berlin 1963, p. 51, fig. 34; K.G. Boon, "Lucas van Leyden", *Encyclopedia of World Art*, vol. IX, 1964, p. 351; E.I. Reznicek-Buriks, "Max J. Friedländer, Lucas van Leyden, herausgegeben von F. Winkler, 1963, Walter de Gruyter & Co (vormals G.J. Göschen'sche Verlagshandlung) Berlin" (book review), *Oud Holland* 80 (1965), p. 244; F. Gorissen, *Ludwig Jupan von Marburg*, Düsseldorf 1969, p. 113; W.S. Gibson, "Lucas van Leyden and his two teachers", *Simiolus* 4 (1970), p. 93, fig. 6; Friedländer, X, 1973, pp. 51, 82, fig. 119; H. Miedema, *Karel van Mander - Den grondt der edel vry schilderconst*, Utrecht 1973, II, p. 504, fig. 47; C. Brown, "Leiden: the Lucas van Leyden Exhibition", *The Burlington Magazine* 120 (1978), p. 782; R. Vos, *Lucas van Leyden*, Bentveld-Maarssen 1978, p. 32, figs. 42, 44, 138, cat. no. 196; M.L. Wurfbain, "De genreschilderijen van Lucas van Leyden (ca. 1490-1533)", *Antiek* 13 (1978-1979), pp. 205-206, fig. 6; J.P. Filedt Kok, "Underdrawing and other technical aspects in the paintings of Lucas van Leyden", *Lucas van Leyden studies (Nederlands Kunsthistorisch Jaarboek 29 (1978))*, pp. 17, 18, 26-33, 52, 120, 125, 143, 162 (note 79), 176 (note 202), 182-183, figs. 2a, 14, 17-23; J.P. Filedt Kok, "Lucas van Leyden exhibitions and recent publications", *Lucas van Leyden studies (Nederlands Kunsthistorisch Jaarboek 29 (1978))*, p. 510 (no. 2); L. Silver and S. Smith, "Carnal knowledge: the late engravings of Lucas van Leyden", *Lucas van Leyden studies (Nederlands Kunsthistorisch Jaarboek 29 (1978))*, pp. 263-264, 288 (n. 56), 293 (n. 106); K. Renger, "Lucas van Leyden, Ausstellung Leiden, Städtisches Museum De Lakenhal, 28. September - 29. Oktober 1978, Lucas van Leyden. Graphik, Ausstellung Amsterdam, Rijksmuseum, Prentenkabinett, 9. September - 3. Dezember 1978", *Kunstchronik* 32 (1979), p. 58; R. Vos, "The life of Lucas van Leyden by Karel van Mander", *Lucas van Leyden studies (Nederlands Kunsthistorisch Jaarboek 29 (1978))*, p. 500 (n. 98); W.S. Gibson, "Lucas van Leyden studies, edited by Jan Piet Filedt Kok, Wouter Th. Kloek and Ilja M. Veldman (Nederlands Kunsthistorisch Jaarboek 29 [1978])" (book review), *Simiolus* 11 (1980), p. 107; S. Ringbom, *Icon to narrative - The rise of the dramatic close-up in fifteenth-century devotional painting*, Doornspijk 1984 (2nd ed.), p. 192; J.D. Bangs, "The Leiden Pieterskerk west end, 1512-1637 - aspects of rebuilding and change", *Bulletin KNOB* 84 (1985), pp. 2-3; J.O. Hand and M. Wolff, *Early Netherlandish painting - The collections of the National Gallery of Art, systematic catalogue*, Washington 1986, p. 142; E. Lawton Smith, *The paintings of Lucas van Leyden, a new appraisal, with catalogue raisonné*, Columbia-London 1992, pp. 89-91, fig. 4.

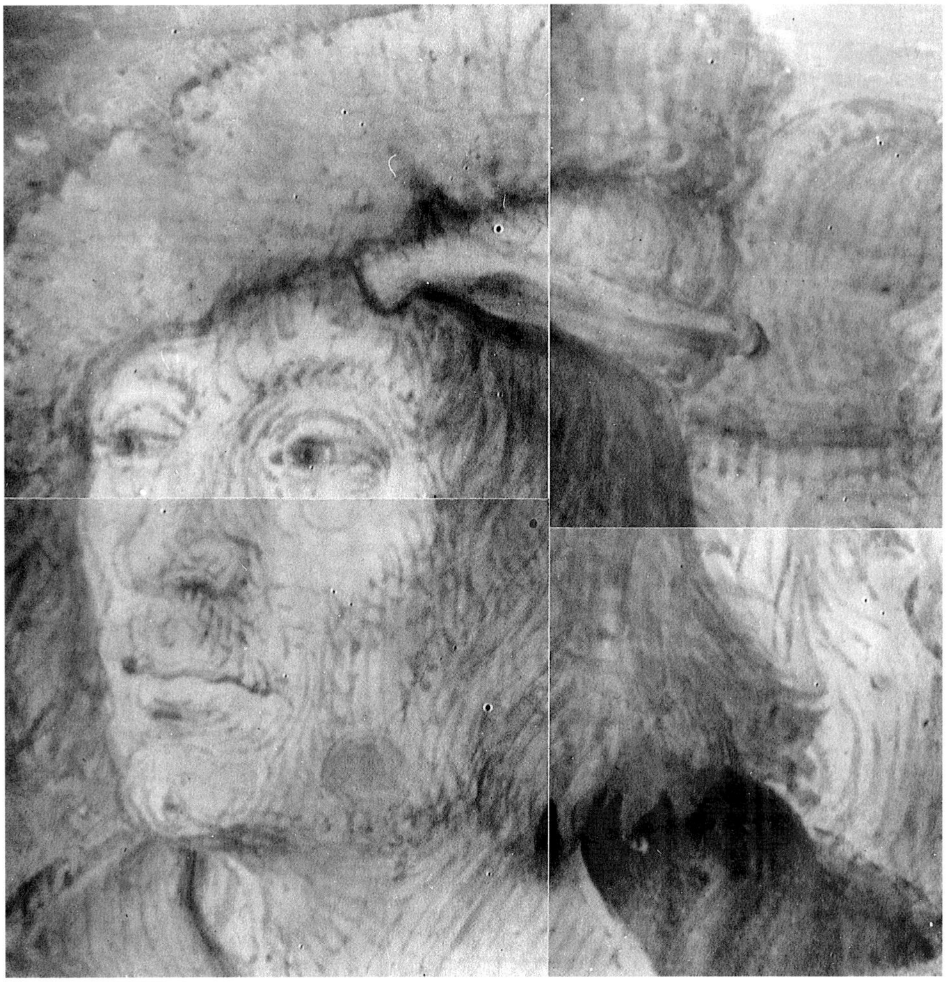

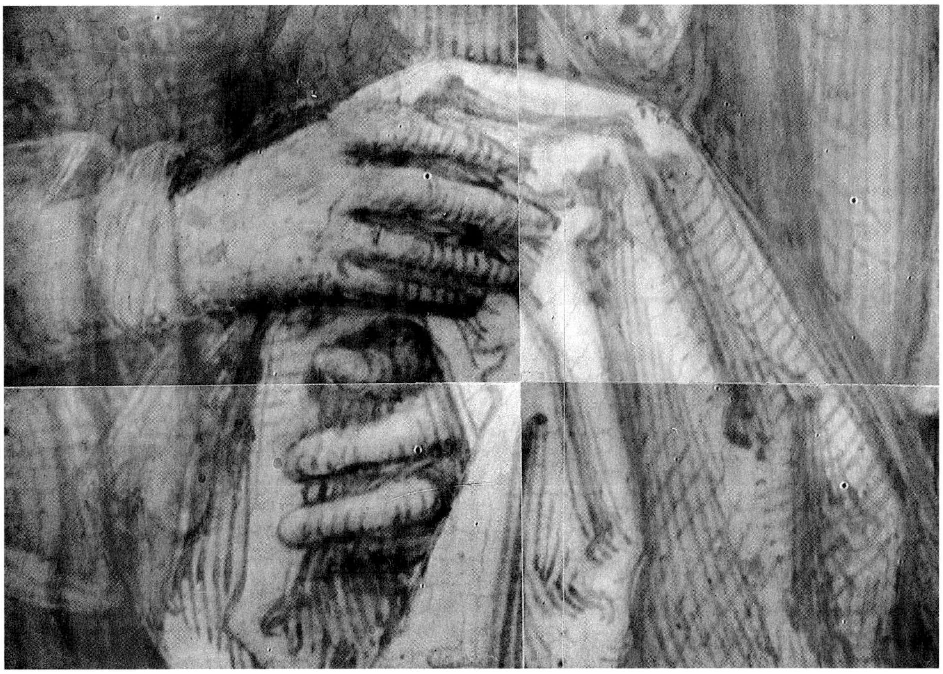

a. Infrared reflectogram assembly showing the face of one of the bystanders

b. Infrared reflectogram assembly showing the hands of Potiphar's wife

The painting illustrates an episode from the life of Joseph as recounted in Genesis 39:1-20. It depicts the moment when Potiphar's wife, falsely accusing Joseph of trying to seduce her, produces his garment as proof. Potiphar, enraged with his faithless servant, makes a condemnatory gesture. The five figures behind Potiphar and his wife may be the members of the household to whom she first maligned Joseph. It is presumed that the youth on Potiphar's left is Joseph,[5] but the Bible makes no mention of Joseph being present at that moment. When Friedländer first published the painting in 1930, some years after it was found in a private collection in Prague, he could not identify the subject with certainty. He considered both *Susannah before the judge* and *Potiphar's wife accusing Joseph* to be possibilities, while the reproduction accompanying the article was entitled *The daughter of Jephta*. Subsequent commentators were also unsure of the subject, until Beets in 1940 identified the figures visible through the window as Joseph being led away by two men. This is indeed in accord with the Bible story, in which Potiphar has Joseph thrown into prison.

Lucas painted the figures with close attention to detail, as evidenced by the variation in their costume and the care devoted to the fabrics. The range of colour is equally varied, with almost imperceptible transitions from light to shadow. Each of the faces has its own individual characteristics, and the hands are very natural. Potiphar, the only figure depicted in "antique" rather than contemporary dress, wears a fur-lined coat over a red gown which, like the white undergarment, is embroidered in gold. His soft yellow and rose headdress has a loose panel at the back which is draped around his head in the manner of a turban. His wife wears a blue dress with a white bodice. An interesting detail is the youth's hand, which seems to rest on the frame.

The composition was first carefully built up in the detailed underdrawing (figs. a, b), which is visible to the naked eye in Potiphar's face. The hand of Lucas the engraver is perceptible here in the variation of delicate shading consisting of precisely placed lines endowing the faces with vitality. A remarkable feature of the composition is the half-length figures and the overlapping, a composition he may have learned from his second teacher, Cornelis Engelbrechtsz, whose *Christ as the Good Shepherd* displays a similar composition.[6]

Various commentators have tried to explain the significance of the reliefs in the background. The nude female figure standing on a globe to the right of the window could represent Fortuna or Venus, signifying the power of women and the vicissitudes of love. The nude boy on the extreme right could be Cupid, god of love, even though he is not winged.[7] In the view of one author, the nude female figure on the far left may depict Temperantia, or Moderation, because she is pouring water,[8] but this is not conclusive. It is more probably Eve tempting Adam, whose figure is just barely perceptible.[9] If these theories are right, the painting refers to the wiles employed by women to attract men. This would be in line with the representations of chess and card players containing similar references which Lucas painted about the same time.[10]

Potiphar's wife, which can be dated around 1512, is an early work by Lucas van Leyden. The dating is based on stylistic similarities with the engravings he produced at that time and on the style of the underdrawing.[11]

Another painting dating from about 1512 is *Daniel convinces the judges of Susannah's innocence* (fig. c), whose composition shows a close affinity with that of *Potiphar's wife*. Much of the space in the two works is filled with half-length figures before a wall bearing reliefs, with an aperture revealing a distant view on the left.

Lucas produced a number of versions of the story of Joseph, such as a series of five engravings signed with "L" and dated 1512 (Bartsch 19-23). In addition, Van Mander reports in the fourth book of his *Schilder-boeck. Het Leven der Doorluchtighe Nederlandtsche / en Hoogduytsche Schilders*, published in Alkmaar in 1604, that in the house of a brewer in Delft, he saw "...several water-colour canvases portraying the story of Joseph....".[12] They were then in poor condition and have since been lost.

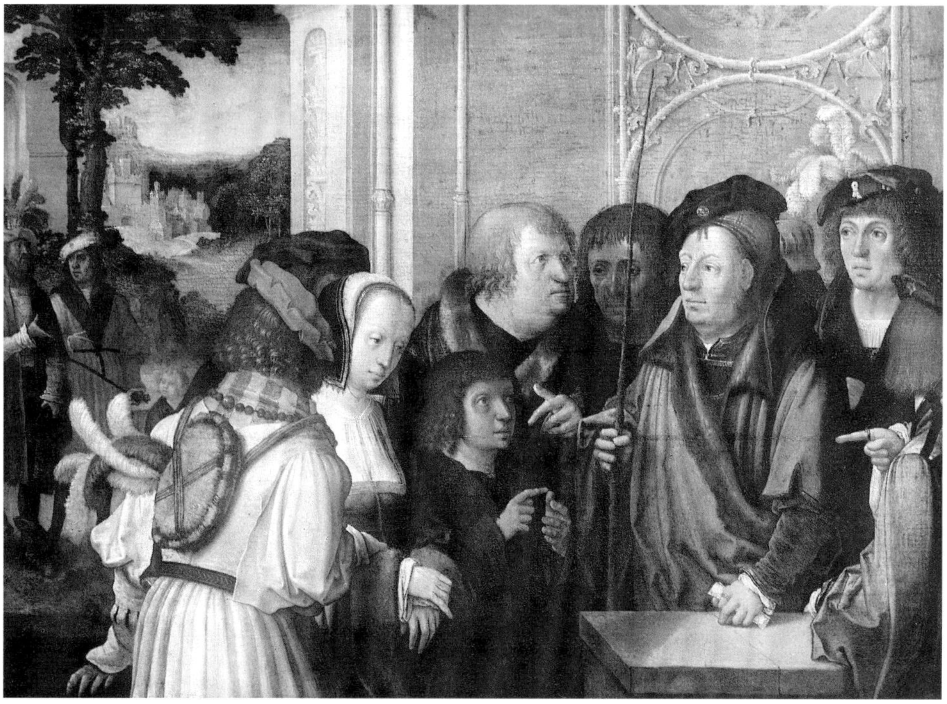

c. Lucas van Leyden, *Daniel convinces the judges of Susannah's innocence*, c. 1512
Panel; 34 x 46 cm
Formerly in Bremen, Kunsthalle (missing since World War II)

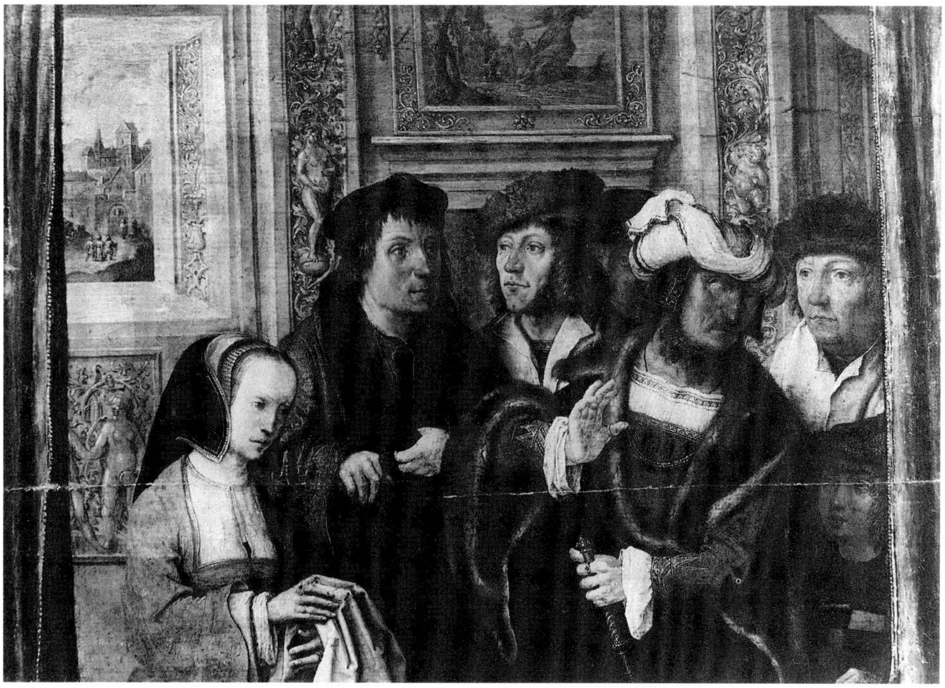

d. Lucas van Leyden, *Potiphar's wife displays Joseph's garment*
Before restoration.

A photograph from about 1930 shows that at that time the top and sides of the Rotterdam painting were extended and it was partly painted over (fig. d). The architectural structure in the background was adorned with a mantel surmounted by a painting, part of a relief was discernible on the right, and a curtain was painted along each of the two sides. The additions and overpainting were removed shortly after 1930.[13] There was a copy in the Semmel Collection in Berlin.[14]
SL

1 Filedt Kok (1979), pp. 26-31. Infrared reflectograms: AB 1541/1-34.
2 Friedländer (1930), p. 499.
3 Note by D.G. van Beuningen on the back of a photograph of the painting. The photograph is in the Museum's file on the painting.
4 See note 3.
5 Friedländer (1930).
6 See cat. no. 54.
7 Silver and Smith (1978) and Wurfbain (1978-79).
8 Wurfbain (1978-79).
9 Silver and Smith (1978).
10 *The chess players*, c. 1508 (Berlin-Dahlem, Gemäldegalerie, Staatliche Museen Preussischer Kulturbesitz); *The fortune-teller*, c. 1509 (Paris, Musée du Louvre); *The card players*, c. 1515 (Madrid, Museo Thyssen-Bornemisza); *The card players*, c. 1517 (Salisbury, Earl of Pembroke Collection).
11 Filedt Kok (1979), pp. 26-31, 36.
12 "[...] eenighe Water-verwe doecken / wesende vervolghens d'Historie van Ioseph [...]".
13 Hannema (1949) mentions a seventeenth-century Flemish painting of a picture gallery showing the panel with a surround, probably that which was removed by the restorers in 1930. As he does not say where he saw it, however, it can no longer be determined to what painting he referred.
14 Friedländer (1930).

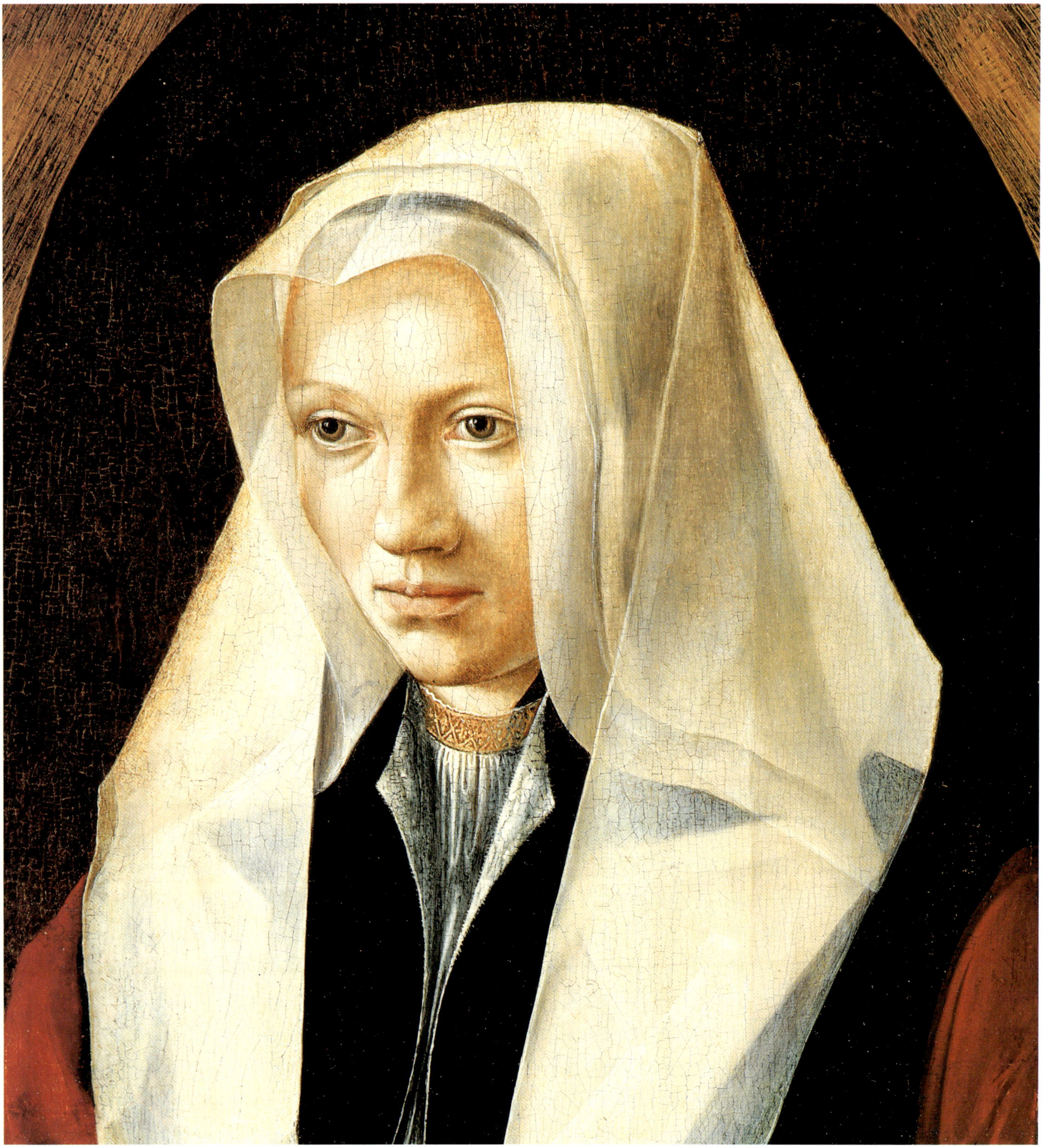

Portrait of an unknown woman

Anonymous
North Netherlandish master
c. 1520-1530

Panel; 26 x 24.4 cm

Physical characteristics: the painting was transferred to a new panel, but it is not known when. It appears to have been sawn off along the lower edge. A small section of what is probably a hand is visible in the lower left-hand corner.

Infrared reflectography:[1] faint traces of a few scattered lines of underdrawing, notably in the cap and round the chin.

Provenance: Goudstikker Gallery, Amsterdam; purchased in 1935 by D.G. van Beuningen, Rotterdam and Vierhouten, for 12,500 guilders; acquired by the Museum in 1958 with the Van Beuningen Collection; inv. no. 2457.

Exhibitions: *Jeroen Bosch, Noord-Nederlandsche Primitieven*, Rotterdam, Boymans Museum, 1936, no. 86, fig. 119; *Meesterwerken uit vier eeuwen 1400-1800*, Rotterdam, Boymans Museum, 1938, no. 11, fig. 43; *Honderd jaar museum Boymans Rotterdam. Meesterwerken uit de verzameling D.G. van Beuningen*, Rotterdam, Boymans Museum, 1949, no. 17; *Drie eeuwen portret in Nederland*, Amsterdam, Rijksmuseum, 1952, no. 85; *Chefs-d'œuvre de la collection D.G. van Beuningen*, Paris, Petit Palais, 1952, no. 55; *Het portret in de oude Nederlanden*, Bruges, Stedelijk Museum, 1953, no. 70, fig. 71; *Middeleeuwse kunst der Noordelijke Nederlanden*, Amsterdam, Rijksmuseum, 1958, no. 129.

Literature: H.P. Bremmer (ed.), *Beeldende Kunst* 23 (1936), pp. 1-2, no. 1, fig. 1; C. Veth, "Boymans: Jeroen Bosch, Van Geertgen tot Scorel, Noord-Nederlandsche Primitieven", *Maandblad voor Beeldende Kunsten* 13 (1936), p. 290, fig.; L. Baldass, "Die Bildnisse des Lukas van Leyden", *Pantheon* X (1937), pp. 206, 208, fig. p. 209; G.J. Hoogewerff, *De Noord-Nederlandsche schilderkunst*, III, The Hague 1939, p. 278, fig. 144; M.J. Friedländer, "Bilder und Zeichnungen in der Sammlung Van Beuningen", *Phoenix* IV (1949), p. 145, fig. 9; Hannema, 1949, no. 17, fig. 43; W. Wegner, "Mittelalterliche Kunst der nördlichen Niederlande - Die Jubiläumausstellung des Rijksmuseums in Amsterdam", *Kunstchronik* 12 (1959), p. 8; cat. 1962, p. 78; M.J. Friedländer, *Lucas van Leyden*, Berlin 1963, p. 62, fig. 49; Friedländer, X, 1973, p. 88, Supp. 173, fig. 125; E.I. Reznicek-Buriks, "Max J. Friedländer, Lucas van Leyden, herausgegeben von F. Winkler, 1963, Walter de Gruyter & Co (vormals G.J. Göschen'sche Verlagshandlung) Berlin" (book review), *Oud Holland* 80 (1965), p. 244; P.W. Parshall, "Exhib. cat. Lucas van Leyden: grafiek", Amsterdam (Rijksprentenkabinet) Sept. 9-Dec. 3, 1978; Rik Vos, "Lucas van Leyden, Bentveld (Andreas Landshoff) & Maarssen (Gary Schwartz) 1978" (book review) *Simiolus* 10 (1978-1979), p. 53; E. Lawton Smith, *The paintings of Lucas van Leyden, a new appraisal, with catalogue raisonné*, Columbia-London 1992, pp. 200-201.

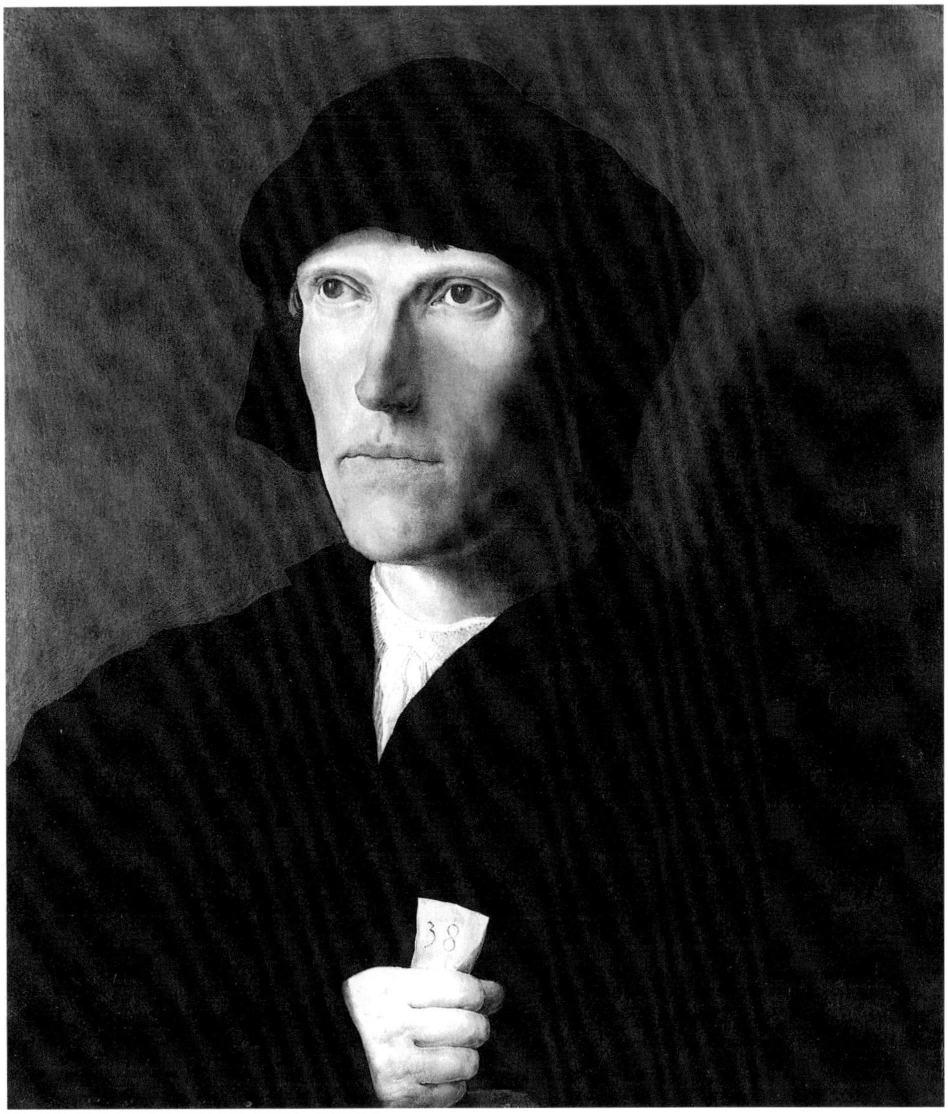

a. Lucas van Leyden, Male portrait, c. 1521
Panel; 46.5 x 48 cm
London, National Gallery

D.G. van Beuningen bought this portrait of an unknown young woman in 1935. Its attribution to Lucas van Leyden had long been generally accepted. It has been compared with the female figure wearing a similar cap in the *Chess players*,[2] and with two female portraits in black chalk by Lucas,[3] which are indeed similar in some respects to this portrait, particularly in regard to the sitters' clothes. Stylistically, there is little resemblance between the two drawings and the painting. Comparison of this portrait with the male portrait generally believed to have been painted by Lucas about 1521 shows a number of distinct differences in their manner of execution (fig. a). The man's face is much more expressive; the transition from light to shadow is more fluid. Despite his dark attire, the folds and sheen of the fabric emerge through the use of subtle tones of black. The background is enlivened not only by the shadow cast by the figure, giving a sense of space, but also by its varied hues. Conversely, in the lady's portrait the lines are stronger and the contrast between light and shadow is more pronounced, rendering the whole less expressive. The near lack of shading in her black dress renders the painting rather flat.[4] On the basis of this comparison, the attribution of the portrait to Lucas van Leyden is open to some doubt. It was probably painted by a North Netherlandish master. The white cap characteristic of women's dress in the first half of the sixteenth century suggests a date around 1520-1530.
SL

1 Scanned by J.R.J. van Asperen de Boer in 1977.
2 Berlin-Dahlem, Gemäldegalerie, Staatliche Museen Preussischer Kulturbesitz, c. 1508, Panel; 28 x 36 cm. The comparison was made by Baldass (1937).
3 Paris, Musée du Louvre, c. 1521, black chalk, 29.5 x 33.5, and Weimar, Schlossmuseum, black chalk, 29.5 x 33.5 cm, signed and dated 1521. Hoogewerff (1939) made the comparison with the Weimar portrait, and Friedländer (1963) with that in the Louvre.
4 See also Lawton-Smith (1992).

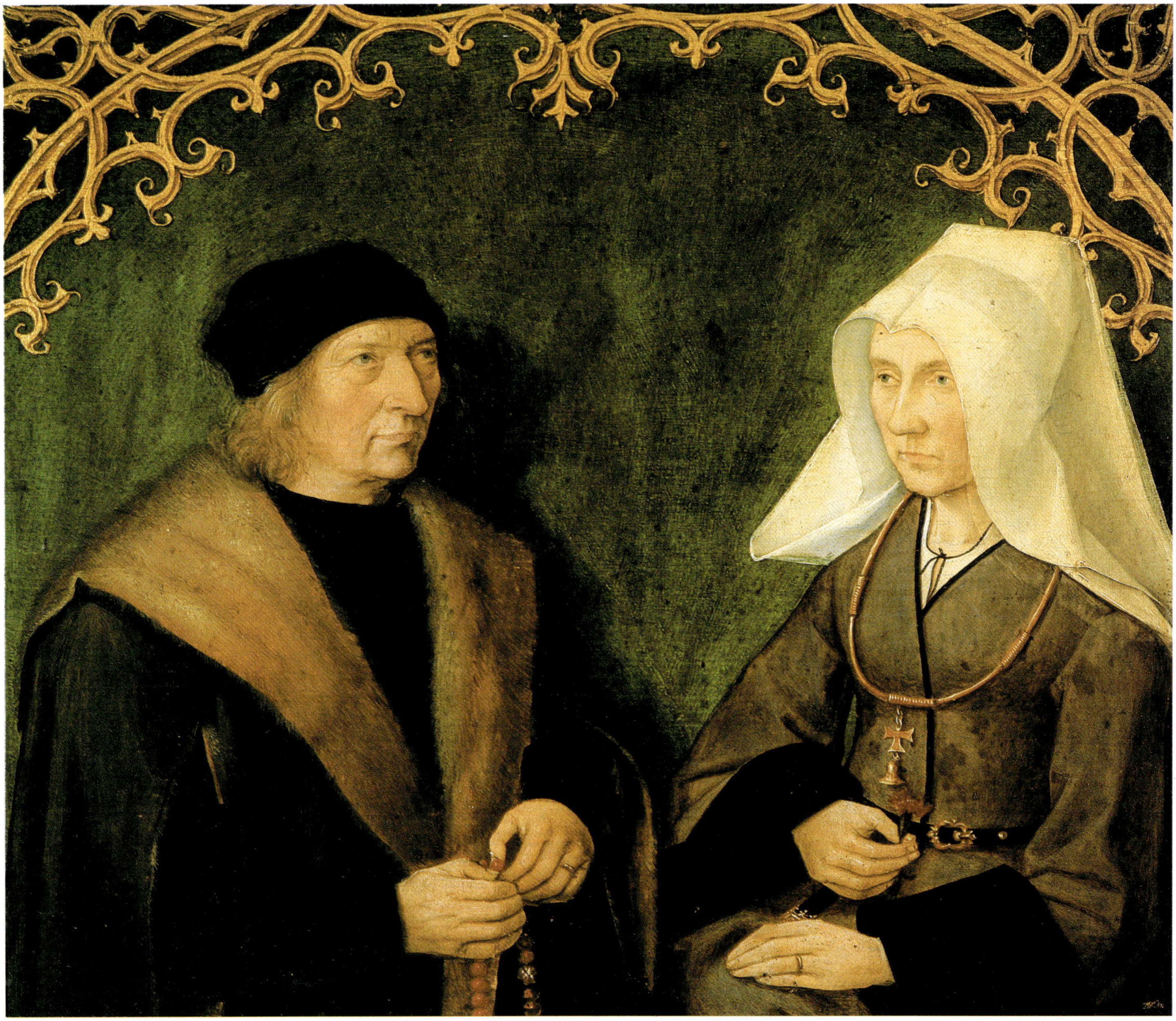

Portrait of Dirck Borre van Amerongen and Maria van Snellenberg

Master of the Amsterdam Death of the Virgin
(active Amsterdam?, Utrecht? c. 1480-1515)

Panel; 21.5 x 38.5 cm
Later inscription on the reverse: DIRCK BORRE VAN AMERONGEN ʘ 1527 MARIA VAN SNELLENBERG ʘ 1540

Physical characteristics:[1] the panel consists of a single plank. The *barbe* is intact on all sides.

Infrared reflectography: no more than a few fine lines visible.

Dendrochronology: the youngest heartwood growth ring dates from 1487. The panel could not have been painted before 1498; it was more probably painted in 1504. See description and article by P. Klein.

Provenance: Art gallery, London, 1923;[2] Klaassen Gallery; bought there in 1938 by D.G. van Beuningen, Rotterdam and Vierhouten, for 20,000 guilders; acquired by the Boymans Museum in 1958 with the Van Beuningen Collection; inv. no. 2464.

Exhibitions: *Catalogus schilderijen, teekeningen en beeldhouwwerken uit particuliere Nederlandsche verzamelingen*, Rotterdam, Boymans Museum, 1938-39, no. 17, fig. XI; *Oude Kunst Tentoonstelling*, Maastricht, Stedelijk Museum, 1939, no. 9, fig.; *Honderd jaar Museum Boymans Rotterdam. Meesterwerken uit de verzameling D.G. van Beuningen*, Rotterdam, Boymans Museum, 1949, no. 22; *Chefs-d'œuvre de la collection D.G. van Beuningen*, Paris, Petit Palais, 1952, no. 59; *Middeleeuwse kunst der Noordelijke Nederlanden*, Amsterdam, Rijksmuseum, 1958, no. 45, fig. 31.

Literature: Friedländer, X, 1932, pp. 118, 138, no. 153, fig. 94; G.J. Hoogewerff, *De Noord-Nederlandsche Schilderkunst*, I, The Hague, 1936, pp. 521-522; Hannema, 1949, no. 22, fig. 49; K.G. Boon, "De meester van het Amsterdamse sterfbed van Maria (werkzaam te Utrecht omstreeks 1480-1500)", *Openbaar Kunstbezit* 2 (1958), no. 32; cat. 1962, p. 84; Friedländer, X, 1973, p. 85, no. 153, fig. 117.

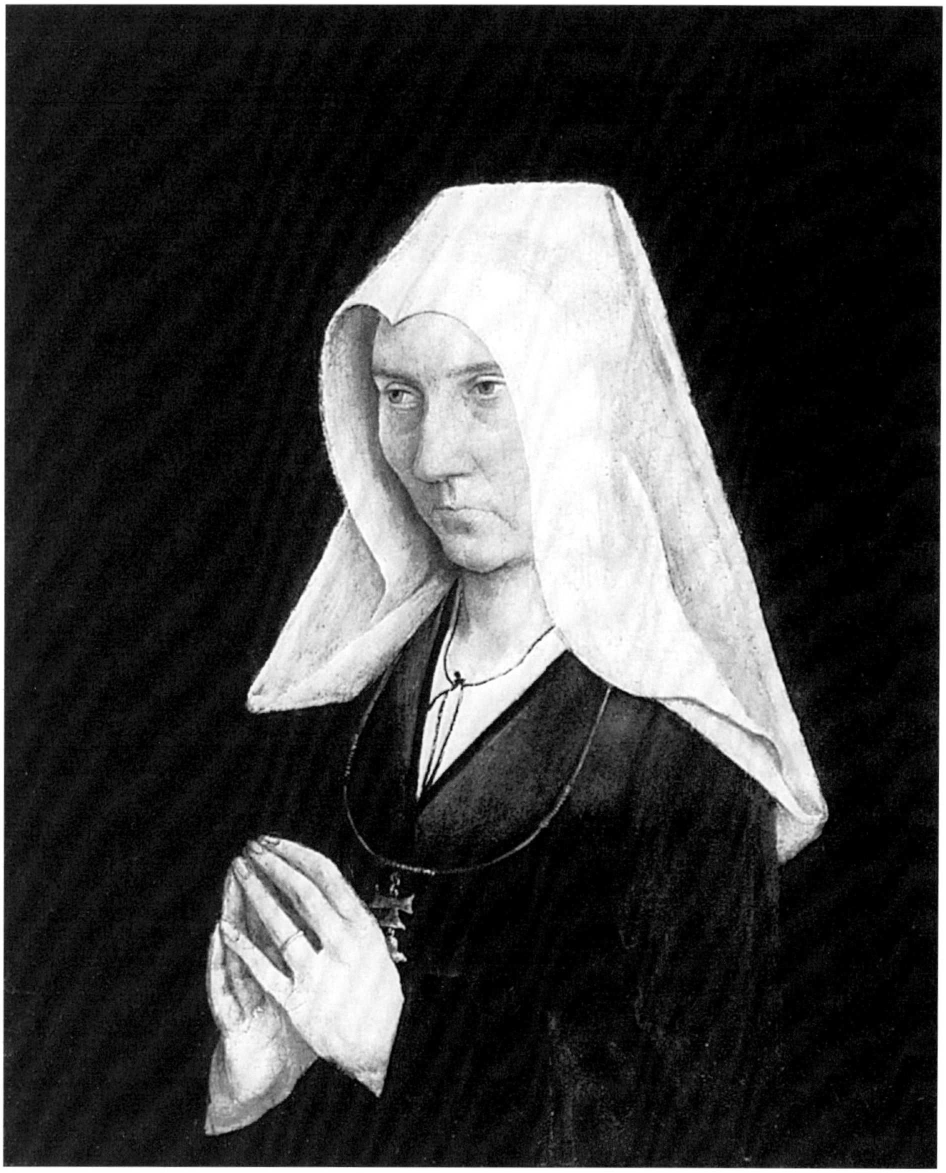

a. Master of the Amsterdam Death of the Virgin,
Portrait of Maria van Snellenberg
Panel; 24 x 19.5 cm
In the collection of Mrs N. Boon-van Leer in 1973

The later inscription on the reverse side of the panel states that it is a portrait of Dirck Borre van Amerongen (d. 1527) and his wife, Maria van Snellenberg (d. 1540). They are richly dressed. He holds a jewelled rosary. Her belt is adorned with a buckle and an orchid. Around her neck she wears a heavy necklace from which are appended the cross and bell emblems of the Order of St Anthony.[3]

In 1932 Friedländer grouped a number of paintings around the *Death of the Virgin*, then in the Hofje der Zeven Keurvorsten, Amsterdam, and in the Rijksmuseum, Amsterdam, since 1944. He named the artist the "Master of the Amsterdam Death of the Virgin", whom he thought had worked in Amsterdam around 1500. In view of the name of the assumed sitter, Hoogewerff thought the artist would have worked in Utrecht, a city close to Amerongen. Boon noted that Dirck Borre was burgomaster of Utrecht, and likewise concluded that the artist was active in Utrecht around 1480-1500, and that the portraits would date from 1510-1515. The works ascribed by Friedländer to the painter comprise the Amsterdam work, two panels in the Rijksmuseum, a painting in Philadelphia and a panel in Antwerp. He added to this group the Rotterdam panel, and a portrait of a woman which in 1973 was in the collection of Mrs N. Boon-van Leer (fig. a). According to Schretlen, an X-radiograph revealing the brocade mantle of a patron saint under the overpainted background proves the latter portrait to be the upper part of a kneeling donor. This is of interest in connection with the Rotterdam panel,[4] for the woman is remarkably like the woman in the Rotterdam portrait, and even wears the same necklace. It seems certain that the sitter in both cases is Maria van Snellenberg.

Dirck Borre van Amerongen, born about 1438, was a member of the furriers guild, a senior officer of the guild in 1475, 1477 and 1483, magistrate of Utrecht in 1471, 1473, 1477 and 1479, and burgomaster of Utrecht in 1475 and 1487. He died at an advanced age in 1527, and was buried in the Buurkerk in Utrecht. Maria van Snellenberg was born around 1465, died in 1540, and was buried, like her husband, in the Buurkerk.[5]

Identifying the artist with Utrecht remains tenuous. Friedländer recognised the Utrecht tower in a triptych ascribed to the Master which at that time was in the Glitza Collection in Hamburg, but thought it probable that it had been used by an Amsterdam artist.[6] One reason in favour of Amsterdam is that the painting in the Rijksmuseum was first in an Amsterdam *hofje*, so it is reasonable to suppose that the patron would have commissioned an Amsterdam painter.

Peter Klein, who conducted the dendrochronological examination, concludes that the last growth ring dates from 1487, so that the panel could have been painted after 1504. This accords with Boon's dating of 1510-1515.
JG

1 Conducted by F.E.D. Hartmann under the supervision of J.R.J. van Asperen de Boer in 1991. Paint samples A 323/1-3.
2 According to Friedländer, X, 1932.
3 With acknowledgements to Professor J. Koldewey and A. van Dongen for the identification of these objects.
4 M.J. Schretlen, "De meester van Delft," *Oud Holland* 40 (1922), p. 17.
5 With acknowledgements to A. Pietersma, head of the archives and library department of the Utrecht Municipal Archives, who in a letter dated 30 December 1993 drew my attention to *De Nederlandsche Leeuw*, 95 (1978), cols. 355, 356, and to an article by C.A. van Kalveen, "De Gildenbeweging van april 1525 en haar voorgeschiedenis," *Jaarboek Oud-Utrecht*, 1972, pp. 93 ff.
6 Friedländer, X, 1932, p. 117.

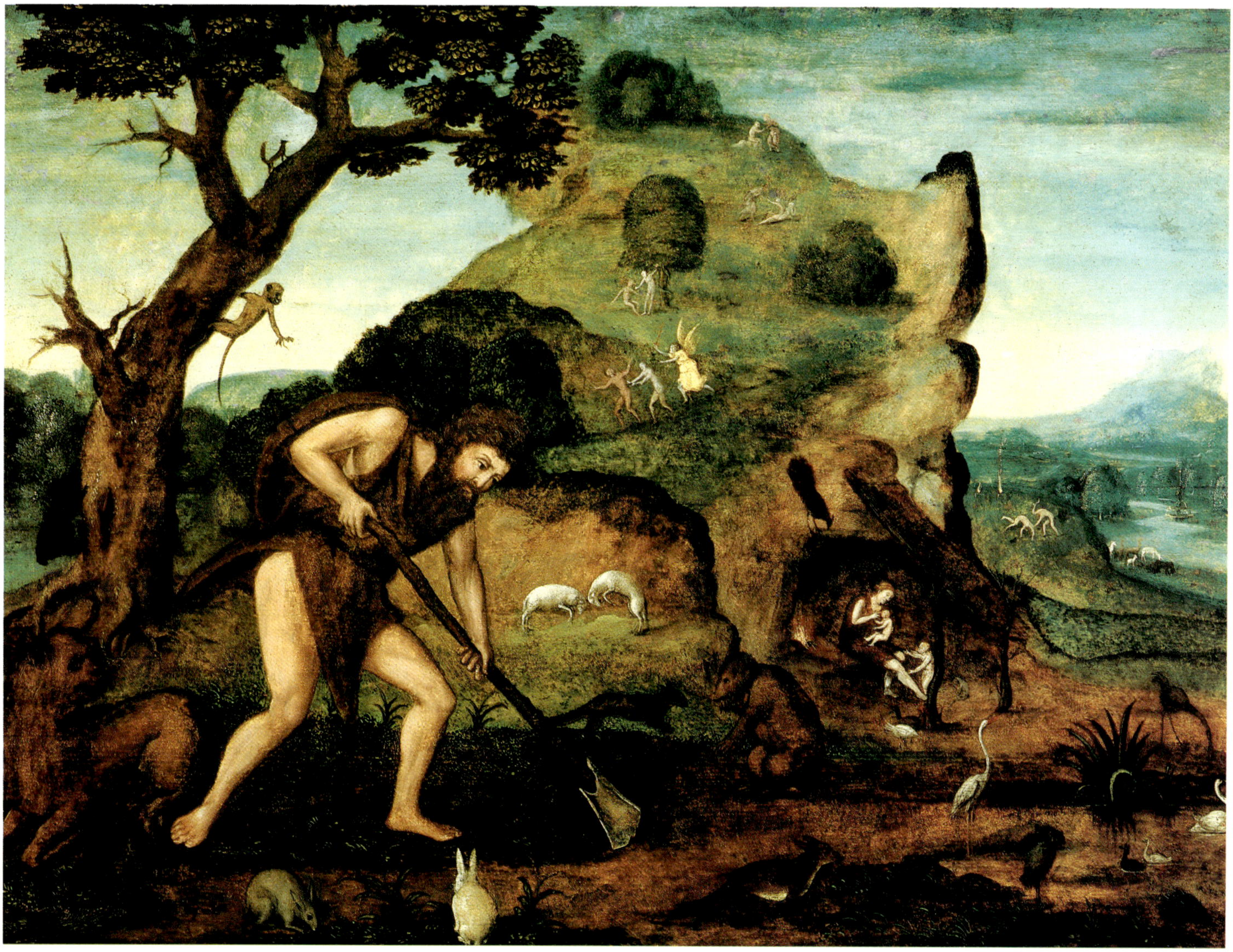

Adam's labour after the Fall

Anonymous
Netherlandish master
c. 1540-1550

Panel; 48.6 x 63.8 cm

This painting was given to the Museum in 1957 by the famous art historian J.A. Emmens. In the foreground of the panel, Adam is tilling the earth with a spade. Behind him, in a hut, we see Eve nursing her youngest son Abel. Beside her stands her first son, Cain.

The hut is built against a mountainside on which scenes from the creation are depicted. They are, in order: the creation of Adam, the creation of Eve from Adam's rib, Eve offering Adam the apple, and an angel driving Adam and Eve from paradise (Genesis 2, 3). Behind and to the right of the mountain, we see the murder of Abel by Cain beside two altars where the brothers had made their sacrifices (Genesis 4).

As punishment for their disobedience, mankind was cast out of paradise and made "to till the ground from whence he was taken." (Genesis 3:23). This is the main theme of the work. In accordance with the biblical description, Adam and Eve are dressed in animal skins (Genesis 3:12). Adam digging the earth with Eve behind him breast-feeding or spinning is a recurring theme in the visual arts of the sixteenth century, particularly in graphic art.[2]

The painting was ascribed to Jan Mostaert by Friedländer in 1951.[3] In the Museum's 1962 catalogue it was described as a work by an artist in the circle of this master. The attribution to Mostaert seems untenable in any case. The awkward figures and the cumbersome composition do not recall the work of this painter. The figure of Adam displays no resemblance to the quite easily recognisable figure-type which Mostaert painted. It is possible that this painting is a copy after a lost work by this master. Mostaert made a panel depicting the first family which closely corresponds to our panel in terms of subject matter (Williamstown, Mass., Clark Art Institute).[4] However, it is equally possible that the Boymans-van Beuningen painting is unrelated to the work of the Haarlem artist. The panel is in poor condition, which makes a good assessment impossible. It is therefore attributed to an anonymous Dutch master in this catalogue. The panel probably dates from around 1540-1550.
FL

Physical characteristics: the panel consists of two vertical planks and is painted up to the edges.

Infrared reflectography[1]: underdrawing is only sporadically visible, consisting of thin, fine lines.

Provenance: P. de Boer Gallery, Amsterdam, 1951; bought by Mr and Mrs J.A. Emmens-Klippus, Hillegersberg; donated to the Museum in 1957; inv. no. 2423.

Exhibitions: *Tentoonstelling van oude schilderijen. Collectie C.V. kunsthandel P. de Boer, Amsterdam*, Rotterdam, Rotterdamsche Kunstkring, 1951, no. 32; *Prisma der bijbelse kunst*, Delft, Prinsenhof, 1952, no. 2.

Literature: Cat. 1962, p. 93.

1 Scanned on 10 January 1994 by J.R.J. van Asperen de Boer.
2 See H. van de Waal, *Drie eeuwen vaderlandsche geschied-uitbeelding 1500-1800*, The Hague 1952, pp. 82-83, 158-159.
3 In exhib. cat. Rotterdam, 1951.
4 See for this painting, P.R. Berk, "Et Adam dilexit Abel: Jan Mostaert's 'First family'", *Oud Holland* XCVI (1982), pp. 201-212.

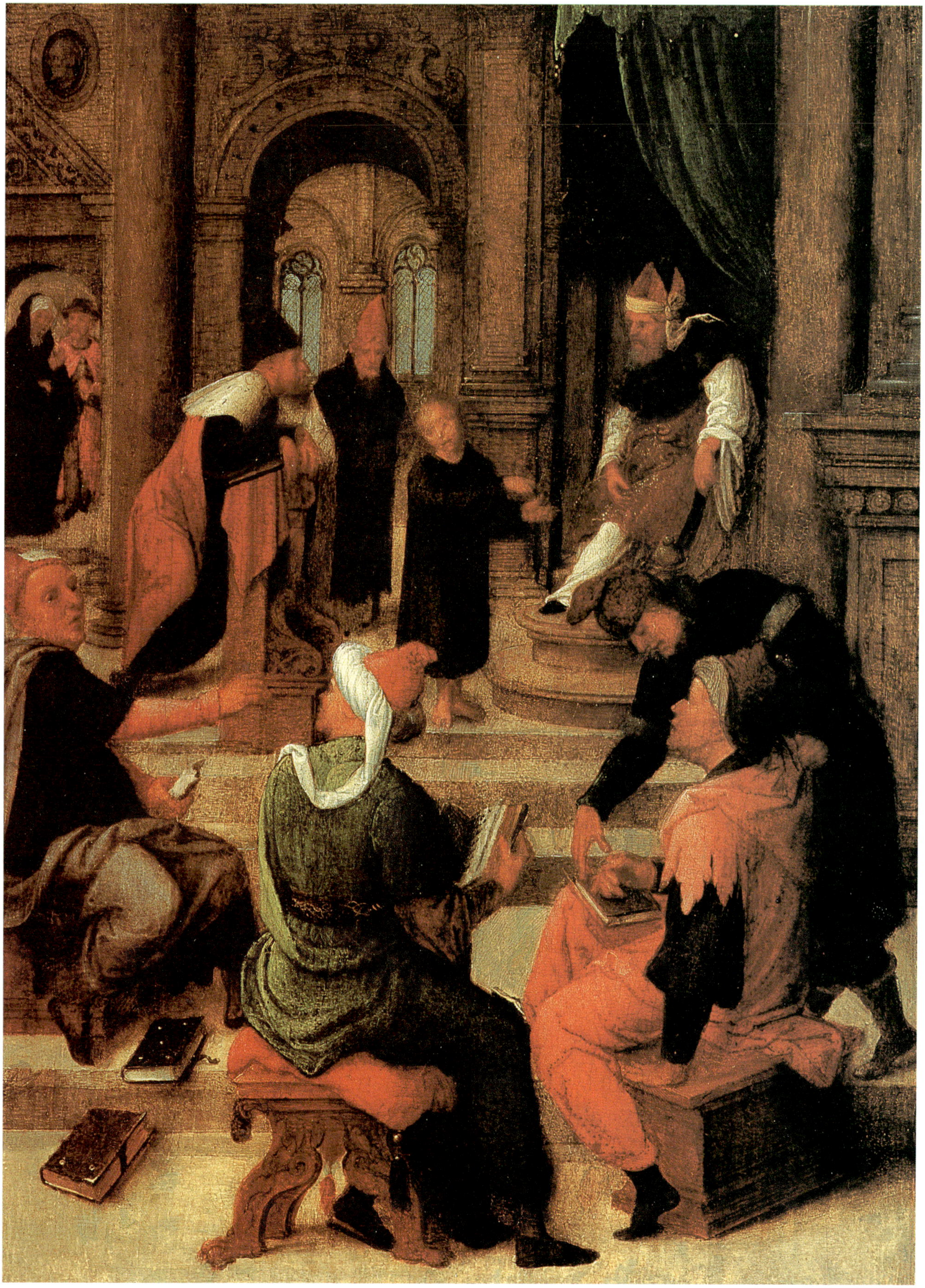

The boy Jesus among the doctors in the temple

Adriaen Ysenbrant
(? -Bruges 1551)

Panel; 29.5 x 21 cm

Physical characteristics:[1] the panel consists of a single plank. The *barbe* can be seen on all sides.

Infrared reflectography: an underdrawing of the entire composition appears to have been transferred to the panel by means of a pricked cartoon.

Paint samples: an intermediate layer was applied to the ground and an underdrawing made on this layer. A cross section of the paint shows black grains on this layer, a further indication of the use of a pricked cartoon for the underdrawing.

Provenance: Grassi Gallery, Rome; Vitale Bloch; D.G. van Beuningen, Rotterdam and Vierhouten;[2] acquired by the Museum in 1958 with the Van Beuningen Collection; inv. no. 2453.

Exhibitions: *Chefs-d'œuvre de la collection D.G. van Beuningen*, Paris, Petit Palais, 1952, no. 53; *Nederlandse primitieven uit Nederlands particulier bezit*, Laren, Singer Museum, 1961, no. 47 (wrongly listed as in the collection of Mrs A.E. van Beuningen-Charlouis, Vierhouten).

Literature: Cat. 1962, p. 159; J.C. Wilson, "Workshop patterns and the production of paintings in sixteenth-century Bruges", *The Burlington Magazine* 132 (1990), p. 524.

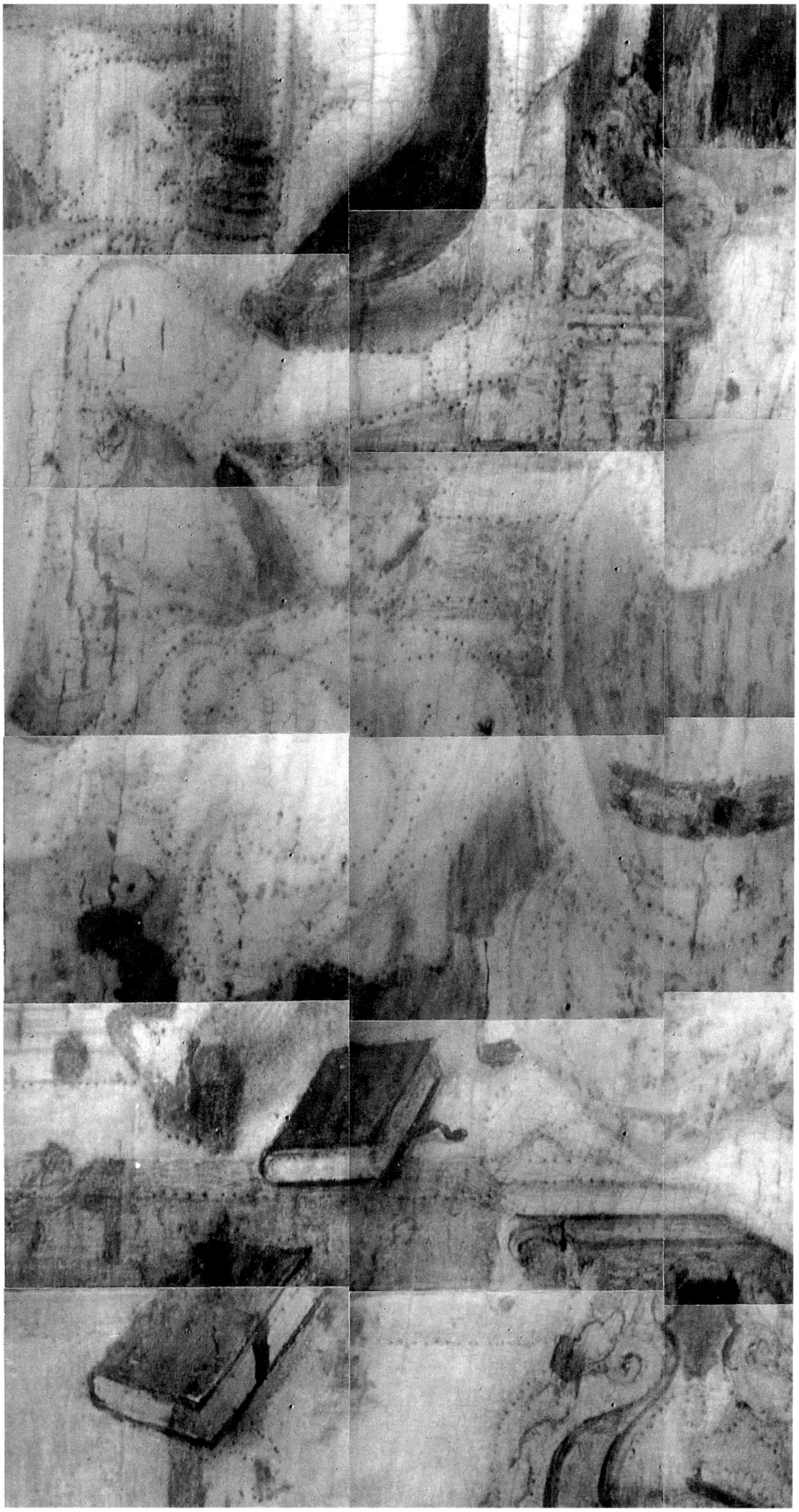

a. Infrared reflectogram assembly

On 17 November 1950 Max Friedländer noted on the back of a photograph of this painting: ".....ein gut erhaltenes, charakterisches Werk von Adriaen Isenbrant".[3] It does indeed seem to belong amongst the paintings attributed to Ysenbrant. When it came into the Museum's possession the paint was beginning to flake and there was evidence of much past restoration.

The panel depicts the boy Jesus amidst the doctors in the temple (Luke 2:40-52). In the left background are the Virgin and Joseph, who have found him after searching for three days.

The composition, with some of the doctors in the foreground and Jesus on a dais in the centre, is identical to that used by Ysenbrant in the *Seven Sorrows of the Virgin* in Onze Lieve Vrouwkerk in Bruges.[4] It was also used by some of his contemporaries.[5]

The subject was popular in the first half of the sixteenth century, especially in the context of the *Seven Sorrows of the Virgin*. So the Rotterdam panel could well have been part of a small polyptych depicting each of the sorrows separately.[6]

The underdrawing of the composition (fig. a) is stippled, indicating that the artist transferred it to the prepared panel from a pricked cartoon. The dots are separate and not, as was often the case, linked by lines.[7] The black dots are not equidistant and are not all of the same thickness as is to be expected in pouncing. The underdrawing was closely followed in applying the paint. One of the few differences is that a clasp on the lowest book was not painted.

Pouncing was often used in the first half of the sixteenth century, and is found in the work of such other artists as Gerard David and Patinir.[8] The technique was especially useful for making copies of a particular design, though this was not the only reason for its application. It was also a good means of accurately laying in a pre-drawn design. No further versions of the Rotterdam work are known.
FL

1 Scientific examination conducted by Astrid van den Berg under the supervision of J.R.J. van Asperen de Boer. Paint samples A 379/1-3. Infrared reflectograms AB 1560/1-AB 1561/13A.

2 The painting does not appear in Van Beuningen's record of purchases. He must have bought it between 1949 and 1952.

3 Photograph in the Museum's file.

4 See Friedländer, XI, 1974, no. 138. The left panel of this diptych, portraying the donors, is no longer in the church but in the Koninklijke Musea voor Schone Kunsten, Brussels. On its reverse is again depicted the *Seven Sorrows of the Virgin*. The composition of *The boy Jesus amongst the doctors* is also the same.

5 For instance by Bernard van Orley in paintings in Besançon (Musée des Beaux-Arts et d'Archéologie), Rome (Galleria Colonna) and Antwerp (Koninklijke Musea voor Schone Kunsten). See Friedländer, VIII, 1972, nos. 89, 94, 95.

6 Cf. Jan Joest van Calcar's altarpiece, the *Seven Sorrows of the Virgin*, in the Palencia cathedral. See Friedländer, IX, 1972, no. 2. It is equally possible that the Rotterdam work was part of a polyptych of the life of Christ.

7 This is a frequent feature of paintings attributed to Ysenbrant, such as the *St John the Baptist* in Budapest. See S. Urbach, "Research report on examinations of underdrawings in some early Netherlandish and German panels in the Budapest Museum of Fine Arts," *Le dessin sous-jacent dans la peinture, colloque VI (1985)*, Louvain-la-Neuve 1987, pp. 50-52, figs. 32, 33.

8 The underdrawing is stippled in several versions of Gerard David's famous *Virgin with the pap spoon*. See M. Comblen-Sonkes, "A propos de la 'Vierge et Enfant à la soupe au lait.' Contribution à l'étude des copies," *Bulletin voor de Koninklijke Musea voor Schone Kunsten te Brussel* I-III (1974-1980), pp. 29-42. See also cat. no. 47.

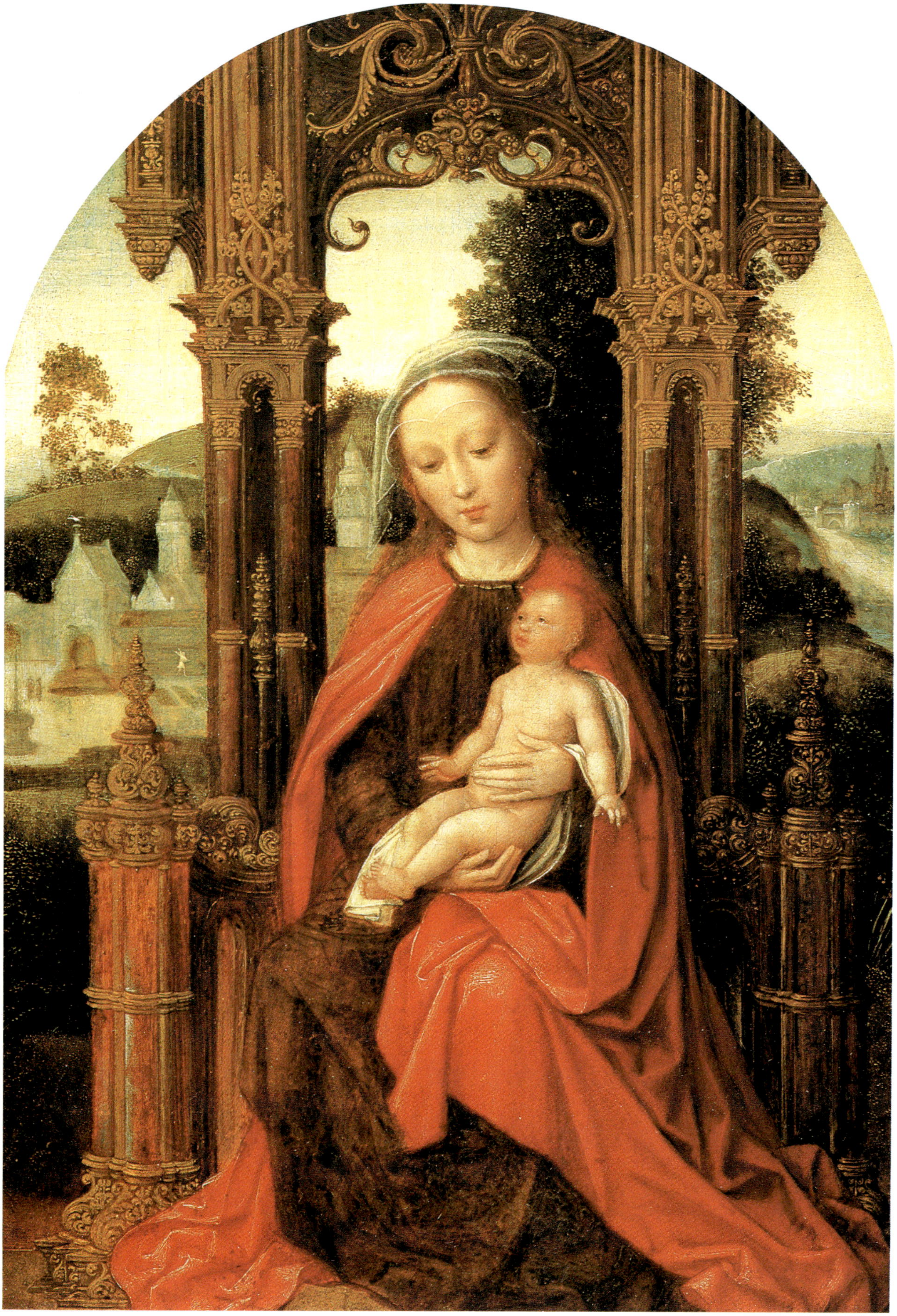

Virgin and Child enthroned, with landscape background

Adriaen Ysenbrant
(?-Bruges 1551)

Panel; 31 x 20 cm

Physical characteristics: the panel consists of a single arched plank.

Infrared reflectography:[1] hatched underdrawing found in the shaded sections of the Virgin's garments.

Provenance: Charles Butler, London, 1896; Warren Wood, Hatfield; Walter von Pannwitz, Haarlem; Knoedler Gallery, London; purchased there by D.G. van Beuningen, Rotterdam and Vierhouten, in 1928 for 24,500 guilders;[2] acquired by the Museum in 1958 with the Van Beuningen Collection; inv. no. 2452.

Exhibitions: *Exhibition of works by the Old Masters [...] Winter exhibition*, London, Royal Academy of Arts, 1896, no. 168; *Winter tentoonstelling van oude kunst uit particulier bezit*, Haarlem, Frans Hals Museum, 1940, no. 36; *Honderd jaar Museum Boymans Rotterdam. Meesterwerken uit de verzameling D.G. van Beuningen*, Rotterdam, Boymans Museum, 1949, no. 15; *Chefs-d'œuvre de la collection D.G. van Beuningen*, Paris, Petit Palais, 1952, no. 52.

Literature: M.J. Friedländer, *Die Kunstsammlung Von Pannwitz*, I, Munich, 1926, no. 19; Friedländer, XI, 1933, no. 172, p. 134; A. Heppner, "Particuliere kunstbezit in het Frans Halsmuseum" *Maandblad voor Beeldende Kunsten* 17 (1940), p. 244, fig. 7, p. 226; Hannema, 1949, no. 15, fig. 38; cat. 1962, p. 159; M. Davis Hill, "The virgin and child attributed to Isenbrandt in the Ackland Art Center", *North Carolina Museum of Art, Raleigh, Bulletin*, IX (1970), pp. 42-51, fig. 2; Friedländer, XI, 1974, no. 172, fig. 131; L.C. Ragghianti, *Dipinti Fiamminghi in Italia 1420-1570*, Bologna 1990, p. 210; M.R. de Vrij, "Adriaen Ysenbrant. De ontwikkeling binnen een serie tronende Madonna's en de authenticiteit van de Tronende Madonna te Rotterdam" *Kunstlicht* 13 (1992), pp. 20-24, fig. 1.

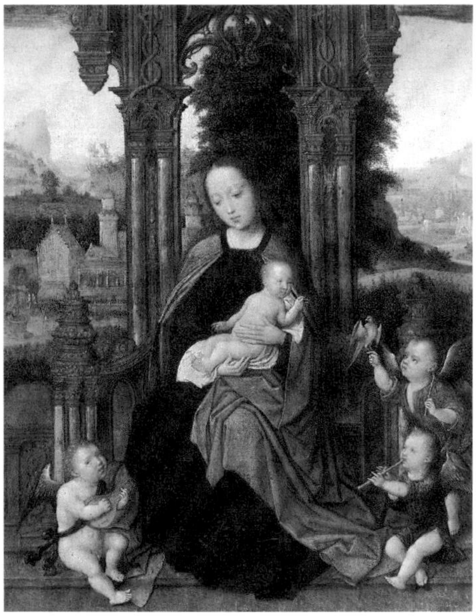

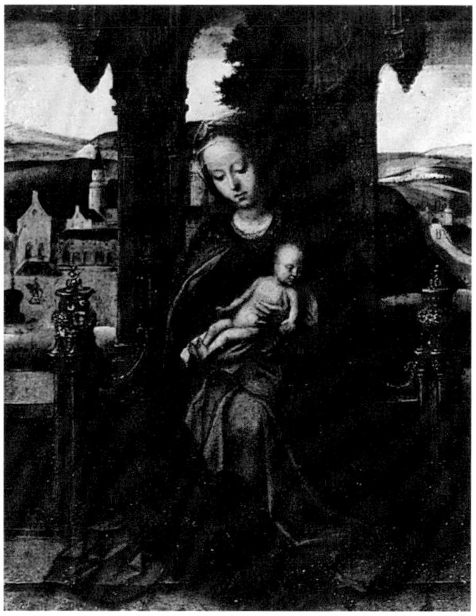

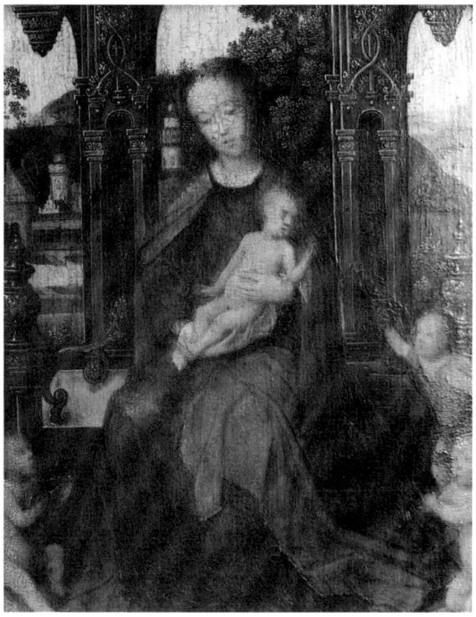

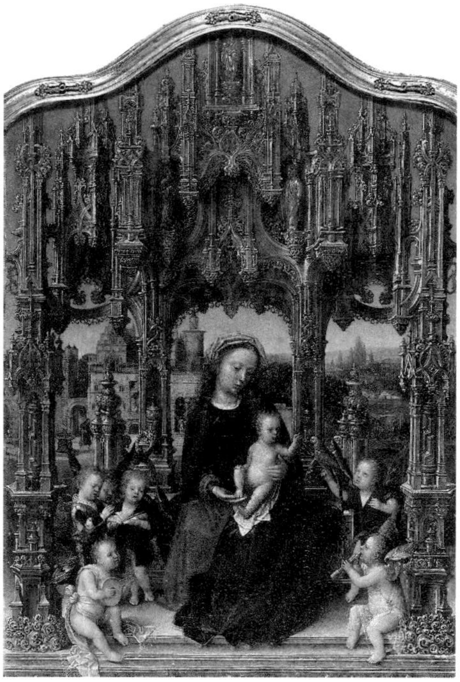

a. Adriaen Ysenbrant, Virgin and Child with angels
Panel; 24 x 19 cm
San Diego (California), San Diego Museum of Art

b. Adriaen Ysenbrant, Virgin and Child
Panel; 26.5 x 20 cm
Palermo, Galleria Nazionale della Sicilia

c. Adriaen Ysenbrant, Virgin and Child with St John and three angels
Panel; 16.5 x 12.3 cm
Madrid, Museo del Prado

d. Adriaen Ysenbrant, Virgin and Child with angels.
Central panel from triptych.
Former Von Pannwitz Collection, Haarlem

The Virgin and Child are seated on a highly ornate throne against a landscape background. The Virgin wears a red cloak over a brown robe which was probably originally blue.

This panel is one of the many paintings of the Virgin and Child attributed to Ysenbrant. At least three other versions of the Rotterdam panel are known. They are in the San Diego Museum of Art (fig. a), the Galleria Nazionale, Palermo (fig. b) and the Prado, Madrid (fig. c).[3] The three are not exactly the same. The details of the throne are different; so too is the posture of the Child. The architecture in the background, on the other hand, has the same structure, and the folds in the Virgin's garments are almost identical.[4] Three angels in the San Diego and Madrid panels do not appear in the others. They are modelled on the central panel of Jan Gossaert's "Malvagna" triptych in Palermo.[5]

The throne, identical in all paintings, derives from the same source.[6] Ysenbrant's familiarity with Gossaert's triptych is known from his copy of it that was formerly in the Walter von Pannwitz Collection (fig. d).[7]

It is difficult to trace the relationship between the works. Those in San Diego and Madrid bear more resemblance to the "Malvagna" triptych and are possibly earlier than the two in Rotterdam and Palermo. The Rotterdam panel appears to be superior in quality to the Palermo panel, with more detail and a more sensitively conveyed bond between mother and child. In the Palermo work the Child is looking into the distance, whereas in the Rotterdam version he and his mother are gazing into each other's eyes. Whether all four are from the hand of Ysenbrant is very much open to question.

A striking difference between the Rotterdam panel and the others is the Virgin's face, which is much rounder.[8] However, it is a facial type found in other works attributed to Ysenbrant.

Establishing precisely what can be ascribed to Ysenbrant gives rise to many problems. No single work can be ascribed to him with absolute certainty. Over the years a large oeuvre has accumulated under the name of this artist who is known only from the Bruges archives and two literary references.[9] Many of these paintings exhibit marked stylistic similarities, and the Rotterdam panel fits into this category. But whether they are indeed the work of Ysenbrant and his workshop remains uncertain.
FL

1 Conducted by Molly Faries in September 1993.
2 According to Friedländer, XI, 1933, p. 134, the panel was in the Perls Gallery, Berlin, in 1930. This date must be wrong, because then it had already been in the Van Beuningen Collection for two years.
3 On the San Diego painting: *European paintings in the Timken Art Gallery*, Timken Art Gallery, San Diego, 1969, no. 17, pp. 52, 53 (fig.), 116; the Palermo painting: G. Cardente, *Collections d'Italie, I. Sicilie* (Les Primitifs Flamands II, répertoire des peintures Flamandes du quinzième siècle 3), Brussels 1968, no. 12, fig.; the Prado painting: *Museo del Prado. Catalogo de las Pinturas*, 1985, p. 339.
4 The posture of the Virgin probably derives from a work by Rogier van der Weyden. See De Vrij (1992).
5 See Friedländer, VIII, 1972, no. 2, fig. 4. The triptych is generally considered to be an early work, dating from around 1511.
6 Ambrosius Benson also appears to have taken Gossaert's throne as a model, see his *St Anna and the Virgin* in the Prado, Madrid. See George Marlier, *Ambrosius Benson*, Damme 1957, no. 1a, fig. XXIII.
7 Friedländer (1926). De Vrij (1992), mentions a second, somewhat more freely executed copy by Ysenbrant of Gossaert's central panel.
8 De Vrij (1992) doubts the authenticity of the Rotterdam panel because of this difference.
9 Jean C. Wilson, "Workshop patterns and the production of paintings in sixteenth-century Bruges," *The Burlington Magazine* 132 (1990), p. 523. She lists some five hundred paintings attributed to Ysenbrant.

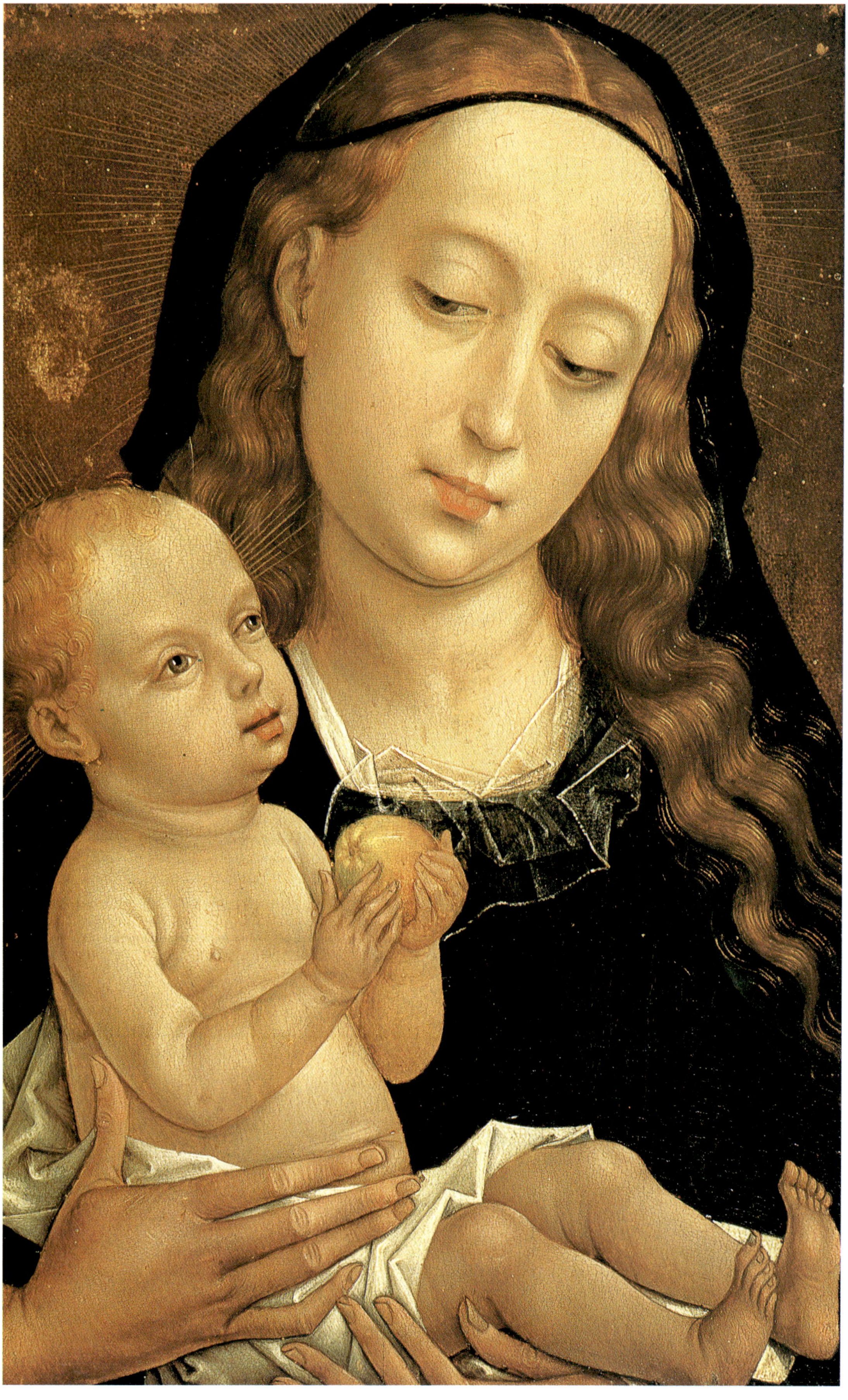

The Virgin with the infant Christ holding an apple

Master of the legend of the Magdalen (?)
(active in Brussels c. 1500)

Panel; 25 x 18 cm

The Virgin Mary is holding the infant Christ before her in both hands. There are golden rays around both heads. Christ is holding an apple. An apple in the hands of Adam would be a symbol of sin. In the case of Christ it signifies redemption. The picture has a gilded background with black stipples.

The painting was attributed to Rogier van der Weyden in both the 1932 sale and in the Van Beuningen Collection. This is quite understandable in view of the panel's excellence. The paint's good state of preservation makes the plasticity of form and refinement of detail all the more convincing.

In 1937 Friedländer wrote that the painting was a characteristic and exceptionally well-preserved work by Rogier van der Weyden.[2] In 1949, however, Hannema expressed the view that it could also have been painted by a member of his school, such as the Master of the legend of the Magdalen. Since then this attribution has been generally accepted. The pseudonym was associated by Friedländer with a group of paintings including *The Magdalen preaching* in the Johnson Collection in Philadelphia. The master was active in Brussels and may be seen as an important link between Rogier and Bernard van Orley.

Baes-Dondeyne claims that characteristic traits of the artist can be seen in the Rotterdam work. These include the parallel lines for Mary's flowing hair, the large hands with extended fingers (with the middle- and ring fingers pressed together), the short dark outlined nails and the gilded background with black stipples.[3] It is particularly interesting that the painting is on fir. This is unusual for works of Flemish origin and might suggest a different provenance, such as Germany.

There are several slightly different versions of this painting. The Hermitage in St Petersburg has an excellent example which is closely related to the Rotterdam painting. Nikouline mentions six other versions, including the one in Rotterdam, in the Hermitage catalogue.[4] In addition to these, there is a version in private ownership in Geneva which was exhibited in Bruges in 1969. The type of painting for which Rogier had provided the prototype was evidently much sought after for private devotion.
JG

Physical characteristics: the panel consists of a single fir plank (see Peter Klein's article in this catalogue). The *barbe* can be seen around the whole painting.

Infrared reflectography:[1] an underdrawing of fine lines is detectable which does not, however, appear to bear any relationship to the actual painting. It may have been the outlines of a cloak.

Provenance: Conde Morra di Loriano, Turin; (?) Claudio Gallo, sale in Milan, 1932, no. 136 (as Rogier van der Weyden); Dr. Wendland, Paris, 1937; purchased by D.G. van Beuningen, Rotterdam and Vierhouten, in 1938 as Rogier van der Weyden for 90,000 guilders; acquired in 1958 with the D.G. van Beuningen Collection; inv. no. 2481.

Exhibitions: *Meesterwerken uit vier eeuwen 1400-1800*, Rotterdam, Boymans Museum, 1938, no. 19a; *Honderd jaar museum Boymans. Meesterwerken uit de verzameling D.G. van Beuningen*, Rotterdam, Boymans Museum, 1949, no. 33; *Chefs-d'œuvre de la collection D.G. van Beuningen*, Paris, Petit Palais, 1952, no. 73; *Anonieme Vlaamse Primitieven, Zuidnederlandse meesters met noodnamen van de 15de en het begin van de 16de eeuw*, Bruges, Groeningemuseum, 1969, no. 73, fig., pp. 273-274.

Literature: Hannema, 1949, no. 33; J.Q. van Regteren Altena, "D. Hannema, Catalogue of the D.G. van Beuningen collection", *Oud Holland* LXVIII (1953), p. 229; cat. 1962, p. 86; V. Loewinson-Lessing, N. Nicouline, *Le Musée de l'Ermitage Leningrad, Les Primitifs Flamands*, Brussels 1965, p. 64, no. 1; K. Arndt, "Altniederländische Meister mit Notnamen", *Kunstchronik* 23 (1970), p. 116; N.N. Nikulin, *The Hermitage catalogue of Western European Painting, Netherlandish Painting Fifteenth and Sixteenth Centuries*, Moscow-Florence 1989, p. 150.

[1] Scanned and recorded by J.R.J. van Asperen de Boer on 20 December 1993 and 17 January 1994. Infrared reflectograms: AB 1562/1A-10A.
[2] Note on the reverse of a photograph in the Museum's archive: "Das umstehend photographierte Bild ist meiner Ansicht nach ein charakteristiches, ungewöhnlich gut erhaltenes Werk von Rogier van der Weijden - M.J. Friedländer, Berlin, d. 16.XI.37."
[3] See exhib. cat. Bruges, 1969.
[4] 1. New York, previously the Reinhardt Gallery, Friedländer, V, 1935, pl. VI; 2. Sale at Sotheby's, London, 2 July 1958, no. 31; 3. Vaduz, collection of the Prince of Liechtenstein, no. 931; 4. Paris, Louvre, inv. no. R.F. 2822; 5. Cologne, Kunstgewerbemuseum, Clemens Collection.

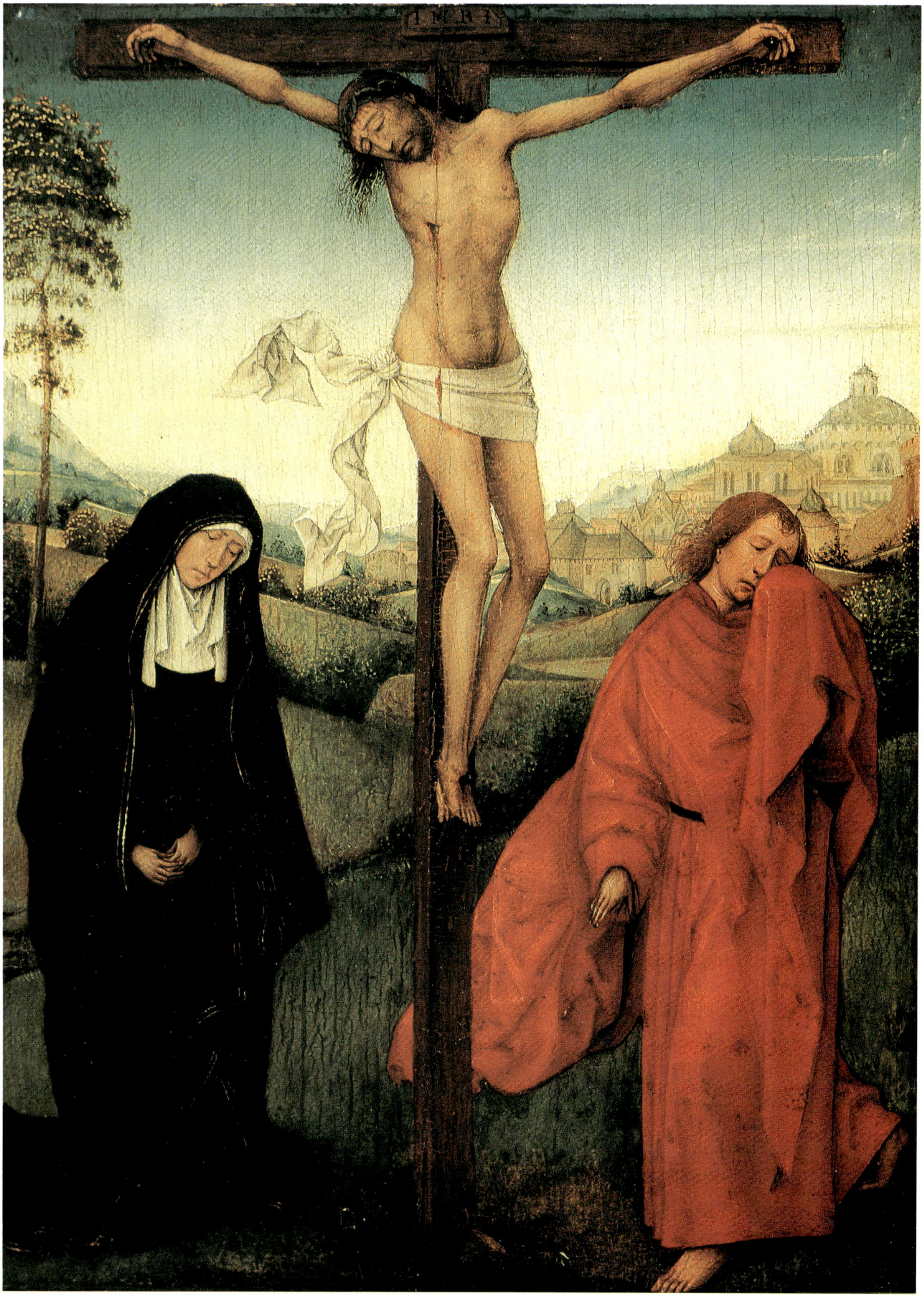

Crucifixion, with the Virgin and St John

Anonymous
South Netherlandish master, Brussels
c. 1500

Panel; 25 x 19 cm

Christ on the Cross is flanked on the left by the sorrowing Virgin, and on the right by the weeping St John. The eastern-style architecture in the background is the city of Jerusalem. L. Baldass attributed this painting in 1932 to the Bruges master, Jan Provoost.[2] Friedländer identified it in 1935 with the Master of the Legend of the Magdalen, active in Brussels around 1500. In the catalogues of the Van Beuningen Collection and Boymans Museum it nevertheless continued to be listed as a work by Provoost. In the 1969 Bruges catalogue, Baes-Dondeyne discusses the attribution to the Master of the Legend of the Magdalen, but concludes that the painting cannot be ascribed to any particular artist. The author states that although the figure of Christ is reminiscent of Rogier van der Weyden, the contorted posture is not, while the tiny hands of the Virgin and St John bear no relation whatsoever to the hands painted by the Master of the Legend of the Magdalen. Baes-Dondeyne concludes that the picture must be attributed to an anonymous master of the Brussels School.

The panel undeniably displays some kinship with the Master of the Legend of the Magdalen, as in the landscape and the refinement of detail. But the hands of the Virgin and St John are singularly weak. So in line with the conclusion reached by Baes-Dondeyne, it is attributed here to an anonymous Brussels master.
JG

Physical characteristics: the panel consists of a single plank. The *barbe* is present along all edges.

Infrared reflectography:[1] shows only what seem to be a few contour lines as underdrawing.

Dendrochronology: the youngest heartwood growth ring dates from 1446. The panel could not have been painted before 1457; it was more probably painted in or after 1471. See article by P. Klein.

Provenance: Canot Collection, Barcelona; S. von Auspitz, Vienna; bought through K.W. Bachstitz Gallery, The Hague, by D.G. van Beuningen, Rotterdam and Vierhouten, in 1932 for 10,000 guilders; acquired by the Museum in 1958 with the Van Beuningen Collection; inv. no. 2477.

Exhibitions: *An Exhibition of the Von Auspitz Collection of Old Masters*, London, Agnew, 1932, no. 12; *Honderd jaar museum Boymans. Meesterwerken uit de verzameling D.G. van Beuningen*, Rotterdam, Boymans Museum, 1949, no. 30; *Chefs-d'œuvre de la collection D.G. van Beuningen*, Paris, Petit Palais, 1952, no. 70; *Anonieme Vlaamse Primitieven, Zuidnederlandse meesters met noodnamen van de 15de en het begin van de 16de eeuw*, Bruges, Groeninge Museum, 1969, no. 66, fig.

Literature: Friedländer, XII, 1935, p. 167, no. 17; Hannema, 1949, no. 30, pl. 37; cat. 1962, p. 107; K. Arndt, "Altniederländische Meister mit Notnamen", *Kunstchronik* 23 (1970), p. 116; Friedländer, XII, 1975, p. 92, no. 17, fig. pl. 12.

1 Conducted by J.R.J. van Asperen de Boer on 24 January 1994.
2 L. Baldass, *Treatise on the Von Auspitz Collection*, a manuscript catalogue of the Von Auspitz Collection in the Museum's file on the work. "This small Crucifixion, painted in glowing colours, takes us to a centre of Flemish painting, to Bruges. It formerly belonged to the Canot Collection at Barcelona. The figure of the Saviour with its lank arms and legs on which the joints are strongly accentuated, its protruding chest and thin waist, is evidently an imitation of some work of Rogier's.....I consider the picture to be an early work before 1500 by Jan Provost....."

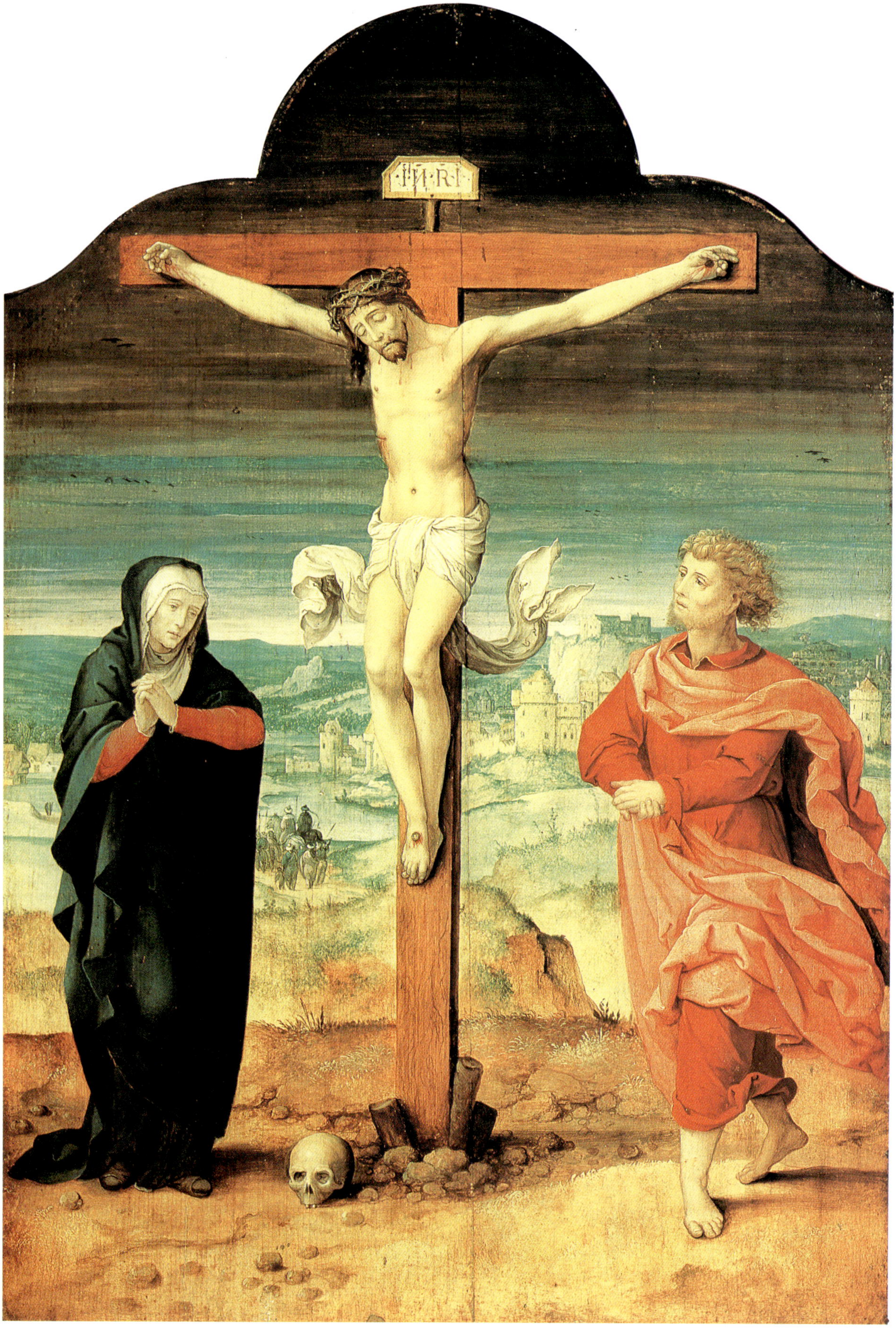
I·N·R·I

Christ on the cross between St John and the Virgin

Master of the Female Half-Lengths
(active in Antwerp c. 1530)

Panel; 72 x 49 cm

When the painting was donated in 1851, it was known only that it was made in the sixteenth century. The attribution to the Master of the Female Half-Lengths was made by P. Haverkorn of Rijsewijk in 1904. The painter did not only produce the female half-length figures from which he acquired his name, but also altarpieces and small religious representations. Friedländer placed the artist in Antwerp, in the first half of the sixteenth century.[2] Typical of his work are the somewhat flat faces and the great attention to the sometimes complex folds of the draperies.

Martens wrote an article about the Rotterdam painting, which he regards as the example for three other paintings, one in the Comte d'Arschot collection in Brussels, one in the Oudheidkundig Museum in Ghent and one in the National Gallery in London. He describes all three as "anonymous Flemish".[3] Martens also identifies the shape of the clouds, which are shown as horizontal lines, as characteristic of the artist. A comparable figure of Christ, with clouds rendered in a similar way, can be seen on a triptych by the painter in the Galleria Sabauda in Turin.[4] Another comparable work is a painting by Joos van Cleve (1480/85-1540) with the same subject in the Museum of Fine Arts in Boston. It is possible that the Master of the Female Half-Lengths was influenced by Van Cleve.[5]
JG

Physical characteristics: the panel consists of two vertical planks. The top edge is curved.

Infrared reflectography: underdrawing with small, thin lines. No hatching.[1]

Provenance: donated by Mr J.L.C. van den Berch van Heemstede, 1851; inv. no. 1919.

Not exhibited

Literature: *Supplement-catalogus van schilderijen enz. in het Museum te Rotterdam, gesticht door Mr. F.J.O. Boymans*, 1854, no. 430; P. Haverkorn van Rijsewijk, *Verslag omtrent den toestand en de aanwinsten van het Museum Boijmans over het jaar 1904*, p. 5; Friedländer, XII, 1935, p. 172, no. 58; cat. 1962, p. 88; Friedländer, XII, 1975, p. 96, no. 58, pl. 35; M. Díaz Padrón, "Nuevas pinturas del Maestro de la Medias Figuras", *Archivo Español de Arte* 210 (1980), p. 173; D. Martens, "Une *Crucifixion* Flamande et sa descendance au XVIe siècle. Lecture d'une séquence de copies", *Koninklijk Museum voor Schone Kunsten Antwerpen, Jaarboek* 1990, pp. 237-270, figs. 1, 20, 22, 24.

1 Scanned and partially recorded on 20 December 1993 and 17 January 1994 by J.R.J. van Asperen de Boer. Infrared reflectograms: AB 1559/26A-36A.
2 Friedländer, XII, 1935.
3 Martens (1990).
4 Friedländer, XII, 1975, pl. 30.
5 Friedländer, IX, 1, 1972, pl. 51, no. 30.

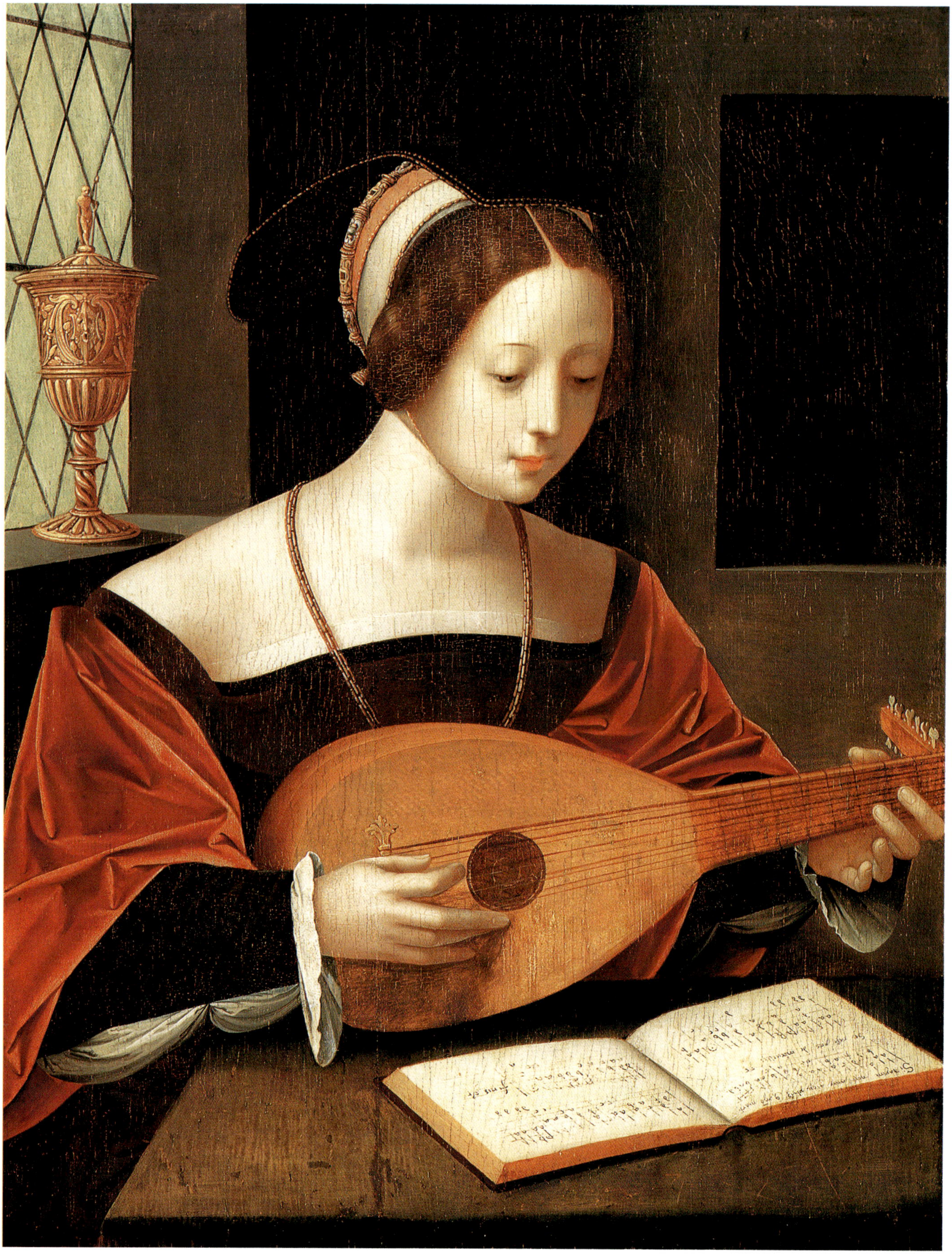

St Mary Magdalene with a lute

Master of the Female Half-Lengths
(active in Antwerp c. 1530)

Panel; 56.5 x 43.5 cm

Physical characteristics: the panel consists of two vertical planks.

Infrared reflectography:[1] no underdrawig could be discerned.

Provenance: legacy F.J.O. Boymans, Utrecht, 1847; inv. no. 1505.

Literature: *Catalogus van schilderijen enz. in het Museum Rotterdam gesticht door Mr. F.J.O. Boijmans*, 1849, no. 206; P. Haverkorn van Rijsewijk, *Verslag omtrent den toestand en de aanwinsten van het Museum Boymans over het jaar 1887*, pp. 17, 18; F. Wickhoff, "Die Bilder weiblicher Halbfiguren aus der Zeit und Umgebung Franz I. von Frankreich", *Jahrbuch der Kunsthistorischen Sammlungen des Allerhöchsten Kaiserhauses* 22 (1901) 5, pp. 221-245, fig. 34; Friedländer, XII, 1935, p. 175, no. 101; cat. 1962, p. 88; Friedländer, XII, 1975, p. 100, no. 101, fig.

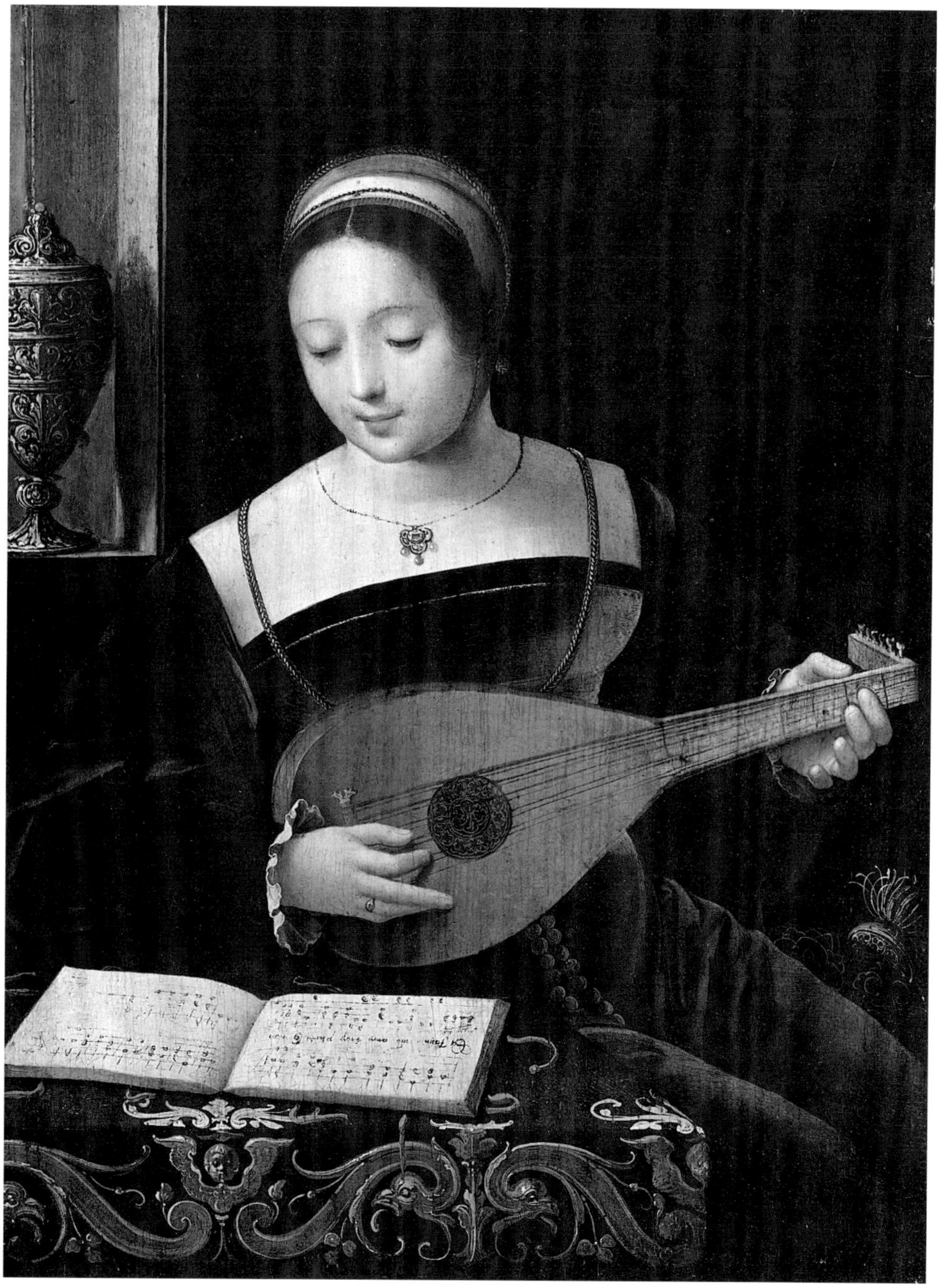

a. Master of the Female Half-lengths, St Mary Magdalene with a lute
Panel; 37.5 x 26.8 cm
Hamburg, Kunsthalle

The elegant, richly dressed young woman is singing and accompanying herself on the lute. A songbook lies before her on the table. On the window ledge stands a covered vase, and a niche is in the wall to her left. She is singing "Si jayme mon amy trop, plus que mon mary se nest pas de mervelles", which may be freely translated as "More than my husband I love my friend, a fool who that a wonder finds". It is a *minnesong* written by Clément Marot, court poet to Francis I of France (1494-1515).[2] It celebrates not marriage, but fidelity to the singer's great love.

Her designation as fools those not understanding that her feelings for her lover are deeper than those for her husband is at first strange. But she is not an ordinary woman: she is Mary Magdalen, identified by her attribute, a pot of ointment. Her song thus acquires an entirely different meaning. Her "friend" is Christ, not a mortal lover. The Magdalene was often portrayed in the sixteenth century in half-length, in sumptuous contemporary dress. She was extremely popular in the Netherlands. Her iconographical identity stems from three Biblical women.[3] The first is Mary Magdalene from whom Jesus exorcised seven devils, the woman who witnessed His death on the Cross and one of the first to whom He appeared after the Resurrection. The second is the unnamed sinner referred to in St Luke, and the third is the highly respected Mary of Bethany, sister of Martha and Lazarus. In the wake of St Augustine, the three Marys were regarded in the West as one and the same person. The combination of Mary Magdalene and the unnamed sinner in the Gospel of St Luke added a special dimension to her person. The unnamed woman, a harlot who turned to Christ in repentance, appeared at the meal in the house of Simon the Pharisee, washed the feet of Jesus with her tears, dried his feet with her hair and anointed them with myrrh from an alabaster jar. It was precisely because of her sinful life that the Magdalene was a saint with whom "sinful mankind" could readily identify. There are various known fifteenth- and sixteenth-century portraits of women who were portrayed as Mary Magdalene.[4] There is no reason to assume, however, that the woman in the Rotterdam panel is a portrait. Her figure is too stereotyped to be a portrait of an actual person.

The work has been ascribed since the late nineteenth century to the Master of the Female Half-Lengths, a painter who worked in Antwerp around 1530.[5] He owes his name to the many women he portrayed in half-length, writing, reading or playing an instrument, accompanied in almost all instances by a jar or bowl of some kind linking the figure with Mary Magdalene. There are a number of versions of this lute-playing woman, all of which are attributed to this master.[6] They differ primarily in their detail, not one being an exact copy of another. The work in the Hamburg Kunsthalle bears the closest resemblance to that in Rotterdam (fig. a). The figure, turned slightly more to the right, plays the same *minnesong* from the same songbook, and even the gown is largely identical.
LH

[1] Conducted by J.R.J. van Asperen de Boer on 20 December 1993.
[2] Wickhoff (1901), p. 235.
[3] J.J.M. Timmers, *Symboliek en iconografie der christelijke kunst*, Bussum 1978, p. 283. See also Liesbeth M. Helmus, *Mechtelt van Lichtenberg toe Boecop (ca. 1520-1598). Een onderzoek naar haar Piëta*, Utrecht Central Museum, Utrecht 1989, pp. 14-16.
[4] The author is currently writing an article on this subject. See also Liesbeth M. Helmus, *op. cit.* (note 3).
[5] P. Haverkorn van Rijsewijk (1887) was the first to suggest this attribution.
[6] Wickhoff (1901) lists six such paintings of a lute-playing woman, describing the Rotterdam panel as the finest. Friedländer lists five. Friedländer, XII, 1975, nos. 98-103, plate 44.

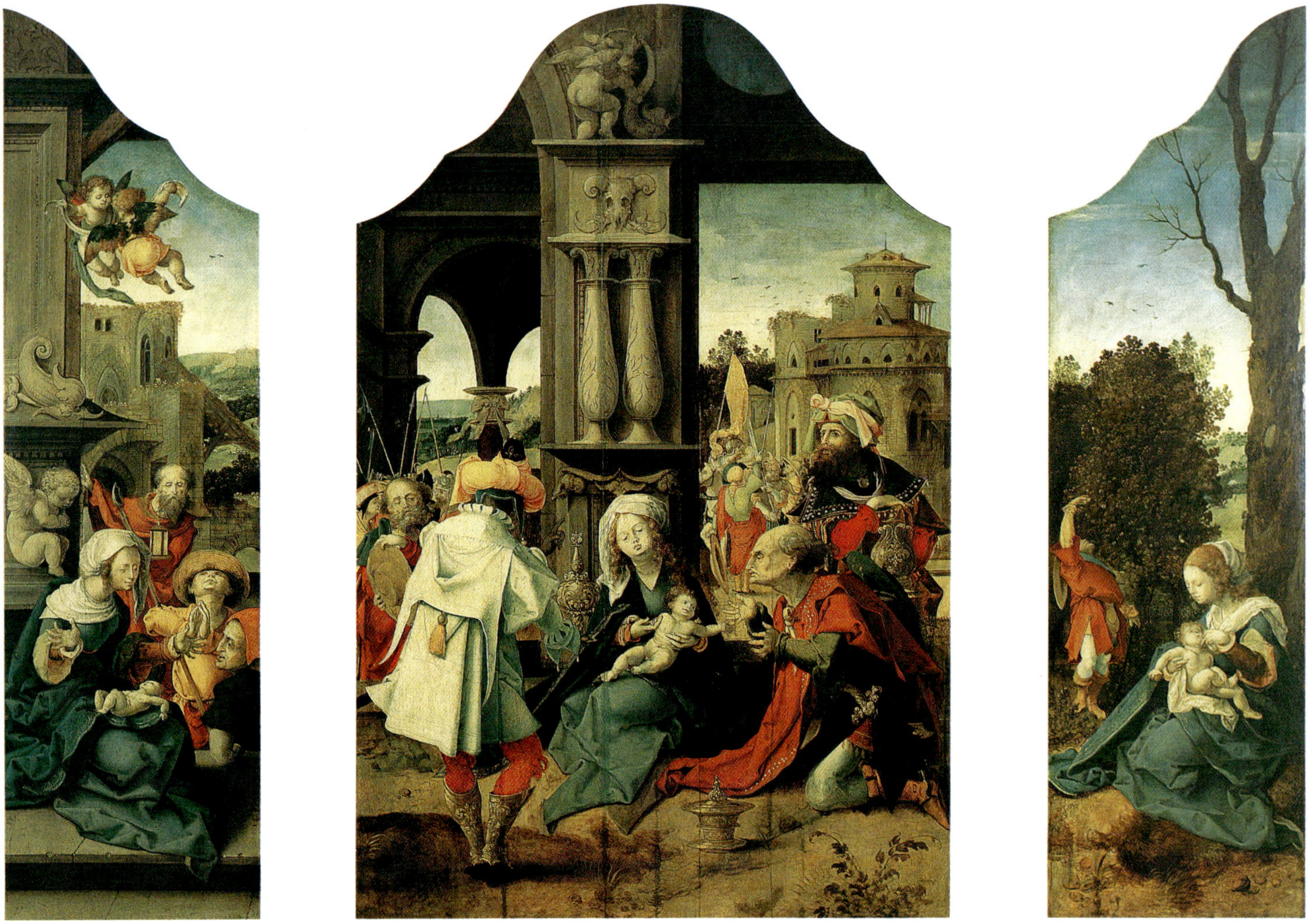

Adoration of the magi (central panel)
Adoration of the shepherds (left panel)
Rest on the flight into Egypt (right panel)

Master of the Lille Adoration
(active Antwerp, c. 1520-1530)

Central panel; 106 x 70 cm
Wings; 106 x 31 cm

Physical characteristics: there is no indication of the wings having ever been painted on the reverse.

Infrared reflectography:[1] highly detailed underdrawing in fine brush strokes. The shaded areas are executed in parallel hatching, sometimes combined with cross-hatching. Many alterations were made at the painting stage, and many elements already painted were subsequently changed. There is some difference in style of underdrawing between the central panel and the wings. See description.

Paint samples: differences can be observed in the paint layer structure of the central panel and the wings.

Provenance: Friedrich Lippmann Collection, Berlin; auctioned in Berlin, Lepke, 26 November 1912, no. 43, fig. 21; sold to A.S. Drey, Munich, for 30,000 marks; Stephan von Auspitz Collection, Vienna; bought in 1932 by D.G. van Beuningen, Rotterdam and Vierhouten, through the K.W. Bachstitz Gallery, The Hague, for 30,000 guilders; loaned to the Boymans Museum, Rotterdam, immediately after it was acquired; acquired by the Museum with the Van Beuningen Collection in 1958; inv.no. 1959.

Exhibitions: *Drei Jahrhunderte Vlämische Malerei 1400-1700*, Vienna, Wiener Secession, 1930, no. 137, fig.; *Honderd jaar Museum Boymans Rotterdam. Meesterwerken uit de verzameling D.G. van Beuningen*, Rotterdam, Boymans Museum, 1949, no. 36; *Chefs-d'œuvre de la collection D.G. van Beuningen*, Paris, Petit Palais, 1952, no. 74.

Literature: G. Glück, *Jahrbuch der Kunsthistorischen Sammlung* XXII (1901); L. Baldass, "Dirk Vellert als Tafelmaler," *Belvedere* 1922, p. 163, fig. 2; M. Conway, *The Van Eycks and their followers*, London 1921, p. 393, fig. XXI.1; F. Winkler, *Altniederländische Malerei*, Berlin 1924, p. 221; A.E. Popham, "The engravings and woodcuts of Dirck Vellert", *The Print Collector's Quarterly* 12 (1925), p. 350; W. Burger, *Die Malerei in den Niederlanden 1400-1500*, Munich 1925, p. 126, fig. 197; Friedländer, XII, 1935, p. 48, no. 139, fig. XX; *Beknopte catalogus van de schilderijen en beeldhouwwerken tentoongesteld in museum Boymans te Rotterdam*, 1935, no. 457; J. Vuyk, "Een onbekende triptiek van Dirk Vellert", *Oud Holland* LXI (1946), p. 20; Hannema, 1949, no. 36, figs. 51, 52, 53; G.T. Faggin, *La pittura ad Anversa nel cinquecento*, Florence 1968, p. 21, fig. 37; G. von der Osten, H. Vey, *Painting and sculpture in Germany and the Netherlands 1500-1600*, Harmondsworth 1969, p. 195; P. Wescher, "Neue Beiträge zum Schaffen des Jan Gossaert", *Wallraf-Richartz Jahrbuch* XXXII (1970), p. 109, fig.79; D. Hannema, *Flitsen uit mijn leven als verzamelaar en museumdirecteur*, Rotterdam 1973, p. 59; Friedländer, XII, 1975, p. 30, no. 30, fig.; exhib.cat. *Trésors cachés des églises de la Nièvre*, Nevers, Palais Ducal, 1990, with no. 76.

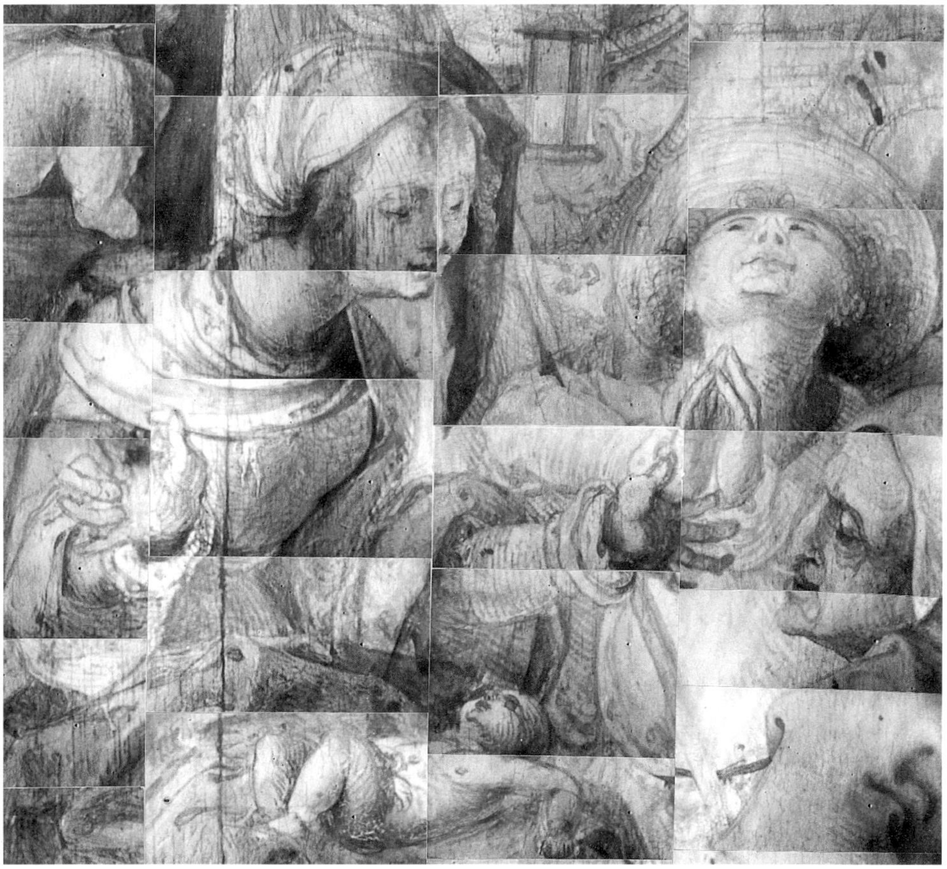

a. Infrared reflectogram assembly showing the Virgin and shepherds on the left panel.

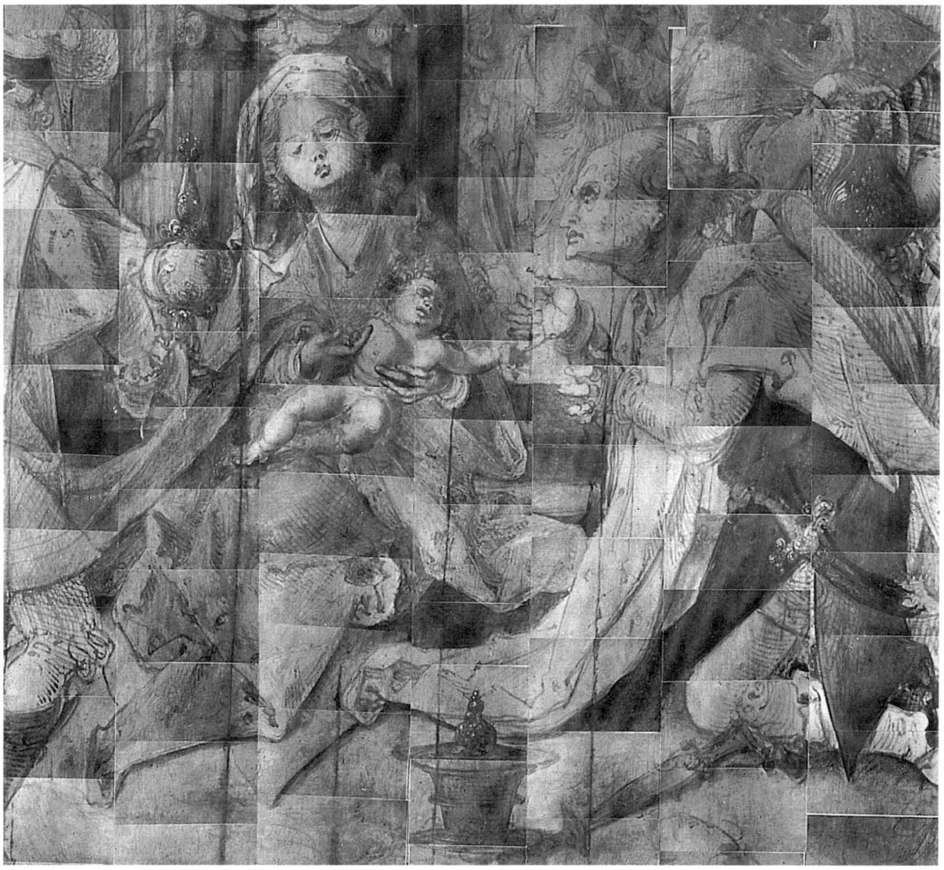

b. Infrared reflectogram assembly of the Virgin and the kneeling king on the central panel.

In 1931 the art dealer Bachtstitz offered the works owned by the Viennese collector Von Auspitz to D.G. van Beuningen. Accompanied by Dirk Hannema, director of the Boymans Museum, he went to Vienna to examine the Collection. Van Beuningen was particularly interested in the Italian bronzes and small paintings. Not without difficulty, Hannema managed to persuade him to buy a number of larger works as well, including this triptych, which he immediately gave to the Museum on loan.[2]

On the central panel is the *Adoration of the magi*, on the left wing the *Adoration of the shepherds*, and on the right wing the *Rest on the flight into Egypt*. Behind the central figures in the *Adoration of the magi* can be seen the kings' retinue. The left wing shows two shepherds in the background, gazing at the sky. The Virgin and Child are depicted in the foreground of the right wing. Behind them Joseph, with an elegant gesture, picks an apple from a tree. This probably relates to a legend in what is called the pseudo-gospel of St Matthew, according to which Joseph tried to pick fruit from a tree during the flight into Egypt. The tree was too high, so Jesus bade it to bow down. The legend was popular in the early sixteenth century, when it was painted by artists such as Joachim Patinir and Gerard David.[3] An equally popular legend was that of the "cornfield miracle," depicted here in the background of the right wing. Passing a cornfield during the flight into Egypt, Jesus changed the green corn into ripe corn. Shortly afterwards, Herod's soldiers asked the peasants if they had seen the Holy Family. Answering truthfully, they said they had seen them before the corn ripened, whereupon the soldiers decided to pursue them no further.[4]

The paint is applied thinly to the panels, and in many places the underdrawing can be seen with the naked eye. The underdrawing is very elaborate, not only of the figures but also of the architectural features. It was rapidly executed with a fine brush. In painting the panels, the artist frequently deviated from the underdrawing, and sometimes changed what he had already painted. The architecture behind the king on the right, for instance, was initially underdrawn and painted quite differently. Another example is the sceptre initially lying before the king on his knees. It was later overpainted and the knee was broadened (fig. b).[5]

The triptych was attributed by Glück to Dirck Jacobsz Vellert (active in Antwerp 1511-1547) in 1901. The artist was entered in the register of the Antwerp St Lucas Guild as a glass painter. He is now known primarily for a few engravings and designs for glass windows. Friedländer shared this view and also attributed various other works, including an *Adoration of the Shepherds* in the Musée des Beaux-Arts, Lille, to Vellert.[6] A few more works were added to his oeuvre in the course of the years.[7] The group as a whole has a readily recognisable character of its own. In each of them the paint layer is rather thin, and the underdrawing can often be seen by the naked eye. The figures are usually portrayed in a dramatic pose, making emotional gestures. The overall impression is one of agitation.

The drawings of Dirck Vellert, however, exhibit different characteristics. The composition is usually balanced and the figures are scarcely ever portrayed in a dramatic manner. The lines and hatching are more composed in feeling than those in the underdrawing of the paintings. This being the case, Ellen Konowitz would seem to be right in her view that this group of paintings does not belong in Vellert's oeuvre. She gave the anonymous artist the name of Master of the Lille Adoration.[8] There seems to be no ground for Wescher's attribution to the young Jan Gossaert.[9] The Rotterdam triptych was probably painted around 1520.
FL

1 Conducted by J.R.J. van Asperen de Boer on 18 January 1991. The infrared reflectogram assemblies were made by F. Visser and S. Bouwman. Paint samples A 333/1-7. Infrared reflectograms: AB 1216-AB 1223/18.

2 Hannema (1973), p. 59.

3 See E.J. Mundy, "Gerard David's 'Rest on the flight into Egypt': further additions to grape symbolism," *Simiolus* XII (1981-1982), pp. 211-222; and R.L. Falkenburg, *Joachim Patinir. Landscape as an image of the Pilgrimage of Life*, Amsterdam-Philadelphia, 1988.

4 See Falkenburg, *op. cit.* (note 3).

5 Other modifications: Left wing: the left leg of the cherub on the left was drawn more to the right; the architecture appears to have been different; the fingers of the Virgin's left hand were slightly changed. Central panel: the feet of the man holding the hat, behind the black king, were first painted but later overpainted with a low wall and the ground, and his eyes were at first drawn differently; the head of the Child was altered, two right eyes appearing on the infrared reflectograms; in the drawing the Child's left leg hung down; the kneeling king was drawn looking more upward, and his sleeves were narrower than in the painting; the whole of the sword hilt was first visible, but was later overpainted with more folds; the underdrawing of the lid of a vase held by the standing king was different from the final version.
Right wing: the head of the Child was turned more towards the Virgin.

6 Friedländer (1935).

7 See Friedländer (1975), p. 135. Besides the paintings in Rotterdam and Lille, the most important work is a triptych, *Ecce Homo*, in Brussels (Musée de l'Assistance Publique), a copy of which was in the Volker Westphal Gallery, Berlin, in 1989. The Brussels painting has a very free underdrawing in black chalk, and it is considerably different in style from the Rotterdam triptych. This can probably be explained by the different materials used. There are marked similarities between the types of figures and the painting technique displayed in the two works (with acknowledgements to Peter van den Brink, Groningen). Vuyk (1946) published another triptych depicting the *Holy Family* in a private collection in Spain, and also drew attention to two wings from a castle in Herdringen that are similar in some respects to a painting in Kremsmünster (Friedländer, XII, 1975, fig. 70). Comparison shows the Herdringen wings to be of a better quality, and they are undoubtedly original, while the Kremsmünster work appears to be a copy. Christie's, Amsterdam, auctioned a triptych attributed to Vellert (no. 97) on 20 June 1989. The work, which was bought by the National Museum, Havana, is painted rather stiffly and does not seem to be by the same artist. An *Adoration of the magi* in St Amand Church in the French town of Saint Amand-en-Puisaye which was published in 1990 (see exhib.cat. *Trésors cachés des églises de la Nièvre*, Nevers, Palais Ducal, 1990, with no. 76) is likewise attributed to Vellert, but lacks the quality of the works in Rotterdam, Brussels and Lille.

8 Ellen Konowitz in exhib.cat., *Antwerpen, verhaal van een metropool*, Antwerp, Hessenhuis, 1993, no. 49, p. 195. She attributes the *Ecce Homo* triptych (Brussels, Musée de l'Assistance Publique) to this artist, but makes no mention of the Rotterdam work.

9 Wescher (1970).

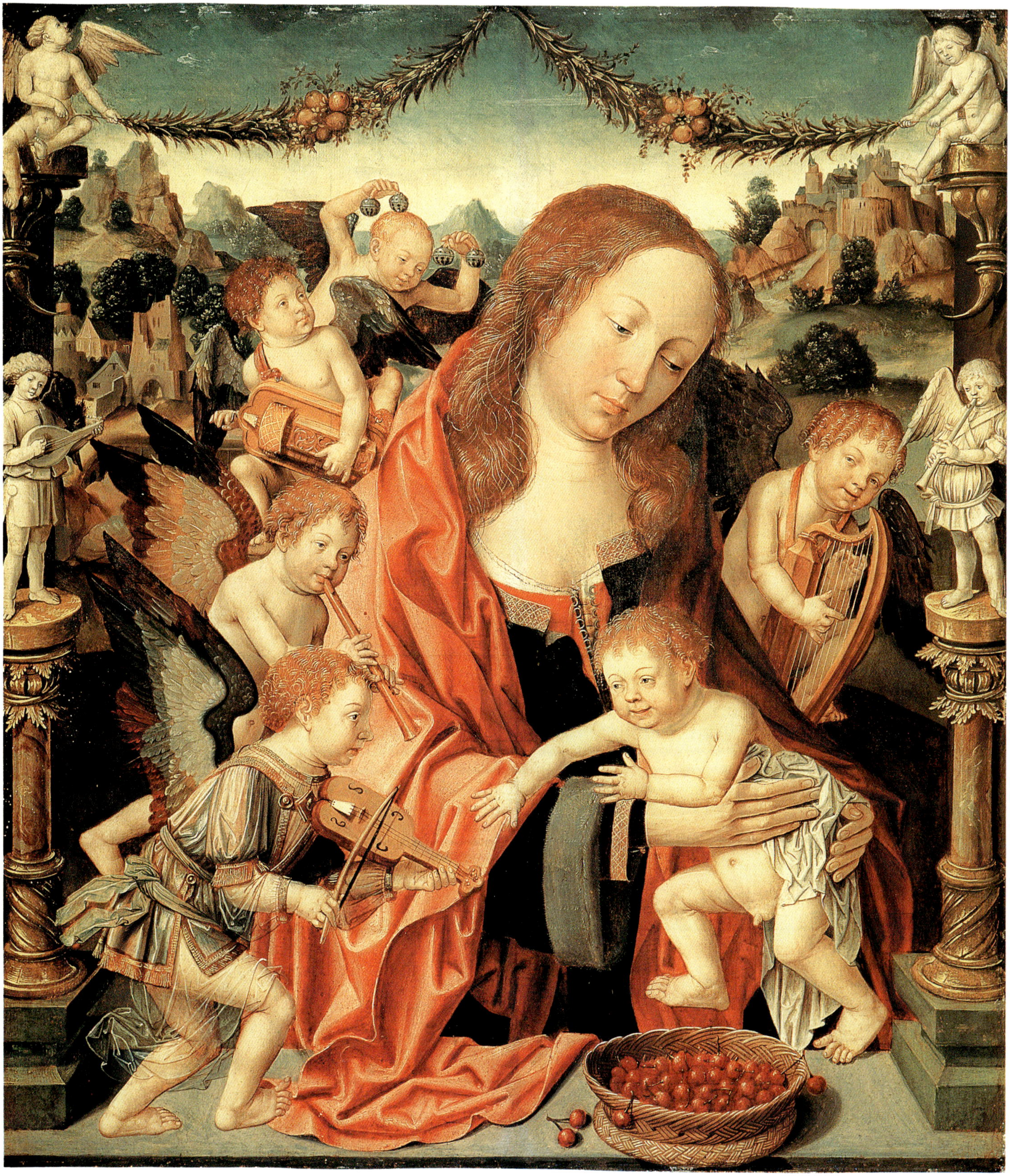

Virgin and Child with angel musicians

Jacob Cornelisz van Oostsanen (group)
(Oostsanen before 1470-
Amsterdam c. 1533)

Panel; 66 x 57.4 cm

Physical characteristics: the panel consists of two vertical planks. The upper left and right corners were originally arched.

Infrared reflectography: extensive underdrawing and square grid in black chalk (figs. a and b).[1] See entry.

Provenance: Harrach, 1902; J. Böhler Gallery, Munich; H.O. Miethke Gallery, Vienna; Courtiers Gallery, Paris; William H. Bennett Collection, 1913; Thomas Agnew Gallery, London, 1922; D.A. Hoogendijk Gallery, Amsterdam, 1929; J. Goudstikker Gallery, Amsterdam, 1935 and 1938; loaned by the Netherlands Office for Fine Arts to the Gemeentemuseum Arnhem, 1952-1988, inv. no. NK 1601; on loan to the Boymans-van Beuningen Museum since June 1988; inv. no. 3170.

Exhibitions:
Exposition des Primitifs Flamands et d'art ancien, Bruges, Hôtel du Conseil Provincial/Hôtel Gruuthuuse, 1902, no. 281; *Woman and child in art*, London, Grosvenor Gallery, 1913-1914, p. 75, fig. 42; *Exhibition of Dutch Art, 1450-1900*, London, Royal Academy of Arts, 1929, no. 40; *Oude Kunst*, Amsterdam, Rijksmuseum, 1929, no. 27; *Jeroen Bosch Noordnederlandse Primitieven*, Rotterdam, Boymans Museum, 1936, no. 93, fig. 91; *Gedenck-clanck* Amsterdam, Stedelijk Museum, 1938, no. 4, fig.; *Herwonnen Kunstbezit*, Utrecht, Centraal Museum, 1946, no. 46; *Middeleeuwse Kunst der Noordelijke Nederlanden*, Amsterdam, Rijksmuseum, 1958, no. 105; *L'art et la musique*, Bordeaux, Galerie des Beaux-Arts, 1969, no. 10.

Literature: M.J. Friedländer, "Die Brügger Leihausstellung von 1902", *Reptertorium für Kunstwissenschaft* 26 (1903), p. 171; F. Dülberg, "Die Ausstellung Altniederländischer Meister in Brügge", *Zeitschrift für Bildende Kunst* 15 (1904), pp. 188-189, 192; M. Conway, *The Van Eycks and their followers*, London 1921, p. 459; K. Steinbart, *Die Tafelgemälde des Jakob Cornelisz von Amsterdam*, Strasbourg 1922, pp. 97-99, fig. 9; F. Winkler, *Die Altniederländische Malerei. Die Malerei in Belgien und Holland von 1400-1600*, Berlin 1924, p. 232; J. Six, "Jan van Hout, Cornelis Buys en Jacob Cornelisz", *Oud Holland* 42 (1925), pp. 7, 9; K. Steinbart, "Nachlese im Werk des Jakob Cornelisz.", *Marburger Jahrbuch für Kunstwissenschaft* 5 (1929), pp. 13, 43, fig. 22; W. Cohen, "Die Madonna mit musizierenden Engeln von Jakob Cornelisz und einige andere Gemälde des Meisters", *Pantheon* 5 (1930), pp. 105, 108, fig.; Friedländer, XII, 1935, p. 193, no. 240; G.J. Hoogewerff, *De Noord-Nederlandsche schilderkunst*, III, The Hague 1939, pp. 117-119, fig. 60; F.W.S. van Thienen, "Jacob Cornelisz. van Oostsanen (ca. 1470-1533)", *Openbaar Kunstbezit* 6 (1962), p. 17a-b, fig.; A.J. de Lorm, *Schilderijen Gemeentemuseum Arnhem*, Arnhem 1965, p. 29, fig.; O. ter Kuile, *500 jaar Nederlandse schilderkunst*, Amsterdam 1970, p. 27, fig. 31; Friedländer, XII, 1975, p. 114, no. 240, fig. 130; J.L. Carroll, *The paintings of Jacob Cornelisz. van Oostsanen (1472?-1533)*, Ann Arbor 1987, pp. 17-18, 37-38, 60, cat. no. 8, pp. 143-150, figs. 18-21.

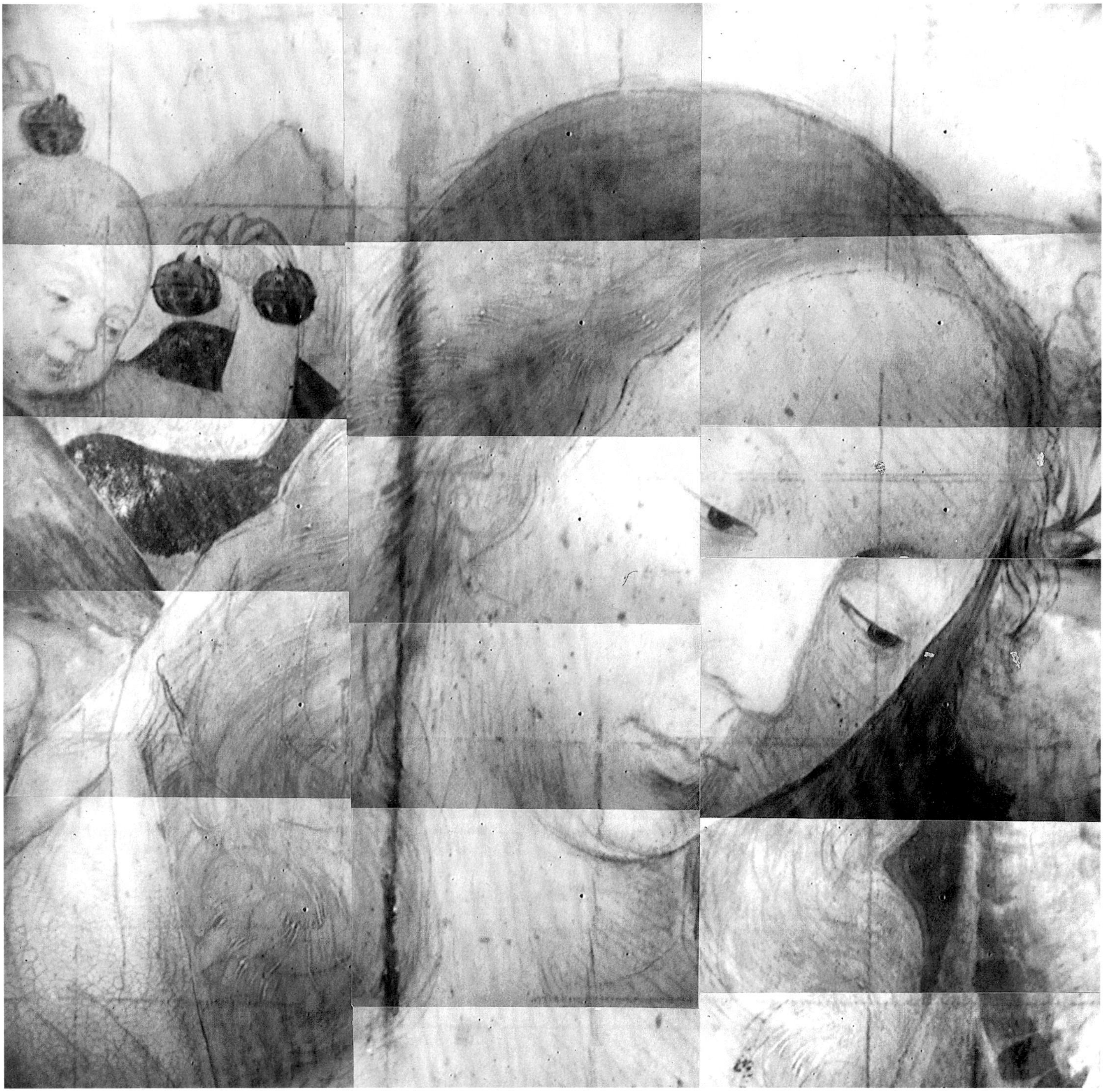

a. Infrared reflectogram assembly. Detail of the Virgin's head.

The Virgin Mary gazes pensively before her, her right hand restraining the infant Christ who is reaching out to an angel playing a fiddle. The Virgin is portrayed in a red cloak rather than the more conventional blue. The angel with the fiddle, shown in a rather fanciful costume, is one of five musician angels frolicking around the Virgin and Child. One of his companions has a set of bells, another plays a lyre, the third a harp and the fourth a flute. The scene is flanked by two columns, each bearing a statue of a musician putto. Two more putti are seated on the consoles in the upper left and right-hand corners of the painting. They are holding garlands of fruit which are fastened together in the middle of the painting, spanning the figures of the Virgin, the Child and angels. In the distance is a mountainous landscape with trees and castles. On the balustrade in front of Mary is a basket of cherries, which may be interpreted as a symbol of paradise and eternal life.[2]

The painting was first shown at an exhibition in Bruges in 1902, when it still formed part of a triptych. The two side panels were dismantled some time between 1913 and 1929.[3] The paintings on the front and reverse of the wings have also been separated from one another, but it is unknown when this was done. The triptych has thus been dismembered to form five separate paintings, which are now in different collections. The paintings that were originally on the inside of the shutters are at the Kunstmuseum in Dusseldorf (figs. c and d); those on the outside are privately owned.[4]

On the left panel is a portrait of the donor accompanied by what are assumed to be his son and late daughter. To show that the girl was no longer alive the artist has made her far smaller than the other figures and placed her in a different picture space from her family. The fact that she is portrayed on the left panel rather than on the right with the women could be to show that she was the child of an earlier marriage. The donor and his son and daughter are depicted with St Peter. The right panel shows three women together with Mary Magdalene in a landscape similar to that in the centre panel. On the outside of the shutters are grisaille paintings with St Peter on the left and John the Evangelist on the right. The main panel is executed in a different style from the wings, and is therefore probably not the work of the same artist.[5]

The centre panel showing the Virgin Mary, the infant Christ and the musician angels has been firmly attributed to the Amsterdam painter Jacob Cornelisz van Oostsanen. It is believed to date from his master years, around 1512-1513.[6] The design was transferred to the panel with the aid of a grid (figs. a and b), which is visible to the naked eye under the paint in Mary's face. The artist would have drawn squares on both the preliminary study and the panel to make it easier to transfer the design. The whole composition was worked out in a detailed underdrawing in black chalk. The figures in the drawing are fairly distinctive in that they are outlined in repeated, faltering strokes. Hatching is used to add shadow to the faces. The painting as such is similar to the underdrawing which corresponds in style to underdrawing in other paintings in this group.[7]

In the first decades of the sixteenth century, Jacob Cornelisz van Oostsanen ran a workshop in Amsterdam, employing apprentices and assistants to help meet the demands of his clientèle. His best known pupil was Jan van Scorel, who joined the studio in about 1512. Jacob Cornelisz was a versatile master whose achievements included woodcuts and designs for windows and embroideries as well as paintings on panel and canvas. Over the years some 180 works have been attributed to him. Carroll recently narrowed his oeuvre down to 27 paintings, the majority of which were made on commission.[8] Over 200 woodcuts made between 1507 and 1528 have also survived. Some of Van Oostsanen's paintings are signed with a symbol flanked by the letters I and A. The same mark appears on work by his brother Cornelis Buys and his cousin Cornelis Buys II, while his son Dirck used a modified version of this signature. Though not one of the great, innovative artists of his day, Jacob van Oostsanen certainly ranks among the most gifted craftsmen of his generation.[9]

1 The examination was carried out by J.R.J. van Asperen de Boer on 11 August 1988. The assemblies were made by I. Sjobbema, who also wrote an unpublished report. Infrared reflectograms: AB 1072-1073/15.

2 R. Falkenburg, *Joachim Patinir. Landscape as an image of the pilgrimage of life*, Amsterdam-Philadelphia 1988, p. 71.

3 The triptych was intact at the exhibition at the Grosvenor Gallery in London in 1913-1914, but only the main panel was on display at the *Exhibition of Dutch Art* in 1929. Carroll (1987), p. 146, believes that the triptych was dismantled in 1922, when it was put on sale at the Thomas Agnew Gallery in London.

4 Kunstmuseum Dusseldorf, Dusseldorf, inv. no. M 1970 13a and 13b, panel, 65 x 23.5 cm (2x). The wings were in the collection of P. de Boer in Amsterdam in 1929, and subsequently in the Girardet Collection in Dusseldorf. They were presented to the Kunstmuseum in 1970. Carroll (1987), p. 143, omits to mention that the paintings on the front and reverse were separated from one another. On this subject, see the correspondence between the Kunstmuseum Dusseldorf and the Boymans-van Beuningen Museum of January 1990.

5 Carroll (1987) suggests that the side panels were either added later or that they were made by a studio assistant who was unfamiliar with the central panel. See also Steinbart (1922), p. 98.

6 Carroll (1987), pp. 37-38 and pp. 147-148.

7 See M. Faries, "Master and pupil. A North Netherlandish example", in *Le dessin sous-jacent dans la peinture*, lecture IX, 1991. *Dessin sous-jacent et pratiques d'atelier* (ed. R. van Schoute, H. Verougstraete-Marcq), Louvain-la-neuve 1993, pp. 101-112, and exhib. cat. *Kunst voor de beeldenstorm. Noordnederlandse kunst 1525-1580*, Amsterdam, Rijksmuseum, 1986, p. 92.

8 Carroll (1987).

9 Carroll (1987) and J.L. Carroll in exhib. cat. Amsterdam, 1986, p. 131 (see note 7).

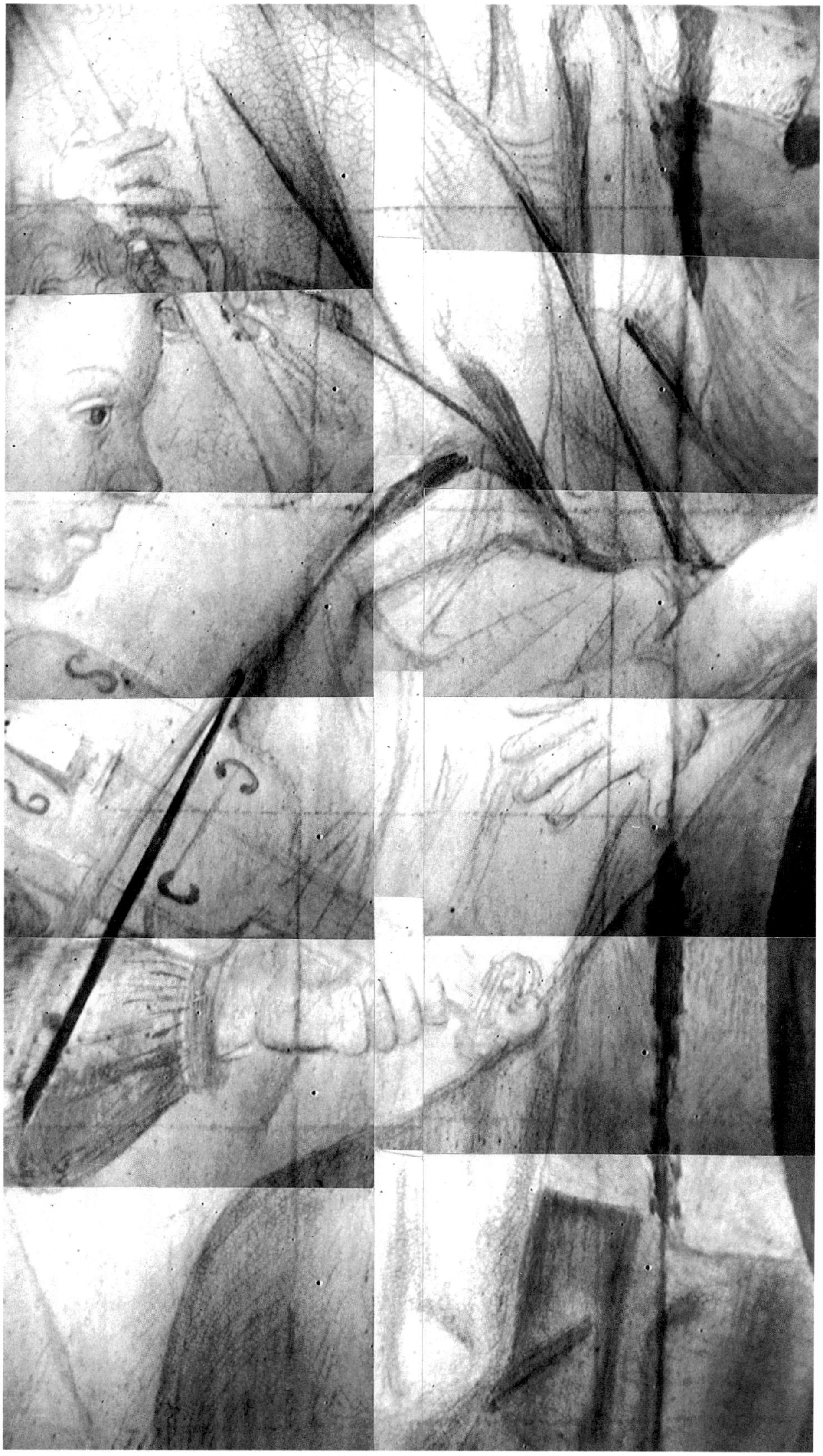

b. Infrared reflectogram assembly. Detail of the Virgin's right arm.

Several versions of the centre panel are known.[10] A copy by a follower forms part of a triptych made for the Sampson family of 's-Hertogenbosch in 1518. The triptych is now at the Roman Catholic Parish of Our Lady in Aarle-Rixtel.[11] Another version dated to about 1515 is at the Bayerische Staatsgemäldesammlungen in Schleissheim.[12] A third copy was also made around the same time, but its present whereabouts are unknown.[13]
LH

[10] Steinbart (1929) and Carroll (1987).
[11] Centre panel; 118.5 x 83.5 cm, shutters; 118.5 x 41.5 cm. See exhib. cat. *In Buscoducis 1450-1629. Kunst uit de Bourgondsiche tijd te 's-Hertogenbosch. De cultuur van late middeleeuwen en renaissance*, 's-Hertogenbosch, Noordbrabants Museum, 1990, no. 124, and A.M. Koldeweij, "'Sicut lilium inter spinas'. Het devies en de insignes van de Illustre Lieve Vrouwe Broederschap te 's-Hertogenbosch", *Antiek* (1990), pp. 515-521. Koldeweij accepts it as an autograph work made before the Rotterdam panel.
[12] Bayerische Staatsgemäldesammlungen, Schleissheim, inv. no. WAF 159. Panel; 84 x 58 cm. Previously at the Gemäldegalerie in Bamburg, inv. no. 3031. See Carroll (1987), p. 144.
[13] See Carroll (1987).

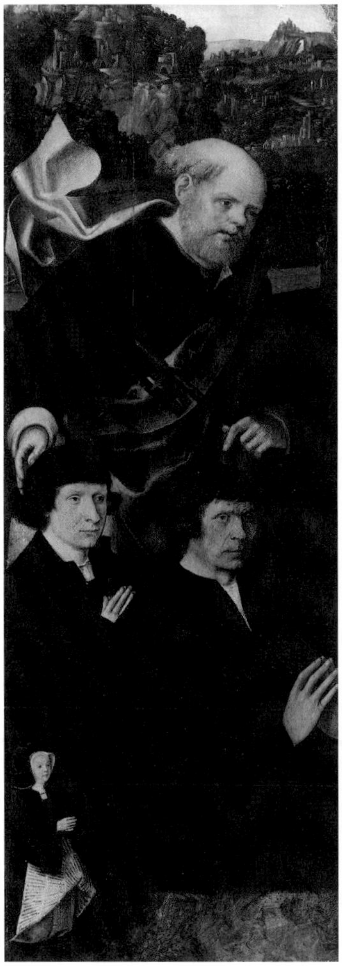

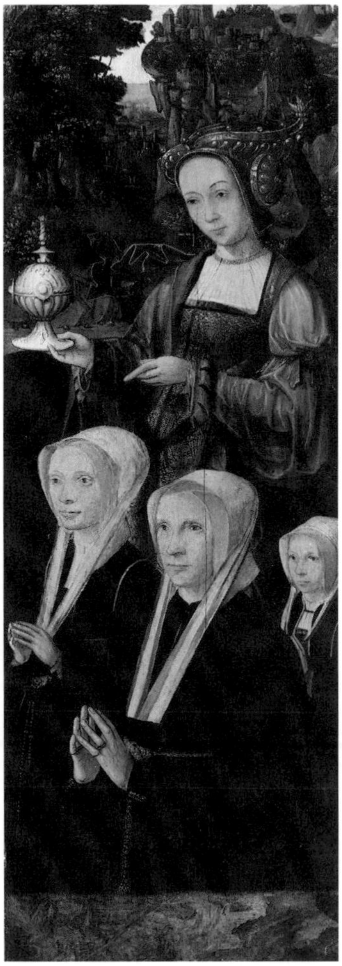

c. Jacob Cornelisz van Oostsanen, St Peter and donors
Originally the left shutter
Panel; 65 x 23.5 cm
Dusseldorf, Kunstmuseum.

d. Jacob Cornelisz van Oostsanen, Mary Magdalene and donors
Originally the right shutter
Panel; 65 x 23.5 cm
Dusseldorf, Kunstmuseum

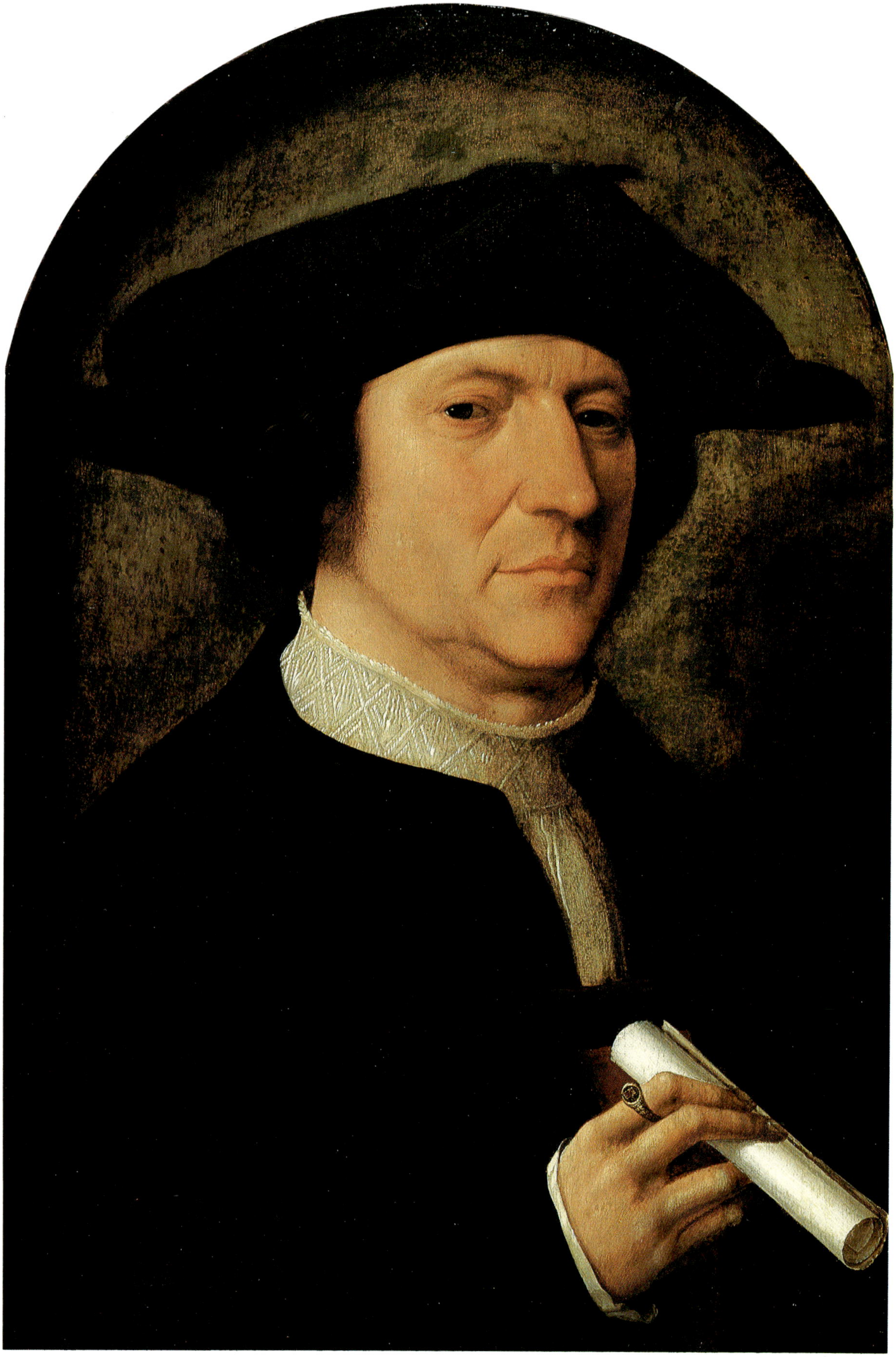

Portrait of Augustyn van Teylingen
Portrait of Josina van Egmond van der Nieuburgh

Jacob Cornelisz van Oostsanen (group)
(Oostsanen before 1470-
Amsterdam c. 1533)

Panel; 51.5 x 34.5 cm / 51.1 x 34.6 cm
Inscription on the frame:
(cat. 69) AVGVSTYN VAN TEYLINGEN/ ANNO 1511
(cat. 70) IVDOCA VAN EGMONT VAN DER NIEVBVRGH/ ANNO 1511

Physical characteristics: each panel consists of a single plank.

Infrared reflectography: (cat. no. 69) a few black chalk lines can just be discerned under the mouth and eyes.[1] An x-radiograph shows that the portrait was executed on top of another painting. The head may have been smaller and slightly lower. (cat. no. 70) A few black chalk lines can be discerned under the mouth and eyes.[2]

Provenance: donated by J.B. Hoogeweegen, 1867; (cat. no. 69) inv. no. 1625; (cat. no. 70) inv. no. 1626.

Exhibitions: *Tentoonstelling van Oudheden*, Delft, 1863, no. 2606; *Noord-Nederlandsche schilderkunst en beeldhouwkunst voor 1575*, Utrecht, Gebouw voor Kunsten en Wetenschappen, 1913, no. 12; *De Abdij van Egmond*, The Hague, Gemeentemuseum, 1934, no. 8, fig. 14; *Rondom de Meester van Alkmaar*, Alkmaar, Stedelijk Museum, 1950, nos. 8 and 9.

Literature: *Verslag omtrent den toestand en de aanwinsten van het Museum Boymans over het jaar 1887*, pp. 12-13; cat. 1892, nos. 193 and 194, p. 26; J. Six, "Nog iets over Moes' Iconographia Batava No 130 en Jan Mostaert", *Bulletin Nederlandschen Oudheidkundigen Bond* 4 (1902-1903), p. 116, fig.; *Verslag omtrent den toestand en de aanwinsten van het Museum Boymans over het jaar 1904*, p. 6; *Verslag omtrent den toestand van het Museum Boymans over het jaar 1909*, p. 9; M.D. Henkel, "Die Neugestaltung des Museum Boymans in Rotterdam", *Zeitschrift für Bildende Kunst* 21 (1910), p. 211, fig. 7; G. Ring, *Beiträge zur Geschichte Niederländischer Bildnismalerei von 15. und 16. Jahrhundert*, 1913, pp. 30-31, 53, 89; W. Cohen, "Die Ausstellung Frühholländischer Malerei und Plastik in Utrecht", *Zeitschrift für Bildende Kunst* 25 (1914), p. 32; N. Beets, "De tentoonstelling van Noord-Nederlandsche schilder- en beeldhouwkunst vòòr 1575", *Onze Kunst* 25 (1914), p. 87; C.H. de Jonge, *Bijdrage tot de kennis van de Noord-Nederlandsche costuum-geschiedenis in de eerste helft van de XVIe eeuw. Deel I. Het mannencostuum*, Utrecht 1916, pp. VI en XX; M. Conway, *The Van Eycks and their followers*, London 1921, p. 461; K. Steinbart, *Die Tafelgemälde des Jakob Cornelisz van Amsterdam*, Straatsburg 1922, pp. 101, 116-19, nos. 53 and 54, p. 157, fig. 10; F. Winkler, *Die Altniederländische Malerei. Die Malerei in Belgien und Holland von 1400-1600*, Berlin 1924, p. 230; C.M.A.A. Lindeman, "A selfportrait by Jacob Corneliszoon van Oostzanen", *The Burlington Magazine* 46 (1925), pp. 29-35, pp. 30, 35, figs. C and D; J. Six, "Jan van Hout, Cornelis Buys en Jacob Cornelisz.", *Oud Holland* 42 (1925), pp. 4-5, 35; J. Six, "Nog eens: Cornelis Buys, Jan van Hout en Jacob Cornelisz", *Oud Holland* 43 (1926), pp. 136-137; F. Dülberg, *Niederländische Malerei der Spätgotik und Renaissance*, Potsdam 1929, p. 163; J.H.H. Kessler, "Het vraagstuk Jacob Cornelisz", *Oudheidkundig Jaarboek* 1 (1932), p. 101; A.B. de Vries, *Het Noord-Nederlandsch portret in de tweede helft van de 16de eeuw*, 1934, pp. 11-12; Friedländer, XII, 1935, pp. 109, 110, 113, 198, no. 290; G.J. Hoogewerff, *De Noord-Nederlandsche schilderkunst*, II, The Hague 1937, pp. 420-422, figs. 204 and 205; G. Knuttel, *De Nederlandsche schilderkunst. Van Van Eyck tot Van Gogh*, Amsterdam 1938, p. 137; G.J. Hoogewerff, *De Noord-Nederlandsche schilderkunst*, III, The Hague 1939, p. 115; P. Wescher, "Jan Scorel und die beiden Cornelis Buys, der Ältere und der Jüngere", *Oud Holland* 61 (1946), p. 83; cat. 1962, pp. 40-41; G. van der Osten, *Deutsche und Niederländische Kunst der Reformationszeit*, Cologne 1973, p. 172; Friedländer, XII, 1975, p. 59, no. 290, p. 119, fig. 155; J. L. Carroll, *The paintings of Jacob Cornelisz. van Oostsanen (1472?-1533)*, Ann Arbor 1987, cat. nos. D9 and D10, figs. 23-24, pp. 313-316.

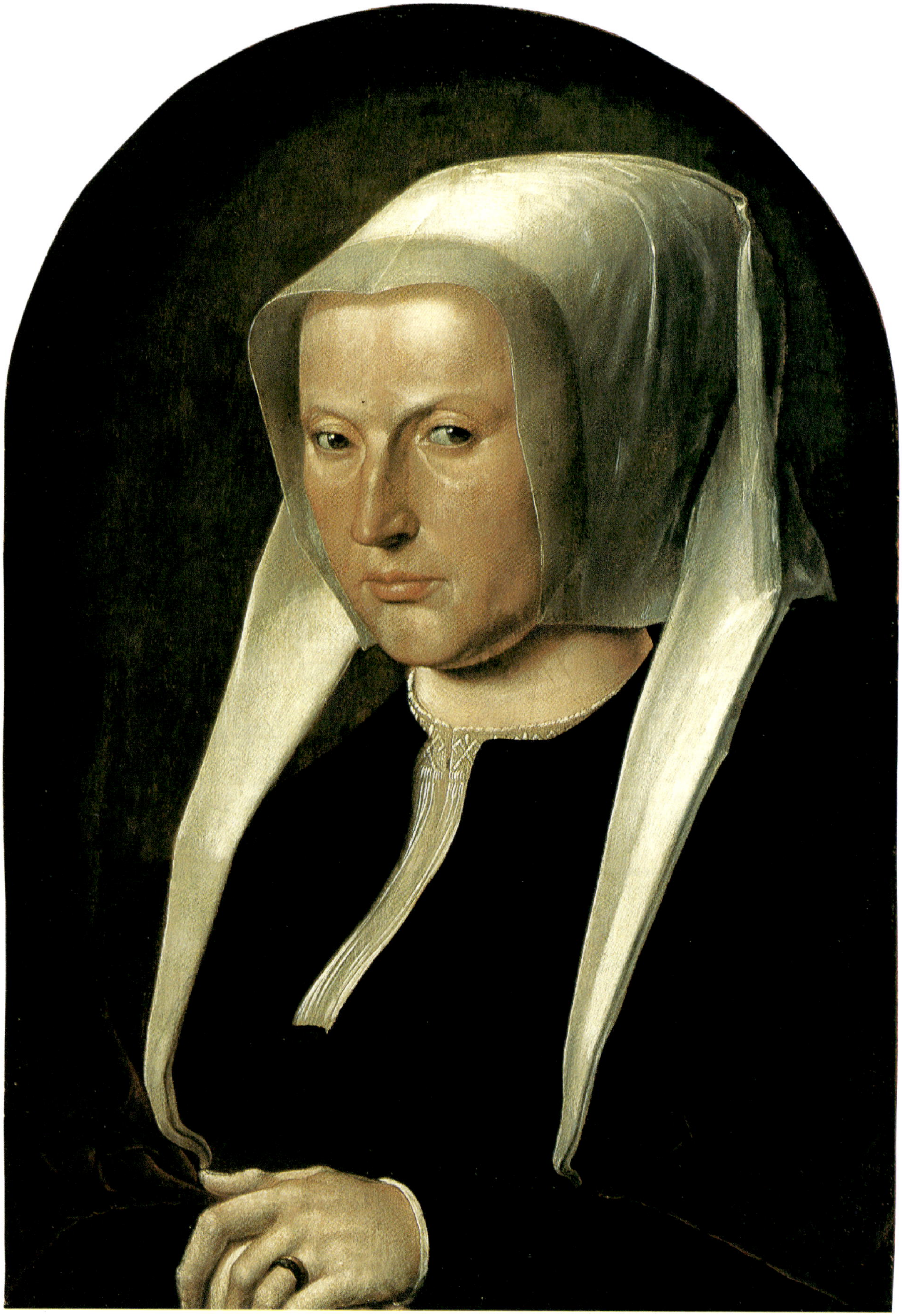

The inscriptions on the frames of these paintings identify them as companion portraits of Augustyn van Teylingen and his wife Josina van Egmond van der Nieuburgh. Van Teylingen, who was born in Le Quesnoy in about 1475, lived and worked in Alkmaar, where he held numerous distinguished posts. He was clerk to his uncle Claes Corff, rent collector of West Friesland, treasurer, burgomaster, pensionary, a member of the *vroedschap* and church warden. He was also the custodian of the Middelhof in Alkmaar, vassal of Egmond and Holland, and the owner of the sexton's houses in Maasland and Oudkarspel. Van Teylingen died on 25 May 1533 and was buried in the Grote Kerk in Alkmaar. On 29 May 1503 he drew up an antenuptial contract with the twenty-year old Joosgen Jansdr van Egmond van de Nijenburg, who was born in Alkmaar on 2 December 1484.[3] Josina and her brothers founded the Van Egmond van de Nijenburg-Van Teylingen Almshouse in Alkmaar as a home for their less well endowed relatives and others in need. Josina died on 8 November 1556 and was buried with her husband in the Grote Kerk.

The couple are portrayed against a green background. The shadows cast by the frames are painted on the panel. The panels were apparently painted in their frames, as the *barbe* is visible on all sides. It is difficult to establish whether the present frames are new, as several authors have suggested. The evidence against this is the fact that during a restoration in 1909 traces of green paint were found on the inside of the frames when the green background was uncovered from under a darker, even layer of paint. It therefore seems reasonable to conclude that the present frames are the originals. During the restoration a layer of black lacquer was removed from the front of the frames, and the inscriptions were touched up.[4] It is uncertain whether these inscriptions were copied over an older text. The date, given as 1511, is also puzzling, since the costumes worn by the sitters only came into fashion about a decade later.[5] The man's hat, for instance, has ear flaps that turn up and can be fastened above the head with ribbons. This style was in vogue between 1520 and 1525.[6] The style of the paintings also suggests a later date.[7] An annotation has been found in the sixteenth-century genealogy of the Van Teylingen family at the national archive in Utrecht which presumably refers to the portraits. The author remarked that although the painting was a good likeness of Van Teylingen, no artist could capture his soul.[8]

A manuscript report at the Boymans-van Beuningen Museum, dated 1868, ascribes both portraits to Jan Mostaert. However, this attribution was set aside in 1904 in favour of Jacob Cornelisz van Oostsanen, a painter who had worked for the Van Teylingens previously. They had ordered a triptych from him in about 1515 which is now at the Staatliche Gemäldegalerie in Berlin-Dahlem (fig. a).[9] The centre panel is a portrayal of the Virgin Mary and Christ. The left panel shows Augustyn van Teylingen and St Augustine, and the right his wife with St Barbara. The two portraits were ascribed to the Amsterdam master partly on the grounds of the attribution of the triptych. Steinbart endorsed the attribution without reservation, but J. Six ascribed them to Van Oostsanen's brother Cornelis Buys, who used the same mark for his signature.[10] Kessler, the only author to agree with this attribution, also accepts the date on the frames.[11] Neither of the portraits appears in the latest monograph on Jacob Cornelis van Oostsanen as an autograph work by the master.[12] Nor is any mention made of the difference in quality between them. The man's face is rendered with far more sensitivity than his wife's, although this apparent discrepancy might be due to the present condition of the paintings. The portrait of Van Teylingen is in fact in a rather better state than its pendant.[13] Though it is of course possible that the commission was given to two different artists, it is hard to image why.
LH

1 Noted by J.P. Filedt Kok on 1 November 1971.
2 Examination conducted by J.R.J. van Asperen de Boer on 20 December 1993. See note 1.
3 1501, clerk to his uncle Claes Corff; 1514 to 1522, rent collector of West Friesland; 1508 and 1533, treasurer; 1509 and 1531, burgomaster; 1516, pensionary; 1508 to 1530, member of the *vroedschap*; 1514 and 1533, church warden. The information cited in the catalogue is from G.J.J. van Wimersma Greidanus, *Kwartieren Greidanus-Jaeger in stamreeksen* (publication due).
4 *Verslag omtrent den toestand van het Museum Boymans over het jaar 1909*, p. 9. Carroll (1987) argues that the frames are not original.
5 Carroll (1987) concludes that a mistake was made when copying an older inscription, and that the date should be 1525.
6 De Jonge (1916), De Vries (1934). See also Conway (1921).
7 Steinbart (1922), Hoogewerff (1939), Friedländer, XII, 1975.
8 "Augustine tuam haec duxit pictura figuram/ Questor sed mentem pinxere non potuit/ Haec Augustini coniunx fuit illa Telingi/ Gnatos bis septem sex est enixta puellas". Utrecht National Archive, Van Attevelt Collection, no. 362 (Van Teylingen file); Central Genealogical Bureau, Ms van Teylingen, 'deductie ende affcompste van den huijse en geslachte van Teijlingen van 993-1583'. See note 3.
9 Carroll (1987).
10 Six (1925 and 1926).
11 Kessler (1932).
12 Carroll (1987).
13 Lindeman (1925) suggests that the woman's portrait was exposed to sunlight for a prolonged period and that it has faded and been otherwise damaged as a result.

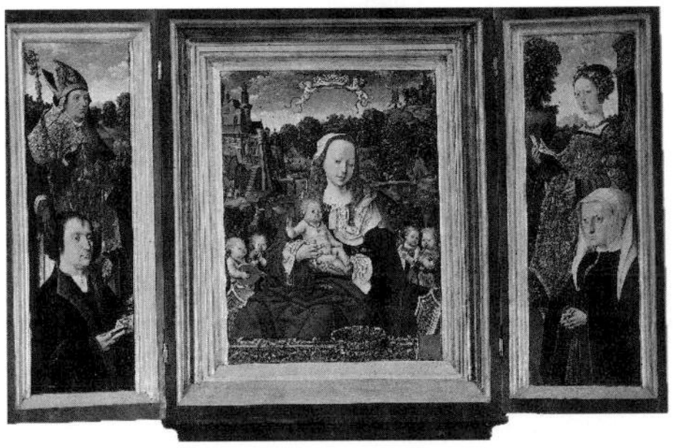

a. Jacob Cornelisz van Oostsanen, Triptych with the Virgin Mary and Child
Left panel: Augustyn van Teylingen and St Augustine.
Right panel: Josina van Egmond van der Nieuburgh and St Barbara
Centre panel; 42 x 32 cm
Side panels; 50 x 17 cm
Berlin, Staatliche Museen Preussischer Kulturbesitz, Gemäldegalerie.

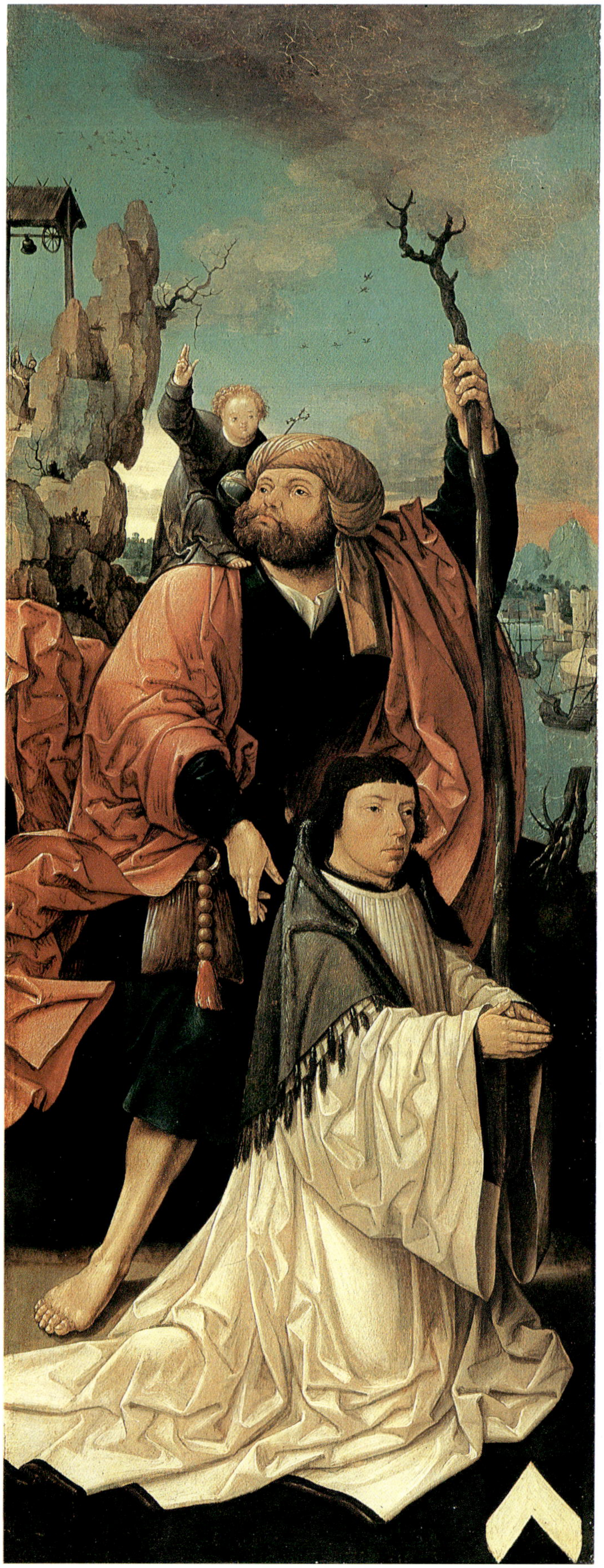

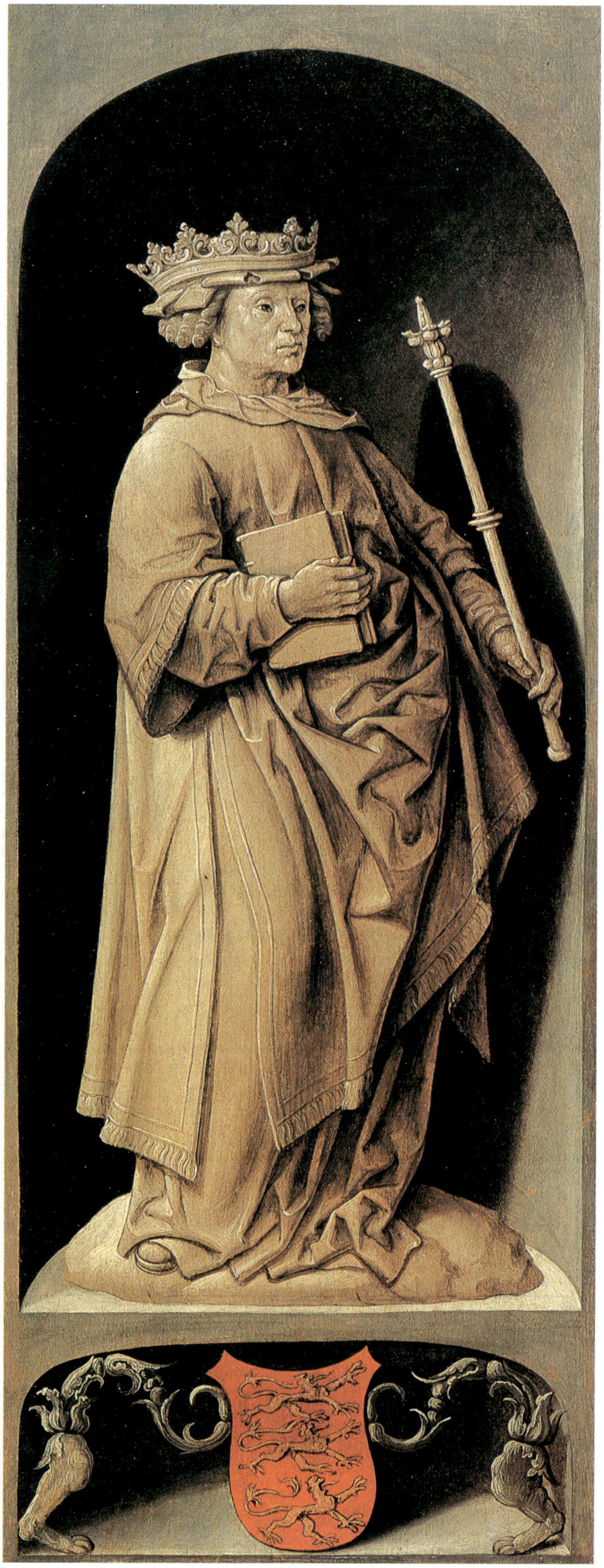

St Christopher and donor/Reverse: Edward the Confessor
St Catherine/Reverse: A canonised Scottish monk

Jacob Cornelisz van Oostsanen (group)
(Oostsanen before 1470-Amsterdam c. 1533)

Panels; 70 x 26.5 cm

Physical characteristics: (cat. nos. 71 and 72) under a raking light an arch can be seen in the sky on the front of the panel. This is where the frame used to be. The sky in this part of the painting was retouched when the frame was removed.[1]

Infrared reflectography: the underdrawing, which is visible to the naked eye, could not be seen under infrared radiation. It may have been executed in dark brown ink.[2]

Provenance: sale, Frank T. Sabin Gallery, London, 1931; J.W. Frederiks Collection, The Hague, on loan from J.W. Frederiks to the Boymans-van Beuningen Museum since 24 August 1966; gift from the J.W. Frederiks Collection, 1994; (cat. 71) inv. no. Br.F.4; (cat. 72) inv. no. Br.F.5.

Exhibitions: *Nederlandsche kunst van de XV en XVIde eeuw*, The Hague, Mauritshuis, 1945, no. 42; *Jan van Scorel*, Utrecht, Centraal Museum, 1955, no. 78; *Nederlandse primitieven*, Laren, Singer Museum, 1961, no. 28 (left panel), no. 29 (right panel).

Literature: Friedländer, XII, 1935, p. 109, fig. 194, no. 247, XLVII (inner sides), XLVIII (outer sides); Friedländer, XII, 1975, p. 115, fig. 138, no. 247; J.L. Carroll, *The paintings of Jacob Cornelisz van Oostsanen, (1472?-1533)*, University of North Carolina, Chapel Hill, 1987 (diss.), p. 325, figs. 105-106.

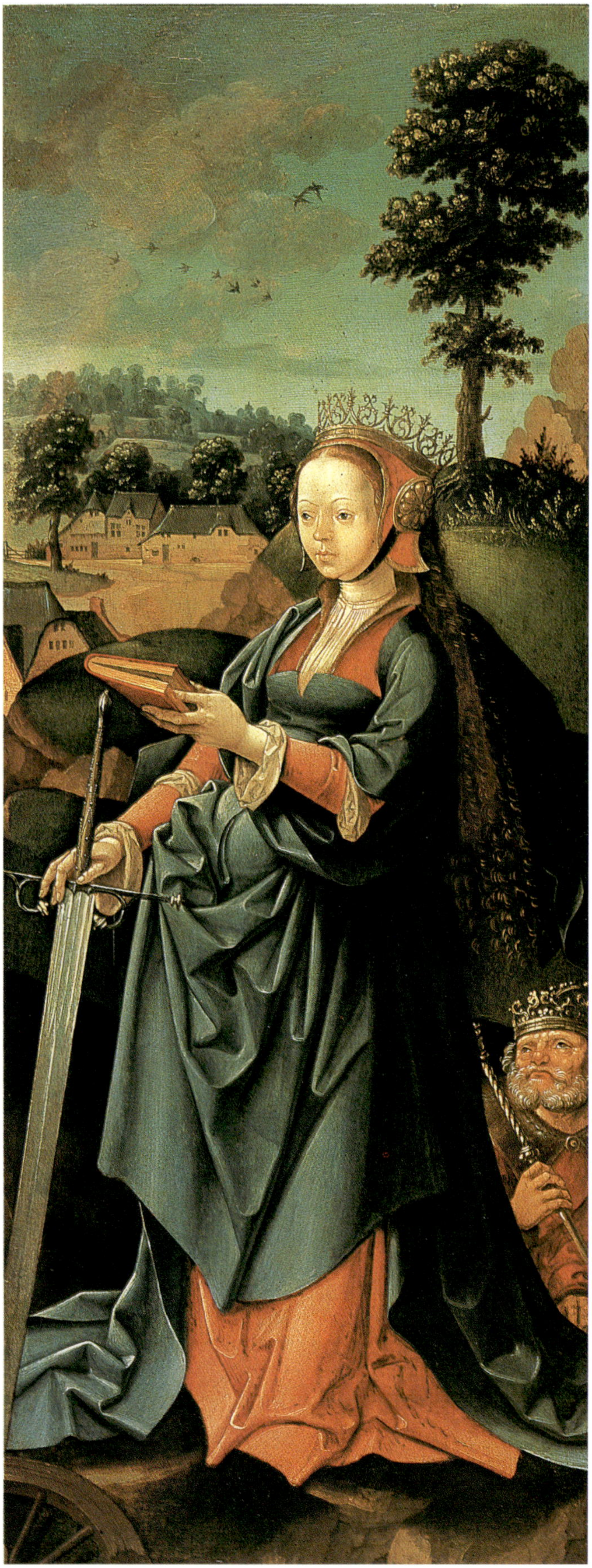

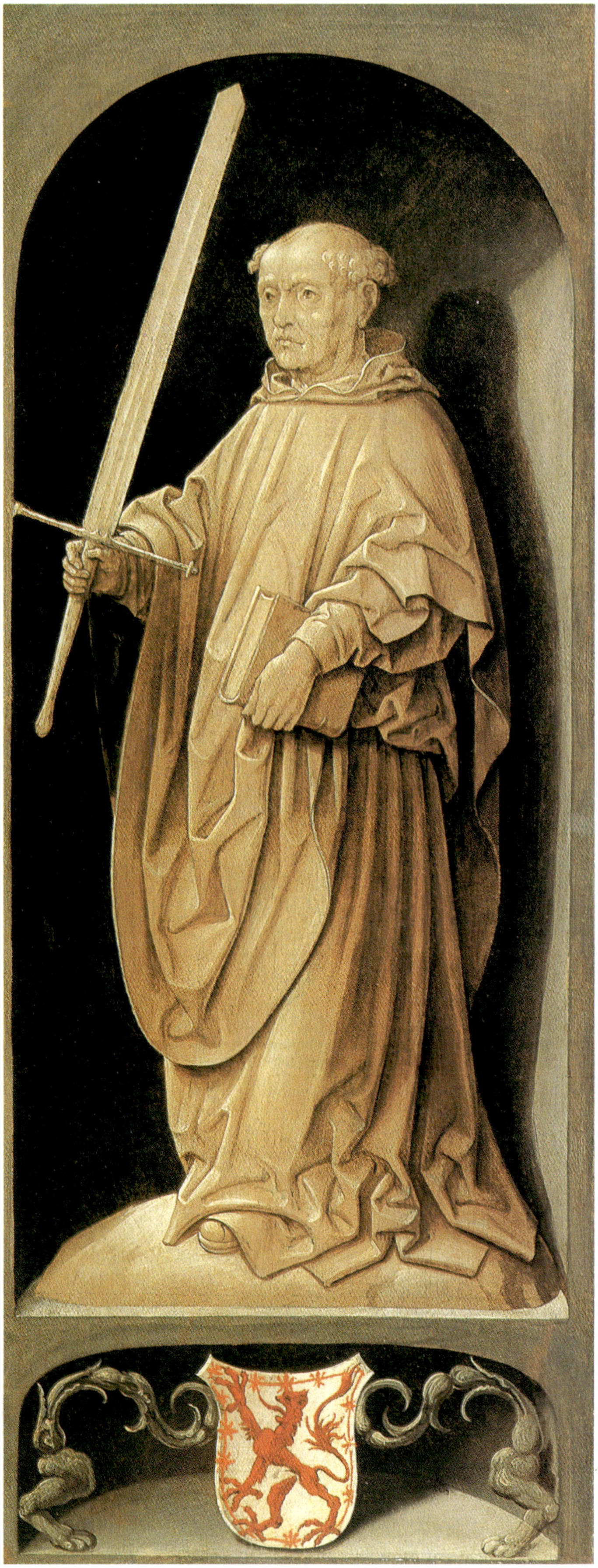

These two paintings were originally the shutters of a triptych. The centre panel has been lost. The left panel shows St Christopher, who can be recognised by the palm tree he uses as a staff, and by the globe and infant Christ he carries on his shoulder. The Saviour's hand is raised in benediction. The popular version of St Christopher's story describes him as a man of huge stature who was guided by a hermit and taught to serve Christ by carrying the poor and weak across a river. One night he carried a small child who grew heavier and heavier with each step he took. The child revealed that he was Christ and that Christopher had therefore been carrying the weight of the world upon his shoulders. Christopher gave protection against unexpected disaster and was the patron saint of wayfarers, pilgrims and crusaders.[3] The hermit can be seen in the left background, ringing a bell to warn St Christopher that Christ is approaching. The hermit is usually portrayed with a lamp or a torch. On the right we see a harbour in the distance, with ships in tranquil waters. The figure kneeling at Christopher's feet must be the donor, but his identity remains unknown. A silver chevron on a black ground is a relatively common family coat of arms in Europe. The man was evidently a canon, as can be seen by his long white choir robe and the ermine almuce draped over his shoulders.[4] He is also wearing a fur-lined undergarment.

The king on the reverse of the panel is wearing a crown and has a sceptre and a book in his hands. He is standing in a niche, under which are the arms of the English royal family.[5] This figure could be the patron saint of England, Edward the Confessor,[6] who was a popular figure in medieval times[7] and the founder of Westminster Abbey.

On the right-hand panel is St Catherine of Alexandria in a stretch of countryside with farmhouses. She wears a crown as a sign of her royal birth, and is depicted with her conventional attributes: a book, a broken wheel and a sword. Behind her on the right is the emperor Maxentius.[9] The legend of St Catherine describes her victory in an intellectual contest with fifty philosophers whom the emperor sent to undermine her faith. The book is therefore a symbol of her wisdom. Catherine was executed on the emperor's orders. The wheel and the sword are the attributes of her martyrdom. She was the patron saint of the dying and of philosophers and theologians.[9] This may explain why she was chosen to decorate the side panel, since the donor, like most canons, would probably have come from an aristocratic family and enjoyed a university education.[10]
St Catherine was extremely popular in the sixteenth century. She appears on several side panels painted by Van Oostsanen, with the Virgin Mary and Child on the centre panel, sometimes accompanied by St Christopher on the reverse of the shutter.[11]

The reverse shows a monk holding a sword in one hand and a book in the other. Although he has never been firmly identified, he is obviously a Scot, because the arms of the Scottish royal family are painted under the niche.[12] A triptych with the English king Edward the Confessor and a Scottish monk on the reverse is highly unusual in Dutch art. The donor was presumably himself an Englishman or someone who had ties with England.

In 1935 Friedländer attributed both panels to Jacob Cornelisz van Oostsanen,[13] and they are indeed similar in many respects to other work by the master. He made several comparable paintings of St Catherine and the emperor Maxentius, for instance. Two examples are the paintings on the outside of the shutters of a *St Jerome altar* (1511) in Vienna, and on the reverse of a diptych in Basel.[14] One of the wings of a triptych from 1517, at the Rijksmuseum in Amsterdam, has a painting of St Christopher. This, too, closely resembles the one in Rotterdam except that Christopher is resting his weight on his right leg rather than his left.[15] Recurrent features in Van Oostsanen's work between 1510 and 1520 are the smooth, immutable faces of his female saints, his bearded male figures, and his angular rendering of drapery.[16] A recent study by Carroll sets out to demonstrate that the Rotterdam panels are not by Jacob Cornelisz van Oostsanen, but the work of an artist she designates as hand A, an unidentified painter employed at Van Oostsanen's studio.[17] While it is evident that other painters had a hand in Van Oostsanen's work, it is curious that the side panels were not compared with the

1 A scientific examination was conducted by Cunera Vergeer under the supervision of J.R.J. van Asperen de Boer in 1994. Paint samples: A 380/1-3; A 381/1-4. Infrared reflectograms: AB 1555/ 9-13.
2 Dark brown ink contains no carbon and is therefore invisible under infrared radiation.
3 L. Réau, *Iconographie de l'art chrétien*, III, Paris 1958, A-F, pp. 304-313.
4 Franz von Sales Doyé, *Die alten Trachten der männlichen und weiblichen Orden sowie der geistlichen Mitglieder ritterlichen Orden*, Leipzig, s.a., pp. 36-42.
5 Michael Malcolm, *Lines of succession. Heraldry of the Royal Families of Europe*, London 1991, pp. 14-17.
6 Also suggested by Godfrey E. Evans (National Museum of Scotland) and David Caldwell (Museum of Antiquities, Edinburgh) in a letter to the Museum of 17 March 1994. Rosalind K. Marshall (Scottish National Portrait Gallery) expressed the same view in a letter to the Museum on 22 March 1994.
7 D.H. Farmer, *The Oxford Dictionary of Saints*, Oxford 1978, pp. 123-125.
8 See cat. nos. 33 and 43.
9 *Op. cit.* (note 3), pp. 262-272.
10 *Utrecht tussen kerk en staat* (Utrecht contribution to medieval studies), Hilversum 1991, pp. 197-225.
11 These representations range from a Virgin and Child, a Holy Family, an Adoration of the Magi, to a scene of St Anne's selbdritt. In the Rijksmuseum triptych from 1517 Rijksmuseum with *The Adoration of the Magi* in the middle, Catherine is on the right wing and Christopher on the reverse of the left.
12 *Op. cit.* (note 5), pp. 36-39.
13 Friedländer, XII, 1935 and 1975.
14 The unsigned *St Jerome altar* is dated 1511. Friedländer, XII, 1975, pl. 134, 135 and p. 115. The diptych shows the *Adoration of the shepherds* on the front and St Lawrence with St Catherine on the reverse; for the painting in Basel, see Friedländer, XII, 1975, fig. 128 and p. 114.
15 *Adoration of the Magi*, Friedländer, XII, 1975, p. 239, fig 128 and p. 114,
16 Carroll (1987).
17 Carroll (1987).

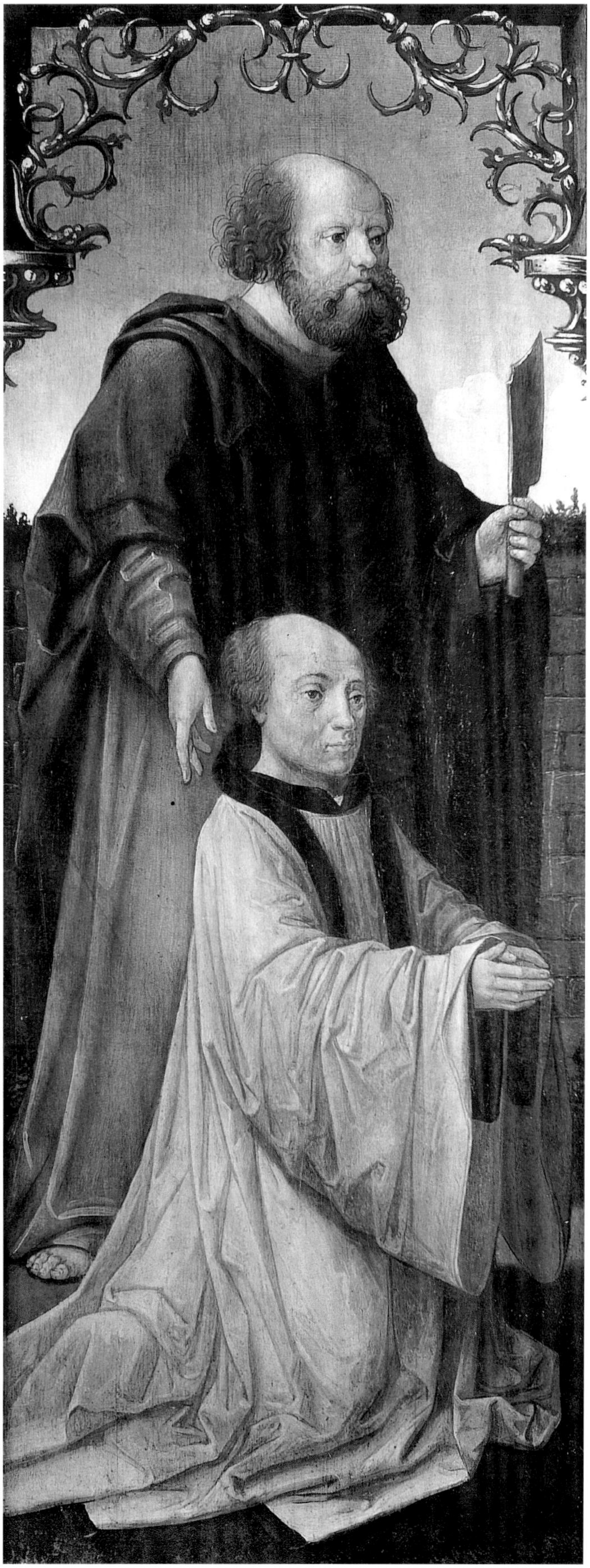

a. Jacob Cornelisz van Oostsanen, St Bartholomew with a donor
Panel; 50.8 x 20.4 cm
Chicago, The Art Institute

Rijksmuseum triptych before being attributed to hand A. Until more is known about Van Oostsanen's studio, it is impossible to draw any conclusions about the authorship of the panels.

Friedländer dates the paintings around 1518. They bear a marked resemblance to the Obervellach altarpiece by Jan van Scorel, who was an apprentice of Jacob Cornelisz van Oostsanen's from 1512 to 1518.[18] Van Scorel's altarpiece is signed and dated 1519.[19] It is therefore quite probable that the Rotterdam panels were painted before this date. In fact, given their similarity to the Rijksmuseum triptych from 1517, they may well have been made around the same time. The Art Institute in Chicago has two panels with figures very similar to those in Rotterdam. Except for the head, the donor on the left shutter is almost identical to the one on the Rotterdam panel (fig. a). The St Bartholomew behind the donor and the St Peter on the right panel are very like the St Christopher in Rotterdam. They are shown in the same position, and the faces and beards are executed in the same style. The Chicago panels must have been made at Jacob Cornlisz van Oostanen's studio, in Carroll's view by the same painter as the Boymans-van Beuningen panels.[20]
CV

18 The effects of Van Scorel's apprenticeship with Van Oostsanen are evident in this panel. The saints on the insides of the wings, for instance, clearly reflect the master's impact. There is a strong similarity between the St Christopher with the infant and the St Christopher on this altarpiece, while further evidence of Van Oostsanen's influence can be seen in the folds of cloth, the treatment of hair, the children's figures and the decoration. See Friedländer, XII, pl. 160-162 and p. 120.

19 Infrared photography shows the date 1519 on the centre panel. See exhib. cat. *Jan van Scorel in Utrecht*, Utrecht, Centraal Museum, 1977, p. 27. This was confirmed by an infrared reflectographic examination in July 1978 by Van Asperen de Boer and Faries (unpublished).

20 The two wings are the only surviving panels of a triptych. The right panel shows St Bartholomew with the donor, and the left St Peter with the donatrix. Saints Andrew and Matthew are portrayed in grisaille on the reverse. The Art Institute, Chicago, inv. nos. 36.240 and 36.241, panel; 50.8 x 20.4 cm (2x).

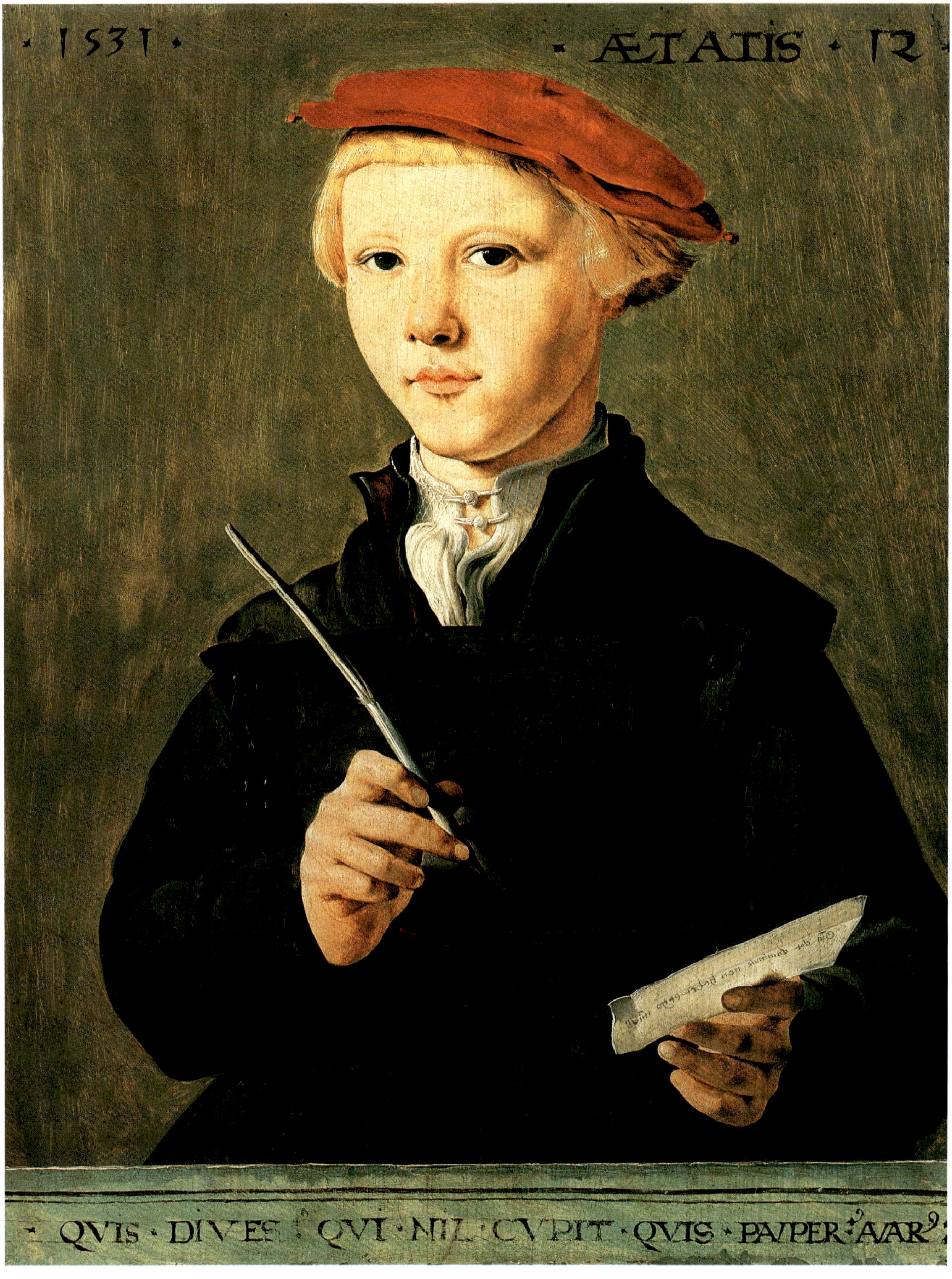
· 1531 ·
· ÆTATIS · 12 ·
· QVIS · DIVES ? QVI · NIL · CVPIT · QVIS · PAVPER ? AVAR

A young scholar

Jan van Scorel
(Schoorl 1496-Utrecht 1562)

Panel; 46.5 x 35 cm
Inscription at the top of the painting: .1531..Aetatis. 12
Inscription at the bottom of the painting: .Quis.dives? Qui nil cupit.Quis.Pauper? Avar
Inscription on the piece of paper in mirror writing: Oia dat dominus non habet ergo mius

Physical characteristics: the panel consists of a single plank. The panel is painted to the edges.

Infrared reflectography: no underdrawing could be discerned.

Dendrochronology: the youngest heartwood growth ring dates from 1520. Five sapwood rings were also found. The tree could not have been felled before 1529. See article by P. Klein.

Paint samples: three cross-sections of paint show only a single layer of paint on a white intermediate layer.[1]

Provenance: Mrs J. van der Hoop, auction Rotterdam, Lamme, 13 and 14 October 1864, no. 75; bought by Lamme for the Boymans Museum for 70 guilders; inv. no. 1797.

Exhibitions: *Tentoonstelling van kinderafbeeldingen*, The Hague, Museum voor Moderne Kunst, 1924, no. 100; *Exhibition of Dutch art 1450-1900*, London, Royal Academy, 1929, no. 34; *Jeroen Bosch Noord-Nederlandsche primitieven,* Rotterdam, Boymans Museum, 1936, no. 110; *Herinnering Kersttentoonstelling 1947-1948,* Rotterdam, Boymans Museum, 1947-1948, no. B, fig.; *Nederlandsche kunst van de XVde en XVIde eeuw*, The Hague, Mauritshuis, 1945, no. 85; *La peinture Hollandaise de Jerome Bosch à Rembrandt*, Brussels, Palais des Beaux-Arts, 1946, no. 98, fig.; *Tentoonstelling Utrecht's kunst in opkomst en bloei 650-1650*, Utrecht, Centraal Museum, 1948, no. 60; *Het portret in de oude Nederlanden*, Bruges, Stedelijk Museum, 1953, no. 71, pl. II; *Dutch Pictures 1450-1750*, London, Royal Academy of Arts, 1952-1953, no. 1; *Jan van Scorel*, Utrecht, Centraal Museum, 1955, no. 39, fig. 42; *Kunst voor de beeldenstorm*, Amsterdam, Rijksmuseum, 1986, no. 72, fig.

Literature: *Beschrijving der schilderijen in het Museum te Rotterdam, gesticht door Mr. F.J.O. Boymans*, 1867, no. 200; L. Scheibler, W. Bode, "Verzeichnis der Gemälde des Jan van Scorel", *Jahrbuch der Königlich Preussischen Kunstsammlungen* 2 (1881), p. 213, no. 271; M.J. Binder, *Studien zur Entwicklungsgeschichte des Malers Jan van Scorel,* 1908, pp. 12-13; C.H. de Jonge, *Bijdrage tot de kennis van de Noord-Nederlandsche costuum-geschiedenis in de eerste helft van de XVIe eeuw,* Utrecht, 1916, p. 37, p. XX, appendix I; J. Six, "De ontwerpers van de Haagsche glasramen", *Oud Holland* 37 (1919), p. 175; M.J. Friedländer, *Von Eyck bis Bruegel*, Berlin 1921, pp. 167, 168, 201; G.J. Hoogewerff, *Jan van Scorel peintre de la renaissance*, The Hague 1923, pp. 72, 133, no. 10, pl. XVII; F. Winkler, *Die Altniederländische Malerei*, Berlin 1924, p. 283; L. Baldass, "Bildnisse des niederländischen Romanismus", *Städel-Jahrbuch* 6 (1930), p. 84, 85; C.H. de Jonge, "Vroege werken van Maerten van Heemskerck", *Oud Holland*, 49 (1932), pp. 157, 159, fig. 8; K. Steinbart, "Das Kasseler Familienbildnis des Jan van Scorel", *Pantheon* 12 (1933), pp. 265, 269; A.B. de Vries, *Het Noord-Nederlandsch portret in de tweede helft van de 16e eeuw*, Amsterdam 1934, p. 22; Friedländer, XII, 1935, p. 135, p. 149 note, p. 206, no. 374, fig. 75; D.T. Enklaar, *Varende Luyden*, Assen 1937, p. 122, fig. 2; D.T. Enklaar, *Uit Uilenspiegel's Kring*, Assen 1940, p. 75, fig. 6; C.H. de Jonge, *Jan van Scorel*, Amsterdam (1940), p. 35, fig. on p. 42; G.J. Hoogewerff, *De Noord-Nederlandsche Schilderkunst*, IV, The Hague 1941-1942, pp. 104-107, 110, 239, fig. 46; K.G. Boon, "Overzicht van de litteratuur betreffende Nederlandsche kunst, verschenen in Nederland van 1942-1946", *Oud-Holland* 61 (1946), p. 157; J. Bruyn Hzn, "Vroege portretten van Maerten van Heemskerck", *Bulletin van het Rijksmuseum* 3 (1955), issue 2, p. 33, note 3; N. van der Blom, "De Latijnse teksten van De Scholier van Jan van Scorel", *Bulletin Museum Boymans* 8 (1957), pp. 91-100; cat. 1962, pp. 128-129; H. Arndt, ""Johannes est stultus. Amen. Kinderzeichnungen eines Lateinschülers aus den Tagen des Erasmus", *Argo Festschrift für Kurt Badt*, Cologne 1970, p. 265, fig. 80; Friedländer, XII, 1975, p. 73, p. 80, note 5, p. 127, no. 374, pl. 196; R. Grosshans, *Maerten van Heemskerck, Die Gemälde*, Berlin 1980, p. 64; E.K.J. Reznicek, "Rainald Grosshans, Maerten van Heemskerck..", *Oud Holland* 97 (1983), p. 42, fig. 2; L. Silver, "Rainald Grosshans: Maerten van Heemskerck...Armin Zweite: Marten de Vos...", *Zeitschrift für Kunstgeschichte* 47 (1984), p. 270; J.C. Harrison, "The Detroit Christ on Calvary and the Cologne Lamentation of Christ: Two Early Haarlem Paintings by Maerten van Heemskerck", *Nederlands Kunsthistorisch Jaarboek* 37 (1986), p. 176, note 8; J.O. Hand, M. Wolff, *Early Netherlandish Painting, The collections of the National Gallery of Art systematic catalogue*, Washington 1986, p. 117, note 31; W. Kloek, "Onderzoek tijdens de tentoonstelling 'Kunst voor de beeldenstorm'", *Bulletin van het Rijksmuseum* 35 (1987), p. 245, fig. 5; J.C. Harrison, *The paintings of Maerten van Heemskerck*, Ann Arbor 1987 (UMI 1991), no. 11.

The boy, whose name is not known, is looking the viewer straight in the eye. He is wearing a dark "paltrok" tunic which is buttoned at the top. In his right hand he is holding a goose-quill pen, with which he has written the text on the piece of paper he holds in his left hand. From the inscription at upper left it seems that the portrait was painted in 1531. The bold lettering at upper right tells us that the boy was twelve years old at the time.

At the very bottom of the panel is what seems to be the front of a writing desk, which bears a Latin text. The author of this text began the inscription on the left leaving big spaces but apparently realised halfway through that he was running out of room and even had to abbreviate the last word. The text means: "Who is rich? He who covets nothing. Who is poor? The grasping miser." The wording in mirror writing on the piece of paper means: "The Lord gives everything, yet does not therefore have less".

Van der Blom devoted an extensive study to these texts. He found the first inscription in a book by Erasmus published in 1514.[2] He was unable to trace the second, although it did recall other passages by Erasmus. It was found as a motto on the bed of Ursula von Lützelstein in Urach castle in Württemberg, probably from around 1585.[3]

Van der Blom combined the first verse, a hexameter, with the verse on the piece of paper, a pentameter, and interpreted the result as a moral. Whilst the text in mirror writing on the piece of paper is almost hidden, the text at the bottom of the painting is written in such bold letters that the latter must represent the actual theme of the painting: the young scholar is being given an important instruction for life, which he is communicating to the viewer.

The boy in the portrait has not been identified, but Van der Blom did put forward an intriguing suggestion. In 1529, Alardus, a former teacher at the Latin school in Alkmaar and a friend of Erasmus, wrote to the then rector that he would send him a son of his sister's as a pupil. Van der Blom considers it possible that the young scholar is the boy who was sent to school in Alkmaar by Alardus.

The attribution of the portrait, which is unfortunately unsigned, has been a problem for some time. When it was bought in 1864 with money from the insurance settlement after the fire at the Museum, it was still ascribed to Jan van Scorel. However, in her article of 1932, De Jonge attributed it to Maerten van Heemskerck. Towards the end of the 1520s, Heemskerck was a pupil of Scorel and their styles were very similar. De Jonge attributed the portraits of Pieter Bicker and his wife Anna Codde which were painted in 1529 and are at the Rijksmuseum in Amsterdam to Maerten van Heemskerck. She considered the Rotterdam painting to be by the same hand on the basis of the use of light and shade and the manner of painting. However, in her 1940 monograph on Jan van Scorel she changed her attribution to this painter with no further explanation. By contrast, Hoogewerff, 1941, asserted that the work could not be by Van Scorel. Bruyn considered the painting to be "definitely by Scorel". Silver and Harrison attribute the work to Heemskerck. Finally, in his book on Heemskerck, Grosshans contends that doubts as to the authorship by Scorel, and in particular the attribution to Heemskerck, are completely misplaced on stylistic grounds.[4]

1 J.R.J. van Asperen de Boer notes that the white intermediate layer could point to Scorel rather than to Heemskerck. Paint samples: A 151/1-3. Infrared reflectograms: AB 265/8-10.

2 Full title: *Opuscula aliquot Erasmo Roterodamo castigatore et interprete. Catonis praecepta. Mimi Publiani. Septem Sapientum celebria dicta. Institutum Christiani Hominis carmine pro pueris ab Erasmo compositum;* in translation: "Some works, improved and explained by Erasmus of Rotterdam. Proverbs by Cato. Maxims from the burlesques of Publius. Famous sayings of the Seven Sages. Instruction of a Christian, written in versus by Erasmus for young scholars". Van der Blom (1957).

3 Van der Blom (1957), fig. 10.

4 Bruyn (1955); Silver (1984); Harrison (1987); Grosshans (1980).

A good comparison for our painting has always been that with the portraits of Anna Codde and Pieter Bicker (see above), now generally accepted as by Maerten van Heemskerck. Another useful comparison is that with another portrait by Heemskerck, of his father Jacob Willemsz van Veen, dated 1532, in the Metropolitan Museum in New York. A beautiful example of Scorel's work from the same period is the *Portrait of a man* from 1529 in the Rijksmuseum in Amsterdam.

What is striking in these comparisons is that Heemskerck is always exceptionally expressive in the rendering of the faces and hands: he paints very pronounced noses and chins, wrinkles in the face, swollen veins in the hands. These are characteristics which we do not find in the Rotterdam painting. In contrast, there does seem to be a much closer resemblance with the *Portrait of a man* by Van Scorel in the Rijksmuseum. Here we see a similar flatness, very similar lighting, and the way in which the hand is painted is virtually identical. It therefore seems justified to maintain the attribution which the painting had when it was purchased in 1864.
JG

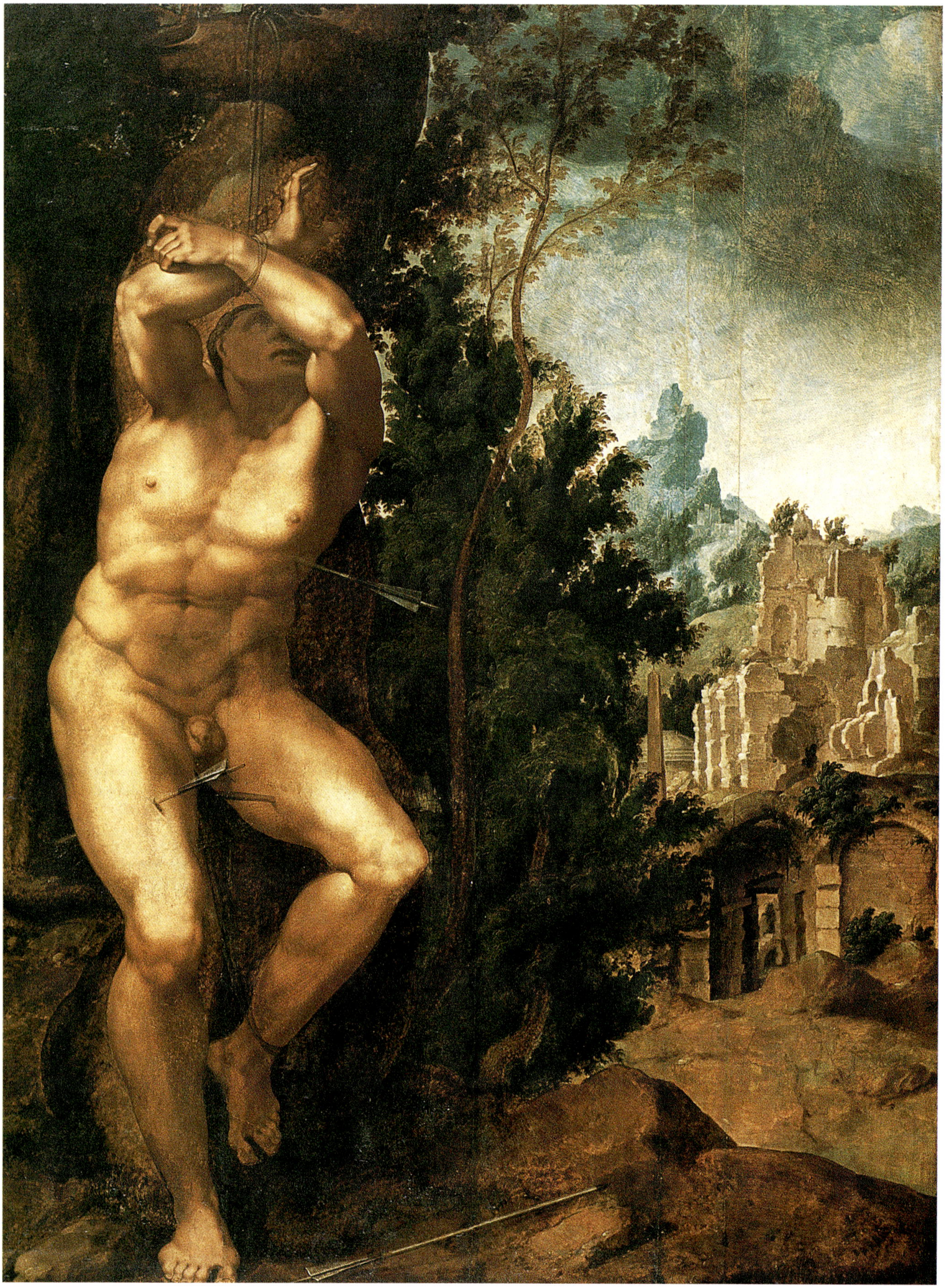

St Sebastian

Jan van Scorel, studio
(Schoorl 1496-Utrecht 1562)

Panel; 155 x 115 cm
Dated: 1542.

Physical characteristics[1]: the panel consists of four vertical planks and is painted up to the edges.

Infrared reflectography: extensive underdrawing visible. See text.

Dendrochronology: three of the four boards are from the same tree. The youngest heartwood growth ring dates from 1521. The panel could not have been painted before 1531; it was more probably painted in or after 1538. The dating therefore seems reasonable. See article by P. Klein.

Paint samples: paint cross-sections show only one layer of paint, with no intermediate layer. The underdrawing was made directly onto the ground.

Provenance: S. Paris, auction London, 5 May 1738, £86; Sir Jacob Bouverie, First Viscount Folkstone; Earl of Radnor, Longford Castle; Grete Ring, London; art market, antiques fair Delft, 1950; acquired by the Museum in 1950; inv. no. 2342.

Exhibitions: *Jan van Scorel*, Utrecht, Centraal Museum, 1955, no. 62, fig. 73; *Jan van Scorel in Utrecht*, Utrecht Centraal Museum, Douai, Musée de la Chartreuse, 1977, no. 48, fig. 95; *Kunst voor de beeldenstorm*, Amsterdam, Rijksmuseum, 1986, no. 117, fig.

Literature: Dr. Waagen, *Treasures of Art in Great Britain*, III, London, 1854, p. 140; Claude Philips, *Art Journal*, 1897, p. 102, fig.; Helen Matilda, Countess of Radnor, William Barclay Squire, *Catalogue of the Pictures in the Collection of the Earl of Radnor*, I, London 1909, no. 95; E.W. (J.C. Ebbinge Wubben), "Een teruggevonden werk van Jan van Scorel?" *Bulletin Museum Boymans Rotterdam* 2, no. 1 (1951), pp. 1-6, fig. 1, 2; F. "Ein wiedergefundenes Gemälde von Jan van Scorel", *Die Weltkunst* 21, no. 13, 1 July 1951, p. 2, fig.; B. Cnattingius, A.L. Romdahl, *Maerten Heemskercks Laurentiusaltare i Linköpings Domkyrka*, Stockholm 1953, p. 22, note 1; cat. 1962, p. 129; J.G. van Gelder, "Jan van Scorel in Frankrijk en Vlaanderen", *Simiolus* 1 (1966-1967), p. 30, fig. 25; H.G. Franz, *Niederländische Landschaftsmalerei im Zeitalter des Manierismus*, Graz 1969, p. 64, fig. 36; G. von der Osten, H. Vey, *Painting and Sculpture in Germany and the Netherlands 1500 to 1800*, Harmondsworth 1969, p. 184, fig. 167; Molly Faries, "Underdrawings in the workshop production of Jan van Scorel", *Nederlands Kunsthistorisch Jaarboek* 26 (1975), pp. 193-199, fig. 74.

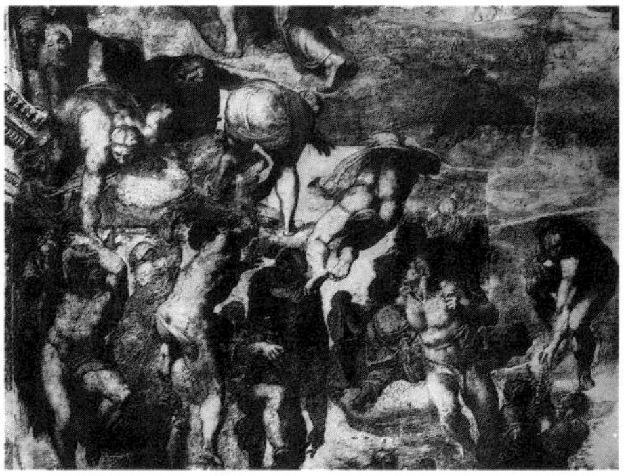

a. Michelangelo, Last Judgement (detail), Vatican, Sistine Chapel.

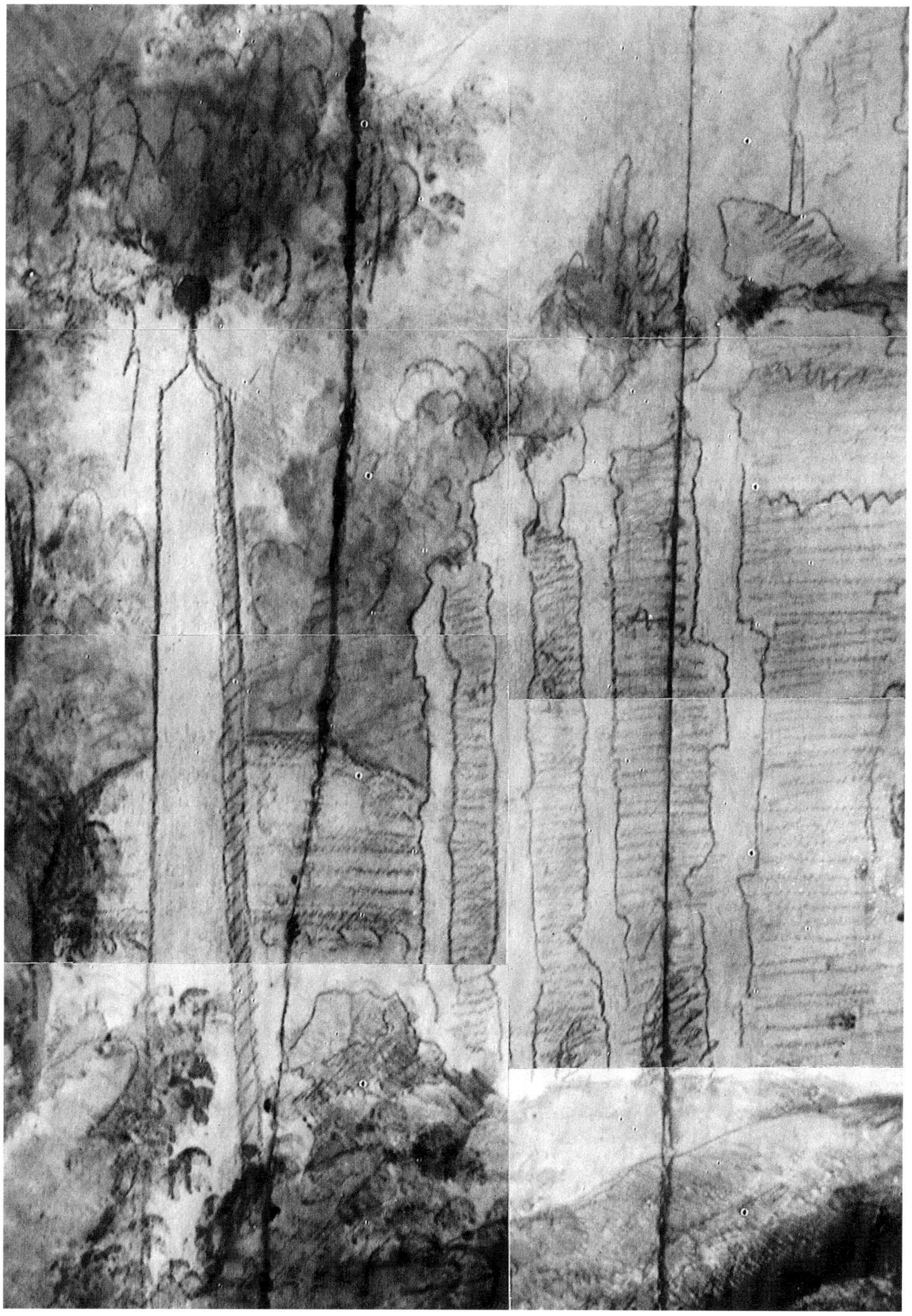

b. Infrared reflectogram assembly showing a detail of the ruins.

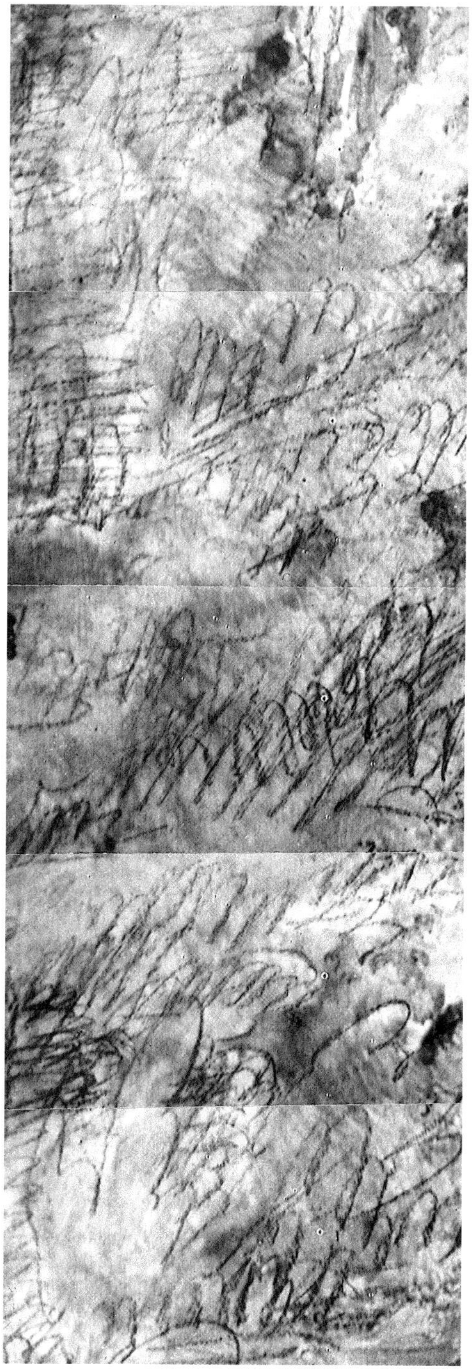

c. Infrared reflectogram assembly showing a detail of the foliage.

In 1854, Waagen described the painting as being by the Italian painter Sebastiano del Piombo, after a design by Michelangelo. In the catalogue of the Earl of Radnor's collection it was noted that the figure of Sebastian was copied from a figure in Michelangelo's *Last Judgement* in the Sistine Chapel, Rome (fig. a). The figure is being raised up as one of the blessed. The same source indicates that the panel was regarded as the work of a Dutch painter and mentions the name of Maerten van Heemskerck. However, the attribution to this painter was considered problematical because the *Last Judgement* was completed in 1541 and Maerten van Heemskerck would have been unable to see it in its finished state whilst living in Rome between 1532 and 1536.

The painting was acquired by the Museum in 1950, whereupon it was extensively publicised by Ebbinge Wubben, who followed Grete Ring in ascribing it to Jan van Scorel. The author pointed to a passage in the book by Aernout van Buchell from 1585-90, which mentions a Sebastian by Jan van Scorel not painted after a living model. This prompts the question whether the Rotterdam painting and this version by Scorel are not identical.[2]

The painting is unsigned but it is dated 1542, one year after the completion of Michelangelo's *Last Judgement*. The painter must therefore have had access to sketches or prints of the great fresco to have been able to make this copy. Van Gelder assumes that Scorel had seen a copy of Michelangelo's cartoon for this figure in the style of a drawing by Stradanus in the Uffizi, Florence from around 1550.[3]

The figure of Sebastian does indeed have the same posture as the floating figure on Michelangelo's fresco. In the painting, the saint's hands are tied together with rope and his body is pierced with arrows. He is standing on a rise backed by thick foliage. In the right background we see Roman ruins and an obelisk. In the right foreground are the lightly-sketched outlines of several archers who were not worked out further.

The figure on Michelangelo's fresco was used as a model by more than one sixteenth-century painter.[4] The manner in which the figure of Sebastian is painted seems to differ from the technique used to render the ruins, a fact which Faries deduced by studying the underdrawing.[5] The broad, bold cross-hatching which forms the underdrawing of Sebastian can easily be seen with the naked eye. We can also see the fluent, curly brush-strokes used, for example, to draw the trees above the ruins.

Faries compared the obelisk and the spherical building behind it with a page from the Roman sketchbook of Maerten van Heemskerck, which could have served as an example for Roman motifs in Dutch paintings. The separation of the motifs, the Sebastian after Michelangelo contrasting with the ruins in the style of Heemskerck, led the author to speak of a compilation. She had already described the painting as "Scorel, studio" and assumes that it was made with assistance from the painter's studio. We shave the view also that the work was probably not executed entirely by the master himself.
JG

1 Paint samples: A 149/1-6. Infrared reflectograms: AB 117/5-25.
2 G.J. Hoogewerff, J.Q. van Regteren Altena, *Arnoldus Buchelius "Res Pictoriae"*, The Hague, 1928, pp. 29-30: "Fecit Sanctum Sebastianum quemdam, non ilum autem ad vivi hominis similitudinem" (He has painted a St Sebastian, but not after a living model).
3 Van Gelder (1966-1967).
4 See *Die Staatliche Gemäldegalerie zu Dresden*, Berlin-Dresden 1929, p. 37, no. 74 (Florentine school); a painting in the Emil Edler auction, E. von Mecenseffy, Vienna, Wawra, 16 April 1918, no. 254 (Vlämisch um 1600, canvas, 106 x 76 cm), probably the same painting which was in the Siegfried Griesser collection, Umhausen on 30 December 1985 (letter to the Museum); according to M. Feilchenfeldt (21 June 1970) there is a small version of the painting in the Escorial in the room of Philip II, as anonymous; a painting in the Sotheby's auction, New York, 21 October 1988, no. 11, fig. (as circle of Jan van Scorel).
5 Faries (1975) and in exhib. cat. Amsterdam, 1986.

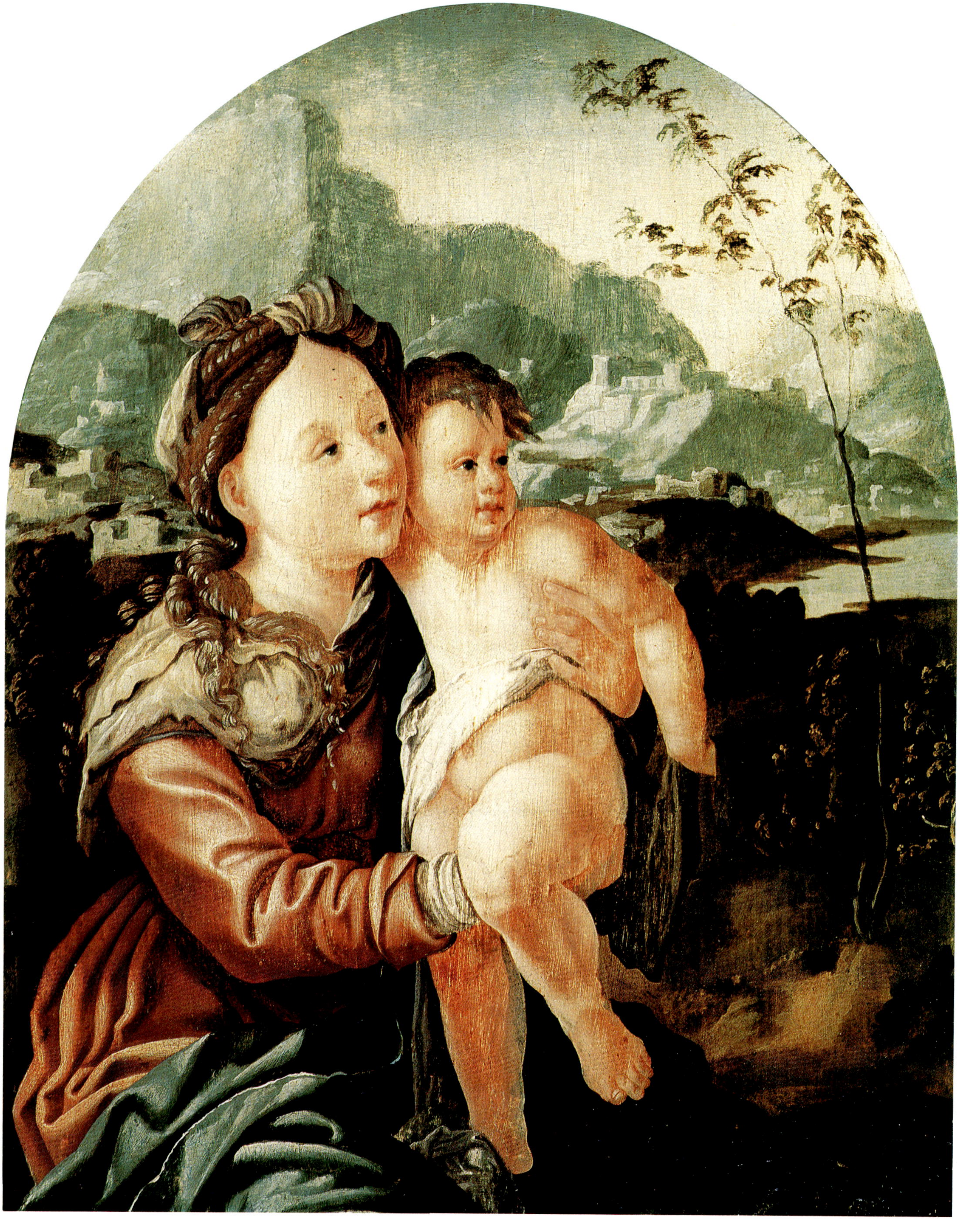

Virgin and Child

Jan van Scorel, circle of
(Schoorl 1495-Utrecht 1562)

Panel; 35 x 26.5 cm

Physical characteristics[1]: the panel consists of a single plank which has been rounded off at the top. The panel is painted to the edges.

Infrared reflectography: a summary underdrawing in black chalk is discernible, most notably in the faces of the Virgin and Child.

Dendrochronology: the youngest heartwood growth ring dates from 1500. The panel could not have been painted before 1511; it was more probably painted in or after 1517. See article by P. Klein.

Paint samples: paint cross-sections show that there is a thick white intermediate layer on top of the ground. There are generally two layers of paint.

Provenance: estate of F.J.O. Boymans, Utrecht, 1847; inv. no. 1798.

Exhibitions: *Jan van Scorel*, Utrecht, Centraal Museum, 1955, no. 58, fig. 69.

Literature: *Catalogus van schilderijen enz. in het Museum te Rotterdam*, 1849, no. 247; L. Scheibler, W. Bode, "Verzeichnis der Gemälde des Jan van Scorel", *Jahrbuch der königlich Preussischen Kunstsammlungen* II (1881), p. 213, no. 270; M.J. Friedländer, *Von Eyck bis Bruegel*, Berlin 1921, p. 201; G.J. Hoogewerff, *Jan van Scorel, peintre de la renaissance Hollandaise*, The Hague 1923, p. 86; G.J. Hoogewerff, "Scorel-parallellen", *Oud Holland* 46 (1929), p. 207, fig. 7; Friedländer, XII, 1924, p. 202, no. 330; G.J. Hoogewerff, *De Noord-Nederlandsche Schilderkunst*, IV, The Hague, 1941-1942, p. 154; cat. 1962, p. 129; Friedländer, XII, 1975, p. 123, no. 330, fig. 180.

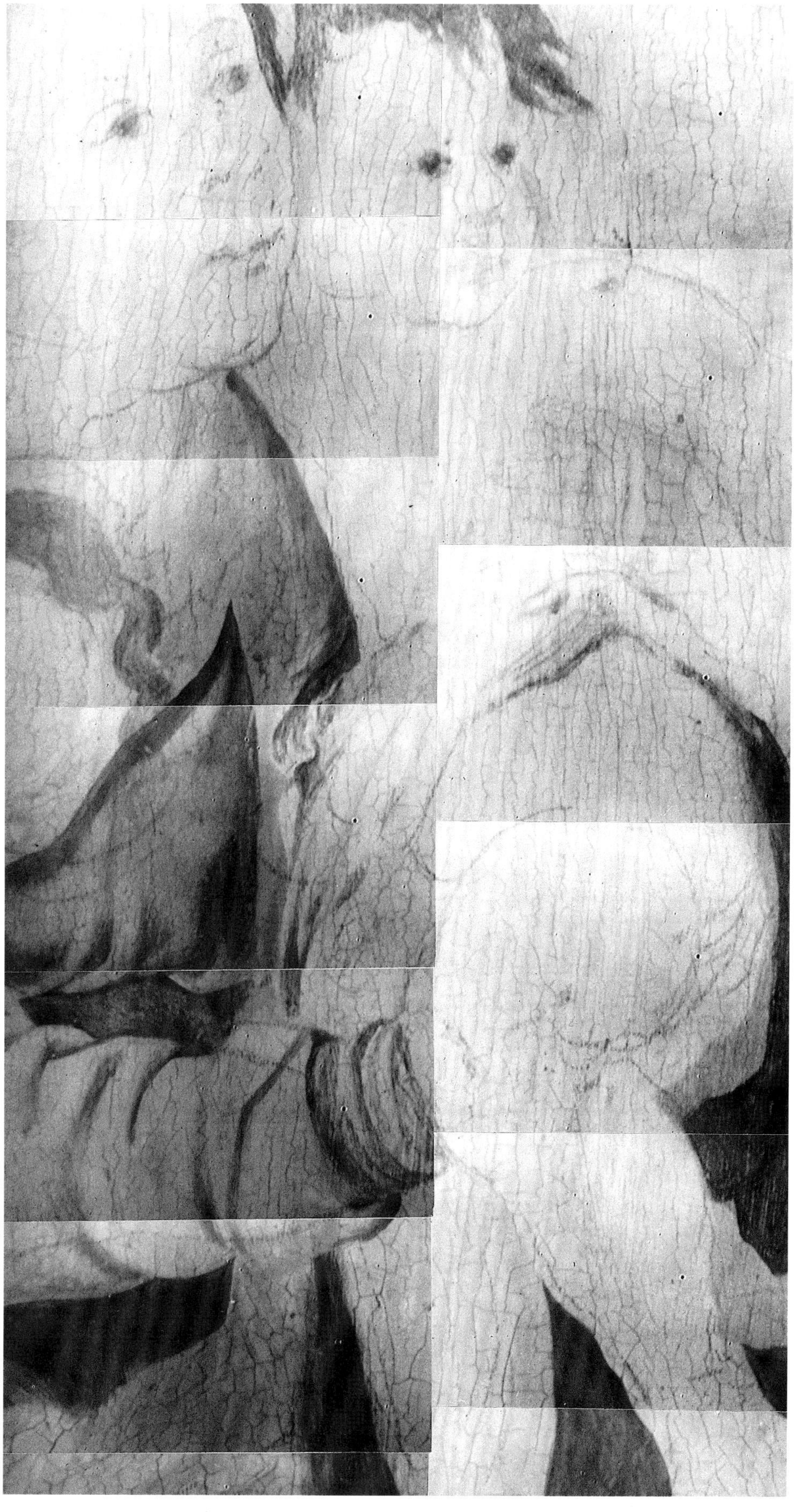

a. Infrared reflectogram assembly. Detail of the Virgin and Child.

The painting shows a Virgin and Child. The infant Christ is standing on one leg and has the other raised. The Virgin Mary is supporting the Child by holding her right hand under its left leg and her left hand around its chest. The figures are both looking to the right and are shown against a background of impressive mountains.

The direction in which both figures are looking might suggest that there was originally a second panel on the right-hand side bearing the portrait of a donor.

The painting was attributed to Jan van Scorel in the Boymans Collection. Hoogewerff was very disparaging about the piece in 1929, dismissing it as "nothing but a free copy after an original work by the master". He compared it with a painting which was then at the Goudstikker Gallery, also showing a *Virgin and Child*, which he did consider to be by Scorel. However, to judge by the photograph, this work, which was in the Heinz Kisters collection in Kreuzlingen, Switzerland, in 1975, is rather weak and could be a copy after the Rotterdam painting. This was also the view of Friedländer, who considered the Rotterdam painting a work by Scorel and the painting in the Kisters collection a free copy.

The painting in Rotterdam underwent a dendrochronological examination which showed that it was probably made after 1517. The fluent, sketchy underdrawing argues against its being a copy (fig. a). Moreover, it can be seen that several small changes were made during the painting process, such as the narrowing of Christ's right leg and the substantial shortening of the Virgin's left forefinger which is on the infant Christ's chest. Underdrawing and alterations point to a creative process. The schematic and careful folds of the Virgin's robe as well as the style of the underdrawing itself, would suggest that the painting is not by the master himself. Even so, many features, such as the postures of the figures, the tousled hair of the Child and the blue landscape indicate a painter very close to Jan van Scorel.
JG

1 Paint samples: A 150/1-3. Infrared reflectograms: AB 265/11-23.

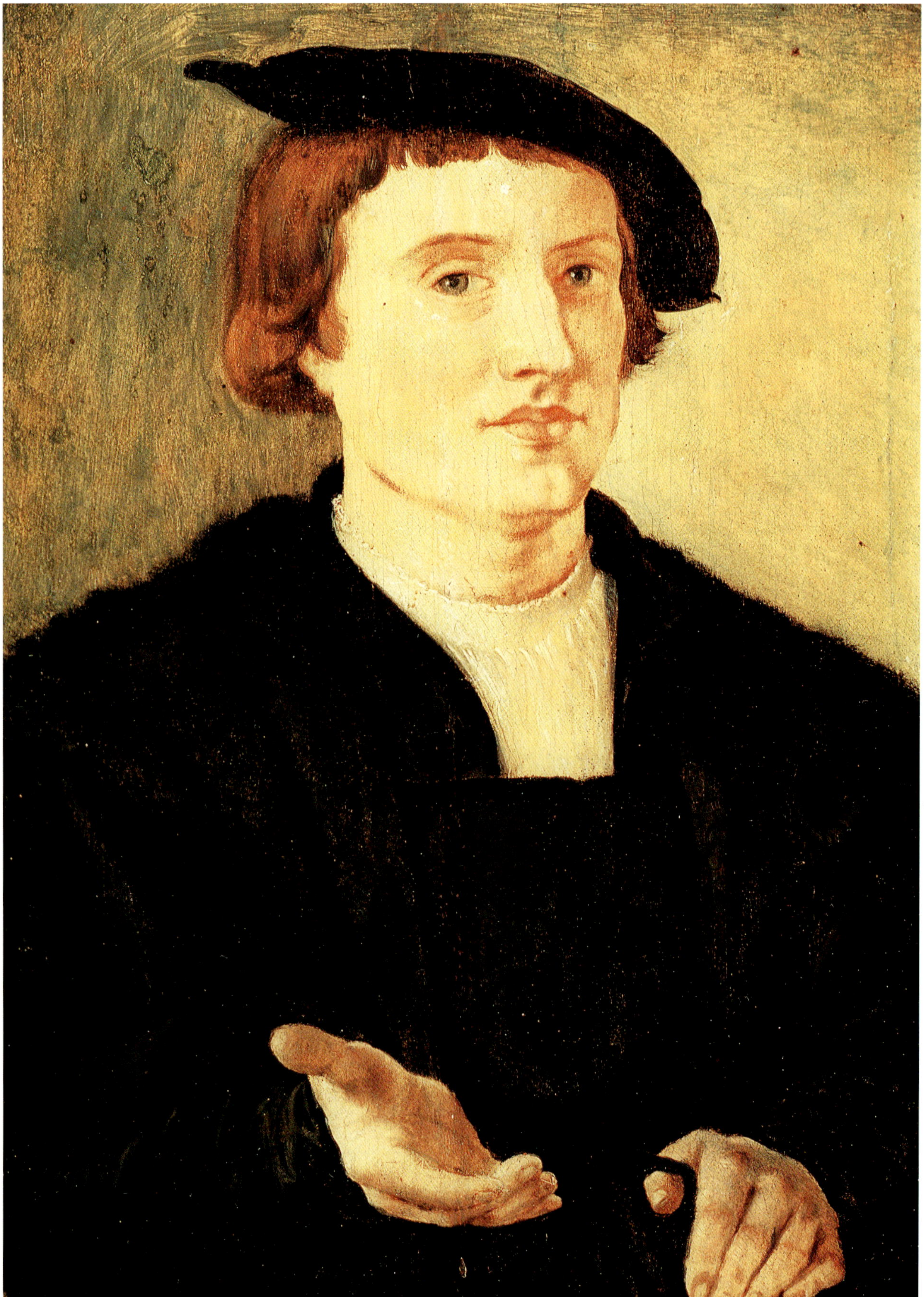

Portrait of a young man

Anonymous
North Netherlandish master
First half of the sixteenth century

Panel; 30 x 21 cm

The young man in this portrait is wearing a fur coat and a flat cap. The thumb of his left hand is hooked through the belt around his waist. With his right hand he is making a gesture as though to address the viewer.

Bloch and Friedländer as well as the Van Diemen Gallery simply described the painting as a portrait by Jan van Scorel. No fewer than three certificates confirming the painting as an original by Van Scorel are preserved in the documentation. They were issued by Cornelis Hofstede de Groot (March 1926), Max J. Friedländer (16 June 1926) and W.R. Valentiner (11 October 1926). However, the link with Scorel is far from clear. The young man's face is exceptionally weak, and the rendering of the clothing suggests a rather undistinguished painter. Because the connection with Van Scorel is tenuous at best, it seems safer to provisionally designate the painting as North Netherlandish, sixteenth century. It may have been painted in the first half of the century.

The painting has been transferred to a new support. Only a very thin part of the original panel has been preserved, which has been glued on to a sturdy plywood base. It is not clear when or why this was done.
JG

Physical characteristics: the painting was transferred to a new panel.

Infrared reflectography: no underdrawing could be discerned.[1]

Provenance: Van Diemen & Co., Berlin, Amsterdam, 1927 and 1928 (advertisement in *Der Cicerone* 20, 2. März Heft, 1928, p. I); acquired by D.G. van Beuningen, Rotterdam and Vierhouten, in 1929 from the Maas Gallery for 30,000 guilders; acquired in 1958 with the D.G. van Beuningen Collection; inv. no. 2480.

Exhibition: *Jan van Scorel*, Utrecht, Centraal Museum, 1955, no. 49, fig. 50.

Literature: V. Bloch, "Vom Amsterdamer Kunsthandel", *Der Cicerone* 19, 1.Okt. Heft, 1927, p. 601; Friedländer, XII, 1935, p. 206, no. 373; cat. 1962, p. 130; Friedländer, XII, 1975, p. 127, no. 373, fig. pl. 195.

1 Scanned on 10 January 1994 by J.R.J. van Asperen de Boer.

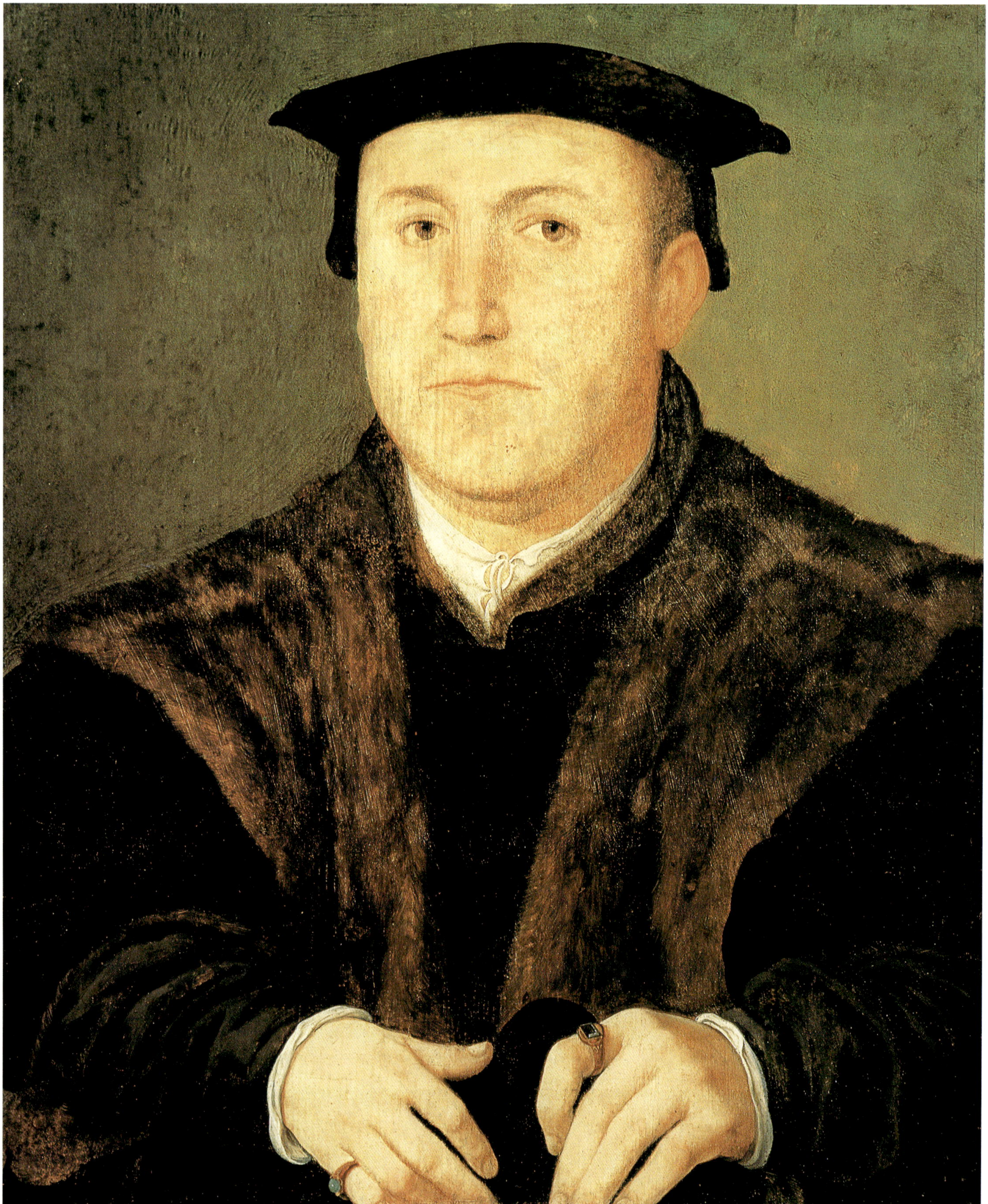

Portrait of a man

Anonymous
North Netherlandish master
c. 1530-1550

Panel; 41 x 34 cm

The sitter is wearing a heavy fur-lined coat and a flat cap. The two expensive rings on his fingers suggest a prosperous figure.

The painting was donated in 1880 as a work by Jan van Scorel. However, in 1892 Haverkorn van Rijsewijk described it as sixteenth century Dutch school, pointing to its resemblance to the *Braspennings banquet* by Cornelis Anthonisz in the Amsterdam Historical Museum. Friedländer nonetheless recorded the painting as a Jan van Scorel; J. Bruyn regarded the portrait as a work by the Master of the Regent Maria.[2] We only know a portrait of Mary of Hungary by this artist, who was identified by Friedländer as Guillaume Scrots. Comparison of the latter painting with the Rotterdam picture does not suggest any great resemblance.[3]

Not only is the portrait, which as Friedländer noted is in a particularly poor condition, relatively difficult to link to Scorel, but an attribution to a different artist also creates problems. The face is very flat and the shoulders are rather badly shaped. The hands are perhaps the best part of the painting. The work has so few distinguishing features that a more precise specification than Northern Netherlands sixteenth century is not possible, except to note that a dating around 1530-1550 is probable.
JG

Physical characteristics: the panel consists of a single plank and is painted up to the edges.

Infrared reflectography: no underdrawing could be discerned.[1]

Provenance: donated by P. de Kuijper, Paris, 1880; inv. no. 1796.

Exhibitions: *Jan van Scorel*, Utrecht, Centraal Museum, 1955, no. 47, fig. 51.

Literature: *Verslag omtrent den toestand en de aanwinsten van het Museum Boymans over het jaar 1880*, p. 5; *Beschrijving der schilderijen en beeldhouwwerken in het Museum te Rotterdam gesticht door Mr. F.J.O. Boymans*, 1883, no. 303; P. Haverkorn van Rijsewijk, *Beknopte beschrijving der schilderijen en beeldhouwwerken in het museum te Rotterdam*, 1892, no. 116; Friedländer, XII, 1935, p. 205, no. 366; cat. 1962, p. 130; Friedländer, XII, 1975, p. 127, no. 366, fig. pl. 194.

1 Scanned on 10 January 1994 by J.R.J. van Asperen de Boer.
2 The opinion is reported in cat. 1962, p. 130.
3 See Friedländer, XIII, 1975, pp. 49-50, p. 116, fig. pl. 130.

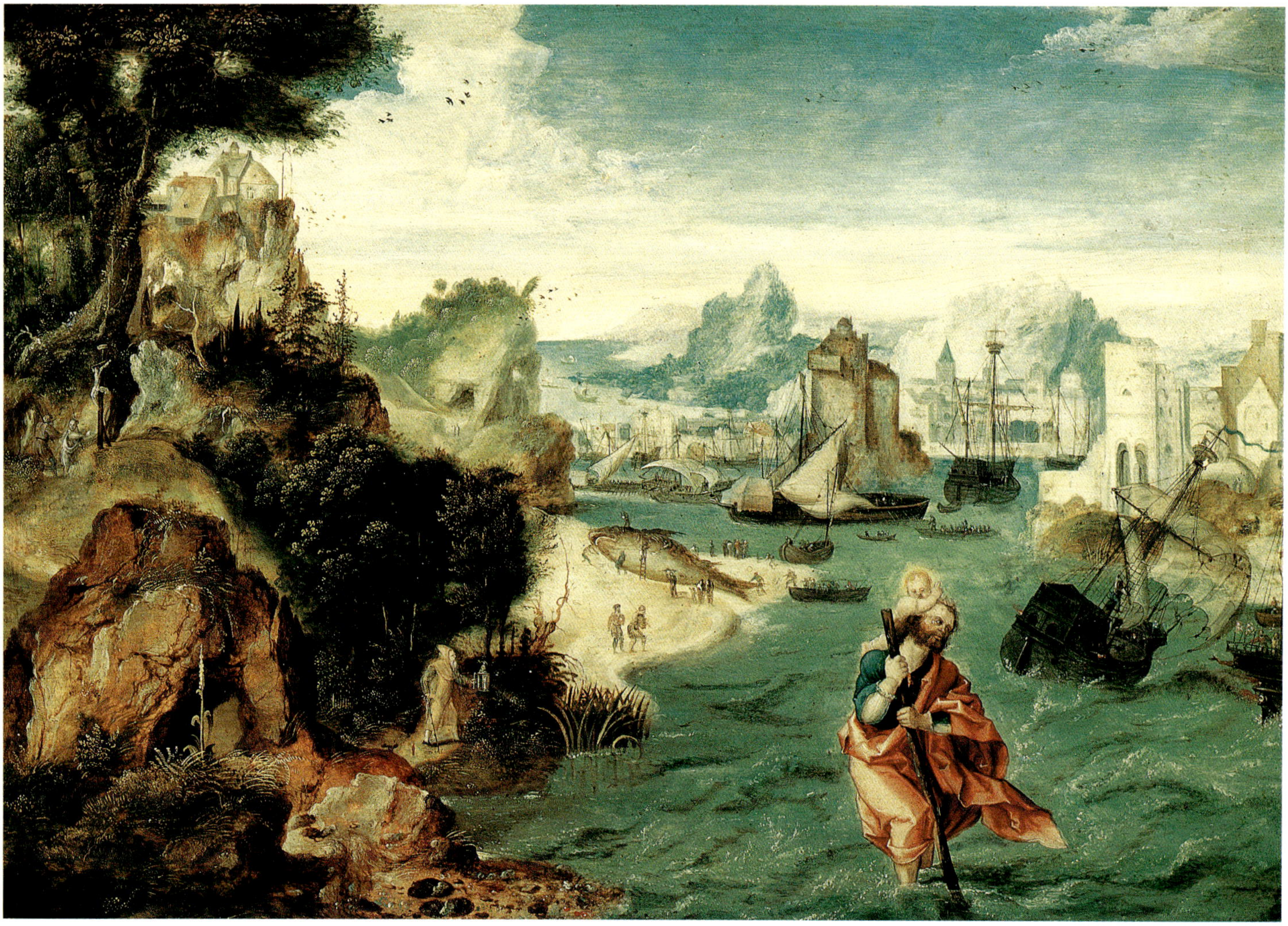

Landscape with St Christopher

Herry met de Bles
(Bouvignes 1500/1510-?)

Panel; 30 x 42 cm

Physical characteristics[1]: the panel consists of one plank.

Infrared reflectography: the painting is completely underdrawn with a dry medium, possibly black chalk (fig. a and b). The landscape and boscage were roughly sketched. The figures, architecture and ships were also sketched freehand, although in rather more detail. Shadows are sometimes indicated by a few separate hatchings. The most detailed part of the underdrawing is St Christopher, where bolder strokes are used than elsewhere. No significant changes were made between the underdrawing and the final painting. The artist did, however, occasionally deviate from the original architectural contours.

Paint samples: cross-sectional analysis of the paint shows that a white intermediate layer was applied to the chalk ground. There are mainly two layers of paint on top. The blue pigment is azurite.

Provenance: Freiherr Von Brenken Collection, Wewer (1904); Richard von Kaufmann Collection, Berlin; sale at Paul Cassirer & Hugo Helbig, Berlin, 4 December 1917, no. 97, fig.; Stefan von Auspitz Collection, Vienna; purchased in 1932 by D.G. van Beuningen, Rotterdam and Vierhouten through the K.W. Bachstitz Gallery, The Hague, for 2000 guilders; acquired in 1958 by the Museum with the D.G. van Beuningen Collection; inv. no. 2437.

Exhibitions: *Kunsthistorische Ausstellung*, Düsseldorf, 1904, no. 189; *Tentoonstelling van Nederlandsche zee- en riviergezichten in de XVIIde eeuw*, Rotterdam, Boymans Museum, 1945-46, no. 11, fig.; *Les Primitifs Flamands*, Paris, Musée de l'Orangerie, 1947, no. 1; *Honderd jaar Museum Boymans Rotterdam. Meesterwerken uit de verzameling D.G. van Beuningen*, Rotterdam, Boymans Museum, 1949, no. 3; *Chefs-d'œuvre de la collection D.G. van Beuningen*, Paris, Petit Palais, 1952, no. 38.

Literature: M. Conway, *The Van Eyck and their followers*, London 1921, p. 356, fig. 4; J. Held, *Dürers Wirkung auf die Niederländische Kunst seiner Zeit*, The Hague 1931, p. 63; Friedländer, XIII, 1936, p. 43, 148, no. 80; C. van de Wetering, *Die Entwicklung der Niederländischen Landschaftsmalerei vom Anfang des 16. Jahrhunderts bis zur Jahrhundertmitte*, Berlin 1938, p. 33-34; Hannema, 1949, no. 3, fig. 33; J.S. Gudlaugsson, "Het Errera-schetsboek en Lucas van Valckenborch", *Oud Holland* XXIV (1959), p. 122, fig. 7; L. van Puyvelde, *La peinture Flamand au siècle de Bosch et Breughel*, Brussels 1962, p. 227; W.S. Gibson, "Herri met de Bles. Landscape with St. John the Baptist preaching", *The Bulletin of the Cleveland Museum of Art* LV (1968), p. 83; Friedländer, XIII, 1975, no. 80, fig.; M. Russell, *Visions of the sea. Hendrik C. Vroom and the origins of Dutch marine painting*, Leiden 1983, p. 12, fig. 15; Exhib. cat. *Sillages Néerlandais: la vie maritime dans l'art des Pays-Bas/Kunst in het kielzog. Het maritieme leven in de Nederlandse kunst*, Paris, Musée de la Marine, 1989, p. 89, fig. 56; W.S. Gibson, *"Mirror of the earth". The world landscape in sixteenth-century painting*, Princeton, New Jersey 1989, pp. 28, 43.

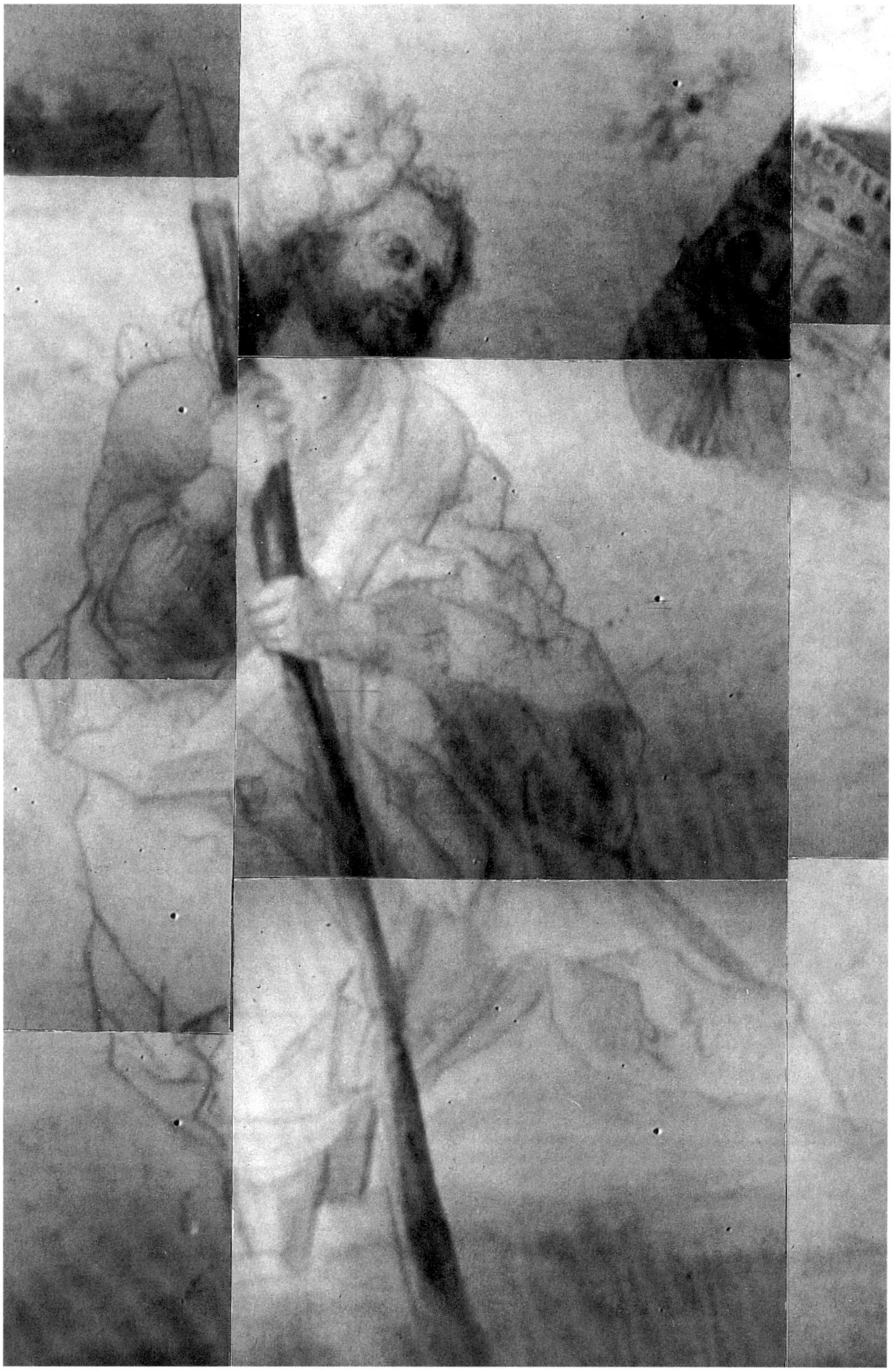

a. Infrared reflectogram assembly showing St Christopher.

The painting depicts the giant Christopher wading through turbulent, foaming waters, carrying the infant Christ on his shoulders. The hermit, who had advised the giant to serve Christ by carrying travellers across the dangerous river, is standing to the left by the river with a lantern in his hand.[2]

In contrast to the water, where a fierce storm appears to be raging, there is not even the hint of a breeze on land. All the trees are bolt upright and motionless.

The artist took the figure of Christopher and the infant Christ from an engraving by Albrecht Dürer (fig. c). The giant is much more formally drawn than the rest of the underdrawing (figs. a and b). This can presumably be explained by the fact that the figure is an exact copy of the print. The staff is longer in both the underdrawing and the print than in the final painting. The artist probably reduced the upper part of the staff to avoid any interference with the boat behind. The hermit is a mirror image of Dürer's print, with the torch replaced by a lantern.

The giant fish lying on the beach was probably inspired by a work portraying St Christopher ascribed to Jan de Cock and dated about 1520.[3]

St Christopher was particularly popular during the fifteenth and sixteenth centuries. He was principally revered as the patron saint of travellers. His legend was regarded as a good example of the difficult and dangerous road which everyone must travel in the journey through life. A number of paintings with Christopher as their subject have thus been interpreted as depicting a truly Christian life.[4] The two pilgrims by a crucifix shown in the painting may also be a reference to man's pilgrimage through life.

The painting in Rotterdam has always been attributed to Herry met de Bles. But the absence of a single signed work makes it difficult to reconstruct the oeuvre of this landscape painter. Van Mander's comment that he signed his work with an owl does not, in any case, seem to hold.[5] An attempt has been made to gain an overall idea of his work using paintings attributed to him in some early inventories.[6]

The spontaneous underdrawing of the present painting is matched by one found on the *Preaching of John the Baptist* ascribed to the painter in the Cleveland Museum of Art.[7] Most authors regard the panel in Rotterdam as an early work probably dating from around 1535-1545.[8]

The painting seems to have been the source of a number of later borrowings by other artists. The ship entering the harbour and the boat on the right heeling over at a violent angle with its sails billowing out appear in a drawing in the so-called "Errera Sketchbook" (fig. d). The same sketchbook contains a drawing featuring a harbour resembling the one in the present painting.[9]

The galley in front of the harbour whose sail is being taken down appears on a panel by an anonymous South Netherlandish master in the Museum in Brussels.[10]
FL

1 Scientific examination conducted by Astrid Kwakernaak under the supervision of J.R.J. van Asperen de Boer in 1990-91. Further details are available in the Museum's file on the painting. Paint samples A 322/1-5. Infrared reflectograms: AB 1213/1-34; AB 1214.

2 See cat. no. 15 for the legend of St Christopher.

3 For further information on this privately owned painting, see G. Unverfehrt, *Hieronymus Bosch. Die Rezeption seiner Kunst im frühen 16. Jahrhundert*, Berlin 1980, p. 269, no. 74. Gibson (1989) ascribes the painting to the Master of the Viennese Lamentation. A print of the painting was published by Dankertsz (see Unverfehrt) around 1550. There is an anonymous sixteenth-century Dutch *St Christopher* in the Pushkin Museum in Moscow depicting a similar giant fish.

4 See R.L. Falkenburg, *Joachim Patinir. Landscape as an image of the pilgrimage of life*, Amsterdam, Philadelphia 1988, p. 106.

5 C. van Mander, *Het Schilder-boeck [...]*, Haarlem 1604, fol. 219.

6 The *Landscape with a mine*, which now hangs in the Uffizi in Florence, was exhibited under the name of Herry met de Bles in the Tribuna in 1603. A *Landscape with the Holy Family*, now in the Oeffentliche Kunstsammlung in Basle, was listed under his name in the Amerbach Collection in 1586. See Friedländer (1936).

7 See W.A. Real, "Exploring new applications for infrared reflectography", *The Bulletin of the Cleveland Museum of Art* 72 (1985), pp. 395-397. A schematic underdrawing has also been found on a work ascribed to Herry met de Bles in the Thyssen Collection. See C. Eisler (ed.), *The Thyssen-Bornemisza collection. Early Netherlandish Painting*, London 1989, pp. 254-255.

8 Gibson (1968, 1989), Russell (1983).

9 See Gudlaugsson (1959). The 'Errera Sketchbook' is in the Koninklijke Musea voor Schone Kunsten van België in Brussels. At least three different artists can be distinguished in the sketchbook. The drawing with the two boats is on fol. 38. The drawing of the harbour, which is not actually identical to the one in the painting, is on fol. 57. The same harbour appears in a drawing (fol. 56) in a sketchbook in the Kupferstichkabinett in Berlin (79C2). There is another comparable drawing with St Christopher in the 'Errera Sketchbook' on fol. 33. For further information on the 'Errera Sketchbook' see, for example, B.L. Dunbar, "Some observations on the 'Errera Sketchbook' in Brussels", *Bulletin Koninklijke Musea voor Schone Kunsten van België* 21 (1972), pp. 53-82.

10 Serck refers to this in an unpublished dissertation on Herry met de Bles. For further details about the painting, see *Musées Royaux des Beaux-Arts de Belgique. Catalogue inventaire de la peinture ancienne*, Brussels 1984, p. 394, inv. no. 4001, as Southern Netherlands, c. 1520-1530, *St Peter walking on the water*, panel; 35,5 x 59 cm.
The same galley also appears in mirror image in a print by the master A.F, *Landscape with St Christopher*. See E.K. Stahl, *Die Legende vom Heil. Riesen Christophorus*, Munich 1920, fig. LIV.

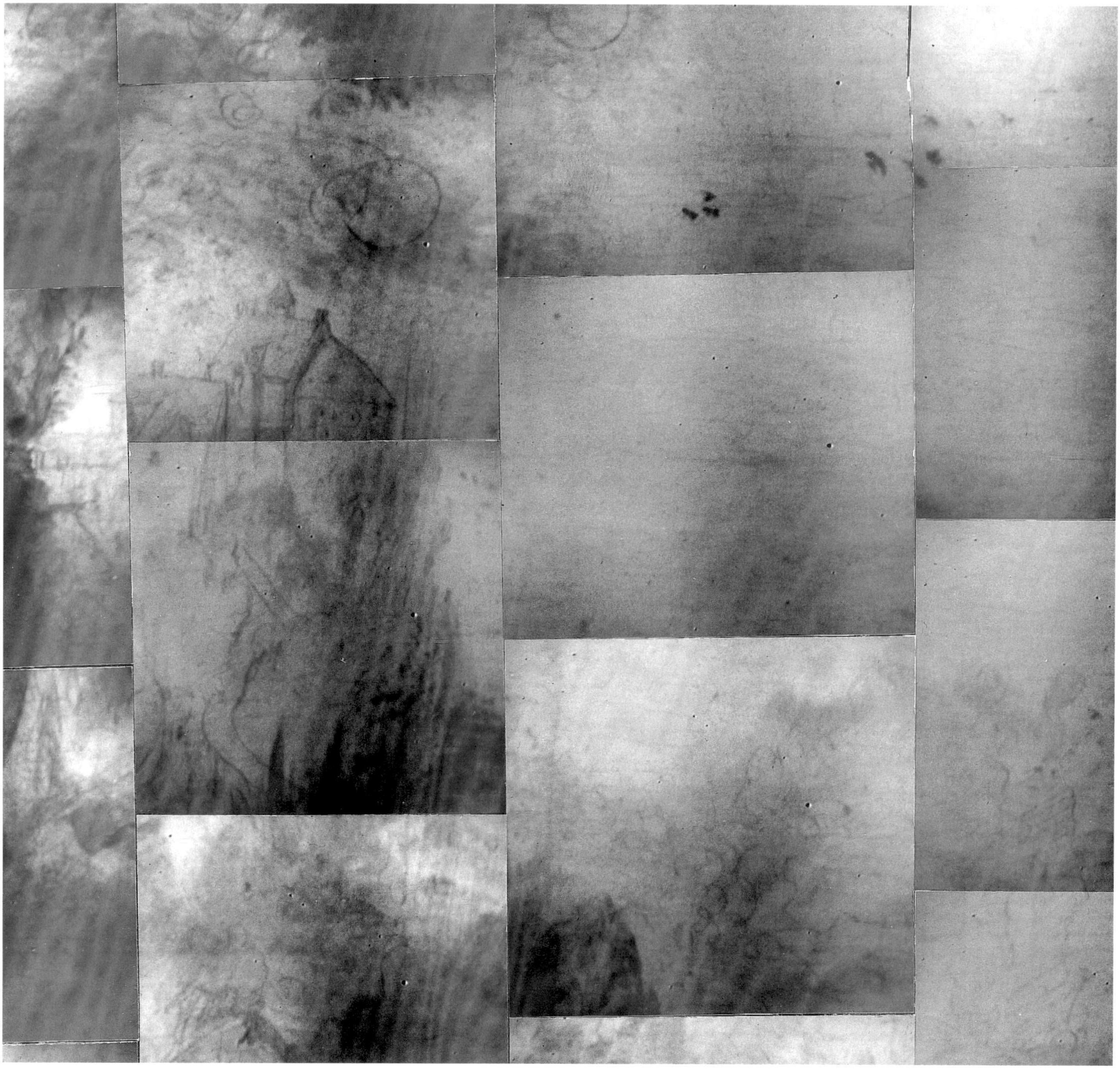

b. Infrared reflectogram assembly. Detail of the landscape at upper left.

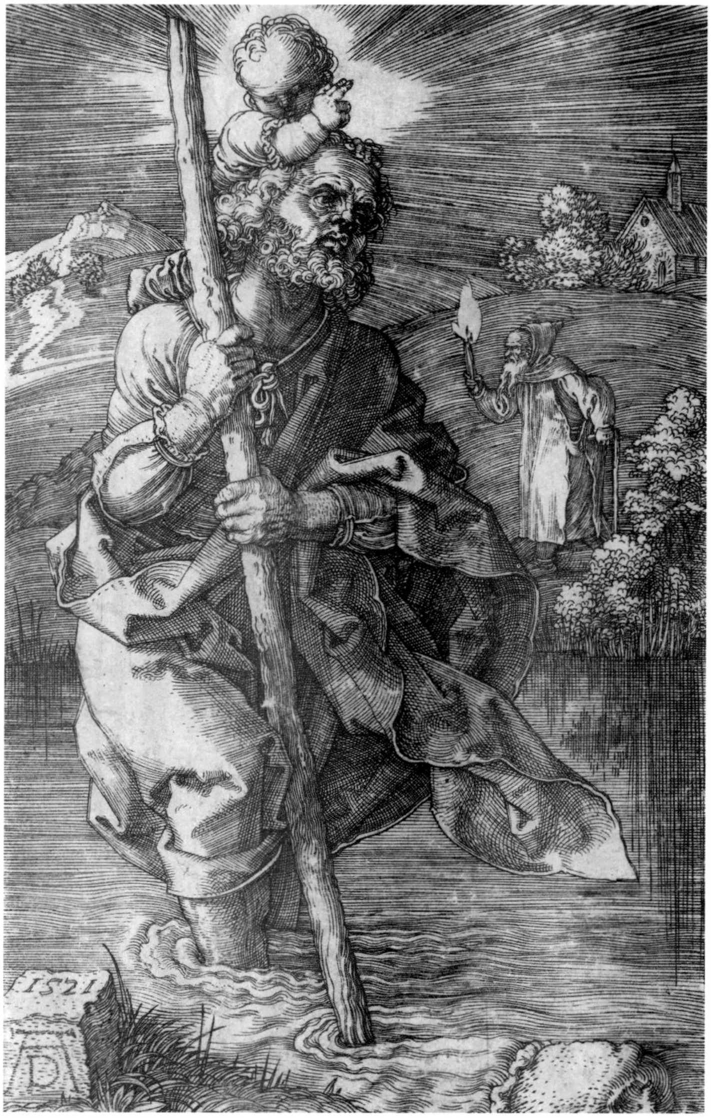

c. Albrecht Dürer, St Christopher
Engraving
(Bartsch 52)

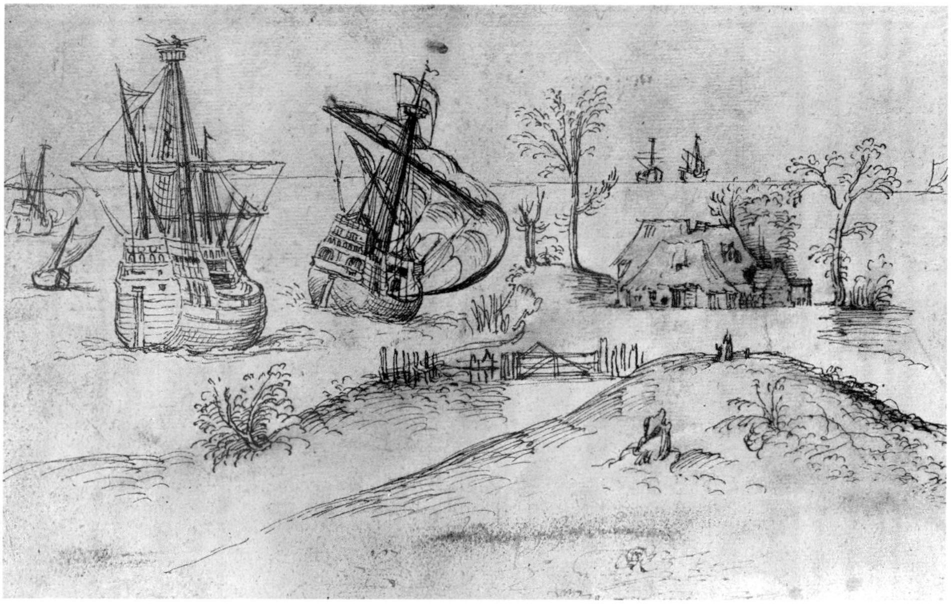

d. Anonymous, *Landscape with ships*
Fol. 38 from the "Errera Sketchbook"
Museum voor Schone Kunsten van België, Brussels

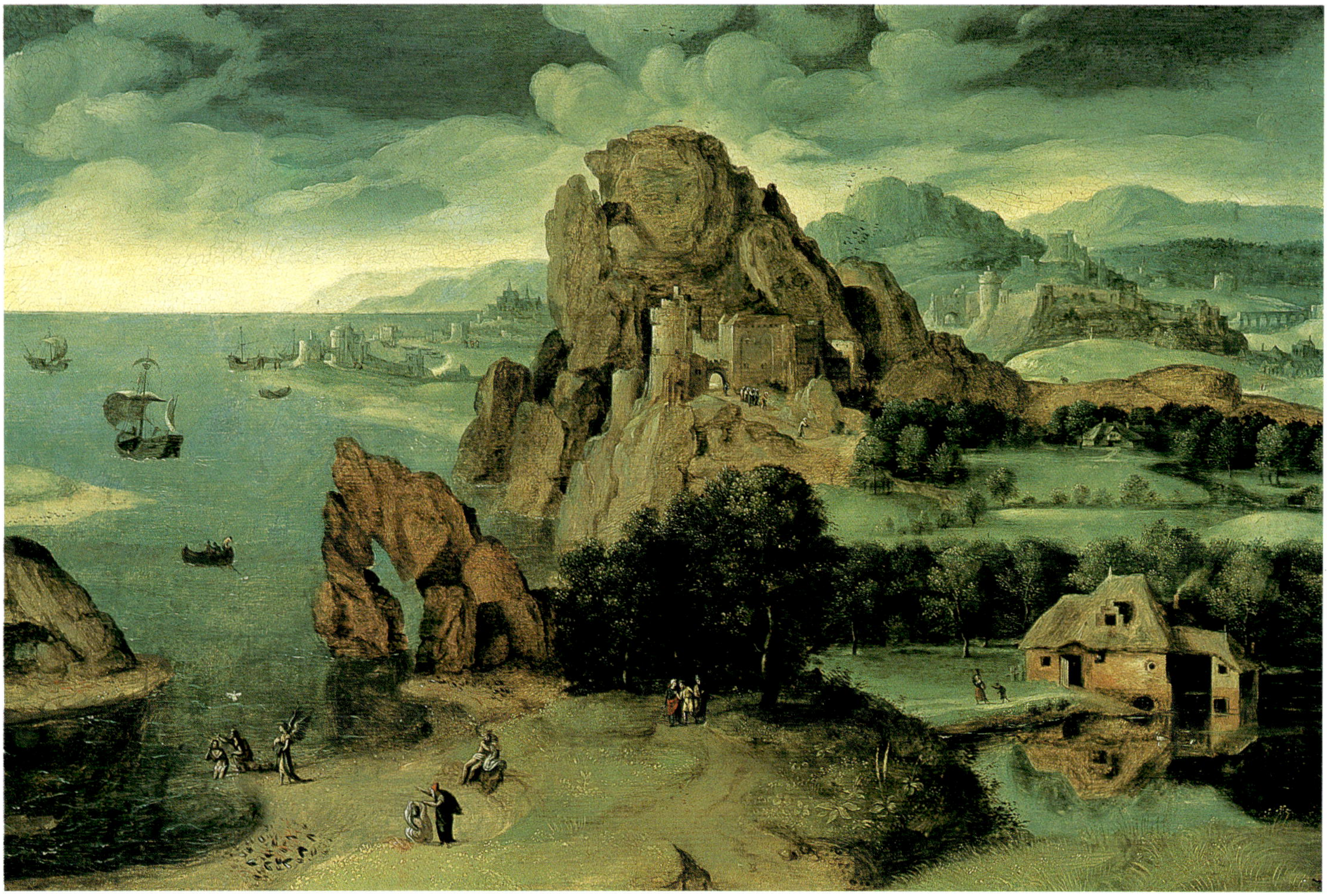

Landscape with the baptism of Christ and the journey to Emmaus

Herry met de Bles, follower of
Antwerp c. 1540-1550

Panel; 37 x 55 cm

The Museum's 1962 catalogue lists this painting as by the School of Joachim Patinir. It is now more accurately identified as modelled on a composition by Herry met de Bles. The landscape in a small panel in the Museo Capidamonte, Naples, depicting *St Peter on the waters* (fig. a) is practically identical to this work. Judging by the photograph, the Naples panel is more finely executed, the work in Rotterdam lacking the precise draughtsmanship so characteristic of Herry met de Bles.

The underdrawing was followed faithfully in paint (fig. b), with no obvious changes. The work is thus possibly a copy of an original composition by Herry met de Bles. It was probably painted around 1540-1550 by a follower of the celebrated landscape painter.[2]

The painting depicts a remarkable combination of scenes from the life of Christ. Hitherto called *Landscape with the baptism of Christ*, which is portrayed in the left foreground, it also shows the journey to Emmaus (Luke 24), with Christ between the two travellers on a wooded path leading to the village where He manifested Himself. In the background we see the earlier events of that day: the disciples leaving the gates of Jerusalem and discovering that the body of Jesus was no longer in the sepulchre. These two interrelated scenes bear no iconographical relation to the baptism of Christ, and consequently at first sight it might seem that the figures of Christ, John the Baptist, the angel and the men taking off their clothes were later additions. There are however two other versions of the painting with similar scenes (figs. c and d),[3] both of which appear to date from the sixteenth century.[4] The figures of the baptism of Christ in the Rotterdam panel must therefore have been added at a very early date, or they may even have been there from the outset. The unusual combination of Christ and the journey to Emmaus with the Baptism of Christ remains unexplained.
FL

Physical characteristics: the panel consists of two horizontal planks.

Infrared reflectography:[1] the underdrawing, executed in black chalk (fig. b), was on the whole followed faithfully. The buildings in the harbour were sketched in outline, to which some alterations were made in paint.

X-radiograph: the line of the horizon was incised.

Provenance: Leegenhoek Collection, Paris; purchased there in May 1953 by D.G. van Beuningen, Rotterdam and Vierhouten, for 15,000 guilders; acquired by the Museum in 1958 with the Van Beuningen Collection; inv. no. 2475.

Literature: Cat. 1962, p. 102.

1 Scanned in its entirety on 20 December 1993. The left half was recorded by J.R.J. van Asperen de Boer on 17 January 1994. The infrared reflectogram assembly was made by Joris Dik. Infrared reflectograms: AB 1557/18A-AB 1558/22A.

2 In a letter to the Museum dated 12 June 1965, P. de Boer suggested an attribution to Matthys Cock. But there are no paintings which can be attributed with certainty to this artist, and the panel displays little similarity with the few drawings signed "Cock". On Matthys Cock, see, for example, H.G. Franz, *Niederländische Landschaftsmalerei im Zeitalter des Manierismus*, Graz 1969, pp. 140-153.

3 One is in the Galleria Borghese, Rome, inv.no. 202. The other was in the S. Hartveld Gallery, Antwerp, until 1938 (photograph in the Netherlands Institute for Art History, The Hague). It was later radically restored and the baptism figures were removed. The painting was in the Brienner Galerie Lodi, Munich, in 1965. A photograph showing it after the restoration is in the Museum's file.

4 In addition, there are three other known versions of the landscape, all on the theme of the calling of St Peter. One is in the Galleria Borghese, Rome (inv. no. 359; panel; 27.5 x 42 cm), listed as by a follower of Joachim Patinir. See L.C. Ragghianti, *Dipinti Fiamminghi in Italia (1420-1570)*, Bologna 1990, no. 281, p. 146. Another was in the Van Merlen Collection, Antwerp, and attributed to Lucas van Valckenborch (panel; 29 x 43 cm). See exhib. cat., *De eeuw van Bruegel*, Brussels, Koninklijke Musea voor Schone Kunsten, 1963, no. 225. The third was in the Gosta Stenman Collection, Helsingfors, in 1925 (photograph at the Netherlands Institute for Art History, The Hague).

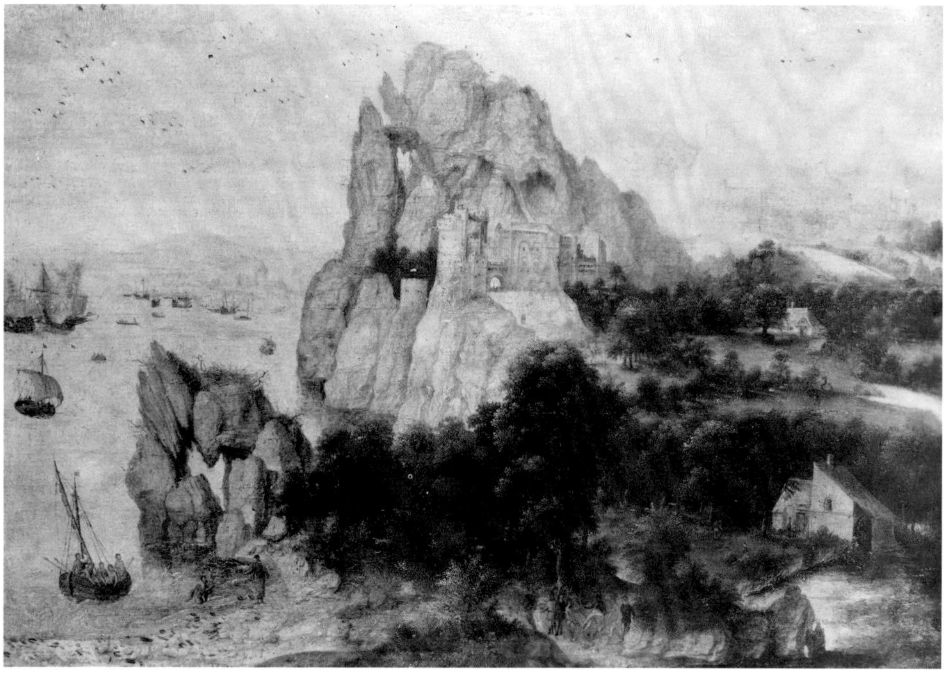

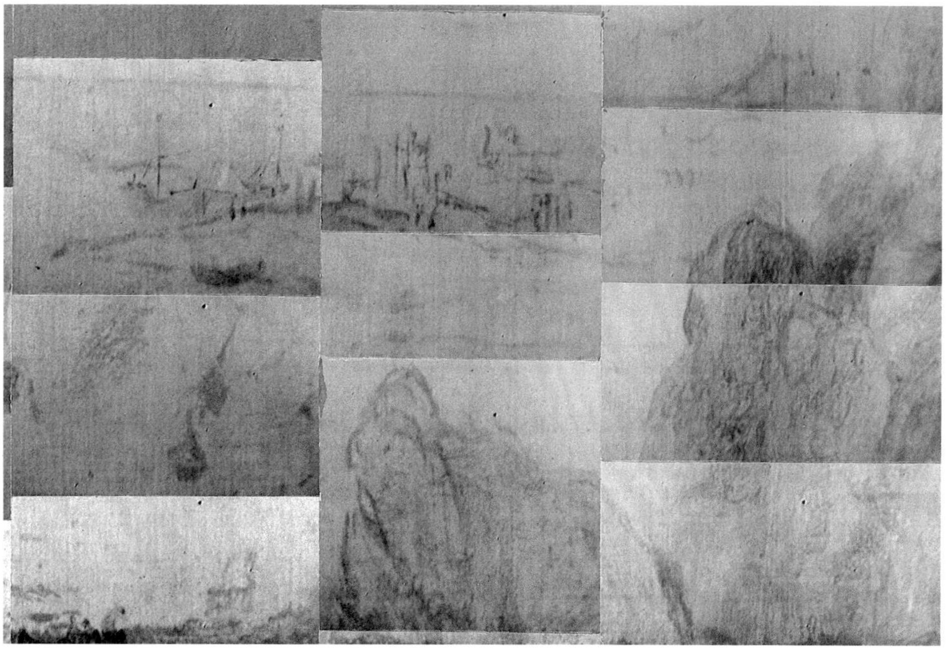

a. Herry met de Bles, St Peter on the waters
Panel; 27 x 36 cm
Naples, Museo de Capidamonte, inv. no. 84484.

b. Infrared reflectogram assembly. Detail of the harbour.

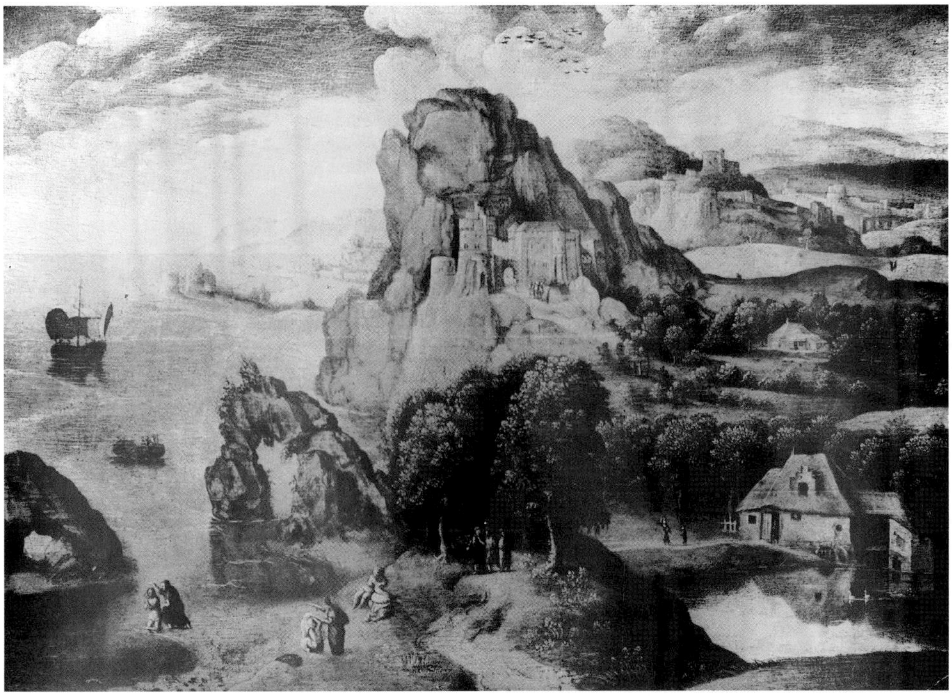

c. Anonymous, Landscape with the Baptism of Christ and the Journey to Emmaus
Panel; 35 x 49.5 cm
The photograph shows the work before restoration.
S. Hartveld Gallery, Antwerp, before 1938; Brienner Galerie Lodi, Munich, in 1965.

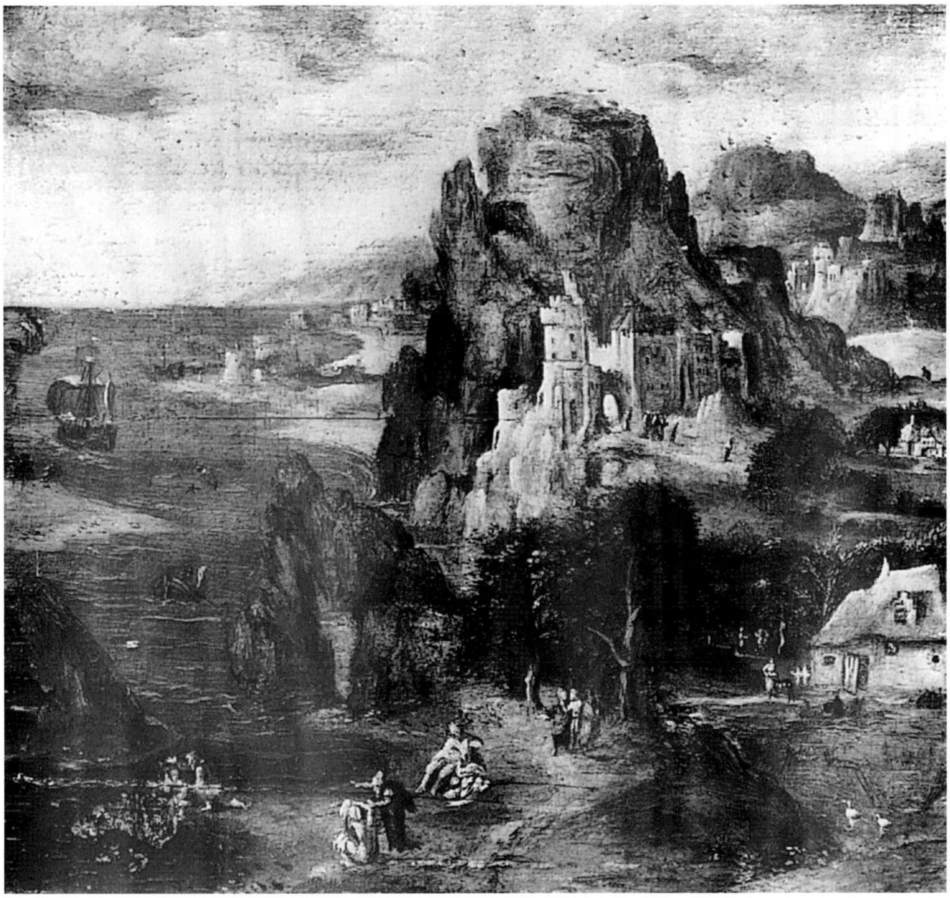

d. Anonymous, Landscape with the baptism of Christ and the journey to Emmaus
Panel; 35 x 56 cm
Rome, Galleria Borghese, inv. no. 202.

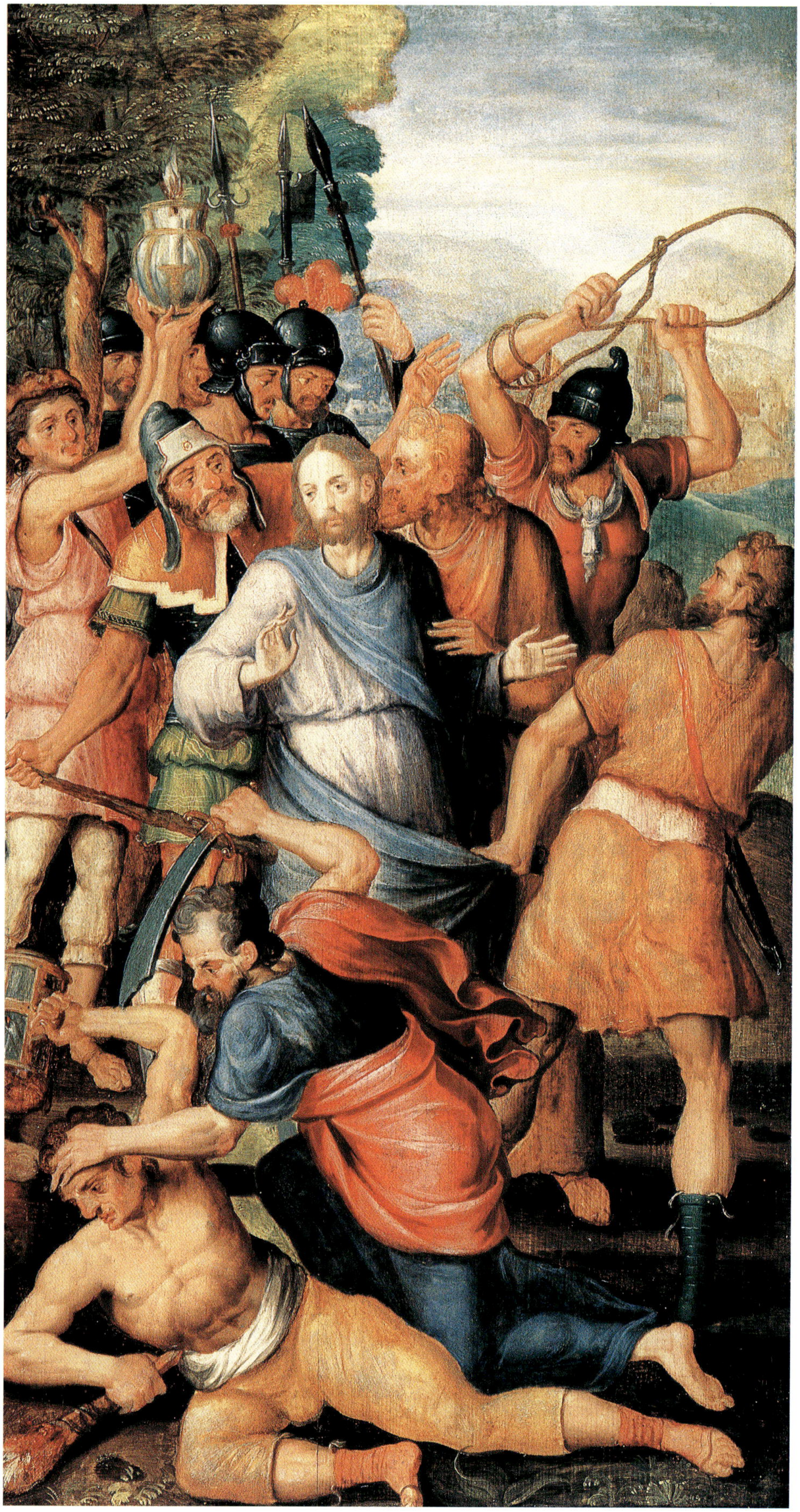

The betrayal of Christ
Reverse: Two priests and a youth by an altar

Lambert Lombard, circle of
(Liège 1505/1506-Liège 1566)

Panel; *79.5 x 42.5* cm

The two panels (cat. nos. 80 and 81), which are also painted on the reverse, were originally part of a larger work.

The first depicts the *Betrayal of Christ* by soldiers and servants of the high priests and Pharisees in the garden of Gethsemane. Judas had said he would embrace Jesus so they would know which person to seize. They carried torches, lanterns and weapons. The Apostle Peter, keeping watch with Jesus, severed the ear of a high priest's slave. The painting shows the moment of Judas' betrayal. In the foreground Peter raises his sword to sever the ear.

The reverse shows two priests kneeling by an altar. The priest on the right is swinging an incense burner. Behind the other priest stands a youth carrying the papal tiara. At the back of the altar hangs a painting of the sacrifice of Ahraham and Isaac, an episode in the scriptures which was traditionally regarded as a prefiguration of the Crucifixion. Both priests look to the right. Their gaze seems to be fixed on something outside the picture, suggesting that there was originally a second panel forming a continuation of the scene. It probably depicted St Gregory, with Christ and the instruments of the Passion above the altar. It would thus represent *St Gregory's mass*, in which he prayed for a sign that would convert an unbeliever. Christ appeared, surrounded by the instruments of the Passion. The story was very popular in the fifteenth and sixteenth centuries and was often painted on the reverse of retables.[2] The two priests may be the donors. The tiara held by the youth is probably that of St Gregory.[3]

Physical characteristics: the panel consists of two vertical planks. The *barbe* is present along all edges.

Infrared reflectography:[1] detailed underdrawing in black chalk.

Provenance: J.W. Frederiks, The Hague, on loan to Boymans-van Beuningen Museum, Rotterdam, since 1966; inv. no. BrF 6.

Not exhibited.

Unpublished.

1 *The betrayal of Christ* was scanned on 20 December 1993 and partly recorded on 17 January 1994 by J.R.J. van Asperen de Boer. The infrared reflectogram assembly was made by Joris Dik. Infrared reflectograms: AB 1558/28A-AB 1559/14A

2 See exhib. cat. *Antwerpse retabels, 15de-16de eeuw*, Antwerp, Cathedral, 1993, nos. 4, 6, 9. See also H.J. de Smedt, "De Antwerpse retabels en hun iconografie: een overzicht van de onderwerpen en veranderingen," in H. Nieuwdorp (ed.) *Antwerpse retabels, 15de-16de eeuw, II, essays*, Antwerp 1993, p. 32.

3 The tiara is often held by someone else, such as on the reverse of Pieter Pourbus' *Triptych of the Brotherhood of St Salvator's*, Bruges, St Salvator Church Museum, and in Albrecht Dürer's woodcut of *St Gregory's mass*. On both works, see exhib. cat, *Pieter Pourbus, meester-schilder 1524-1584*, Bruges, Memling Museum (Sint-Janshospitaal), 1984, pp. 161-166.

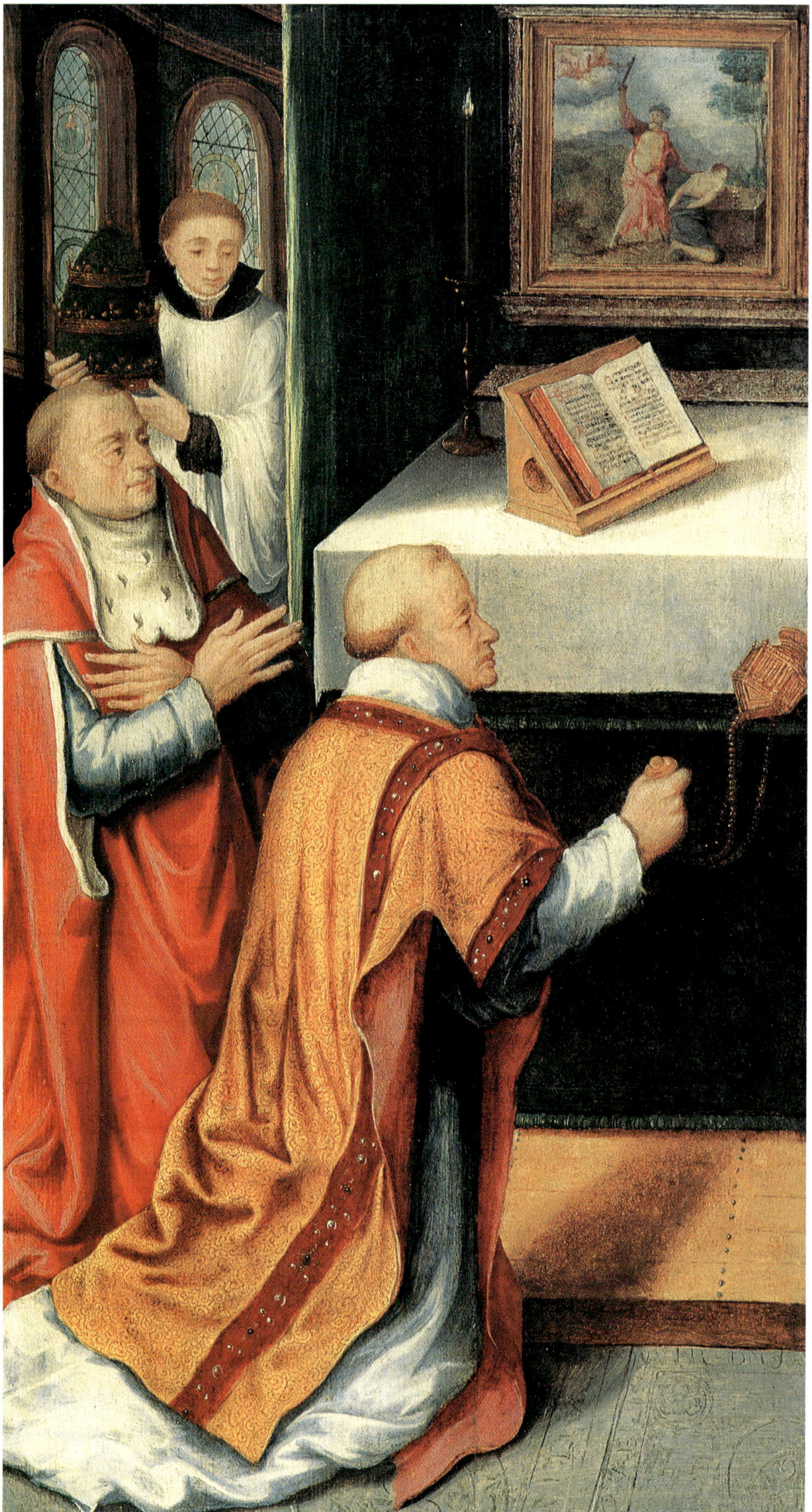

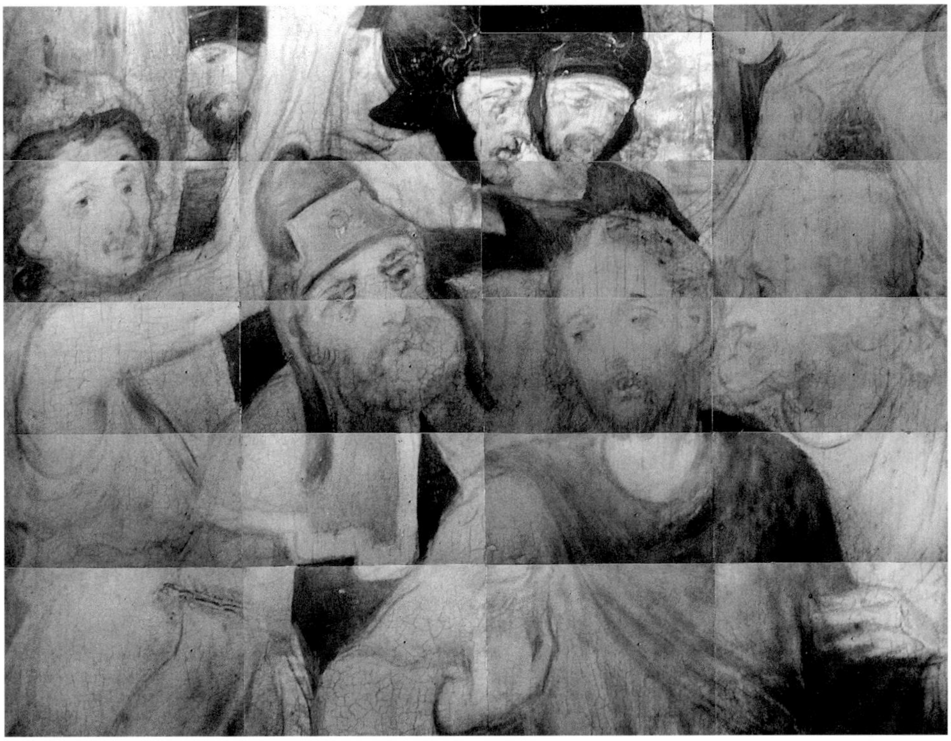

a. Infrared reflectogram assembly. Detail of the betrayal of Christ.

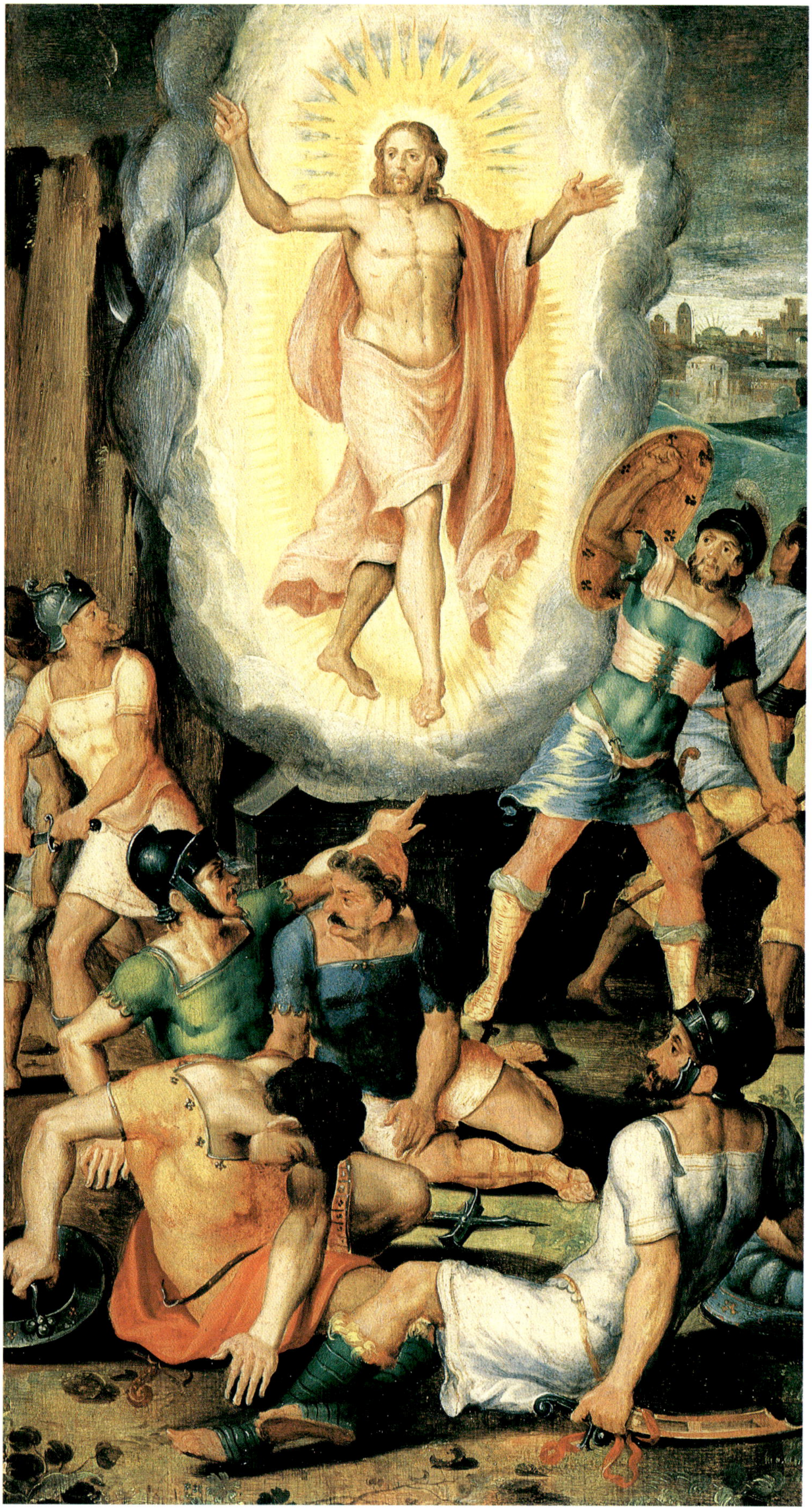

The resurrection of Christ
Reverse: St Martin with a beggar and St Clare

Lambert Lombard, circle of
(Liège 1505/1506-Liège 1566)

Panel; *79.5 x 42.5 cm*

The second panel depicts *The resurrection*. Christ, surrounded by an aureole, rises from a sarcophagus as the guards look on with awe.

The reverse of this panel shows two saints in a landscape. The saint on the left is St Martin, bishop of Tours. He was often portrayed with a crippled beggar at his feet. In this painting he deposits a few coins in the beggar's bowl. On his left stands St Clare, who was usually depicted in a grey habit and white cap covered by a black veil. The monstrans in her hand signifies her expulsion of the Saracens from Assisi. She holds a bishop's staff as the founder of her order.[4]

As noted above, the two panels must originally have been part of a polyptych, but its precise nature is uncertain. It could have been a pentaptych, with two panels on either side of the central panel. The subject was undoubtedly the Passion of Christ, centred on the Crucifixion, which was probably painted but could also have been carved. The *Betrayal of Christ* will have been at the far left, and *The resurrection* on the inside right. When the wings were closed, the two central panels showed *St Gregory's mass*, flanked on the right by *St Martin and St Clare*, and on the left presumably by two other saints. Such a combination of themes was common on sixteenth-century retables with a carved central panel and painted wings.[5]

When they came to the Museum on loan, the two panels were thought to derive from the Utrecht school. In 1967 Ms Van Gelder-Jost suggested their attribution to Pieter Pourbus.[6] Despite some similarities with this artist's work, they cannot however be identified with him.[7] In technical terms, they are definitely too weak to be associated with the Bruges master.

Physical characteristics: the panel consists of two vertical planks. The *barbe* can be seen along all edges.

Provenance: J.W. Frederiks, The Hague, on loan to Boymans-van Beuningen Museum, Rotterdam, since 1966; inv.no. BrF 7.

Not exhibited.

Unpublished.

4 On the iconography of these two saints, see I.M. Veldman and L.D. Couprie (eds.) *Hall's iconografische Handboek*, Leiden 1992, pp. 66, 231-232.
5 See note 2. The themes of retables show little variation, though their sequence is often different.
6 Letter dated 10 March 1967 in the Museum's file on the panels.
7 Cf. the Pourbus *Resurrection* in Belfort, Musée de Belfort, and that in the Groeninge Museum, Bruges. See exhib. cat. *Pieter Pourbus, meester-schilder 1524-1584*, Bruges, Memling Museum (Sint-Janshospitaal), 1984, pp. 46, 183.
8 See G. Marlier, "Lambert Lombard et les tapisseries de Raphael," in *Miscellanea Jozef Duverger*, Ghent 1968, fig. 1; and G. Denhaene, *Lambert Lombard*, Antwerp 1990.
9 The three paintings are the *Baptism of Christ*, *Christ healing the lame man* and the *Resurrection*, all measuring 117 x 71 cm. *The resurrection* is signed and dated "I. Robionoi fecit a 1560". They are in the Musèe des Beaux-Arts, Verviers. *Christ healing the lame man* can be traced back to a drawing by Lombard in the Metropolitan Museum, New York. See Denhaene, *op. cit.* (note 8), pp. 229, 234.
10 Quite a number of works similar to the *Resurrection* and *The betrayal* were painted in the second half of the sixteenth century. On the *Resurrection* see, for example, D. de Vos, *Stedelijke Musea Brugge. Catalogus schilderijen 15de en 16de eeuw*, 1979, pp. 70-71. *The betrayal* appears to be modelled primarily on works by Albrecht Dürer.
11 D. Lampsonius, biography of Lombard written in 1565. Quoted in exhib. cat., *Lambert Lombard et son temps*, Liège, Musée de l'Art Wallon, 1966, p. 53.

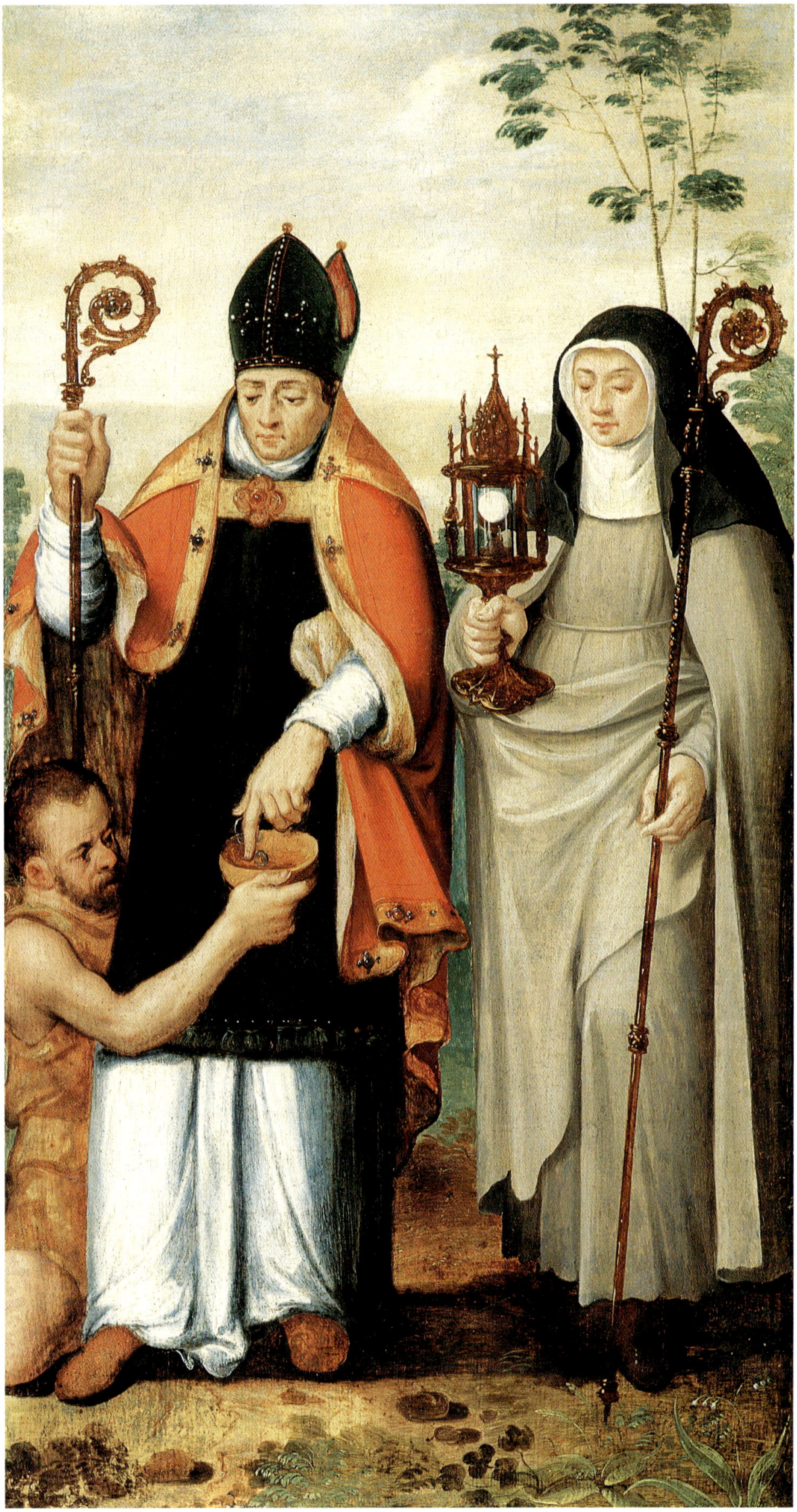

Their origin is more likely to be the circle of Lambert Lombard. The *Betrayal of Christ* is remarkably similar in some respects to a painting of the same subject in the Saint Denis Church, Liège, which derives from his circle.[8] Moreover, details of the Rotterdam panel, such as the weaponry and the man holding aloft a torch pot, have their origins in classical antiquity, and Lombard and his pupils were deeply interested in classical elements of this kind.

A virtually identical *Resurrection* was painted by the unknown artist Jean de Robionoy (fig. b). It is part of a series of three, of which one, *Jesus healing the lame man*, is based on a drawing by Lombard.[9] Given the style, it is conceivable that the two other works in De Robionoy's series were also based on this artist's work, so that the same could apply in respect of the Museum's two panels.[10] Lombard is known to have made his drawings available to "artists less gifted than he on the points of invention and drawing".[11] The painting style being somewhat different from that of the work attributed to Lombard and his studio, the Rotterdam panels are however more likely to be the work of a follower. Some corrections were perceived in the underdrawing of the *Betrayal*, the right arm of the soldier holding the rope, for instance, being drawn in several different ways. The underdrawing appears to have been reproduced in paint without further alteration.

The two panels probably date from around 1560, the year on one of the paintings by De Robionoy referred to above.
FL

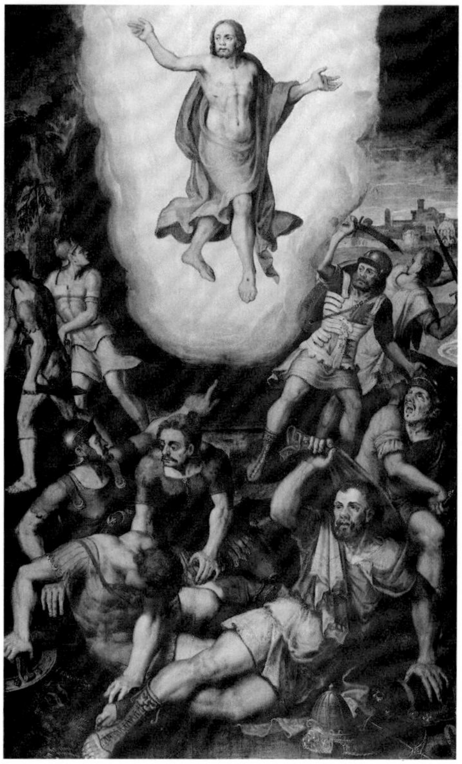

b. Jean de Robionoy, The resurrection, 1560
Panel; 117 x 71 cm
Verviers, Musée des Beaux-Arts.

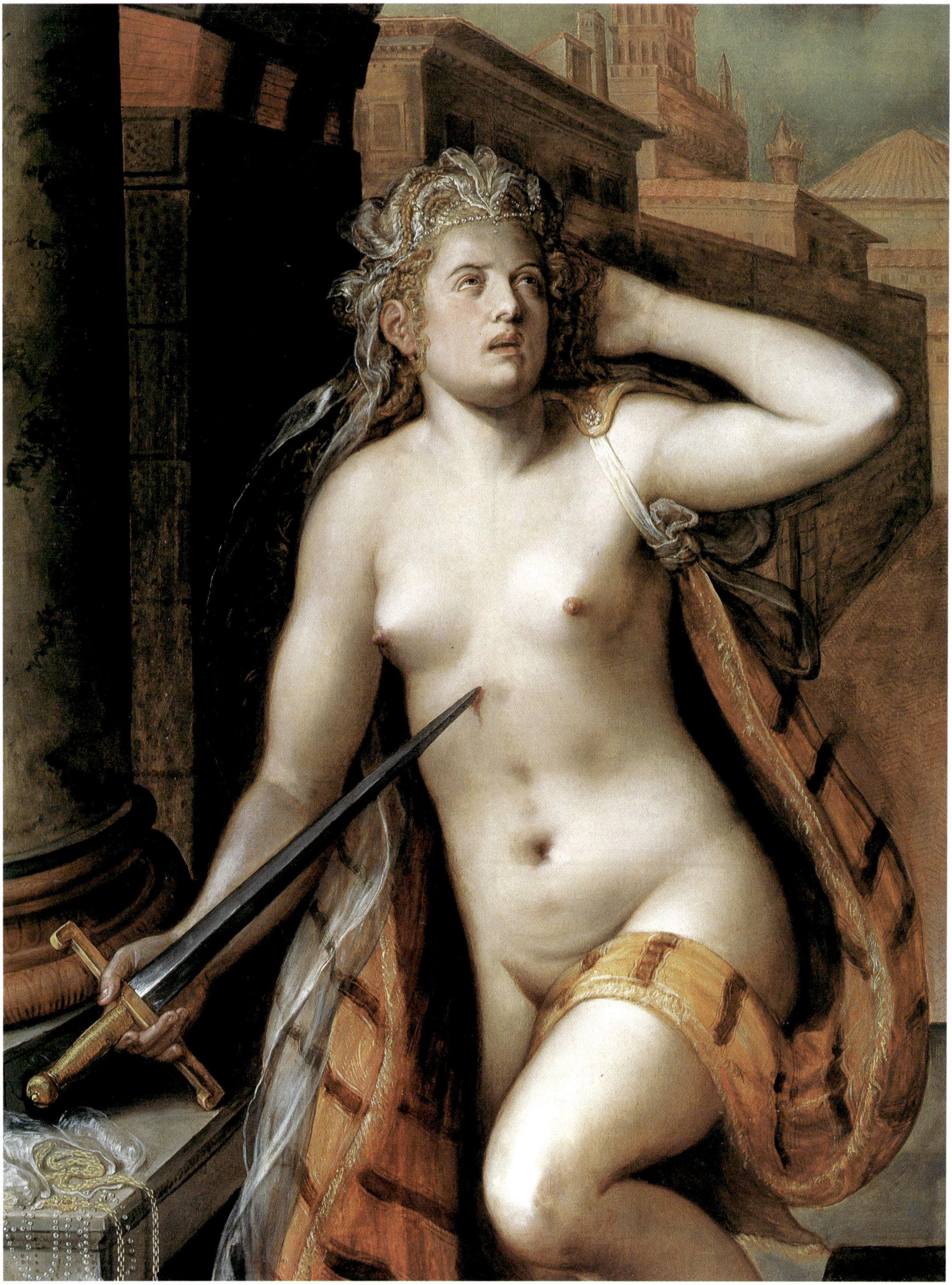

Death of Lucretia

Frans Floris
(Antwerp 1519/20-Antwerp 1570)

Panel; 125 x 94 cm

In Roman legend, Lucretia was the wife of Tarquinius Collatinus. She was dishonoured by Sextus, the son of the king Tarquinius Superbus. Next morning, having avowed her dishonour in the presence of her family, she stabbed herself. The legend was related by Ovid and others.[6]

The tale of Lucretia was a favourite theme of artists. She is almost always depicted nude. Frans Floris was one of the first northern painters to adopt the Italianate nude figure as the principal subject of a work.

The inventory of the art dealer Herman de Neyt (1588-1642) lists a Lucretia by Floris, but whether it is the Rotterdam panel is uncertain. The painting auctioned at Rotterdam in 1875 could be our painting, even though it was described as from "the Italian School of the seventeenth century".

Donated to the Museum in 1880, it was listed in the 1883 catalogue as a work by Frans Floris, an attribution subsequently universally accepted.

Van de Velde refers to a drawing in the Louvre, Paris, with four studies for the *Death of Lucretia* which could be preliminary studies for the painting (fig. a).[7] He also notes a resemblance between the drawings and the painting and a print by Marcantonio Raimondi, though the resemblance is not very marked.[8] In addition, he points to a sketch in oils of the head of a woman which in 1930 was in the S. Hartveld Collection, Antwerp, and which could be a study for the painting (fig. b).[9] A second such sketch in the Musée des Beaux-Arts in Quimper (fig. c)[10] appears to have served the same purpose.

Opinions differ on the dating of the panel. Zuntz puts it around 1555; Van de Velde considers this to be too early, preferring a date around 1565. If this is correct, it is a fairly late work by the artist.
JG

Physical characteristics: the panel consists of four vertical planks.

Infrared reflectography:[1] no underdrawing could be discerned.

Provenance: possibly Herman de Neyt (Antwerp 12 March 1588-Delft 8 September 1642);[2] possibly Johannes de Renialme, Amsterdam, (d. 1657)[3]: not in the Dufresne auction, 1770;[4] possibly Lamme auction, Rotterdam, 31 May-2 June 1875, no. 11;[5] donated by J.A. Nahuys, 1880; inv. no. 1940.

Not exhibited.

Literature: *Beschrijving der schilderijen en beeldhouwwerken in het Museum te Rotterdam, gesticht door F.J.O. Boymans*, Rotterdam 1883, no. 364; D. Zuntz, *Frans Floris, ein Beitrag zur Geschichte der Niederländischen Kunst im XVI. Jahrhunderts*, Strasbourg 1929, pp. 46-47, 68, 101; Friedländer, XIII, 1936, p. 154, no. 149; W. Sumowski, "Zwei Werke der Floris-Schule im Stralsunder Museum", *Oud-Holland* 74 (1959), p. 109; cat. 1962, p. 51; C. van de Velde, *Frans Floris (1519/20-1570), Leven en Werken*, Brussels 1975, no. 183, fig. 96; Friedländer, XIII, 1975, p. 86, no. 149, fig. 77; J. Foucart in exhib. cat. *Tableaux Flamands et Hollandais du Musée des Beaux-Arts de Quimper*, Paris, Institut Néerlandais, Quimper, Musée des Beaux-Arts, 1987, no. 15; E. Duverger, "Aantekeningen betreffende de Antwerpse schilder en kunsthandelaar Herman de Neyt (1588-1642)", *De zeventiende eeuw* 6 (1990), p. 72.

1 Partly scanned by J.R.J. van Asperen de Boer on 10 January 1994.
2 According to Duverger (1990), p. 72. See J. Denucé, *De Antwerpsche "konstkamers," inventarissen en kunstverzamelingen te Antwerpen in the 16e en 17e eeuwen*, Amsterdam 1932, p. 97: "Een Lucretia van Floris, op een acht stuyvers maet, get. no. 537" (A Lucretia by Floris, eight stuyvers size, marked no. 537).

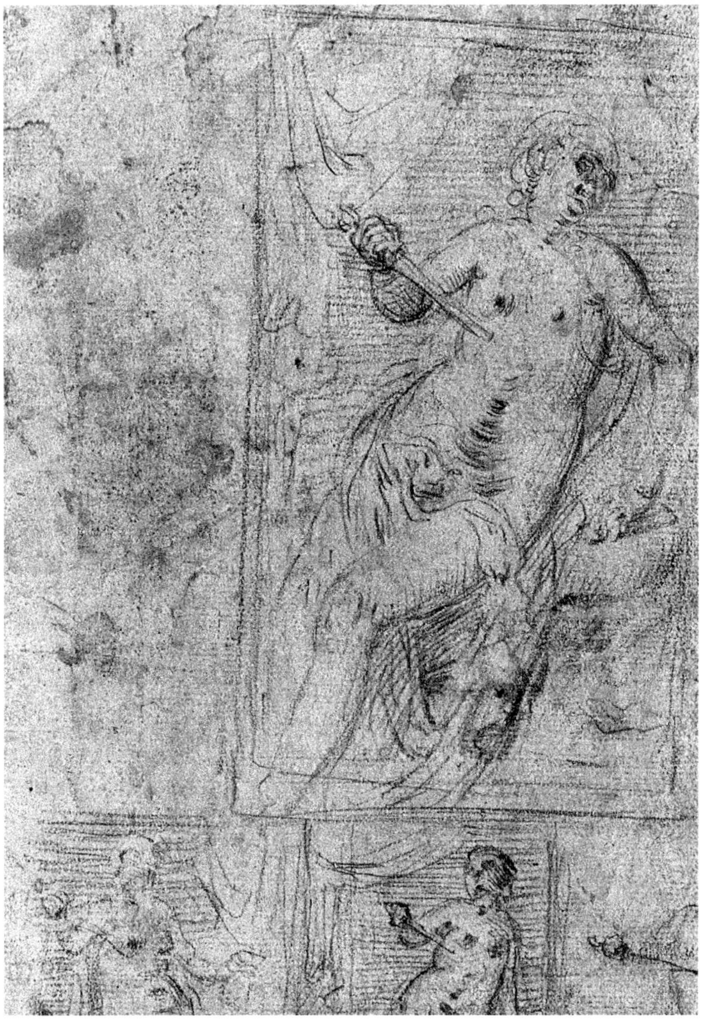

a. Frans Floris, Studies for the Death of Lucretia
Chalk; 22.5 x 16 cm
Paris, Cabinet des dessins du Musée du Louvre

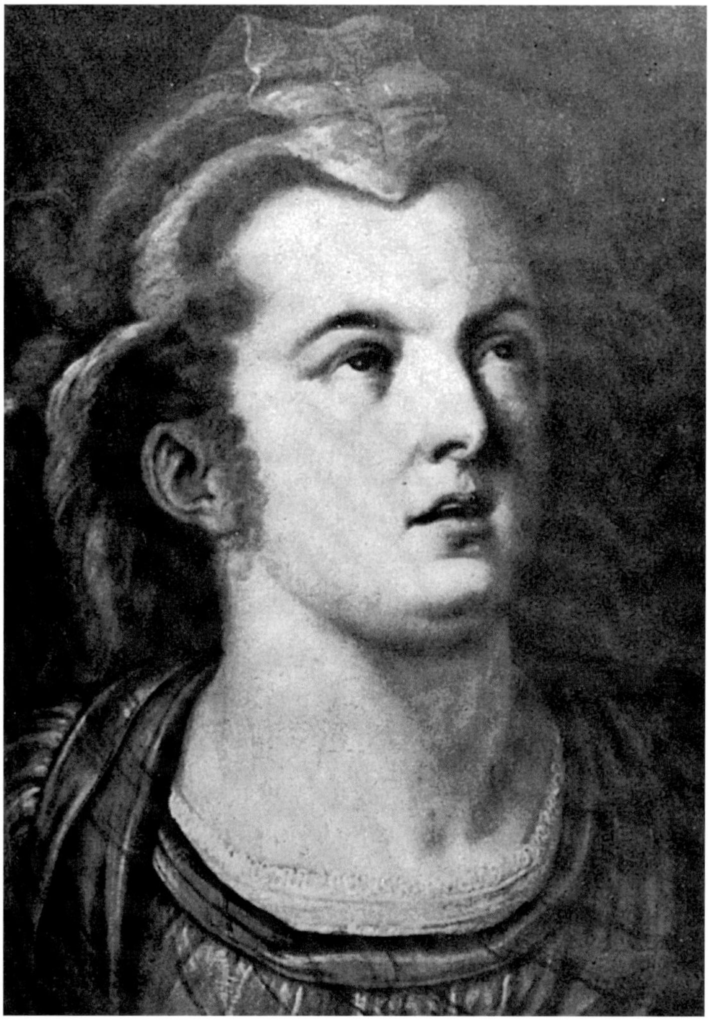

b. Frans Floris, Head of a woman
Panel; measurements unknown
Whereabouts unknown (in 1930 in the S. Hartveld Collection, Antwerp)

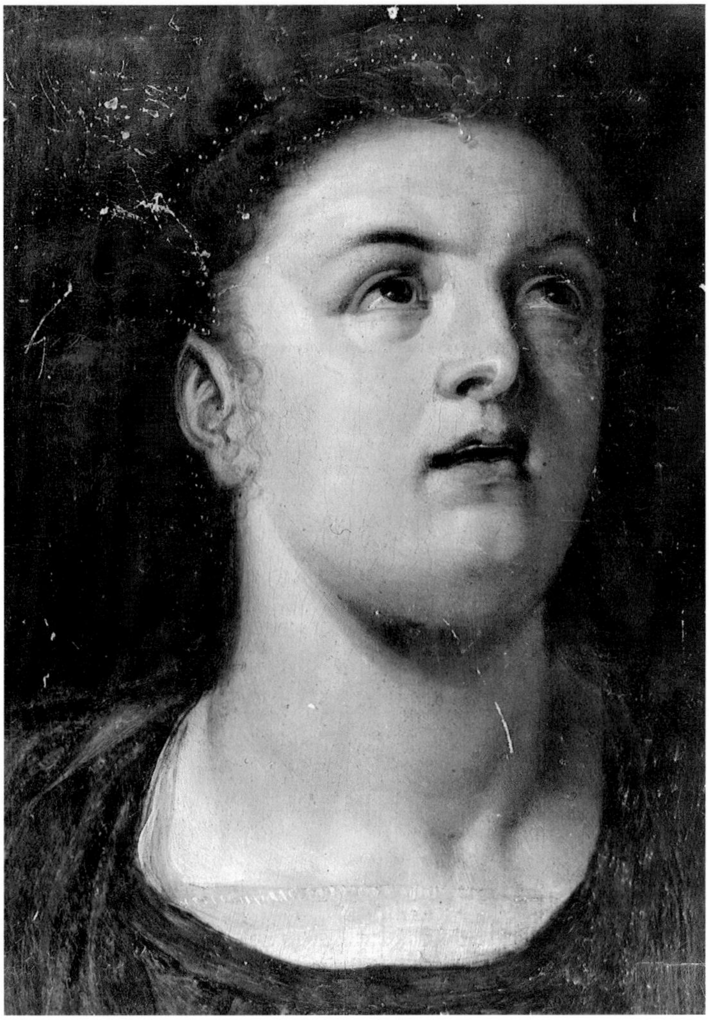

c. Frans Floris, Head of a woman
Panel; 44 x 31.5 cm
Quimper, Musée des Beaux-Arts

3 Zuntz (1929), p. 46, mentioned the inventory of art dealer De Renialme. In her view, it was not certain that this painting was the *Lucretia* it listed. She referred to A. Bredius, *Künstlerinventare* I, 1915, p. 235, no. 240: "A Lucretia by Frans Floris 300 guilders".

4 It has invariably been stated that the painting was in the F.I. Dufresne auction, Amsterdam, 22 August 1770, no. 9. But this was a work by Guido Reni, "Lucretia, height 89, width 62 inch; it is greater than life-size; she is on her knees and about to thrust the dagger into herself. Very fine and accurate drawing and pure of colour, painted on *linen*" ("Lucretia, Hoog 89, Breed 62 duim; Dezelve is meer dan Levensgrootte verbeeld. Zy is rustende op haar knien en als gereed om zich met een Dolk te doorsteeken. Zeer schoon en juist van Tekening en helder van Coloriet, op *Doek* geschildert."

5 As "Ecole Italienne du 17e Siècle. Lucresce. Bois. Haut 125 cent. Larg. 93 cent".

6 Ovid, *Fasti*, II, verses 831 ff.

7 Van de Velde (1975), no. T 53, verso, fig. 152; F. Lugt, *Musée du Louvre, Inventaire Général des dessins des écoles du nord*, Paris 1968, no. 305.

8 For the print, see *The Illustrated Bartsch*, 26 (previously 14, 1), New York 1978, p. 188, no. 192-1(155).

9 Van de Velde (1975), no. 182, fig. 95.

10 See Foucart (1987).

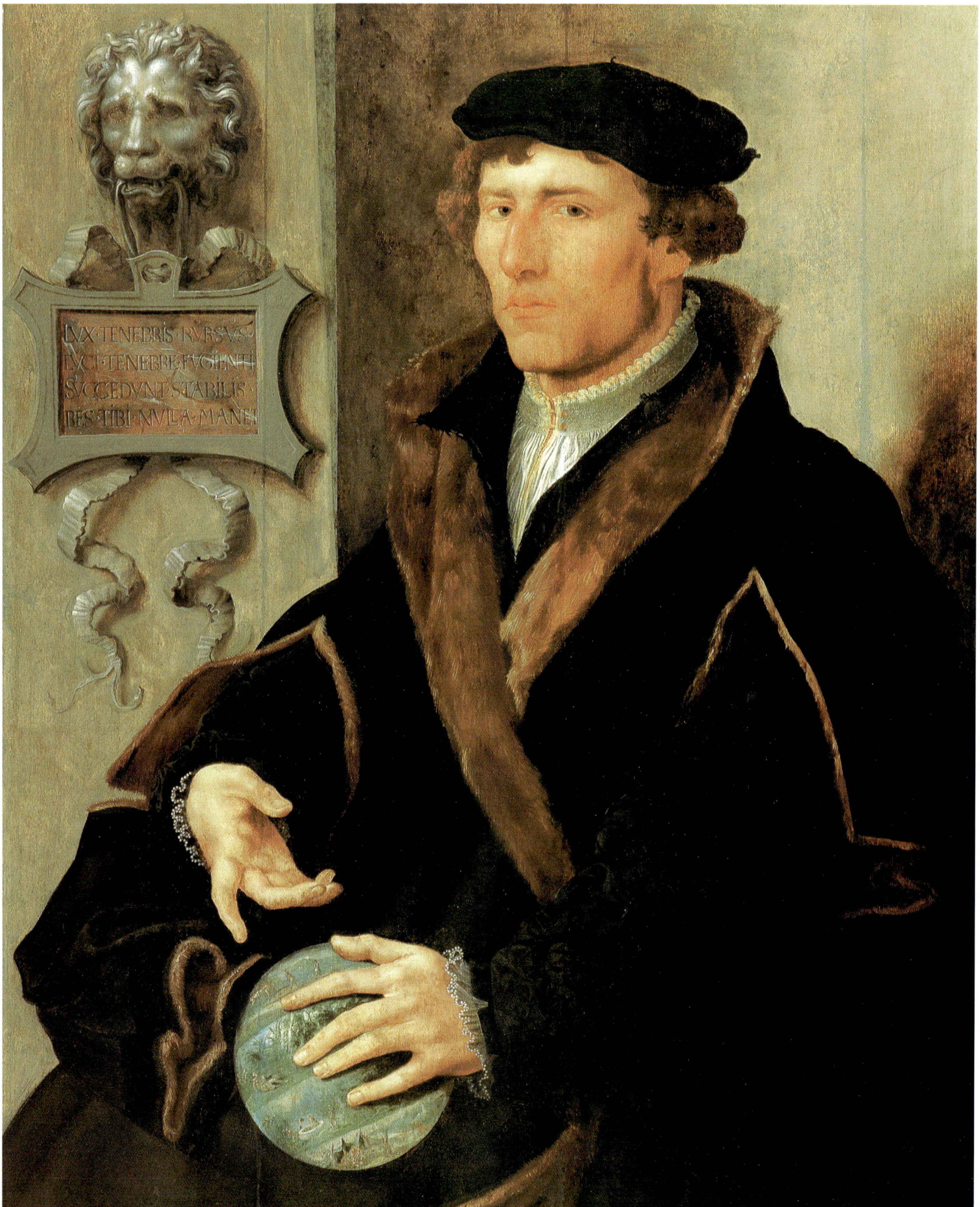
LVX·TENEBRIS·RVRSVS·
LVCI·TENEBRE·FVGIENTI
SVCCEDVNT·STABILIS·
RES·TIBI·NVLA·MANET

Portrait of Reinerus Frisius Gemma

Maerten van Heemskerck
(Heemskerk 1498-Haarlem 1574)

Panel; 104 x 83.5 cm
Inscription on the cartouche, left: lux.tenebris.rursus/luci.tenebre. fugienti./succedunt.stabilis./res.tibi.nulla.manet.

Scholars have long been puzzled not only by the identity of the painter of this portrait but also by that of his subject. Passavant and Waagen described it as a portrait of Luther painted by Holbein. Woltman argued that the sitter was not Luther at all, and that the artist was in any event Georg Pencz. Scheibler and Bode, on the other hand, gave the attribution to Jan van Scorel.[3] The portrait was published in the *Art Journal* of 1897 as a work by Joos van Cleve, and was subsequently listed as such in the 1909 catalogue of the Earl of Radnor's collection. The present attribution to Heemskerck was first proposed by Winkler in 1924 and has never been challenged since. Today the work is widely regarded as one of Heemskerck's finest portraits, dating from 1540-45.

A life-size, relatively young man gazes out at the observer, impressive in his elegant fur coat and beret-like hat. His right hand draws our attention to the sphere on his lap, which he holds in place with his left hand. The sphere is divided into horizontal bands representing the four seasons. Spring, the top band, is signified by a peasant ploughing a field and another sowing seed; the second band, summer, is a figure, probably a woman, lying under tall trees; autumn is symbolised by harvesters gathering fruit and tossing it into a bowl, and winter is a scene of figures around a campfire with tents nearby. A sturdy lion's head holds a large cartouche in the top left hand corner, with two ribbons curling down. The Latin inscription means: "Light moves in darkness, darkness follows upon the fleeting light; nothing shall you find enduring". E. Gombrich was unable to trace any record of the quotation, but associated it with the writings of Ovid and Lucretius.[4] Grosshans discovered several comparable texts by Catullus and other authors.[5] Bruyn suggested that it might be an extremely free interpretation of a passage from the Book of Job (17:12).[6]

Nothing was known about the identity of the sitter until J. Roegiers, senior librarian at the Catholic University of Louvain, recently recognised him as Gemma Frisius,[7] and referred to A. de Smet's comprehensive biography.[8] Gemma was born in Dokkum on 8 December 1508, and died in Louvain on 25 May 1555. A distinguished astronomer and astrologer, he was also professor of mathematics and medicine at the university of Louvain, a designer of globes and mathematical instruments, and the author of several treatises on geography and mathematics. His portrait was engraved by various artists including Jan van Stalburch (active in Louvain 1555/1562). An inscription on the print reveals that the engraving was made in Louvain in 1557, two years after Gemma's death (fig. a). When seen in reverse, as it is reproduced here, Van Stalburch's print is remarkably similar to the painting.[9] Both show Gemma in a fur-lined gown with wide openings for the arms, and a flat, beret-like hat. He is viewed from roughly the same angle. In the engraving, however, he is holding a globe in both hands whereas the painter has him pointing to a sphere illustrating the four seasons. The cartouche containing a Latin inscription is in the same place in both works.

At the age of six Gemma suffered a crippling disease which left him in poor health for the rest of his life. He spent his youth in Groningen before moving to Louvain, where he enrolled at the university in 1526. He wrote several books and formed a friendship with Joannes Dantiscus (1485-1548), an emissary of the king of Poland. Gemma was the first

Physical characteristics: the panel consists of four vertical planks.

Infrared reflectography:[1] no underdrawing could be discerned.

Provenance: Earl of Radnor, Longford Castle, at least after 1814; Agnew Gallery, London; acquired by D.G. van Beuningen, Rotterdam and Vierhouten, in 1936 for £1,000; donated to the Museum by the Rembrandt Foundation and D.G. van Beuningen;[2] inv. no. 1347.

Exhibitions: *Jeroen Bosch Noord-Nederlandsche primitieven*, Rotterdam, Boymans Museum, 1936, no. 122, fig. 148; *La peinture Hollandaise de Jérôme Bosch à Rembrandt*, Brussels, Palais des Beaux-Arts, 1946, no. 13; *De triomf van het Maniërisme*, Amsterdam, Rijksmuseum, 1955, no. 63.

Literature: J.D. Passavant, *Kunstreise durch England und Belgien*, Frankfurt 1833, p. 136; J.D. Passavant, *Tour of a German artist in England*, I, 1836, p. 294; G.F. Waagen, *Kunstwerke und Künstler in England*, II, Berlin 1838, p. 265; Dr Waagen, *Treasures of art in Great Britain*, III, London 1854, p. 139; G.F. Waagen, *Galleries and cabinets of art in Great Britain*, London 1857, p. 360; A. Woltmann, "Holbein und Quentin Massys in Longford Castle", *Zeitschrift für Bildende Kunst* I (1866), p. 201; L. Scheibler, W. Bode, "Verzeichniss der Gemälde des Jan van Scorel", *Jahrbuch der Königlich Preussischen Kunstsammlungen* II (1881), p. 213; C.P., *Art Journal*, 1897, p. 104; Helen Matilda, Countess of Radnor, William Barclay Squire, *Catalogue of the pictures in the collection of the Earl of Radnor*, London 1909, no. 145; F. Winkler, *Die Altniederländische Malerei*, Berlin 1924, p. 288; A.B. de Vries, *Het Noord-Nederlandsch portret in de tweede helft van de 16de eeuw*, Amsterdam 1934, pp. 27, 125; Friedländer, XIII, 1936, pp. 82, 160, no. 228, fig. XLIII; *Museum Boymans Rotterdam Catalogus 1937*, no. 187; G.J. Hoogewerff, *De Noord-Nederlandsche Schilderkunst*, IV, The Hague 1941-42, pp. 356-358, fig. 168; G.J. Hoogewerff, *De Noord-Nederlandsche Schilderkunst*, V, 1947, p. 159, no. 72; cat. 1962, p. 63; *Agnew's 1817-1967*, London 1967, fig.; B. Haak, "De vergankelijkheidssymboliek in 16e eeuwse portretten en 17de eeuwse stillevens in Holland", *Antiek* 1 (1967), pp. 28-30, fig. 6; G. von der Osten, H. Vey, *Painting and sculpture in Germany and the Netherlands 1500-1600*, Harmondsworth 1969, p. 186; G. von der Osten, *Deutsche und Niederländische Kunst der Reformationszeit*, Keulen

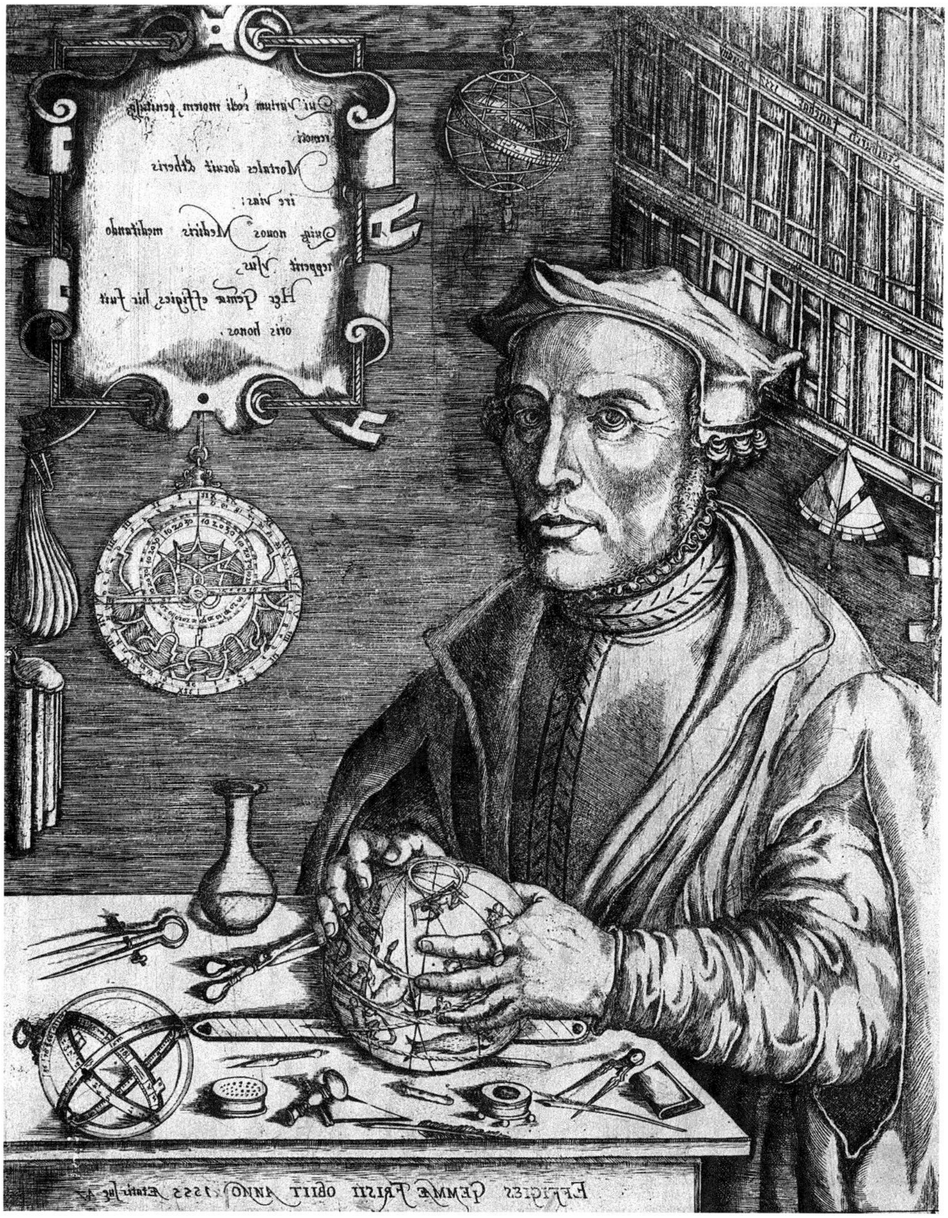

a. Jan van Stalburch, Portrait of Gemma Frisius
Engraving
Rotterdam, Maritiem Museum "Prins Hendrik"
Reproduced in reverse

scholar in the Netherlands to display an interest in the theories of the Polish astronomer Nicolaus Copernicus (1473-1543). He designed two globes, the second in collaboration with his pupil Gerard Mercator and several other colleagues. Gemma was acquainted with the most illustrious scholars of his day. Now that the identity of the sitter is known, the sphere and its representation of the four seasons takes on a different meaning. The seasons of course, like the Latin inscription, allude to the swift passage of time, but the shape of the sphere also resembles the globes Gemma made, as can be seen in Stalburch's print. It therefore seems likely that the sphere was intended to proclaim that Gemma was a man of learning.

It is difficult to imagine why this monumental portrait of a Louvain scholar should have been painted by an artist from Haarlem. We can in any event conclude that it was considered too important to entrust to a local master. J. Roegiers has suggested that the eminent Dantiscus may have commissioned the work to commemorate one of the leading scholars of his day.
JG

1973, p. 189; Friedländer, XIII, 1975, pp. 45, 92, no. 228, fig. pl. 116; R. Grosshans, *Maerten van Heemskerck, Die Gemälde*, Berlin 1980, pp. 64, no. 38, Table IV, fig. 59; J. Bruyn, "Oude en nieuwe elementen in de 16de-eeuwse voorstellingswereld", *Bulletin van het Rijksmuseum* 35 (1987), p. 152, fig. 16; J. Bruyn, "Old and new elements in 16th-century imagery", *Oud Holland* 102 (1988), pp. 104, fig. 16; J.C. Harrison, *The paintings of Maerten van Heemskerck. A catalogue raisonné*, 1987 (UMI 1991), no. 33.

1 The painting was scanned by J.R.J. van Asperen de Boer on 10 January 1994.
2 A note under the year 1936 in D.G. van Beuningen's purchases ledger reads: "Maarten v. Heemskerk Agnew £ 1000 portret Boymans gegeven", indicating that D.G. van Beuningen presented the painting to the Museum. According to the annual report, however, it was also a gift from the Rembrandt Foundation.
3 Passavant (1836 and 1839), Waagen (1838, 1854, 1857), Woltmann (1866), Scheibler, Bode (1881).
4 Letter to the Museum, 17 November 1948.
5 Grosshans (1980).
6 Bruyn (1987, 1988).
7 The author wishes to thank Ms Elly Bos, curator at the Prins Hendrik Maritime Museum in Rotterdam, for her help in obtaining further information and for the photograph of the print by Stalburch.
8 A. de Smet, "Gemma Frisius", in *National biografisch woordenboek* 6, Brussels 1974, pp. 315-331.
9 Hollstein, 28, p. 43, no. 17.

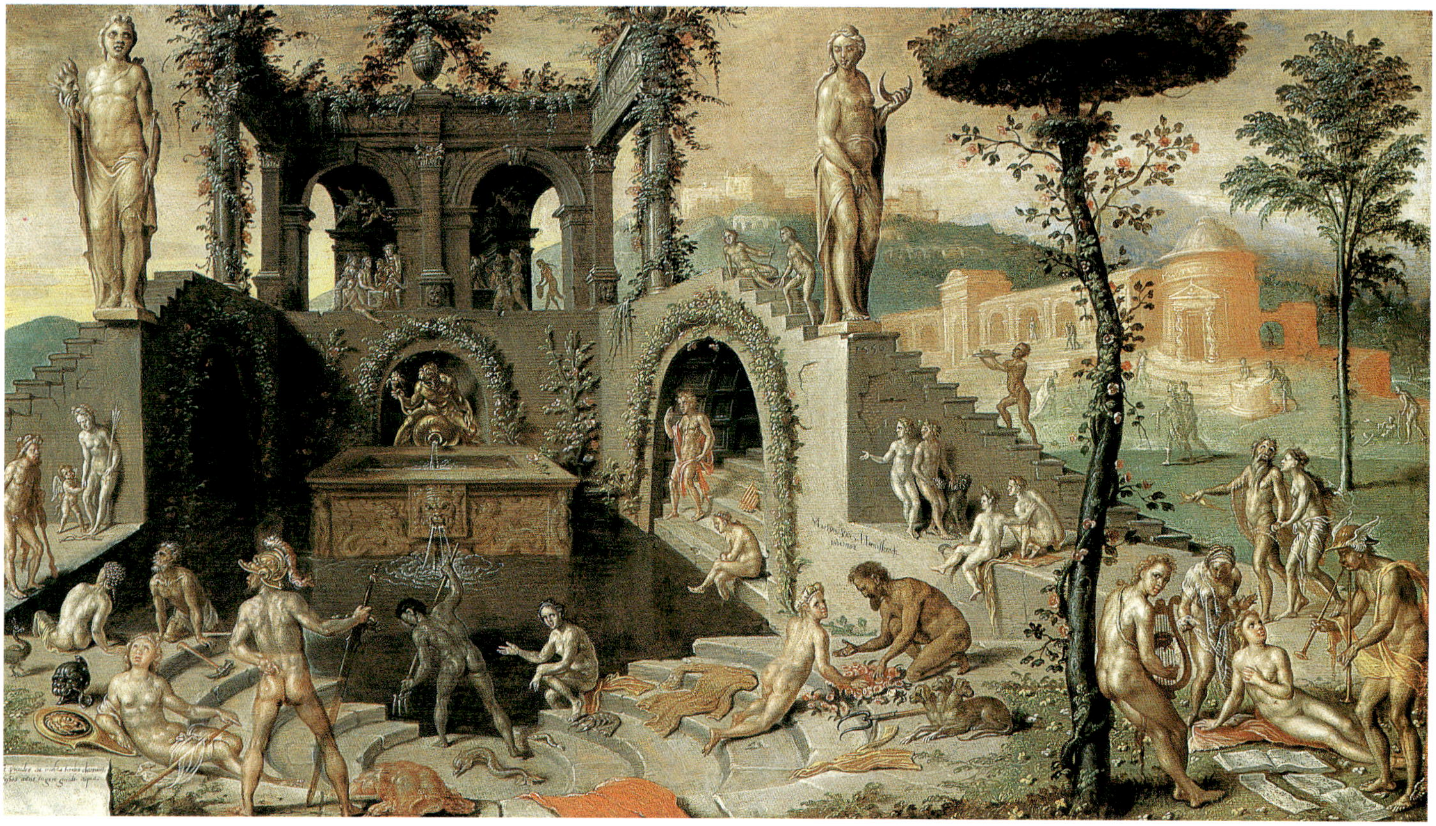

The gods of Olympus

Maerten van Heemskerck
(Heemskerk 1498-Haarlem 1574)

Panel; 56 x 98 cm
Signed and dated: Martyn Van.Heemskerck. / inventor / 1556.

In 1978 the Erasmiaans Gymnasium presented this painting to the Boymans-van Beuningen Museum on loan.
It is a picture of gods and goddesses amusing themselves around a pool on Mount Olympus. Apollo is on the right, one buttock leaning against a tree with decorative foliage and a creeper encircling its trunk. He plays a lyre and looks out at the observer. The figure in the winged helmet, further to the right, is Mercury, playing two flutes. Between them are two muses who appear to be singing from the music books lying open on the ground. Jupiter, with lightning in his right hand strolls past behind the group, escorting a goddess on his left. Further back, at the edge of the pool, is the goddess Ceres with an ear of corn in her hair and a sickle. Her hand is resting on the back of a young boy, whom Veldman has tentatively identified as Jupiter's son Iasion. In the distance we see Bacchus leaning against a step, with vine leaves in his hair, grapes in his hand and a panther at his side. His wife Ariadne is standing near by. To the left of the tree in the foreground is Pluto with the three-headed dog Cerberus. Pluto and Proserpina are making a garland of flowers. Neptune, halfway up the staircase, is fishing with a trident. Grosshans suggests that the woman crouched beside him and pointing to him could be his wife Aphrodite.[3] On Neptune's left, and also seen from the back, is the helmeted Mars holding a sword. The woman with the lance directly in front of him is Minerva. Behind Minerva, Vulcan with his hammer emerges from the water. Juno with her peacock is seated at the edge of the pool beside him. In the foreground on the far left is Hercules, with his lion skin and club. Leaning against the staircase behind him are Venus, holding an arrow in her hand, and her winged son Amor. Arches rise up on either side of the rectangular pool. Seated on the stairs of the arch on the right and trailing her foot in the water, is a goddess with a pan flute, whom Schrier identifies as Syrinx.[4] He also suggests that the man descending the stairs beside her is her partner Pan. The large statues on the staircases flanking the pool personify the sun, with a staff in the left hand and a wreath of sunbeams in the right, and the moon, holding a sickle moon in her right hand. A surprising omission from this illustrious company, as Schrier has observed, is the important goddess Diana. He suggests however that she might be represented by the large statue of the Moon, with which she is always identified. In a renaissance-style building behind the pool are ten people who appear to be banqueting. Even more figures can be seen on the stairs on the right and in the distance. They too are probably gods. There are more buildings as well, in the right-hand background and on the mountain in the distance. On a deceptively realistic sheet of crumpled paper on the left of the painting are two lines of Latin verse. The poem is a distich, consisting of one hexameter and one pentameter, which may be rendered as follows. "The Pieridic Muses, the exalted throng of gods, delight in bathing their weary limbs".[5] There is space on the paper for another two lines, but nothing more can be seen. Unfortunately it has not yet been possible to trace the verse to a classical source. Heemskerck, however, was acquainted with such Haarlem luminaries as Hadrianus Junius and Dirck Volckertsz Coornhert, who may have given him the poem.
Veldman points out that the pool is in the shape of a nymphaeum of the type used for relaxation in Roman times. Heemskerck would have seen the ruins of these pools in the course of his travels through Italy. The painting must have been ordered or bought by a Haarlem intellectual who shared Heemskerck's fascination with classical antiquity.
JG

Inscription on the cartouche, left:
Musae pierides ac inclita turba deorum.
Defessos artus tingere gaudet aqua.

Physical characteristics: the panel consists of a single plank. The left and right sides are in their original unpainted condition.

Infrared reflectography: no underdrawing could be discerned.[1]

Provenance: unknown German or Austrian collection:[2] Harald Petri (consul general of Sweden in Antwerp), sale Amsterdam, Mensing, 30 November-3 December 1926, no. 66; Dr H. Burgerhout (1870-1959), pupil at and later president-curator of the Erasmiaans Gymnasium, Rotterdam, bequeathed by him to the gymnasium; loaned to the Museum in 1978 to mark the 650th anniversary of the Erasmiaans Gymnasium; inv. no. 2964.

Not exhibited

Literature: Ilja M. Veldman, *De Olympische goden op een schilderij van Maerten van Heemskerck uit 1556*, Rotterdam, Boymans-van Beuningen Museum, 16 December 1978-28 January 1979; R. Grosshans, *Maerten van Heemskerck, Die Gemälde*, Berlin 1980, no. 83, fig. 116; Ilja M. Veldman, "De Olympische goden op een schilderij van Maerten van Heemskerck uit 1556", *Hermeneus* 52 (1980), pp. 214-222; O.J. Schrier, "Vermoeide goden op de Olympus? Over een schilderij van Maerten van Heemskerck", *Hermeneus* 53 (1981), pp. 283-288; N. van der Blom, "Ten derde male. Van Heemskerck's Olympus (1556)", *Hermeneus 55* (1983), pp. 294-296; J.C. Harrison, *The paintings of Maerten van Heemskerck. A catalogue raisonné*, II, Virginia 1987 (UMI 1991), no. 83.

1 Scanned by J.R.J. van Asperen de Boer on 10 January 1994.
2 A cutting from an auction catalogue with text in German is attached to the back of the panel.
3 Grosshans (1980).
4 Schrier (1981).
5 See Schrier (1981) on the distich.

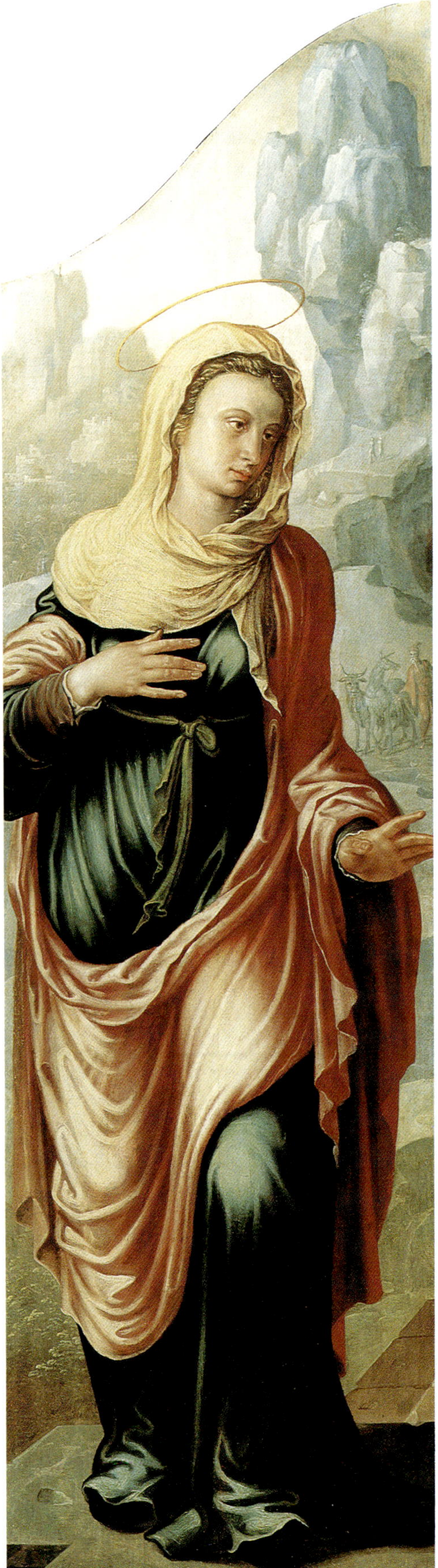

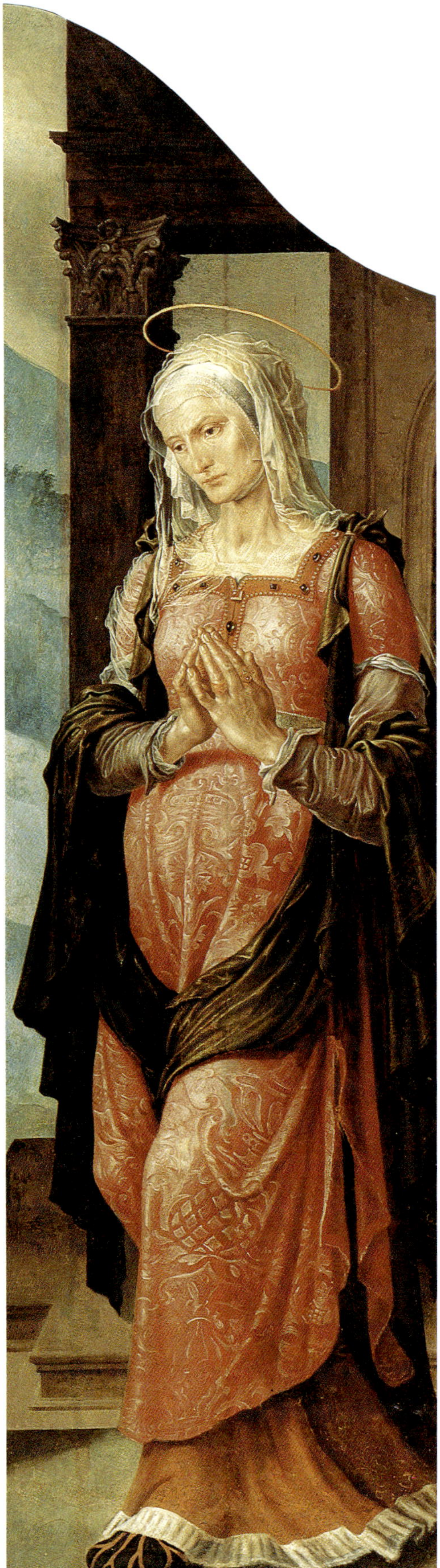

The Virgin Mary
St Elizabeth

Maerten van Heemskerck
(Heemskerk 1498-Haarlem 1574)

Panel; 175 x 50 cm
Cat. no. 86 signed on the plinth: Mae...va.../Heemskerck Inventor; dated on the stairs: 1550.

These two paintings (cat. nos. 85 and 86) were originally on the outside of the shutters of an altarpiece. When closed, the shutters formed an illustration of the Visitation. Luke 1:39-56 describes Mary's visit to her cousin Elizabeth and relates how the child that Elizabeth was carrying leapt in her womb on hearing the Virgin's greeting. This child was to be John the Baptist. The left shutter shows the Virgin with her hand over her breast. Elizabeth, on the right, is portrayed as an older woman with her hands clasped in front of her. The right-hand panel is dated 1550 and has Maerten van Heemskerck's signature on the step. Grosshans maintains that parts of the left shutter have been badly damaged by restoration and overpainting, leaving little evidence of Van Heemskerck's hand. He sees most of the harm in the area around the Virgin's face. In our view, however, there is nothing noteworthy about the condition of the paint layers. Rather, the piece simply seems to have been made by a different artist. There is a marked difference in the rendering of the complexions of the two women and in the fabric of their garments. The figure of Elizabeth is worked out in Van Heemskerck's characteristically detailed style, which is especially evident in her robe. The Virgin, by contrast, is rendered in large, relatively undifferentiated planes of colour, which create a more voluminous impression. The most plausible conclusion therefore seems to be that the right shutter, which is signed by Van Heemskerck, was painted by the master himself, and that the left one was the work of an assistant.

Grosshans suggests that two paintings at the Musée des Beaux-Arts in Strasbourg[2] were originally on the reverse of the Rotterdam shutters;[3] in other words, they would have been the inward-facing sides of the shutters. He identifies a painting of Adam and Eve as the reverse of the panel with the Virgin, and one of Gideon with the fleece (Judges 6:36-40) as the back of the painting of Elizabeth. If this hypothesis is correct, the original altarpiece must have had two side panels and a large centre panel which, according to Grosshans, would have illustrated the Nativity. This, however, means that the shutters would have opened to reveal the unusual combination of Adam and Eve on the left and Gideon with the fleece on the right.
JG

Physical characteristics: both panels (cat. nos. 85 and 86) consist of two vertical planks.

Infrared reflectography: no underdrawing could be discerned.[1]

Provenance: private owner, France; bought by W.M van der Vorm from A. Weinberger, Paris, in December 1960 for 60,000 new French francs; presented by W.M. van der Vorm in 1961; (cat. 85) inv. no. vdV 36; (cat. 86) inv. no. vdV 37.

Not exhibited

Literature: D. Hannema, *Beschrijvende catalogus van de schilderijen uit de kunstverzameling Stichting Willem van der Vorm, Westersingel 66, Rotterdam*, Rotterdam 1962, nos. 36 and 37, figs. 1-3; R. Grosshans, *Maerten van Heemskerck, Die Gemälde*, Berlin 1980, p. 51, no. 70, figs. 101-102.

1 Partially scanned by J.R.J. van Asperen de Boer on 10 January 1994.
2 Grosshans (1980), no. 71, figs. 103-104.
3 Grosshans (1980), no. 71, figs. 103-104.

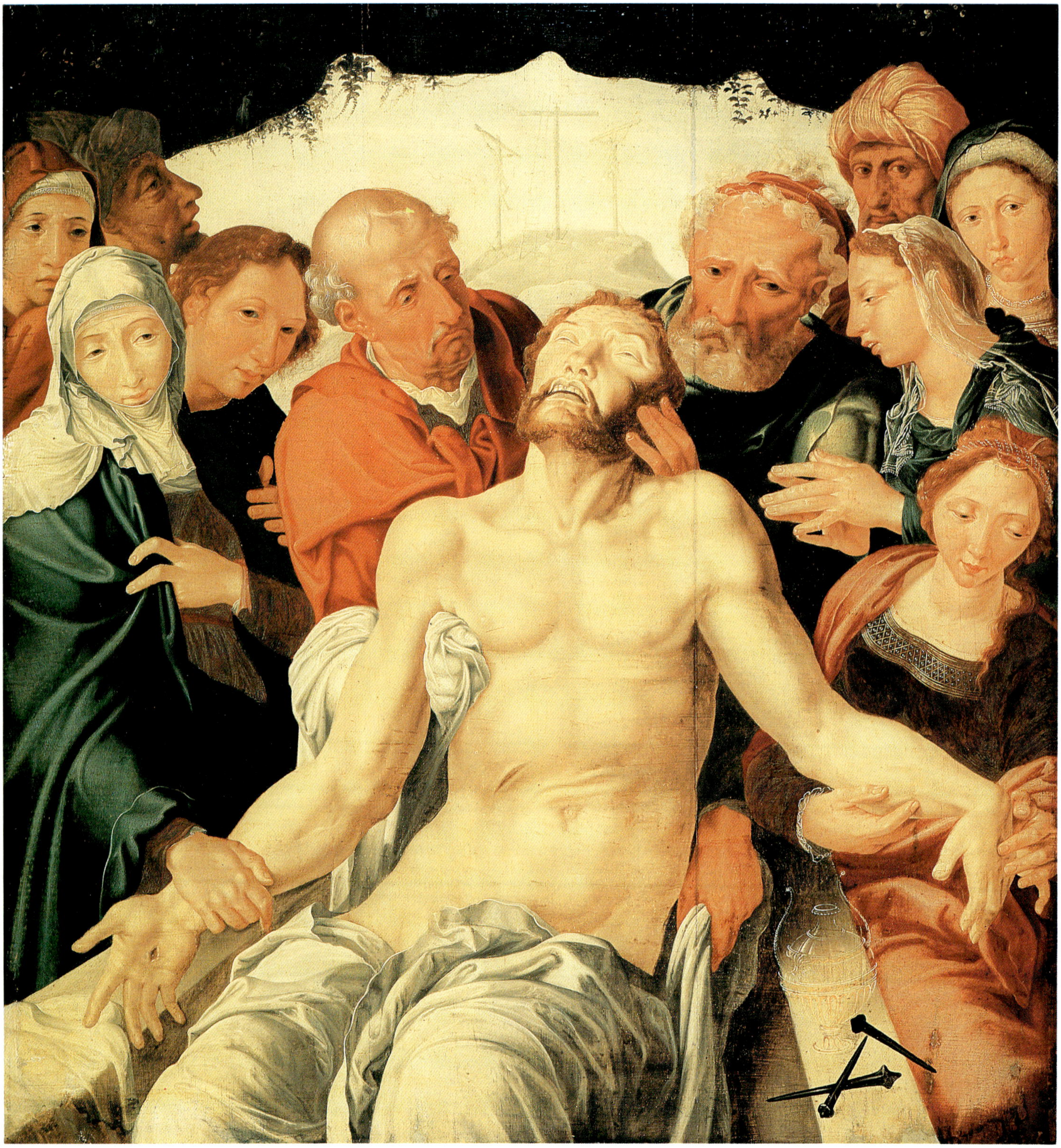

The Entombment of Christ

Maerten van Heemskerck, studio
(Heemskerk 1498-Haarlem 1574)

Panel; 88 x 79 cm

The body of Christ is shown at the moment of burial. He is supported by Nicodemus, who has his right hand under Christ's armpit and is holding the shroud with his left. On the right is Joseph of Arimathea, supporting Christ's head with his left hand. To the left stands the Virgin, who is holding up Christ's right arm. Beside her we see the head of the young John the Evangelist. In the right foreground Mary Magdelene is supporting the arm of Christ with her right hand. She has laid her left forefinger over the wound in his hand. Behind her we see Mary Cleophas and Mary Salomé. The heads of a woman and a man are shown in the left background, as is the head of a man on the right who is looking at the viewer. The three crosses can be seen in the background.

At the auction of the Boymans Collection in 1811 the painting was ascribed to Albrecht Dürer, in the 1849 catalogue to Hendrik Aldegraaf. In the catalogue of 1867 it was described as a piece by Maerten van Heemskerck, apparently by the then director of the Museum A. Lamme.

Preibisz regarded the painting as a weak, old copy after a painting now in the Accademia Albertina, Turin (fig. a).[2] Hoogewerff, by contrast, believed that the Rotterdam painting, which he dated ca. 1540-1545, was the original and considered the painting in Turin a good replica.[3] He also noted that a slightly different copy after the *Entombment* by Barent Graat (1628-1709) is at the *Statie der paters Augustijnen*, the premises of the order of St Augustine in Amsterdam (128 x 137 cm). Baldass believed that two panels with portraits of donors, which at the time he was writing were combined to form one painting, had originally belonged to the Turin painting. These panels have since been separated and are now at the Kunsthistorisches Museum in Vienna (fig. b).[4] Grosshans discusses the Turin painting, which he regards as an autograph piece by Heemskerck, at some length. Grosshans agrees with Baldass and sees the Viennese panels as belonging to the Turin painting,[5] and includes a reconstruction of this original triptych.[6] He regards the Rotterdam painting as a replica of the painting in Turin, made soon after the original in the studio of Heemskerck, possibly even with his help. Harrison shares this opinion.[7]

The painting displays great refinement, for example in the rendering of the glass in the foreground, great expressiveness in the figures and relatively rich colours. These features suggest that the painting was made by an artist very close to Heemskerck. The opinion of Grosshans is therefore endorsed here.
JG

Physical characteristics: the panel consists of three vertical planks.

Infrared reflectography: no underdrawing could be discerned.[1]

Dendrochronology: the youngest heartwood growth ring dates from 1516. The panel could not have been painted before 1527; it was more probably painted in or after 1533. See article by P. Klein.

Provenance: F.J.O. Boymans, auction Utrecht, 31 August 1811, no. C 34; estate of F.J.O. Boymans, 1847; inv. no. 1291.

Not exhibited.

Literature: *Catalogus van schilderijen enz. in het museum te Rotterdam*, 1849, no. 3; *Beschrijving der schilderijen in het museum te Rotterdam gesticht door Mr. F.J.O. Boymans*, 1867, no. 81; L. Preibisz, *Martin van Heemskerck, ein Beitrag zur Geschichte des Romanismus in der niederländischen Malerei des XVI. Jahrhunderts*, Leipzig 1911, p. 77 with no. 45, p. 108 note 39; Friedländer, XIII, 1936, p. 158, no. 202; G.J. Hoogewerff, *De Noord-Nederlandsche Schilderkunst*, IV, The Hague, 1941-1942, pp. 347-350, fig. 162, V, The Hague, 1947, p. 156, no. 27; cat. 1962, p. 63; G. von der Osten, H. Vey, *Painting and Sculpture in Germany and the Netherlands 1500-1600*, Harmondsworth 1969, p. 186; J. Richard Judson, *Dirck Barendsz. 1534-1592*, Amsterdam 1970, p. 61; Friedländer, XIII, 1975, p. 90, no. 202, note 43, fig. pl. 103; R. Grosshans, *Maerten van Heemskerck, Die Gemälde*, Berlin 1980, p. 56, p. 158, no. 44, fig. 67; J.C. Harrison, *The paintings of Maerten van Heemskerck-a catalogue raisonné*, 1987 (UMI, Ann Arbor 1991), 2, no. 55.

1 Scanned on 10 January 1994 by J.R.J. van Asperen de Boer.
2 Preibisz (1911).
3 Hoogewerff (1941-1942).
4 L. Baldass, "Bildnisse des Niederländischen Romanismus", *Städeljahrbuch* 6 (1930), p. 85.
5 Grosshans (1980).
6 Grosshans (1980), cat. nos. 42, 43 and 44, figs. 63-67 (reconstruction fig. 66).
7 Harrison (1987).

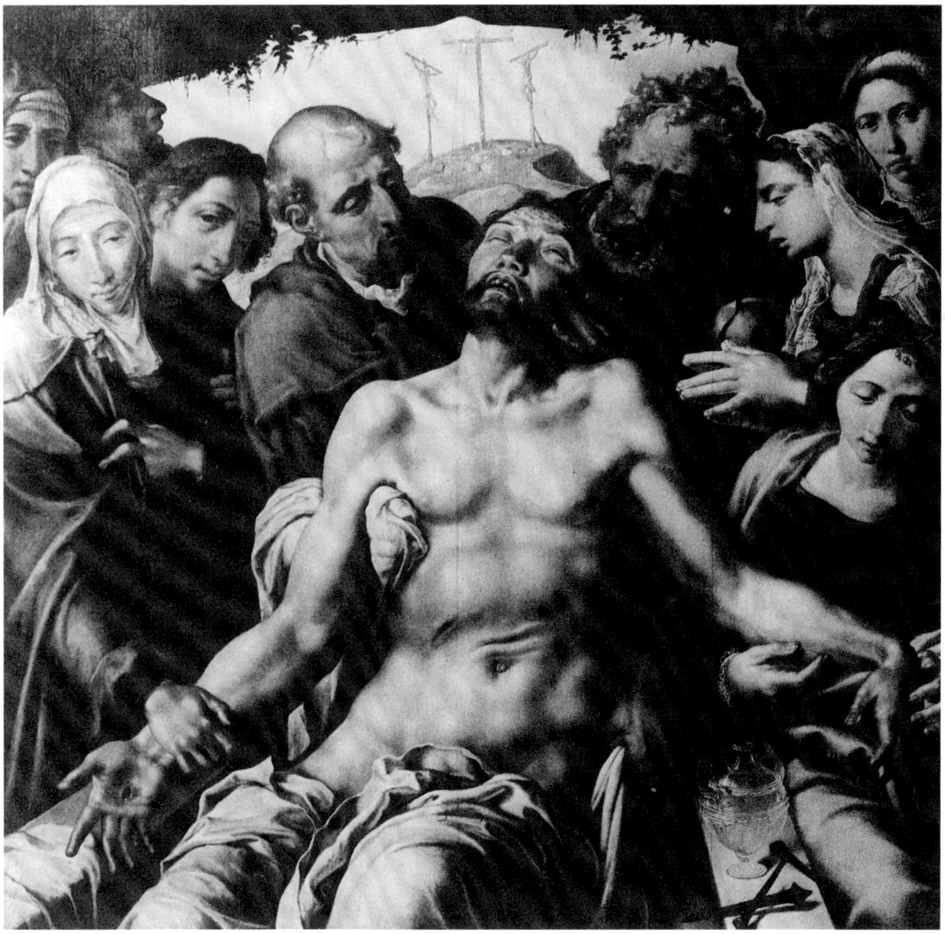

a. Maerten van Heemskerck, The Entombment
Panel; 78 x 79 cm
Turin, Accademia Albertina

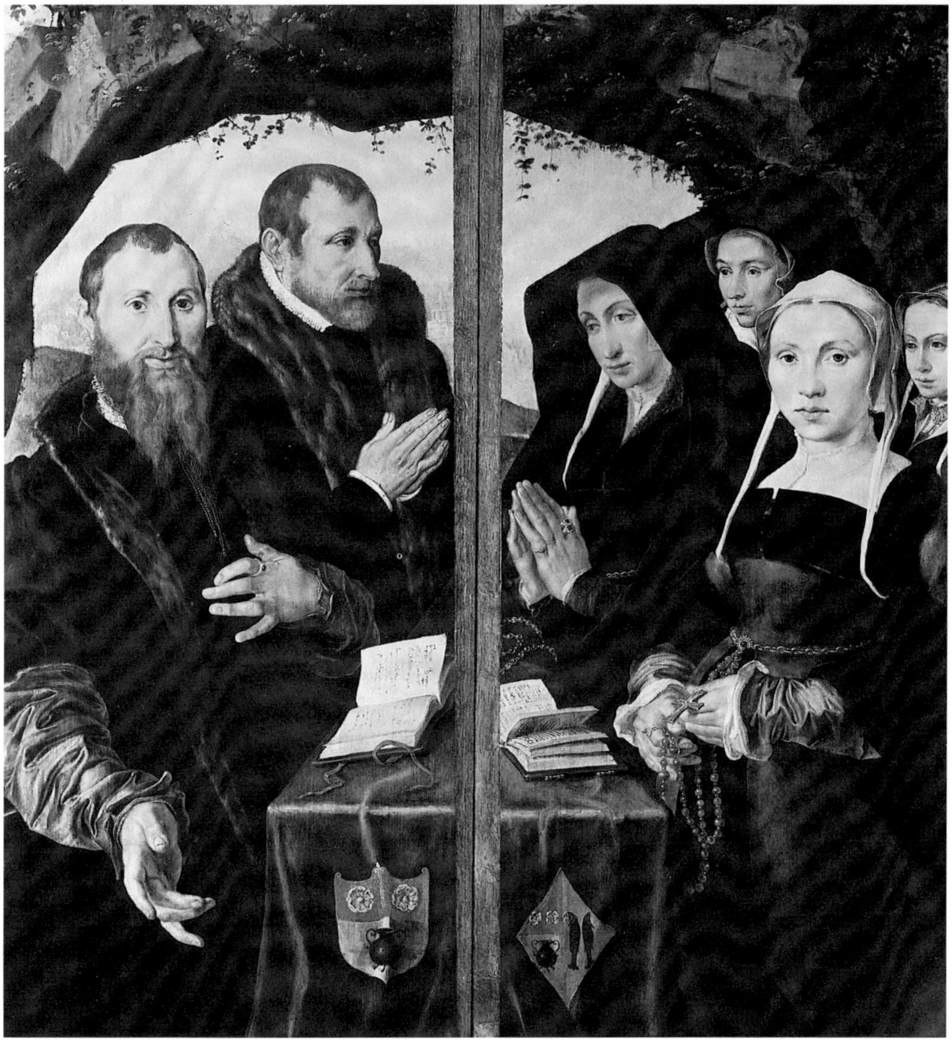

b. Maerten van Heemskerck, Two altar wings with donors
Panel; (both) 80.5 x 37 cm
Vienna, Kunsthistorisches Museum

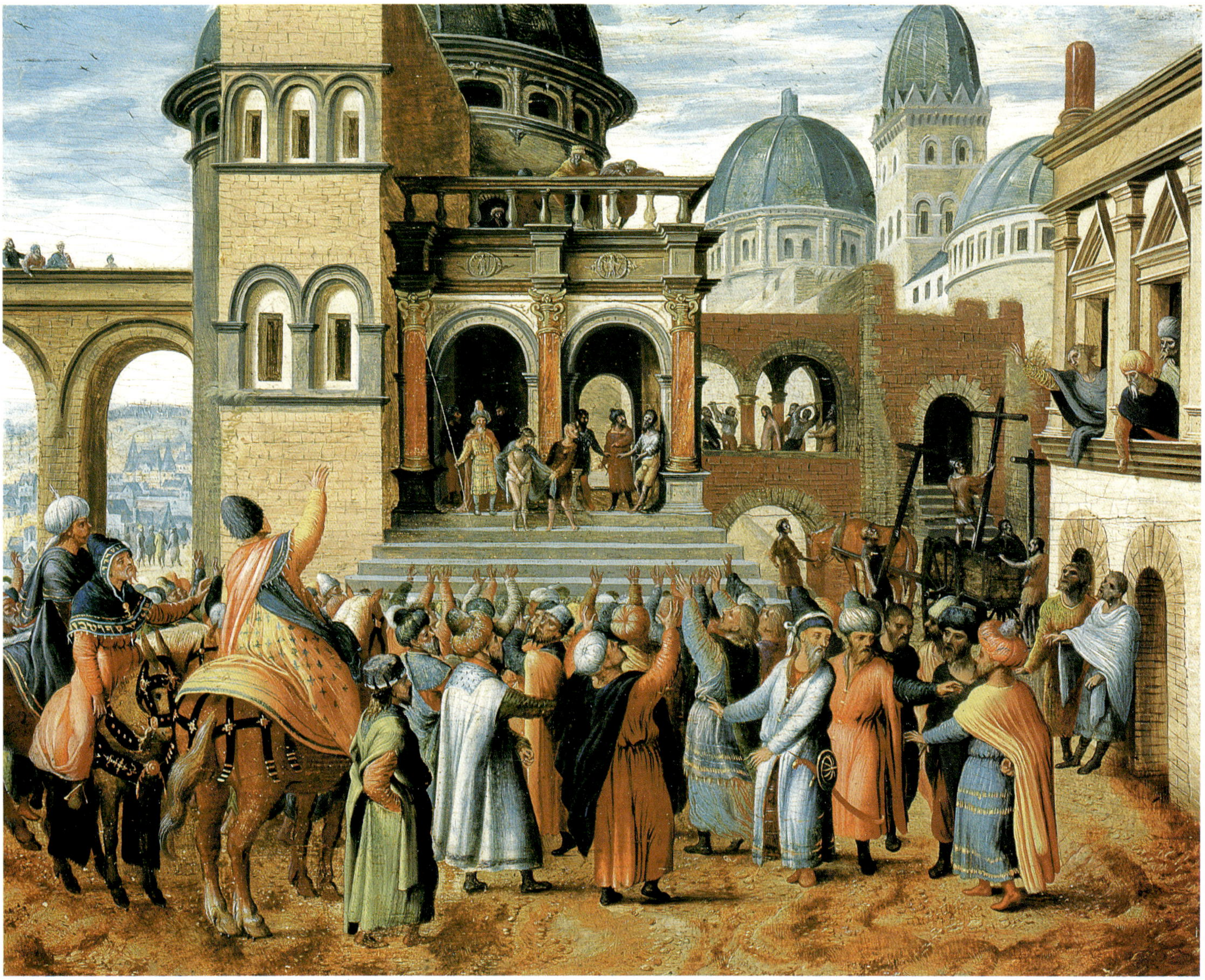

Ecce Homo

Anonymous
South Netherlandish master, Antwerp
c. 1540

Panel; 28 x 23 cm

Physical characteristics: the panel consists of a single plank.

Infrared reflectography:[1] underdrawing can be discerned in only two places. The outlines of two additional small figures are visible – on the balustrade in the upper left-hand corner – who were not included in the final painting (fig. c). The man in the foreground on the right could also have been included in the underdrawing.

Provenance: V. Bloch, London; D. Hannema, Rotterdam, 1939; J.W. Frederiks, The Hague; since 1968 on loan to the Boymans-van Beuningen, Rotterdam; gift from the J.W. Frederiks Collection, 1994; inv. no. S 35.

Exhibitions: *Nederlandsche Kunst van de XVde en XVIde eeuw*, The Hague, Mauritshuis, 1945, no. 22.

Literature: *Catalogue of some Early Flemish Pictures in, or formerly in, the possession of Vitale Bloch*, London 1939, fig. 9; *The Bob Jones Collection of Religious Paintings*, Vol. II, Greenville, South Carolina 1962, no. 158, p. 272; D. Kreidl, "Die religiöse Malerei Pieter Aertsens als Grundlage seiner künstlerischen Entwicklung", *Jahrbuch der Kunsthistorischen Sammlungen in Wien* 68 (1972), p. 52, note 44; M.B. Buchan, *The paintings of Pieter Aertsen* (diss.), New York University 1975, pp. 59, 193; *Museum Ridder Smidt van Gelder, Catalogus I, Schilderijen tot 1800*, 1980, p. 15; H.G. Franz, "Landschaftsbilder als kollektive Werkstattschöpfungen in der Flämischen Malerei des 16. und frühen 17. Jahrhunderts", *Kunsthistorisches Jahrbuch Graz* 18 (1982), p. 170; W. Kloek, "Pieter Aertsen en het probleem van het samenstellen van zijn oeuvre", *Nederlands Kunsthistorisch Jaarboek* 40 (1989), p. 12, 24, note 4.

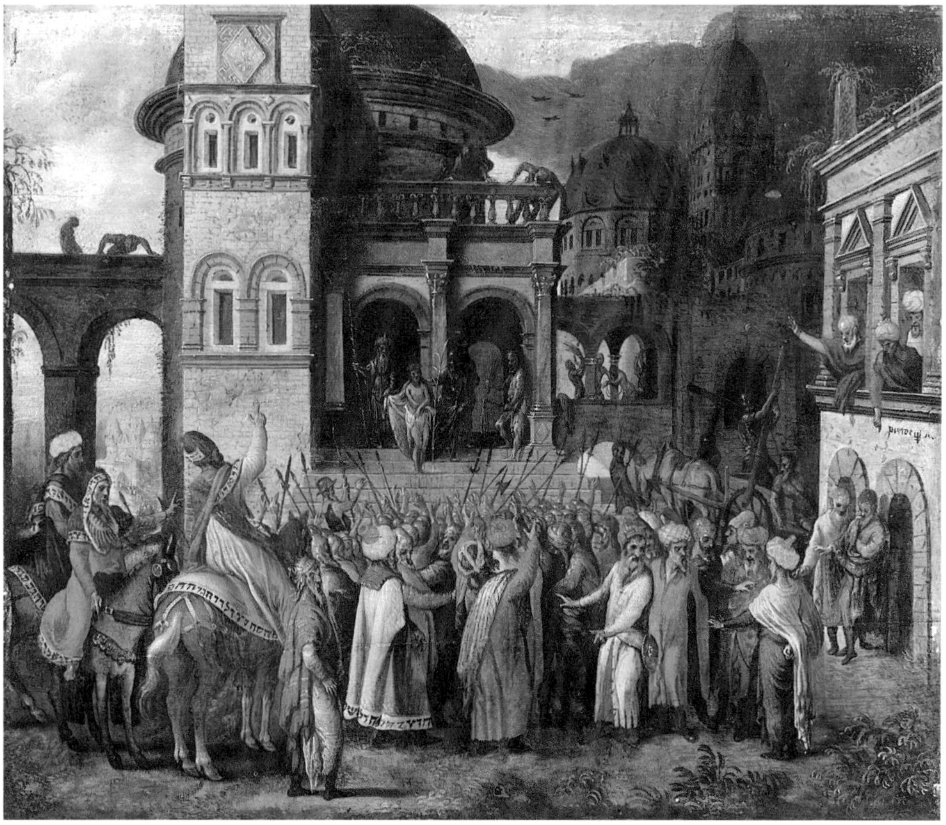

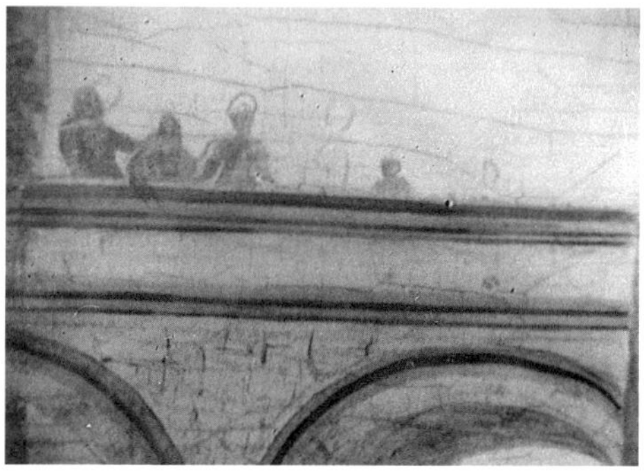

a. Pieter Aertsen, Ecce Homo
Panel; 24.3 x 27.8 cm
Antwerp, Smidt van Gelder Museum

b. Anonymous, South Netherlandish master,
Ecce Homo
Panel; 23 x 28.5 cm
Bob Jones University, Greenville, South Carolina

c. Infrared reflectogram of the balustrade.

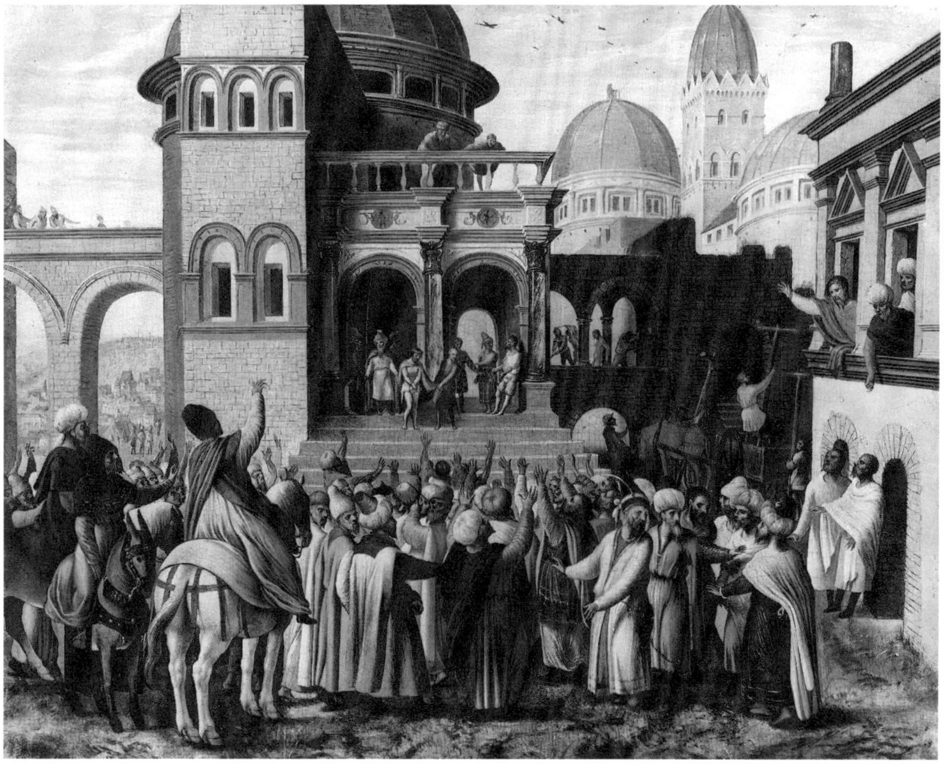

Christ is being shown to the people on the steps of a Renaissance-style court of justice. Behind him is Pilate, wearing a turban and holding a long judge's staff. The crowd assembled in front of the steps have their hands raised to indicate that they wish to see the Saviour crucified, whilst a group of men are already loading the three crosses onto a cart.

As Pilate displayed Christ to the crowd, he uttered the words "Ecce Homo" – behold the man (John 19:5, 6). In addition to this main theme, two other scenes from the Passion are depicted. Christ is being flogged in one of the palace galleries and, in the background on the left, the crucifixion is shown.[2]

At least four other versions of this painting exist – in Antwerp (fig. a), Greenville (fig. b) and two private collections.[3] Of these, only the panel in Antwerp by Pieter Aertsen is signed. It is probably one of his earliest works, painted between 1545 and 1550. The signature does not necessarily mean that Aertsen designed the composition himself.

It seems much more likely that Aertsen used one of the versions mentioned above as an example, or even a version that is now lost.[4] The relationship between the other four versions is difficult to establish.

Infrared reflectography carried out on the panel in Rotterdam shows that two small figures were drawn on the balustrade on the left which were not eventually painted (fig. c). This underdrawing would seem to indicate that the panel is either the original version or a copy of another which did include the two figures concerned.

The paintings in Greenville and Rotterdam have been attributed by most authors to the so-called Brunswick monogrammist.[5] This attribution is based on their similarity to a panel of his with the same subject in the Mauritshuis in The Hague.[6] This resemblance, however, only involves the architecture and the composition; the figures are painted quite differently. Given the affinity of the painting in The Hague with the Brunswick monogrammist's principal work, one or more other artists must have been responsible for the panels in Greenville and Rotterdam.[7]

Both paintings must have been made in Antwerp around 1540.[8] The composition and the figures indicate that whoever made the first version was familiar with the work of Antwerp artists such as Jan van Hemessen, Herry met de Bles, Pieter Coecke van Aelst and the Brunswick monogrammist already mentioned.[9]
FL

1 Scanned and recorded by J.R.J. van Asperen de Boer on 17 January 1994. Infrared reflectograms: AB 1561/33A-36A.

2 Louise Tillemans expresses the view, in the catalogue of the Ridder Smidt van Gelder Museum (1980), that one of the two figures on the right is Barabbas who is being released from his dungeon. It is more likely, however, that both men are simply onlookers.

3 For details of the other four versions, see Kloek (1989). The four other versions are: a. Antwerp, Smidt van Gelder Museum: panel; 24.3 x 27.8 cm. Signed by Pieter Aertsen, inv. no. Sm. 949;
b. Greenville, South Carolina: Bob Jones University;
c. Auctioned on 9/12/1970, no. 21 in Paris at the Palais Galliéra;
d. Private collection in London (previously P. de Boer Gallery, Amsterdam)

4 For further details see, in particular, Kloek (1989), p. 13. Also see R. Genaille, "Réflexions sur le maintien des sujets religieux dans les tableaux de genre et de natures mortes au XVIème siècle", *Jaarboek van het Koninklijk Museum voor Schone Kunsten Antwerpen 1989*, pp. 268-270 (Genaille incorrectly states in a footnote that the painting in Greenville is owned by the Rijksmuseum).

5 Kreidl (1972) and Franz (1982) for example. Franz thinks that the Brunswick monogrammist was responsible for the figures only and that another artist painted the architecture.

6 See B. Broos, exhib. cat. *Liefde, list & lijden. Historiestukken in het Mauritshuis*, The Hague, Mauritshuis, 1993-94, p. 339.

7 The Rotterdam panel generally shows more attention to such details as clothing and architecture. The man in the foreground on the left next to the horse is absent from the painting in Greenville, although he is present, in somewhat altered form, in Aertsen's panel.

8 Kloek (1981) originally thought that the work in Greenville was by the Master of Paul and Barnabas, but later changed his mind (see his note 18). He ascribes two other works to the painter of the Rotterdam panel and gives him the rather cumbersome title of 'Master of the Entry into Jerusalem in the Graefe Collection'. The two other paintings are: *Christ's entry into Jerusalem*, sale at Christie's, London, 11 December 1986, no. 41 (former Graefe collection), and a *Marriage at Cana*, in 1989 in the Fisher Gallery, Los Angeles (former Armand Hammer collection).

9 According to the Bob Jones University catalogue, Greenville (1962), Gudlaugsson thought that their version had been painted by Van Hemessen. Franz originally expressed the view that it came from the circle of Herry met de Bles – in *Niederländische Landschaftsmalerei im Zeitalter des Manierismus*, Graz 1969, pp. 89-90. In 1982 he attributed the works in Rotterdam and Greenville to the Brunswick monogrammist. Doubts remain, however, about both attributions.

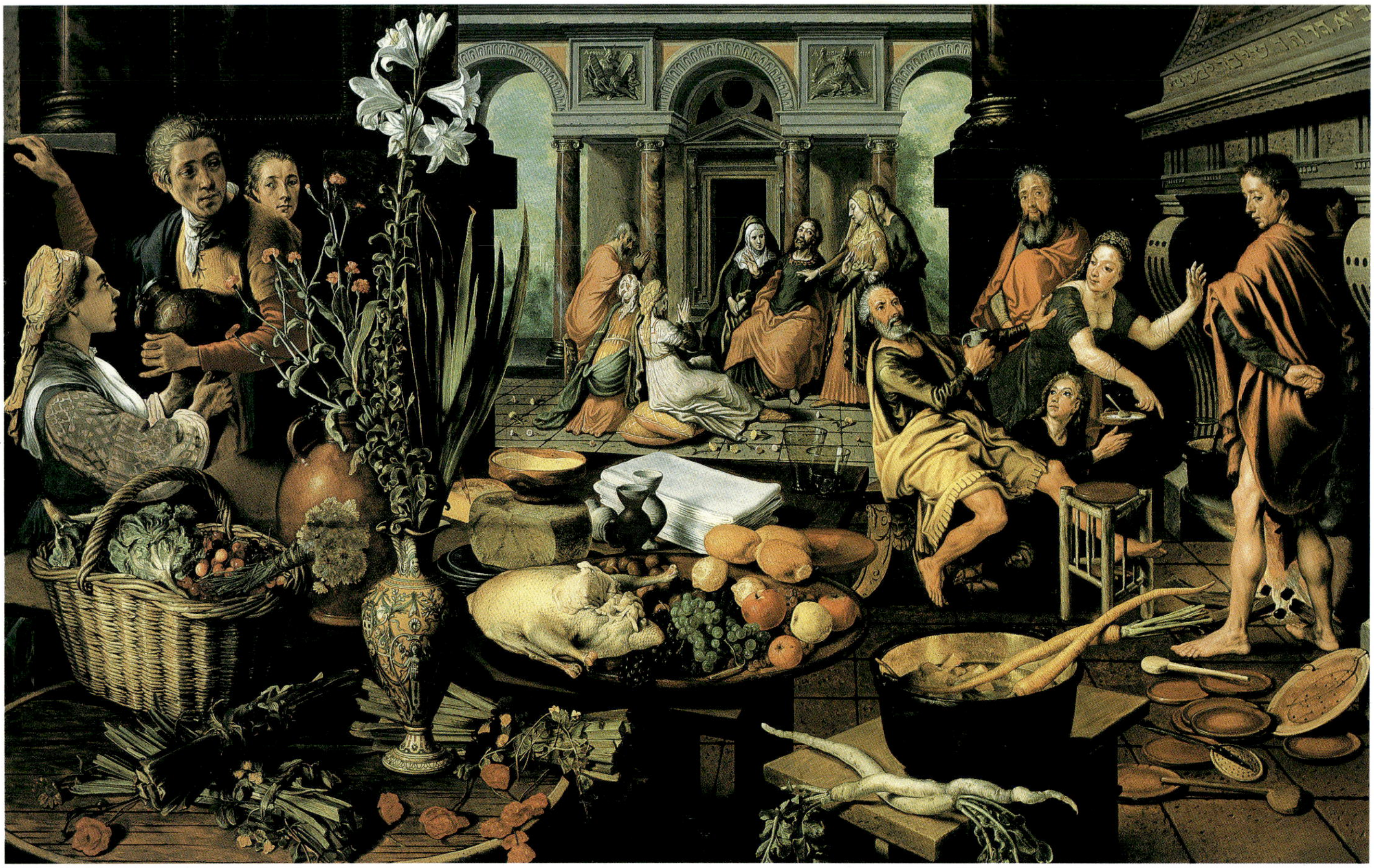

Christ in the house of Martha and Mary

Pieter Aertsen
(Amsterdam 1507/1508-
Amsterdam 1575)

Panel; 126 x 200 cm
Signed in the round window above the door in the background: PA, with a trident between the two letters.
Dated on the edge of the large rectangular table: 1553.27. julius.

Physical characteristics:[1] the panel consists of five horizontal planks and is painted up to the edges.

Infrared reflectography: parts of the underdrawing are visible to the naked eye. The painting is extensively underdrawn. See text.

Paint samples: an intermediate layer was applied to the ground with a broad brush. The underdrawing was made on this intermediate layer in black chalk, after a partial square grid in red had been applied on to the intermediate layer. One of the pigments identified was smalt, discoloured in the cornflowers.

Provenance:[2] private collection, Amsterdam, 1926; Pauli, Gottschewski and Schaeffer Gallery, Berlin, 1927; bought in 1931 by D.G. van Beuningen, Rotterdam and Vierhouten, for 5,500 guilders[3]; loaned by him to the Museum in the same year; acquired with the D.G. van Beuningen Collection in 1958; inv. no. 1108.

Exhibitions: *Kersttentoonstelling*, Rotterdam, Boymans Museum, 1931-1932, no. 3, fig. III; *Het stilleven*, Amsterdam, Goudstikker Gallery, 1933, no. 3, fig. 5; *115 stillevens, 1480-1933*, Rotterdam, Boymans Museum, 1933, no. 1; *Nederlandsche kunst van de XVde en XVIde eeuw*, The Hague, Mauritshuis, 1945, no. 32, fig. 32; *Honderd jaar Museum Boymans Rotterdam. Meesterwerken uit de verzameling D.G. van Beuningen*, Rotterdam, Boymans Museum, 1949, no. 1; *Chefs-d'œuvre de la collection D.G. van Beuningen*, Paris, Petit Palais, 1952, no. 35, fig. 4; *De triomf van het maniërisme. De Europese stijl van Michelangelo tot El Greco*, Amsterdam, Rijksmuseum, 1955, no. 13; (Y. Bruijnen), *Pieter Aertsen. Vier schilderijen doorgelicht*, Rotterdam, Boymans-van Beuningen Museum 1990, pp. 29-36, fig.

Literature: I.Q. van Regteren Altena, "Nieuwe Pieter Aertszens. I", *Oud Holland* XLIII (1926), pp. 214, 215, fig. 1; N.N., "Sammler und Markt", *Der Cicerone* XIX (1927), fig. on p. 556; M. Klar, "Eine Antwerpener Majolikakanne auf einem Gemälde von Pieter Aertszen" *Pantheon* I (1928), pp. 212-214, fig.; E. Zarnowska, *La nature-morte Hollandaise*, Brussels-Maastricht 1929, pp. 3,4, fig. 4; *Verslag omtrent de toestand en de aanwinsten van het Museum Boijmans over het jaar 1931*, fig.; *Beknopte catalogus van de schilderijen en beeldhouwwerken tentoongesteld in het Museum Boymans te Rotterdam*, 1935, no. 3a; Friedländer, XIII, 1936, no. 307; R. van Luttervelt, *Kunst van Nederland. Schilders van het stilleven*, Naarden 1947, p. 4, fig 1; G.J. Hoogewerff, *De Noord-Nederlandsche Schilderkunst*, IV, The Hague 1941-1942, p. 510; T.H. Lunsingh Scheurleer, "Pieter Aertsen en Joachim Beuckelaer en hun ontleeningen aan Serlio's architectuurprenten", *Oud Holland* LXII (1947), pp. 127-128; B.J.A. Renckens, "Een ikonografische aanvulling op 'Christus bij Martha en Maria' van Pieter Aertsen", *Kunsthistorische Mededelingen van het Rijksbureau voor Kunsthistorische Documentatie 's-Gravenhage* 4 (1949), pp. 30-32, fig. 1; Hannema, 1949, no. 1, figs. 60, 61; M.L. Hairs, *Les peintres Flamands de fleurs au XVIIe siècle*, Amsterdam-New York-Houston, 1955, p. 9; I. Bergström, *Dutch still-life painting in the seventeenth century*, London 1956, p. 19, fig. 16 (translation of the book published 1947); R. Genaille, "La peinture de genre aux anciens Pays-Bas au XVIe siècle", *Gazette des Beaux-Arts* XXXIX (1952), p. 250; R. Genaille, "L'oeuvre de Pieter Aersten", *Gazette des Beaux-Arts* XLIV (1954), pp. 276, 281, 282, no. 12, fig. 8; R. Genaille, *La peinture Hollandaise*, Paris 1956, p. 20; E. Greindl, *Les peintres Flamands de nature morte au XVIIe siècle*, Brussels 1956, p. 12; R.H. Wilenski, *Flemish Painters*, London 1960, p. 482; P. Pieper, "Ludger Tom Ring D.J., Die Hochzeit zu Kana", *Niederdeutsche Beiträge zur Kunstgeschichte* II (1962), p. 222, fig. 149; cat. 1962, p. 35; J. Bruyn, "Some drawings by Pieter Aertsen", *Master Drawings* 3 (1965), pp. 355, 358, fig. 2; R. Genaille, "D' Aertsen à Snyders: maniérisme et baroque", *Bulletin Koninklijke Musea voor Schone kunsten van België* XVI (1967), pp. 85, 86, fig. 5; H.G. Franz, *Niederländische Landschaftsmalerei im Zeitalter des Manierismus*, Graz 1969, p. 124; G. von der Osten, H. Vey, *Painting and sculpture in Germany and the Netherlands 1500-1600*, Harmondsworth 1969, p. 306; P.K.F. Moxey, "Erasmus and the iconography of Pieter Aertsen's 'Christ in the house of Martha and Mary' in the Boymans-van Beuningen Museum" *Journal of the Warburg and Courtauld Institutes* XXXIV

(1971), pp. 335-356; D. Kreidl, "Die religiöse Malerei Pieter Aertsens als Grundlage seiner künstlerischen Entwicklung", *Jahrbuch der kunsthistorischen Sammlungen in Wien* 68 (1972), pp. 81-82, fig. 56; D. Hannema, *Flitsen uit mijn leven als verzamelaar en museumdirecteur*, Rotterdam 1973, p. 60; A. Grosjean, "Toward an interpretation of Pieter Aertsen's profane iconography" *Konsthistorisk Tidskrift* XLIII (1974), pp. 133-34, fig. 13; Friedländer, XIII, 1975, no. 307, fig. 153; M. Braman Buchan, *The paintings of Pieter Aertsen* (diss.), New York 1975, pp. 75, 101, 102, 198, no. 10.; K.P.F. Moxey, "The 'humanist' market scenes of Joachim Beuckelaer: Moralizing exempla or 'slices of life'", *Jaarboek van het Koninklijk Museum voor Schone Kunsten Antwerpen* 1976, pp. 150-152, 163, 165, fig. 38; K.P.F. Moxey, "Reflections on some unusual subjects in the work of Pieter Aertsen", *Jahrbuch der Berliner Museen* 18 (1976), p. 60; I. Bergström e.a., *Natura in posa. La grande stagione della natura morta Europea*, Milan 1977, p. 173, fig.; R. Genaille, "Pieter Aertsen, précurseur de l'art Rubénien", *Jaarboek van het Koninklijk Museum voor Schone Kunsten Antwerpen* 1977, pp. 16, 37, no. 21, fig. 12; K.P.F. Moxey, *Pieter Aertsen, Joachim Beuckelaar and the rise of secular painting in the context of the reformation* 1977 (diss. Chicago 1974), pp. 3, 44-50, 98, 235, fig. 7; R.H. Fuchs, *Dutch Painting*, London 1978, pp. 27-28, fig. 13; E. Munkgaard, *Mad; Kunst*, Albertslund 1981, pp. 20-21, fig.; L.D. Couprie, "Broodjes met betekenis", *Openbaar Kunstbezit* 1981, pp. 14,15, fig. 13; K.M. Craig, "Pieter Aertsen and 'The Meat stall'", *Oud Holland* 96 (1982), p. 15, note 34; K.M. Craig, "Pars ergo Marthae transit: Pieter Aertsen's 'inverted' paintings of Christ in the house of Martha and Mary", *Oud Holland* 97 (1983), pp. 30-39, fig. 2; G. Irmscher, "'Ministrae voluptatum': stoicizing ethics in the market and kitchen scenes of Pieter Aertsen and Joachim Beuckelaer", *Simiolus* 16 (1986), pp. 227-229, fig. 6; exhib. cat. *Joachim Beuckelaer*, Ghent, Museum voor Schone Kunsten, 1986-1987, p. 146; H. Buijs in: exhib. cat. *Kunst voor de beeldenstorm*, Amsterdam, Rijksmuseum, 1986, p. 345, fig. 227a; C. Grimm, *Stilleben. Die Niederländischen und Deutschen Meister*, Stuttgart-Zürich 1988, pp. 29-32, fig. XI; P. Skira, *Still life: A history*, Geneva 1989, pp. 66-69, fig.; R. Genaille, "Réflexions sur le maintien des sujets religieux dans les tableaux de genre et de natures mortes au XVIème siècle", *Jaarboek van het Koninklijk Museum voor Schone Kunsten Antwerpen* 1989, pp. 286, 287, fig. 10; W. Kloek, "Pieter Aertsen en het probleem van het samenstellen van zijn oeuvre", in: *Pieter Aertsen (Nederlands Kunsthistorisch Jaarboek 40 (1989)*, pp. 5, 9, fig. 3; R.L. Falkenburg, "'Alter Einoutus': Over de aard en herkomst van Pieter Aertsens stillevenconceptie", in: *Pieter Aertsen (Nederlands Kunsthistorisch Jaarboek 40 (1989)*), p. 44, fig. 15; H. Buijs, "Voorstellingen van Christus in het huis van Martha en Maria in het zestiende-eeuwse keukenstuk", in: *Pieter Aertsen (Nederlands Kunsthistorisch Jaarboek 40 (1989)*), pp. 94, 95, 101, 114 (n. 1), 118 (n. 24), fig. 1; J.M.C. Boreel, F.W.H. van Zon-Christoffels, "Enkele aspecten van de schilderspraktijk in het atelier van Pieter Aertsen natuurwetenschappelijk nader bekeken", in: *Pieter Aertsen (Nederlands Kunsthistorisch Jaarboek 40 (1989)*), pp. 167, 170, 173, 175, 176, 179, 180, 182, 187, 189, 195 (n. 49); Z. van Ruyven-Zeman, "Monumentale glasschilderkunst in de kathedraal van Granada. Teodoro de Holanda, de Meester van de verloren zoon en de relatie tot Pieter Aertsen", in: *Pieter Aertsen (Nederlands Kunsthistorisch Jaarboek 40 (1989)*, p. 273; L. Stone-Ferrier, "Gabriel Metsu's 'Vegetable Market of Amsterdam': seventeenth-century Dutch market paintings and horticulture", *The Art Bulletin* 71 (1989), pp. 434-435, note 22, fig. 8; L. Stone-Ferrier, "Market scenes as viewed by an art historian", in: D. Freedberg, J. de Vries (ed.), *Art in history. History in art. Studies in seventeeth-century Dutch culture*, Santa Monica 1991, p. 33; W.A. Brandenburg, "Market scenes as viewed by a plant biologist", in: D. Freedberg, J. de Vries (ed.), *Art in history. History in art. Studies in seventeeth-century Dutch culture*, Santa Monica 1991, p. 65, fig. 6; A.P.E. Ruempol, A.G.A. van Dongen, *Pre-industriële gebruiksvoorwerpen/ Pre-industrial utensils 1150-1800*, Amsterdam-Rotterdam 1991, p. 285, fig.

During a journey which Jesus undertook with his disciples, he visited the house of Martha. Her sister Mary sat down at the feet of the Saviour and listened to his words. Martha, however, was occupied with serving the guests. She therefore asked Christ if he thought it right that Mary did not help her. He answered "Martha, Martha, thou art careful and troubled about many things: But one thing is needful: and Mary hath chosen that good part, which shall not be taken away from her" (Luke 10:41-42).

Aertsen depicted the story in the background of his painting. Christ is sitting by a loggia. In front of him, on the ground sits Mary. Martha is standing to the right of Christ pointing to the scene in the foreground. To the left of Christ sits his mother Mary, wearing a nun's habit. The Virgin is not mentioned in the biblical passage but was sometimes depicted on paintings of this theme.[4] The other figures in the background cannot be identified with any degree of certainty.

The biblical scene only occupies a small part of the painting. The first thing which attracts attention is the still life in the foreground, divided over three tables. On the round table stands a majolica jug, probably made in Antwerp, containing carnations and white lilies.[5] Beside the jug is a basket with cherries, cabbage and cornflowers. Further to the right, on a small table, stands a copper kettle, blackened with soot, containing carrots and parsnips.[6] To the right of the still life, five people are grouped around a fireplace. It has been convincingly demonstrated that they are four of Christ's disciples and probably Marcella, Martha's maid. The seated man with a jug in his hand must be Peter and the youth kneeling beside him is probably John.[7] On the fireplace is a Hebrew inscription which does not seem to have any meaning.[8] Who the three figures on the left are is unclear. They are usually thought to be members of Martha's kitchen staff, and are the only figures shown wearing contemporary clothing.

Aertsen based the palatial architecture on woodcuts from *Reglen van Metselrijen [...]*, Pieter Coecke van Aelst's Dutch translation of Sebastiaan Serlio's work (Antwerp 1549). Both the fireplace and the doorway in the background were reproduced almost exactly from this publication.[9] Aertsen repeatedly used compositions based on a large still life in the foreground and a biblical scene in the background.

In the first half of this century, art historians regarded the biblical scenes in the background as of secondary importance.[10] It was generally accepted that the artist was mainly interested in the still life in the foreground. Observers did not link the still lifes with the religious stories. The notion that the biblical scenes had a moralising or didactic function first emerged in the 1940s. Since then, our painting has been the subject of countless studies.

In general, there is agreement that the still life and the figures in the foreground refer to Martha's choice. The extent to which this choice was viewed negatively by Aertsen's contemporaries is, however, a point of debate. Traditionally, Mary stood for the 'vita contemplativa' and Martha for the 'vita activa'. The teaching of the church presents the 'vita contemplativa' as the highest attainable. The 'vita activa' was less elevated, but certainly not blameworthy. This suggests that the still life and the figures in the foreground should also not be interpreted in a negative way. The supporters of this reading point out that the painting includes reliefs of Aaron and Moses. Like Martha and Mary, Aaron and Moses were taken to represent the contemplative and active life, respectively.[11]

On the other hand, some art critics believe that the foreground has a clearly negative meaning. They see the over-lavish still life and the behaviour of the apostles as images of a worldly and sinful life. They interpret both Moses and Aaron as representing the law of God, rather than referring to the two modes of life mentioned above.[12] The two schools of thought meet in the view that the panel is a kind of 'painted metaphor'. The eye must see beyond the attractive still life to find the religious message. In the same way, the human soul must reach beyond material, worldly things to find the true faith. The view that all Aertsen's paintings with biblical scenes in the background have such a general moral meaning has recently been contested. Instead, it has been suggested that the

1 For a detailed report on the examination of the materials see exhib. cat. Rotterdam, 1990. Paint samples: A 113/1-5. Infrared reflectograms: AB 119/14-36, AB 120/18-37, AB 123/ 5-10, AB 1130-AB 1134/10, AB 123a/1-36.

2 Nothing can be said with any certainty about an earlier provenance. Aertsen painted various works of this subject. However, the descriptions in old inventories are so summary that it is not clear which versions are being referred to. According to Van Mander's *Schilderboeck*, Haarlem 1604, the painter Cornelis Cornelisz of Haarlem owned "a Martha" ("een Martha", fol. 244 r.). At the auction of the estate of Johan Chrisostomus de Backer in 1662, a "Mary and Martha by Lange Pier" ("Maria en Martha van Lange Pier") was sold to Dr. Dedel in Delft for 83 guilders, see F.D.O. Obreen, *Archief voor Nederlandsche kunstgeschiedenis*, 5th volume, Rotterdam 1882-83, p. 295. In 1615, the estate of Claes Pietersz van Vierhuyzen included "A picture of Mary and Martha" ("Een stuck van Maria an Martha"), see N. de Roever, "Pieter Aertsz: gezegd Lange Pier, vermaard schilder", *Oud Holland* VII (1889), p. 18.

3 Hannema (1973), p. 60, recounts that the original asking price was 6,500 guilders. Because the Museum had no money, Hannema asked Van Beuningen to buy the piece and loan it to the Museum. Van Beuningen apparently replied "Things are bad in the harbour [...] but if that chap will sell it for 4,500 I'll do it" ("Het gaat beroerd in de haven [...] maar als de vent het voor vijf en veertig honderd wil verkopen zal ik het maar doen"). Van Beuningen's purchase book shows that he bought it for 5,500 guilders.

4 See for example Buijs (1989), p. 94.

5 See for this jug, Klar (1928).

6 The utensils on this painting can be identified as follows: The standing man on the far left is holding a stoneware pitcher from Cologne (mid-sixteenth century). On the large rectangular table are a stoneware jug with a pewter lid from Frechen (mid-sixteenth century). Beside it, under a cheese, are several pewter trenchers (probably Netherlands, mid-sixteenth century). On the cheese is an earthenware bowl (first half of the sixteenth century, Netherlands). Beside it stand three conical stoneware beakers from Siegburg (first half of the sixteenth century). The two glasses are a beaker of forest glass on the left (German, first quarter of the sixteenth century) and on the right a berkemeier of forest glass (German, first half of the sixteenth century). The large dish on the table is probably Dutch earthenware (sixteenth century). On the small table stand a kettle of brass and wrought iron (Netherlands sixteenth century). Beside it on the floor are several wooden trenchers, a brass skimmer and probably a colander. Peter is holding a small stoneware mug from Raeren (first half of the sixteenth century). With thanks to Alexandra van Dongen, curator of pre-industrial utensils.

7 Moxey (1971).

8 See Craig (1983), p. 38, note. 30. There is also Hebrew lettering on Jesus' cloak.

9 See Lunsingh Scheurleer (1947) and Moxey (1977), p. 47, note 1.

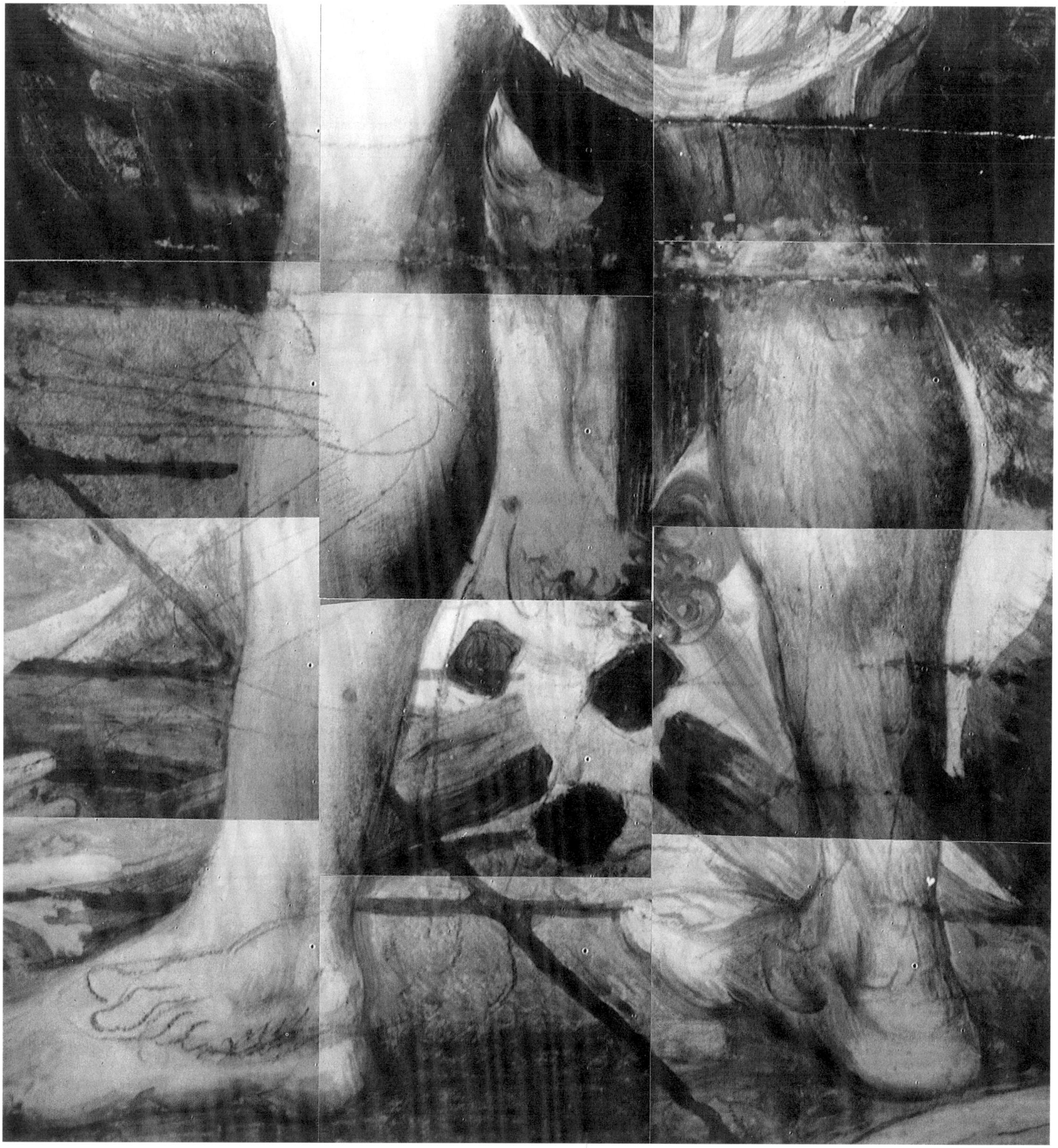

a. Infrared reflectogram assembly. Detail of the standing man on the right at the fireplace.

paintings are a satire on the kitchen staff and the traders shown selling meat, fish and the like. The wealthy burghers, who bought the paintings would have seen the works as a satire on the lower classes who had no sense of important matters.[13] Such an interpretation would seem untenable for our painting. The three figures on the left, who may be kitchen staff, would be essential to the painting on such a reading of its meaning. It is therefore odd at the very least that these are the only figures which were not or scarcely underdrawn.[14]

The underdrawing is free and sketchy (fig. a). Parts of a red grid over which the still life on the rectangular table is painted are visible to the naked eye. Due to the red, this grid does not show up in the infrared reflectogram assembly. The red grid probably does not extend beyond the still life.

X-radiographs show that Aertsen made a number of changes when painting. The figure closest to the viewer by the fireplace on the right-hand side, for example, was originally smaller.[15] The sketchy underdrawing and the numerous changes to both the underdrawing and painting makes it very likely that this painting is autograph, at least to a large extent. Aertsen may have had help with the still life, for which we know a grid was used. However, changes are also visible in the still life. The majolica jug, for instance, was originally drawn higher. The panel is generally regarded as one of Aertsen's most powerful paintings.

The painting bears a strikingly specific dating, 27 July 1553. It has been suggested that this date is linked to the feast-days of Mary Magdalene, who was generally identified with the Mary in the story, and Martha. The saint's day of the former was on 22 July, that of the latter on 29 July. The painting in Vienna with the same biblical scene in the background which was painted the year before, is dated 25 July.[16]

A free copy of our painting was owned by the Heim Gallery in London. The panel also served as a source of inspiration for a number of paintings of the same subject by Joachim Beuckelaer.[17]
FL

10 See for a summary of the literature on Aertsen: K. Moxey, "Interpreting Pieter Aertsen: The problems of 'Hidden Symbolism'", in: *Pieter Aertsen (Nederlands Kunsthistorisch Jaarboek 40 (1989))*, pp. 29-39.

11 See Moxey (1977) and Craig (1983). Oddly, Craig links Moses with the contemplative life and the priest Aaron with the active life.

12 See especially Buijs (1989).

13 Irmscher (1986).

14 A few small traces are visible in the faces. It is possible that the three figures are underdrawn with a material which, like the red grid of the still life, is not visible to infrared reflectography. Even then, the question remains why a different medium was used for those three figures alone. See Boreel, Van Zon-Christoffels (1989), p. 180.

15 See further exhib. cat. Rotterdam, 1990 and Boreel, Van Zon-Christoffels (1989).

16 Moxey (1977), p. 45, refers to an archive document which apparently indicates that two birthday masses were held for Aertsen and his wife in the church of the 'White Sisters' or the order of the Penitents of Mary Magdelene.

17 For the various versions of the subject by Aertsen and Beuckelaer see especially Buijs (1989), p. 114, note 1.

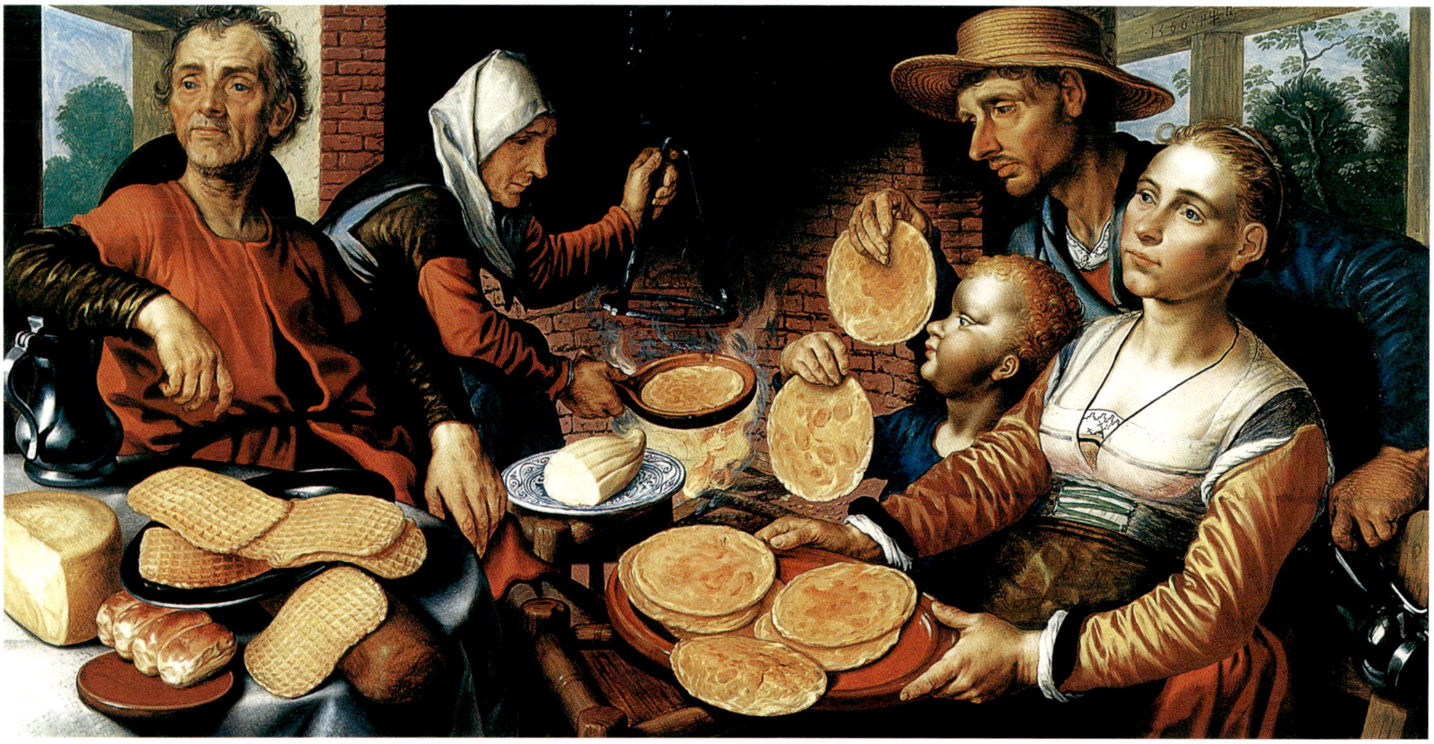

The pancake bakery

Pieter Aertsen
(Amsterdam 1507/1508-Amsterdam 1575)

Panel; 86 x 170 cm
Signed and dated at the top right on the cross-beam of the window: 1560 PA, with a trident between the letters.

Physical characteristics[1]: the panel consists of three horizontal planks, and is painted up to the edges.

Infrared reflectography: the underdrawing is partly visible to the naked eye. The representation is confidently drawn. The underdrawing was faithfully followed during the painting process. The contours are sometimes rendered with long, fluent lines and sometimes with short, broken lines. There are many of the short zigzag lines, indicating shadow in the paint, which are so typical of Pieter Aertsen (fig. a). See the text.

Dendrochronology: the youngest heartwood growth ring dates from 1535. Sapwood was found in two of the planks. The youngest sapwood growth ring dates from 1543. The panel could not have been painted before 1546; it was more probably painted in or after 1552. The dating of 1560 therefore seems reasonable. See article by P. Klein.[2]

Paint samples: an intermediate layer containing lead white has been applied to the ground. The underdrawing was made on this intermediate layer. The pigments identified included smalt.

Provenance: Cornelis van der Geest Collection, Antwerp, ca. 1628; possibly Hendrick Gras collection, Amsterdam 1648[3]; possibly Barbara Carel collection, Amsterdam, 1678[4]; possibly auction Amsterdam, 7 June 1708[5]; J. Goudstikker Gallery, Amsterdam, 1922-1926; bought from the Gallery by the Museum in 1926 for 15,000 guilders; inv. no. 1006.

Exhibitions: *Udstilling af aeldere og nyere Hollandsk malerkunst*, Copenhagen, 1922, no. 1, fig. 1; *Dutch and Flemish pictures from the Goudstikker collection*, New York, Anderson Gallery, 1923, no. 1; *Collection Goudstikker d'Amsterdam*, The Hague, Pulchri Studio, 1923, no. 2, fig.; *Nederlandsche stillevens uit vijf eeuwen*, The Hague, Gemeentemuseum, 1926, no. 1; *Collection Goudstikker d' Amsterdam*, Rotterdamsche Kunstkring 1926, no. 1, fig.; *Kunst voor de beeldenstorm*, Amsterdam, Rijksmuseum 1986, no. 228, fig.; (Y. Bruijnen), *Pieter Aertsen. Vier schilderijen doorgelicht*, Rotterdam, Boymans-van Beuningen Museum 1990, pp. 37-39, fig.

Literature: I.Q. van Regteren Altena, "Nieuwe Pieter Aertszens. I", *Oud Holland* XLIII (1926), pp. 216, 217, fig. 2; *Verslag omtrent den toestand van het Museum Boymans te Rotterdam over het jaar 1926*, pp. 2, 3, fig. 2; *Beknopte catalogus van de schilderijen en beeldhouwwerken tentoongesteld in Museum Boymans te Rotterdam*, 1935, no. 2; Friedländer, XIII, 1936, p. 170, no. 331; G.J. Hoogewerff, *De Noord-Nederlandsche schilderkunst*, IV, 1941-1942, p. 538; E. Greindl, "Einige Stileigentümlichkeiten an den Werken des Pieter Aertsen und Joachim Beuckelaer", *Pantheon* XXX (1942), p. 154, fig.; H.E. van Gelder, *W.C. Heda, A. van Beyeren, W. Kalf*, Amsterdam, p. 6, fig.; R. Genaille, "La peinture de genre aux anciens Pays-Bas au XVIe siècle", *Gazette des Beaux-Arts* XXXIX (1952), p. 250; R. Genaille, "L'œuvre de Pieter Aertsen", *Gazette des Beaux-Arts* XLIV (1954), pp. 278, 284, no. 32, fig. 11; R.H. Wilenski, *Flemish Painters*, London 1960, p. 482; E. Trautscholdt, "De oude koekebakster, Nachtrag zu Adriaen Brouwer", *Pantheon* 19 (1961), p. 187; cat. 1962, p. 17; R. Genaille, *L'Art Flamand*, Paris 1965, p. 88, fig. XXIV; R. Genaille, "D'Aertsen à Snyders: Maniérisme et Baroque", *Bulletin van het Museum voor Schone Kunsten van België* XVI (1967), p. 83; G.T. Faggin, *La Pittura ad Anversa nel cinquecento*, Florence 1968, p. 36, fig. 93; F. Baudouin, "De 'Constkamer' van Cornelis van der Geest, geschilderd door Willem van Haecht", *Antwerpen* 15 (1969), p. 12; G. von der Osten, H. Vey, *Painting and sculpture in Germany and the Netherlands 1500-1600*, Harmondsworth 1969, p. 306, fig. 273; C. Grimm, *Frans Hals; Entwicklung, Werkanalyse, Gesammtkatalog*, Berlin 1972, p. 62, fig. 30; D. Kreidl, "Die religiöse Malerei Pieter Aertsens als Grundlage seiner künstlerischen Entwicklung", *Jahrbuch der Kunsthistorischen Sammlungen in Wien* 68 (1972), p. 98; G. von der Osten, *Deutsche und Niederländische Kunst des Reformationszeit*, Kassel 1973, p. 303; D. Hannema, *Flitsen uit mijn leven als verzamelaar en museumdirecteur*, Rotterdam 1973, p. 61; Friedländer, XIII, 1975, no. 331, fig. 163; M.B. Buchan, *The paintings of Pieter Aertsen* (diss. New York 1975), pp. 150-152, no. 32, pp. 212-213; K.P.F. Moxey, *Pieter Aertsen, Joachim Beuckelaer, and the rise of secular painting in the context of the reformation* (diss. Chicago 1974), London-New York 1977, pp. 24-25; R. Genaille, "Pieter Aertsen, précurseur de l'art Rubénien", *Jaarboek van het Koninklijk Museum voor Schone Kunsten Antwerpen* 1977, no. 49, pp. 60-61; J. Briels, "Amator Pictoriae Artis. De Antwerpse kunstverzamelaar Peeter Stevens (1590-1668) en zijn constkamer", *Jaarboek van het Koninklijk Museum voor Schone Kunsten Antwerpen* 1986, p. 203; W.Th. Kloek, W. Halsema-Kubes, R.J. Baarsen, *Kunst voor de beeldenstorm*, The Hague 1986, p. 123, fig.; R.L. Falkenburg, "'Alter Einoutus': Over de aard en herkomst van Pieter Aertsens stillevenconceptie", in: *Pieter Aertsen (Nederlands Kunsthistorisch Jaarboek) 40 (1989)*, p. 49, fig. 26, n. 68, p. 65; J.M.C. Boreel, F.W.H. van Zon-Christoffels, "Enkele aspecten van de schilderspraktijk in het atelier van Pieter Aertsen natuurwetenschappelijk nader bekeken", in: *Pieter Aertsen (Nederlands Kunsthistorisch Jaarboek) 40 (1989)*, pp. 167, 170, 173, 176, 184, 185, 187, 191, n. 22, p. 193, figs. 30-32, 36; M. Bijl, M. Zeldenrust, W. Kloek, "Pieter Aertsen in het restauratie-atelier van het Rijksmuseum", in: *Pieter Aertsen (Nederlands Kunsthistorisch Jaarboek) 40 (1989)*, pp. 213, 231.

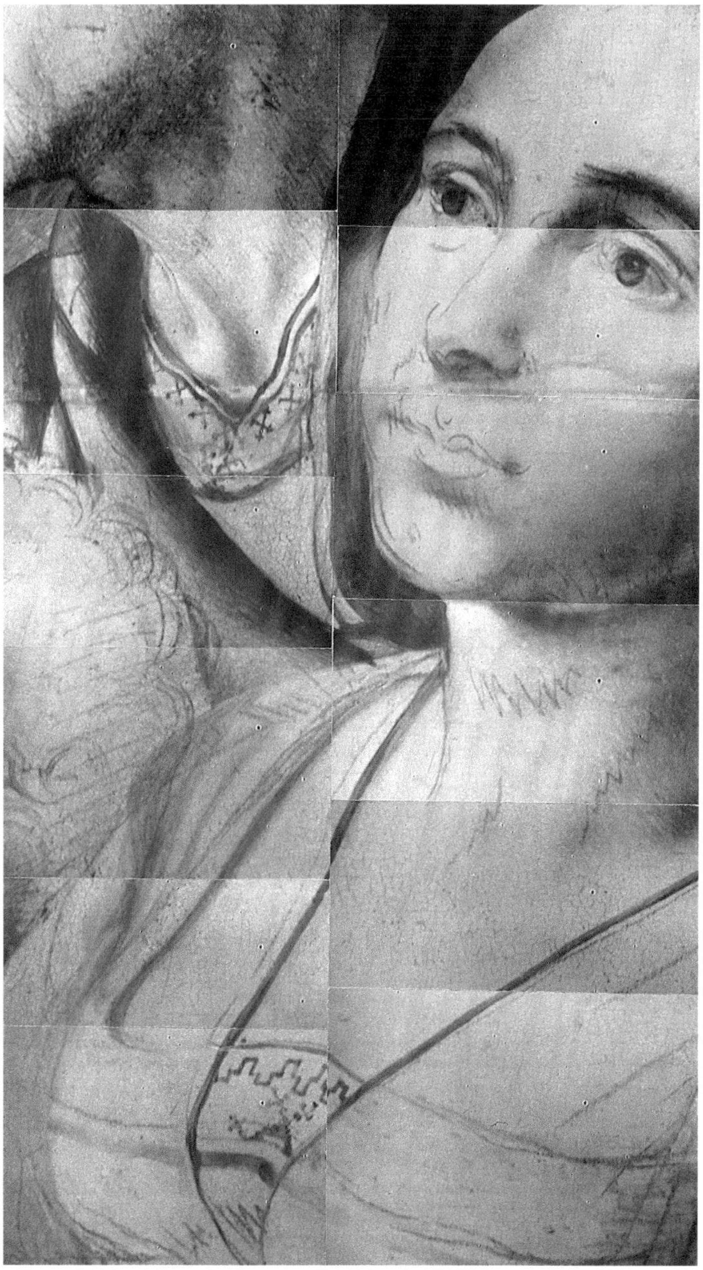

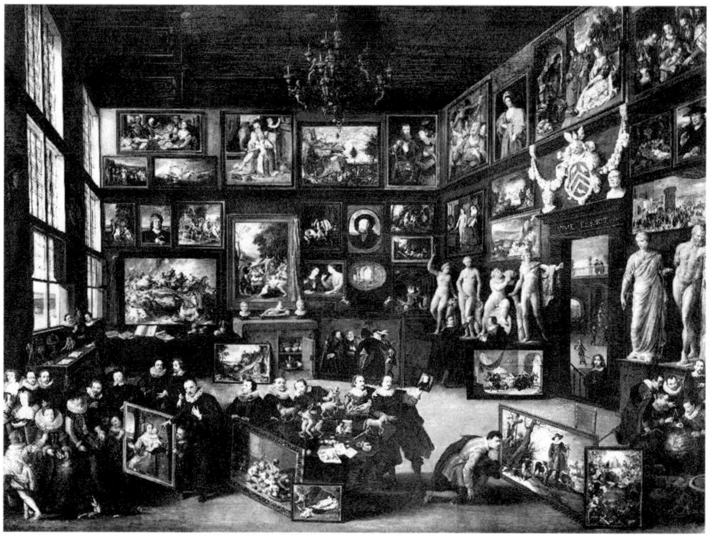

a. Infrared reflectogram assembly. Detail of the woman in the right foreground.

b. Willem van der Haecht, Cornelis van der Geest's art cabinet, 1628
Panel; 100 x 130 cm.
Antwerp, Rubenshuis

Five figures are seated by a fireplace. An elderly man is seated on the left, resting his right arm on a pewter jug. On the table in front of him are waffles on a pewter plate, bread and bread rolls on a wooden trencher, and a cheese. The woman behind him is holding a stoneware skillet containing a pancake. She has a stand in her left hand. On a stool in front of her is a majolica plate with a large piece of butter on it.[6] A woman in the right foreground is holding a large plate of pancakes. Behind her are a small boy and a man, both holding pancakes in their right hands.

Pancakes and waffles were traditional fare at winter feasts in the sixteenth century, and were especially popular on Shrove Tuesday. In the seventeenth century our painting was described as "a Shrove Tuesday, where substantial pancakes are fried".[7] It therefore seems likely that Aertsen was depicting this particular feast day. In contrast to most portrayals of people feasting before Lent, our panel contains no signs of immoral behaviour or excessive revelry. The atmosphere here is better described as sedate. It is difficult to be sure whether, as has been suggested, this mood is meant to be ironical.[8] The idea that the man on the right is making an erotic gesture because the jug which he is holding in his right hand is pointed at the woman in front of him, seems very far-fetched. In this interpretation, the man on the left with his arm resting on the jug would represent failure in love. In other paintings by Aertsen and his followers which show figures making waffles and pancakes, the erotic allusions are much more obvious.[9] The lack of such references makes it unclear whether our painting had a moralistic or satirical meaning. With its monumental figures, the panel is a good example of Aertsen's work from the period around 1560.

The painting has an extensive underdrawing (fig. a)[10] which was followed faithfully during the painting. As with so many of Aertsen's works, it is likely that his studio assistants helped the master to paint it, although it is difficult to know to what extent.

Aertsen's panel was most probably in the possession of Cornelis van der Geest of Antwerp around 1628. A very similar painting appears in Willem van der Haechts's *Cornelis van der Geest's art cabinet* made in 1628 (Antwerp, Rubenshuis, fig. b).[11] However, in this painting Aertsen's panel is depicted as being wider on both sides. On the left side of the table are a beaker and a bread roll which do not appear on the Rotterdam panel. There would seem to be three possible explanations for this discrepancy. Firstly, the Rotterdam panel may have been reduced on both sides some time after 1628. However, no signs of sawing have been found on either side.[12] Secondly, Aertsen could have made two very similar versions, which only differed slightly in width. This is unlikely, however, because the painting owned by Van der Geest is known to have been signed and dated in exactly the same way as our work.[13] Thirdly, it is possible that Van der Haecht did not copy Aertsen's painting exactly but made it seem wider than it was in reality. This explanation in fact seems the most plausible, since it is known that Van der Haecht did not adhere exactly to the dimensions of other paintings which he portrayed.[14]
FL

1 See exhib. cat. Rotterdam, 1990. Paint samples: A 112/1-7. Infrared reflectograms: AB 123/17-AB 124/33.

2 The measurement was taken by Dr. P. Klein, Hamburg and published by him in: Bijl, Zeldenrust, Kloek (1989), p. 231.

3 See N. de Roever, "Pieter Aertsz: gezegd Lange Pier, vermaard schilder", *Oud Holland* VII (1889), p. 20, estate of Hendrik Gras, director of the Dutch West India Company, "A painting of a pancake bakery" ("Een schilderij sijnde een pannekoeckebackerij").

4 On 16 November 1678, Barent Graat and Jan Rosa evaluated paintings belonging to Barbara Carel, widow of Jeronimus Ranst, including a "pancake baker by Lange Pier, 45 guilders" ("een pannekoekbakker van Lange Pier *f* 45,-", Steenman, notary, Amsterdam; notes, Bredius, Netherlands Institute for Art History). In view of the use of the male form, this was probably a different painting.

5 See G. Hoet, *Catalogus of naamlyst van schilderyen [...]*, I, The Hague 1752, p. 124, "24. Two excellent pieces by the same [Lange Pier], a farmer with chickens and a woman making pancakes 43-0" ("24. Twee kapitale stukken van dito [Lange Pier] een boer met Hoenders en een Pannekoekenbakster 43-0"). In view of the pendant, this was probably a different painting.

6 The plate shows a resemblance to surviving butter dishes which have a pewter pin in the middle to hold the butter in place. With thanks to Alexandra van Dongen, curator for pre-industrial design.

7 "een Vastenavont daermen strugins [struiven] backt", see Briels (1980). The description is by Peeter Stevens who made notes in his copy of Van Manders's *Schilderboeck* from 1625 onwards. The painting was then owned by Cornelis van der Geest, see also below. The note by Stevens that the artist had portrayed himself in the painting together with his wife and child is less likely to be correct.

8 This is suggested by Buijs in exhib. cat. *Kunst voor de beeldenstorm*, 1986. Falkenburg (1989) believes that 'paradoxical encomium' is the basis of Aertsen's concept of his peasant portrayals. He argues that the 'classical' and 'respectable' presentation of 'humble' subjects, such as peasants is meant to be ironical.

9 See exhib.cat. Amsterdam, 1986.

10 Boreel, Zon-Christoffels (1989) believe that different styles of underdrawing are used in our painting. They argue that the underdrawing of the woman on the right and, for example, the hand of the man on the right correspond with Aertsen's style. The underdrawing of the head of the man on the left, by contrast, they regard as deviating in style.

11 See for this painting Baudouin (1969) and J.S. Held, "Artis Pictoriae Amator: an Antwerp art patron and his collection", in: J.S. Held, *Rubens and his circle*, Princeton, New Jersey, 1982 (previously published in *Gazette des Beaux-Arts* L (1957)).

12 See exhib. cat. Rotterdam, 1990. It is quite possible that the traces of sawing have disappeared over the years.

13 See Briels (1980).

14 That Van der Haecht was rather unreliable with respect to the dimensions of the paintings he portrayed is underlined by the panel by Cornelis van Dalem with a rocky landscape which hangs on the same upper row as the Aertsen in Van der Haecht's piece. This painting was about 54.5 x 68 cm, that is less tall than the Aertsen. However, in Van der Haecht's painting the Van Dalem seems to be over twice as tall as the Aertsen. See for the Van Dalem, F. Grossmann, "Cornelis van Dalem re-examined", *The Burlington Magazine* XCVI (1954), p. 46.

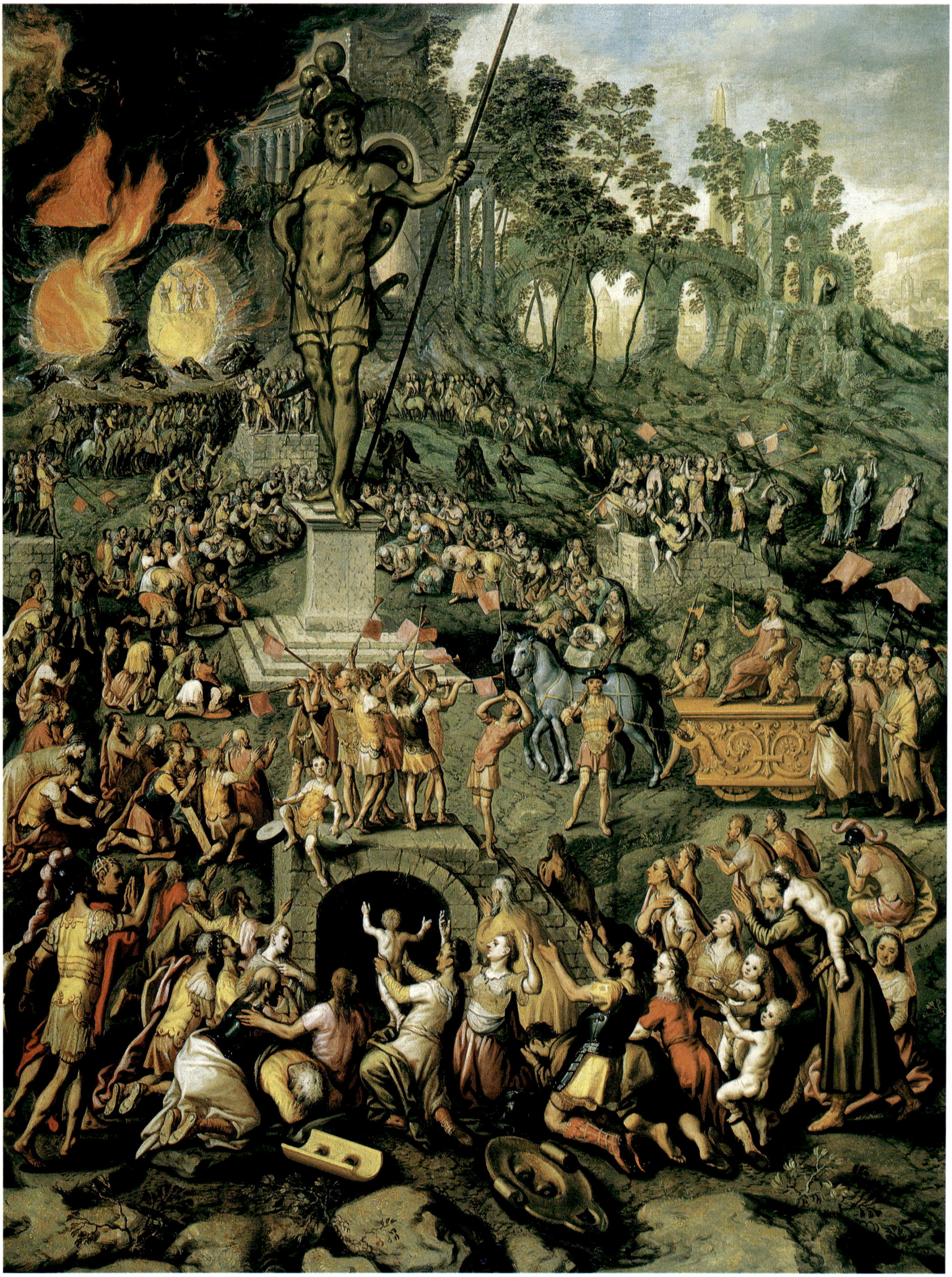

Worship of the statue of Nebuchadnezzar

Pieter Aertsen
(Amsterdam 1507/1508-
Amsterdam 1575)

Panel; 114 x 85 cm
Signed at bottom left with a trident

Physical characteristics:[1] the panel consists of three vertical planks. The panel is painted up to the edges.

Infrared reflectography: a grid was drawn with black chalk with squares of 3.5 x 3.5 cm. The underdrawing is extensive and fluent. See text.

Dendrochronology: the youngest heartwood growth ring dates from 1542. Sapwood was found in two of the planks. The youngest sapwood growth ring dates from 1546. The panel could not have been painted before 1553; it was more probably painted in or after 1559. See article by P. Klein.

Paint samples: a white intermediate layer was applied onto the ground. The underdrawing was done on this intermediate layer. The pigments identified are azurite and malachite.

Provenance: probably the painting which was auctioned on 30 September 1622 in Amsterdam with the estate of Jan Vincentsz Coster as "1 piece by Lange Pier of the Blazing Furnace"[2]; bought by Jacques van der Laen for 162 guilders; possibly the painting which was auctioned in 1639 with the estate of Willem Calschuyr as "a painting of worshippers before Baal"[3]; Pieter Loquet collection, Amsterdam; his auction 22 September 1783, Amsterdam, no. 191[4]; bought by Carré for 18.10 guilders; anonymous German collection; G.C.A. Basch Gallery, Rotterdam; bought from the Gallery by A. van Veen, Rotterdam; donated by him to the Museum in 1926; inv. no. 1007.

Exhibitions: (Y. Bruijnen), *Pieter Aertsen. Vier schilderijen doorgelicht*, Rotterdam, Museum Boymans-van Beuningen, 1990, pp. 24-28, fig.

Literature: *Verslag betreffende de aanwinsten en den toestand van het Museum Boijmans te Rotterdam in 1927*, p. 3, fig.; P. Wescher, "Der Maler Pieter Pietersz. und sein Werk", *Oud Holland* XLVI (1929), p. 157, fig. 2; Friedländer, XIII, 1936, p. 167, no. 297; G.J. Hoogewerff, *De Noord-Nederlandsche Schilderkunst*, IV, The Hague 1941-1942, pp. 523-525; R. Genaille, "L'œuvre de Pieter Aersten", *Gazette des Beaux-Arts* XLIV (1954), pp. 272, 281, no. 11; R.H. Wilenski, *Flemish Painters*, London 1960, p. 482; cat. 1962, pp. 17, 18; D. Kreidl, "Die religiöse Malerei Pieter Aertsens als Grundlage seiner künstlerischen Entwicklung" *Jahrbuch der Kunsthistorischen Sammlungen in Wien* 68 (1972), p. 80, fig. 53; Friedländer, XIII, 1975, no. 297, fig. 148; D. Freedberg, "The problems of images in Northern Europe and its repercussions in the Netherlands", *Hafnia. Copenhagen papers in the history of art* 1976, pp. 38-39, fig.; K.P.F. Moxey, "Reflections on some unusual subjects in the work of Pieter Aertsen", *Jahrbuch der Berliner Museen* 18 (1976), pp. 70-76, fig. 9; K.P.F. Moxey, *Pieter Aertsen, Joachim Beuckelaer, and the rise of secular painting in the context of the reformation*, New York-London 1977 (diss. Chicago 1974), pp. 243-249, fig. 67; M. Braman Buchan, *The paintings of Pieter Aertsen*, New York 1975 (diss.), pp. 106-107, 201-202, no. 15; R. Genaille, "Pieter Aertsen, précurseur de l'art Rubénien", *Jaarboek van het Koninklijk Museum voor Schone Kunsten Antwerpen 1977*, p. 35, no. 19, fig. 11; D. Freedberg, "De kunst en de beeldenstorm, 1525-1580. De Noordelijke Nederlanden", in exhib. cat. *Kunst voor de beeldenstorm*, Amsterdam, Rijksmuseum, 1986, p. 61, fig. 20; H. Buijs, in exhib. cat. *Kunst voor de beeldenstorm*, Amsterdam, Rijksmuseum, 1986, p. 409; D. Freedberg, "Aertsen, Heemskerck en de crisis van de kunst in de Nederlanden", *Bulletin van het Rijksmuseum* 35 (1987), pp. 236-238, fig. 9; D. Freedberg, *Iconoclasm and Painting in the revolt of the Netherlands 1566-1609*, New York-London 1988 (diss. Oxford 1972), pp. 188, 189 fig. 2; N.N. Nikulin, *The Hermitage. Catalogue of Western European painting: Netherlandish painting, fifteenth and sixteenth centuries*, Moscow-Florence 1989, p. 26; J.M.C. Boreel, F.W.H. van Zon-Christoffels, "Enkele aspecten van de schilderspraktijk in het atelier van Pieter Aertsen natuurwetenschappelijk bekeken", in: *Pieter Aertsen (Nederlands Kunsthistorisch Jaarboek) 40 (1989)*, pp. 167, 168, 170, 173, 175, 176, 182, 183, 187, 189, fig. 1, 25; M. Bijl, M. Zeldenrust, W. Kloek, "Pieter Aertsen in het restauratie-atelier van het Rijksmuseum", in: *Pieter Aertsen (Nederlands Kunsthistorisch Jaarboek) 40 (1989)*, p. 214; P. van den Brink, "Het Petrus en Paulus altaarstuk van Pieter Pietersz in Gouda. Verslag van een natuurwetenschappelijk onderzoek", in: *Pieter Aertsen (Nederlands Kunsthistorisch Jaarboek) 40 (1989)*, p. 240; M. Aston, *The King's Bedpost. Reformation and iconography in a Tudor group portrait*, Cambridge 1993, p. 75, fig. 56.

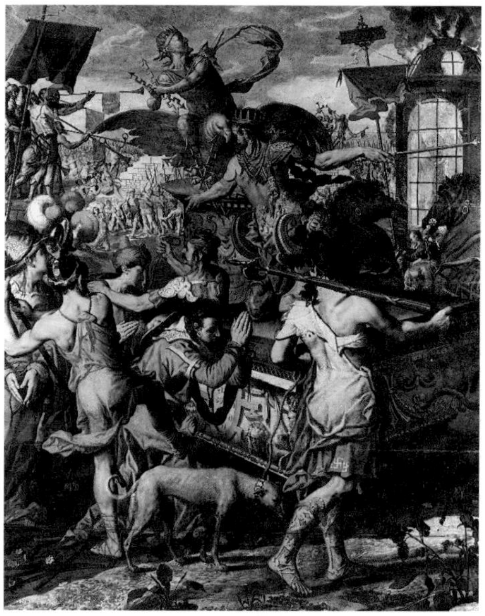

a. Pieter Pietersz, The three young men in the blazing furnace, 1575
Panel; 222.8 x 182.2 cm
Haarlem, Frans Hals Museum

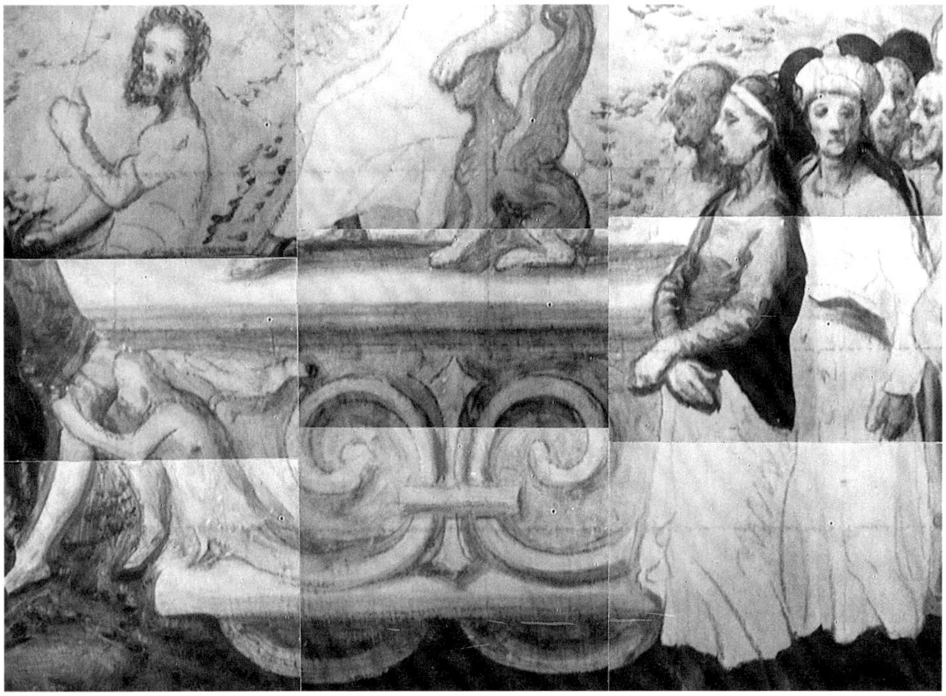

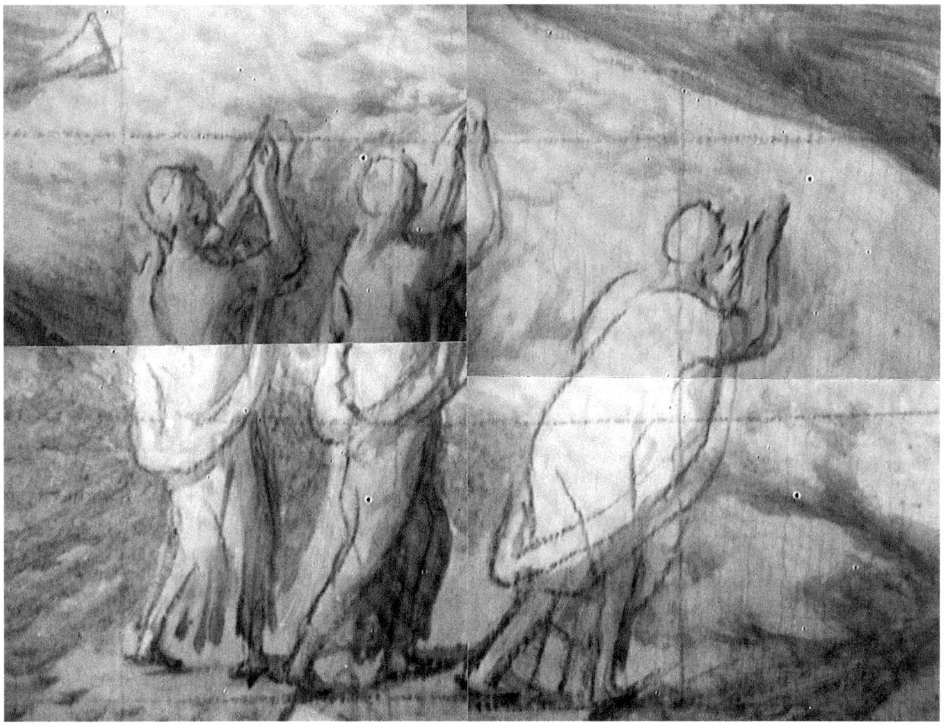

b. Infrared reflectogram assembly. Detail of Nebuchadnezzar's carriage.

c. Infrared reflectogram assembly. Detail of the three young men on the right.

King Nebuchadnezzar ordered that a giant golden statue be erected on the Dura plain in the province of Babel. All the administrators of the province were summoned for its dedication. The king commanded that everyone should kneel down and worship the statue upon hearing the sound of the horn, flute, zither, lute, harp, bagpipes and other instruments. Sadrach, Messach and Abednego, the administrators of the province of Babel, refused to obey this decree. Nebuchadnezzar had the three young Jewish men bound and cast into a furnace, but they remained unharmed and walked through the flames together with a fourth person who was recognised as a "son of the gods". After witnessing this miracle, the king praised the god of the three young men. He issued a proclamation that anyone who spoke disrespectfully of their god should be cut to pieces and his house destroyed (Daniel 3:1-30).

Aertsen followed the biblical text closely. The idol in the centre of the picture is being worshipped by a multitude of people. The musicians are playing on four raised platforms. The king is approaching from the right on a richly decorated carriage. Behind him stand three people, presumably the young men, their faces upturned to the heavens in prayer. In the left background, Sadrach, Messach and Abednego are shown amid the roaring flames, together with the angel.

The subject is very rare in sixteenth-century visual art. A series of four engravings by Philips Galle after a design by Maerten van Heemskerck from 1565 tells the story of the three young men.[5]

Writers do not agree about the dating of Aertsen's painting. It has been variously dated early, that is around 1552, but also around the early 1560s.[6] The dendrochronological examination supports the latter dating, i.e. around 1560. In any case it seems clear that the painting was made on the eve of the Iconoclasm in 1566. A number of authors have asked what the artist and/or his patron meant by the painting. At the time when the panel was painted, a fierce debate was raging about the veneration of religious images. The story of the three youths was cited by Protestant writers as proof that God rejected the worship of images. Catholic authors saw the episode only as the story of a heathen king worshipping a heathen image. They saw no connection to the veneration of Christian images.[7]

It seems almost unthinkable that a painting with such a rare subject should not have had some bearing on this debate. Aertsen was a Catholic painter, but that tells us little. Around the same time, another devout Catholic painter, Heemskerck, designed several series of prints with inscriptions critical of the practice of worshipping idols.[8]

In 1575 Aertsen's son, Pieter Pietersz, was commissioned by the Haarlem bakers' guild to paint the same subject of the three young men as an altarpiece for the church of St Bavo (fig. a).[9] This painting emphasises the miracle in the furnace more than Aertsen's piece, but the idol is nevertheless clearly visible. This indicates that the subject was not irreconcilable with the Catholic faith.

Like Heemskerck's series of prints, Aertsen's painting was intended as a criticism of the wrongful use of images. It is difficult to determine whether the panel has a further meaning.

The painting has extensive underdrawing including a squared grid (figs. b and c). Even the smallest figures have been underdrawn. With the exception of the decoration on the carriage, the painter did not deviate from the underdrawing. The very dark shadows were painted using a black pigment. As with many of Aertsen's works, it is probable that the master was aided by a studio assistant. The faithful following of the underdrawing, which was definitely by Aertsen, adds weight to this view.
FL

1 The scientific examination was supervised by J.R.J. van Asperen de Boer and was published by Yvette Bruijnen in exhib. cat. Rotterdam, 1990. Paint samples: A 111/1-2. Infrared reflectograms: AB 119/1-13, AB 120/1-6.

2 "1 stuck van Lange Pier van de Gloeiende Oven", see N. de Roever, "Pieter Aertsz: gezegd Lange Pier, vermaard schilder", *Oud Holland* VII (1889), p. 19.

3 "een schilderij van Baal, daar hij aangebeden wordt", see Roever, *op. cit* (note 1).

4 See Buchan (1975).

5 Ilja M. Veldman, *The New Hollstein. Dutch & Flemish etchings, engravings and woodcuts 1450-1700*, I, Roosendaal 1993, nos. 170-173, pp. 147-149.

6 Genaille (1954), dates it around 1552 and compares it to the *Christ bearing the cross* dated in that year which was formerly in Berlin. Buchan (1975) dates it in the mid-1550s and compares it to the *Triptych with the seven joys of Mary* dated 1554, in Zoutleeuw. Buijs (1986) dates it in the late 1550s or early 1560s.

7 See Moxey (1976).

8 See Saunders (1978-1979) and Freedberg (1986 and 1987).

9 See for this painting Buijs (1986).

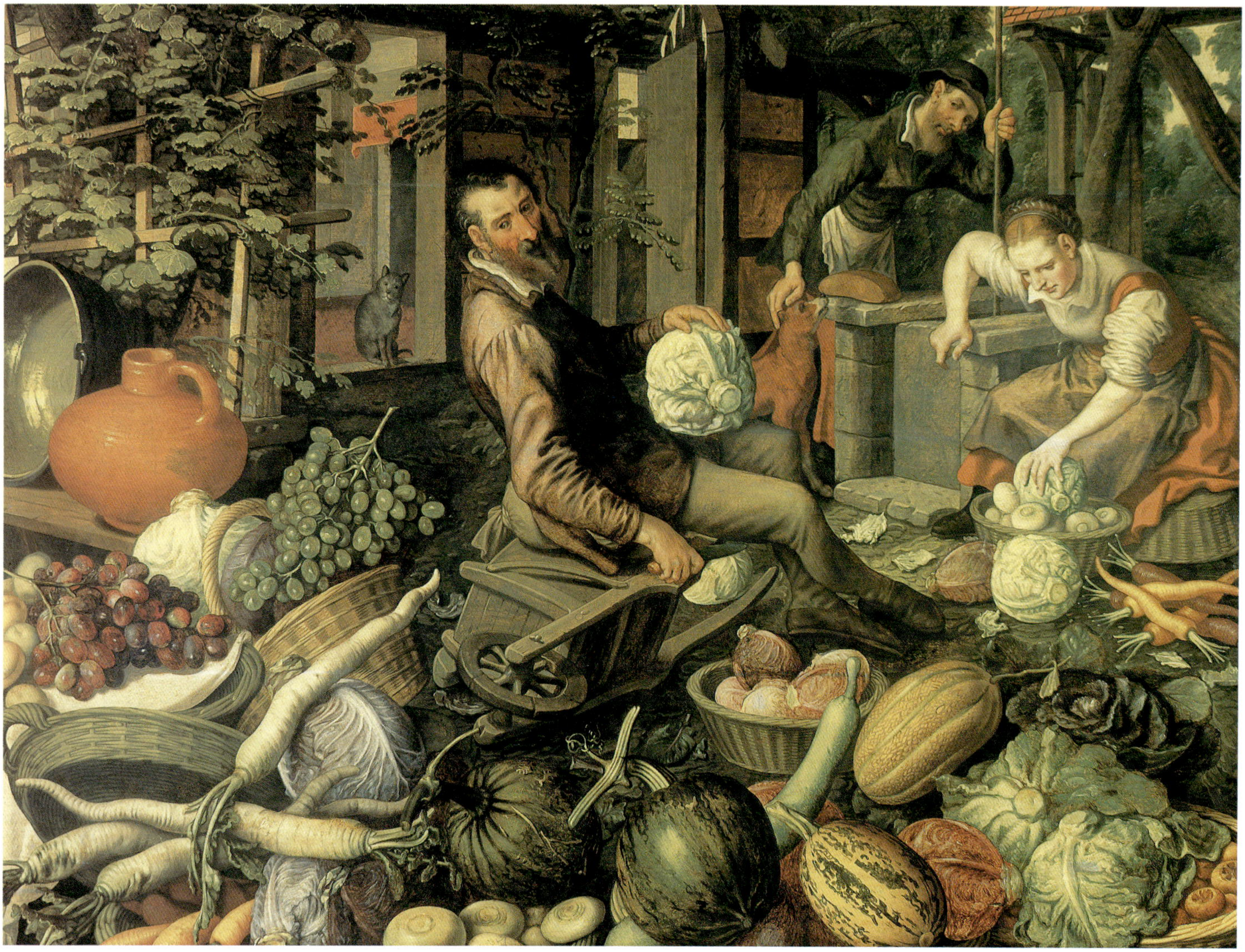

After the harvest

Pieter Aertsen
(Amsterdam 1505/1507-Amsterdam 1575)

Panel; 102.5 x 134 cm

Physical characteristics:[1] the panel originally consisted of four horizontal planks. In a radical restoration carried out between 1967 and 1971, P.F.J.M. Hermesdorf removed the planks and transferred the ground and paint layers to a linen backing. The report on the operation states that it was necessary to halt the ongoing flaking. In addition, heavy shrinkage was causing the ground layer to become detached from the wood.

Infrared reflectography: an extensive underdrawing in black chalk. See description.

Paint samples: pigments identified are smalt, lead white and azurite. There was no intermediate layer containing lead white. The underdrawing was applied directly on the ground.

Provenance: Bruno Beroll, Vienna; Jagenau Gallery, The Hague; bought there by D.G. van Beuningen, Rotterdam and Vierhouten, in 1939 for 7500 guilders; inv. no. 2436.

Exhibitions: *Honderd jaar Museum Boymans Rotterdam. Meesterwerken uit de collectie D.G. van Beuningen*, Rotterdam, Boymans Museum, 1949, no. 2; *La Nature Morte de l'Antiquité à nos jours*, Paris, Musée de l'Orangerie, 1952, no. 11; *Chefs-d'œuvre de la collection D.G. van Beuningen*, Paris, Petit Palais, 1952, no. 36; (Y. Bruijnen), *Pieter Aertsen. Vier schilderijen doorgelicht*, Rotterdam, Boymans Museum, 1990, pp. 40-44.

Literature: E. Greindl, "Einige Stileigentümlichkeiten an den Werken des Pieter Aertsen und des Joachim Beuckelaer", *Pantheon* XXX (1942), p. 154; Hannema, 1949, no. 2, fig. 59; Ch. Sterling, *La Nature Morte de l'Antiquité à nos jours*, Paris 1952, fig. 32; R. Genaille, "L'œuvre de Pieter Aertsen", *Gazette des Beaux-Arts* XLIV (1954), p. 287, no. 52; cat. 1962, p. 18; R. Genaille, "D' Aertsen à Snyders: maniérisme et baroque", *Bulletin Koninklijke Musea voor Schone kunsten van België* XVI (1967), p. 86, fig. 6; G.T. Faggin, *La Pittura ad Anversa nel cinquecento*, Florence 1968, p. 114, fig. 94; D. Kreidl, "Die religiöse Malerei Pieter Aertsens als Grundlage seiner künstlerischen Entwicklung", *Jahrbuch der kunsthistorischen Sammlungen in Wien* 68 (1972), p. 105, fig. 76; M.B. Buchan, *The paintings of Pieter Aertsen* (diss.), New York 1975, p. 171, no. 43; K.P.F. Moxey, "The 'humanist' market scenes of Joachim Beuckelaer: moralizing example or 'slices of life'", *Jaarboek van het Koninklijk Museum voor Schone Kunsten Antwerpen* 1976, p. 159, note 121; R. Genaille, "Pieter Aertsen, précurseur de l'art Rubénien", *Jaarboek van het Koninklijk Museum voor Schone Kunsten Antwerpen* 1977, p. 75, no. 67, fig. 44; exhib. cat. *Joachim Beuckelaer*, Ghent, Museum voor Schone Kunsten, 1986-87, pp. 142-143, fig.; R.L. Falkenburg, "'Alter Einoutus': Over de aard en herkomst van Pieter Aertsens sillevenconceptie", in: *Pieter Aertsen (Nederlands Kunsthistorisch Jaarboek 40 (1989))*, pp. 52-54, fig. 22; J.M.C. Boreel, F.W.H. van Zon-Christoffels, "Enkele aspecten van de schilderspraktijk in het atelier van Pieter Aertsen natuurwetenschappelijk nader bekeken", in: *Pieter Aertsen (Nederlands Kunsthistorisch Jaarboek 40 (1989))*, pp. 167, 186-187, 191, 192, figs. 6, 37; W.A. Brandenburg, "Market scenes as viewed by a plant biologist", in: D. Freedberg, J. de Vries (eds.), *Art in History. History in Art. Studies in seventeeth-century Dutch culture*, Santa Monica 1991, pp. 65-67.

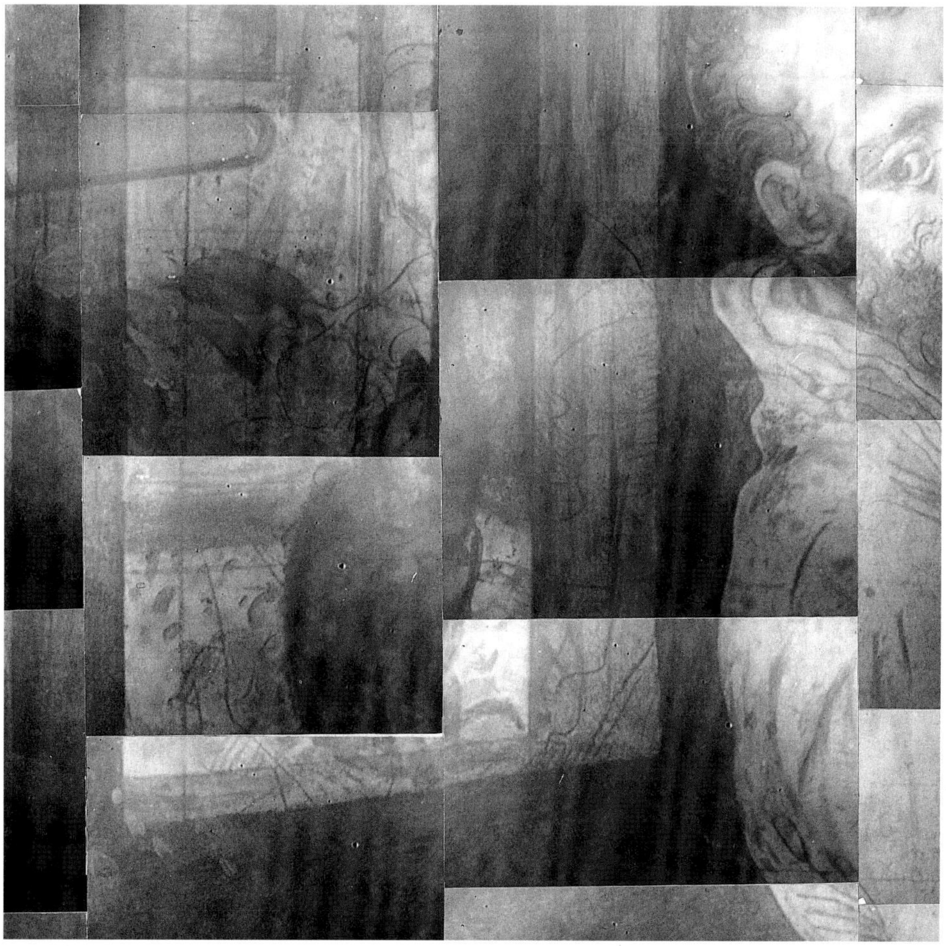

a. Infrared reflectogram assembly. Detail of the man at the window who is not shown in the painting.

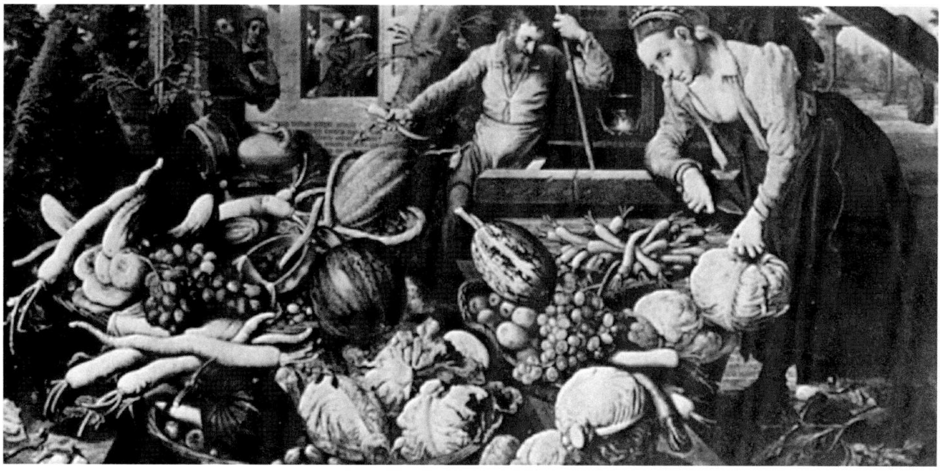

b. Pieter Aertsen, Market scene
Panel: 83 x 169 cm
Stockholm, Hallwyl Museum.

The foreground is an elaborate still life of vegetables and fruit like cabbage, pumpkins, grapes, parsnips, turnips and medlars. Behind them a man holding a cabbage is seated on an overturned wheelbarrow. On the right, a man and woman are working beside a well. A cat is sitting on a window ledge of the house visible in the background.

The painting was traditionally called *A fruit and vegetable stall*, but *After the harvest* seems preferable because there is nothing to indicate that the produce is for sale; the figures look more as if they are cleaning it.

Like so many of Aertsen's paintings, this has been the subject of iconographical study. It is assumed that it is filled with erotic significance, that the well and the cabbage, turnips and parsnips all have a sexual connotation,[2] even though there are no clear indications that this is so. Other pictures by this artist are more explicit, often through the figures' gestures. One art historian sees the chaotic arrangement of the still life in the foreground as deliberately consistent with the country-life genre.[3] According to the same author, the rustic on the wheelbarrow is borrowed from Italian painters, his elegant, "classical" posture and the sprawling still life being an ironic comment on "elevated composition art". But it is very much open to question whether the artist's motives were so complex. The panel itself displays no evidence of any such intellectual significance.

The elaborate underdrawing is executed in black chalk.[4] It is closely followed in the painting, save for the window on the left, in which a man was to be seen (fig. a). He was replaced by the cat. The man in the underdrawing appears to be very like the figure leaning out of a window in an Aertsen painting in the Hallwyl Museum, Stockholm (fig. b).[5] He was probably left out of the Rotterdam painting for compositional reasons. A similar still life can be seen in the Stockholm picture, in which some of the fruit and vegetables, such as the grapes, the pumpkins and the parsnips, are in fact identical in form and size.

The same farm produce is reproduced in other works by Aertsen. It is therefore extremely likely that cartoons were used in the artist's workshop.[6] Models must have been available for certain compositional elements, such as the heaped parsnips, or individual vegetables and fruit. The cartoon, blackened on the back, would be placed on the prepared panel, and the contours traced with a sharp instrument. It has been suggested that the rather muddled appearance of the still life in this painting (and others by Aertsen) is the result of such a working method.[7]

It may be deduced from the use of cartoons that Aertsen worked with assistants. It is difficult to determine precisely what was painted by the artist himself.

The Rotterdam panel is generally thought to be a late work from around 1567-1569, a date based on the *Fruit and vegetable seller* in Berlin (Staatliche Museen Preussischer Kulturbesitz), which is dated 1567.[8]
FL

1 See exhib. cat. Rotterdam 1990, and Boreel, Van Zon-Christoffels (1989). Paint samples: A 110/1-6. Infrared reflectograms: AB 1134/13-AB 1136/22, AB 1236/1-28.
2 See exhib. cat. *Joachim Beuckelaer*, Ghent 1986-87.
3 Falkenburg (1989).
4 The underdrawing is similar to that of the *Adoration of the Magi* and a *Kitchen piece* in the Rijksmuseum, Amsterdam. See Boreel and Van Zon-Christoffels (1989).
5 The description of Boreel and Van Zon-Christoffels (1989), who see in the figure a haloed saint with a scroll, is unlikely.
6 See Y. Bruijnen, "Fruits and vegetables: new information on workshop practice of Pieter Aertsen", *Oud Holland* (forthcoming).
7 See note 6.
8 Genaille (1954), Buchan (1975).

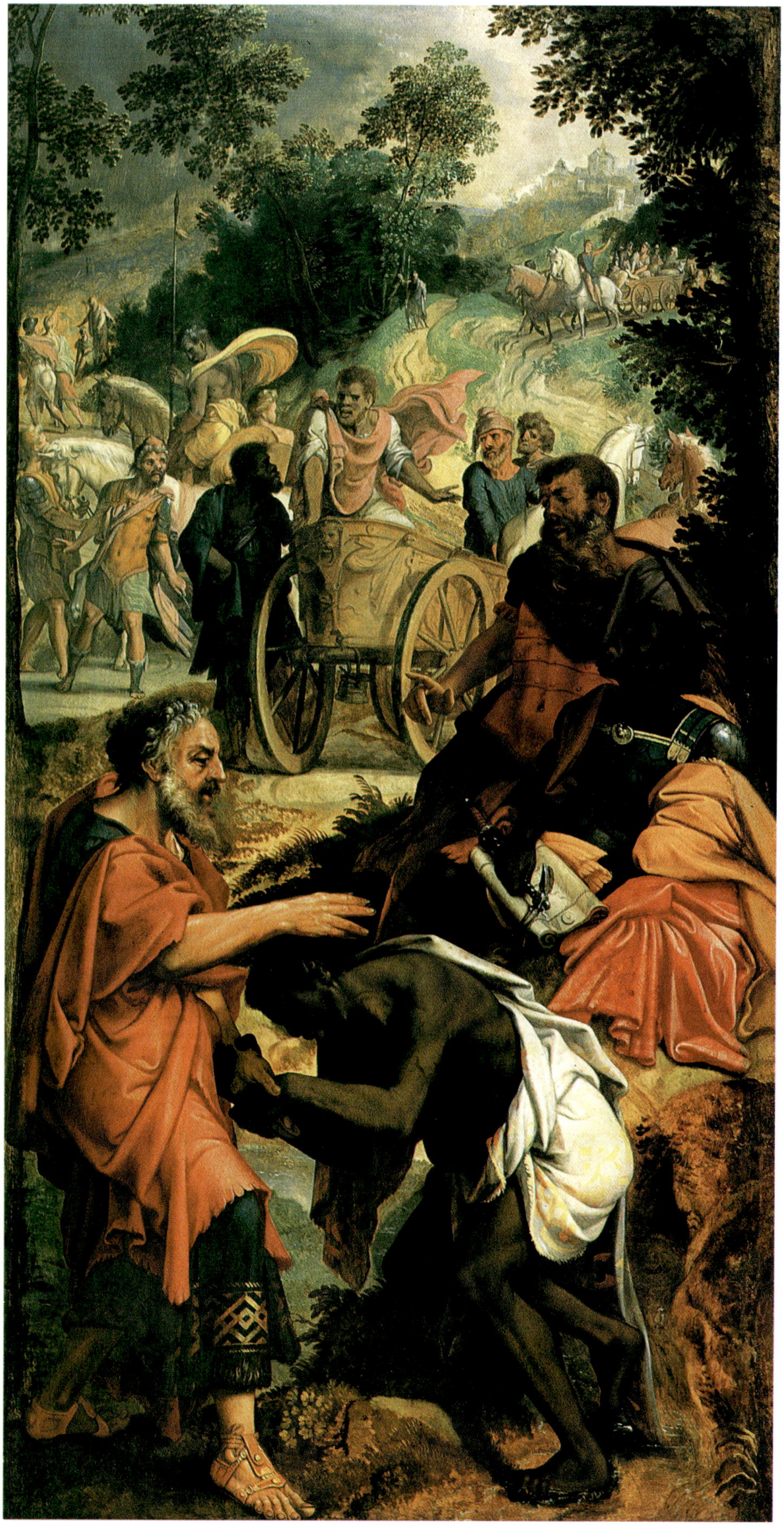

The baptism of the eunuch

Hansje van Elburg
(Elburg-Antwerp (?), after 1560)

Panel; 186.5 x 99 cm

Physical characteristics: the panel consists of four vertical planks. The *barbe* can be seen at the side- and lower edges. The panel has been sawn off along the upper edge.

Infrared reflectography:[1] parts of the the underdrawing are visible to the naked eye. It is freely executed, probably in black chalk.

Provenance: ordered around 1560 by the Antwerp fishmongers' guild to form the left-hand panel of their altarpiece in Antwerp Cathedral; in the cathedral until at least 1798; W.A. Engelbrecht, Rotterdam; donated by him to the Boymans Museum in 1938; inv. no. 2121.

Exhibitions: *Bijbelsche Kunst*, Amsterdam, Rijksmuseum, 1939, no. 128a

Literature: *Verslag omtrent den toestand en de aanwinsten van het Museum Boijmans over het jaar 1938*, p. 2, fig. V; N.N., "Ein Pieter Aertsen für das Museum in Rotterdam", *Weltkunst*, 20 November 1938; G.J. Hoogewerff, *De Noord-Nederlandsche schilderkunst*, IV, The Hague 1941-42, pp. 523, 539, fig. 247; J.J.M. Timmers, *De religieuze schilderkunst*, Naarden 1947, p. 30, fig. 35; R. Genaille, "L'œuvre de Pieter Aertsen", *Gazette des Beaux-Arts* XLIV (1954), p. 287; J. Bruyn, "Niet Lange Pier maar Cleen Hansken", *Bulletin Museum Boymans-van Beuningen* XVII (1966), pp. 2-12, 39, fig.; M. Braman Buchan, *The paintings of Pieter Aertsen* (diss. New York) 1975, p. 228, no. 14 R; W. Kloek, "Pieter Aertsen en het probleem van het samenstellen van zijn oeuvre", *Pieter Aertsen (Nederlands Kunsthistorisch Jaarboek)* 40 (1989), The Hague 1990, p. 25, note 25, p. 26, note 28; W. Kloek, "De tekeningen van Pieter Aertsen en Joachim Beuckelaer", *Pieter Aertsen (Nederlands Kunsthistorisch Jaarboek)* 40 (1989), The Hague 1990, p. 145, K.G. Boon, *The Netherlandish and German Drawings of the XVth and XVIth centuries of the Frits Lugt Collection*, Paris 1992, p. 6.

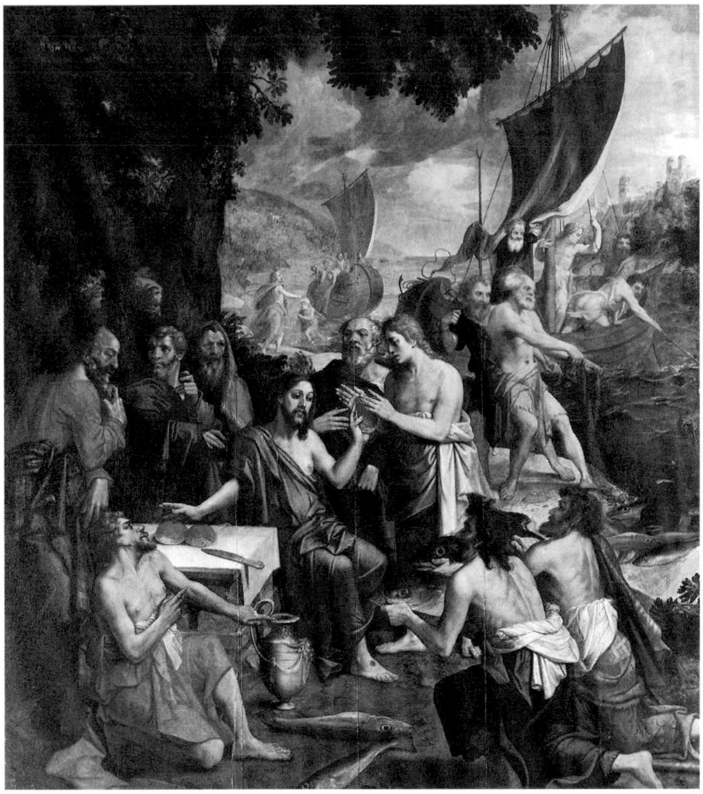

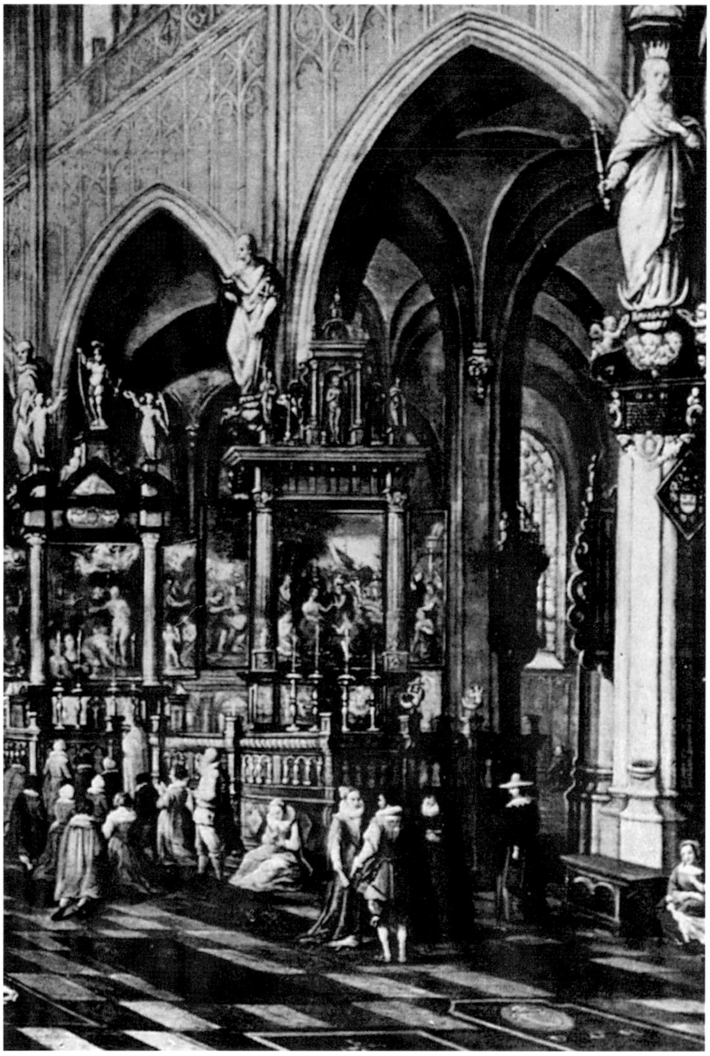

a. Hansje van Elburg, The miraculous draught of fishes
Panel; 190 x 167 cm
Antwerp Cathedral

b. Anonymous, View of Antwerp Cathedral, c. 1630 (detail)
Panel; 74 x 103 cm
Whereabouts unknown

On his way to Jerusalem the apostle Philip met the chamberlain of the Queen of Ethiopia, who was reading aloud from the book of Isaiah. The chamberlain invited the apostle to take a seat next to him in his carriage. The Moor continued reading and asked Philip the meaning of a particular passage, Isaiah 53:7, 8. He explained that it was a reference to Jesus Christ. When they came to some water, the chamberlain asked the apostle if he would baptise him (Acts 8:27-39).

In the foreground the panel shows Philip performing the baptism. In the background on the right the preceding events – the joint reading of the Bible – are depicted. In the background on the left is what appears to be a third portrait of Philip, this time preaching.

When the painting arrived at the Museum in 1938, it was attributed to Pieter Aertsen. This remained the case until 1966, when it was shown beyond reasonable doubt that the true artist was in fact Hansje van Elburg.[2]

Van Mander made the following comment about Hansje van Elburg in his *Schilderboeck*: "In the year 1535 Hans van Elburg, or little Hans, came to the guild in Antwerp, where his Fish Merchants' Altar stood in the church of Our Lady, where St Peter fishing is shown".[3] The centre panel of the altarpiece is still in Antwerp Cathedral (fig. a). It originally had two wings, both of which were probably removed in the nineteenth century. A *View of Antwerp Cathedral* by an anonymous artist shows that the wings depicted scenes from the lives of the apostles Philip and James who were, in addition to Peter, patron saints of the fishmongers' guild (fig. b).[4] The right wing portraying James has been lost, but the other one is undoubtedly the painting dealt with here. The panel in Antwerp is 190 cm high and 167 cm wide. The curious way in which it has been trimmed along the right and lower edges indicates that it was once larger. The Rotterdam panel has always been 99 cm wide, which suggests that the width of the centre panel was probably reduced by about 30 cm. The panel in Rotterdam, like that in Antwerp, must originally have been higher.

The back of the Rotterdam panel is a uniform grey. X-radiographs show that the grey paint in fact conceals a monumental male figure, standing barefoot on a stone ledge, wearing a large cloak and holding a book in his right hand. The entire head is missing, however, because the top of panel has been sawn off. It seems likely that the figure was a portrait of the apostle Philip.

It is no surprise that the panel was originally attributed to Pieter Aertsen, given the close stylistic relationship between the two painters. Indeed Hansje probably based his work on a lost painting by Aertsen. The Custodia Foundation has a drawing attributed to Aertsen with the same subject which is very similar to the work in Rotterdam (fig. c).[5] The original design of the painting showed an even greater similarity. The hand of the bearded figure on the right, for example, was initially outstretched, as in the drawing (fig. d). The artist subsequently made the hand point forwards.

Archive records show that the altar of the Antwerp fishmongers' guild must have been made after 1538.[6] Hansje van Elburg drew inspiration for the centre panel from an engraving by Pieter van der Heyden based on a design made by Lamberd Lombard in 1556.[7] A painting by Joachim de Beuckelaer, dated 1563, seems in turn to have been influenced by the work by Hansje van Elburg.[8] This implies that the triptych was probably made around 1560.
FL

[1] Carried out by J.R.J. van Asperen de Boer on 24 January 1994. Infrared reflectograms: AB 1564/9A-26A.
[2] Bruyn (1966). Genaille (1954) rejected Aertsen as the artist, but did not suggest an alternative.
[3] C. van Mander, *Het Schilderboeck*, Haarlem 1604, fol. 205 v. "In 't Jaer 1535. quam t'Antwerp in 't Gildt Hansken van der Elburcht, by Campen/ geseyt Cleen Hansken. Van hem was aldaer in onse Vrouwen kerck den Visch-vercoopers Altaer/ daer Petrus doende was met vischen [...]".
[4] Bruyn was the first to identify the painting as the wing of the centre panel in Antwerp. See Bruyn (1966).
[5] Pen, brush, chalk; 373 x 199 mm. Paris, Custodia Foundation (F. Lugt Collection), Institut Néerlandais (inv. no. 1983-T. 11). Kloek (1989), p. 145, considers the drawing to be by one of Aertsen's studio assistants. Boon (1992) believes that it is by Aertsen himself. A grid in red chalk was added to the drawing, indicating that the design was in fact most probably carried out. It is, therefore, unlikely that the drawing is a preparatory study by Hansje van Elburg himself.
[6] Bruyn (1966).
[7] See Kloek (1989) and G. Denhaene, *Lambert Lombard. Renaissance et humanisme à Liège*, Antwerp 1990, pp. 234-235, figs. 314, 315. Kloek states mistakenly that the engraving is dated 1566.
[8] Bruyn (1966). The painting is now in the J. Paul Getty Museum, Malibu, California.

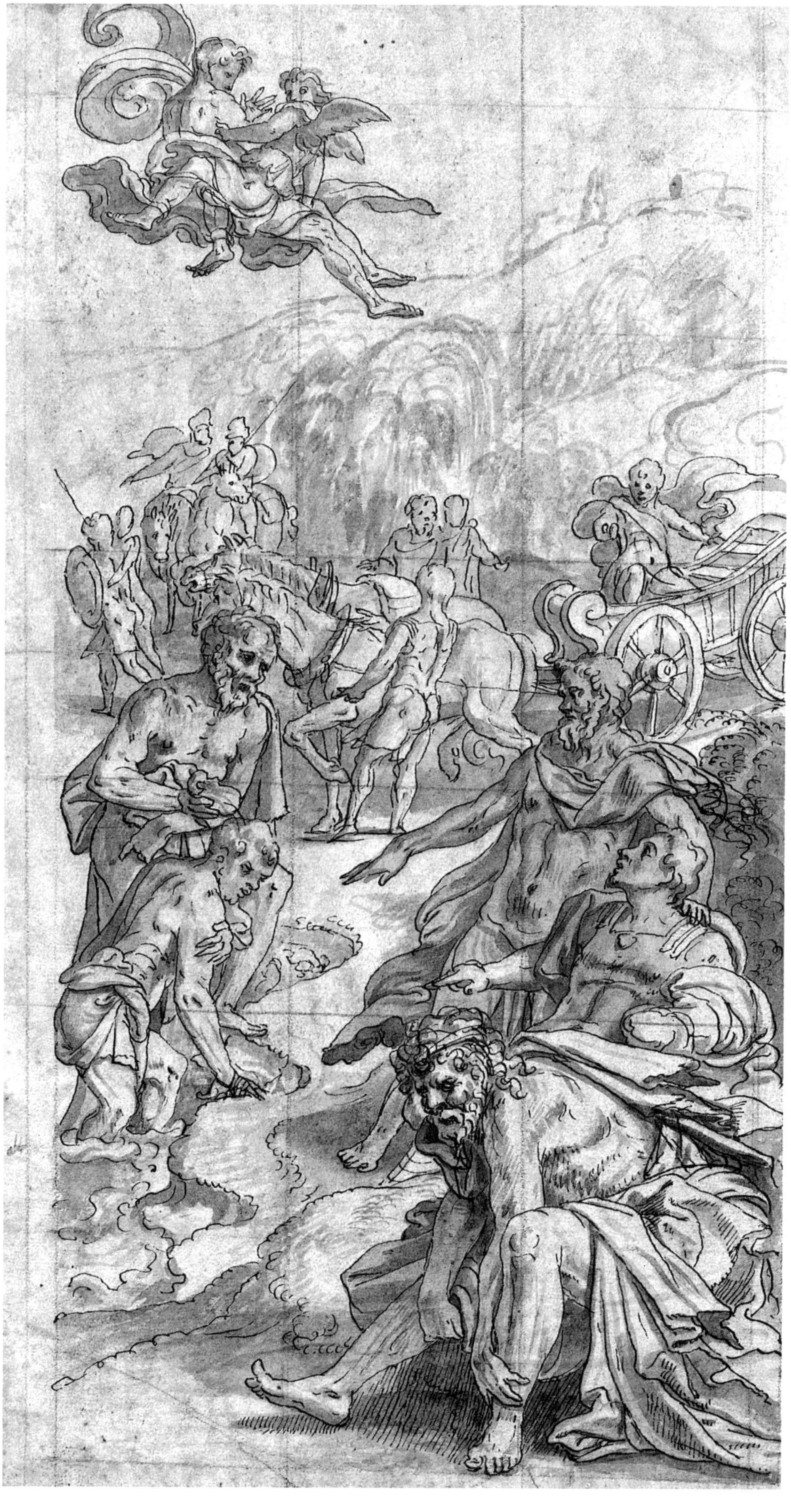

c. Pieter Aertsen (?), The baptism of the eunuch
Pen, brush, chalk on paper; 373 x 179 mm
Paris, Custodia Foundation (inv. no. 1983-T.11)

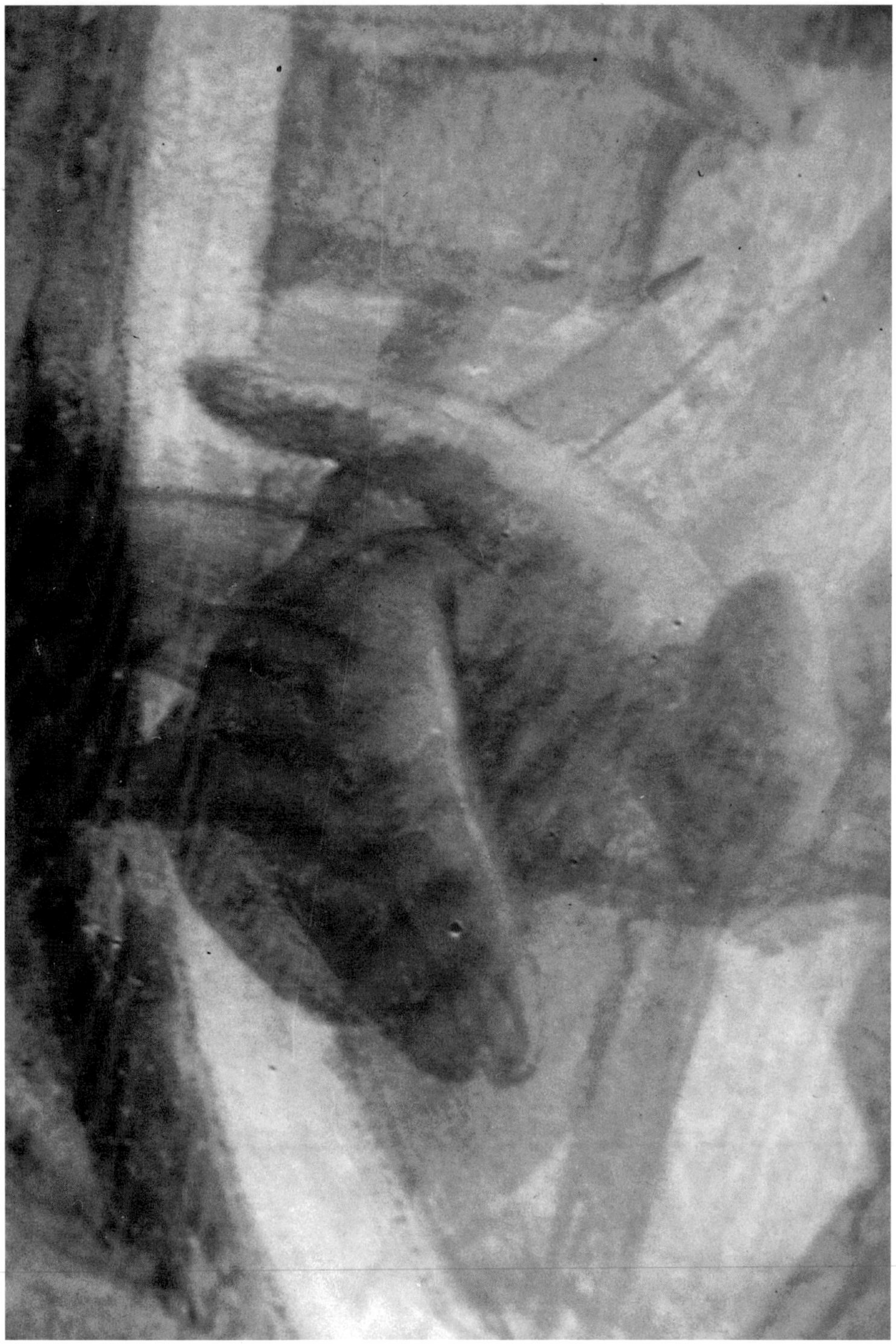

d. Infrared reflectogram showing modifications in the hand of the bearded man on the right.

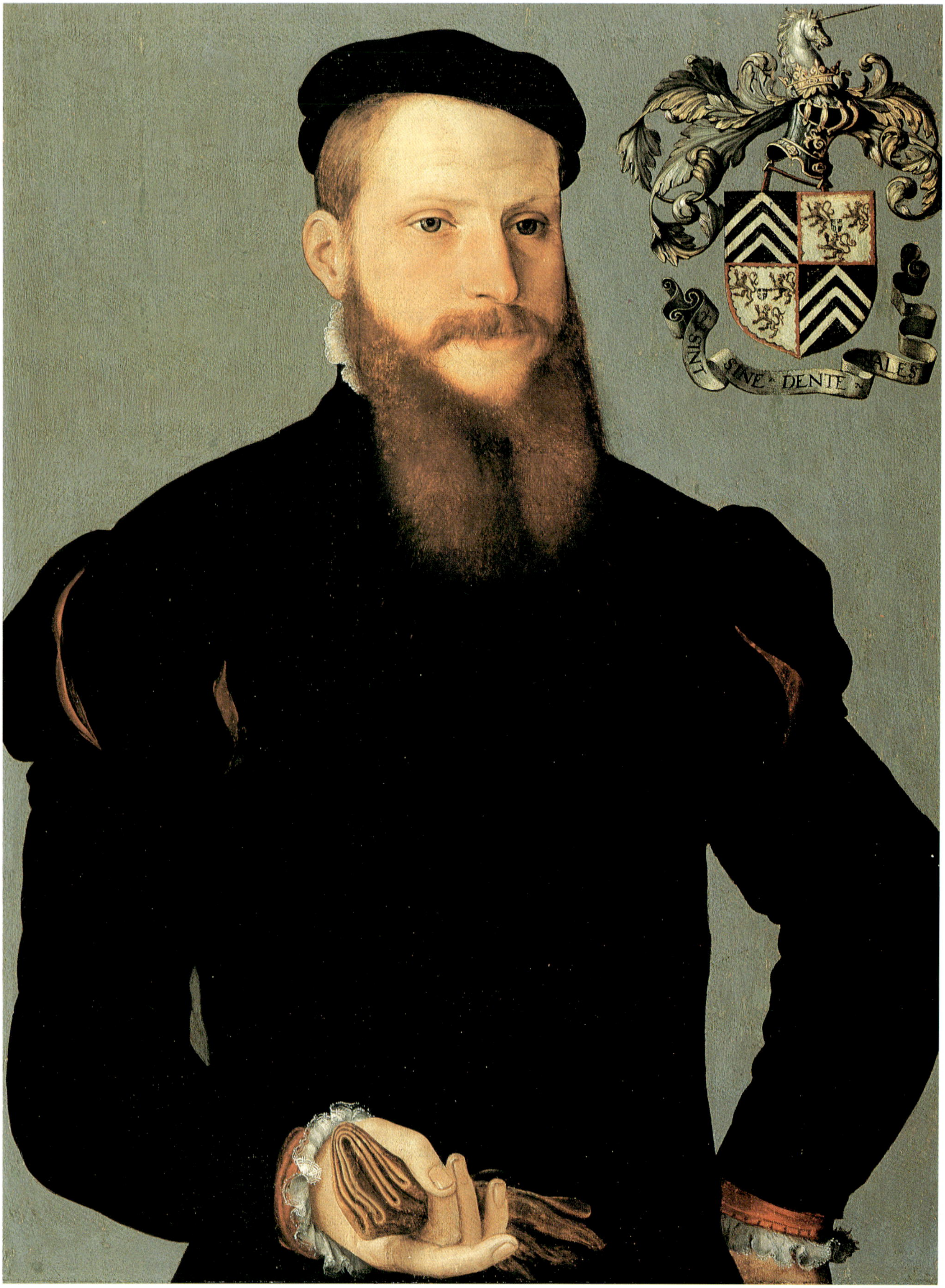
SINT
SINE DENTE
ALES

Portrait of Joris (?) van der Heede

Pieter Pourbus
(Gouda 1524-Bruges 1584)

Panel; 64 x 46.5 cm
Inscription: SINT SINE DENTE SALES

This is a full frontal portrait of a man in black against a blue-grey background. In his right hand he holds a glove. In the upper right corner is a coat of arms with the device SINT SINE DENTE SALES (Your temper be not hurtful). The coat of arms belonged to the branch of the Van den Heede family related to the Lannoy family. They lived in Oudenaarde and Bruges.[2] Through the coat of arms the sitter was identified in 1880 as Joris van de Heede (d. 1569),[3] son of Willem van den Heede (d. 1540) and Jeanne van der Crucen. He married Levina de Baenst and, after her death in 1541, Eleonara van der Beken. His birth date can be no later than 1520.

His costume dates the work to around 1555-1560. If it is indeed a portrait of Joris van den Heede, he would then have been aged about 40, as seems likely from the painting.

But this identification is by no means certain. As the coat of arms and device were also borne by other members of the family, it could equally well be a portrait of one of his brothers, Willem and Jan, or of Daniel van den Heede, a relative who died in Bruges in 1559.[4]

The underdrawing consists of fine lines executed in black chalk. The only alteration made during painting was to place the top of the ear slightly higher (fig. a).

The catalogue of the 1867 auction at which the Museum bought the painting described it as a portrait of a man attributed to Pieter Pourbus. But evidently this was not accepted because the Museum's catalogue for the same year placed it in the category of anonymous masters. In the 1902 catalogue it was attributed to Joos van Cleve on the authority of A. Bredius. The entry in the 1907 catalogue remained unchanged, but with a note stating that some authorities considered it to be a work by Pourbus. Pieter Pourbus was cited as the artist in the 1916 edition, and there has been no further doubt since then. Indeed, since 1907 there has been universal recognition of the resemblance between this work and Pourbus' signed portrait of Jan van Eyewerve dating from 1551 (Groeninge Museum, Bruges).[5]
FL

Physical characteristics: the panel consists of two vertical planks.

Infrared reflectography:[1] black chalk underdrawing could be discerned under the head, hand and lace. See description.

Provenance: Rotterdam auction, 8-11 March 1867, no. 22; bought there by the Museum; inv. no. 1681.

Exhibitions: *Pieter Pourbus, meester-schilder 1524-1584*, Bruges, Memling Museum (Sint-Janshospitaal), 1984, no. 17, fig.

Literature: G. Ring, *Beiträge zur Geschichte Niederländischer Bildnismalerei im 15. und 16. Jahrhundert* (Beiträge zur Kunstgeschichte XL), Leipzig 1913, pp. 57, 58; F. Winkler, *Die Altniederländische Malerei. Die Malerei in Belgien und Holland von 1400-1600*, Berlin 1924, p. 290; Friedländer, XI, 1933, p. 114; G. Marlier, "Le maniérisme dans l'art de Pierre Pourbus", *Jaarboek der Koninklijke Museums voor Schoone Kunsten van België* II (1939), p. 85, fig. 12; R.-A. d'Hulst, "Pieter Pourbus, portretschilder van de Brugse burgerij uit de tweede helft der 16de eeuw", *Gentse bijdragen tot de Kunstgeschiedenis* XIII (1951), pp. 220, 253, figs. 2, 3; J. Schouten, "De nieuwe Pourbus in Gouda", *Nederlands Kunsthistorisch Jaarboek* X (1959), p. 62, fig. 5; cat. 1962, p. 106; L. van Puyvelde, *La peinture Flamande au siècle de Bosch et Breughel*, Paris 1962, p. 278; Friedländer XI, 1974, fig. 197.

1 Scanned on 10 January 1994 and partly recorded by J.R.J. van Asperen de Boer on 17 January 1994. The infrared reflectogram assembly was made by Joris Dik. Infrared reflectograms: AB 1554/30A-AB 1555/8A.
2 Exhib. cat. Bruges, 1984.
3 *Beschrijving der schilderijen en beeldhouwwerken in het Museum te Rotterdam gesticht door mr. F.J.O. Boymans*, 1880, no. 357.
4 See note 2.
5 *Beknopte catalogus der schilderijen en beeldhouwwerken van het Museum te Rotterdam geheeten naar den stichter Museum Boijmans* 1907, no. 14. It was thought at that time to be a portrait of J. Fernagant. On the identification of Jan van Eyewerve, see exhib. cat. Bruges, 1984, no. 16.

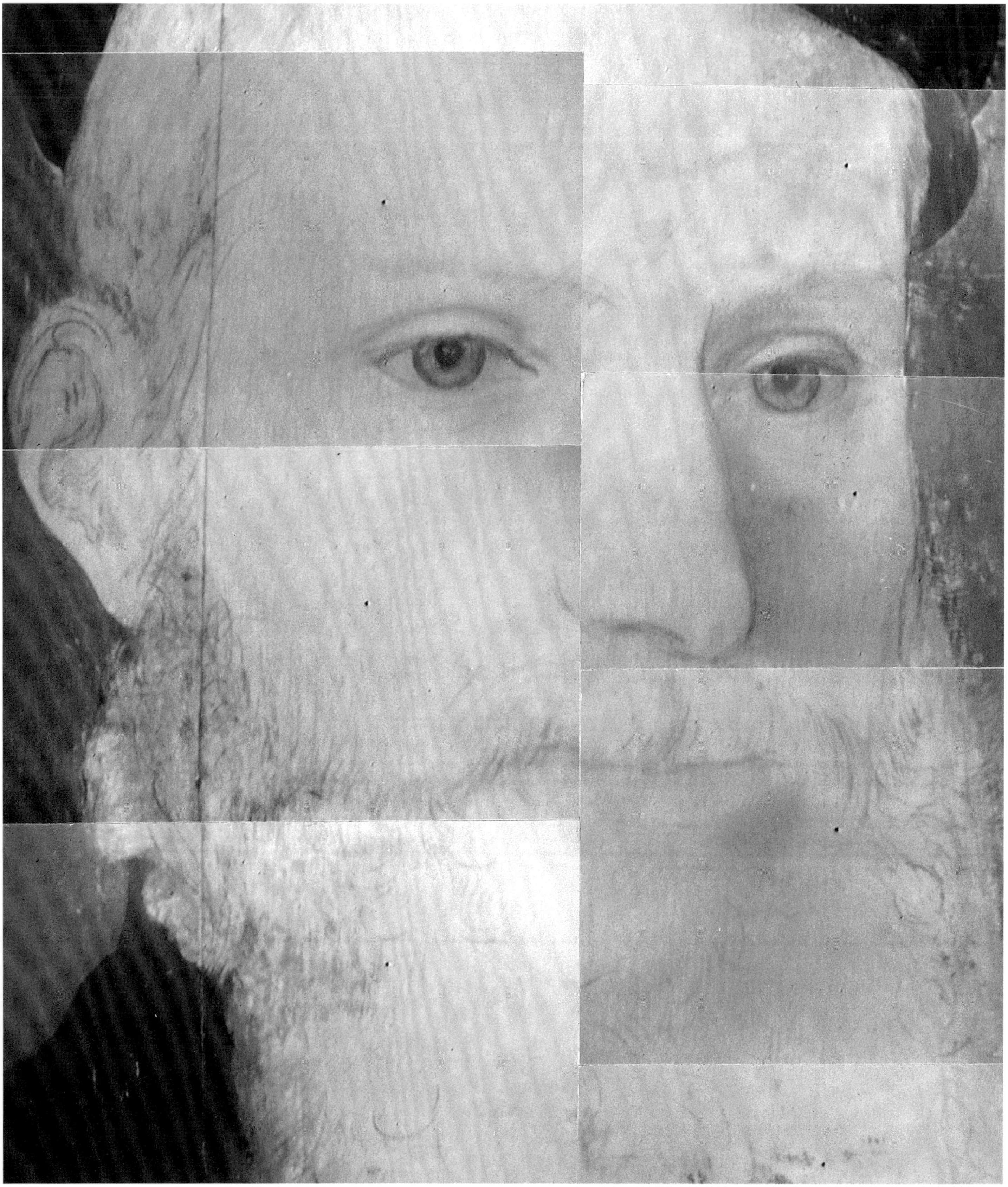

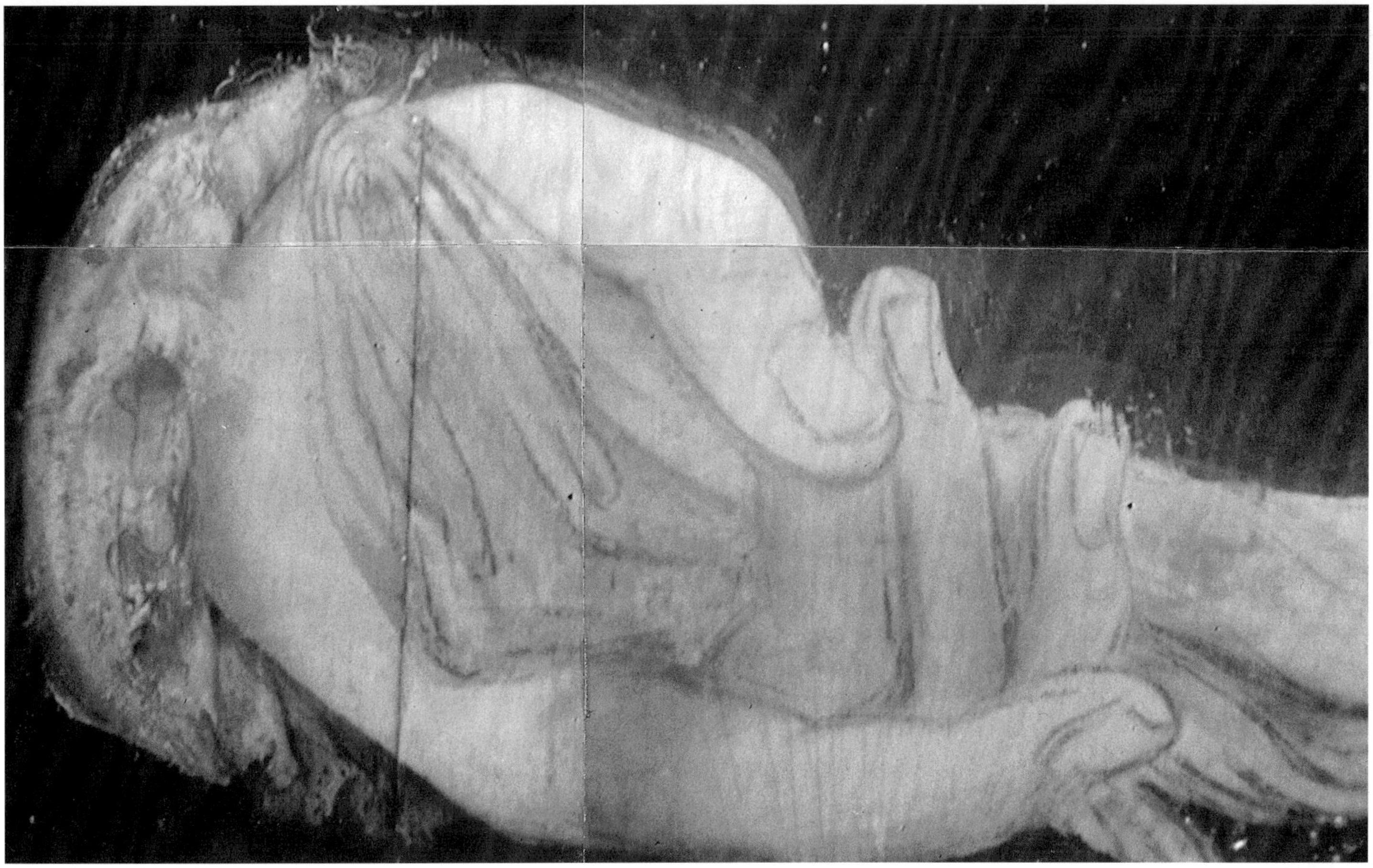

a. Infrared reflectogram assembly showing a detail of the head.

b. Infrared reflectogram assembly showing a detail of the right hand.

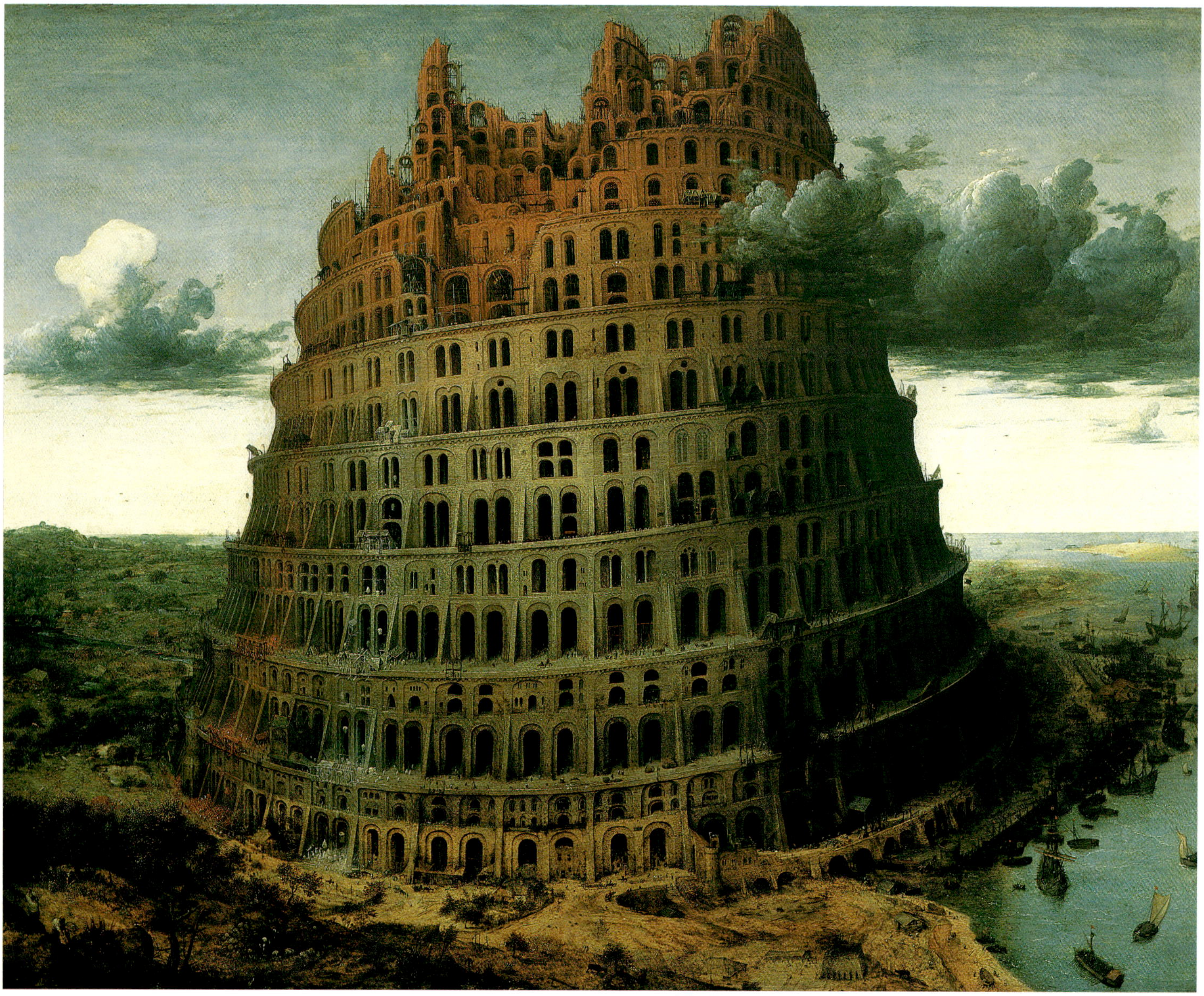

The tower of Babel

Pieter Bruegel the Elder
(1526?-Brussels 1569)

Panel; 59.9 x 74.6 cm

Physical characteristics: the panel consists of two vertical planks. Some time after the panel was made, two strips roughly 1.5 cm in width were added to the left and right edges. The panel is painted up to the edges.

Infrared reflectography:[1] some underdrawing could be discerned in the contours (fig. a) and some storeys of the tower. The clouds and the line of the coast were also underdrawn. Some ships were underdrawn but not painted (fig. b, c).

Dendrochronology: the youngest heartwood growth ring dates from 1539. The panel could not have been painted before 1550; it was more probably painted in or after 1556. See article by P. Klein.

Paint samples: paint sample analysis has shown that the air contains smalt and lead white and the clouds a blue copper pigment.

Provenance: Emperor Rudolph II, Prague, 1604[2]; possibly in the Van den Branden Collection, Antwerp, around 1650[3]; Empress Elisabeth Farnese, Madrid, from ca. 1714[4]; the painting re-surfaced in 1935 at the Paris gallery of E. Jonas and F. Kleinberger; bought by N. Beets and the Gallery P. Cassirer of Amsterdam; bought by D.G. van Beuningen, Rotterdam and Vierhouten, in 1936, for 120,000 guilders; acquired by the Museum in 1958 with the Van Beuningen Collection; inv. no. 2443.

Exhibitions: *Meesterwerken uit vier eeuwen 1400-1800*, Rotterdam, Boymans Museum, 1938, no. 1a, fig. 44; *Nederlandsche kunst van de XVde en XVIde eeuw*, The Hague, Mauritshuis, 1945, no. 36, fig. 24; *Honderd jaar Museum Boymans Rotterdam. Meesterwerken uit de verzameling D.G. van Beuningen*, Rotterdam, Boymans Museum, 1949, no. 9 fig. 55; *Chefs-d'œuvre de la collection D.G. van Beuningen*, Paris, Petit Palais, 1952, no. 43, fig. 20; *Bruegel, een dynastie van schilders*, Brussels, Koninklijke Musea voor Schone Kunsten, 1980, no. 3, fig.

Literature: C. van Mander, *Het Schilderboeck*, Haarlem 1604, fol. 233 v.; G. Glück, "Peter Bruegels des Aelteren 'kleiner' Turmbau zu Babel, *Jahrbuch der Kunsthistorische Sammlungen in Wien* X (1936), pp. 193-196, fig.; Friedländer, XIV, 1937, pp. 26, 59; G. Jedlicka, *Pieter Bruegel, der Maler in seiner Zeit*, Erlenbach-Zürich-Leipzig 1938, pp. 157-166, 520, 521; C. de Tolnay, "La seconde Tour de Babel de Pierre Bruegel l'Ancien", *Jaarboek der Koninklijke Museums voor Schone Kunsten van Belgie* I (1938), pp. 113-121; *Katalog der Gemäldegalerie (Führer durch das Kunsthistorische Museum, nr. 8)*, Vienna 1938, p. 25; J.B. Knipping O.F.M., *Pieter Bruegel de Oude*, Amsterdam 1945, p. 36; Hannema, 1949, no. 9, figs. 54-58; G. Glück, *Das grosse Bruegel-Werk*, Vienna 1951, pp. 42-43;; V. Denis (ed.), *Tutta la pittura di Pieter Bruegel*, Milan 1952, p. 31, figs. 57-59; R. Genaille, *Bruegel l'Ancien*, Paris-Brussels 1953, pp. 87-88, fig. 40; O. Benesch, "Die grossen Flämischen Maler als Zeichner", *Jahrbuch der Kunsthistorischen Sammlungen in Wien* 53 (1957), p. 20; J. Lassaigne en R.L. Delevoy, *La peinture Flamande de Jérôme Bosch à Rubens*, Geneva 1958, p. 52; F. Klauner, "Venezianische Landschaftsdarstellungen von Jacopo Bellini bis Tizian", *Jahrbuch der Kunsthistorischen Sammlungen in Wien* 54, (1958), p. 128; R.I. Delevoy, *Brueghel*, Geneva 1959; J.G. van Gelder, "Pieter Bruegel de Oude (ca. 1525 – 1569), De toren van Babel", *Openbaar Kunstbezit* 3 (1959), no. 40; H. Minkowski, *Aus dem Nebel der Vergangenheit steigt der Turm zu Babel*, Berlin 1960, pp. 54-55; L. van Puyvelde, *La peinture Flamande au siècle de Bosch et Breughel*, Paris 1962, p. 84, figs. 56, 57; cat. 1962, p. 34; J.H. Ronday, *Pieter Bruegel de Oude*, The Hague 1962, p. 41; exhib. cat. *De eeuw van Bruegel*, Brussels, Koninklijke Musea voor Schone kunsten, 1963, p. 170; M. Fryns, *Pierre Brueghel l'Ancien*, Brussels 1964, fig. 44; Z. Wazbinski, "'La construction de la tour de Babel' par Bruegel le Vieux", *Bulletin Musée National de Varsovie* 5, 1964, pp. 112-121; O. Benesch, *The art of the renaissance in Northern Europe*, 3rd edition (1st edition 1955), London 1965, pp. 147, 148; G.W. Menzel, *Pieter Bruegel der Aeltere*, Leipzig 1966, pp. 60, 61, fig. 38; G. Arpino and P. Bianconi, *L'Opera completa di Bruegel* (classici dell'arte 7), Milan 1967, no. 47, fig.; F. Ragette, "The tower of Babel", *Aramco world*, Jan.-Feb. 1967, pp. 18-23; H.A. Klein and M.C. Klein, *Pieter Bruegel the elder*, New York 1968, p. 74; C.D. Cuttler, *Northern Painting from Pucelle to Bruegel*, New York and others, 1968, p. 476; exhib. cat. *Bruegel, de schilder en zijn wereld*, Brussels, Koninklijke Musea voor Schone Kunsten, 1969, with no. 20; B. Claessens and J. Rousseau, *Onze Bruegel*, Antwerp 1969, p. 144, fig. 40.; R. H. Marijnissen, *Bruegel, le vieux*, Brussels 1969, pp. 14, 44, 46.; G. Marlier, *Pierre Brueghel le Jeune, édition posthume mise au point et annotée par Jacqueline Folie*, Brussels 1969, p. 96; G. von der Osten and H. Vey, *Painting and sculpture in Germany and the Netherlands 1500-1600* (The Pelican history of Art), Harmondsworth 1969, p. 303; R.H. Marijnissen and M. Seidel, *Bruegel*, Brussels 1969, p. 99, figs. 98-102; R.H. Marijnissen, *Werken van Bruegel uit Nederlands en Belgisch openbaar bezit*, 1969, p. 82, figs. 8-9; W. Stechow, *Pieter Bruegel the Elder*, New York 1970, p. 86, fig. 18; A. Wied, "Lucas van Valkenborch", *Jahrbuch der Kunsthistorischen Sammlungen in Wien* 67 (1971), pp. 192, 204; E.G. Grimme, *Pieter Bruegel, Leben und Werk*, Cologne 1973, p. 109; F. Grossmann, *Pieter Bruegel, Complete edition of the paintings*, 3rd revised edition (1st edition 1955), London 1973, p. 194, figs. 60, 63, 65; exhib. cat. *Pieter Bruegel der Ältere als Zeichner*, Berlin, Staatliche Museen Preussischer Kulturbesitz, Kupferstichkabinett, 1975, pp. 35, 106.; D. Ronte, *Pieter Bruegel*, Weert 1975, fig. 34; F. de Poli and E. Baccheschi, *I geni dell'arte, Bruegel*, Milan 1976, p. 55.; W.S. Gibson, *Bruegel*, London 1977, pp. 91, 96, 97; A. Prater, *Pieter Bruegel der Ältere*, Munich 1977, pp. 50-53; H.A. Klein, "Pieter Bruegel the elder as a guide to the 16th-century technology", *Scientific American*, March 1978, pp. 134-140; Kees Broos, "Raakvlakken tussen kunst, wetenschap en techniek", *Openbaar Kunstbezit* 1978, p. 103; J.C. Klamt, "Anmerkungen zu Pieter Bruegels Babel-Darstellungen", in: *Pieter Bruegel und seine Welt, ein Colloquium*, O.V. Simson and M. Winner (eds), Berlin 1979, pp. 43-49.; W.S. Gibson, *Bruegel*, Paris 1980, p. 63, fig. 59; J. Briels, "Amator Pictoriae Artis, de Antwerpse kunstverzamelaar Peeter Stevens (1590-1668) en zijn Constkamer", *Jaarboek van het Koninklijk Museum voor Schone Kunsten Antwerpen* 1980, pp. 197, 206; *Flämische malerei von Jan van Eyck bis Pieter Bruegel d.Ä, Katalog der Gemäldegalerie, Kunsthistorisches Museum Wien*, 1981, pp. 78-79; S.A. Mansbach, "Pieter Bruegel's towers of Babel", *Zeitschrift für Kunstgeschichte* 45 (1982), pp. 43-56; K. Roberts, *Bruegel*, Oxford 1982 (1st edition 1971), no. 15; H. Gassner and V. Ritter, *Fragen an ein Bild*, Berlin 1987, pp. 8-21.; S. Grieten, "De iconografie van de toren van Babel bij Pieter Bruegel: traditie, vernieuwing en navolging", *Jaarboek van het Koninklijk museum voor Schone Kunsten Antwerpen* 1988, pp. 127-136.; W.S. Gibson, *"Mirror of the earth", The world landscape in sixteenth-century Flemish Painting*, Princeton-New Jersey 1989, pp. 67-68, fig. 5.17.; A. Wied, *Lucas und Marten Valkenborch (1535 – 1597 und 1534-1612)*, Freren 1990, pp. 31-34; U. Kultermann, "La ciudad Caïda", *Goya* 217-218 (1990), p. 90; H. Minkowski, *Vermutungen über den Turm zu Babel*, Freren 1991, p. 175, fig. 215.

Bruegel made at least three paintings of the Tower of Babel. One is in Rotterdam, while a larger rendering of the same subject is at the Kunsthistorisches Museum in Vienna (fig. d). A third version has been lost, and is known only from the inventory of the miniaturist Giulio Clovio from 1577. It was painted on ivory and was definitely made in Rome.[5]

The story of the Tower of Babel is related in Genesis 11:1-9. It describes how the people of the land of Shinar used brick and lime to build a city and a tower which was supposed to reach up to heaven. But the Lord intervened and prevented the builders from completing the tower. He scattered them abroad and confounded their speech, so that humankind, which had been united by a single, common language, was divided into nations who were no longer able to understand one another. "Babel" is the Hebrew word for "confusion". According to Flavius Josephus (Book I, 4), the command to build the tower was given by Noah's great-grandson King Nimrod. Joseph condemns the arrogance of this act much more strongly than the bible.

The painting in Rotterdam differs from the work in Vienna as there is no city to be seen. Although this conflicts with the biblical account, it corresponds with Sibille's version of the story, which Josephus cites. She relates that a city – Babylon – was built only after the tower had been destroyed. The fall of Babylon is described at length in Revelations 18 and 19. The prosperous trading city was demolished in one hour in punishment for its sins which "reached unto heaven".

Most writers interpret the painting as a symbol of pride which is destined to fall,[6]. Some have suggested that it may also refer to the fall of Rome,[7] mainly because Bruegel's tower is clearly based on the Roman Colosseum. He was not the first artist to use this classical theatre as the model for the Tower of Babel, as Cornelis Anthonisz portrayed it in an etching of the same subject in 1547.[8] The view has also been advanced that Bruegel's painting was meant as a warning to the merchants of Antwerp,[9] while Klamt interprets it as an indictment of the arrogance of the Catholic church. He contends that a procession of worshippers can be seen on one of the galleries, and that they are carrying a red canopy, which could point to the presence of the Pope.[10]

On the other hand, the tower is shown under construction rather than after its fall, prompting some art historians to attach a positive meaning to the painting,[11] and various writers have noted that the Tower of Babel represents the source of all languages. Such a meaning would have been particularly appropriate to Antwerp, which was a centre of trade for merchants from all corners of the globe.[12] The piece is generally accepted as a late work, and if this is correct Bruegel would have been living in Brussels when he painted it.

Many authors have commented on the subtle use of colour. Whilst the bricks near the top of the tower are still bright red, those lower down have started to weather. This suggests that construction has been underway for a long time. There are also two unusual colour accents on the left of the painting. In one part, the builders can be seen hoisting chalk, and both they and the structure itself are smeared white. Slightly to the left there is a hoist for bricks, which have left a similar vertical streak, but in red.

Although the attribution to Pieter Bruegel the Elder is generally accepted, the dating is controversial. Glück believes it was made before the version in Vienna, which is dated 1563.[13] Most authors, however, are inclined to follow De Tolnay's argument that it is a later work.[14] Comparison between the landscape in this painting and the countryside of *The magpie on the gallows* in Darmstadt, which is dated 1568, appears to confirm this. The panel must in any event have been made before 1568, for the *Tower of Babel* which Lucas van Valckenborch painted in that year would be inconceivable without Bruegel's example (Munich, Alte Pinakothek, fig. e). Van Valckenborch's interpretation of the scene includes a portrayal of Nimrod marching in a procession at lower right. It is possible that the Rotterdam painting once showed the same motif, but that the panel was

1 Scanned and recorded by J.R.J. van Asperen de Boer on 11 May 1992. Paint samples: A 337/1-3. Infrared reflectograms: AB 1429/17-AB 1431/11.
2 Mander, C. van, *Schilderboeck*, Haarlem 1604, fol. 233 v.
3 In his copy of Van Mander's *Schilderboeck* (1618), Peeter Stevens (1590-1668) wrote: "Ditto cleyn toren van Babilonien heb [ik] gesien tot Brussel toebehoort hebbende de Raetsheer vanden Branden" (I saw this small Tower of Babel belonging to Councillor van den Branden in Brussels). Stevens began annotating his copy of the *Schilderboeck* in 1625. See Briels (1980), he believes that the painting may have been taken by Swedish soldiers when they plundered Prague. He suggests it was for a time in the collection of Christina of Sweden, before coming onto the Antwerp art market where it was acquired by Van den Branden. Stevens's note in his *Schilderboeck* is written in the past tense, which suggests the painting was already in different hands by then. Briels notes that the inventory and subsequent auction of the paintings of Gillis van Coninxloo in Amsterdam in 1607 included "a large Tower of Babel by Pieter Bruegel the Elder". Since he describes it as a "large" *Tower*, it would seem that this does not refer to our painting.
4 On the reverse is a stamp with the coat of arms and the inscription "ELISABETH DEI GRATIA HISPANIARVM REGINA" of Empress Elisabeth Farnese, the second wife of King Philip V of Spain. Elisabeth became Empress in 1714, and this is therefore the earliest date on which the stamp could have been used. The painting is described as no. 310 in the inventory of Elisabeth Farnese drawn up in the La Granja de San Ildefonso Palace in 1746. The number 310 is still visible on the reverse of the panel. The painting is described as follows: "310: Una Pintura arig[ina]l en Tabla de mano de Brugul, que rep[resen]ta la Torre de Bavilonia: tiene dos tercias y un dedo de alto; tres quartas, y seis de ancho. Marco dorado como el antecedente." With thanks to José Gabriel Moya Valgaìon and Juan Martínez of the Departamento de Conservacion of the Palacio Real in Madrid.
5 First noted by De Tolnay, *Pierre Bruegel l'ancien*, Brussels 1935, p. 61.
6 For example Glück (1951), Marijnissen (1969), Grossman. (1973).
7 For example Wazbinski (1964).
8 See for this etching, exhib. cat. *Kunst voor de beeldenstorm*, Amsterdam, Rijksmuseum, 1986, no. 157. This points to an illustration from 1534, in which the Colosseum was also used as a model for the tower, as a possible source of inspiration for Cornelis Anthonisz.
9 Menzel (1966).
10 Klamt (1979).
11 For example Genaille (1953) and Fryns (1964).
12 Gibson (1977).
13 Glück (1936).
14 De Tolnay (1938).
15 After restoring the panel in 1989-1990, P.F.J.M. Hermesdorf surmised that it had been reduced on all sides. This remains open to question. In the 1746 inventory of Elisabeth Farnese the dimensions correspond fairly closely with those of the current panel (see note 4).
16 See Minkowski (1991).

reduced and that this part of the picture was therefore lost.[15] Besides Lucas van Valkenborch, his brother Marten and several other painters have drawn inspiration from the Bruegel in Rotterdam or works based on it.[16] In contrast to the *Tower of Babel* in Vienna, however, no exact copies of the piece are known.

The x-radiographs show that Bruegel made some changes during the painting of the panel, particularly in the contours of the tower.
FL

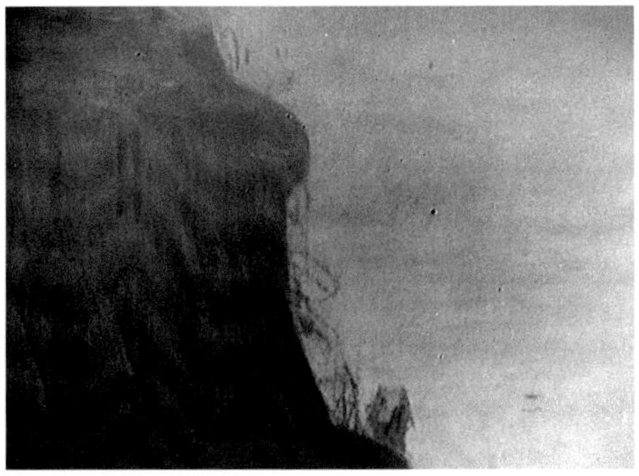

a. Infrared reflectogram showing the contours of the tower.

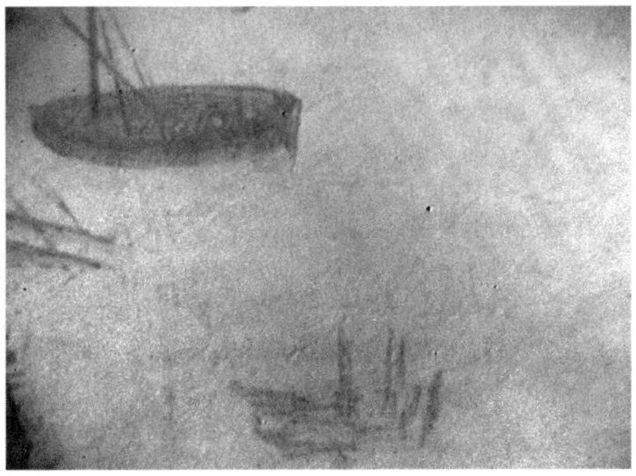

b. Infrared reflectogram showing a ship which was not painted

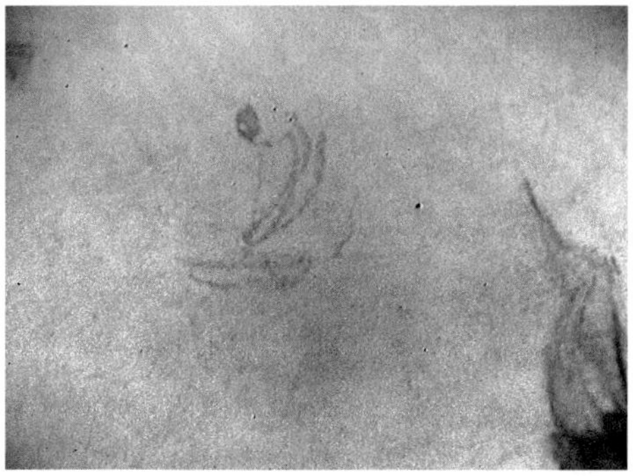

c. Infrared reflectogram showing a ship which was not painted

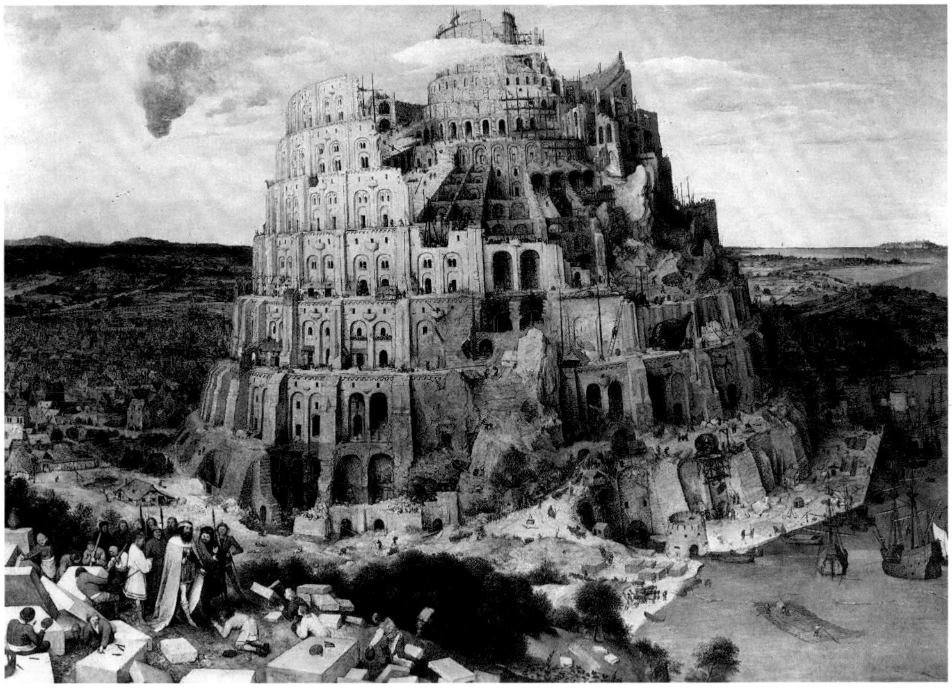

d. Pieter Bruegel the Elder, The Tower of Babel, 1563
Panel; 155 x 114 cm.
Kunsthistorisches Museum, Vienna

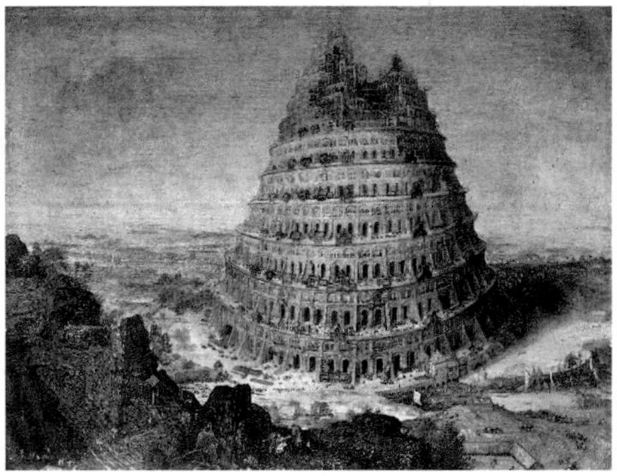

e. Lucas van Valckenborch, The Tower of Babel, 1568
Panel; 21 x 29 cm.
Alte Pinakothek, Munich.

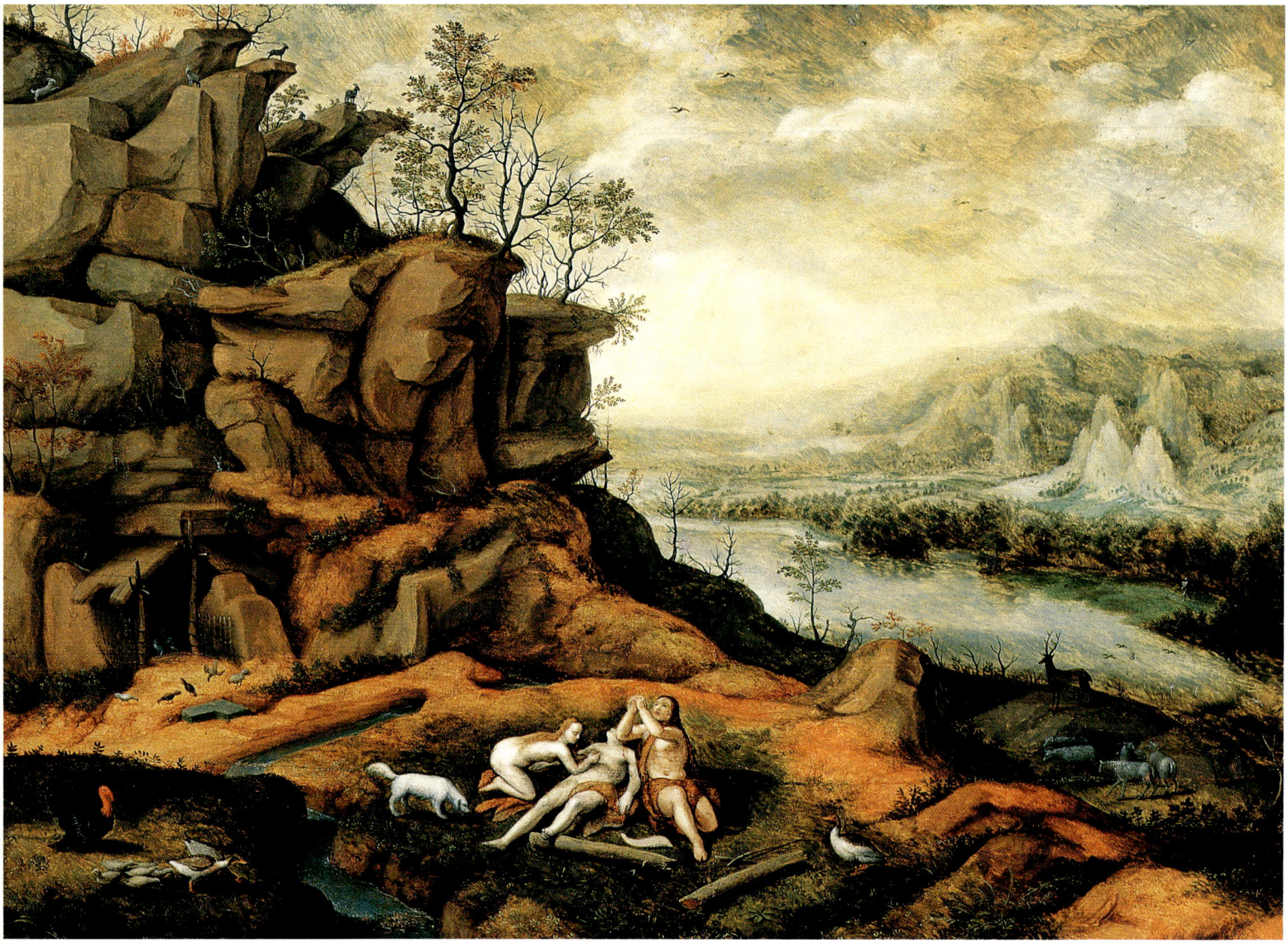

Landscape with Adam and Eve lamenting over the body of Abel

Cornelis van Dalem, after
(Antwerp c. 1530-
Bavel, near Breda 1573)

Panel; 51.5 x 69.5 cm

Physical characteristics: the panel consists of three horizontal planks. The panel is painted up to the edges.

Infrared reflectography: no underdrawing could be discerned.[1]

Provenance: C. Benedict Gallery, Paris, 1937; purchased by the Museum in 1937; inv. no. 2095.

Literature: *Verslag omtrent den toestand en de aanwinsten van het Museum Boymans over het jaar 1937*, pp. 3-4; *Museum Boymans. Beknopte catalogus schilderijen en beeldhouwwerken*, 1937, no. 104a; F. Grossmann, "Cornelis van Dalem re-examined", *The Burlington Magazine* 96 (1954), p. 47, fig. 8; Ch. Sterling, "Cornelis van Dalem et Jan van Wechelen", *Studies in the History of Art, dedicated to William E. Suida on his eightieth birthday*, London 1959, p. 282; cat. 1962, pp. 43-44; H.G. Franz, *Niederländische Landschaftsmalerei im Zeitalter des Manierismus*, Graz 1969, pp. 224-225, fig. 396; D. Allart, "Un paysagiste à redécouvrir: Cornelis van Dalem (Anvers, avant 1534? – Bavel, 1573)", *Revue Belge d'Archéologie et d'Histoire de l'Art* LXII (1993), pp. 103, 127, 129-130, fig. 14.

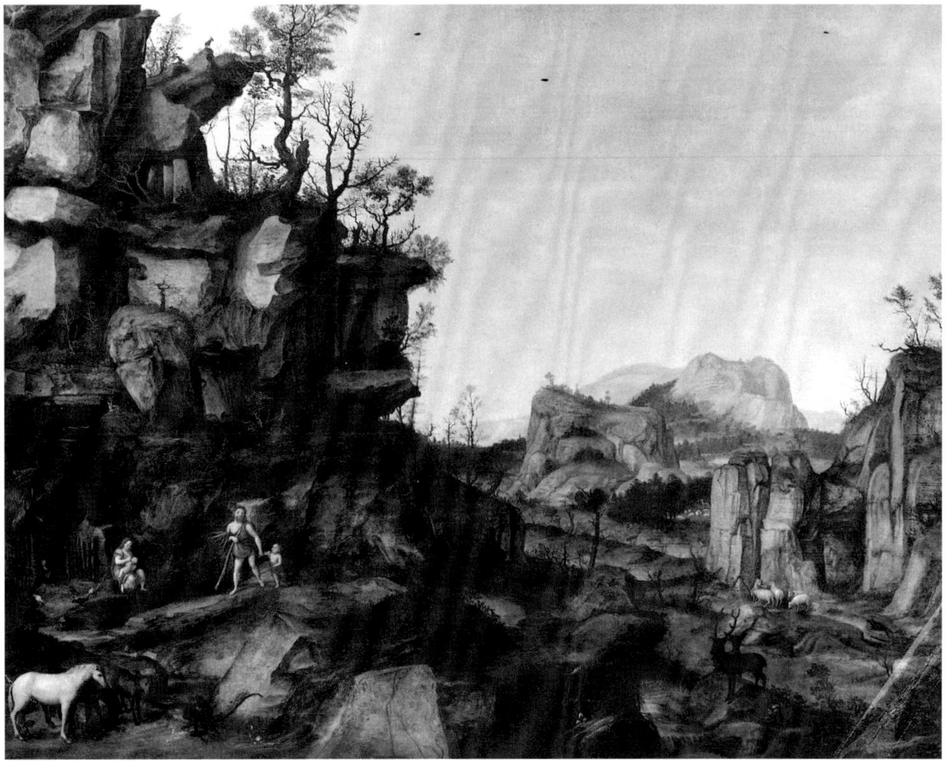

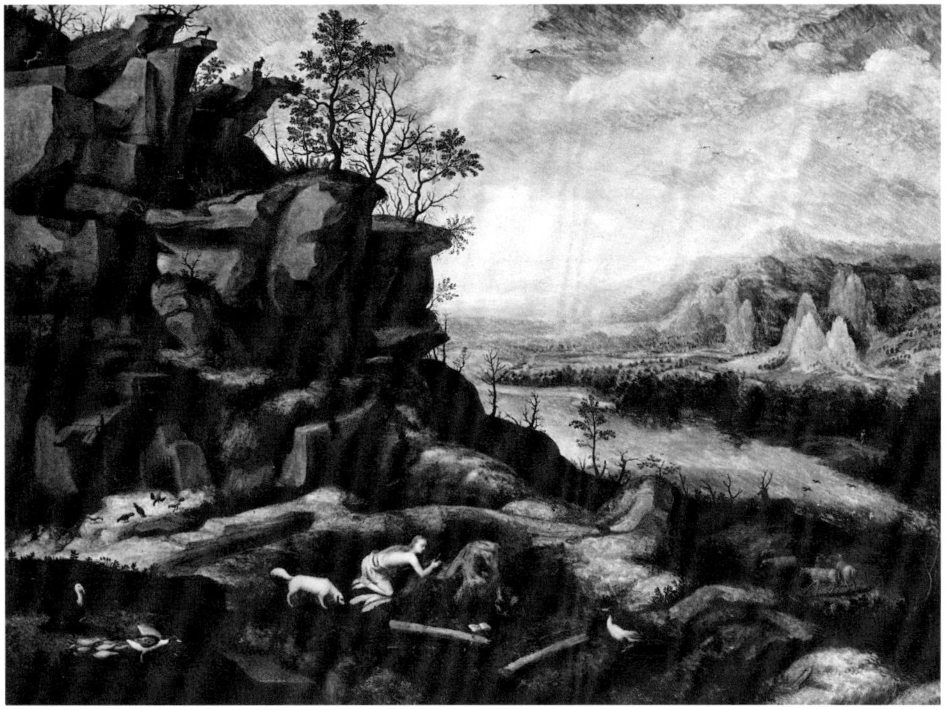

a. Cornelis van Dalem and Hans van Wechlen,
Landscape with Adam and Eve
Panel; 75.6 x 96.5 cm
Stanford, The Stanford Museum and Gallery

b. The Rotterdam painting before restoration.

Genesis 4 tells how Abel was killed by his brother Cain. As a punishment, God turned the murderer into a wanderer and fugitive on earth.

The painting shows the body of Abel in the foreground, amid a rocky river landscape. On either side of Abel are his mourning parents, Adam and Eve. Before them lies the jawbone of an ass. In the sixteenth century this was assumed to have been the murder weapon.[2] The wandering Cain is shown as a small figure in the right background.

Numerous animals are portrayed in the landscape, including sheep, deer, rabbits and ducks. The presence of a turkey is noteworthy because this native of the Americas was not introduced to western Europe until around 1520-1530.

The lamentation of Adam and Eve is not described in the bible, but the scene does recur in the visual arts, for example in the work of Lucas van Leyden.[3]

A small hut stands against the rocks. The appearance of this primitive structure has been linked to a treatise by the classical writer Vitruvius. In the first chapter of the second volume of his treatise on architecture, he describes how early man built huts of clay and wood. Some sixteenth-century editions of Vitruvius include illustrations showing structures which bear some resemblance to the hut in the painting.[4] A painting by Jan Mostaert depicts a similar landscape with rocks and huts.[5]

The Rotterdam painting was purchased in 1937 as an original work by Cornelis van Dalem. The nobleman Van Dalem was, according to Van Mander in 1604, a "fine painter of rocks". He painted for pleasure and only rarely.[6] It is therefore not surprising that few paintings are known by him. A number of his works show rocky landscapes which strongly resemble the one in our panel.

Most authors nonetheless have doubts about the attribution to Van Dalem.[7] The painting is of a lesser quality than other works which are known to be by him. A correct judgement is made more difficult by the poor condition of the painting.

The Rotterdam panel is probably a copy after a composition by the master himself. In Stanford there is a slightly larger painting by Van Dalem, *Landscape with Adam and Eve*, in which the rock formation on the left is virtually identical to that in the Rotterdam painting (fig. a).[8] The bearings of several of the animals are also literally the same. The panel in Stanford is of a noticeably higher quality. The figures in the American painting were probably painted by Hans van Wechlen.

The question remains whether the maker of our work based his painting on the American panel and changed the landscape and the story. Or, it is also possible that he worked after a painting by Van Dalem which is no longer known and which resembles our panel even more closely. The painting is undoubtedly a contemporary copy, and was made around 1560-1570, possibly in Van Dalem's own studio.

When the painting re-emerged on the art market in 1937, a rock had been painted over the figures of Abel and Adam. Eve had been changed into a kneeling Mary Magdalene (fig. b).
FL

1 The painting was partly scanned on 10 January 1994 by J.R.J. van Asperen de Boer.

2 See A.A. Barb, "Cain's murder-weapon and Samson's jawbone of an ass", *Journal of the Warburg and Courtauld Institutes* 35 (1972), pp. 386-389 and the literature listed there.

3 See A. Pigler, *Barockthemen*, I, Berlin 1974, p. 23, The engraving by Lucas van Leyden is Bartsch 6 and is dated 1529.

4 See Grossmann (1954) and H. van de Waal, *Drie eeuwen vaderlandsche geschied-uitbeelding 1500-1800*, The Hague 1952, pp. 85-86.

5 See the famous painting in the Frans Hals Museum in Haarlem. The connection with Van Dalem's work was made by Grossman (1954). See for a recent interpretation of the representation in Mostaert's painting, C.D. Cuttler, "Errata in Netherlandish art: Jan Mostaert's 'New World' landscape", *Simiolus* 19 (1989), pp. 191-197.

6 "Fraey schilder van rotsen", C. van Mander, *Het Schilderboeck*, Haarlem 1604, fol. 205 r., 268 v., 269 r. The work of Van Dalem was first highlighted by Ludwig Burchard in an article "Der Landschaftsmaler Cornelis van Dalem", *Jahrbuch der Preuszischen Kunstsammlungen* 45 (1924), pp. 66-71. Important new details about the life of Van Dalem were published in C. van de Velde, "Archivalia over Cornelis van Dalem", in: *Miscellanea Josef Duverger*, I, Ghent 1969, pp. 237-246.

7 Grossmann (1954) queries whether the work is by a studio assistant or is an early piece by the master himself. He surmises the former. Sterling (1959) first pointed out the resemblance with the painting in Stanford. He puts forward the possibility that the Rotterdam work was painted by a pupil of Jan van Wechelen, Hans de Boeys, who is known only from documents. Van Wechelen himself several times painted figures in works by Van Dalem (see E. Brochhagen, "Zu Hans van Wechlen und Cornelis van Dalem", *Münchner Jahrbuch der Bildenden Kunst* XIV (1963), pp. 93-104.) Franz (1969) calls it a copy or a studio piece. Allart (1993) also thinks it is probably a studio piece.

8 See for this painting Sterling (1959). The painting was purchased in 1962, see *The Art Journal* XXI (1962), pp. 198, 200.

Organisation:
Friso Lammertse

Translators:
Elizabeth Berkhof-Haig
Marcel de Jong
Yvette Rosenberg
Andrew Ross
Cat. nos. 3, 28, 29 were written in English

Project supervisor:
J.J. van Cappellen

Photographs:
T. Haartsen
and others

Design:
8vo, London

Printing:
Snoeck-Ducaju & Zoon, Gent

Colour lithographs:
Daiichi Process PTE Ltd.

ISBN 90-6918-137-1

Corporate members of the Boymans-van Beuningen Museum:

ABN AMRO Bank N.V.
CALDIC
Internatio-Müller NV
DURA BOUW ROTTERDAM B.V.
CROON elektrotechniek
Rollins Hudig Hall Nederland
Koninklijke Nedlloyd Groep N.V.
Unilever
Loyens & Volkmaars
Koninklijke Econosto N.V.
Koninklijke Pakhoed N.V.
MeesPierson N.V.
Gimbrère en Dohmen Software B.V.
Hollandsche Beton Maatschappij bv
Credit Lyonnais Bank Nederland N.V.
Moret Ernst & Young
Nauta Dutilh
Architektenburo Visser en Beerman B.V.
Siemens Nederland N.V.
PTT Telecom District Rotterdam
Bakker Beheer Barendrecht BV
Mobil Oil B.V.
Nationale Nederlanden
Van der Vorm Vastgoed B.V.
Heineken Nederland B.V.
Vakschool voor Bakkerij- en
Hotelpersoneel
Glaxo B.V.
HAL Investments B.V.
KPMG Accountants Belastingadviseurs
Consultants
EOE-Optiebeurs
Société Générale de Surveillance
(Nederland) B.V.
Stichting Organisatie van
Effectenhandelaren te Rotterdam
Accountants- Administratieconsulenten voor
Bouwbedrijven SCAB B.V.
Hagé International B.V.
Horst Makelaars
Nidera Handelscompagnie b.v.
Automobielbedrijf J. van Dijk & Dochters b.v.
KOEN VISSER GROEP